KANSAS PLACE-NAMES

ALLEN ALMA ALMENA ALTAMONT ALTA VISTA ALTON ALTOONA AMERICUS ANDALE AN

ABBYVILLE ABILENE ACRES ADAMSVILLE ADMIRE AGENDA AGRA ALBERT ALDEN ALEXANDER
LMENA ALTAMONT ALTA VISTA ALTON ALTOONA AMERICUS ANDALE ANTHONY ARCADIA ARGON
CITY ARLINGTON ARMA ASHERVILLE ASHLAND ASSARIA ATCHISON ATHOL ATLANTA ATTICA ATWO
STA AURORA AXTELL BAILEYVILLE BALDWIN CITY BARNARD BARNES BARTLETT BASSETT BATESVI
A BAXTER SPRINGS BAZINE BEATTIE BELLE PLAINE BELLEVILLE BELOIT BELPRE BELVUE BEND
CT BENNINGTON BENTON BERN BEVERLY BIG SPRINGS BIRD CITY BISON BLAINE BLOOM BLOOM
UE MOUND BLUE RAPIDS BLUFF CITY BOGUE BONITA BONNER SPRINGS BREWSTER BRIDGEPORT
BROOKVILLE BROWNELL BUCKLIN BUFFALO BUHLER BUNKER HILL BURDEN BURDETT BURLINGAME
TON BURNS BURR OAK BURRTON BUSHONG BUSHTON BYERS CAIRO CALDWELL CALVERT CAMBRIDGE
US CANEY CANTON CARBONDALE CARLTON CARNEIRO CASSODAY CAWKER CITY CEDAR CEDAR BLUFFS
AR POINT CEDAR VALE CENTRALIA CHANUTE CHAPMAN CHARLESTON CHASE CHAUTAUQUA CHENEY CH
KEE CHERRYVALE CHETOPA CIMARRON CIRCLEVILLE CLAFLIN CLAY CENTER CLAYTON CLEARWATER C
ENTS CLIFTON CLIMAX CLONMEL CLOVERDALE CLYDE COATS COFFEYVILLE COLBY COLDWATER COLLY
OLONY COLUMBUS COLWICH CONCORDIA CONWAY CONWAY SPRINGS COOLIDGE COPELAND CORNING
TTONWOOD FALLS COUNCIL GROVE COURTLAND COYVILLE CRESTLINE CUBA CULLISON CULVER CUMM
CUNNINGHAM DAMAR DANVILLE DEARING DEERFIELD DE GRAFF DELIA DELLVALE DELPHOS DENISON D
ON DERBY DE SOTO DETROIT DEVON DEXTER DIGHTON DILLWYN DODGE CITY DORRANCE DOUGLASS DO
DOWNS DRESDEN DUNDEE DUNLAP DURHAM DWIGHT EARLTON EASTON EDGERTON EDMOND EDNA EDS
DWARDSVILLE EFFINGHAM ELBING EL DORADO ELGIN ELKADER ELK CITY ELK FALLS ELKHART ELLINW
ELLIS ELLSWORTH ELMDALE ELMO ELSMORE ELWOOD ELYRIA EMMETT EMPORIA ENGLEWOOD ENSIGN
ERPRISE ERIE ESBON ESKRIDGE EUDORA EUREKA EVEREST FAIRVIEW FALL RIVER FLORENCE FONTANA
D FORMOSO FORT DODGE FORT SCOTT FOSTORIA FOWLER FRANKFORT FREDERICK FREDONIA FRONTEN
ULTON GALATIA GALENA GALESBURG GALVA GARDEN CITY GARDEN PLAIN GARDNER GARFIELD GARNE
AS GAYLORD GEM GENESEO GEUDA SPRINGS GIRARD GLADE GLASCO GLEN ELDER GODDARD GOFF GO
ND GORDON GORHAM GOVE GRAINFIELD GRANTVILLE GREAT BEND GREELEY GREEN GREENLEAF GREEN
RG GRENOLA GRIDLEY GRINNELL GYPSUM HADDAM HAGGARD HALFORD HALSTEAD HAMILTON HAMLIN H
VER HANSTON HARDTNER HARLAN HARPER HARRIS HARTFORD HARVEYVILLE HAVANA HAVEN HAVENS
HAVILAND HAYNE HAYS HAYSVILLE HAZELTON HEALY HEPLER HERINGTON HERNDON HESSTON HIAWAT
CKOK HIGHLAND HILL CITY HILLSBORO HILLSDALE HOISINGTON HOLCOM HOLLENBERG HOLTON HOLY
D HOME HOPE HORACE HORTON HOWARD HOWELL HOXIE HOYT HUDSON HUGOTON HUMBOLDT HUNNE

ATCHISON ATHOL ATLANTA ATTICA ATWOOD AUGUSTA AURORA AXTELL BAIL

John Rydjord

LLE ABILENE ACRES ADAMSVILLE ADMIRE AGENDA AGRA ALBERT ALDEN ALEXANDER

KANSAS
PLACE-NAMES

A ARGONIA ARKANSAS CITY ARLINGTON ARMA ASHERVILLE ASHLAND ASSARIA

UNIVERSITY OF OKLAHOMA PRESS : NORMAN

BY JOHN RYDJORD

Foreign Interest in the Independence of New Spain (Durham, N.C., 1935)
Indian Place-Names (Norman, 1968)
Kansas Place-Names (Norman, 1972)

Rydjord, John.
    Kansas place-names.
    Bibliography: p.
    1. Names, Geographical—Kansas.   I.   Title.
F679.R9   917.81   79–177346
ISBN 0–8061–0994–7

Copyright 1972 by the University of Oklahoma Press, Publishing Division
of the University. Composed and printed at Norman, Oklahoma, U.S.A., by
the University of Oklahoma Press. First edition.

*To my Wife, Lillian
and to our children: John, Marilyn, and Robert*

PREFACE

WHAT'S IN A NAME? is a question asked more often than answered. This has been particularly true of place-names. Europeans have been far ahead of Americans in the study of place-names, but the organization of the American Name Society and its publication of a quarterly called *Names* are evidence of a growing American interest in place-name studies.

When I retired as Dean of the Graduate School of Wichita State University in 1958, I had several topics available from which to choose a research project. Kansas was at this time having several centennial celebrations and so I chose to make a study of Kansas place-names as a contribution to the revived interest in Kansas history. I have asked the question, "What's in a Kansas place-name?" The answers have not always been available and many of the sources have been dimmed by time. The collection and organization of a vast amount of scattered material has been a stimulating challenge. I hope that the results will be of interest not only to students of place-names but also to the general public.

The scope and variety of Kansas place-names are universal. There are many aspects to the study of nomenclature: it may be researched from the perspective of geography or topography, philology or etymology, philosophy or folklore. But a broad study of this scope lends itself to the historical approach, and that should be, at least theoretically, all-inclusive. There is a close relationship between historical events and Kansas place-names.

To identify a place-name one must determine where it came from, the language used, who used it, why, and when. This book is more concerned about the source of a name than in its perpetuation. Thus the names of many dead towns are included. It may be observed also that when a post office was closed, its name could be used for another location. It was not uncommon for a name to be used several times.

The subject could be organized as a dictionary or encyclopedia or divided topically with some chronological sequence. A dictionary approach would destroy the topical and historical sequence. Mark Twain

vii

purportedly disliked the dictionary because, he said, it was constantly changing the subject. Less legitimate may be the complaint of the student who objected to the use of the dictionary because it had no index. While this study is not a narrative, there is some sequence; and because chapters are organized around topics, readers may browse about to find the information to fit their interests. I hope that the index will make this work as useful as a dictionary.

This task was greater than I had anticipated. What had been intended as two chapters on Indian names became a separate book of twenty-six chapters entitled *Indian Place-Names*, published by the University of Oklahoma Press in 1968. Although the general study occupied several years—years consisting of many seven-day weeks—it has been a stimulating and rewarding experience. After twelve years of work, partially interrupted by two years of teaching at other universities, the broader work is now completed. While it is comprehensive, one dare not say it is definitive.

In expressing appreciation for support and aid, I should mention studies of others that have been the most helpful. Among these are Robert W. Baughman's *Kansas Post Offices*, the mimeographed report on Kansas place-names by Wayne E. Corley, newspaper articles by journalists who have been interested in place-names, professional works on place-names, and, above all, the publications of the Kansas State Historical Society in Topeka. The scholarly work of this organization, under the able direction of Nyle Miller and his competent and helpful staff, deserves special recognition.

The staff of the Ablah Library of Wichita State University has been most co-operative. Special mention of those who have been helpful in obtaining material would include Downing P. O'Harra, Merle J. Paulson, Michael Heaston, and Thoburn Taggart, Jr. I have also received excellent assistance from the Library staff on the third floor where my study is located: Mr. Phillip Shih, who is distinguished for his courteous help; Mrs. Florence Wurst, who always brought in every new book on names that came to her attention; and Miss Beatrice Paddock, who has aided in identifying the possible source of strange names, especially Biblical names.

I am also grateful to the University Administration for permitting me to retain a study in the Library. I wish especially to thank President Clark D. Ahlberg and Vice-President John B. Breazeale for providing financial assistance. Professor Margaret L. Jantze and Mrs. Mary Wilkes of the Department of Business Education have been most co-operative in recommending student secretaries, and none better than Vickie Christensen, who was remarkably alert in detecting errors and who typed the final copy of the manuscript with efficiency. There are many others who have been helpful. Dr. Robert D. Oursler, a former student, did some volunteer typing for me. Dr. Francis W. Schruben and Jerry Riseley collected material from Rooks County. For a critical reading of individual chapters, I am indebted to Professors Allen M. Cress and Henry Malone and my daughter, Marilyn (Mrs. G. C. Belden). I am especially grateful to Professor Robert W. Mood for his critical reading of the whole manuscript. Thanks are also due to Mr. G. C. Belden for his assistance in preparation of the maps.

Finally, names get lost and errors creep in, and there must be no better way of escaping responsibility than to put the blame on the gremlins.

Wichita, Kansas   JOHN RYDJORD
May 17, 1972

CONTENTS

	Preface	*page vii*
I.	Introduction	3
II.	Sun, Water, and Weather	9
III.	Hills, Highlands, and Lowlands	21
IV.	Prairies and Prairie Flowers	36
V.	Trees	43
VI.	Bees, Birds, and Beasts	59
VII.	Natural Resources	74
VIII.	Economic Imprint	81
IX.	Castilian Names in Kansas	89
X.	French and Indian River Names	104
XI.	Additional French Names	119
XII.	Names from Old England	134
XIII.	Scotland and Sir Walter Scott	151
XIV.	Welsh and Irish	163
XV.	Deutsch and the Dutch	172
XVI.	Scandinavian Names in Kansas	185
XVII.	Names from Slavic Sources	192
XVIII.	Orient and Africa	197
XIX.	Greek Place-Names in Kansas	204
XX.	Italy and the Roman Empire	215
XXI.	Bible Names in Kansas	223
XXII.	Saints	238
XXIII.	Preachers	244
XXIV.	Secondhand Names from New England	249
XXV.	New York, New Jersey, and Neighbors	259
XXVI.	Names from the Old Northwest	273
XXVII.	Midwest and Westward	290
XXVIII.	Names from the Southern States	300
XXIX.	Bogus Legislature	308
XXX.	Kansas State Officials	323
XXXI.	Lincoln and His Associates	341
XXXII.	Presidents and Their Associates	351

XXXIII.	The Fourth Estate	363
XXXIV.	Political Nomenclature	371
XXXV.	Generals and County Names	377
XXXVI.	Private Rooks and Men of Rank	397
XXXVII.	The Soldier State	409
XXXVIII.	Lo, the Poor Indian	423
XXXIX.	Names from the Santa Fe	439
XL.	Railroad Roster	451
XLI.	Cherchez La Femme	464
XLII.	Potpourri	479
	Appendix	491
	Notes	496
	Bibliography	564
	Index	595

Maps

Kansas Names from the British Isles	150
German Names in Kansas	183
Kansas Names from the Bible	236
Bible Names in Kansas	237
Kansas Names from New York	272
Kansas Names from Illinois	289
Military Names for Kansas Counties	396
Indian Tribes Contributing Place-Names to Kansas	438
Names Associated with the Santa Fe Railroad	450

KANSAS PLACE-NAMES

CHAPTER I

INTRODUCTION

CAPTAIN JOHN SMITH once made a pertinent observation about the relationship between geography and history. "For as Geography without History," said he, "seemeth a carkasse without motion; so History without Geography is a vagrant without Habitation." Place-names deal with both geography and history and may serve as a bond between the two.

The first observations of a new land usually concern its geography. The comments on Kansas by Zebulon M. Pike and by Stephen H. Long were not favorable. Their reports created public opinion which stimulated government policy. The land was believed to be unfit for white settlement, but that did not mean, as Pike suggested, that it was not sufficient for Indians. No solution to the conflict between white men and Indians on the advancing frontier east of the Mississippi existed until it was suggested that the Indians could be moved to Kansas. There they could live in peace "forever," unmolested by aggressive and greedy whites. These opinions served as the justification for the Indian removal policy.

Kansas already had Indians and Indian names, but removal brought to Kansas many tribes with new names which served as a source for geographical designations. These gave color and distinction to Kansas place-names, and, as John Smith might have appreciated, they combined history and geography.

One might begin the naming process, as the Indians did, by using descriptions of nature. The geographical diversity of Kansas gave the natives a wide variety of natural objects to be named. Descriptive names were applied to trail-markers and campsites. River bottoms were identified as muddy, sandy, or rocky; water was fresh or salty, sweet or bitter; rivers were long, short, crooked, or straight; they were wet or dry; they were red, yellow, blue, or green-gray. Streams were lined with willows, cottonwoods, or oaks; and on their waters were ducks, geese, or swans. All these and more were sources for descriptive place-names.

Incidents were also recorded as place-names. There was, for example, the place "Where they ate the squashes river," and that was on

3

the Republican. Cheyenne Bottoms and Blood Creek were named for Indian battles, as was Pawnee Rock.

Kansas pioneers were well aware of the importance of geographical features and used practically every descriptive name the Indians had used. Whether in selecting a homestead or a townsite, the pioneers' choice was based largely on geography. The soil, resources, communication, and view were prime factors in deciding on a location and naming it. Whether it be Fairview in English, Belvue in French, or Olathe in Indian, Pretty Prairie in English, Belpre in French, or Muscotah in Indian, the impressions of the name-givers were the same.

The Spaniards were the first Europeans to see Kansas. They did not stay long enough to leave many permanent names. Yet the foreign sound and simplicity of the Spanish names appealed to the Kansas settlers, even though they could not always pronounce them correctly. Santa "Fay" might become Santa "Fee," but who would object? Most of the Spanish names were derived from place-names in other areas, especially Spain, Mexico, and California.

After the Spaniards came the French. They knew how to adjust to the life of the Indians. They made treaties with them, traded with them, married them, and learned their languages. Indian names already in use in Kansas, notably river names, were transmitted to us by the French. They put Indian names into written form. To some frontiersmen, the French language was as unintelligible as the Indian language. The French spelling was generally changed by pioneers to fit the phonetics of frontier English, losing thereby, the meaning.

The French name which caused the most difficulty was Marais des Cygnes, a translation of an Indian name which meant "marsh of the swans." While some might prefer to use the simpler name of Osage for the French name, the state legislature passed a law which made Marais des Cygnes the legal name, and woe be to those who dare break the law. Not until the Marais des Cygnes crosses the border into Missouri can the name Osage be used legally. There is a fondness for the difficult but familiar French name.

Some of the French pioneers left their own names on the map. A few French names came directly from France or Canada; others, like Paris or Bourbon, came from other American states.

American settlers kept in touch with the world through the postal system. Thousands of post offices were established, many of them only a few miles apart. Altogether there were, at one time or another, over four thousand post offices, all of which had to be named. Many were given more than one name. Popular names that were dropped when a post office was closed were quite often revived for other post offices.

4

The name-givers could certainly agree with Shakespeare's Falstaff, who wished he knew where an adequate supply of names might be had.

Kansas pioneers were notorious promoters of new towns. Horace Greeley said that it took only three houses to make a city in Kansas. Some "towns" had only one house and others never got beyond the plan on paper. Almost every post office expected to become a town, and almost every town expected to become a city. The nucleus for a town could be a post office, a blacksmith shop, or a hotel with a tavern; if it had all three, it was on its way to become a city. The boom in town-building stirred the speculative interests of those who would make an easy buck. Farming was hard work, a gamble, and seldom profitable. Speculation in town lots seemed to promise the quickest return. Whole towns were built, bought, and sold.

A stranger coming across the prairies of Kansas stopped to talk to a man who was plowing. "Ain't you laying off them corn rows quite a distance apart?" he asked the plowman. "Man alive," was the answer, "them ain't corn rows over there. They's streets an' alleys, an' this here's a city. You are right now a-straddlin' the corner uv Commercial Street and Emporium Avenue . . . ."[1] We know not what he named it, but having names for the streets, he must have had one for the "city" as well.

So many towns were planned and started that settlers worried lest there be too little land left for farming. The territorial legislature in 1859 passed a resolution stating that every alternate section of land should be set aside for farming.

In their search for place-names, the name-givers had great latitude, but postmasters and town promoters frequently started with their own names or those of relatives, friends, and sweethearts. There was a post-master whose name was Post, but the post office in Gray County named Post was not named for a postmaster. When a postmaster opened a post office in his home in Marshall County, he named it Home.

All post office names had to be approved by the Post Office Department to prevent duplication. The department could also suggest names and was often requested to do so. The clerks in the Postal Department naturally used the names of people they knew—fellow-clerks, and, as one suggested, the names of "practically all of the kids and babies" in the neighborhood. No wonder there are so many girls' place-names whose origins remain unknown.

As the Kansas population increased, political events and politicians' names served as a convenient source for place-names. This was especially true in naming counties. There was, however, a conspicuous difference between names chosen in eastern Kansas before the Civil War and those selected in western Kansas after 1865. In 1855 the first county names were chosen to fit the political bias of the "Bogus Legislature," as the first territorial legislature was called because it was dominated by Missourians and other proslavery representatives. After the Civil War, the bias shifted, and the legislature chose names of the men who represented the victorious North. Several of the earlier names, unacceptable to the victors, were replaced. Most prominent among the new county names were those of officers in the Union army. But politicians' names, from presidents to postmasters, were widely used as place-names.

Military officers' names were popular because of the tremendous impact of the Civil War. After the war, they continued to be in the public eye because of the Indian wars or because the officers had gone into politics. The higher the rank, the more popular the name. John C. Rooks was the only private soldier to have his name given to a county. Forts were logically named for military men, and the names of Forts Leavenworth, Riley, Ellsworth, and Wallace were eventually applied to counties and towns.

Historical events, notably battles, were used as place-names in Kansas. History books were filled with names and dates of battles on the questionable assumption that if these were known, the student knew history. Kansas has or has had a Bunker Hill, a Bennington, and a Lexington from the American Revolution; a Shiloh, a Bull Run, and an Appomattox from the Civil War; a Buena Vista and a Cerro Gordo from the Mexican War; and even a Zulu from the Zulu War in Africa in 1879.

After the Civil War two great forces attracted people to Kansas: free land and railroads. Railroad builders were hard put to find enough names for the hundreds of towns and stations along their tracks. They used the names of railway officials and their own wives and children. Many a farmer's name was also used as a station name, especially if he had donated land for a right-of-way or for a townsite. Santa Fe investors from Newton, Massachusetts, named Newton, Kansas.

Advertisements for free land and promotion by railroads brought in great waves of European immigrants. Many foreigners preserved a sympathetic tie with Europe by adopting familiar town names for their Kansas towns. Kansas place-names reveal the origins of many of the state's people, but not all European names came directly from Europe. Westphalia, for example, was named for Westphalians from Iowa, Paris by Parisians from Kentucky.

Like the Europeans, immigrants from other states brought their home-town names with them. Most of these second-hand names came from the eastern states and more from Ohio and Illinois than any other state. As Forty-Niners drifted back eastward, some of them, like Governor Charles Robinson, remained in Kansas. These adventurers introduced California place-names to Kansas.

An interesting result of the variety in the backgrounds of people settling in Kansas is reflected by the universality of its place-names. One may see from the classical and Biblical references the way in which the education, religion, and culture of a people were reflected in the choice of place-names. In the mid-nineteenth century Americans took pride in their knowledge of the classics. Greek and Latin were still college requirements and enough filtered down to the frontier to make classical names acceptable. Together with Biblical names were pagan names like Odin and Valhalla.

The repetition of previously used place-names was both tedious and confusing, but it was difficult to find a name which had not been used. There were some that showed originality in expressing a mood or emotion. Kansas has also had whimsical names like Ego and Pride, Discord and Bonaccord, Utopia and Monotony.

Names were occasionally created or coined. New names could be made by modifying old ones. Rivalry over whose name should be given to a town could be settled by using parts of both names. The names of Anderson and Dale were combined to make Andale, and those of Warren and Keeney were combined to make WaKeeney. Nonchalant was a word which was made into a place-name by adding a vowel to make it Nonchalanta, a name in Ness County. The initials of T. E. Scott were attached to his surname to name a town Tescott.

Names, like everything else, have been subject to change. Even the Old English names have undergone a long evolution. These changes may be referred to as erosion but are commonly called "corruption." A kindlier term would be simplification.

Names suffered from frequent changes in spelling, as might be expected with Indian and foreign names. But incorrect spelling could cause some confusion. One town in Geary County was named Batcheller for a man who was not a bachelor. But the town's name was spelled Bacheller, Bachelor, Batcheller, Batchellor, and Batchelor. The problem of spelling was solved by changing the name to Milford. The United States Board of Geographic Names recommended combining names. It would change El Dorado to Eldorado, but in this it failed. Nor did it succeed in changing La Cygne to Lacygne. Oklahoma, however, was successful in changing Abe Lincoln to Abelincon, an alteration of questionable merit.

Names were as ephemeral as the post offices. Even a short-lived post office might have several names, all to be lost or adopted for other places. Some post offices moved about so much that they might be called "peripatetic." The coming of the railroads made many a post office and town move to the tracks; others died where they were. Their original names could be retained as a station-name or could be replaced.

The second great factor in eliminating the post office was the introduction of the Rural Free Delivery, that great boon to the farmers. This removed more place-names than any other factor. In western Kansas only a few of its many names now remain on the map. Some of this decline was due to the coming of the automobile, after which the country store and post office were no longer essential. Wallace and Greeley counties have no towns left that are not located on railways or main highways. The nineteenth-century maps have fascinating lists of names of towns that have not survived. Cecil Howes has recorded 135 ghost towns in Shawnee County alone.

One sentence in a Kansas guide illustrates the wide divergence in the choice of Kansas place-names. Referring to 1854, when Topeka was founded, it says: "Before the year was out Palmyra, Louisiana, and Brooklyn were begun along the Santa Fe Trail, with Prairie City, Baldwin City, and Hickory Point in its close vicinity; on the Oregon Trail (locally known as the California Road) Franklin and Wakarusa appeared."[2] Palmyra was an ancient city of Syria dating back to Solomon's time; Louisiana is a name honoring a French king for the province which once included Kansas; Brooklyn is the Dutch name of a New York city; Santa Fe is the Spanish name of the town which marked the end of the best-known trail in the country; Prairie City and Hickory Point are Kansas descriptive names; Baldwin City was named for an Ohio educator who founded Baldwin College; Oregon was the territory which drew pioneers to the Pacific coast before gold diverted both interest and the trail to California, a place with a Spanish name; Franklin honored one of the greatest statesmen in American history; and Wakarusa was an Indian name from the Sioux tribes in Kansas.

Names were frequently taken from events. Covert Creek in Osborne County had been named for a pioneer who was killed by the Indians. Four streams supposedly took their names from the statement, "Indian kill Covert, Carr got away." So they were named Indian Creek, Kill Creek, Covert Creek, and Carr Creek.[3]

"There is no place in the world where nomenclature is so rich, poetical, humorous, and picturesque as in the United States of America," said Robert Louis Stevenson. The opinion has since been shared by many others, including H. L. Mencken. One might add that there is probably no state in the Union with such a rich variety of place-names as the state of Kansas.

8

CHAPTER II

SUN, WATER, AND WEATHER

IN THE BEGINNING God created the heavens and the earth." On the little solar satellite called Earth, a dust speck in the universe, emerged a myriad of features to be named. The crust of the earth experienced a succession of geological eras. The wind, weather, and sun have changed the surface to give it characteristics to be described. Weather and water are closely linked with the sun, as are day and night and time. For all these phenomena, man has developed a descriptive vocabulary, and out of this vocabulary Kansas chose many of its place-names.

An ambitious town in Sedgwick County took a universal outlook, added "a" to the word cosmos, and named itself Cosmosa. The name lasted less than a year and became Park City, the name of a town near Valley Center.

Brown County had a place named Discord. Discord was discontinued and its post office was moved to Comet, a neighboring place which anticipated a great future. Comets usually flash and then fade away. This one lasted fourteen years.

The earth is believed to have left the sun like a comet but it is now generally referred to as a globe. A town in Douglas County, first named Marion and then Washington, was finally named Globe.

The globe must rotate to give the earth its rising sun and sunset, its night and day, and its light and dark. Time is also marked by the sun and measured from midday, or the meridian, when the sun is at its zenith. Time was the name of a post office in Crawford County, later moved to McCune. Light was the name of a place in Smith County, but only for one summer. Time may be checked by an hourglass, and Hourglass in Cheyenne County functioned twice as a post office, lasting only a few months. No place was named Sundial, but Osborne County had a post office named Dial, a name that is generally associated with a timepiece. Zenith was the name proposed for a town in Reno County. But A. A. Robinson renamed it Sylvia for his daughter. Then he gave the name of Zenith to the next station to the west.[1]

Greenwich in England is a center from which one measures time and distance. This name migrated to Connecticut and to Greenwich in

Sedgwick County, Kansas. As for measurement, Rooks County had a place named Survey, and Crawford County had a post office named Base Line.

In Kansas the Sixth Principal Meridian was used as the base for surveys. Meridian in Sumner County was promoted by a group from Wichita to become the county seat, but Wellington won and Meridian died. Finally, there was a place named Parallel on the line between Washington and Riley counties. The Rand McNally map of 1879 showed it on the Riley County side. It was supposed to be on the first standard parallel. There was also a Parallel Trail from Atchison to Denver.

Although Christians have repudiated sun worship, they do worship on Sun Day. Men appreciate the sun, and a number of Kansas place-names are identified with it. Cloud County had a place named Sunday but the name was changed to Hollis.

In Barber County, a cowboy town was named simply Sun, later changed to Sun City. Jefferson County had a place named Rising Sun. Both Republic County and Sumner County had places named Sunset. There were many variations of sun names between Sunrise and Sunset. Wabaunsee County even had a Sunbeam. For a short time Ford County had a place named Sunshine. Sedgwick County has a Sunny Dale and Sumner County had a Sunny Slope. Of all the names pertaining to the sun, Sunnyside was the most popular. The name was used as one word in Butler, Dickinson, and Wichita counties, but Montgomery County made it Sunny Side.[2] A station on the Union Pacific in Wallace County is named Sunland. Sunny Dale, Sunland, and Sun City are the only sun names that remain.

One of the phenomena of the relationship between the sun and moon is the eclipse. Coffey County had a post office named Eclipse. It lasted a decade and was then changed to the Biblical name of Antioch. Eclipse may, of course, have been used to mean "to surpass."

Ten times as bright as the sun is the star Altair. In Thomas County, Altair is a little station. Thrice the name of Star was adopted, first in Graham County, then in Greenwood County, and finally in Stevens County. These were small stars and passed into oblivion. The Star in Stevens County twinkled but a moment and then its light went out, or, in more prosaic language, its post office was "rescinded" in 1912, the very year it opened. In Cherokee County, the place called New Memphis was renamed Starvale and then changed to Star Valley.

Lone Star in Sumner County and in Douglas County had a Texas connection, as did Lone Star Township in Rush County. But the Lone

Star School in Rawlins County was given this name because it stood "like a lone star out on the prairie."[3]

The sun is a controlling factor in weather, which also contributed place-names. Hot Hill in Ottawa County was named in August, 1872. By September the heat must have subsided. Cooler heads had the name of the post office changed to Ada to honor the wife of Jacob B. Lane, the postmaster.[4] Equally hot must have been the place named Calorific, a station in Wyandotte County.[5]

One might seek respite from the heat in a town named Cool in Cloud County, only to discover that the town, also called Cooltown, was named for Joseph Cool, a pioneer.

The sun evaporates water and returns it to the earth as rain. Rainbelt in Meade County was beyond the rainbelt area and had its name changed to Jasper. There were also such thirst-quenching names as Artesia and Springlake.

Among the weather names were thunder, lightning, hail, hurricane, and, occasionally, rainbow. It was natural that Thunderbolt Creek should be a branch of Lightning Creek. Lightning Creek was described as being crooked and winding, with a double fork that earned it the name "Forked" Lightning Creek. During a thunderstorm, according to legend, several Osage hunters were killed when they took shelter under a tree. From this incident, Lightning Creek could have been named.[6] The source for the name of Thunderbolt Creek in Crawford County could have been Chief Thunderbolt of the Ottawas. When the Chief refused to sign away the lands of his people, the negotiators plied him with liquor and then guided his hand for his signature on a treaty which he vainly repudiated.[7]

Near Station Number 9 on the Smoky Hill Trail, a tornado overturned "many heavy freight wagons, blew a light buggy into fragments, tore up boxes, and scattered dry-goods for several miles . . . ." The place was consequently named Hurricane Hill.[8] In Grant County, not far from Rainbelt, another place was called Hurricane. The hurricane name came from the Caribbean where natives spoke of those devastating storms as *Huracan*, the "evil spirit." In contrast to Hurricane, Mitchell County had a place named Zephyr, and Crawford County had a Breezy Hill post office.

Linn County had a Hail Ridge post office, Labette County had a Snow Hill post office, and Montgomery County had a Snow Creek. Lincoln County had a post office named Dewdrop.

After a storm, the sun breaks through the clouds and catches the colors of the spectrum in the drops of rain or mist, producing the rainbow. Chingawassa Springs in Marion County was also known as Rainbow Lake.[9] In Wilson County a branch of Fall River was named Rainbow Creek, and Cowley County had a Rainbow Bend.

There was a geological period when Kansas was under water. The quarries in eastern Kansas from Moline to Ottawa reveal strata that contain a variety of sea-shells and coral. In western Kansas, the cretaceous layers contain petrified fish and other forms of primitive sea life. During the Tertiary period, there was a phase known as the Miocene, during which much of life evolved. Miocene means "recent," but that is by geological time. Leavenworth County had a station named Miocene.[10]

Many fossil remains of coral, sponge, and shells are found in Greenwood County, and there, where the shell-rock is exposed, were post offices named Shell Rock and Shell Rock Falls. There, too, is Shell Rock Township.

Benjamin Franklin Mudge, professor of natural science at Kansas State University, was impressed by the fossil remains of the large lizards found in Phillips County. He suggested naming a stream "Salurian Creek," and the place where he collected fossils "Salurian Point." Perhaps he had in mind the Silurian period, too early for the Saurians. In keeping with the fossil remains in the area, a stream was named Saurian Creek.[11]

In the cretaceous country of Russell County a stream was named Fossil Creek. On its banks was the Fossil Creek Station of a stage line and later of the railroad. Eventually the name was shortened to Fossil. Lacking popular appeal except to the fossil hunter, Fossil was changed to Russell. The street through which U.S. Highway 281 runs is still called Fossil Street as a reminder of the original name of the town.

Kansas has many streams, thousands of springs, and a few natural lakes, supplemented by man-made reservoirs. Its two large river systems, the Kaw and the Arkansas, are important for its water supply. The Smoky Hill and the Kaw are occasionally rampaging streams which flood the rich lowlands, and the Arkansas occasionally diminishes to a little rivulet, barely moistening its sandy bottom. During such a dry spell, a reporter for the *Wichita Eagle* found occasion to announce: "The Arkansas wet its bed again last night."

Oasis is an old Greek word which meant "a fertile or green spot in a waste of desert." In Kansas, Saline County was the first to have a place named Oasis. A second Oasis was located in Logan County, and a post office in Smith County was twice named Oasis. The name was evidently popular; as soon as one Oasis post office was closed, another chose the name.

Springs had a special appeal to travelers and settlers. These natural fountains supplied man with not only liquid to quench his thirst but also medicine for his many ailments. The chemical contents of the springs were carefully checked for their medicinal values, especially for their level of Epsom salts. "We cure when doctors fail" was the slogan of some health resorts. Most of the waters of medicinal springs were ill-tasting, but patients were led to believe that "the worse the taste, the quicker the cure."

Springs were named with as much care or abandon as the creeks, rivers, and towns. Many of their names became the names of towns, townships, and post offices. Baughman listed thirty-four post offices whose names ended with Spring and sixteen more names which started with Spring.[12] Of the six places named Springfield, all were named after another Springfield, with the possible exception of Springfield north of Newton, now defunct.[13] Names of springs were descriptive, like Big Springs; associated with events, like Wagon Bed Springs; or identified by a personal name, like Bonner Springs. A spring called Old Fountain in Miami County was renamed Fontana. Big Springs near Lawrence was named "from several large springs from which beautifully clear water in abundance gushes forth," said Julia Lovejoy in 1858.[14] The place had been known as "Coon Hollow Camp."[15] Also with emphasis on size were Big Indian Spring in Sherman County and Jumbo Spring in Greeley County.

Early travelers were fully aware of the need for water. Ben Jones discovered Diamond Springs when he traveled ahead of George Sibley to survey the Santa Fe Trail, and Sibley first named it Jones' Spring. Colonel St. George Cooke called it "A true Diamond of the Desert," and "a Pearl of the Prairie . . . ."[16] But it was better known as "Diamond of the Plains or Diamond Spring." Sibley, who camped there in June, 1827, said: "I made requisition of 'Big John' Walker and his carving implements . . . to inscribe on the stooping elm 'Diamond of the Plain'."[17] The town named Diamond Springs, also called Diamond City, was located about five miles from the famous oasis. Diamond Springs was the source for the name of Diamond Creek and Diamond Valley Township. Diamond Springs post office was moved to Six Mile Creek, but Diamond Springs is still a railway station in Morris County.

"Big John" Walker, a guide on Sibley's second survey of the Santa Fe, was a Sac chief from Wisconsin. He discovered a spring "bubbling from the roots of a branching oak." He brought its cool water to Major Sibley, who instructed him to carve "Big John's Spring" on an oak tree. Big John Creek is east of Council Grove. Little John Creek, a branch, should have been named the Little Big John Creek.[18] One writer suggested that the spring was called Frémont Spring.[19]

Lost Springs in Marion County is about fifteen miles west of Diamond Springs. The spring, which flows from a bluff, occasionally becomes dry and therefore "lost." Lost Spring was a trading post on the Santa Fe Trail and is now a railway station at the junction of the Santa Fe and Rock Island.[20] Its Indian name, Nee-nee-oke-pi-yah, was also supposed to have meant "lost spring." To the Spaniards it was Agua Perdida.[21]

The Cimarron was like Lost Springs in that its surface water disappeared during the dry spells. A dry stretch west of the Arkansas made it essential for travelers on the Santa Fe Trail to reach water at the Cimarron. Water was equally important for cattle drovers. Mr. Hardesty, a rancher near Coolidge, discovered that water could be obtained by digging into the dry sand of the river bed. Finding an abandoned wagon nearby, his men dug a pit in the sand and lowered the wagonbox into the depression, where water gradually seeped in.[22] The place had several names, such as Cimarron Springs, Lower Cimarron Springs, Wagon Bed Springs, and Wagon Springs.[23]

Two springs on the Fort Wallace Trail in Greeley County combined to make an attractive camping place for travelers. A barrel was dug in at the spring to retain an adequate supply of water, so this one was named Barrel Springs.[24]

Lieutenant Julian R. Fitch was a member of the surveying group that laid out the Butterfield stage line along the Smoky Hill. Fitch's Meadows west of Big Spring Station was named for him. Not far away was Louisa Springs, believed to have been named for Fitch's wife. Lieutenant Fitch is also credited with naming several stations in the area, including Grinnell Springs, not far from the present town of Grinnell. Smoky Hill Spring was about thirty-six miles farther west.[25]

The town of Chautauqua, with its Iroquois Indian name, was first called Chautauqua Springs. These springs were noted for their "miraculous cures." Like many others, this one declined when the state legislature stopped cure-all advertising in 1903.[26]

Wakonda was probably the most famous spring in Kansas. The Kansa Indians called it Ne-Woh'kon-daga or Ne Wakonda, "the great spirit springs." The *Wakon* was in the Siouan language the "great spirit" and "the creator."[27] Because of its minerals, the spring was also called the Great Spirit Salt Spring. It was assumed by the Indians that its minerals had great medicinal value, and this attribute was later exploited by the white man, even to the point of making beer from its waters. The place called Waconda Springs has become part of man-made Lake Waconda.

According to legend, Wakonda was the name of an Indian maid

who had helped a wounded warrior of a rival tribe. The two fell in love, but only with the approval of the respective tribes could they obtain permission to marry. One council which met to consider the problem of breaking tribal traditions broke instead into open conflict and war. The young Indian lover was shot while standing on the rim of the spring and fell into its deep water. Seeing this, Wakonda plunged into the spring to join her lover in death. From then on, many Indian tribes have come to Ne Wakonda to perform their rituals and to seek health from its healing waters.[28]

Seven springs on the Sumner-Cowley County border were known to the Ponca Indians as Geuda, meaning "healing waters."[29] They could have been named Seven Springs, as were those in Scott County. Seven Springs near Kansas Falls on the Smoky Hill are also called Mair's Springs. Indians came many miles to seek the healing influence of Geuda Springs and, like Waconda, it became a health resort for white man as well as red. Geuda was expected to become as well known as Saratoga in New York or the Hot Springs of Arkansas.[30] Some of the springs near the Geuda area were called Salt Springs and had sufficient saline content to make salt.[31]

Sulphur Springs in Cloud County became a post office name in 1875 and later a railway station named Emery.[32] Selzer Springs near the Butler County border should have been Seltzer if it had reference to a chemical. Selzer Springs was the source for the water of Four Mile Creek, known to Wichita residents as the old "Swimming Hole."[33]

Pioneers sought the healing waters of Cave Springs in Elk County, and they planned to make it a "future metropolis." It did have a press and a three-story hotel, but it failed during the depression of 1893 and is now only a relic on the Bert Doze Ranch.[34] Butler County also had its Cave Springs, the name of a station on the Frisco Railway. Only Spring Township is left of this name.[35]

One of the springs in the Baxter Springs area had the unusual name of Calybeate. Who but a chemist would know that Calybeate referred to iron salts?[36]

Merrill Springs, located south of Topeka near Carbondale, were named for M. D. Merrill, a former book publisher from Rock Island, Illinois, who had come to Kansas for his health. Merrill was told that the springs on his farm contained beneficial minerals. He was cautious and had a St. Louis chemist check their mineral content. The springs were declared to have curative minerals "beneficial in healing many ailments through the regulation of the alimentary tract and by means of baths." The Indians had, of course, known this for a long time. Kansas pioneers were told that the springs would cure everything from dyspepsia to insomnia. Backed by Dr. Thomas Lindsay of Topeka, Merrill Springs became so popular that a horse-drawn bus carried Topekans to the spa, where a three-story hotel had been built to accommodate visitors.[37]

Creeks are spring-fed all over Kansas and the simplest and most obvious name for such a creek is to call it Spring Creek. Spring Creek in Doniphan County had its name changed to Kickapoo Creek. According to an early record, forty-four streams were named Spring Creek and to these may be added one Spring Branch and a Spring Brook Township. Six townships were named Spring Creek. A Chautauqua County post office was twice named Spring Creek. The name survived until 1907.

Spring River, "one of the prettiest streams in the state," cuts the southeastern corner of Kansas on its way to Missouri.[38] Eugene Ware thought the Indians named it.[39] The French called it Pomme de Terre.

Spring Creek was fed by the waters of Baxter Springs from which it got its name. The Baxter part of the name came from A. Baxter, or possibly J. Baxter, who was a Universalist missionary, although people who disagreed with him called him a "cantankerous infidel." Baxter Springs was long a popular campsite on the military road.[40]

When the Donner party stopped at the Independence Crossing of the Big Blue on the California Trail, Edwin Bryant was impressed by its "magnificent prairie" and a scenic view which produced a "wild ecstacy of admiration." There, above a waterfall, was a spring which Bryant named Alcove Springs.[41] It became the first home station of the Pony Express. What disparity there must have been between the appreciation of the beautiful scenery along the Blue in Kansas and the desperation of the Donners in the unconquerable snow of the Sierras in California.

Many of the springs had descriptive names, such as Rock Creek Springs, south of Junction City where the Rock Springs Ranch has a 4-H Club summer camp. Rock Springs in Saline County is now Arcola. Spring Valley became the name of a township and post office in McPherson County. Round Springs post office and Round Spring Township were located in Mitchell County. There were other springs characterized by their contents such as Wea Tar Spring and Dale's Oil Spring in eastern Kansas where the Kansas oil industry got started.[42]

The following names may illustrate the wide use of the word "spring" in place-names. There were Crystal Springs in Harper County and Mud Springs in Douglas County, Twin Springs in Finney County, and a Twin Springs post office in Linn County. There was a Springdale in Leavenworth County and a Spring Dale in Sumner County, a Springvale in Pratt County, a Springville in Washington County, Spring Hill in Johnson County, Spring Lake in Meade County, and a Springside in Pottawatomie County. Spring Valley was first a name in Leavenworth County and then in McPherson County. Spring Place in Johnson County was changed to Glenwood.[43] There was a Cold Spring in Allen County and another in Ness County. Doniphan County once had a Cold Spring station on the Pottawatomie Trail.[44]

But no post office in Kansas was named Hot Springs. Kansas might have imitated a procedure in California where the wind in the desert turned the windmill so fast and with so much friction that the water came up hot. So the real estate men named the place "Desert Hot Springs."[45]

Equally important among the names of springs were those named for people, but not all people were equally important. A name like John Brown Spring is interesting, even when the name was possibly used mistakenly. The Orville C. Brown Spring was named for "Osawatomie Brown," one of the founders of Osawatomie. Governor Hoch is accused of making a double error when he christened the battleship *Kansas* with water instead of champagne and said the water came from the John Brown Spring at Osawatomie, when actually it was Orville C. Brown Spring water. If it were from a John Brown Spring, it would have been from Linn County and not from Miami County.[46] As for using water for the christening of a ship named for Carry Nation's Kansas, one may accept its propriety without assuming that the iron-clad *Kansas* remained permanently dry.

Moodyville Springs, named for Sargent and Ben Moody in Pottawatomie County, wisely shortened its name to Moody Springs. Fuller Springs in Ness County was named for John Fuller. Baptiste Springs was named for Baptiste Peoria, a well-known Indian interpreter.[47]

When pioneers in Brown County found a number of skulls scattered about, they assumed they had found the site of a battle, so they named the place Skull Springs.[48]

A post office in Seward County had its name changed from Harwoodville to Fargo Springs. The Harwoodville came from the Harwood Ranch. Fargo Springs was named for C. H. Fargo, a shoe manufacturer of Chicago, who owned some land in the area.[49] Neither Fargo Springs nor its rival Springfield survived, but Fargo's name remains on a township.

Chingawassa or Shingawassa Springs northwest of Marion was said to be named for a Kansa chief, but there was also an Osage chief named Shingawassa, better known as Black Dog. The Marion Belt and Shingawassa Springs Railroad indicates the importance of this popular resort. As the place declined in popularity, it became a quarry and consequently was renamed Quarry or Quarry Siding.[50] It was a productive quarry, and much of the stone in the State Capitol came from Chingawassa Springs or Quarry.[51]

Shallow Water was named for a place where water could be found within twenty feet of the surface. It is in the area where White Woman Creek runs underground. Shallow Water, south of Scott City, advertised the available water in the "Shallow Water Empire."[52] There is also a Lake Township in Scott County, but the lake is named Dry Lake.

One might think that Kansas is too flat to have waterfalls, but its long slope from Colorado does provide enough rocky ledges to have a few short falls and several rapids, providing water power for mills. Most of these have contributed to the list of appealing place-names in Kansas. Kansas Falls west of Junction City was at the end of the mail route in 1858, and it became a post office and town. It was a popular camping ground but is now only a name on a railroad.[53]

Fall River, flowing out of the Flint Hills, has given its name to Fall River in Greenwood County and to Elk Falls in Elk County. Valley Falls on the Delaware River gots its name to replace the unpopular name of Grasshopper Falls. Neosho Falls and Neosho Rapids in Woodson County and Lyon County were named for the Neosho River. The "riffles above this town is responsible for the name" of Neosho Falls.[54]

The Verdigris, a fast-flowing stream as it leaves the Flint Hills, was the source for naming Shell Rock Falls and the Verdigris Falls in Greenwood County. This county also had a post office named Twin Falls. These are in the scenic area on the eastern slope of the Flint Hills.

The Solomon Rapids on the Solomon River in Mitchell County was the source for Solomon Rapids Township and a station named Solomon Rapids on the Union Pacific. Ballard Falls or Ballard's Falls on the Little Blue in Washington County was named for D. E. Ballard, who was active in organizing the county.[55] There, too, were Granite Falls and Marble Falls.

Ozro Falls was the name of a post office in Chautauqua County. It was located on the Caney River but later discontinued. Later the name was revived as Ozro for a station east of Cedarvale. No other place in the world has such a name, it seems. Being in a Norwegian community, Ozro may have a Scandinavian origin.[56] Pioneers in Chautauqua County believe it was a personal name.

The creeks in Kansas form a vast drainage system which resembles the branches of a tree, converging in the Kaw and the Arkansas, which join the Mississippi to disgorge into the Gulf of Mexico. The Indians, explorers, and pioneers named the creeks for some association with events, people, and description. There was much repetition of tree names and descriptive names such as sand, rock, crooked, straight, long, short, dry, wet, or muddy.[57] Irene Paden, tracing the pioneer routes of the prairie schooners, was annoyed by the repetition of names. "A noticeable rift in my otherwise sweet disposition," said she, "is due entirely to the maddening habit of using the same name again and again, so characteristic of early travelers."[58]

While driving alongside a stream in the mountains one may easily fall victim to the illusion that it flows uphill. On the Mormon Trail beyond the Big Blue, a stream flowing into the Republican was called Uphill Creek. A creek on the level would not be a creek but a slough, yet Morris County had a creek named Level. With such deceptive names, it is not strange that a creek which flows into the Cheyenne Bottoms has been named Deception Creek. It seemingly disappears.

Some creeks were named by the mile and some by their length or distance from a given point. These names ran from One Mile Creek east of Fort Riley to One Hundred and Forty-two Mile Creek in Lyon County. Map makers found it convenient to write "142 Creek." Two Mile Creek was two miles from the flagstaff at Fort Leavenworth. Seven Mile Creek nearby was seven miles in length. Eight Mile Creek on the Oregon Trail was a station with a tavern where David Harley served beverages for thirsty travelers. Similar mileage names were given to the creeks and stations near Fort Riley. In Clay County a series of converging creeks is called Five Creeks, numbered consecutively. Even a township is named Five Creeks. On the Santa Fe Trail, One Hundred and Ten Mile Crossing was on One Hundred and Ten Mile Creek, the estimated distance from Independence, Missouri, or Sibley. It was actually less. One Hundred and Ten Mile post office was one of the candidates for the state capital.[59] It did receive one vote. Creeks named by the mile were found all across the state and with a great deal of repetition. There were eleven creeks named Four Mile.

Among the more interesting men for whom creeks were named was P. M. Thompson, a buffalo hunter known as "Smoky Hill Thompson." Thompson Creek flows into the Smoky Hill from the south in Ellsworth County. According to the stories told about Thompson, he not only killed buffalo, "he plowed with buffaloes, harnessing them with rope made of their own hair." The buffalo calves he owned were lost in a buffalo stampede.[60]

Switzler Creek, which the Santa Fe Trail crossed beyond "142 Mile" Creek, was named for a pioneer "who was run over and killed by a wagon, while descending the eastern bank . . . ."[61] The Switzler Crossing was near the present Burlingame.

Names could be used for effect, as illustrated by "Horned Toad"

Harry, who, upon entering a saloon in Caldwell, announced his residence as "the headwaters of Bitter Creek near Pizon Rocks in Rattlesnake Bend."[62] As for Bitter Creek, that was genuine and became the name of a Sumner County post office.

Kansas is well drained by its streams, which leave few lakes. Silver Lake, west of Topeka, was created by the Kaw cutting off an oxbow bend. It was the center of an Indian community and occupied by white settlers before the territory was open to settlement. Most of these white men married Indian women and their children acquired Indian lands. Silver Lake in Silver Lake Township was both a post office and railway station. [63]

McPherson County has two lakes. One had the Swedish name of Lake Farland, and the other was named Lake Inman for Major Henry Inman. These are connected by Blaze Fork of the Little Arkansas, and this connection gave rise to their name as "Chain Lakes."[64]

Most lakes in Kansas now are reservoirs created by control of the watershed. Many of these are state park lakes or county lakes and bear the names of the county or nearest town. There are, for example, El Dorado City Lake and Bluestem Lake. McKinley Lake in Linn County was named for M. C. McKinley, a member of the Izaak Walton Club, who promoted the lake.[65] Lake McKinney is a part of the Kearny County State Park and was named for J. R. McKinney, a pioneer in the sugar beet industry.[66] This lake is a part of the irrigation system. Lakeview in Douglas County had an attractive name but no lake to view. Another case where the name has no water connection is Lake City in Barber County. This one got its name from Reuben Lake, a pioneer who settled there in 1873 with his son Riley.[67]

Early place-names in Kansas indicate that explorers and pioneers were impressed by the presence of water. The Indians were always conscious of the need for water. The French were constantly aware of it.

CHAPTER III

TON BURNS BURR OAK BURRTON BUSHONG BUSHTON BYERS CAIRO CALDWELL CALVERT CAMBRI

HILLS, HIGHLANDS, AND LOWLANDS

US CANEY CANTON CARBONDALE CARLTON CARNEIRO CASSODAY CAWKER CITY CEDAR CEDAR B

LOCAL NOMENCLATURE," said a writer many years ago, "while more immediately related to geography, is also intimately and indissolubly connected with history."[1] From place-names, we may learn much about the topography and general environment of Kansas. And although it is occasionally elusive, there is behind each name a history and a personal reaction to nature.

The first impressions of Kansas, reported by Zebulon Pike and Stephen H. Long, were not favorable. It took some time to dispel the impression that Kansas was a desert, fit only for prairie dogs and Indians. Kansas later severed Colorado from its western edge because the land between was uninhabitable. The Dust Bowl created by the hot, dry years of the "dirty thirties" seemed to support the desert reputation. The impressive agricultural production of Kansas has, however, disproved the opinion that Kansas is only a dusty plain. Those who are skeptical about the conquest of the desert should read *Deserts on the March*, by Paul B. Sears.

Much of Kansas is almost flat, but the variety of its topography is indicated by its descriptive place-names. The names of its hills, highlands, bluffs, mesas, and mounds should call attention to the irregular, upland character of the country. In the flowery words of John J. Ingalls:

> The stranger who crossed our borders for the first time at Wyandotte and travelled by rail to White Cloud would with consternation contrast that uninterrupted Sierra of rugose and oak-clad crags with the placid prairies of his imagination. Let him ride along the spine of any of those lateral "divides" or water-sheds whose "level leagues forsaken lie, a grassy waste, extending to the sky."[2]

Yet he was describing only one corner of Kansas.

Some writers have divided Kansas, like Gaul, into three geographical parts: the eastern portion with its wooded streams, the highlands of the Flint Hills, and the High Plains in the west. Kansas is wearing down from the west, exposing lower strata as one moves eastward. It is 4,135

21

feet in altitude on its western border and drops to a mere 700 feet at its lowest level in Montgomery County. There is, however, too much variety in its topography to limit the description of Kansas to simply three divisions.

Northeastern Kansas has a glacier drift which has brought gravel and Lake Superior agates all the way to Topeka. The hills of southeastern Kansas have been called the Osage Cuestas, using the name of its Osage inhabitants and the Spanish *cuestas* for "hills." There we find the Cherokee Lowlands, the Chautauqua Hills, and the Osage Plains. West of these are the Flint Hills, running from north to south.

The north-central area is cut by the Smoky Hill and the Kansas River and their tributaries. The Arkansas River has made its own lowland valley across the west with a bend to the north and then a sharp turn southward into Oklahoma.[3] It once flowed through the Cheyenne Bottoms and joined the Kaw on its way to the Missouri. Then the river was diverted from the south and made a big bend and headed for Oklahoma and Arkansas.[4] That is how Great Bend got its name.

One-third of western Kansas is in the High Plains and the shortgrass country. There the cactus may flourish but the buffalograss kept it from becoming a desert. South of the central valley of the Arkansas is a region dominated by the Dakota sandstone which contributed the names of the Red Hills and the Red Fork of the Arkansas. The sand and salt in the streams, the color of the water and the soil, the trees along the stream beds, and the hills all suggested descriptive names for the area.

When Kansas was a territory, it encompassed the eastern slope of the Rockies. After statehood it lost the mountain country, once known as "the gold fields of Kansas." There are still a few uses of "mountain" and many uses of "mount" as a part of place-names. Most of these names are descriptive; others are borrowed names which have no relationship with the topography of Kansas. Mount Vernon, Mount Hope, and Mount Gilead are in no way related to local highlands.

There are highland areas in Kansas which have regional names of distinction, such as the Flint Hills, the Smoky Hills, the Blue Hills, the Gypsum Hills,[5] and the Ozarks. These names are well known, yet they need interpretation.

The Ozarks border on eastern Kansas, but the Kansas ridges which are called the Ozarks were highlands between the watershed of the Neosho and the Osage, northeast of Yates Center and extending through Coffey County into Anderson County. These hills are called the "Ozark Mountains of Kansas." More modest and realistic writers have referred to these highlands as the "Ozark Ridge" or the "Ozark Range." From the summit of the Ozark Mountain, said Isaac Moffatt, one may look for miles over receding hills, woodlands, and valley.[6]

In Anderson County, Ozark also became the name of a town, a township, and a post office.[7] This area on the watershed was also called the Narrows. The railroad called it the Great Divide and from this a post office was named Divide. Its name was changed from Divide to Colony when it was settled by an organized colony from Ohio and Indiana.[8]

The Flint Hills form a broad north-south strip east of the central part of Kansas. "Commenced our march at seven o'clock," said Captain Pike, "and passed some very rough flint hills."[9] The Flint Hills name was applied to the limestone hills by the settlers and spread to cover the whole range. Flint Hills has been called a misnomer by those who prefer "Blue Stem Hills." The hills are in the bluestem grass country and the name frequently used in the twenties was "Kansas Bluestem Region." Even the name "Limestone Pastures" is more meaningful than "Flint Hills," and it has also been suggested that the name could well be the "Bluestem-Limestone Pastures." This is, of course, too long. It leaves out the flint, but it is descriptive, appropriate, and accurate. The name adopted by the Kansas State Board of Agriculture in 1929 was "The Blue-Stem Pasture Region of Kansas." So it is, but no one is likely to substitute that for what is more readily called the Flint Hills.[10] The cattlemen know the richness of the bluestem grass of the area and the value of the limestone. It is the leaching of the Permian limestone which leaves the harder chert and flint that justifies the Flint Hills name.[11] In Elk County the Flint Hills became Flint Ridge. In Greenwood County a post office was named Flint Ridge and later Flintridge.

The Indians found the Flint Hills attractive, and there they collected the nodules of "blue" flint which they shaped into a variety of implements. But the white man found these hills to be "the most beautiful scenery of serenity and quiet." According to Rolla Clymer of El Dorado, the Flint Hills were characterized by "a stillness and tranquility." Another referred to the hills as "Peace on Earth."[12]

The Smoky Hills may have been named for the smoke from Indian camps in the valley of the Smoky Hill River, or possibly for the smoke-like mist that settled in the valley.[13] These hills were also called the Smoky Hill Bluffs. Like mountains, hills tend to look blue in the distance, especially towards evening. These hills near Lindsborg are now known as the Coronado Heights. In the Salina area Iron Butte, Soldier Cap, and North Pole Mound are found as individual names among the Smoky Hill Buttes.[14]

The Blue Hills in Mitchell County were named for the blue-gray coloring of the exposed Pierre shale. That this was once an ocean bottom is indicated by the number of scaphites, ammonites, and shark's teeth found in the area. The natives knew them as the Blue Hills and so did the Spaniards. Pedro Vial, exploring the Santa Fe Trail from the south in the 1790's, gave the hills the Spanish name of La Loma Azul.[15] The Blue Hill post office took its name from the Blue Hills, as did the Blue Hill Creek, the Blue Hills School not far from Tipton, and Blue Hill Township.[16] To the north of the Blue Hills is a large hill called Lone Hill.

Rooks County has several hills which were conspicuous enough to have been given individual names, and one of these was called Blue Hill, from which another Blue Hill post office got its name. The highlands in Rooks County also included the names of Sugar Loaf Mound, Twin Mounds, Mount Horeb, and a place called Highhill.

The Blue Hill on the Missouri border evoked this eloquent outburst by Max Greene: "Overlooking the confluent rivers, Blue Hill, in flowing vestments of verdure, stands as in priestly benediction of the nuptials of the lordly Kanza with his impetuous and willing bride."[17]

Important among the highlands was Bluemont, the site of Blue Mont or Bluemont College, now Kansas State University at Manhattan. Bluemont has a magnificent view of the Big Blue, which joins the Kaw at Manhattan. John C. Frémont, who once camped at its base, is given credit for naming Blue Mont.[18] It is only 215 feet high and scarcely measures up to its name. It could be a feeling of restraint that caused people to add the word "hill" to the "mont."

Other college names continue the use of "Mont" or "Mount," but only the wildest stretch of the imagination could justify the names on the basis of geography. Marymount at Salina has no great geographical eminence; Fairmount College in Wichita is "Fairmount on the Hill" in its college song. Since it is on the rise of land above the bottom lands of the Arkansas River, it has a moderate claim to a "hill" description, but certainly no "mount." Highland College in Doniphan County may be added to the list, but the name came from Illinois and not from its elevation. In listing the Kansas college names, one may see their emphasis on highlands: Mount Oread, Bluemont College, Fairmount College, Marymount College, Mount Scholastica, and Highland College.

A surprisingly wide choice of names was used for the highlands of Kansas. They included mount, mountain, mound, ridge, bluff, butte, peak, point, and summit. Each of these had its own description to give it distinction, and yet there was also some confusing repetition.

The Bible furnished a long list of place-names in Kansas which use the word "mount." Among them are such familiar names as Mount Gilead,

Mount Horeb, Mount Zion, and others.[19] Some were borrowed from eastern states, like Mount Oread, the beautiful setting of the University of Kansas. Mount Oread, with its New England source, is much more attractive than earlier descriptive names of "Hog Back Point" and "The Devil's Backbone." Unpopular as these might be, a station west of Hays was named Hog Back.

Local interest inspired the names of Mount Jesus, Mount Sterling, Mount Mitchell, and Mount Prospect. In Riley County, Mount Prospect was across the river from Bluemont. The "Prospect" evidently referred to the view which was said to be "perfectly enchanting."[20] Mount Helen and Mount Ida were named for Kansas women.

Kansas had nineteen post offices whose names began with Mount, but none starting with Mountain. Yet the mountain name was used. Marshall County has a Mountain Creek, which flows into Horseshoe Creek from the south. In writing about "Pike's Pawnee Village," a pioneer spoke of locating an Indian village on "Boat Mountain, south of the White River."[21] He may have referred to White Rock Creek. The use of mountain as a name would appear to be a misnomer, but Boat Mountain may be defended as a descriptive name. Guthrie Mountain in Bourbon County was only two hundred feet high. The Guthrie name was that of a man who was hanged by vigilantes there.[22]

No state should be without a high point which could be named Lookout Mountain. There were two in Kansas. The one in Doniphan County was a spur of the Devil's Backbone above Wolf Creek. In Chautauqua County, Lookout Mountain was once considered as a prospective townsite for Cedarvale. It is believed locally that the name was suggested by Civil War veterans.[23] This is the one in Kansas which looks most like a mountain, according to Arch O'Bryant, a *Wichita Beacon* columnist. The valley from which Cedarvale was named was also called Lookout Valley. These highlands of Chautauqua County have been called "Table Mounds" and described as "the crowning glory of Chautauqua County."

Any high point, especially if it appeared to be the highest, could be named Summit, although Ness County had a Highpoint and Greenwood County had a Hilltop. South of Hilltop is Climax, also said to be named for its summit. Near Leavenworth, Moore's Summit, named for Captain Crawford Moore, a local landowner, had its name shortened to Summit.[24] Hall's Summit in the Ozark range of Coffey County was also shortened to Summit. A railway station on the Santa Fe in Cowley County is called Grand Summit. Both Butler County and Osage County had high points named Summit. On the watershed between the Blue and the Republican, the highest point in Washington County had its name changed from Linn to Summit.[25] Ellsworth County has a Summit Spring, and a high point on the railway east of Ellsworth was for a time known as Summit Siding.[26]

Avoiding repetition of Summit was possible by substituting its Greek name. As linguists know, there is a lot of Greek in our English. The first Akron was in Douglas County and the next one in Dickinson County. In Cowley County, Akron replaced the name of Little Dutch. It is not on a summit but in the lowlands of the Walnut Valley. So the name was far from being descriptive and was most likely borrowed from Akron, Ohio. Acme, once the name of a town southwest of Abilene, is another Greek word for "top" or "highest point."

Rome was built on seven hills, each with its own distinctive name and its own history. Repetition was not uncommon in the naming of hills, as we have seen in the use of blue, but the many names for the hills gave variety to the place-names in Kansas. These descriptive terms could be color, such as blue, black, white, green or red; contour, like flattop, round, mushroom, or mansard; atmosphere, such as fragrant, pleasant, or breezy; and, finally, the highlands, whatever name was used, could be associated with people or places, such as Osage Hills, Chicago Mound, or Hall's Summit.

Hills were named for pioneers who may have left no other record, although names of distinguished men were also used. There is Hodgson's Hill in Wabaunsee County, supposedly a site for buried treasure.[27] Sleigh's Hill near Oxford was a limestone quarry. Then there was the more famous Cody Hill in Leavenworth County where "Buffalo Bill" Cody lived and where his mother ran a hotel after his father had been killed by proslavery men. The hotel on a hill was named "Valley Grove House."[28] There was a place in eastern Kansas called Anatomy Hill because so many personal names in the community were the same as the names for parts of the human body, such as Hart, Foote, Shinn, and Legg.[29]

Names like Hill City and Hillsboro were names derived from people and not topography. Both towns were named for the owners of the townsites. W. R. Hill was the landowner of the Hill City site in Graham County. He was a popular man and yet he aroused considerable criticism when he helped to promote the Negro town of Nicodemus.[30]

Hillsboro in Marion County was named for John G. Hill, who not only owned the townsite but also served several terms as its mayor. Both Hill City and Hillsboro were located on slight rises and this would doubly justify their names.[31] For a short time, two other towns were named Hillsboro. One was in Linn County, changed to Potosi; and the other, in Morris County, changed to Dunlap.

Rocky Hill was once the county seat of Lincoln County. There the Rocky Hill dam was seriously damaged by the "cantankerosity" of a flood on the Saline.[32] There was a Stony Hill in Norton County, a Silica Hill in Meade County, and a Silver Hill in Linn County.

Breezy Hill in Crawford County was an appropriate name where the Kansas zephyrs are likely to blow into a breeze at any time. Fragrant Hill in Dickinson County must have come from the fragrant appeal of flowers. Marshall County had a Cottage Hill. Similar descriptive names were Hillside in Phillips County, Hillside Farm in Harvey County, and Hillsdale in Miami County. Then there were hills named for their trees: Walnut Hill in Bourbon County, Maple Hill in Wabaunsee County, Oak Hill in Clay County, and a Poplar Hill in Dickinson County.

The borders of Kansas creeks and rivers form into bluffs, giving Kansas six Bluff Creeks. They flow into the Cimarron, the Smoky Hill, Rock Creek in Lyon County, Onion Creek in Montgomery County, and the Big Blue in Pottawatomie County, and one flows out of Harper County into the Chikaskia in Oklahoma. That one was called Pa-ha-bee by the Indians who named it for its "bluffs."

Bluff City in Harper County was named for Bluff Creek. It was first named Bluff, then Bluff Creek post office, and finally Bluff City. It is not a "city," and some call it simply "Bluff," but the name remains as Bluff City. There was a place named Bluffville on Bluff Creek in Ellsworth County. Sumner and Harper counties have townships named Bluff. To give its altitude distinction, a bluff near White Cloud in Doniphan County was named Crest of Bluff. Crest of Bluff is meticulous rather than redundant.

Like the hills, the bluffs were occasionally named for people. There was Weibly Bluff in Neosho County, named for John C. Weibly, a pioneer. The view was superb from its top, and the Osages had used it for a lookout.[33]

Red Bluff in Clark County was a town started by promoters from Winfield. Being only four miles from Protection it lost its postal service. There were red bluffs and a Bluff Creek in the area, which justified both names.[34] A post office in Meade County was named Redbluff in 1903. The Red Bluffs west of Topeka got their name from "the peculiar light brown of the soil," said Max Greene. The color was more brown than red, suggesting a "mulatto color."[35]

Granite Bluff was a post office in Phillips County, where there is also a Granite Township, but it may be a misnomer. The chief outcrop of granite in Kansas is Red Dome near Yates Center in Woodson County. The word "granite" in Granite Creek in Cloud County also appears to be inaccurate.[36] Perhaps the quartzite or sandstone looked like granite.

Man-made hills are generally called mounds, and these may be associated with Indian structures. But in Kansas mounds and hills were terms which were used interchangeably. The mounds in Montgomery County have been described as "peak-shaped" and others as "capped with almost level plain." This explains a name such as Table Mound, which was also known as Walker's Mound for a local settler.[37] White Mound near White Rock Creek in Jewell County in north-central Kansas was named for the near-white limestone. It left its name on White Mound Township. Flat Top Hill in Clay County is also called Table Mound.[38]

Bender Mounds in Labette County call attention to a notorious family of murderers named Bender. Under the guise of frontier hospitality, travelers seated at their supper table would lean against a curtain behind which a member of the family waited with an axe or club. The Bender Mounds are small hills west of Parsons.[39]

There are other personal names of mounds such as Jacob's Mound in Chase County, named for a preacher; and Wadsworth Mound, which might better have been named John Brown's Mound, because it was from this vantage point that the vigilant Brown kept watch for Border Ruffians.[40] The Wadsworth may have been J. F. Wadsworth, elected assessor of Anderson County in 1858.[41]

Potato Mound on a branch of the Pottawatomie was the meeting place for a number of Border Ruffians from Missouri. After John Brown and the "Pottawatomie Rifles" drove the Border Ruffians out, Potato Mound became known as Battle Mound.[42]

Moundville in Linn County had its name changed to Mound City. Mound Valley was named for a row of hills in Labette County. Miami County had a Mound Creek. Pioneers living in Miami County on Mound Creek in Mound Creek Township liked this name well enough to have their post office name of Trenton changed to Mound Creek.[43]

Cherry Mound in Anderson County, a post office and station on the Humboldt stage line, was named for Cherry Creek. It is now only the name of a church and a community center.[44]

At Mound Ridge the mound is barely visible. First the township was named Mound Ridge. Names proposed for the town included Christian Othea and Hill City. Then Mound Ridge, changed to Moundridge, was suggested by D. P. Jones, who was directing the building of the Missouri Pacific Railway in the area.[45] The mound or ridge which supposedly justified the name was only a slight elevation above Black Kettle Creek.[46]

Sugar Mound in Linn County got its name from the sugar maple. The post office changed the name to Mound City.[47] Sugar Loaf Mound in Rooks County was named for its shape. For this name, the post office deleted the Mound. Sugar Bowl Mound in Norton County was a local landmark with an impressive view on the divide overlooking the Prairie Dog.[48] Tea Pot Mound near Matfield Green is named for its shape. There may be oil in the area, but no Tea Pot Dome of unsavory fame. Walker's Mound was later changed to Table Mound.[49]

Paint Creek in McPherson County enters the Smoky Hill from the south near Lindsborg. There were the Paint Creek Mounds where Coronado encountered the Wichita Indians. The Paint Creek Mounds may be a good introduction to names associated with color.

Like the Blue Hills, mounds were also given the name of this favorite color. Places named Blue Mound were at both ends of the state. In Linn County, the postmaster, who had the distinguished name of John Quincy Adams, named Blue Mound because "from a distance it looks blue." The post office moved about the neighborhood to four different sites, keeping the same name except for a few days when it was called Babcock.[50] Mound City in Bourbon County was named for another Blue Mound, but the "city" did not survive. Mound City in Linn County did.[51] The Blue Mounds in Cherokee County remained only a topographical name. Blue Mound near Blue Jacket's Crossing of the Wakarusa was named for its "darkly timbered" slopes.[52] The Blue Mounds in Wallace County were near the Colorado border. Verdi Mound also has a color designation even though it is only the "green" half of the Verdigris, "green-gray" in French. The Verdi Mounds are near Neodesha.

Chief Little Bear, or Metsoshinka, established his Osage village at the base of a mound between Fall River and the Verdigris. He took his tribe to the Little River near Wichita for their summer hunts. There Little Bear, a portly and friendly chief, enjoyed the hospitality of John Ross as long as the coffee and flour held out. The chief lies buried at Little Bear Mound near Neodesha.[53] Little Bear Creek in Barber County may also be named for the Osage chief.

Hills and mounds frequently come in pairs, and such combinations called for appropriate names. There were Twin Mounds in at least seven counties: Cloud, Marshall, Norton, Osage, Wilson, Douglas, and Lincoln. Twin Mounds in Norton County was a voting district.[54] Twin Mound was a post office in Douglas County, but Twin Mounds in Wilson County was too near to Fredonia to get a post office. Only in Lincoln County were the Twin Mounds identical. Henry Inman was so impressed by the similarity of the Twin Mounds that he said that "they are so exactly similar, even to two patches of limestone on their southwestern slopes, that their name would immediately suggest itself to a stranger, for never were twins born so perfect in resemblance as these dual masses of disrupted rock."[55]

Finally, there was Half Mound Station in Jefferson County. As a post office it became Halfmound. It has lost its official status as a station and as a post office and is again Half Mound.

"Twin" could be descriptive of buttes as well as mounds. Twin Buttes in Barber County west of Medicine Lodge, which are actually mesas, give a distinct character to the scenery of Kansas. There, too, were the Mansard Buttes. Twin Buttes are in the rugged country referred to as the "Cedar Mountain."[56] Before they were depleted by pilfering fence-post cutters, the dark cedars gave the hills a black appearance. One geologist, looking for fossils west of Sun City, called the highlands "Black Hills."[57]

In approaching the highlands south of Mount Oread, one traveler wrote:

> Before us are the Wakarusa Buttes, from whose summits, conspicuous far out over the swells of verdure, rising in terraced gardens, is the Divide traversed by the Santa Fe Trail and separating the head springs of the Osage from the Wakarusa Valley into which it descends in a series of long strips resembling the slopes of parapets, their platforms changing direction, and forming angles like walls of a bastion.[58]

Below the Wakarusa was the Santa Fe Ridge that the rails followed towards Emporia.[59]

There were many interesting names known locally, such as Soldier Cap Mound, North Pole Mound, and Iron Mound in the Smoky Hill Buttes. There is a Round Mound in Trego County, and another farther south called Round House. Osborne County had a post office named Round Mound. Gove County had an eminence where the "Hackberry sweeps by the base of Round Top."[60]

Wabaunsee County had a Chalk Mound post office but only the Chalk part of the name remains. Jewell County, too, had a Chalk Mound, named for "the soft, white, magnesian limestone on its surface." Its single elevation rising abruptly from the plains was called "a curiosity."[61]

Buffalo Mound is the highest point in Wabaunsee County and deserves the distinction of a name. It was no longer buffalo country when settled but the name may have come from its shape, even though, as one historian said, the "shape bears a stronger resemblance to the back of a dromedary than to anything else."[62]

Townships frequently retained names that post offices lost. One township was named Mound City, two were named Mound Valley, and four were named Mound. Miami County had a Mound Township, a Mound Creek, and a Mound Creek post office. In Wilson County, a place was called West Mound and a post office was named Mound Springs.

Bluffs and cliffs retained their higher positions because of the harder rock which they contained. This was especially noticeable of the mesas or table rocks. Their names could consequently be simply rocks and distinguished by an adjective. Pawnee Rock, one of the best-known markers on the Santa Fe Trail, was an outcrop of Dakota sandstone. It was located near Fort Larned in the buffalo-hunting territory of the Pawnees. Its Pawnee name came supposedly as a result of a battle between the Pawnees and Comanches.[63]

Travelers carved their names in the soft sandstone of the rock, making it look like a hotel register. It was called Red Rock, Painted Rock, and some called it Rock Point. As a natural fortress it became known as the "Prairie Citadel."[64] Settlers have used much of the rock for building material, but what is left of it has now been preserved as a state park through the efforts of the Women's Kansas Day Club.[65]

Point of Rocks on the Cimarron not far from Elkhart was another well-known landmark on the Santa Fe Trail. It had the reputation of being a "famous resort for outlaws" and was known as "Robber's Roost." It has since been the location of a ranch whose buildings are sheltered by the rocks.[66] Nearby was a post office named Taloga which had its name changed to Point Rocks. There was another Point of Rocks near the old site of Fort Mann west of Dodge City.[67]

There were strange formations of eroded rocks in the "badlands" of Kansas. Best known for their strange formations were the Monument Rocks. While surveying for a stage line, Lieutenant J. R. Fitch thought one of these rocks looked like a group of English castles, and so, as he said, "We named it Castle Rock." When the Butterfield stage came through, the station there was named Castle Rock Creek Station.[68] One mile south is Pinnacle Rock.

A fascinating formation of two tall pillars and a capstone in Lincoln County had the appearance of a table and was, of course, named Table Rock. It was composed of soft Dakota sandstone on which were many inscriptions. Now even the rock has gone. There, too, was a Table Rock Creek.[69]

Twenty-eight creeks, seven townships, and three post offices were named Rock Creek. Even the popular Sand Creek name was repeated only twelve times. The three counties having Rock Creek post offices were Pottawatomie, Jefferson, and Lyon. The little town of Rock in Cowley County is in Rock Township and must have taken its name from Rock Creek. Rock Creek post office in Pottawatomie County had its name changed to Louisville. Lyon County later had a post office named Rock Creek. After it closed in 1871, Cooks Ford in Jefferson County changed its name to Rock Creek.

Wabaunsee County had a Rocky Ford for a couple of years, and Riley County now has a railway station named Rocky Ford. On the Military Road from Leavenworth to Fort Riley, a town between Rock Creek and the Vermillion was named Rock City.[70]

Like the Senecas in New York who got their name from a stone near their village, places in Kansas were also named stone. Norton County has a Stony Hill. Cherokee County had a Stone City, Rice County had a Stone Corral, serving both as fort and post office, and Smith County had a Stone Mound. Leavenworth County now has a town named Stone.

Northeastern Kansas is known as the Glacier Uplands.[71] Farther west are the Blue Hills Uplands. Jewell County had a post office named Upland, and after it was closed, a post office in Dickinson County was named Upland.

The hills above the Missouri River in Doniphan County are sufficiently high to justify the use of the name Highland. But Highland was named by William Sugg for Highland, Illinois, the home of Swiss settlers, whom he hoped to encourage to emigrate from there to Kansas.[72] The town was settled on the site of S. M. Irvin's Indian mission. Highland College was founded there. Two distinguished names are associated with this college: Abraham Lincoln once donated $100 for the college, and George Washington Carver was denied admission to it. Highland Station in Doniphan County had its name changed to Sparks, for John Sparks, a local pioneer.[73]

Rocks and hills were trail-markers, fortifications, and observation points as much for the Indian as for the white man. Indian Guide Hill south of Peabody was exactly what the name implied.[74] The highest point in Leavenworth County was named Pilot Knob, and, to make it higher, the Indians had piled rocks on top of it. The Knob evidently served as a guide for the Indians in the area, and its panoramic view was said to be magnificent.[75] Farther south are the Indian Hills, the name of an attractive residential section of Kansas City. Norton County also has a rock-capped hill called Pilot Knob. It was a famous landmark and afforded a good view, but it is now a bit worse for wear.[76]

When many arrowheads were found on a hill in McPherson County, it was assumed that it was the site of an Indian battle, and the place was named Battle Hill,[77] from which Battle Hill Township took its name. Lone Rock in Lincoln County marks a place where Indians fought a battle against railroad workers. Osage Rock in Comanche County was the site of another Indian battle.

Indian Mound north of the Arkansas River, near the Upper Ford and not far from Chouteau's Island, was another hill associated with the Indians. Burnett's Mound, also called "Webster's Peak," south of Topeka was named for Abraham Burnett, a Potawatomi chief, who lies buried on this beautiful 230-foot-high hill. Burnett married the daughter of William Greiffenstein of Wichita. The mound has another Indian name more Indian than Burnett. It was called Shunganunga Mound for Shunganunga Creek.[78] Little Bear Mound or Bear Mound, was also named for the burial place of a chief.[79]

The Arikara Hills in Comanche County are associated with the Arikara River which cuts the northwestern corner of Kansas. The Chippewa Hills in Franklin County were named for the Chippewa or Ojibway Indians from Michigan who were given a reservation in the area.[80]

A group of Osages known as the Big Hill band got their name when they took refuge on a hill to escape a flood in Missouri. Because of this incident, the French named them Gross Côte. From the Big Hill band came such names as the Big Hill Creek in Montgomery County and Big Hill post office in Labette County.[81]

Highlands are perhaps more conspicuous than plains, but the plains of Kansas have a certain distinction when the wheat fields take on the appearance of ocean waves. What was at first West Plains in Meade County is now just Plains in West Plain Township. Plainville in Rooks County describes an area which is not far removed from canyons, mounds, and hills.

Wyckoff Bottoms near Neosho Rapids was the name of bottom land where the grass grew so high that one man said he had to stand on his companion's shoulders "to see the trees and get the right direction." Nearby was the town of Wyckoff, also written Wycoff.[82] Atchison County had Rush Bottoms, which gave its name to Rushville,[83] and a place called Musser's Bottom, named for Joe Musser.[84]

In addition to French Bottoms at Kansas City, Missouri, and French Ridge in Coffey County, Kansas, there was also a Dutch Flats in Ness County. Collar's Flats in Clark County were probably named for Henry or "Hi" Collar, who settled near Mount Jesus.[85] Plum Creek Flats are in Rice County, and Big Flats are in the Sharp's Creek area of McPherson County. Even in the rough Riley County area, lowlands near the place planned for the state capital were called Pawnee Flats. The Missouri Flat in Sumner County would indicate a Missouri settlement. Scott County had a place called Beaver Flats.

Where there are hills there are naturally dales, vales, and valleys. Nearly all the names of valleys have additional descriptive names, but four post offices were named just Valley. These were in Greenwood County, Clark County, Hodgeman County, and in Trego County. Other uses of the name incorporated names of trees, resulting in Oak Valley and Ash Valley. What had been New Memphis in Cherokee County became Star Valley and later Starvale.

Valley Center, a name which was once proposed for Wichita, was adopted for a town in the valley of the Little Arkansas. Valley Falls was the name which replaced Grasshopper Falls because of its greater popular appeal. Mound Hill, Labette County, escaped its redundant name by becoming Mound Valley, being in the valley of Pumpkin Creek.[86]

A number of names describing dales, such as Andale, Zeandale, Carbondale, Sylvandale, and Hillsdale, may be included in other categories. A few were named for pioneers. Zimmerdale lies between Hesston and Newton near East Emma Creek. It was first called Truesdale for W. J. Truesdale, a Mennonite who had proposed having the Mennonite School of the West established there before Hesston was chosen as its site. The Truesdale family had land in Edwards County and there they promoted a town which was then named Truesdale. The Truesdale in Harvey County had its name changed to Zimmerdale for Martin Zimmerman, substituting the "dale" from Truesdale for the "man" in Zimmerman.[87] Glendale and Dellvale are attractive names but the glen, the dell, and the vale vary little in meaning. In Sherdahl, Republic County, the name has a Scandinavian form; in Liebenthal, Rush County, it has a German form. Cowley County once had a place named Dale and Wallace County had a post office named Dale.

All a place needed to have political influence was a name. Springdale, described as an "imaginary town," received twenty-four votes for county seat of Jewell County. "Failing of selection for this honor, Springdale never was born."[88] But its name was attractive enough to have deserved not to die. It could not have become a post office, however, since there was already a Springdale in Leavenworth County.

That part of Kansas known as the High Plains is located in the western third of the state. There are other flat areas, such as the one within the broad valley of the Arkansas River. The towns named Plains in Meade County and Plainville in Rooks County are both logically in the High Plains country. Plains was first called West Plains but being located in the west, that part of the name became superfluous. When Judge Darland suggested the name of Plainville, he did not expect to have it accepted, but it was and is there still.[89] Names like Argonia and

Abilene may also mean "plains" but these names were not chosen to fit the plains of Kansas.

The Kansas pioneers suffered from almost every conceivable hardship, but still they tried to create the impression that Kansas was a pleasant land. Five townships were named Pleasant and seven were named Pleasant Valley. Pleasant Valley in Lincoln County was neither in Pleasant Township nor in Valley Township. To these we add the towns named Pleasant Ridge, Pleasant Green, and Pleasant Grove, Pleasant Spring, and Pleasant View, Pleasant Hill, and Pleasant Dale, and there was also a Pleasant Run. Pleasant Plain in Osborne County had its name changed to Deliverance. Pleasant Grove was so popular that it was used as a place-name in Phillips, Greenwood, and Douglas counties, but only the one in Douglas County survived. A town founded in Atchison County by Thomas Fortune, inventor of a traction engine, was named Mount Pleasant, but this was changed to Locust Grove and then to Potter.[90] After Pleasant Hill died in Osborne County, the name was revived as Pleasanthill in Franklin County.[91] One can only conclude that the hills and valleys, ridges and runs, were pleasing to the eyes of the pioneers.

Such a wide variety of geographical place-names challenged the assumptions of many who believed that Kansas was a plain from one end to the other. The change in point of view may be illustrated by a comment by Horace Greeley. He liked Kansas better than he had expected and said, "The soil is deeper; the timber is more generally diffused; the country more rolling, than I had supposed."[92]

CHAPTER IV

AR POINT CEDAR VALE CENTRALIA CHANUTE CHAPMAN CHARLESTON CHASE CHAUTAUQUA CHE

PRAIRIES AND PRAIRIE FLOWERS

KEE CHERRYVALE CHETOPA CIMARRON CIRCLEVILLE CLAFLIN CLAY CENTER CLAYTON CLEARW

SINCE THE TIME OF CORONADO, the "sublime Prairie Wilderness" of Kansas had been compared to a vast ocean. Captain Pike thought that the prairies were unfit for cultivation and should be left to the "uncivilized aborigines."[1] It was said of Walt Whitman, who traveled across Kansas, that, "Much as the grandeur of the mountains impressed him, the impression of the plains will remain longest with him." There he found "America's characteristic landscape."[2] Kansas was nicknamed the "Prairie Queen."

Pioneers from the East thought that timber was essential for home-building. This "wooden psychology," as Walter Prescott Webb called it, stopped the advance of the frontier on the Missouri border for a quarter of a century. Then it occurred to some that if the prairie could support buffalo, it could also support cattle. Pioneers learned that houses could be built of limestone and prairie sod as well as wood. As the pioneers penetrated the plains, they found the prairies attractive, and "prairie" became a popular descriptive word used in many Kansas place-names.

Senator Ingalls spoke of the "grassy quadrangle which the geographers call Kansas."[3] The most conspicuous grasses were tall bluestem in the east and buffalograss in the western short-grass country. Some used the term Grand Prairie only for western Kansas,[4] but Brown County had a Grand Prairie post office, a competitor of Prairie Springs. When Hiawatha became the county seat, both towns with the Prairie names died.[5] Montgomery County had a post office named Grass in the 1880's and also a place named Prairie Spur.

Republic County made the widest use of the Prairie name; it had post offices named Prairie Plain, Prairie Grove, and Prairie Home, and it had a Prairie Dell School and a Prairie Center.[6] Doniphan County had a place named Prairie Grove, but the name was replaced by Bendena.[7] The name of the Prairie Dell School in Republic County was repeated in Graham County and in Russell County. Johnson County had a Prairie Center post office and still has a Prairie Village, as does Butler County. In Douglas County, Prairie Center was nearly equidistant from four neighboring towns.[8] A place near Baldwin was named Prairie City, but was also called Palmyra or Hickory Point.[9] Shawnee County had its Prairie Hill School, and Chase County had a Prairie Hill community. Prairie View was first used as a post office name in Jefferson County; after it was closed, there was a Prairieview post office and a Prairie View Township in Phillips County. An association of mechanics from Kentucky established a town in Osage County which they named Prairie City. After one of its town officers was accidentally killed, the place was abandoned and the town was sold for taxes.[10]

By adding an adjective to prairie, the pioneers created such names as Rolling Prairie Township in Morris County and Rolling Prairie post office in Lane County. In Leavenworth County, a place which had been surrounded by "a circuitous fringe of timber" was reasonably named Round Prairie.[11] High Prairie in Leavenworth County was changed to Bowling or Boling. A logical source for the name of Boling could have been L. S. Boling of Lecompton, a state bank examiner and one of the founders of the extinct town of Buffalo in Davis County.[12] Chase County had a High Prairie Church and a High Prairie School.[13] Eden Prairie was the name of a church and a post office in McPherson County.

Pretty Prairie was sufficiently popular to be used as a place-name in English, French, and Indian languages. Mary Newman Collingwood, a widow with nine children, left Indiana in 1872 for Kansas and settled south of Hutchinson. There the "wide prairie looked so beautiful that she called the place Pretty Prairie."[14] Quite similar is the French name of Belpre, given to a town in Edwards County. Prairie is a French word and describing a township in Rush County as Belle Prairie makes it doubly French.

Muscotah, the name of a town in Atchison County, is an Indian name which comes from the Prairie band of the Potawatomis or Kickapoos. Muscotah was said to mean "prairie on fire," but it has also been interpreted to mean "beautiful prairie."[15] A Delaware village on Soldier Creek near Topeka was called Chach haa-hogeree, interpreted by George Remsburg to mean "prairie village."[16]

To these names we may add a couple of Prairie Creeks, one in Jefferson County and the other in Sumner County. A Prairie Branch Creek flows into the Wildcat in northeastern Sedgwick County.

The bluestem grass of the Flint Hills is a rich grass for fodder, and cattle are shipped in by the thousands to grow fat on it. The Bluestem Hills have several kinds of grass and also a variety of bluestem. There is a popular report that "a beef steer two or three years old may go into the pastures so scrawny that it is said he would 'have to stand twice in the same spot to make a shadow,' and in two months be so fat that he waddles when he walks . . . ."[17] Russell County had a post office named Blue Stem, indicating how far west the bluestem grew. After a decade, the name was changed to Lucas. A tributary of the Chikaskia in Kingman County was named Blue Stem Creek and Butler County has a Bluestem Lake.

Hay came from the prairies of Kansas and was occasionally used as a place-name before it was changed to something the public considered more appropriate. Promoters from Oswego and Indiana settlers who arrived there in 1869 did not have time to finish roofing their homes, and for winter they covered the rafters with hay.[18] The Indians called the place "Haytown." The residents may not have had a roof over their heads, but they prospered.[19]

Xenia in Bourbon County was once called Hay.[20] A community center which became Milan in Sumner County was first known as "Haytop." The pioneer name for the Little Blue, which flowed into the Big Blue in Missouri, was "Hay Cabin Creek," "Creek of the Hay Cabins," and "Hay Creek." The name was given because there were "Camps of Straw built on it," said William Clark. Since the camps were built of straw and not hay, the stream was also known as Straw Hill River.[21]

Then there is the story about the origin of the name Tonovay. Settlers estimated that a hayrack contained "a ton of hay." This was changed phonetically to Tonovay, now the name of a town in Greenwood County.[22]

There were areas in Kansas which were described collectively by optimists as a "Garden of Eden." "So beautiful" is the southwestern portion of Ellsworth County, read one report, "that it has been given the name of 'Green Garden,' " now the name of the local township. Nearby was the Garden Valley post office in Valley Township, bordering on Green Garden Township. The optimism was obvious, particularly in the name of neighboring Prosper, a post office which did not.[23] Green Valley on the border of Rice County had its name changed to Cain.[24]

In western Kansas, a place in Finney County was known to railroad men as Fulton for Captain J. R. Fulton, who donated land for a Santa Fe station. Fulton built a home which became a hotel named the Occidental House, fitting for the West, but he called it the "Accidental Hotel." Local residents would have named the town Fulton, but that name had been pre-empted by a town in Bourbon County.[25] Only Fulton Street honors the name of the founder of the town.

Mrs. Fulton was fond of flowers and she carried buckets of water to bring them to bloom. One day, so the story goes, a tramp looked up at the hot western sun and decided that it was time for his coffee break. He stopped at the Fulton house and Mrs. Fulton kindly gave him some coffee. He asked her what was the name of the place. When she replied that it had no name, the tramp looked at her flowers and said, "Why don't you call it Garden City?" So, in this land of soapweed and sagebrush, a town which has bloomed ever since was named Garden City.[26] "Buffalo" Jones imported a carload of trees to shade its streets, one of which is named Jones Street.[27]

Finney County has a Garden City Township. Harvey County, calling itself the "garden of Kansas," had a town named Garden City, which disappeared but left a township named Garden. Cherokee and Harper counties also have townships named Garden. In Sedgwick County, a place with the English name of Southwick Glen was renamed Garden Plain, which is now also the name of a township.

Just as the town of Orchard, a suburb of Arkansas City, could introduce places named for fruit, so the place named Floral, also in Cowley County, should introduce the places named for flowers. Barber County had a Flower Pot Mound, named for its shape and reputedly haunted.[28]

Associated with prairies and gardens are such names as Pleasant Green, Rolling Green, Bowling Green, and College Green. Pleasant Green was a post office in Phillips County. In Sumner County, Rolling Green had its name changed to Millerton and is now a railway station. College Green was in Sedgwick County. Bowling Green in Franklin County was a name borrowed from Kentucky.

The name Bloomington might suggest a borrowed name from college towns in Indiana or Illinois, but one book on names gives the following information: "The beautiful setting of its site on the south branch of the Solomon River suggested a name for this farming village—'Blooming Valley,' and newcomers named the settlement 'Bloomington.'"[29]

According to a 1578 account, the sunflower "groweth in the Weste India, the whiche is called America, and in the country of Perowe."[30] There are those who say that the sunflower was not native to Kansas and that sunflower seeds were brought in on the dirt attached to the wheels of freighters' wagons. Yet Captain John Bell, traveling down the Arkansas River in 1820, found the river bank "covered with sunflowers and high plants."[31] James R. Mead reported sunflowers growing ten feet high in the Saline Valley.[32] Every plowing, even of sod, seemed to produce a crop of sunflowers all over the state. One may wonder if the wheels of freight wagons could have spread the flower so far and so fast. The sunflower was also known as the helianthus because of its efforts to turn its face to the sun or because its "golden-rayed heads are likened to the sun." It has also been called "Indian Sun" and "Chrysanthemum Peruvianum."[33] It was raised for its seeds, which served as food for poultry, and, after Russians settled in Kansas, as a tasty tidbit for people.

The Iowa Legislature created a stir when it described the sunflower as a noxious weed. According to a Kansas comment: "Call it gaudy, coarse and self-asserting, if you will—it is persistent, hardy, bright, ever reaching upward and turning its face toward the light, and so is an emblem of a true Kansan."[34]

The first Kansas place to be named Sunflower was in Mitchell County. More recently the Sunflower Ordinance Plant near DeSoto, known as "Sunflower Village," resulted in another Sunflower post office.[35] Kanorado, 4,026 feet high, was long accepted as the highest point in Kansas, but recently a point was discovered in Wallace County which was thirteen feet higher and named Mt. Sunflower.[36]

The sunflower has not been important as a place-name but after a Kansas delegation to a convention in Colorado wore sunflowers as an emblem, the state legislature declared in 1903 "that the helianthus or wild native sunflower is hereby made, designated and declared to be the state flower and floral emblem of the state of Kansas."[37]

Wild roses gave color to the Kansas landscape and names for streams and towns. There was a Rose Creek and a Rose Creek Township in Republic County, another Rose Creek near Pond Creek Station in Wallace County, and a Rose Bud Creek in Kingman County. There was a post office named Rose in Woodson County, now a Missouri Pacific station. The railroad suggested that Rose was probably "named for someone's wife, daughter, mother, or sweetheart."[38]

But the rose could be associated with a hill, a mont, a dale, or a valley. The town of Rosedale, now in Kansas City, was named by railroad promoters for the abundance of roses along the track.[39] Rose Hill in Neosho County was possibly named for "Squire Rosa," its first postmaster.[40] He moved it to the railway at Galesburg.

The place named Weaver in Osage County became Rosemont. Anderson County had a Rosyvale in 1860, and Clay County had a Rose Vale a few years later, changed to Springfield and now defunct. Stafford County had a post office named Rose Valley, Dickinson County had a Rose Bank, and Cherokee County still has a Roseland.

Roseport in Doniphan County was named for Richard Rose. When the community discovered that Rose was a former convict, it expelled him. The town was reorganized by John B. Elwood of New York and renamed Elwood. J. H. Lowery loved flowers and planted so many on his place that it was called "the Rose Farm." Consequently, when a town was established there, east of Wichita, it was named Rose Hill.[41]

Pansy was first a place-name in Gray County and later a place in Finney County where it was changed to Loyal; and Franklin County also had a post office named Pansy. The Violet post office in Osborne County changed its name to Downs. Rice County once had a place called Violet Springs.

Verbena in the sand hills of Grant County was promoted by J. W. Dapport and named for "a wild flower that grew in profusion in the sandy soil."[42] It did not become a post office, nor did the Verbena promoted in Labette County.[43] The Verbena in Grant County was surely named for the flower which responds so remarkably well to a rain shower in the desert, but one may be less sure of the source for the Verbena in Labette County. Even a dictionary concludes its definition of verbena by stating: "a feminine proper name."

There are several kinds of goldenrods in Kansas, including the noble goldenrod, the giant goldenrod, and the common goldenrod, each contributing to the golden colors of Kansas in the late summer. Lincoln County has a railway station named Goldenrod, a name rarely used as a place-name.

The lily family of flowers has forty species and has supplied three place-names for Kansas: Lily, Sego, and Mariposa. There was a place named Lily in Morris County and another in McPherson County. The possibility of Lily's being a girl's name, shortened from Lillian, is there, but Lily was more likely a flower name. The sego lily is a lovely three-petaled flower of different colors. Reno County had a place named Sego. The Mormons found its bulb edible and nourishing, and Utah chose it as the state flower. The sego is also referred to as the Mariposa. But this was also the Spanish name for butterfly, and that name, as it was used in California for John C. Frémont's ranch, was the most logical source for the Mariposa name in Saline County, Kansas.

The spatterdock is a member of the waterlily family; one kind is called the cowlily. A stream following the Arkansas past Kinsley was known as Spatterdock Creek and a "puddlesome slough." Some thought this was De Mun's Creek and Coon Creek. It was named by Captain John R. Bell who came across the creek in 1820. His description fits better for Ash Creek than Coon Creek, which Bell called Dumun's Creek.[44]

When reporting on Kansas, Albert Richardson said that he saw whole fields of wild onions south of the Marais des Cygnes.[45] These prairie onions, with bulb roots topped with balls of starlike flowers, were related to the lily. Onion Creek post office in Osage County took its name from Onion Creek; it is now Osage City. There was an Onion Creek branch of the Verdigris in Montgomery County and another joining Elm Creek in Wabaunsee County.

The Caney River was named for the abundance of cane in the area, and the town of Caney was named for the river.

The vine may be more closely associated with woods than prairies, but there were creeping vines like the wild morning glory and the woodbine bush. Ottawa County had its Vine Creek, and there Sara D. Seeley, postmistress, named the Vine Creek post office.[46] Although it was situated on Vine Creek, the town's name was, after fifteen years, changed to Vine. And Ivy, another vine, was the name of a post office in Lyon County.

Among the vines was the woodbine, an ornamental shrub, variously referred to as the Virginia creeper and honeysuckle creeper. Several states have used Woodbine as a place-name, as has also Dickinson County, Kansas. It has been suggested that Woodbine in Kansas was named from a line in a popular Civil War song: "Gone where the Woodbine twineth."[47]

Fern is the name of a plant best known for its growth in woodland country, but there are ferns even in open prairies. Fern was a post office in Sherman County, and Wilson County had a place named Ferndale. Franklin County has beautiful fern imprints in a stratum which is approximately fifty million years old.

Although cactus may have its hostile spikes, it does have attractive flowers. In western Kansas, the rose-pink flowers of the star cactus and the waxlike flowers of the prickly pear give a touch of beauty to the pastures and prairies. Cactus Creek got its name from the colorful wild cactus growing in the valley in eastern Norton County, and there a post office named Cactus served for years.[48]

CHAPTER V

TREES

P EOPLE MAY APPRECIATE trees for their beauty or for their utility. "The primeval forests," said William Mitchell, pioneer Linn County newspaperman, "were the glory of this [Kansas] country. Great oaks, giant cottonwoods, great white 'ghostly' sycamores, magnificent walnuts, valuable hickory and ash—this original growth of trees would more than equal the market value of all the land in the country now."[1] From the side of Mount Tamalpais, Muir Woods give one an impression of only a mass of forest green, but from the park entrance, each tree takes on a distinct character and each has its own history. In Kansas, the variety of trees give them distinction; this becomes obvious as one sees the trees individually.[2] Indicative of the mixture are such names as Elmdale on the Cottonwood, Lone Elm on Cedar Creek, and Green Elm on Hickory Creek.

East of the Mississippi and along the first tier of states west of it, trees were abundant and wood was plentiful for buildings and furniture. West of the 95th Meridian, trees grew only along the life-giving streams. Land that could not support trees was considered worthless, or almost worthless—it could be given to the Indians. But even the Indians, who also treasured trees, would travel hundreds of miles to get wood for their bows. Settlers selected homesteads along streams as much for wood as for water.

There were those who were disturbed over the destruction of the beautiful trees that gave distinction to the Kansas landscape. When L. Stillwell wrote about *The Giant Elm* in Neosho County, he spoke of trees being ruthlessly slaughtered by the first settlers, concluding:

> *Thou canst not censure more than we*
> *The vandal hand that laid thee low;*
> *For any fool can fell a tree,*
> *But it takes a god to make one grow.*[3]

Settlers recognized the value of trees and planted thousands. It has been estimated that seventy-five years after its settlement, Kansas had more than 230,000,000 trees.[4]

43

Horace Greeley, a most observant traveler, found the area around Lawrence "heavily timbered with elm, yellow oak, black walnut, hickory, cottonwood, sycamore, basswood, etc." He might have named a few more, except for his proclivity to end such lists with "etc." The pioneers, he said, relied mostly on hickory, oak, and black walnut, since the elm, cottonwood, and sycamore warped badly when sawed into boards.[5]

Trappers, traders, and other travelers, like the Indians before them, found landmarks and trail guides along streams and frequently identified them by their trees. In eastern Kansas there were many varieties from which to choose a name, but as one moved westward, only the hardy cottonwoods, ash, and the cedars were conspicuous. Broad terms were occasionally used to identify a site, such as "timber," or "forest," or "grove," and as a result we have places named Big Timbers, Sylvan Grove, and Forest City. Osborne County had a town named Arbor and Bourbon County had a town named Woodland.

Timbers was a word widely used in naming streams and towns in Kansas. Big Timber Creek in Rush County runs through Big Timber Township. Another Big Timber Creek in Norton County flows into the Solomon. There was also a Big Timber Creek in Cheyenne County, and Frémont followed a Big Timber Creek near Concordia in Cloud County. There was a Big Timber in Meade County, a place so sparsely wooded that it had only a Lone Tree. The town of Timber Hill in Labette County was started by George W. and William Blake and named for "a brush covered hill in the vicinity."[6]

Forest and wood were also used in a descriptive combination for place-names. A town in Nemaha County was named Woodlawn. Bourbon County had a place named Woodland, and not far away, Crawford County had a Drywood Creek and a post office named Drywood. Names like Woodsdale, Woodstock, and Woodston, have in most cases evolved from earlier place-names or personal names.

There was a Forest Hill in Lyon County and Linn County had a Forest Mills. Forest City is a dot on the map in Barber County and Forest Lake Station is a place in Wyandotte County. Homewood in Franklin County was first called Forest Home. Russell County had a post office named Forest.

As a place-name, grove was much more popular than either timber or forest. The most historic grove was surely Council Grove on the Neosho. The Indians were accustomed to assembling there for good fellowship after the hunting season. There George Sibley met the Osage Indians to negotiate a treaty for opening the Santa Fe Trail. "I suggested

44

the propriety of naming the place Council Grove," said he.[7] When Kit Carson camped there, he "took two or three pieces of dressed buffalo skin, and wrote the name 'Council Grove.' " He nailed them on a tree later known as "Council Oak." Carson is also said to have carved his name on the "Kit Carson Oak." Custer found shelter under an elm called "Custer's Elm."[8] The Kit Carson tree near Halstead was also an elm. Long famous was the oak in Council Grove where travelers left letters in the hollow of a tree which became famous as the Post Office Oak. The American Forestry Association has placed these trees in the Hall of Fame for Trees.[9] Council Grove has also been known as the Post, Neosho Crossing, Council Spring, and the Grove. Council Grove Creek, though bordered by oaks, is named Elm Creek.[10]

Park City was said to have been given its appealing name for "the mythical trees that shaded the broad streets."[11] Park City disappeared, but the name was revived for a suburb north of Wichita, built above the low meadows of the Arkansas River.

One of the first stations on the Santa Fe Trail out of Westport was at a clump of trees called Elm Grove and Lone Elm. The Lone Elm was said to be three feet thick but was unable to withstand the immigrant's ax. The place was more of a camp than a community and did not become a post office as did the Lone Elm in Anderson County. It did become a voting center where its six or seven families somehow cast 1,600 votes in 1857.[12] Elm Grove was also known as Caravan Grove, Round Tree Grove, and Round Grove, and at one time it was written "Round (Caravan) Grove."[13] Other clumps of trees on the trail were referred to as "Left-hand Grove" and "Right-hand Grove,"[14] fitting if there were only one-way traffic. Elm Grove in Washington County had its name changed to Barnes to honor Earl Barnes, a popular writer of history textbooks. Round Grove in the same county was renamed Greenleaf, not for any arboreal connection, since Greenleaf was the name of a railroad man.

The elm, called a "Fountain of Green," has won distinction as a place-name for historical sites in the East. The Washington Elm in Cambridge and William Penn's Treaty Elm in Pennsylvania are examples. The naming of the Lincoln Memorial Tree, "under whose shade the crowds sat to hear Lincoln speak" in Kansas, may raise a question. It was the first week in December when Lincoln spoke in Kansas, and at each town he had a hall from which to speak. Little or no shade was available from the trees in December, when it was so cold that Lincoln borrowed a buffalo robe to keep warm on his buggy ride from Elmwood to Troy.[15]

Bismarck Grove north of Lawrence was a name which honored the

45

German chancellor. An Old Settlers celebration held there in 1879, with Edward Everett Hale as the main speaker, drew a crowd of over 25,000. Walt Whitman, greatly interested in Kansas, agreed to come provided he was "not asked to speak nor eat any public dinner."[16]

A grove in Brown County which served as a landmark on the California Trail was named Pilot Grove.[17] A favorite camping place for the Latter Day Saints was located about three miles from Atchison and named Mormon Grove. "It stands on high ground in the prairie," said a New York correspondent, "and is of young hickory trees, which can be seen at a great distance."[18] It was an outfitting station, and three thousand Mormons left there for the West in 1855.[19]

Many places in Kansas were identified by the elm. Lone Elm in Johnson County was on Cedar Creek, but Green Elm in Crawford County was on Hickory Creek. Elm City in Labette County dropped the "City" part of its name. In Barber County, Elm Mill is in Elm Mills Township. Elmdale is on the Middle Creek of the Cottonwood, and for a time Middle Creek was its name. Two townships were named Elm, one in Allen and the other in Pratt County; and three townships were named Elm Creek. There were two streams referred to as Elm Branch rather than Elm Creek, but there were thirteen streams named Elm Creek. A mount on which grew many elms was the source of the name of Elmont in Shawnee County.[20] In Jewell County, Elm Creek must have had better willows than elms, since the two peddlers suspected of murder were hanged on a willow tree on Elm Creek.[21]

Plums were plentiful in Kansas and were appreciated by the pioneers. Even Coronado praised them. The *Sumner County Press* of Wellington reported in 1874: "Thousands of bushels of wild plums are ripening on the Arkansas and Chikaskia rivers." Plum Creek flows into Cow Creek in Rice County and fourteen miles below were two buttes on the Santa Fe Trail "with a luxuriant growth of Plum bushes" from which the Plum Buttes got their name. Near there "Buffalo Bill" Mathewson had his trading post. The buttes eroded during dry years and were then called "Bald Buttes."[22] On a map of the route to the Kansas gold fields in 1858, this place was also listed as "Holes in the Prairie."[23] A Bohemian colony settled on the upper part of the Creek in Plum Creek Flats. Plum Creek Township in Mitchell County evidently took the name of Plum Creek flowing into the Solomon. A place in Jackson County was called Plum Station even though it was not on a railroad. Atchison County had a Plum Grove, a name later changed to Oak Mills. After all, plums could be picked but an oak would need a saw mill. Frederic Remington's ranch in northern Butler County was near a place called Plum Grove, a "flourishing village" with "two inhabitants—man and wife."[24]

The first Mulberry Grove was in Crawford County where the name was shortened to Mulberry. The second Mulberry Grove, near Windom in Rice County, was named by Nathan Boone, who was there looking for the murderers of Chávez, the Spaniard for whom Jarvis Creek was named.[25] Butler County also had its Mulberry Grove. Mulberry in Clay County had its name changed to Riverdale, and later Mulberry became a post office name in Saline County. Governor Geary said that he had camped on "an old Indian camping-ground, upon Mulberry Creek, where there is an abundance of wood, water, and grass."[26] This was in Wabaunsee County. E. Valentin de Boissiere planted twenty acres of mulberry trees for his silk industry at Silkville.[27]

Both the wild black cherry and the chokecherry grew well in eastern Kansas. Cherokee County had a Cherry Creek and a place called Cherry, later changed to Mineral. Montgomery County has a Cherry Creek, a Cherry Township, and a town named Cherryville, Cherry Vale, and then to Cherryvale. Cherry Creek and Cherry Mound were names in Anderson County. Woodson County had a Cherry Creek as did Cheyenne County in the west. Cherry Creek in Labette County had its sawmill, where "much of the handmade cherry furniture, . . . which is now considered antique, was produced from timber grown in that valley."[28]

There was a Peach Creek tributary of the Republican in Washington County and there, too, was the Peach Creek post office. Peach Grove in Clay County was only two years old when the Colorado locusts invaded Kansas. These hungry locusts ate not only the leaves of the peach trees but also the fruit, leaving the bare seeds hanging on bare limbs.[29]

Locust Grove in Atchison County, first named Mount Pleasant, was not named for the ravenous locusts but for the honey locust, a native tree. For a few years there was a place named Locust in Greeley County.

The "beech is all that we want a tree to be," said an authority on trees.[30] This tree was especially abundant in the Old Northwest, but not in Kansas. Yet Graham County had a place named Beech Grove in 1879; two years later the name was changed to Fremont.

Birch was used as a post office name on the Sedgwick-Reno County border until 1894. Anderson County has a station named Birch, named for the tree, which in Kansas would most likely be the river birch or the red birch.

When apple orchards and peach orchards were planted in southern Kansas, a suburb of Arkansas City was named Orchard. The town of Pomona was laid out by H. Wheaton adjoining an apple orchard and named to memorialize the "queen of fruit," the apple.[31] Cherokee County and Chase County had places named Fruitland.

Sylvan Grove appears to be redundant, but such is the attractive name suggested by William C. Buzick, a local editor in Lincoln County.[32] When Sylvan Grove, a part of Twin Groves, moved to the railway, it kept its name. Marshall County once had a town named simply Sylvan, and Labette County had a place near Timber Hill called Sylvan Dale.

Pine wood was generally shipped to Kansas from the East and was quite expensive. A scattering of pine names would indicate the presence of some pine trees. Butler County once had a Pine Grove. Lincoln County had a Pinon from the Spanish *piñon*. The Pine School in Republic County was so named because it was built from pine.[33]

The ailanthus, related to the sumac, has been called the Tree of Heaven. Three times the name of Ailanthus has been given to a post office in Ottawa County, giving it the character of a perennial, but nevertheless it died each time. Ailanthus Grove in Norton County lasted only from May to December, 1879.

Pawnee Fork had the normal mixture of elm, ash, cottonwood, wild cherry, and plum. It also had the "toothache tree," and if that strange name is not comprehensive enough, it was also called "Sting-tongue, pigeon tree, spitberry, and more commonly, prickly ash, and if not an ash, then a prickly elder."[34] Two branches of the Pawnee had tree names, Plum Creek and Hackberry Creek. Pawnee County must have been fairly well wooded judging by the names of its townships: Pleasant Grove, Brown's Grove, Walnut, and Ash Valley, and this is supported by the name of Saw Mill Township. Brown's Grove was named for Gallatin Brown, a local pioneer. After a decade the post office name was changed to Burdett, but Brown's Grove is still the name of the local township.[35]

One pioneer traveling along the Marais des Cygnes said that he had "nooned" at "Cold Water Grove." McPherson County had a place named Groveland and Shawnee County had a place named Grove. Pleasant Grove was the name of a post office in Doniphan County and later, one in Phillips County.

Seldom was an object more conspicuous as a landmark than a lone tree, and as such, it became a trail-marker and a campsite. Cowley, Osborne, and McPherson counties had post offices named Lone Tree. There was a Lone Tree Crossing of the Arkansas above Kinsley, another near Dodge City, and a third at the Cimarron Crossing. An immense cottonwood on the trail near Garden City was known as the Lone Tree. Six surveyors were killed by Indians near a large cottonwood tree in Meade County in an event known as the "Lone Tree Massacre."[36] North of Winfield a railway station bore the name of Lone Tree. John Barnum, who lived in Sedgwick County before

Wichita was born, said that he had a store at the "Lone Tree" settlement, most likely north of Durfee's Ranch. He also referred to the Little Arkansas Treaty as the "Lone Tree Treaty."[37]

Like the cottonwood, the willow was a hardy tree which followed the streams for moisture. When Edwin Way Teale returned to Wichita to hike on familiar paths along the Arkansas, he chose a willow tree to illustrate his book *Journey into Summer*. Thoreau's impression of the willow tree was expressed in these words:

> *Ah, Willow! Willow!*
> *Would that I always possessed*
> *Thy good spirit.*[38]

A favorite resting place along the Santa Fe Trail was at Willow Springs in Douglas County, and there a township and a post office were named Willow Springs. The post office had been named Davis, Willow Springs, and Akron, but under none of these names did the town survive. Cherokee, Greenwood, Wilson, and Mitchell counties have streams named Willow Creek. "Our next place to rest the milk cows," said Mrs. Olive A. Clark, traveling through Mitchell County, "was at Willow Springs, . . . on the present site of Beloit . . . ."[39] In western Kansas the creek that flows into the Smoky at Big Timbers was named Willow Creek. The willow names that survived were Willowdale Township in Dickinson County and Willowdale, formerly Peters, a town in Kingman County.

The immortal oak is one of the best-known trees in the world. It has a special place in history as the sacred tree of the Druids. To avoid simple repetitions in naming places, people added the variety of the particular oak, such as Jack oak, "Black Jack," and burr oak, often spelled "bur oak." Other distinctions were made by applying oak to a valley, hill, ridge, or grove. The abundance of oak trees in Kansas made the oak a popular place-name. Logan Grove, named for General John A. Logan by Captain Ralph R. Henderson, was a homestead south of Junction City which contained over 92,000 oak trees.

The Jack oak or "Black Jack" grew well in eastern Kansas but did not have a good reputation; it was "too large for a shrub and too small for a tree."[40] Black Jack Creek was named by Mexicans and then the local post office was named for the creek. John Brown called the Battle of Black Jack "the first regular battle fought between Free-State and proslavery men in Kansas." As such, it has also been called "the first battle of the Civil War."[41]

The oak migrated westward, especially along the northern streams. Travelers along the Blue in Washington County were "attracted by the great woods, the beautiful oak groves, and a scattering of black walnut trees, an occasional elm or hackberry."[42] There were, however, only four streams named Oak Creek, all in the central part of Kansas. Even as far into the southwest as Seward County, there was once a place named Oak City, later changed to Tyrone. In Smith County there was another Oak City, an Oak Creek, a Middle Oak Creek, a West Oak Creek, an Oak Township, and an Oakvale. Jewell County has an East Oak Creek and there was the post office named Little Oak.

James McCormick, the postmaster, had a farm on Burr Oak Creek and he named Burr Oak in Jewell County.[43] Burroak Township in Doniphan County also had a Burr Oak Bottom.[44]

Oakland is so popular as a place-name that the name may be found in more than half of our states. A few, like Oakland in California, were named for the oak, while others lost their meaning. Both Jewell and Kingman counties had post offices named Oakland, and Oakland is the name of a suburb of Topeka. Oakland Township in Clay County had an Oak Hill post office.

Jefferson and Seward counties had places named Oak, and Smith County had an Oak Township. Other places were given the oak name with descriptive variations: Oak Grove in Pottawatomie County, Oak Mills in Atchison County, Oak Ridge in Elk County where there was also an Oak Valley. The creek entering Elk River at Oak Valley was called Hickory Creek. There is still an Oakwood in Linn County, and Rawlins County in northwestern Kansas had an Oak Ranch post office.

Historically, the cedar tree owes its fame to the Cedars of Lebanon, which furnished the timber for Solomon's temple a thousand years before Christ. Kansas has its Lebanon as well as its cedars.

The red cedar was the only coniferous tree native to Kansas. It was especially conspicuous in western Kansas where it had few trees with which to compete. Altogether, thirteen post offices have used the name of Cedar in one form or another, and there were eleven Cedar Creeks. The one in Doniphan County was called the "River Poke," "Pape," and "Pappie" by members of the Lewis and Clark expedition. It was supposedly named for a Spaniard who accidentally shot himself while lifting his rifle from a boat.[45] Cedar Creek in Cowley County served as the name of a post office. Five townships and four post offices have been named Cedar. To these we may add a Cedar Bluff post office in Anderson County, changed to Shannon, and a Cedar Bluffs post office in Decatur County. There was also a Cedar Bluff and Cedar in Rooks County. A cairn on Cedar Bluff in Clay County was set up to mark the site for the English settlers who established Wakefield.[46] As a final honor, Cedar Crest is the name of the governor's home in Topeka.

Other variations are derived by combining cedar with ford, falls, grove, junction, point, vale, ville, and gulch.[47] Marshall County had a Cedar Falls. Cedar Grove in Geary County was a post office but not Cedar Grove in Chase County. Cedar Point was a post office in Chase County but not Cedar Point in Neosho County. O. H. Drinkwater, who cut cedar posts in the area while "moonlighting" as postmaster, named Cedar Point in Chase County.[48] It was only a mile south of Cedar Grove Station and the station survived, but it was given its neighbor's name of Cedar Point. In Cedar Township, Jackson County, a place was named Tippinville for Welwood Tippin, its first merchant. It received its mail from North Cedar. After two decades, North Cedar had its name changed to Denison.[49] Johnson County once had a station at the crossing of the Santa Fe and the Kansas City and Western named Cedar Junction.[50] In 1876 a big dance was held at Charlie Posson's new barn on Cedar Gulch on the Prairie Dog in Norton County.[51]

Cedar Vale in Chautauqua County was named by J. R. Marsh for the trees in the scenic valley of Cedar Creek. The view from "White Oak Bluff" or "Lone Tree Hill" is most attractive. One year after Cedar Vale was named, a post office in Smith County was named Cedarville. The similarity of the two names was too great, so Cedarville deleted the "ville" and became Cedar.[52]

An abundance of cedars grew on the north side of the bluffs of the Smoky Hill River in Trego County, and there the Cedar Bluff Reservoir has become an attractive fishing center. Cedars were also plentiful along Cedar Creek in Barber County, where the red rock mesas made a colorful background for the dark green cedars.

Cedars were useful as durable fence posts, and many of the trees were destroyed by the pioneers. The red cedar was sufficiently green in the winter to serve as a Christmas tree. The hardy cedars withstood the elements until the heat, dust, and drought of the thirties destroyed many of them, together with the elm and ash. Yet they have not suffered as complete a destruction as the more famous Cedars of Lebanon, of which only four hundred remain, leaving denuded mountain slopes and eroded land fit only for a "goat economy."[53] The obituary or memorial for one Kansas cedar read: "Pioneer cedar which died in 1935 at the age of 235 years."[54]

The ash was named by such patriotic colors as red, white, and blue; and, there was, of course, a green ash. The white ash, also called the American ash, was found in eastern Kansas, but the red ash followed the watercourses westward. The wood of the red ash made good boat oars and ball bats. The ash tree in Kansas was sufficiently abundant to justify the name of Ashland, but in fact, this name came from Henry Clay's home in Kentucky.

Ash Point in Nemaha County served as a stage stop near Guittard's on the way to Marysville.[55] John O'Laughlin, the postmaster and store-keeper, also dispensed Kentucky Bourbon. The place was called "Uncle John's Store," but because of its liquid provisions, dry travelers called it "the Oasis."

The ash must have been conspicuous in Rooks County with its Ash Creek, Ash Creek post office, Ash Grove, Ash Grove School, and Ash Grove post office. The first store in Rooks County was called Ash Rock, later changed to Raceburg. The township kept the Ash Rock name. Ash Creek in Pawnee County flows through Ash Valley Township on its way to the Arkansas north of Larned. The stream was extremely crooked and was first called Crooked Creek, but its new name was "probably suggested by ash and elm that shaded the creek."[56]

The sycamore is an impressively tall tree which grew over a wide area in Kansas. Cross sections of its sturdy trunk have been used for butcher blocks, now collector's items for those who have the room for such bulky antiques. The sycamore peels its bark and belongs to the group called "strip-teasers."[57] Covered by large leaves in summer, the sycamore limbs remain half concealed and half revealed in winter.

Several sites commemorated the sycamore tree. There is a Sycamore Springs in northeastern Kansas, where both Indians and immigrants were accustomed to stop for refreshment, and another Sycamore Springs in Butler County. There are two Sycamore Creeks in Montgomery County and a Sycamore railway station.[58] Chautauqua County had a post office named Sycamore. Butler County, with townships named Plum Grove, Walnut, and Hickory, also had one named Sycamore. Montgomery County has both a township and a town named Sycamore. Chapman's Creek was briefly known as Sycamore Creek.[59]

Indians used hickory nuts to a make a milky liquor called *powcohicora*, and from this word, the hickory is believed to have derived its name.[60] Its wood is hard and tough; similar characteristics earned Andrew Jackson the nickname "Old Hickory."

"I saw more good hickory this day than in any former day of my life," said Horace Greeley, traveling south from Olathe.[61] In Franklin County, Hickory Creek is next to Walnut Creek, and in 1859, the local post office was also named Hickory Creek. There also was Hickory Grove. Other Hickory Creek names are found in Coffey, Crawford, and Elk counties. There was a Hickory Point in Jefferson County and another in Douglas County. Hickory Point in Douglas County was well known as a battle site in the Kansas conflict in which James H. Lane participated. The proslavery group fought under a black flag but soon waved a white flag. Then they negotiated peace, drank together, and parted amicably.[62] One could appreciate peace in a place with the expressed opinion that there was "no richer nor more beautiful spot on the continent."[63] Except for Butler County, all the hickory names were in eastern Kansas. Butler County used the Hickory name for a creek, a township, and a post office.

It has been said that "the tree that one knows so well yet does not know at all, usually proves to be the Hackberry."[64] Its clusters of small twigs are known as the "witches broom." The hackberry, or hagberry, as it was called in Scotland, is also known as the sugartree. Its name was used as a place-name in four counties—Labette, Republic, Barber, and Gove. Hackberry post office in Labette County lasted a little over one year. In Gove County the Hackberry Creek gave its name to Hackberry Mills which was shortened to Hackberry for a couple of years; and then, in 1881, it again became Hackberry Mills. Now, however, the name is again Hackberry. North, Middle, and South Hackberry creeks flow out of Logan County to enter the Smoky Hill in Trego County. There is a short Hackberry Creek flowing out of Kansas in Barber County and another running into the Pawnee River in Hodgeman County.

The heavily wooded south fork of the Pawnee River was the nearest good supply of firewood and timber for the soldiers at Fort Atkinson near Dodge City. Mules were used to draw the logs up from the river bank. When buffalo hunters saw these logs, they named the stream Sawlog Creek.[65] There, in Hodgeman County, is also Sawlog Township. The woods were a mixture of ash, elm, box elder, cottonwood, and hackberry, but most of the logs were hackberry.

An enterprising Indian with an inventive mind started a sawmill near Wyandotte City. The Indians were so impressed by the machine that produced board lumber that they gleefully shouted, "Heap split log!" Splitlog then became the name of the sawmill owner, the "millionaire Indian." The stream on which Splitlog's Mill was located was henceforth known as Splitlog Run. Splitlog's home was known as Splitlog Hill and a street in Kansas City is now named Splitlog.[66] Sawlog and Splitlog share the distinction of being original, unusual, and meaningful place-names.

The linden or linwood is called by some the basswood. It is noted for the sweet and penetrating odor of its flowers. The bees love it for its superb honey, and the white linden is called a bee tree. A place named Stranger for Stranger Creek and then Journey Cake or Johnny Cake for a Delaware Indian had its name changed to Linwood by Senator W. A. Harris,[67] who admired the linwood trees in the area.

The "magnificent maple" had many attractive assets, and eastern Kansas became fully aware of its value. In addition to its wood, the tree produced maple sugar and maple syrup and furnished shade. In the autumn, the yellow and gold and orange-red leaves gave a splash of brilliant color to the Kansas scene that could rival the colors in New England.

The Indians taught the Pilgrims how to get sugar from the maple tree. One might ask how the Indians learned about it. According to legend, an Indian woman asked her husband to get a pail of water. Irked by the thought of such a menial task, he didn't move. The woman put the pail under a maple tree and waited. The brave, sullen and silent, finally picked up his tomahawk and started to walk away. As he passed the maple tree, he gave it an angry whack with the weapon. When his wife, much later, picked up the pail, she saw the white liquid, thought it was water, and cooked her venison in it. Then she discovered the sugar.[68]

The maple name was used as far west as Clay and Cowley counties. In Cowley County, Maple Creek formed a branch of Pole Cat Creek. A Cowley County town named Clarence from April to December, 1872, had its name changed to Maple City. Clay County had a Maple Grove in 1877, and the next year, Pottawatomie County also had one. Maple Hill in Wabaunsee County joined the two words to make Maplehill and then changed back to Maple Hill. George Fowler from "Pine Ranch" promoted Maple Hill with railway excursions and free beer.[69] In Allen County a town was named Maplewood. Mrs. Kathryn Blair in Bourbon County named the town of Eldora and, with a woman's privilege, changed her mind and renamed it Mapleton. The town was colonized by Vermonters who must have been happy to see the familiar sugar maple.[70] Although the town was named for its maples, its tavern "had frame, siding, shingles, and interior finish entirely of black walnut . . . ."[71]

The word "sugar" in eastern Kansas place-names was generally associated with the sugar maple. Sugar Loaf in Rooks County was, however, named for the appearance of a hill. In Linn County, Sugar Mound (Mound City) was named for the sugar maple. Anderson County had a Sugar Valley, for years dormant as a post office, which in 1894, was revived under the name of Sugarvale. Sugar Creek flows through Sugar Creek Township in Miami County into Linn County. Reporting on Governor Geary's travels, someone said that his "party" came to "Sugar Mound and camped on Little Sugar Creek, well timbered with oak, hickory, walnut, and sugar maple." Here was a long list of names from which to choose, yet the sugar maple won.[72] The post office named Sugar came from the same sweet source.

The elder tree in Kansas was the ash-leaved maple, commonly called the box elder. When Leslie Snow wrote to his sister from Glen Elder in Mitchell County, he described it as "a town whose name savors of mountains and trees, but with lamentable absence of both."[73] The box elder provided the name, but it is no longer as popular a tree as it was in the nineteenth century.

One of the branches of the Caney is called Paw Paw Creek and for a time there was also a Paw Paw post office named for it.[74] The name is associated with two kinds of trees, one tropical and the other found in south-central states. The name was Papaw, according to some, and Papaya, the corruption of an Indian name. It has been listed as of both French and Goajira Indian origin.[75] The paw paws were not plentiful according to the views of one disappointed pioneer:

> *Don't tell me of your corn and wheat—*
> *What do I care for such?*
> *Don't say your schools is hard to beat,*
> *And Kansas soil is rich.*
> *Stranger, a year's been lost by me,*
> *Searchin' your Kansas siles,*
> *And not a paw paw did I see,*
> *For miles, and miles, and miles.*[76]

The laurel from the East and the redwood from California also served as names in Kansas. The laurel, also called the sassafras tree, gained the reputation of having valuable medicinal qualities among the English who first came to America. Captain John Smith sent a shipload back to England. After its medicinal value was disproved, its leaf was still used for flavoring. The laurel was not a Kansas tree, yet Hodgeman County has a town named Laurel. Far removed from the redwoods of California and the petrified redwood trees of Florissant, Colorado, was the place named Redwood in Dickinson County, Kansas.

There are two varieties of catalpa trees in Kansas, one, according to the Kansas State Board of Agriculture, having "no economic value," and the other classified as "a highly valuable decorative tree."[77] One would not assume that it was native to Gove County, but the post office named Catalpa was there.

Ford County had a post office in 1878 named Hazelwood. The hazel shrub or tree is noted more for its nuts than its wood. They are frequently called filberts, having been named for St. Philibert's Day, August 22, when the nuts ripen in France. The pigmentation of these nuts gave us the name for the hazel color.

The redbud, a tree that ushers in the beauty of spring, is well represented in southern Kansas. In Oklahoma, it is so popular that it was adopted as its state tree. It has been called the Judas tree because it was from a related redbud tree that Judas hanged himself.[78] In southern Kansas it has inspired the redbud tour in spring. Father Eugene Bononcini referred to his parish in eastern Kansas as the "Red Bud."[79] In Cowley County, the Red Bud post office has strangely retained its name as two words.

The buckeye name may be found in Kansas, but most, if not all, of the Buckeye place-names came from Ohio, the "Buckeye State." Kansas was on the border of the buckeye country. The buckeye was named for its seed, which looked like the eye of a deer.[80] The nut from the buckeye had a special charm, according to tradition, and many a Kansas farmer carried a buckeye in his pocket to ward away rheumatism, as had the people of Ohio.[81] Buckeye names were especially noticeable in Dickinson County.

Of all the trees in Kansas, the cottonwood had the greatest prestige, but the black walnut had the greatest value. A walnut log exhibited by Kansas at the St. Louis World's Fair was eighty-four inches in diameter and nearly five hundred years old.[82] Walnut was used as a descriptive name in Kansas more frequently than the name of any other tree, surpassing even the cedar. Creeks, rivers, and towns were named for this precious tree. Fourteen townships and eighteen creeks were given the Walnut name. Settlers were not immediately aware of the commercial value of the walnut wood, but they eventually discovered a good market in Europe. The walnut was a most practical and useful wood for such local essentials as ox yokes, axle timbers, and gun stocks, as well as furniture and houses. Eugene F. Ware, poet and politician, said he had built for himself a "black walnut shanty." He got the walnut logs free for hauling them away from a neighbor's farm.[83]

When Captain John R. Bell came to the Great Bend country in 1819, he spoke of it as a "civilized" country because it had "pastures" for horses, shaded by "cottonwood, elm, black walnut, ash, mulberry and coffee nut trees," trees which he greeted as "old friends."[84] Walnut Creek, which joins the Arkansas near Great Bend, was called Ash Creek by the Indians, since it was there that they gathered ash saplings for lodge poles. Another tributary is called the Little Walnut or, more frequently, the "Dry Walnut." By contrast, the Big Walnut is called the "Wet Walnut." A community on the Walnut in Rush County was called the Walnut Creek Settlement, and as a town it became Walnut City. The name was later changed to Rush Center to compete with La Crosse for the County seat. Rush Center lost.[85]

The Walnut River flowing southward out of Butler County joins the Arkansas River at Arkansas City. The valley has a variety of trees but it was correctly named for the "abundance of walnut trees which grows along its course."[86] One of the four names for Arkansas City was Walnut City. This name was abandoned when it was discovered that farther upstream in Butler County a post office was already named Walnut. The first post office name of Leon on the Little Walnut Creek was Little Walnut.

Walnut Station in Crawford County shortened its name to Walnut in 1877. Crawford County had a Walnut Creek post office, as did Barton County. The latter was located at the second site of Fort Atkinson. Bourbon County has a post office named Walnut Hill. The first Santa Fe station north of Wichita was once called Walnut Grove. Walsburg in Riley County was elusively named for Walnut Creek.

The hardy cottonwood tree deserves recognition for its resistance to changing weather, winds, and drought. Few trees in the East could endure such hardships, but the western cottonwood took root along the streams all the way across the state, standing conspicuously alone or in attractive groves. It was the fastest-growing tree in Kansas, the largest, and the most popular. It furnished shade, shelter, and kindling. One venerable cottonwood in Smith County was reported to be three hundred years old.[87] Another which was cut down near Fort Riley was nine feet in diameter.[88] Hollenburg's Cottonwood Station for the Pony Express was named for his Cottonwood Ranch.[89] The cottonwood is a member of the poplar family. Poplar Hill in Dickinson County was the only post office that used the name of the poplar trees. The Alameda of Kingman County was from a Spanish name for the poplar.

Travelers on the Santa Fe Trail were pleased by the appearance of cottonwood trees growing along a stream in Marion County with "its crystalline ponds mirroring the trembling leaves of the tree whose name it bears."[90] Another referred to the Cottonwood Creek as "a little stream charming beyond all description."[91] On Emory's map of 1844, the name was written "Cotton Wood," as was the common practice of the pioneers. The Cottonwood is a fair-sized river but it has also been called Cottonwood Creek and Cottonwood Fork. This became the most noted Kansas landmark to honor the cottonwood tree.

Chase County, where several branches of the Cottonwood merge before joining the Neosho near Emporia, has used the name in various ways. Cottonwood Valley, Cottonwood City, Cottonwood Station, Cottonwood Falls, and North Cottonwood Falls have all been names in the same neighborhood.

The town at the two-foot falls of the Cottonwood was naturally named Cottonwood Falls. Sam Wood, who came there as publisher of the town's first newspaper, is also credited with having named the falls.[92] When another town was started a mile to the north, it adopted the same name but added direction as North Cottonwood Falls. This was too long and the Santa Fe Railway called it simply Cottonwood Station. Then the post office changed the name to Strong to honor William Barstow Strong, president of the Santa Fe Railroad.[93] Not until 1951 was it changed to Strong City.

Chase County once had a trading post called Cottonwood City which was the terminus of a mail route from Cottonwood Falls.[94] The place called Cottonwood Valley, also in Chase County, had its name changed to Cedar Point. Cottonwood Falls was divided into two names for townships, one named Cottonwood and the other Falls. Three creeks were named Cottonwood in three other counties. Big Cottonwood Grove, the last station of the Butterfield stage in Kansas, was a famous landmark and campsite for both red men and white.[95] Shady Bend in Lincoln County and Shady Brook in Dickinson County were both named for their shade trees.

Cottonwoods provided shade for thousands of travelers. Having "spread its shade like a benediction over the land," the stately cottonwood has been characterized as "the best native tree in the state," a tree that was "stately even in death." It has been called the "Pioneer Tree of Kansas," and was deservedly chosen to be state tree.[96]

CHAPTER VI

BEES, BIRDS, AND BEASTS

IN THE OPEN COUNTRY of Kansas were many living creatures. Some provided entertainment for pioneers; others were hunted for sport or for food. Still others were pests. Speaking of the Manhattan area, Isaac Goodnow reported seeing wild turkeys, prairie chickens, quail, rabbits, deer, wildcats, and wolves.[1] Pioneers seldom had to hunt buffalo, because, said one, "they usually came to us."[2] Captain John R. Bell encountered a different sort of game on the Arkansas River, commenting, "Julian killed a turkey and a skunk, the last we threw away."[3] Many of these animals left their names on the land.

Like larger species, the bee, busily gathering nectar for its sweet honey, provided a place-name. Bee was the name of a post office in Montgomery County. When settlers found a bee tree near a stream in Greenwood County in 1856, they named the stream Honey Creek.[4] Wyandotte County had another Honey Creek, and what had first been Slough Creek, twenty-two miles west of Leavenworth, also became known as Honey Creek.[5]

Butterfly was for a short time the name of a place in Kingman County. Mariposa in Saline County was probably named for Frémont's Mariposa Ranch in California. In Spanish, *mariposa* means "butterfly."

Among the insects, none was more annoying than the mosquito, and none more dangerous than the female with striped legs, carrier of dreaded malaria. In Colorado a clerk read a report on a new town; and in the blank for the proposed name, he found a dead mosquito. With such material evidence the place was named Mosquito. In Kansas the obnoxious mosquito justified the use of its name for streams in Doniphan, Jackson, Nemaha, Atchison, and Marshall counties. Mosquito Creek in Franklin County was near the site of the Potawatomi Massacre.[6]

The Grasshopper River was named long before the grasshopper invasion of 1874. It was probably an Indian name which the French translated to Sauterelle, generally written Soutrelle, although Isaac McCoy spelled it phonetically as "Sotrael." The name was translated into English as Grasshopper River. The grasshopper name was unpopular and again became Soutrelle. The French name was meaningless to most people, and Sol Miller, the salty editor from White Cloud, called it "Sowtail." Other jokers made it "Cowtail." Sensitive to such derisive names, the community along the Soutrelle asked for a change, and the Grasshopper name was restored. But this proved to be a mistake.

In 1874 came the invasion of the Colorado locusts, insects identified as either "short-horned" or "long-horned." "Language is too poor to paint the scene of desolation wrought by the grasshopper in 1874," said one who tried.[7] Men were drafted from the ages of twelve to sixty-five to kill grasshoppers in what amounted to war. A grandmother chided her granddaughter about having to eat grasshopper soup if she went to Kansas, but the little girl said: "If daddy can eat grasshopper soup, I can too."

But the grasshoppers drove Kansans away by the thousands. The insect's name became so obnoxious that in 1875 the legislature changed the Grasshopper River to Delaware River, Grasshopper Falls to the more attractive Valley Falls, and Grasshopper Falls Township to Delaware Township. But there is still a Grasshopper Township in Atchison County and there, too, is Grasshopper Creek.[8]

Orbitello is a name that quickly sends one to the dictionary, but the results are even more confusing. The name looks like *orbitale*, a zoological term for the geometric spiders, or "orb-weaver," the spider that weaves a circular web. Orbetello is a town in Tuscany. Orbitello, whatever its origin, was for two decades the name of a post office in Lincoln County.

A proper introduction to birds may be the egg, accepting, of course, the debatable assumption that the egg came first. Butler County once had a place named Ovo,[9] and that should refer to egg or *ovum*, the female germ cell. The place had been called Whitewater, located about twelve miles northeast of the present Whitewater.

Butler County once had a Bird Creek and a place named Cage. Bird City in Cheyenne County was not named for birds but for John Bird, founder of the "City." The town was first named Bird Town and then changed to Bird City.[10] Rawlins County had a town named Bird on Beaver Creek, but beavers must have been more obvious than birds because its name was changed to Beaverton. Tennessee has its Bird Crossroad; Ohio, its Bird's Run; Kentucky, its Bird Wood; Pennsylvania, its Bird-in-hand; but only Kansas had a Bird Nest, the name of a post office in Pawnee County.

The bird sanctuary of Cheyenne Bottoms is a favorite summer home of the redwing blackbird, and there a place is named Redwing.

No bird's name was used more widely as a place-name in Kansas than Turkey. The turkey was attractive, abundant, and appetizing. G. Webb Bertram, a pioneer, said that in 1870 he had seen a thousand turkeys a day for several days near the junction of the North and South Solomon.[11] The turkey, domesticated by the Aztecs and Zuñis, was given a place in American history when the Pilgrims ate it for their first Thanksgiving dinner. Benjamin Franklin wished the turkey rather than the eagle had been chosen as the bird to represent our country. The turkey, he said, was " a much more respectable bird" and "a bird of courage."[12]

Turkey Creek in McPherson County was especially important on the Santa Fe Trail. Branches of Turkey Creek were called Dry Turkey Creek (now Dry Creek), Spring Turkey Creek, and Running Turkey Creek. A creek near Wichita was once called Standing Turkey Creek. Seventeen Turkey Creeks and three Turkey Creek townships are indicative of the popularity of the bird and its name. Turkey Creek post office in Bourbon County was changed to Uniontown because its settlers were Union men.[13]

The graceful swan became best known through the French translation of an Indian name for the stream called Marais des Cygnes, "marsh of the swans."[14] This was the source for the naming of the La Cygne post office in Linn County and Swan River post office in Osage County. Swan Township in Smith County and Swan post office in Harper County were most likely named for the bird, but that does not preclude the possibility of their having been named for a person; there was once a Wea Chief named Swan.

Atchison County had a Curlew on the Santa Fe "Pollywog" railroad. The curlew was said to be of the *Scolopacidae* family, but is more familiar as a member of the snipe family.

Most hunters included the prairie chicken on their list of game birds. One man in Davis (Geary) County reported having killed 660 prairie chickens in one month in 1863.[15] On the Santa Fe Trail there was a stream near 142 Mile Creek which was named Prairie Chicken Creek but was also called "Chicken Creek."[16]

Grouse Creek joins Silver Creek in Cowley County, and there also was the Grouse Creek post office. The Indians were more impressed by the geese than the grouse they saw there, so they named it Me-her, "goose-creek." Also associated with the grouse was the post office in Cowley County named Glen Grouse and then Glengrouse. It, too, was on upper Grouse Creek and opened a year after the post office named Grouse Creek closed.

The name of Leoti was rejected for a post office in Wichita County because it was too much like the name of Leota in Norton County. The community could not agree on a better name until Milton Brown saw a picture of a prairie grouse with its species name, *bonasa*. He liked the name, recommended it, and the townspeople accepted it, as did the Post Office Department. It was not likely to be duplicated. The ambitious townspeople gave it prestige by calling it "Bonasa City." Yet when the Leota post office in Norton County was closed, Congressman S. R. Peters had the Leoti name restored.[17]

Ducks were plentiful enough to name eight streams Duck Creek. All of these were in eastern Kansas except Duck Creek in Ford County.

Streams named Goose Creek were mostly in south-central Kansas. One Goose Creek was a branch of Silver Creek in southern Reno County; another, a branch of Sand Creek, was in neighboring Kingman County. In western Kansas, a Goose Creek flows into the Smoky Hill in Wallace County. There, too, was a Goose City.

Eagles and hawks were important in the ecology of Kansas. Ame Cole observed a high point in Norton County which he called "Eagle Point" because "Bald Eagles frequently soared above its summit." Ame piled stones on its top to make it even higher.[18]

When Ely Moore, Jr., was heading for a crossing of the Kaw at Dry Ford near Lawrence, his Indian guide got drunk and Moore had to get new directions. He was told by the captain of a California train to follow the California Trail to "Coon Point" and head north to the river at "Bald Eagle," now Lecompton. Many bald eagles nested there in several immense sycamore trees on both sides of the Kaw.[19] Moore crossed the river on a huge sycamore log which its owner called a "ferry" and had named the "Fairy Queen." William R. Simmons, the ferryman, was the first settler at Bald Eagle, and Moore calls him the "founder of Lecompton." According to the story of his love affair with Miss Mandy Wilcox of Indiana, Simmons had reasons for going to Kansas. "William," Mandy lisped, "when I said Yes to you un's, I were plum in earnest: when I say No to you Un's I are plummer. William I are anchored to another feller." William, in tears as he unfolded the story, still spoke of her as "the honeyest peach that ever blossomed along the Wabash—she were."[20] Where he settled in sorrow at Bald Eagle, Lecompton was built.

Four townships named Eagle were in Kingman, Harper, Barber, and Sedgwick counties, all adjoining one another in south-central Kansas. But in Sedgwick County, Eagle Township was named for Murdock's newspaper, *The Wichita Eagle*.[21] Eagle Creeks were flowing into the Saline, Neosho, and Smoky Hill. Those in Lyon and Rooks counties became post office names. Barber County had a post office named simply Eagle, as did also Pottawatomie County, but the latter Eagle had its name changed to Laclede. In northern Kansas, Clay County had an Eagle Bend post office, and Smith County had an Eagle Rapids. Eagle Tail Station on the Kansas Pacific Railroad had been an Indian crossing of the Smoky Hill and a stage stop. It is now Sharon Springs. Eagle Springs was to be the name of a planned town for Doniphan County.[22] As the majestic eagle has gradually disappeared, so have the post offices using its name.

Some hawks so closely resemble the eagle in flight and habits that the two are not easily distinguished. Kansas had no post office named Hawk, but it did have a Hawkeye in Decatur County and a Hawkswing in Linn County. Hawkswing, said a local historian, was "probably a poetic name bestowed by Indians . . . ."[23] The Hawkeye can, of course, be associated with Iowa or with an Indian chief. The Black Hawk post office in Osborne County was most likely named for the famous Sac and Fox chief, Ma-ka-tai-me-she-pia-kiak, or "Black Sparrow Hawk."[24]

Another of the soaring birds was the vulture, not a popular bird, yet when Captain John R. Bell saw a large number of them at what is now Pawnee River, he named it Vulture Creek.[25]

There were several people in Kansas history named Crow, but when a creek was named Crow Creek it was likely to be for that big black bird which the farmers try to keep away from their fields. Montgomery County has a Crow Creek flowing into the Verdigris. Phillips County had a Crow Creek post office and later a Crow post office, probably from the same source. Crow Springs was, however, named for O. W. Crow, a Finney County pioneer.

Oriole was for ten years the name of a post office in Smith County and then, in 1882, it was changed to Sherwood. It was most likely named for the colorful Baltimore Oriole, although Bullock's Oriole is also found in Kansas, especially in the west.

"Whipperwill" Creek, now Peter's Creek in Doniphan County, was named, said Sergeant Ordway of the Lewis and Clark expedition, when "a whiper will [sic] perched on the boat for a short time . . . ."[26]

Owls of several varieties were found in Kansas, but the barn owl, also called "monkey-faced" owl, and the barred owl were the most common. The owl name was given to one township and four creeks. A stream flowing into the Neosho was the source for naming Owl Creek Township in Woodson County. One Owl Creek had an outlet in the Big Walnut in Crawford County, one into the Little Osage River in Linn County, and another into the Saline in Lincoln County.

When Zebulon Pike passed through the Flint Hills, he "observed," as he said, "buffaloes, elk, deer, cabrie, and panthers." Pike used the old form for the pronghorned antelope when he wrote "cabrie." As for the panther, whether it is called cougar, mountain lion, or puma, each region has its own name for this cat. Panther Creek flows into Grouse Creek in Cowley County, a county which also named creeks Badger, Beaver, Otter, and Wild Cat.[27]

When James R. Mead named Paradise Creek he spoke of it as "a paradise of game—buffalo, elk, black-tailed deer in bunches of fifteen or twenty, turkeys in abundance, beaver, otter, and hungry wolves in gangs."[28] The names of these animals all became Kansas place-names. Not only did Mead then name Paradise Creek, but he also named other streams in the area.

After a hunting expedition southeast of Dodge City, Colonel Richard I. Dodge reported the killing of 127 buffalo, 2 red deer, 11 antelope, 154 turkeys, 5 geese, hundreds of ducks (mostly teal), 32 grouse, 9 hawks, 3 owls, 2 badgers, 7 raccoons, and 11 rattlesnakes. There were many more animals killed, a total of 1,262 in twenty days. Nowhere in the world, said Dodge, could one find a greater variety of wildlife.[29] The list above refers only to species whose names became place-names in Kansas.

The Spaniards spoke of the Quivira country as the land of Los Cibolas or *bufalo*, also called "Crooked-backed oxen." Kansas was in the heart of the buffalo country. As the white population grew in eastern Kansas, the buffalo were concentrated in a north-south range on the High Plains. General Phil Sheridan said that he had seen a herd ninety miles long.[30] Mead once saw buffalo pass steadily for three weeks, night and day.[31] Some said they numbered in the billions, but a figure in the millions is generally accepted .The Grand Duke Alexis of Russia was given a royal buffalo hunt by Sheridan, Custer, other military officers, Buffalo Bill Cody, and the ever present journalist, James Gordon Bennett. Great crowds gathered at Wallace, not to hunt buffalo, but to see the "Rooshun feller" who had come so far just to shoot "buffeler."[32]

The civilization of the Plains Indians was built around the buffalo. It provided food, shelter, utensils, and ornaments. From the buffalo, the Indian took not only his sustenance but also the basis of his culture.

The supply seemed endless. Then came greedy and wasteful white men who destroyed this generous gift of nature. Buffalo Bill Mathewson, Buffalo Bill Cody, and Buffalo Jones earned their living and their names as hunters. Buffalo Bill Cody killed 4,280 buffalo with a gun named "Lucretia Borgia."[33] To these men, killing was a business.

There are those who remind us that the buffalo is actually the American bison, but in the vocabulary of the American public, buffalo is the

64

accepted name. Only in Rush County did Bison become a place-name and only after Buffalo was rejected.[34]

It was natural that the buffalo name should be applied to the creeks where the animals were first seen, and one of the first to be named Buffalo Creek was a branch of the Verdigris in Wilson County. There Chester Gould, the first postmaster, named the town Buffalo, a "common-place and unromantic name," said Alexander Wetmore.[35] But this was on the eastern border of the buffalo country. There had also been a place named Buffalo and "Buffalo Hollow" in Doniphan County.[36] One Buffalo Creek flows into the Republican River in Jewell County and another into the Smoky Hill in Ellsworth County. Barton, Cloud, and Jewell counties had townships named Buffalo. Wabaunsee has a hill named Buffalo Mound. In Gove County, Buffalo was a temporary place-name for a town first named Hill Gove, then Buffalo Park; it is still Buffalo Park, but the post office is just Park. A little business community near Fort Dodge was called Buffalo City and Buffalo Station. Its main interest of selling whisky to soldiers notwithstanding, it was later named "Buffalo Capital" for its position as the greatest western shipping center for buffalo hides and bones.[37] From there over five million buffalo hides were shipped. "This singularly uninspired name," said one critic, "was objected to by the post office, which already was wrestling with half a dozen Buffalo Cities, Creeks, Hills, Rivers and Villes."[38] He might also have mentioned a Park, a Junction, and New Buffalo. The town of Yuma in Cloud County had first been named Buffalo Junction for the terminal of a branch railroad.[39]

Also in the buffalo country of western Kansas was a county named Buffalo. Changes were made in both names and boundaries, and most of Buffalo County became Garfield and was later absorbed by Finney County. Logical though the name had been, it lost in the conflicts over county boundaries. While it was still Buffalo County, a post office there was named New Buffalo and then Buffalo Center.

Perhaps the best known of four Cow Creeks in Kansas is the one flowing into the Arkansas at Hutchinson. This one was probably named for the buffalo by the Indians. It was called "Cold Water or Cow Creek" by Joseph Brown, the surveyor.[40] A branch of Cow Creek was called "Bull Crick," where a traveler in 1821 said he had killed "Buffelow Bulls."[41] Cow Creek, in the area of the Quivira villages, was an important crossing on the Santa Fe Trail. There was for a time a station and a Cow Creek store at the crossing. Speaking of its name, the founder of Hutchinson said that he "rejoices in the practical, if not the poetical name of Cow Creek."[42]

The first travelers and hunters in Kansas noticed the number of deer and elk in the unspoiled country. Both red deer and black-tailed deer were found in Kansas. Phillips County has a Deer Creek Township crossed by Deer Creek, flowing into the North Fork of the Solomon. The branch of a Deer Creek in Allen County gave its name to a township. Marshall County has a Deer Creek, a Fawn Creek, and a Game Creek. Barber County had a Deerhead post office in Deerhead Township. Kearny County has a town named Deerfield. There was a post office named Fawn in Montgomery County, shortened from its first name of Fawn Creek; and Labette County had a Deerton.

Buck Creek in eastern Jefferson County enters the Kaw near Buck Creek station on the Union Pacific. Buck Creek in Montgomery County flows into Elk Creek below Elk City. Bourbon County had a Buck Run.

When Mead named Beaver Creek, he might as easily have named it Elk Creek, since "here," he said, "I shot two fat elk from a passing bunch."[43] Many of the early travelers and settlers spoke of their seeing the stately elk in Kansas, especially in the eastern portion. Elk River, flowing into the Verdigris in Montgomery County, was the source for several names. When Howard County was divided, the northern part was named Elk County for Elk River. The river has also given its name to Elk Falls and Elk Falls Township in Elk County and Elk City in Montgomery County. Chase County had a town named Elk.

In the Western Hemisphere the elk is an American deer; in England it is a moose. In reality it is a Wapiti, an unfamiliar name to most people and used as a place-name only in Colorado and Wyoming. Eight creeks in Kansas were named Elk, surpassing by one the number named Antelope or Deer. Except for Elk Creek in Norton County, all were in the eastern half of Kansas where the elk could find safety in the timber and brush along the streams.

Townships named Elk are located in Cloud and Osage counties, and Elk Creek Township is in Republic County. The majestic elk shed their impressive horns annually, and the finding of an elk horn could well inspire a name. In Lincoln County, Elkhorn Creek flows into the Saline River. There, too, is Elkhorn Township.

Vast herds of antelope were seen in western Kansas. One frontiersman said that he saw two thousand of the "graceful animals in a single herd near Dodge City."[44] The antelope on the High Plains of Kansas was the pronghorn or American antelope, not the true antelope. When frightened, the pronghorn sped away, exposing its white-patch rump as a danger signal. Seeing the divided leather patch on the cowboy pants of Charles Russell as he walked away, the Blackfoot Indians were reminded of the antelope and named the artist Ah-wah-cous, "horns that fork."[45] The English name for the antelope came originally from the Greek word meaning "horned animal." The Indian name was more specific when it identified the antelope as "horns that fork."

We have the comments of two journalists, Horace Greeley and Albert Richardson, to indicate the admiration people had for the antelope. Greeley said antelope were the only animals he had seen on the High Plains "that might boast of either grace or beauty." Watching them moving across the hillsides, Richardson concluded that the antelope was "the best living illustration of the poetry in motion."[46] But antelope made good food, were easily shot, and were gradually exterminated.

The place where the first antelope were generally seen on the Santa Fe Trail was in Marion County, site of the only post office to have been named Antelope.[47] Seven creeks were named for the antelope, most of them in central Kansas. Clark County had an Antelope Valley. Graham County has an Antelope Lake hidden in its state park. Antelope Springs were in Davis (Geary) County. Wonsevu in Chase County is believed to be an Indian name for antelope.

Bears were not abundant in Kansas, but the creeks named Bear indicate where they were seen. These streams are all in southwestern Kansas. One flows into the Medicine Lodge River; a second into the Cimarron in Clark County; and two streams from Colorado named Buffalo and Horse Creek join to make Bear Creek, which disappears south of the sand dunes in Kearny County. Aubrey's route to the Cimarron was by way of the Bear Creek Pass.[48]

Nearly all early travelers, from Lewis and Clark on, mentioned the gray wolf, the big black wolf, also called a "buffalo wolf," and the coyote, or prairie wolf. The Wolf River that Lewis and Clark described had already been named Rivière de Loup by the French, a translation from its Indian name.[49] One explorer referred to it as the "River de Loup."[50] The source of this river is in Wolf River Township in Doniphan County, the location of the Wolf River post office.[51]

After a morning's hunt in the Saline Valley, James R. Mead found a pack of "big wolves, nearly white, and resembling sheep," tearing into his buffalo meat. He poisoned several with strychnine, and there, near Sylvan Grove, he named Wolf Creek. He named the branches West Fork Wolf Creek, Wolf Creek, and East Wolf Creek.

There were twelve widely scattered Wolf Creeks in Kansas. Because of rocky bluffs and an abundance of wolves along a stream in Bourbon County, it was named Wolf Pen Creek. Black Wolf in Black Wolf Township, west of Ellsworth, was named for Black Wolf Creek which is believed to have been named for an Indian called Black Wolf. There is also a station named Wolf, terminal of a short railway west of Garden City.[52]

The coyote, whose name came from the Nahuatl, or Aztec, language in Mexico, was known as the prairie wolf in Kansas. Although bounties have been paid for killing them, coyotes are still present in fairly large numbers. Coyote was the name of a temporary terminal in western Kansas during the building of the Kansas Central. In 1868 it was a post office in Ellis County, and in 1874 there was another Coyote post office in Phillips County. In Chase County a creek known as Prather's Creek had its name changed to "Yowl Creek on account of the yowling of the coyotes near its head waters."[53] Some called the prairie wolves "singing coyotes."

Fox is used as a personal name, a tribal name, and an animal name. Fox Creek and the Fox post office in Chase County were named for Edward Fox, a local pioneer.[54] The Fox post office, first in Harper County and then in Kingman County, could have been named for the red fox.

The polecat is not really a cat, and the "pole" part of the name comes from *poule*, meaning chicken. By dropping the "u" from *poule*, the name of this chicken-stealer becomes polecat. Odoriferous as he might be, the polecat was nevertheless trapped for his fur. Two creeks were named Polecat Creek, one flowing into the Walnut in Cowley County and another flowing into the Ninnescah in Sedgwick County. Using the word skunk may not make the animal smell worse, but the term makes one more aware of the odor. Graham County had a Skunk Creek flowing into the South Fork of the Solomon. As a part of the language, skunk is a denigrating characterization.

The badger is distantly related to the skunk, and, like skunk, badger has become a part of our vocabulary. "Badgering" means to "pester" or "harass." Although Wisconsin is known as the Badger State, the burrowing animal is found all over the West. Streams named Badger Creek are mostly in eastern Kansas. Badger Creek flows into the Neosho in Greenwood County, into Slate Creek in Sumner County, and into the Walnut in Cowley County. Badger Creek post office, also called Badger City, was in Lyon County.[55] Badger, like other animal names, could be a surname. A town planned for Cherokee County was named Badger for William P. Badger, an Indian agent who seemingly lived up to his name.[56]

The wildcat, also called a lynx or bobcat, was a genuine member of the cat family. When cared for as kittens, wildcats grow up to be as devoted and loving as domestic cats. But hunters have taken delight in killing these cats. They are still being killed in fairly large numbers. Six streams are named Wildcat in as many counties. One Wild Cat Creek flows out of Riley County and enters the Kaw at Manhattan. This creek gave its name to the Wild Cat post office and Wild Cat Township. The Wild Cat post office had its name changed to Keats.

Although yellow-haired porcupines were present in Kansas, especially along wooded bluffs, the only place named for this animal was Porcupine Creek, a branch of Limestone Creek in Jewell County.

The raccoon was a night-prowler known to the eastern Indians as the *Aroughcun*, as Captain John Smith spelled it.[57] This was conveniently simplified to raccoon and later to "coon." Nine streams in Kansas have been named Coon Creek. Most of these are in eastern Kansas, but one of the better-known Coon Creeks flows into the Arkansas River below Kinsley. This was once called De Mun's Creek, for one of Chouteau's companions, and then Clear Creek by Major Sibley.[58] It had another name, according to the report of J. Fowler, a pioneer. "We gave this the name of Buffelow Crick from one of our Horses Being Swamped With the meet of a Buffelow on Him and these anemels Being very plenty Heare."[59] The "Buffelow" name was not official, and the creek is now Big Coon Creek joined by Little Coon Creek.

The opossum, like the raccoon, lost the first syllable of its name. There were places called Possum Hollow in Atchison County, Possum Trot near Winchester in Jefferson County and in Chautauqua County, and Possum Creek in Bourbon County.[60]

The playful otter with its appealingly soft fur was evidently plentiful across the whole state of Kansas. Of the nine streams named for the otter, six were in the eastern half of Kansas. Yet in western Kansas, there were said to be thousands of beaver and otter on the Prairie Dog. "Uncle Dan" McLaren was a hunter and trapper who came to Norton County in 1870 and in that year caught eighty otters. The stream he named Otter Creek flows into the Solomon from the north.[61] There was an Otter Creek flowing into the Walnut in Rush County. Because of the abundance of otters in the Pawnee Fork the Indians called it Otter Creek.[62] Pottawatomie County had an Otter Lake.

Cowley County had a township named Otter, and Greenwood County had a township named Otter Creek for a local stream flowing into Fall River. In Clay County a post office was named Otter Creek, and the little stream flowing into the Republican River from the south was also called Otter Creek.[63] Pottawatomie County had a post office named Otter Lake. Republic County, which had an Otter Creek, also had a Beaver Creek.

Beaver pelts were so popular and so valuable during pioneer days that much of Kansas was explored by trappers in search of these fascinating rodents. The beaver is known as an engineer, builder, and architect. Long before the federal government promoted the building of dams, the beaver built reservoirs on Kansas streams; but settlers showed little appreciation for this control of the water flow. The animal was virtually exterminated in most of Kansas by the turn of the century, but newspapers reported the sale of over five thousand beaver pelts in Kansas in 1968–69, indicating a remarkable recovery.[64] Beaver are now found along streams and even in such populated areas as Douglas County.[65]

There were eleven Beaver Creeks in Kansas, an equal number of Beaver Townships, generally named for the creeks, seven post offices using the name Beaver, and one town named Beaver with no post office. The Oregon Trail crossed the Kaw near Beaver Creek.[66] Cloud County had the only post office named Beaver Creek. When James R. Mead's expedition to the valley of the Saline first camped on a small creek, the hunters found many beaver dams. With no formal ceremony, said Mead, "We named that Beaver Creek."[67]

All of the townships named Beaver were in the northwestern part of the state, except for Beaver Township in Cowley County, which had a Beaver Creek and a town named Beaver. Five post offices were named Beaver in northwestern Kansas. Beavertown in Miami County was without a post office and is listed only among "Extinct Towns."[68] Similar to Beavertown was the name of Beaverton, which replaced the name of Bird in Rawlins County. Beaverview was also in Rawlins County. Scott County had a Beaver Flats.

When Lieutenant Colonel William H. Lewis pursued Chief Dull Knife, who was leading his Cheyennes from the reservation back to the North, Indians "posted themselves on the tops of conical hills which bordered a canyon on Punished Woman's Fork or Famished Woman's Fork, later known as Ladder or Beaver Creek . . ."[69] The stream was named Ladder Creek when some hunters found an abandoned ladder nearby.[70] But with so many names from which to choose, the combined streams are now listed under the name of Beaver. The North Fork of the Beaver joins the Little Beaver to enter the Middle Beaver, then joins the South Fork of the Beaver in Rawlins County and crosses Beaver Township in Decatur County, continuing on to the Republican River in Nebraska. The river was aptly named, but there were probably as many beaver in the parallel streams of the Sappa and Prairie Dog.[71]

Kansas was prairie dog country, and a popular pastime of pioneers was target practice which they called "varmint hunting." The gregarious prairie dogs lived in colonies called towns. When a community became overcrowded, small groups, or just a couple, moved out to start a new town. Horace Greeley, a sharp observer, said that the prairie dog was "the funny fellow of these parts—frisky himself, and a source of merriment to others."[72] The Indians called the animal Wishtonwish to imitate his sound. Lewis and Clark called the prairie dog a "barking squirrel." Some swindlers seeking to sell bonds for development of new counties even included prairie dog villages as human dwellings. One animal town was said to be listed as "the home of John and Mary."[73]

On June 23, 1843, John Charles Frémont came to a beautiful wooded branch of the Republican in western Kansas where he found a large number of prairie dog towns. He named it Prairie Dog Creek.[74] This creek begins in Thomas County and meanders through four counties on its way to join the Republican in Nebraska. In Sheridan County it left its name on Prairie Dog Township, and in Decatur County it crossed another Prairie Dog Township. Bob Anderson opened a post office which was named Anderson in Pratt County. Because of a prairie dog town to the south, the post office was known locally as "Dogtown."[75]

Although the striped gopher was quite common on the prairies, its name was limited to one town, Gopher in Logan County, but within a year it was changed to Winona, an Indian name.

Kansas had a large jackrabbit population. Now the number is kept down by the automobile, and rabbit round-ups are no longer necessary. Many farmers have satisfied their hunger with "rabbit pie." Only Rabbit Creek in Miami County honors the Kansas jackrabbit.

Like the beaver, the mole was a busy animal. Moles helped to aerate the soil and aided cultivation despite the efforts of farmers to exterminate them. The name of Mole Hill in Dickinson County[76] might refer to a small hill rather than to the animal.

The mole may have named a hill, but the lonely mouse left its name on Mouse Creek, which flows into Big Hill Creek in Montgomery County.

The turtle family furnished the terrapin to represent it as a place-name. A place called Rural Springs in Kingman County, probably a good hang-out for freshwater turtles, had its name changed to Terrapin, the "aristocrat of the marshes."

Frogs and terrapins live much alike. Frogs are fancy fly-catchers and are food for snakes and occasionally for man. Surveyors in Coffey County found frogs so abundant along a stream that they lived on frog legs and named the stream Frog Creek.[77]

Joe Field, a member of the Lewis and Clark expedition, was bitten by a rattlesnake near Fourth of July Creek, and there "Joe Field's Snake Prairie" was named. The Missouri River bluffs are known as "Rattlesnake Hills."[78] Only two streams in Kansas were identified by the name of this deadly serpent. A long Rattlesnake Creek flows from Ford County to the Arkansas River in Rice County. This furnished the name for Rattlesnake post office, now Hudson, in Stafford County. The other Rattlesnake Creek is a branch of Salt Creek in northern Lincoln County. The stream named Pioneer Creek flowing into the Cimarron in Clark County had its name changed to Snake Creek. Another Snake Creek flows into the Ninnescah in Kingman County. Snake Hill in Lyon County took its name from a snake hunt in which 4,150 reptiles were killed in five days.[79] Another report tells of Walter Battice being born at "Rattlesnake Hill" in the Sac and Fox reservation.[80]

Names of animals which were not native to Kansas were also used. We find such names as Moose Hill, Wolverine, and Cariboo. But Moose Hill in Brown County was named for a pioneer, W. H. Moose.[81]

The wolverine is a northern animal, and Michigan is known as the Wolverine State. There are now few of these vicious wolverines left south of Canada. Yet Wolverine is the name of a tributary of the Marmaton, whose French name is something of a puzzle, although possibly it was named for the prairie dog. The Wolverine was named for the "many wolves" in the area.[82] Inaccurate though the name may be, the explanation is plausible.

Equally remote was the caribou, yet Butler County had a Cariboo post office near Potwin on the Whitewater. The caribou, cousin of the reindeer, is an Alaskan animal.

Pike was too modest when he said, "I believe there are buffalo, elk, and deer sufficient on the banks of the Arkansas alone, if used without waste, to feed all the savages in the United States territory one century."[83] The key to this livelihood was, "if used without waste." Had this been done, Pike could well have extended his prediction to two centuries. White hunters destroyed the enormous food supply in a matter of two decades, leaving the Indian destitute. But there were white men who also regretted the destruction of prairie wildlife.

No American song dealing with buffalo, deer, or antelope is better known than "Home on the Range." It was the favorite song of Franklin D. Roosevelt; Admiral Byrd sang it to the penguins in the Antarctic; and it was recorded by many, including folklorist John Lomax. One may accept the statement that "it was literally sung around the world."[84] There has been considerable controversy over its authorship, but credit has been given to Daniel E. Kelley and to Dr. Brewster Higby. Dan Kelley lived at Gaylord and Brewster lived in a dugout on Beaver Creek, both near the geographical center of the United States in Smith County. The lyrics portray an idyllic frontier life of "the good old days," and in 1947 the Kansas Legislature made "Home on the Range" the official state song.[85] Kansas place-names, like that song, are also reminders of the life on the range.

CHAPTER VII

NATURAL RESOURCES

KANSAS IS REMARKABLY RICH in natural resources. It has lush grasses, rich soil, and subsurface wealth in the form of salt, coal, lead, zinc, and oil and gas. It has cretaceous material for cement, gypsum for plaster, and volcanic dust for soap and cleanser. Whatever the product, its location may be identified by a place-name.

Kansas is not noted for precious metals or gemstones, but that fact did not prevent pioneers from using place-names which would imply the presence of gold, silver, diamonds, and rubies. These must not be taken literally. Gem is a word which refers to a precious stone, but it may be used to describe anything that is precious. Thomas County had a post office and station named Gem, but its source was not a precious stone. It was named for the Gem Ranch, which was, no doubt, precious to its owner. As for Ruby, a name used in both Sedgwick and Harper counties, the name was probably that of a girl. The diamond in Diamond Springs, a popular stop on the Santa Fe Trail, described the sparkle in its bubbling waters. Diamond Island, not far from Leavenworth, was named for its rhombic form.[1] There is a stone called the "Kansas Diamond," but like the Herkimer Diamond of New York, it is only clear quartz.

When a New York correspondent rode out from Abilene to see four thousand acres of ripening wheat owned by T. C. Henry, he exclaimed: "What a magnificent golden belt!"[2] The place named Golden Belt in Lincoln County picked up the name for the golden grain belt of central Kansas. As for gold, there was some in Kansas streams, washed all the way from the gold fields in Colorado. It did show color, but placer mining on the Smoky Hill did not prove to be profitable.[3] The gold mine shown on an 1857 map by Le Page du Pratz as being at the future site of Wichita proved to be only a teaser, as did the placer mines.[4] But Butler County had a place named Oro, and that means "gold" in Spanish.

Silver as a name was widely used in Kansas, but in no case did it refer to the metal. Silver Lake near Topeka had a silvery appearance. Silverdale in Cowley County got its name from Silver Creek, which had no silver. The quarry for the attractive building stone called Silverdale was located there. Silver City near Independence was associated with mining but not silver mining. A fiery-looking amber mica called phlogophite was mined nearby.[5] Neither Silver Creek in Chase County nor Silver Spring in Nemaha County was named for the metal. Kansas, with no silver, had nine creeks named Silver.

Argentine, now a part of Kansas City, has a name which refers to silver, but its smelter, the source of its name, processed mostly copper. Chalcopyrite, or copper pyrites, was found in southeastern Kansas; but Copper Creek is in Kingman County.

Several places in Kansas, in Norton and Harper counties especially, have deposits of volcanic ash. In Norton County it has been used to manufacture soap, glazes for pottery, and even toothpaste. Lava, the name of a place in Sherman County, was near this profitable deposit of volcanic material.

Volcanic ash or lava is in some places called silica. It is composed of small particles of glass.[6] Some of the settlers were sufficiently knowledgeable to use Silica as a place-name. The first Silica was a post office in Phillips County. There was also a Silica between Chase and Ellenwood in Rice County. It is still an active railroad station. Meade County has an eminence called Silica Hill.

The erosion of the Rocky Mountains has deposited several layers of gravel, sand, and good soil in Kansas. One has only to read the list of streams named Sand to realize how completely Kansas was covered by this rich wash from the Rockies. Gannett listed twelve Sand Creeks and three named Sandy Creek. Meade County in the south and Norton County in the north had townships named Sand Creek.[7] The vast deposits of sand, especially in the Arkansas River valley, have been a great resource for road building and other cement construction.

Captain Pike deplored the lack of wood in Kansas but said, "Time may make discoveries of coal mines which would render the country habitable."[8] Eastern Kansas has an abundance of coal, and some has been found in other areas. No resource has contributed more Kansas place-names. The coal field extending from Republic County to Cloud County gave rise to the place named Minersville in the former and Minersville post office in the latter.[9] There was a Mineral Point, now Amiot, in Anderson County.

The Tri-State mining area includes the southeastern corner of Kansas, northeastern Oklahoma, and southwestern Missouri. Cherokee is the corner county of Kansas, and there a town was named Mineral. A railroad station was later identified as West Mineral, and so the Cherokee County town became East Mineral. For almost two months in 1898 there was also a Mineral City nearby. Mineral Township had a place named Stripville, for the local practice of strip mining. Chautauqua County had a Minersview. There was also a Mine Creek near Kansas City noted for a battle in the Civil War.

Place-names such as Coalburgh, Coal Centre, Coal Creek, Coalfield, and Coalvale advertise the abundance of coal in Kansas. All of these, except Coal Creek, are or were in eastern Kansas.[10] To the list we may add a Carbon in Jackson County, a Carbondale in Bourbon County, another in Osage County, and a Cokedale in Cherokee County. Carbondale in Osage County was promoted by T. J. Peters of the Santa Fe and was the first town to furnish profitable freight for the Santa Fe Railroad.[11] A post office named Coalvale was in Crawford County near a Braidwood and McLusky Coal Company mine. Another place in Osage County was called Carbon Hill. Also in that county was a place called Coal Bank.

When Lieutenant J. R. Fitch was making the survey for the Butterfield route along the Smoky, he reported: "We found a fine coal bed on what we named Coal Creek" west of Ellsworth.[12] This name did not become official, but six counties had streams named Coal Creek. A stream in Ottawa County had been known as "Hard-Crossing Creek" until an inch-thick seam of coal was discovered in its bank. To call attention to it, a coal company changed the name to Coal Creek. This was the only Coal Creek to give its name to a post office.[13] Coal Canyon was named for a nine-inch seam of fuel in Russell County.[14]

A town first named Folsom in Cherokee County changed its name to Carbona. When the "b" was deleted from the name it became Carona and any reference to carbon or coal was lost.[15]

Scammon and Wier City in Cherokee County were named for coal miners, as were Arma and Croweburg in Crawford County. Scammon was first named Stilson and then Scammonville for four Scammon brothers from Illinois. Wier City was named for T. M. Wier, who gave forty acres for a townsite. Arma honored Arma Post who was also in the coal business. Croweburg was named for the Crowe Coal Mining Company. Radley, in Crawford County, was named for H. H. Radley, secretary of the Girard Coal Company.[16]

The town of Empire City was located on a ridge atop a mining empire in the Galena area. To its first name of Empire, residents added the superfluous appendage of City, hoping to surpass in splendor the rival town of Galena.[17] The rivalry between Empire City and Galena began when a German farmer named Egidius Moll sold the same forty acres of his worthless farm to three different bidders, causing no end of confusion. Taking advantage of the rival claims, the Galena Mining and Smelting Company promoted a town, to be named Cornwall, on Short Creek near the farm. The town was actually known as Short Creek because of its location, but optimistic miners renamed it Bonanza. Several minerals were mined in the area. One of them, lead, was the source for the name of Galena.[18] Red zinc, or sphalerite, crystals were called either ruby or "black jack." Galena was consequently dubbed "The City that Jack built."[19]

Gypsum may take many forms, ranging from alabaster to satin spar and selenite. It is found from Medicine Lodge in the south to Blue Rapids in the north. Gypsum comes from a Greek word meaning "plaster" or "chalk." Used decoratively in ancient Egypt, it is today processed for cement, plaster of paris, and plaster board.[20] Well known are the so-called "Gyp Hills" in the Medicine Lodge area, where the red rocks make an attractive contrast with the dark green cedar trees.

Gypsum Creek east of Salina became the source for the name of the town now called Gypsum City. It "swallowed up" an earlier town named Pliney. Seven thousand tons of gypsum were shipped from its mill to Chicago in 1892 for buildings in the World's Fair.[21] Below Gypsum Township is Gypsum Creek Township in McPherson County. "Gyp" Creek, as it is called in Sedgwick County, was the source for the name of Gypsum Township.

The boom town that grew around the plant of the Portland Cement Company in Allen County was named Concreto.[22] Even the town with the Spanish name of Yocemento in Ellis County referred to the cement made from the cretaceous material in the area.[23]

Greenwood, Sumner, and Rooks counties had enough shalelike slate to have streams named Slate Creek. The stream below the Ninnescah in Sumner County was called *Ne-san-a-cha-had*, the Indian name for Slate Creek, its present name.[24] A resident of Rooks County said that the Slate Creek there was named from "great outcrops of slate all along the stream." From this name, both a post office and a school were named Slate Creek.[25]

Long before the settlers became aware of subsurface salt deposits, the Indians knew about the salty content of Kansas streams. The French knew enough about Indian languages to recognize when Indians named a stream for its salt. The best known of these is the one the French called the Grand Saline, a fork of the Smoky Hill. The Siouan tribes had called it Ne Miskua. All of the rivers south of the Arkansas were at some time or another called Saline.[26]

In one list of place-names in Kansas, Saline and Salt were used thirty times.[27] The first was used for the Grande Saline River, Saline County, and the town of Salina. Only Ellis and Saline counties have townships named Saline, but there were twelve Salt Creek names, three named Salt Marsh, and one Salt Spring. Saline County had a Saline Valley post office. There are twenty-five Salt Creeks, four counties have townships named Salt Creek; and Leavenworth, Cloud, and Reno counties had Salt Creek post offices.[28] Salt Marsh, the first post office in Republic County, had its name changed to Seapo.[29] There was sufficient salt in Salt Marsh, Stafford County, for the settlers to manufacture salt.[30] Greenwood County had its Salt Springs, and Mitchell County had a place named Saltville. Sumner County had a post office named Salt City, probably for the mineral waters of Geuda Springs.

The salt industry began when the oil boom in eastern Kansas spread to the central part of the state. Oilmen often ended their drilling "with nothing but rock salt to show for their operations." But the discovery of layers of salt several hundred feet thick was in itself a bonanza. Hutchinson, the center of the salt industry, is known as "Salt City."

Supposedly one reason for the delay in settling Kansas was the scarcity of lumber there. Yet lumber mills were scattered widely over Kansas and were common in the eastern half. Most of the mills were run by water power although some used horsepower.[31] Any stream that could turn a water wheel might become the site of a grist or a lumber mill and the source for a name. Names like Splitlog and Sawlog were associated with lumbering.

Mill Creek in Bourbon County was named for the first sawmill in southeastern Kansas. It was constructed in 1843 and furnished lumber for the officers' quarters at Fort Scott.[32] The Mill Creek post office there had its name changed to Devon. The mill on Mill Creek in Doniphan County was built by the government for the Indians, who "showed their ingratitude," said George Remsburg, "by burning it down."[33] There were ten other streams named Mill Creek, and Washington County has a Mill Creek Township.

Geary County had a Milford post office on the east side of the Republican River and a Milford Station on the west side, both in Milford Township. Milford had first been named Batcheller, also spelled Bachelder.[34] Annoyed by the people's inability to spell Batcheller, which was a questionable spelling in the first place, the postmaster changed the name to Milford.

The New England Emigrant Aid Society sent several mills to promising Kansas towns. Drunken ruffians dumped the one destined for Quindaro into the Missouri River. It was recovered and sold to the "Bachelder" Town Company.[35] This was the mill that named Milford, which was best known as headquarters for Dr. John Brinkley's medical and political practices. It is now known for the Milford Dam.

Mill Creek in Wabaunsee County was the home of the Kansa Chief E-ya-no-sa, "Big Both Ways."[36] The East Branch Mill Creek flows through Mill Creek Township.

Horace Greeley, concerned by the shortage of lumber, thought that limestone was among "the chief blessings of Kansas."[37] It was not long before pioneers learned how to saw limestone into serviceable building material. While traveling in the Winfield area, a pioneer noted the limestone bluffs which "furnish an abundance of limestone for all purposes of building and fencing."[38] Limestone was a good substitute for lumber and could be used to build houses, barns, railway stations, courthouses and so forth. In midwestern Kansas fence posts were made from limestone.[39] Only in Washington County was a post office named Limestone.

Limestone Creek was a likely source for the name of Limestone Township in Jewell County. In this area of northern Kansas the limestone was of an exceptionally light color and was called Whiterock. This was a source for the name of the White Mound post office and the White Mound Township in Jewell County.

John Galbraith established a sawmill and opened a saloon on White Rock Creek in Republic County, the nucleus for a post office. The first name proposed for the post office was Pinhook. Located near the White Rock Bluffs and White Rock Creek, it was, however, named White Rock. Republic, Smith, and Lane counties have townships named White Rock. Most of the roads in the area are built with this limestone.[40]

The town of Cameron in Norton County was named for its first storekeeper. There was already a Cameron in Kansas, so the storekeeper changed the name of the town to Clayton because of the clay on the roads in the area.

There were, in addition to timber and limestone, other types of natural building material available to pioneers in Kansas, including prairie sod and adobe. There was a Sodville in Ness County and an Adobe in Seward County. In southeastern Kansas brick manufacturing was a major industry. In Montgomery County a post office was to be named Brickton, but the name was rescinded.

There was a great deal of interest in radium after its discovery in 1898. Radium metal was developed in 1910, and in that year the Wellsville post office in Stafford County had its name changed to Radium.

Terra cotta is an Italian term which is descriptive of a reddish clay used for making pottery. The town of Terra Cotta, formerly Mullins Siding, borders on the red Dakota sandstone country of Ellsworth County.[41] Brick manufacturing in the area may have inspired the name. Terra Cotta is not necessarily an unattractive name, although one writer

79

said that it was "a name which disfigures the maps of two states and the District of Columbia."[42] When he lived in Kansas, Frederic Remington[43] had a horse named Terra Cotta, called "Terry" by the artist's friends.[44]

Barber County had an Amber Creek and a post office was named Amber. The translucent fossil from ambergris is not common in Kansas, but George Jelinek has discovered amber not far from Ellsworth.

To these resources may be added alum, sulphur, and niter. Alum Creek post office had its name changed to Carneiro. Several Springs may have contained sulphur, but only in Cloud County did Sulphur Springs become a post office name.[45] Niter in Wyandotte County was luckily not named Saltpeter.

The presence of tar was obvious in Kansas, judging from such place-names as Wea Tar Pits, Beaver Tar Springs, and Won-zop-peach Tar Springs, all in Miami County.[46] There was some prospecting as early as 1860, and experimental drilling revealed a useful source of natural gas in the tar pits area. A suburb of Iola in Allen County was called Gas City, and its post office name was Gas.

The presence of oil in Kansas was known long before it was exploited. The oil and gas boom in the 1890's was the beginning of a profitable business.[47] Not far from the town of Gas was a town named Petrolia. Both are now the names of railway stations. Oil City in Butler County was named in 1877, perhaps as a hint of things to come.[48] Butler County also had a post office named Oil Valley. A suburb of El Dorado was called Oil Hill. Observing a booming oil town east of Douglas, Harry Gore said, "Magna means great, so we'll call it Magna City." It is now a ghost town.[49] Skelly is a well-known name in oil, and when oil was discovered on "Poverty Ridge" in Kingman County, the place was named Skellyville.[50]

CHAPTER VIII

DWARDSVILLE EFFINGHAM ELBING EL DORADO ELGIN ELKADER ELK CITY ELK FALLS ELKHART

ECONOMIC IMPRINT

ELLIS ELLSWORTH ELMDALE ELMO ELSMORE ELWOOD ELYRIA EMMETT EMPORIA ENGLEWOOD

NATURE WAS KIND to Kansas. Prairies and wooded streams gave sustenance and shelter to its natural game. The Indian hunter found sufficient food and shelter to live a reasonably carefree life in this "prairie quadrangle." Then came the white man, also dependent on nature and its beneficence. But too often the white man, bent on the subjugation of nature, destroyed it. Following the explorers, travelers, and hunters were the ranchers and farmers who struggled for a living while feeding the nation.

The small farmer left his mark on the land. Many community names in Kansas were associated with the state's rural economy. The small farmer has now been largely replaced by big ranchers, suitcase or absentee farmers, and "gentlemen farmers." Post offices have been abandoned, but a few place-names remain as a reminder of the farmer's frontier.

In many parts of Kansas post offices and stations preceded towns, but each could be the nucleus of a town. Towns and post offices were not separated from the rural life but were a part of it. Even today, when less than 10 per cent of the population is living on farms, over 30 per cent is classified as rural.

As for the method of naming, an old German farmer in Nebraska was known for his habit of saying, "W'y not," to any suggestion. When a railroad company hesitated to put its station on his farm, he raised the usual "W'y not?" When the farmer won the station, the railroad named it Wynot.[1] And why not? North Carolina has a town named Why Not.

When the ranchers and farmers occupied Kansas, domestic animals replaced wild game. The Texas longhorns and wild horses served as a transition between the two. It is believed that the Cimarron, a river whose name meant "wild," was named for Texas longhorns.[2]

The horse was the Spaniards' most valuable contribution to the Indians. Eastern Kansas had a Wild Horse Creek flowing into the Grasshopper and another into Big Stranger. It is possible that one of these was named for the Pawnee chief named Wild Horse.

Wild horses roamed western Kansas and the Oklahoma Panhandle as

81

late as 1903.[3] Wild Horse Lake was on the Santa Fe Trail in Haskell County.[4] A camping place on the Fort Wallace Trail in Greeley County was known as Wild Horse Corral. A band of wild horses south of Goodland was led by a shiny black stallion named Black Kettle.[5] Creeks named Wild Horse in central Kansas were in Kingman, Stafford, and Ness counties. The Wild Horse name was best represented in Graham County where there was a Wild Horse Creek, a Wild Horse Township, and a Wild Horse post office.

"Hunting wild horses in Western Kansas was the chief occupation of the first settlers in the region," one historian has said.[6] A draw in southern Lane County was used to corral horses and was called Wild Horse Canyon. Another such natural corral near Colby was also called Wild Horse Canyon. The most famous of the western horse hunters, the Fulton brothers, founded Garden City. Horse Creek in Norton County was named because several horses perished in a blizzard there.[7]

The Spaniards called the wild horses *mesteños*, meaning "wild," or possibly "graziers." Anglo-Americans adopted the name and made it mustang. In Comanche County a branch of the Salt Fork is called Mustang Creek. There, too, are found Cavalry Creek and Mule Creek.

The king of Spain once gave George Washington a pair of mules as a royal gift. It was a singular and significant gift but not a surprising one in view of the fact that there was a time when America had to import the sturdy animals. Mules were invaluable in transporting people and products to the West, but still they were not popular, and names to honor them are not common. Yet that hardy, obstinate animal gave its name to several creeks, notably Big Mule Creek and Little Mule Creek in Barber County. There was another Mule Creek in eastern Ellsworth County, from which Mule Creek post office took its name.

The Indians, who spoke of the horse as a "walking dog," are believed to have had some kind of horse in mind when they named Shunganunga Creek south of Topeka. There is no agreement on the description of the horse, but *shunga* would suggest reference to a small horse, perhaps a pony or even a race horse.[8]

The story of the naming of a town in Elk County concerns a girl who owned a pony named Polo. She was riding Polo when the pony stopped at a railroad crossing. The railway workers heard the girl's exclamation or appeal: "You-Polo!" From this, it was said, the town of Upola was named.[9] In Wilson County a Pony Creek flows into the Verdigris, and Brown County had a Pony Creek post office.

When Emporia speculators promoted a town on Grouse Creek in Cowley County, they named it Dexter, after a race horse owned by Robert Bonner of the *New York Ledger*.[10]

82

There were more places named for cattle than for horses in Kansas. Ellis County once had a post office named Stockrange. Five years after it was closed in 1895, the name was adopted for a town in Trego County. This was cattle country, and not far away in Rooks County, a cattle center was to be named "Stocktown," but "happily," said one McNulty, a local resident, "they modified it." They deleted one letter and made it Stockton,[11] causing some to assume that the town was named for Stockton, California.

In Riley County, Stockdale was named to honor the livestock industry. It had been Henryville, named for pioneer postmaster Henry Condray, whose son Mincher was a successful stock raiser.

Both Bull City in Garfield (Finney) County and Bull's City in Osborne County were named for men named Bull. In Garfield County, Bull City was changed to Cowland.

A Missouri band with the slogan, "Lawrence must be wiped out," came to a small stream which, said one commentator, "rejoiced in the classic name of Bull Creek."[12] Big Bull Creek, which joins the Marais des Cygnes, has been described in glowing terms as ". . . the most picturesque piece of water on the plain, . . . with lofty trees growing to the water's edge,—and with a gentle serpentine course, it looks charmingly romantic!"[13]

The Cow name could be confusing if one had not specified whether the source was a buffalo cow or a domestic cow. Three times on one page the historian of Reno County asked the question: "Who named Cow Creek?" He gave no answer.[14] It has been assumed, however, that Cow Creek was named by the Indians for the buffalo cow. Eastern Kansas has a Cow Creek in Crawford County and another in Shawnee County.

When Chief Dull Knife fled across Kansas to escape from the reservation, his Cheyenne followers slaughtered many cattle. So many were found in one canyon in northwestern Kansas that it was called "Hundred Head Canyon."[15]

In Ellsworth County a town with the prestigious name of Attica became Bosland. The railroad is said to have named it Bosland as a cattle terminal after the genus name "Bos," meaning "cow."[16] One writer supposed the name was as "attractive to the cattle as the co-boss, co-boss, of the milkmaid to the cows."[17] Bosland, however, became Wilson, named for Isaac Wilson, an Iowa man who established the town, and not for Hiero T. Wilson, as some suggest.[18]

A stream a few miles west of Wichita was called Crooked Creek by the Indians. When a number of cattle on the Chisholm Trail died from Texas fever, they were skinned and their hides left to dry on the banks of the creek. Travelers then named the stream Cowskin.[19] James R. Mead wrote about traveling to Cowskin Grove where "Dutch Bill" Greiffenstein had his trading post.[20] A post office there called Cowskin was later moved to Waco, a place named for the Waco Indians, Caddoans related to the Wichitas.

Cattle ranching in Kansas was closely associated with the packing business. Armourdale, now absorbed by Kansas City, was named for the Armour Packing Company. Morris in Wyandotte County was named for packer Nelson Morris of Chicago.

The first camping place west of Ellsworth was called Ox Hide. The name has also been written Oxhide and Oxide. According to Henry Inman's account, the place was named from a yoke of oxen "found dead with yoke still on them." It was assumed their owner had been killed by the Indians.[21] The omission of the "h" in Oxhide made it the name of a chemical compound.

A place named Cowboy in Hodgeman County crossed the line and became the Cowboy post office in Ness County. There was also a place named Cowboy in the ranch county of Barber County, together with a place named Roundup. Ellsworth County had a Range, and Ottawa County had a Widerange.

When pioneers and travelers spoke of food, they frequently mentioned salt pork and bacon. There is a Hog Creek in Greenwood County and a Pig Creek in Wilson County.

The Homestead Act of 1862 contributed greatly to the rapid settlement of the Midwest. In Nebraska, Homestead was made a National Monument. In Kansas, Homestead was a post office in Chase County, and then it became the name of a school. It is now a cemetery.[22]

The pioneers of Rush County were honored in 1878 by a post office named Pioneer. Nearly two decades later, after the pioneers were old settlers in eastern Kansas, a place in Johnson County was named Pioneer. Rush, Graham, and Rice counties have townships named Pioneer.

A farmer's home could serve as a community post office and thus become the nucleus for a town. Home City, a busy farm center in Marshall County, was known locally as the "Biggest Little City in this area." The first postmaster, Gottlieb Messell, had the post office in his home, and it was therefore popularly known as "Home" post office. Then it was moved to a new location and called Duver for Chris Duver, the postmaster in 1882.[23] A search for an official name to replace Home produced the names of several local citizens. Dexter was suggested for Thomas Dexter but was rejected because Kansas already had a Dexter. Then Blockerville was proposed for James Blocker, Duvertown for the postmaster and promoter, and Lewisville for "English"

Bill Lewis. The men modestly declined these proposals, and the town was again named Home. It was reorganized in 1884. The new promoter, George W. Van Camp, added "City" to the name, and Home City it remained.

Small towns were built to support a rural population. Williamstown post office in Jefferson County had its name changed to Rural. Chase County had a place named Rural at the turn of the century, and Kingman County had a Rural Springs post office, which was moved to a place called Terrapin.

There was a place named Farmer in Wyandotte County but its name was changed to Turner. The place named Farmer in Wabaunsee County lasted only a month. There was another Farmer in Rice County. Wabaunsee and Rice counties have townships named Farmer, and McPherson County had a place named Farms. There were four farmer names with suffixes to indicate towns: Farmersburg in Chautauqua County, Farmersville in Osage County, Farmington in Dickinson, Republic, McPherson, and Atchison counties, and Farmer City in Wichita County, which later merged with Leoti.[24] Hillside Farm was a post office in Harvey County but its life was short. It was closed three times in four years.[25]

One might assume that names that fit the farmer's vocabulary were associated with farming. Coffey County had a place named Section. Acres in Clark County could have another source. Some may be surprised, however, to find in Graham County a township named Allodium, a term for holding land free from obligations. It once referred to freedom from feudal duties among Teutonic peoples.

Agricola is a puzzling name since it may refer to a Roman general, a German minerologist, an artist, a composer, or simply to agriculture. When Agricola replaced Hardpan in Coffey County, the new name was supposed to have been suggested by a visiting teacher. The teacher might have been exhibiting his classical learning or suggesting a name to fit agriculture.[26] Agricola was certainly preferable to Hardpan, a word that could imply soil erosion.

One of the first farmers in Kansas was Daniel Morgan Boone, grandson of Daniel Boone. He was the government farmer for the Kaws near American Chief's village. His son, also named Daniel, said, "I broke twenty acres of land . . . on Mission Creek."[27] A town there was named Plow Boy or Plowboy. Its name was later changed to Redpath, honoring a journalist and free-state politician. As for Boone, there was a Boon in Sumner County and a Boonville in Coffey County.

Even machinery could provide place-names. Tractor in Scott County is the name of the International Harvester Company experimental station.[28] In the Cedar Bluff area of the Smoky Hill, Indians killed a crew transporting a thresher. Then they burned the machine and dumped it into a canyon. The canyon has since been known as Thresher Machine Canyon.[29]

The name Richfield was a bit of optimistic advertising by a pioneer who wrote home about "the rich fields in Morton County." It was a name based on "visions of future fortunes," said a Kansas guidebook.[30] Richland, a station on the Missouri Pacific in Shawnee County, was more appropriately named. The names of seventeen Richland townships are said to be based upon descriptions by pioneers.

In Sedgwick County, Maize was a name approved by the votes of nine of the fourteen residents of the town.[31] There was a time, before winter wheat became the main crop, when Kansas was considered a corn state like Nebraska and Iowa. Maize is but another name for corn. It was one of the most valuable food products given to the world by the American Indian, but it is not a common place-name. There was a Cornhill in Butler County.

Popcorn Creek was the source for the naming of Pop Corn post office in Osage County.[32] Critics said that Kansas was too hot to raise popcorn because the corn would pop before it could be harvested. According to one story, a farmer going out to inspect his popcorn crop saw his field completely white. He thought it was snow and froze to death.[33] There are those who still insist that popcorn has popped from the Kansas heat, setting fact against fiction.[34]

Zeandale in Riley County was a post office in Zeandale Township. It was named by J. H. Pillsbury.[35] This region along the Kaw was known as the Zeandale Bottoms. Zea is the Greek word for grain. Equally unusual was the use of the Greek word spica as a place-name. It meant an "ear of grain or wheat," but spica has also been used to mean "a sharp point." Spica was once on the map between Colby and Oakley.

The confusion surrounding "Coyne or Corn Creek" in Chase County was solved by changing it to Rogler Creek, for pioneers in the valley of the South Fork of the Cottonwood.[36]

Milo was the name of a post office in Lincoln County. Milo is "erroneously" called "milo maize," according to one dictionary. Milo is the grain from which sorghum is made, and Sorghum was the name of a place in Rice County. It later became Bushton, named for the attractive bushes at the townsite. A valley in northeastern Chautauqua County is known as "Sorghum Hollow."[37]

The feterita is a grain sorghum. Seemingly an Arabic name from the Sudan, Feterita was popular enough to become a place-name in Stevens County, where it is a station on the Santa Fe.

When Mennonites introduced winter wheat from Russia, Kansas became one of the most productive wheat states in the nation. The first Kansas town to be named Wheatland was in Douglas County, but that was in 1856 when wheat was not yet important. The name was more appropriate in McPherson County, where the town of Bachelor was renamed Wheatland in 1876. Townships are named Wheatland in Barton, Dickinson, Ellis, and Ford counties. On the high plains of Gove County, Grainfield continues to advertise the economy of Kansas. Golden Belt was a term used for the central Kansas wheat-producing area, but it was also used as the name of a post office in Lincoln County.

A little suburb south of Wichita was named Oatland. The town had languished, but under the auspices of the Missouri Pacific it was revived as an eighty-acre townsite and renamed Oatville.[38]

Among the popular domestic plants used for fodder was alfalfa, also called lucerne. Alfalfa was first imported from South America and called "Chilian clover." Alfalfa is an Arabic word meaning "the best feed." It was introduced into Kansas by John Gishweller, who bought the seed in Ogden, Utah, and planted it in Norton County.[39] The county consequently had a post office named Alfalfa. Sheridan County has a place named Lucerne. The latter may, however, have a Swiss source.

Like alfalfa, clover is a member of the pea family. It restores nitrogen to the soil and supplies forage for domestic animals. The red clover from Europe is the most common in Kansas, but there are many varieties of clover with such names as bird-foot clover, bur clover, prairie-clover, and owl's clover. Red Clover, or Redclover, was for many years the name of a post office in Johnson County. Chautauqua County has a Cloverdale on the Big Caney. The Caney was supposedly named for its reeds, canes, and cattails.

Edward Janzen, who came from Green Garden, Illinois, and lived in Green Garden Township in Ellsworth County, referred to a stream called Peas Creek.[40] Settlers in Doniphan County named a place Beanville.[41]

The economy of Kansas inspired many place-names. A post office in Rush County was named Economy, but it lasted only a few months.

A place in Dickinson County once sacred to the Indians was named successively Hoffman's Mill, Hoffman Falls, and Enterprise Mills. It was a good mill site, and several enterprising men built mills there. An Abilene editor called it the "City of Mills." When the town was incorporated, it was named Enterprise for its "industry and progressivism." In keeping with this "commercial enthusiasm," a town in northern

Dickinson County was named Industry.[42] Ellsworth County had a place named Work, and Wilson County had a place named Rest.

One may be impressed by the optimism of the men who named the towns of Empire, Empire City, and Wall Street. Empire in McPherson County loomed large like a mirage in the morning, said one pioneer.[43] It is now a township name. Empire City in Cherokee County was named by S. L. Cheney "on account of the town topping a ridge." It is now neither a "city" nor an "empire" but only a name near the mining town of Galena.[44]

The people who named Wall Street in Allen County must have allowed their dreams to rise to the pinnacle of imaginary affluence. The speculative appeal of a roller coaster stock market was dampened by the depression of 1893 and the poverty that followed. Wall Street did not survive the Populist revolt in Kansas. Farmers had little respect for the speculators of New York's Wall Street.

Money Creek was the name of a stream flowing into the Grasshopper on the Leavenworth Road.[45] Cash City in Clark County is a name with a monetary ring to it, but the name came from Cash Henderson, a Wichita merchant who promoted the town. Lyle Merritt's newspaper was named the *Cash City Cashier*. There was a Coin in Gove County and a Nickel in Kiowa County.

In Republic County a town named Prospect died when Courtland acquired its postal service.[46] The cemetery perpetuated the name. Prospect in Sedgwick County could not live up to its name until stimulated by the Prospect Plant of the Cessna Aircraft Company. There the dreams of Clyde Cessna were made a rich reality by Dwane L. Wallace, his nephew. Residents in Farmer Township in northern Rice County must have been optimistic when they named their town Prosper. Bushton was its rival, and, as one pioneer put it, "Bushton grew and Prosper died."[47]

It may be a common desire to want equity in a world full of inequities. Most people would prefer to be rich, although many have accepted their poverty with little complaint in the past. Judging from their place-names, Kansans must have recognized these attitudes and conditions. Anderson County had a place named Rich. A year after it was hit by the depression of 1893, the name was changed to Equity. Poverty Ridge was not far from Hardscrabble in Pratt County.[48] Success, a post office in Russell County, was off the beaten path, and after three decades, it evidently became a failure.

CHAPTER IX

ERPRISE ERIE ESBON ESKRIDGE EUDORA EUREKA EVEREST FAIRVIEW FALL RIVER FLORENCE FOI

CASTILIAN NAMES IN KANSAS

D FORMOSO FORT DODGE FORT SCOTT FOSTORIA FOWLER FRANKFORT FREDERICK FREDONIA FR

THE SPANIARDS WERE THE FIRST Europeans in Kansas. But they did not stay, and most of their place-names were eventually forgotten or replaced. American settlers found Spanish names to their liking and put them back on the map. The source for Spanish names were many and varied. Coronado's travels in Kansas, contact with Cuba, war with Mexico, the Santa Fe Trail, the Forty-Niners in California, and the writings of Washington Irving and William H. Prescott all contributed to the supply of Spanish names for Kansas. A few were descriptive labels and some were repetitions of Spanish names used in other states.

Before considering bona fide Spanish names, we might examine the names of two distinguished Italians in the Spanish service, Christopher Columbus and Amerigo Vespucci. Columbus, or Cristóbal Colón, was one of the world's greatest place-name givers, and it is not surprising that his name was the source for place-names in half of the states of the Union. On the recommendation of Senator Joseph Foos, the Ohio town of Franklinton had its name changed to Columbus "to honor that faith in the future, the courage and persistence of Christopher Columbus."[1] When A. L. Peters named Columbus in Cherokee County, he named it for his home town in Ohio, indirectly honoring the great explorer.[2]

Columbus in Kansas was located in a township named Simancas, after the university town in Spain where the Royal Council met and rejected Columbus's first request for support of his expedition into the Atlantic. Simancas in Spain was also the birthplace of Francisco Vásquez de Coronado.

In Kansas, the name of Columbus was first used in Atchison County for a town located in Rush Bottom. The residents later chose the name of Rushville over Columbus.[3] There was a Columbus City in Doniphan County. It was also called Columbia, a name still retained for the local school.[4]

One of the Indian traders in Kansas before 1854 had the distinguished name of Christopher Columbia. He and his associates from Council Grove established a town south of Emporia and named it Columbia. It was temporarily the county seat of what was then Madison County. Rival towns caused it to decline, and Emporia replaced it as a post office.[5] Columbia's name remains on a street in Council Grove. The Columbia north of Paola bore that name only briefly. Theretofore it was called Ten-Mile; presently it is Hillsdale.[6] In Ellsworth County, another post office was named Columbia. It closed in 1901,[7] but the name is retained on a local township.

Amerigo Vespucci, a contemporary of Columbus, was the victor in what might be called the competition to name the New World. Impressed by Amerigo's explorations and writings about the New World, Martin Waldseemüller, a German geographer, put the name of Amerigo and America terra on the map. The early form of the name was probably Amala-reiks, believed to be of Gothic origin. In Old High German it became Amalrich. *Amal* was interpreted to mean "labor" or "toil," and *rich* or *reich* meant a domain or empire. The name has been interpreted to mean: "The man who ruled because he labored for the benefit of his people." After the Goths brought the name to northern Italy, it was modified, and Amelrigo became Amerrigo and Amerigo on its way to becoming America.[8]

The name America was first given to Brazil and then spread to the whole of the New World, including Kansas. Americus, north of Emporia, was located in a lovely setting of "undulating prairie" and named for the "celebrated explorer Americus Vespucci." A member of the town company was named Columbia. The founders of Americus had planned a jail and courthouse to resemble a Spanish castle with a touch of Morisco architecture, but these plans remained "Spanish castles in air."[9]

On his way through Nemaha County, George Duffield, a pioneer cattle driver, said he had traveled through the "Town of America." To gain distinction, the "Town of America" became America City; it is still not a city, except in name.[10] A geological stratum is also referred to as "the Americus beds." So this Gothic name became a place-name in Kansas.

When the Conquistadors explored the Spanish Borderlands, they gave us three popular names, two of which became names of states. In the East was the land of La Florida, discovered by Ponce de León on the day of the Feast of the Flowers and named for that celebration. In the West was California, named for a mythical queen in a romantic novel. The land was thought to be ruled by lovely Amazons whose image stirred the romantic ambitions of a Don Juan like Hernando Cortez. Between California and La Florida lay Quivira, vague and vast in the heart of North America, and its center was in Kansas. Quivira was a part of the "Northern Mystery." There, according to legend, lived a remarkable people whose wealth and refinement could be measured only by the reality of Montezuma's empire or the fertile imagination of adventuresome Spaniards.[11]

When primitive people came upon a big river, they simply named it "Big River." That is how the Mississippi got its name, and the Yukon, and the Niger in Africa. And so did the Spaniards name the Río Grande, adding del Norte to identify the one from the north. In southern Spain, where the Arabs came upon a big river, they named it Guadalquivir. *Guad*, a modification of *wad* or *wadi*, meant "river" or "water," and *quivir* meant "big."[12]

In Kansas, Vásquez de Coronado was looking for a rich civilization on a big river which he first called the Guadalquiver. But Guadalquiver was unwieldy, and in typical fashion the Spaniards shortened it to "Quivir" and "Quivira." Pedro de Castañeda, Coronado's best chronicler, spoke of their dash to the "River of Quivira." Suceso, another chronicler, said: "After proceeding many days by the needle...it pleased God...that we found the River of Quivira...."[13] Father José Antonio Pichardo said that the Spaniards entered the lands which Coronado called "the province of Guadalquivir; and his followers La Quivira."[14] Some spoke of this land as "Gran Quivira."

The name of the river was given to the land, and the name of the land was given to the people. That is how the Pawnee tribe known as the Wichitas became known as the Quivira Indians. Some have tried to find an Indian origin for the Quivira name from Kirikquis and Kirikurus, Pawnee names for the Wichitas.[15] But the Arabic word used by the Spaniards appears to be more logical.

Early map makers spread Quivira far and wide, but it seems to fit best in the Great Bend area of the Arkansas River in Kansas. Discussing the name of Junction City, George Martin once said, "In the early '80's quite a number of people wanted the town called Quivira."[16] The Santa Fe Railroad promoted a summer resort southwest of Kansas City and named it Quivira. The post office spelled it "Quivera."[17]

Because Coronado first discovered the Big River in Kansas near Ford on the feast day of Saint Peter and Saint Paul, he or the chronicler Jaramillo named it El Río de San Pedro y San Pablo. It was a common practice of the Spaniards to use religious names as place-names. Since the name was too long, some called the stream the "Peter and Paul" River. It was next abbreviated by deleting Paul. In 1775, over two hundred years after Coronado's crossing, the Spanish governor of Texas suggested sending soldiers to the "Río San Pedro" to keep a watchful eye on the encroaching French.[18] Later Spanish explorers gave the river new names which were equally ephemeral. Father Pichardo was "positive" that the Río de San Pedro y San Pablo was the same as the "río de la Santissima Trinidad," or Holy Trinity.[19] On Delisle's map of 1700, the Missouri appears to be only an extension of the Arkansas named "S. Jerome" and "R. de S. Francisco." [20]

Napestle, also spelled Napeste, was most likely a Ute name generally applied to the upper part of the Arkansas.[21] In 1787, Pedro Vial traveled the Santa Fe Trail eastward, and his journal tells of his search for "the Napeste River," which, he said, "we call in French the Arkansas River."[22] As late as 1811, Alexander von Humboldt, a fine linguist, referred to it in three languages as "Le Río Napestle." In eastern Louisiana, he said, it was identified with "l'Arkansas."[23]

Ulibarri also gave the river a Spanish name and a saintly name. "As an honorable memorial to his Christian zeal," he said of Governor Francisco Cuerbo, he gave the river the "name of his saint, calling it the Río Grande de San Francisco." This name was used in addition to the Indian name when he referred to it as the "Napestle or Río Grande de San Francisco."[24] Another combination was used when the Pawnees were reported to have hunted all the way to the "River of San Francisco de Arkanzas." That was the name Governor Miró used in 1785.[25]

When Juan de Oñate came to the Arkansas River in 1601, probably near the junction of the Walnut at Arkansas City and not at Wichita, he called it El Río del Robrodal, "the river of the Oak Trees." This is apparently a variation of *robledal* or *robledo*, meaning "oak grove." *Robles* means "oak," referring particularly to the deciduous oak, in contrast to the live oak which was called *encina*.[26]

Of the major rivers in Kansas, only the Cimarron has preserved its Spanish name. This river, which begins in New Mexico, cuts across a corner of Colorado, and meanders through Kansas and Oklahoma, has been unruly and exasperating. "All that it lacks is water," said one pioneer historian.[27] It has been misnamed, misspelled, and misplaced, and it has been confused with its neighbors.

Elliot Coues noted that the Cimarron had been called: "Red Fork; Saline r.; Grand Saline r.; Jefferson r.; Nesuketong, Nesuketonga, Nesuhetonga, Newsewketonga r.; Cimmaron, Cimarrone." In addition, it was frequently spelled both "Semerone" and "Cimarone," especially by early American explorers. One listed a trail station on the "Semiron."[28]

Even as late as 1839 one map, referring to it as the "Cimarone," had it flowing into the Arkansas River near Dodge City. The Catton Map of 1855, the Morse and Gaston Map of 1856, and the J. G. Wells Map of 1857 show the Cimarron flowing into the Salt Fork. Another had it disappearing in the sands of the southwest. This could explain its being called "Cimarron or Lost River."[29]

In Spanish, the word *cimarrón* means "wild" or "unruly." It is generally applied to animals, but Indian bands who had drifted away from their people were called *cimarrones*. The term *maroon* for escaped slaves had the same source. The Cimarron, said Elliot Coues, "means something unreclaimed . . . and it is applicable to an animal, a person, a place, etc. It designated the wild sheep of the Rocky Mountains (*Ovis montana*), gave name to one of the largest branches of the Arkansaw."[30] The full name of the river was Río de los Carneros Cimarrón, and this explains its early translation as "River of the Wild Mountain Sheep." Rocky Mountain Sheep or Big Horn were abundant at the river's source near Raton, New Mexico. When abbreviated to Carne de Cimarrón, it meant, "meat of the wild animals," whatever they might be.[31]

South of the Cimarron River was the grazing land of the Texas longhorns. They had migrated from the Mexican mining country; they were lost "wanderers," "wild" and "unruly." Eventually these critters, these "cimarrones," reached the river to which they perhaps gave their name. This is one interpretation, and a logical one, yet the mountain sheep theory may be equally valid.[32]

According to the folklore of the country, a cook for a cattle outfit camping on the river had some difficulty cooking his beans until they were done. After supper he decided to cook them longer and told the night watchman to keep an eye on them. The watchman fell asleep, the fire went out, and in the morning the crotchety cook found the beans still unfit to serve. In disgust he threw the whole pot into the river and shouted, "Simmer on, darn you; simmer on!" And that, they say, is how the Cimarron was named.[33]

It was the traveler on the trail to Santa Fe who made the Cimarron famous. At the "Cimarron Crossing" of the Arkansas River the trail headed toward the Cimarron River. That explains why the town of Cimarron is located on the Arkansas River instead of on the Cimarron. A township named Cimarron is also there. Other Cimarron townships are located in Clark, Gray, Meade, and Morton counties. Seward once had a Cimarron Township.

Spaniards seldom used names of their leaders as place-names, but later American settlers revived and preserved many of these names. Kansas might well have been named either Quivira or Coronado. Chroniclers in Coronado's expedition spoke well of Kansas. "The country has a fine appearance," said Jaramillo, "the like of which I have not seen anywhere . . . ." Kansans have shown their appreciation by trying to perpetuate the name of Coronado. First there was a post office named

Coronado southwest of Wichita, but it lasted only five years. In Wichita County, near the western border of Kansas, the flourishing town of Coronado reported a population of 1,500 and a hotel with the historic name of Vendome. But Coronado became involved in a county seat conflict with Leoti and lost. It is still the name of a little station on the Missouri Pacific. On the assumption that Coronado reached eastern Kansas, the town now called Bonner Springs was once named Coronado Springs.[34]

During discussions about a new name for Davis County, which honored Jefferson Davis, George Martin proposed the name Coronado. Significant and most appropriate was the naming of Coronado Heights near Lindsborg. These Smoky Hill Buttes, as they are also called, were on the border of the Quivira country and probably not far from the terminal of Coronado's historic trek into Kansas.

Fray Juan de Padilla accompanied Coronado to Kansas. When he returned later as a missionary to the Indians, he was killed, probably a victim of Indian rivalry. Mount Padilla near Council Grove was named for the first Christian martyr in Kansas.[35]

Hernando de Soto, a contemporary of Coronado's, did not reach Kansas, but he discovered the Mississippi and probably reached Arkansas. His name was given to a town between Lawrence and Kansas City.

Less known is Penalosa, a place formerly named Lotta, northwest of Kingman. Penalosa is believed to have been named in memory of a governor of New Mexico whose full name was Don Diego Dionisio de Peñalosa Briceño y Berdugo. The governor is reported to have come to the "kingdom of Quivira," but this is not based upon a reliable report. He was discredited and expelled from New Mexico, whereupon he offered to sell information about Quivira to Louis XIV of France.[36]

A later governor of New Mexico named Antonio Valverde y Cosio earned a place in Kansas history by leading an expedition across the Arkansas River in 1719 to check the French advance southward. His name appears to be the most likely source for the name of Valverde Township in Sumner County, but unfortunately for Kansas, Don Antonio's reputation was not much better than that of Peñalosa.[37] His three-syllable name was reduced to two by the Americans, and it is occasionally spelled "Valverd" to conform to pronunciation. The name means "green valley." During this time the Spaniards established a post at an Apache ranchería and called it El Quartelejo, "the little barracks." Its location, long debated, is generally accepted to be at the site of the ruins in Scott County State Park.[38]

Cortez conquered Montezuma, emperor of the Aztecs. The Spaniards made a desperate effort to spell this Aztec name and made considerable progress from Motenczoxiatzin to Monctezumo to its popular form of Montezuma. The name was so completely associated with gold that Americans used it to refer to money. Montezuma, Kansas, lost its county seat contest and its railroad, was almost destroyed by a prairie fire, was parched by the unrelenting sun, and was declared dead; yet it was revived and it survived.[39] The founders of Montezuma in Gray County were evidently familiar with the story of the Mexican conquest, because they named their streets for historical figures associated with it.[40]

Hernando Cortez did not visit Kansas, but he had been anxious to lead the expedition to the "Seven Cities of Cibola." Suspicious of Cortez, the viceroy gave the command to Coronado. Yet Graham County paid fleeting respect to the most colorful of the Conquistadors by naming a town Cortez.

The names of four Spanish provinces have become place-names in Kansas: Salamanca, Zamora, Granada, and Valencia. Salamanca, associated with Columbus, has already been discussed. Granada, which means "pomegranate," was well known from Washington Irving's popular account of *The Conquest of Granada*. Pleasant Springs in Nemaha County had its name changed to Granada in 1865 because of its Granada Hotel.[41] Granada is still the name of the local township.

Valencia, a small station west of Topeka, was named for a kingdom in Spain noted for its moderate Mediterranean climate and its oranges. When Livy spoke of it, he called it "Valentia," and with that spelling it could mean "brave," "heroic," or even "boastful."

Zamora in Spain was the name of a province, a town, and a family. It was the province made famous in the medieval epic *El Cid*, which depicts the adventures of one of Spain's greatest fictional heroes and rascals. Citizens of the province, comparing its prestige with that of Rome, boasted, *No se gano Zamora en una hora:* "One does not win Zamora in an hour." In Kansas, Zamora became a place-name competing with the French name of Aubrey in Hamilton County. Cram's map of 1883 listed the town as "Zamora or Aubrey."[42] It might better have been listed as Zamora *and* Aubrey, since the post office named Zamora was in the town of Aubrey. In 1885 the town became Kendall, named for brothers who were local merchants. A nearby ranch organized by six railroad workers was named the Zamora Cattle Company, and its brand was consequently Z6. Zamora was the middle name of Mrs. F. M. Kelley, wife of one of the six ranchers. Zamore in Gray County is one of the extinct towns of Kansas.[43]

Toledo, one of the great cities of Spain, is noted for its cathedral and its sword blades. It was a worthy subject for El Greco's artistic brush. For nearly twenty years Chase County had a post office named Toledo in Toledo Township, both named for the Ohio city which had been named for Toledo, Spain.[44]

Throughout their history, Americans have had a keen interest in Cuba. Its "Ten Years' War" against Spain aroused much sympathy. In 1868, the year the war started, a post office in Republic County was named Cuba. It was to have been named for Obadiah Baird, owner of the townsite, but enthusiastic descriptions of Cuba presented by a recent visitor made the townspeople change their minds.[45] That the town was named for a Bohemian named Kuba has been suggested, and Cuba was called "The Bohemian Capital of Kansas."[46]

Columbus gave Cuba several names. He first called it Juana to honor the Spanish prince, Don Juan, according to Washington Irving.[47] It is more likely that this name was to honor Juana, the daughter of Ferdinand and Isabella, whose psychological problems caused her to be called "Juana la Loca." Columbus also called the island Fernandina to honor Ferdinand. Next he called it Santiago for the patron saint of Spain. Then, as one said, "almost in a cry of despair," he called it Ave María. But from the natives he picked up the name Cuba, which possibly meant "province" or "their country," and applied it to a cape as Cabo de Cuba. Cuba soon became the name of the whole island,[48] which was widely known as the Pearl of the Antilles.

A year after Cuba, Kansas, was named, a place was named Havana in Montgomery County. In Cuba, Havana or La Habaña, the short name for San Cristóbal de la Habaña, was known as the "Key to the New World and Bulwark of the West Indies." An earlier Havana had been established in Osage County, but its residents, German and French settlers from St. Louis, quarreled and abandoned the town.[49] Havana, Kansas, is believed to have received its name from Havana, Illinois.[50]

In Chautauqua County a community petitioned the post office department to be named Matanzas. Although pleasing to the ear, the name means "slaughter" or "massacre." But its meaning was probably unknown to those who proposed it. A province in Cuba is named Matanzas, and Matanzas Bay in Florida commemorates the Spanish slaughter of a French Huguenot colony. The Kansas petition for the name was so poorly written that the post office department asked the neighboring postmaster at Peru for clarification. The postmaster saw a chance for a practical joke and told the post office department that the name was "Jay Hawk." The residents of Jay Hawk were perplexed and had the name changed to Matanzas. Confusion ended when the town just "up and died."[51]

After exploring the islands, the Spaniards moved on to the mainland of Latin America. There they discovered a large stream the natives called

Orinoco, "the river." Similar to Orinoco is the post office name of Oronoque in Norton County. It resembles Oronoco, the name of a tobacco brought to Virginia from the Orinoco Valley.[52]

The Isthmus of Panama, far from being a convenient land-link between the two Americas, was, until completion of the canal, an annoying barrier. Many of the Forty-Niners chose to cross Panama in preference to crossing the Great Plains or sailing by way of the Strait of Magellan to California. The isthmus had a river called the Atrato. The name had been written Tarena and then Dariena before it became Darien, the name of a bay, a peak, and a town. The full name of this dirty, disease-ridden town was Santa María de la Antigua del Darién.[53] Americans called it Darien, a name already made famous by John Keats, who spoke beautifully but mistakenly of Cortez, not Núñez de Balboa, discovering the Pacific from a peak there. For a short time Cowley County had a post office named Darien.

The name of the Pacific Ocean also appealed to Kansas name-givers. There was a Pacific City in Douglas County and another in Nemaha County.[54]

West of Orinoco was the land of El Dorado, and below Darien was Peru. Ever since the Spaniards had explored northern Latin America in search of El Dorado, "The Gilded One," the name has become a synonym for gold or riches. The legend of El Dorado was based on an Indian ritual in Colombia in which an Indian chief was anointed with oil and sprinkled with gold dust before he dove into the sacred waters of Lake Guatabita to offer the metal to the god of the waters. Sir Walter Raleigh, who searched for the rich kingdom, popularized the story of El Dorado. In the words of Hubert Herring, "The legend of El Dorado titillated the fancy of the conquerors . . ." who "were eager to find a king so richly endowed that he could substitute gold dust for bath salts."[55]

El Dorado in Kansas was located on the trail to California, "the El Dorado State." It has been suggested that this juxtaposition could have influenced the naming of the town. But according to Joseph Cracklin, a pioneer, it was named as a result of an exclamation like "Eureka!" In Cracklin's words:

> I would say the name of El Dorado is two Spanish words and signifies "The Golden Land." The beautiful appearance of the country upon our arrival at the Walnut, suggested the name, and I exclaimed, "El Dorado," and when the town site was selected, the name was unanimously adopted. I proposed the name and Mr. Thomas Cordis seconded it.[56]

El Dorado's wealth from "black gold" has prompted the suggestion that it be nicknamed "Oildorado."[57]

The editor of the *Walnut Valley Times* spelled "Eldorado" as one word, and so it was on early maps. When a new editor acquired the *Times*, he changed the name to "El Dorado." This caused much discussion, but the townspeople accepted the change. Both the post office and the United States Board of Geographical Names recommended that it be written as one word, but to no avail. A clerical error supported by popular usage is said to be the cause for making it El Dorado.[58] Butler County, with its El Dorado, also had places named Oro, the Spanish word for gold, and Ophir, another symbol of wealth. A man in Norton County found a bottle labeled "strychnine" at Skull Creek, but its contents were gold nuggets. They were valued at only $19.00, enough perhaps to stimulate gold fever and inspire the name of Oro.[59]

Fourteen places in the United States were named Peru before the name reached Kansas, where it was used three times. William H. Prescott's *Conquest of Peru* had made the name familiar. Settlers from Peru and La Salle in Illinois came to Howard County, now Chautauqua, and their votes for using the home-town names in Kansas were evenly divided. The decision was left to E. R. Cutler, president of the town company. He broke the tie by voting for his "old home town of Peru."[60] Peru was a Quechua name which Garcilaso de la Vega said came from *pelu*, meaning "river."[61]

Lima, the name of the Peruvian capital, also came to Kansas from Illinois. The name is said to have come from Rimac, a river name which referred to an oracle as "one who speaks."[62] It was made a place-name in Kansas three times. In Clay County, Lima was replaced by Wyoming Valley; in Elk County, not far from Peru, Lima's life was brief; and in Allen County, Lima passed into history without even becoming a post office.[63]

La Paz, meaning "the peace," is a popular name in Latin America, but occasionally it is a misnomer. In Cuba, after the Spaniards had treacherously destroyed an Indian village, they named it La Paz. Of the nine places named La Paz in Latin America, the best known is Bolivia's largest city and occasional capital. La Paz in Kansas was the name of a post office in Elk County. There is now a Lapaz on the Union Pacific Line near the Colorado border, the only Lapaz in the United States.

Potosí is the name of fabulously rich mining towns in Mexico and Bolivia. In Mexico it is called San Luis Potosí. The Indian name for the Cerro de Potosí in Bolivia was Potojchi, meaning "a loud voice" or "thunder" warning people to stay away.[64] Because of the miserable life of the miners, Bolivians called it "that accursed hill." When La Mothe Cadillac, French governor of Detroit, discovered a rich lead mine in Missouri, he named it Mine à Breton. Moses Austin, who came to Missouri with his son Stephen to mine for galena, changed the name to Burton, but this later became Potosi, a synonym for great wealth.[65] Linn County probably took this strange name from Missouri. Located near the spot where the French had discovered galena,[66] the town had its name changed to Pleasanton to honor a general. Potosi Township is still there.

From Ecuador came the name Quito, an Inca or Quechua name for one of the capitals of the Inca Empire. Although it is correctly spelled on the maps, a Butler County historian spelled it phonetically as "Key Toe."[67]

The first Spanish explorers sent southward from Peru had to cross the Atacama desert of northern Chile. When they reached the rich green valley of central Chile, its contrast with the desert was so great that they called it Valparaiso, "valley of paradise." Kansas had a Valparaiso in Stevens County, but in two years its name was changed to Moscow, a name no more fitting than the first.

Sonora is the name of an important state in Mexico. It may refer to the natives in the area, to a plant, or to a river. When Mexicans from Sonora set up camp in the gold fields of California, their community was called the "Sonorian Camp," later simplified to Sonora.[68] Both Nemaha and Lyon counties had places named Sonora, and a post office was named Sonora in Harper County.[69]

Toluca, the name of a prominent market town west of Mexico City, was for thirteen years the name of a post office in Haskell County. The name is associated with one of the ancient Indian gods. Taxco, meaning "a ball court," is the name of a silver-mining town south of Mexico City, now noted for its artistic silversmiths.[70] It has long been the name of a railway station in Sheridan County, where it is spelled Tasco.

Among the names commemorating the Mexican War were Palo Alto, Camargo, Cerro Gordo, and Buena Vista. Palo Alto, meaning "tall trees," was the name of the battle fought near Matamoros on the lower Río Grande that precipitated the Mexican War. Palo Alto was once the name of a post office in Neosho County. Camargo is located between Matamoros and Monterrey.[71] It may have been named for Ignacio Camargo, a revolutionary leader executed in 1810. In Kansas a post office near the Nebraska border of Smith County was named Camargo.

General Zachary Taylor, known as "Old Rough and Ready," defeated Santa Anna at the Battle of Buena Vista near Monterrey, but both claimed victory and Taylor became a war hero. The town now named Hoisington was first called Buena Vista, "good view."[72]

Cerro Gordo meant "big hill" or "big mountain." It was there that General Winfield Scott, with the aid of Robert E. Lee, brought his troops around a mountain so rough that "a goat could not flank it" and defeated Santa Anna, who was supposed to block the way to Mexico City. For fifteen years Cerro Gordo was the name of a post office in Jewell County.

The Sedgwick County town of Derby was orginally named El Paso. It was near a crossing on the Arkansas River called Sand Ford. Later a ferry and then a bridge spanned the river there. The name was logical. El Paso in Texas was located where the Spaniards crossed the Río Grande on the trail to Santa Fe. It has been said, however, that John Hufbauer, founder of the town, named it for a town near his home in Illinois. According to one story, the name was changed to Derby by the Santa Fe Railroad after a shipment of hogs intended for El Paso, Kansas, ended up in El Paso, Texas.[73] Utility companies in Derby have retained the El Paso name, and a new shopping center has been named El Paso Village. A year after El Paso changed its name, a post office was named El Paso in Edwards County.

Another Río Grande border town is Laredo. In Rice County the town named Lerado has transposed vowels, but the pronunciation would indicate that it was phonetically the same as Laredo in Texas. In Arkansas it is written Larado. A logical source for the name was the Spanish seaport of Laredo.[74]

Many of the California names adopted in Kansas had a Spanish origin, including Spanish versions of some Indian names. The California town of Yerba Buena became San Francisco and was abbreviated to "Frisco" as a Kansas place-name. Additional Spanish names from California included Monterey, Mariposa, and Benicia.[75]

Purely Spanish names such as Esperanza, Bonita, and Chico, although found in California, were not necessarily Californian in origin. Esperanza, meaning "hope," was the name of the Oneida communal experiment in Neosho County.[76]

Bonita is a Spanish word meaning "pretty good" or "passable." It is the diminutive of *bueno*. It has also been used to mean "attractive" or "beautiful." The town named Bonita in Johnson County had earlier been named Alta. The name was changed to Bonita because "the surrounding country is one of the prettiest scenes to be found in the prairies of eastern Kansas"[77] south of Olathe. Olathe is an Osage word which also means "beautiful."

Among the Spanish descriptive names are Alta, Altamont, and Alta Vista. Alta, meaning "high," was so named because it was the highest point on the Frisco railroad in Johnson County.[78] In Harvey County a town first named Valentine changed its name to Alta.[79]

Altamont in Labette County replaced Elston, named for a pioneer family. Having lost their bid to make Elston the county seat, the community's Illinois settlers renamed it for Altamont, Illinois.[80] Altamont is a "high mount" in neither Illinois nor Kansas.

Alta Vista was more appropriately named since it was on the divide between the Kaw and the Neosho where there was a "high view." The place had been named Pike and later Cable City, and for a time it was Pike post office in the town of Alta Vista, also written Altavista.[81]

Loco, meaning "crazy," was twice used as a place-name in southwestern Kansas. It may have referred to the loco weed so dangerous to cattle. Chico is also a California place-name, but it could have been used in Kansas as a descriptive name meaning "little." A pioneer settlement on Chico Creek near Galena was called Chico, and not far from Baxter Springs was one called Chico Spring. Even when spelled Checo, it conforms to Spanish pronunciation. The name was later given to a post office in Saline County, replacing the name Bridge.[82]

Sandago in Stafford County appears to be an abbreviation of San Diego. *Diego* or *Diago* is Spanish for James, and Diago, with the loss of an "i," was also the origin of Dago. This is not unlike Igo, once a place in Rooks County, which was possibly Iago for James.[83]

Frisco, an abbreviation of San Francisco, was temporarily the name of a town in Norton County. More garbled is the name Jarvis. Don Antonio José Chávez, a wealthy member of a distinguished family in Santa Fe, was traveling to Missouri with a wagonload of merchandise and $10,000 in specie and bullion when he was murdered by a band of Texas robbers at a small creek in Rice County. The creek, flowing into the Little River, was consequently named Chavez Creek. It has also been called Difficult Creek and "Chavez or Owl" Creek. The Spanish name, spoken and heard in English, gradually evolved into Chavis and Garvis and finally became thoroughly Americanized as Jarvis. East of Lyons there was once a place called Jarvis View.[84]

Carneiro was the name of a place once known as Alum Creek Station near Kanopolis. When Alum Creek Station became an important sheep-shipping center, Edward W. Wellington, a large sheepman of Tescott, had its name changed to Carneiro.[85] In Spanish *carneiro* means "sheep," "mutton," or "sheepfold."

In Ellis County, settled by Hungarians and Russian-Germans, there was a place with the Spanish or Latin name of Yocemento.[86] The chief product of the town was cement made from the local cretaceous lime-stone, which may be referred to as *yacimiento*. As transitions go, the change of vowels from yacimiento to yocemento is typical. But because the cement plant was promoted by I. M. Yost, it has been suggested that the name evolved from combining "Yo" for Yost and "cemento."[87]

The strange name of Jarbalo is also an illustration of a phonetic tran-sition from Spanish to English. When a Mexican was stuck in the mud on Big Stranger Creek near Leavenworth, local settlers helped him out. The Mexican looked back and described the place as El Lugar de Diablo, "place of the devil" or "a devil of a place." *Diablo* was the only word grasped by the settlers and the river-crossing henceforth carried that name. To those who did not have an ear for Spanish, it became Jarbalo. When a town was built there, the residents, possibly unaware of its meaning, looked at the garbled name "with indulgence" and named it Jarbalo. "The Mexican," said one commentator, "swearing in a strange language, probably never knew that he had named a town in the sunflower state."[88]

The Santa Fe Trail across Kansas made the name Santa Fe common-place. The full name of the town at the end of the trail was La Villa Real de la Santa Fe de San Francisco. The Santa Fe, or "Holy Faith," did not always refer to Saint Francis, and in this case the identity was completely lost.

Near the east end of the Santa Fe Trail in Johnson County a station was called Little Santa Fe.[89] In Haskell County a town named Santa Fe, formerly Star City, served as the county seat for thirty-three years.[90] When the Santa Fe railway by-passed the town, residents moved to Sublette and Satanta. Americans seldom used the Spanish pronunciation of Santa "Fay," preferring to pronounce it "Fee." Andrew Sublette called it "Santafee," and one who did not recognize its meaning wrote it "San Tafee."[91]

Linguistically and politically, Portugal was so closely linked with Spain that Portuguese names may be included with the Spanish. Lisbon, the capital of Portugal, was once a Phoenician outpost on the Iberian Peninsula. Called Olispia in ancient times, it became Lisboa in Portu-guese and Lisbon in English. The name possibly referred to a fortress, but it has also been said to have evolved from Olissipo or Ulysses.[92] Lisbon, Kansas, merged with Hewins in Chautauqua County and lost its name.[93] Hewins was named for a politician who owned a large cattle ranch. In 1889 there was a short-lived Lisbon in Gove County and a New Lisbon in Logan County. When the "New" became superfluous, the railway station on the Union Pacific became simply Lisbon.[94]

The Kansas names of Brazilton and Amazon may be associated with

Portugal's South American empire. Brazil was the name given to the red dyewood that Portuguese explorers brought back from the New World. They also brought parrots called *papagayos*, and so the region was named the land of the Papagayos and Brazil. But Brazil is also a patronym, and in Kansas, Brazilton in Crawford County was probably named for Thomas Brazil, owner of the townsite.[95]

The Arkansas flows through Finney County, and, although the river does not resemble the Amazon, the county had a post office with that name. The name probably came from an irrigation ditch called the Amazon.[96] The Amazon River was named when Francisco de Orellana, the first to sail it to the Atlantic, discovered female warriors among the natives. The name for such women goes back to Greek mythology.

It was not unusual for Kansans to adopt Spanish names because they were attractive, but attractiveness gave no assurance of survival. There is, however, a station southwest of Burlington in Coffey County with the life-inspiring name of Viva. In Spanish, *viva* is the loyal cry for king or commoner which means "Long live!" There are still a number of Spanish names on the Kansas map, and one might wish them a resounding "Viva!"

CHAPTER X

FRENCH AND INDIAN RIVER NAMES

INDIANS NAMED THE RIVERS of Kansas long before white men came. They were close to nature, and variations in the topography of the land served as their road signs. Their riparian life made the rivers an important feature of their geography, and each river or stream had its distinguishing characteristics. Indians used the color of the water or the banks, the salt in the water, trees along the shore, the width or length of the riverbed, or an event in the area as sources for a river's name. Many of these names were preserved by the French, who were remarkably adept at sensing the meaning of Indian names. Taking an Indian woman as a wife was not only good domestic economy, they learned, but it also provided excellent training in linguistics.

There was, however, little consistency in French spellings of Indian names. The phonetic spellings of Indian names by Frenchmen caused no end of trouble for the English-speaking people. Indian names, as the French used them, were modified, simplified, or corrupted by American pioneers. The meaning of the names was frequently lost as a result. There were, however, those who could translate the French names correctly. The French language has been preserved in names like Marais des Cygnes, Verdigris, Saline, Marmiton, Loup, and La Bette, and with modification, Republicaine; all but Marmiton and Labette were French adaptations of Indian names.

When Marquette and Joliet descended the Mississippi, they heard of a tribe beyond the Missouri called the Kansa, and that name appeared on the map of 1673.[1] This marked the introduction of a new name to the Western world, a name which has been given many interpretations and has at last become the familiar name for one of our fifty states.

The spirit of the winds was important in the life of the Indian. From Longfellow we learn that Mudgekeewis, the West Wind, was the father of Hiawatha. The East Wind was Wabun, like Wabaunsee, meaning "the dawn." Among the Siouan tribes, it was the Kansas, the Tadje unikacinga, who were "the keepers of the rites pertaining to the wind." The gens which performed the ceremony for the spirit of Wakon, the

104

South Wind, could well have been the source for the Kansa name.[2]

The Kansas were also called Smoky, Smoky Water People, Smoky Wind People, and Fire People. But they were best known as the South Wind People.[3]

It is astonishing that a simple name like Kansas could be spelled 80 different ways. Some would make it 120, but the last figure includes variations of both Escansaques and Arkansas. The Escansaques were probably Apaches on the Oklahoma border and had nothing in common with Kansas. Including Arkansas is perhaps more logical. The Arkansea were Quapaws who had once lived with the Kansas on the Wabash before the tribes separated at the mouth of the Missouri. They may have the same origin.

That Spaniards and Englishmen would change the French name is not strange, but the French themselves showed no consistency in spelling Kansa. Joliet, who traveled with Marquette, is supposed to have spelled it Kausa. On Guillaume Delisle's map of 1718, the name was Cansez. Two years later, Bernard de La Harpe referred to the natives as Canci and Cannecis.[4] Others wrote it Chanchez, Canchaz, and Cansez. Émile Lauvrière, a French historian, spelled it six different ways in one volume. George Sibley called the Kansas "Konsees," because "they call themselves so . . . ."[5]

Both the French and Anglo-Americans occasionally shortened the name to one syllable. Sergeant Patrick Gass referred to the "old town de Caugh" as the place where the Lewis and Clark expedition spent the Fourth of July. But he also spelled the name Kanzas. Other short forms were Quans, Caw, and Cah, and from these was derived the present form of Kaw. Some have been critical of the abbreviated form; one writer, who considered it absurd, even criticized the Indians for permitting its use. Historically, it has been common to use both Kansas or Kaw to refer to the Indian tribe. But in popular usage, the Kansa Indians, like the Kansas River, which has become known as the Kaw,[6] are more often known by their short name.

The United States Board of Geographic Names declared that the river should be called Kansas, not Kanzas or Kaw, but the people of Kansas, by popular choice and usage, have made Kaw the name of the river. Floyd B. Streeter, writing for the *Rivers of America Series*, used *The Kaw* for his title.

When the time came to name the state, Americans had a choice of the many French forms of Kansas and an option to add variations of their own. Most residents probably pronounced it "Kauzas," but it was popularly spelled Konzas, according to Stephen H. Long and others. With passage of the Kansas-Nebraska Act which opened the territory to settlement in 1854, the official name became Kansas. The name had been on the map earlier, and a map of 1836 showed Kansas as a region for a new Kansa Indian reservation.[7] Stephen A. Douglas may have given the name to Kansas Territory, but Senator David R. Atchison of Missouri is believed to have suggested the name to him.[8] Even after it was officially designated, some writers continued to spell it Kanzas. Edward E. Hale preferred that, partly to avoid confusion with Arkansas.[9]

The Kansas River is called Kansas or Kaw only after the Republican joins the Smoky Hill at Junction City. Above this confluence, the Indians had their own names for the Smoky Hill, including Oke-see-sebo and Chitolah. The latter was an attractive name, and twice the Chitolah name was given to Kansas towns.[10] Among the Pawnee names for the river was Ka-i-urs-kuta, or Yellow Banks.[11] The Kiowa called it the Pe P'a, or Sand River. Several maps showed it as the Sandy or Sandy Hill Fork.[12] It was also known as the Shallow River and Shallow Water,[13] names used later for a branch of White Woman Creek.

When Sieur de Bourgmont traveled up the Kaw in 1724 to negotiate a treaty between the eastern tribes and the High Plains Indians, he found the Comanches living upstream and named that part of the river the Padouca, or Padoncah. This was said to be the Siouan name for the Comanches. Before the end of the century, the Spaniards had also accepted the name, using it in conjunction with their own and calling it the river of the "Comanches o Padocas."[14] There are also suggestions that the Padoucas were Apaches.[15]

Eventually the upper part of the river received the descriptive name of Smoky Hill. Perhaps the name did come from its Pawnee name Rahota katit hiburu, which means "Big Black Forest River" or "Big Timbers," but it is unlikely. The Cheyennes, however, called it by a similar name, Tse manot ohe, meaning "Bunch of Trees River."[16]

Zebulon Pike used its French name, La Touche de la Côte Bucanieus. Elliott Coues suggested that *touche* was probably a typographical error for *fourche*, or fork. The *côte* was the hill or divide, and *bucanieus* refers to smoke.[17] Pike's reference was surely to the French name for the Smoky Hills. These "Smoky Hills or Smoky Buttes," said Coues, were the source for the name of the river.[18] On Brue's map of 1833, the stream was identified in French as Branche de la Montagne a la Fumée.[19] Smoke from the Indian camps along the river contributed to the haze on the Coronado Heights. So the Côte Bucanieus, the "smoky hills," west of Salina and Lindsborg gave the river its name.

Albert Richardson, a New York journalist, wrote that the Smoky Hills were "wrapt in the softest veils—a dim and dreamy haze."[20] Whether the name came from the cottonwoods of the Big Timbers, from prairie fires or Indian campfires, or from the gray-blue haze hovering about the hills on a cool morning or a calm evening, the name has won a sympathetic interest from strangers and has a sentimental attachment for settlers.[21]

Smoky Hill was used as a name for towns in Dickinson and Mitchell counties. Detroit in Dickinson County was originally Smoky Hill, and Detroit is also a French name. In Ellis County the names were joined to become Smokyhill. Four townships were named Smoky Hill. The one in McPherson County borders on Smoky View Township in Saline County.

Lewis and Clark found the Wolf River already named by the French. They had merely translated its Sioux name of Shun-ta-nesh-nanga to Rivière du Loup. It has also been suggested that it was named for the Pawnee Loup clan living on the Loup River in Nebraska. Lewis and Clark, while camping on Diamond Island, reported, "A large wolf came to the bank and looked at us this morning." Its presence would justify the use of the Loup name.[22] A town near Ottawa named Le Loup later became La Loup.[23]

The Missouri River is so correctly characterized and so well known as the Big Muddy that it has been assumed that Missouri meant "big muddy." The best authorities have rejected this interpretation. It is more likely that Pekitanoui, Marquette's name for the river, may be translated to mean "muddy water."[24] It was named Pekitanoui by the Illinois Indians. Some Sioux called it Katapan Mene Shoska and Mini Sose, also translated to mean "muddy water" or "turbid water." Others called it Niutachi and Nudarcha. The Osage called it Ni-sho-dse, and this, too, may mean "muddy water" or "smoky water."[25]

Marquette made a distinction between Pekitanoui, the name of the river, and Ouemessourit, the name of the Indians living along the Missouri. *Ouemessourit* is a word which is said to be associated with pirogues or canoes. The Algonquians of Illinois referred to the natives as Misssou-li-an, or "canoe people." They were also called the "wooden canoe" people, and this was evidently the original meaning of Missouri.[26]

The "wild Miz-zou-rye" had several names before the English version was adopted. The Spaniards called it Río Misuri. On Mathew Sutter's map of 1735, it was shown as Le Missouri ou Riv. d. S. Philippe on the north side of the river, and as Le Riv. des Osages ou des Missouri on the south side. The French name of St. Philippe was soon dropped, and its Osage designation became the name of a southern tributary of the Missouri. It has also been called the Yellow River and the River of the West.[27]

When Marquette and Joliet stopped at the mouth of the Arkansas

River, they found a native village which they listed on their map as Akansea. As a river name, Akansa was to compete with the Indian name of Napeste, or Napestle, and with many Spanish names. For a time the names were used jointly. On his journey from Santa Fe to St. Louis, Pedro Vial traveled along the Arkansas River and referred to it as the "Napeste River which we call in French the Arkansas River."[28]

The French also called the Arkansas the Rivière d'Osark and Rivière des Arks. The land of the Arkansa Indians was referred to as Aux Arkansa and eventually became Ozark. When the French spoke of the "Arkansaw" Indians as the Beaux Hommes, the English assumed that they were the "Bow" Indians, an unintentional reference to the *bois d'arc*. One index listed the Arkansas River under the following names: "Acansas, Akansas, Arcansas, Arcos, Ares, Chinali, La Zorca, Río Napeste or Napestle, Río Grande de San Francisco."[29] We return, however, to Marquette's map for the reference to the Akansea as the source for the Akansa or Arkansas name.

The spelling and pronunciation of Arkansas varied widely. A popular spelling of the name was Arkansaw, used by Schoolcraft, Longfellow, and Elliot Coues. In 1872 the "best authorities," said the *Wichita Eagle*, pronounced it "Ar-kan-saw."[30] But in Colorado and Kansas, the word was pronounced with the accent on the second syllable and sounding the final "s." In Oklahoma the river name is pronounced with a French accent,[31] as it is in the state of Arkansas, where no variation is tolerated. Formerly, any other pronunciation was attributed to "Damn Yankee Books."[32]

Marsh Murdock avoided the difference by nicknaming the Arkansas the "Rackensack."[33] Some Frenchmen called it the Marne for the famous river in France. American explorers called it "that American Nile." The Osage called it Ne Shudse, the "Red River."[34] The Red Fork of the Arkansas retained the name describing its Dakota sandstone color.

The Little Arkansas was at first the name given to the Red Fork or Salt Fork, a southern branch of the Arkansas. The Indians spoke of the Salt or Red Fork as Ne Shudse Shunga, making it "Little Red River." The Union Pacific Railway map of 1866 still listed it as "L. Arkansas." The Little River on the left bank of the Arkansas was known as the Little Arkansas by 1821.[35] Even though it is the Little Arkansas today, it is generally spoken of as the Little River. A town by that name in Rice County was named for the Little Arkansas River.[36]

The promoters of the town which became Arkansas City originally formed a Walnut City Town Company. Finding another Walnut City in Butler County, they decided to name their new town Delphi. Later the company chose to name it Cresswell for the postmaster general, but

Cresswell was the name of a post office in Labette County. Cowley County kept the Cresswell name for a township.[37]

Senator Edmund G. Ross, whose vote in the impeachment trial of President Andrew Johnson saved him from dismissal, recommended the name of Arkansas City. The town is given the Kansas pronunciation, but the French pronunciation has continued to plague the community and confuse outlanders. Announcers at the 1970 Tournament of Roses Parade, for example, referred to the "Arkansaw City" marching band. The city, which had already had four names, could bear the anonymity and mispronunciation no longer. Popularly, it was called Ark City, and after the Tournament of Roses incident, a movement arose to make that its official name. But some feared that the public would draw a connection with Noah's Ark and that the town's historical relationship with the Arkansas River would be forgotten. There were, of course, more practical, if prosaic, reasons for not changing the name.

The Indians knew of the salt in the streams of western Kansas and named several of them accordingly. The Pawnee word for salt was *kait*, and the Siouan word was *skua*. The meaning was occasionally hidden by variations in spelling.

Before the French named the Solomon River, it already had the descriptive name of Nepaholla, "water on a hill." The source for this name was the spirit spring Ne Wakonda. The river was also called the Wiskapalla, or Wisgapalla, said to mean "salt water on a hill."[38]

When the Mallet brothers first reached the Solomon, they must have encountered difficulties since they gave it the French name of Rivière de Soucis, meaning "river of worries."[39] It soon became known, however, as the Solomon or Solomon's Fork. But for whom was it named? It has been suggested that the river was named for a man named Solomon on Truteau's expedition, or for Everett Solomon on Frémont's expedition. Said one wag, it was "probably Solominized from some early Jewish trader at Solomon City,"[40] but that was obviously a wrong conclusion. Captain Pike tried to find its source in the French word *salement*, which means "dirty."[41] The Indians, after all, had named the Republican River the "filthy" or "dirty" river, or something similar. A simple solution was offered when someone suggested the name came from Solomon of the Bible.

The Solomon was very probably named for a French official. The officials who sent the Mallet brothers across Kansas and gave them their instructions were "Messr. de Bienville, Governor, and Salmon, Intendent of Louisiana."[42] The change from Salmon to Salamon to Solomon was a simple one, not unlike transformations in other names.

When the Mallet brothers came to the Saline River, they called it

Rivière de la Fleche, or "river of the arrow," without any explanation. But its salt content was so obvious that the Indians named it Ne Miskua, or "salt river." This the French understood and translated, giving the stream the name of Saline. They were impressed by its size and called it the Grande Saline, and, in typical fashion, omitted the second part of the name, confusing it with all the other rivers named Grande in the country. But then the Grande was dropped and the name again became Saline. There was also a Petite Saline, now called Salt Creek.[43]

A county was named Saline, and its county seat, founded by William A. Phillips, was first named Saliena, which Phillips said was a "fancy" of his.[44] The name became Salina, perhaps more Spanish than French. This name had already been given to five counties in the United States.

Southwest of the Arkansas River, streams "were deeply tinged with red, and . . . slightly brackish," according to Major Sibley.[45] The Indians had named them as Sibley described them. The Ne-shudse was a "red river." The French named these rivers Grande Saline, Fort Saline, the Little Saline, Saline Creek, and Rock Saline. Pioneer travelers and early map makers found it difficult to distinguish between the numerous Salines. Some of the streams were later identified by restoring their native names or by translating the names into English, retaining, however, their Indian descriptive meaning.

Ninnescah has been translated to mean good water, spring water, running water, white water, and clear water. Post offices named Goodwater and Clearwater were the accepted translations of the Indian name. When the Ninnescah was spelled "Ninnesquaw," which was probably correct phonetically for Ninnescua or Ninneskua, the last syllable meant "salt." But the translation, as used for the town of Clearwater, is undoubtedly more popular. The Indian name certainly does not mean "knee-deep-to-a-squaw," as the school children along the Ninnescah translated it. Ninnescah has been the name for two post offices. The one in Cowley County became Bushnell. In Kingman County, Ninnescah was destroyed by a tornado. To replace it, James D. Cunningham promoted a town on his farm by the railroad and offered two lots to anyone settling there.[46] Thus the ill wind that blew away Ninnescah caused the founding and naming of Cunningham.

One of the rivers below the Ninnescah had the Indian name of Chikaskia and was probably also called Shawakospah or Shawakoskah. The *pah* could refer to a hill, but *skah* could mean "white." A. B. Stubbs was of the opinion that it should have been "Shah'-ga-skah," and this, he said, meant "white finger nails." If, however, the name had been spelled Chikaskua, it could be translated to mean the "white salt river." In addition to being the name of a river, Chikaskia was the name of townships in three counties. Sumner County once had a Chikaskia post office.[47]

Bluff Creek flows into the Chikaskia below the Oklahoma border. It had two Indian names, Pahabe, also spelled Pah-har-be, and Ne-shu-che-sink. *Paha* meant "hill" in the Siouan language, and must have referred to the bluffs along Bluff Creek. The name Ne-shu-che-sink described the river as "water, red, little," making it the Little Red River.[48] The description was accurate, but the name has been more appropriately applied to the Red and the Salt Fork of the Arkansas. The Lewis and King Map of 1805 called this river both the "Red Salinas" and "Ne chu se chin ga."

The Little Red River was also called the Nescatunga. It was said to mean "Big Salt Fork," but that is spelled Neskuatunga. The upper part of the stream was called the Rock Salt River[49] and was probably confused with the Cimarron. The middle part of the stream was called the Red Salinas, combining the names for the Red and Salt Fork of the Arkansas. The lower part was given an Indian name which meant "Big Red River."[50] For a time the river combined Indian and French names as the "Neskuetonga or Grand Saline." Eventually the Saline became the Salt Fork, and on the Rand McNally Map of 1876, it was called the "Salt or Nescutunga." What was the Neskuatunga to the Indians and the Grande Saline to the French became the Salt Fork of the Arkansas to the Anglo-Americans.[51]

The Pawnees who came south of the Arkansas for salt and game gave the streams descriptive names which resembled their Osage and French names. When a river had the taste of salt, they spoke of it as Kai' it tu.[52] Pawnees called the Salt Fork of the Arkansas Kits Kait, meaning "salt river."

The Cimarron was another of the salt rivers, according to the Osages, who called it Ni-Ckiu-Ega-Shki-Bi, which Mathews translated to mean "Cut-Rock-Salt-Waters."[53] Pedro Vial referred to the Cimarron as "the San Guillemo River." [54] This river lost its original and descriptive name and retained its Spanish name of Cimarron, meaning "wild" or "unruly."[55]

Of all these salty red rivers that the French called Saline, three now have English names: the Red Fork, the Salt Fork of the Arkansas, and Bluff Creek. The Indian name of Nescatunga for the whole Salt Fork is now relegated to a single branch flowing into the Salt in Comanche County. The Ninnescah and the Chikaskia have had their Indian names restored.

The Osage River was named for the Osage Indians, who were closely related to the Kaws. The two main tribal divisions were Big Osage and

Little Osage, and the rivers on which they lived were also called the Big and the Little Osage. The Osages moved up these Missouri streams into Kansas. The Osage name, spelled Wah-Sha-She, with many variations, meant the "water people" and "sky people."[56] The French name of Ouzhaghi and Ousage became Osage.

John Robidoux reportedly told some Linn County residents the legend of the naming of Marais des Cygnes. This was a story from Longfellow's narrative poem *Evangeline*. Crossing the country in search of Gabriel Lejeunesse, her lover, Evangeline became friendly with the Indians of eastern Kansas and heard from them the lover's tale of Osa and Coman. Osa was the granddaughter of White Hair or Pahuska, an Osage chief. Coman, a Comanche dressed in the finest of Indian costumes, came to visit. The handsome Coman fell in love with the beautiful Osa, but White Hair, happy in his wooded country, did not want to see Osa live in the prairies of the West. Nevertheless, she stepped into Coman's canoe to defy her grandfather. The river was turbulent and the canoe disappeared as if drawn under by a powerful spirit. Then, as the people watched the tragedy, two white swans came gliding down among the vines and flowers. They are seen there every year. Evangeline said, *"C'est le marais des cygnes"*: "It is the marsh of the swans."[57]

Indians named the junction of the Big and Little Osage rivers Mi'xa-chau-tse, a place "where white swans are plentiful." The French knew that Mi-xa-cka meant white swans and named the stream Marais des Cygnes. The Kansas part of the Grand River or Big Osage thus became known by that name. The French name may have been first used by Charles Du Tisné.[58] Some would use the English translation in preference to the formidable French; others would preserve the French name despite its foreign look, its seemingly impossible spelling, and its difficult pronunciation. Isaac McCoy wrote it "Miry Desein," Governor Geary made it "Mary de Zene," and John Brown, Jr., spelled it "Meridezene." Many writers thought Marais should have been Mary, Marie, or Maria. It was also called "Old Aunt Mary." John Greenleaf Whittier referred to the stream as Swan River, but he used the French "Le Marais du Cygne" for the title of a poem.[59] Champions of the French name appealed to the Kansas Legislature to preserve it, and a law was passed to make Marais des Cygnes official. The Kansas jurisdiction ended at the Missouri border beyond which the river retained its Osage name.[60]

Osage as a name appeared in Osage City, which was in Osage County, and Osage Centre. The latter had its name changed to Lyndon. The Osage City name in Neosho County was one of six names replaced by the name of Chanute. Osage also disappeared from Bourbon County.

Osage County was first named Weller. With the assignment of lands for the Indians in Kansas, the Osages received a reservation along the southern border which became known as the Osage Strip.

The Neosho was another of the many rivers which the French named Le Grande. In early days it was also called the White River. Even in Spanish it was the Río Blanco.[61] Captain Pike called it the White, but Elliot Coues said, "This White or Grand r. of Pike is the Neosho."[62] In 1823 the Reverend Benton Pixley traveled up "the Grand river (Neosho) or Six Bulls."[63] Others, including S. H. Long, also referred to it as the Six Bulls.[64] This appears to be an Indian name, and one may wonder if there is any connection between it and the name of Chief Seven Bulls, the Osage who was one of the signers of the Little River Peace Treaty. The White River has shared three names at once: "The Grand, Neosho, or Six Bulls."[65]

Gradually the Neosho name took precedence over the others, but not until it went through several French forms was it accepted in English. Victor Tixier, a French student who traveled through the Osage country, said that a trail led him to the Nion-chou, which was also the name he gave to an Osage village which had earlier been called Manrihabotso, meaning "the village which scrapes the sky."[66] The French name of Nion-chou became Niocho and then went through many English variations such as Neozhoo and Ni-u-sho before it became Neosho.

There is little agreement on the meaning of Neosho. The first syllable means "water." Neosho has been interpreted to mean, variously, "clear water," "dirty" or "muddy water," and "river with pot-holes."[67] Legend has it that when an Osage band in search of a good site came to the Neosho, one brave rode into the stream where his horse stumbled in a pothole. Thus it was called the "pot-hole river." The chief arrived, the story continues, after the Indians and their horses had muddied the stream. His comment was something like "Ne oshode!" meaning that the water had been made murky by the soft mud from the bottom. This may be only a legend, but it explains the name.[68] Mathews gave a more elaborate interpretation by Osages who described the color of the Neosho as "Water-Like-the-Skin-of-a-Summer-Cow-Wapiti."[69]

Neosho was widely used as a place-name. Because Major Jackson Dorn, for whom Dorn County had been named, had joined the Confederacy, the Kansas Legislature substituted the name of Neosho for Dorn.[70] Neosho City was one of two sites of the Vegetarian Colony in Allen County. This "hydropathic establishment," as it was called, was poorly prepared for frontier life. The people deserted and the town died.[71] In Lyon County, Neosho City encountered both local and state competition for the name. Neighboring Florence merged with new Neosho City, only to discover that Coffey County already had a post office by that name. Two local men searched for a new name. One looked up at the blue sky, which reminded him of Italy, and suggested that they name the town Italia. This was its third name but not its last. One pioneer commented on the confusion, saying, "Many a time I have walked to Florence to get mail addressed to Italia post office."[72] The town later became Neosho Rapids. Neosho Falls was named for the rapids of the Neosho in Woodson County. Five townships in the Neosho Valley were given the Neosho name.

Flowing into the Neosho is Ogeese Creek. This name came from the French pronunciation of Auguste or Auguste. Both Indians and Anglo-Americans stumbled over the name. One variation appeared in a reference to a claim jumper on "Auguste Creek, in Neosho County, which the people insist upon spelling and pronouncing 'Ogees.' "[73] Father Schoenemaker wrote it "Auguste Creek (now corrupted into Ogeese Creek)."[74] Another said the name referred to Auguste Capitaine, called "Captain Ogee" by the Indians.[75] His father was French and his mother was Osage. It was also suggested that the creek was named for "Jean Auguste."[76]

The junction of the Marmiton River and the Little Osage was named We-Ts's-U-zhe, or Wa-Tsi-Uzi, meaning "Snake-with-Mouth-Open," by the Osages. Another Osage name for the Marmiton River was Wah-tse-pa-i'n, supposedly translated by the French to mean "town crier." One translation would make it "Town Crier or Scullion River."[77] But the *pa-i'n* would indicate that it referred to Pawnee and possibly meant Pawnee Creek.

The Marmiton was named by the French in 1837. The word is difficult to define. Indian pottery was found on the banks of the river. Because the French name for pots and pans is *marmite*, it has been suggested that this discovery could have been the source for the name. A scullion or cook's boy is called a *marmiton*, and here again we have an association with pots and pans.[78] The stream could have been named for prairie dogs since the French frequently called them marmots, as did Catlin.[79] The word marmot was occasionally used to refer to "a little monkey" or even to "a puppet." But there were no "little monkeys" in Bourbon County. Prairie dogs may not have looked like little monkeys, but they were entertaining enough to be called "little monkeys." Thus, the name might refer to pots and pans, to the scullion who cleaned pots and pans, or to prairie dogs acting like little monkeys and called marmots.[80]

Having heard the French name, Americans tried to imitate the pronunciation of Marmiton and spelled it Marmitaw and Mommytaw.[81] When two companies promoted towns by this name, one spelled it Marmiton and the other Marmaton. The towns were about three miles and one vowel apart.[82]

The Verdigris had a distinctly French name, which was a translation of its Osage name of Wa-Ce-Ton-xo-E, or "Wasetihoge," as Elliot Coues wrote it.[83] Mathews translated this to mean "Grey-Green-Bark Waters." The French reversed the colors and called it *verdi*, "green," and *gris*, "gray." As Verdigris, it still referred to its clay banks with the green-gray color of sycamore bark.[84] A western branch was called the South Verdigris until the town promoters of Eureka changed its name to Fall River.[85] There was also a Little Verdigris which became the North Caney. The main stream had been called the Vermillion by some map makers,[86] but its more distinctly French name of Verdigris has remained, suffering at the hands of those who write it "Verdigrease"[87] and pronounce it with a final "s," which the French left silent.

Verdigris was the temporary name of a Lyon County post office near the source of that river. Verdigris City was a town in Montgomery County. Greenwood County had a post office named Verdigris Falls. It was changed for a few years to Kenton and then became Verdigris Falls again. Verdi in Ottawa County may refer to a famous Italian composer, but the Verdi in Wilson County was most likely an abbreviation of Verdigris.[88]

Both Kansas and Minnesota had rivers named Monecato from which the towns of Mankato in both states got their names. *Monecato* means "blue earth," and in Minnesota, the Blue Earth River retained its name. Isaac McCoy knew the Blue in Kansas by its Indian name of Monecato, but Thomas Say knew it as the Blue Earth River. Lieutenant Tidball in 1853 called it correctly the Blue Earth River.[89] There was a transition on Soulard's map of 1795 which listed it as R. Agua Azul in Spanish, changing it to Blue Water. Perrin du Lac gave it the same interpretation when he called it "R. d'(e) l'Eau Bleu."[90] Explorers evidently assumed that water, not earth, was blue, but in this case, as in the case of the Verdigris, the Indians had named the river for clay from its banks, which they used for pigment. Pike used the French name of L'eau Bleu in 1807, but William Clark's map of 1809 nevertheless called it Blue Earth River.[91] In transition, both the "earth" and the "water" were dropped, and the river is now known only as the Big Blue. As the largest tributary of the Kaw, it is occasionally confused with the Blue flowing into the Missouri near Kansas City.[92] The phonetic transition from French may also be confusing, as one may see in Oklahoma where L'eau Bleu became Loe Blue and Low Blue.[93]

Also characterized by color was Sappa Creek in northwestern Kansas, which has retained its Siouan name meaning "dark" or "black." With a similar description, the Red Vermillion was called the Egoma Saba by the Indians. The *saba*, like *sappa*, referred to black. The French named it the Vermillion River, and the Americans added the redundant "Red." It was named for its red sandstone bottom.[94] Meriwether Lewis came nearer to the Indian name when he called it "Blackpaint River."[95] There is still a stream named the Black Vermillion which flows into the Big Blue.

French explorers and traders encountered Pawnee tribes in both Kansas and Nebraska and adopted the Indian name for Pawnee, spelling it Pani and Pahni. One of the names for the Pawnee was Pariki, referring to the manner in which the Pawnees made their greased hair stand up like horns. *Pariki* was said to mean "horns." The Siouan name of Padani was closer to the French form of Pahni, as was the Osage name of Pa-l-n or Pa-I'n.[96] The French names were also given to the four divisions of the Pawnee tribe: the Loup, the Pahni Republicaine, the Pahni Pique, and the Tapage.

A stream flowing into the Arkansas River from a popular Pawnee hunting area was named the Pawnee Fork. Not far from its confluence with the Arkansas is the famous landmark known as Pawnee Rock.

There was a Pawnee Trail from the Big Bend of the Blue towards the Great Bend of the Arkansas. There are names along the trail such as Pawnee Bend and Pawnee Gap.[97] Osage County in eastern Kansas once had a Pawnee post office, changed later to Hyatt for James A. Hyatt, owner of the townsite, and then to Hyatsville as a railway station. Bourbon County had a Pawnee Station which was probably named for Pawnee Creek, which runs through Pawnee Township.[98]

In Davis (now Geary) County the town which Governor Reeder promoted to become the territorial capital of Kansas was named Pawnee City. It was abandoned by the legislature after a brief session. Secretary of War Jefferson Davis extended the Fort Riley military reservation to include the Pawnee townsite, thereby giving the newborn capital its deathblow. "Governor Reeder's Town," as it was called, had a bad reputation because it was promoted by both military and political speculators.[99] After it was deserted it became known as Pawnee-on-the-Reserve.

West of the Blue Earth or the Big Blue are the Republican, Solomon, and Saline forks of the Smoky Hill River, all named by the French. Strange as it may seem, the Republican Fork was named for a Pawnee tribe called the Kitkehakis. These Pawnees had left their relatives on the Platte and settled on the Republican, just inside the Kansas border.

Frank North thought the first name meant "on a hill," which George Hyde questioned. Hyde translated Kitskakis as *kitsu* or *kizu* for "water" and *kakis* as "rapids" or "swift."[100]

The Republican River valley was a favorite grazing place for the buffalo. Thousands rested in the shade on the river's tree-lined banks or partook of its cooling waters. The Kitkehakis, annoyed by the pollution caused by the buffalo, named it Ki-rara-tu or Ki-ra-ru-tah, meaning "filthy water," or, as Grinnell translated it, "Manure River."[101] The Osages referred to it as the "Buffalo-Dung River."[102] The French gave it a more refined name when they called it the Republicaine.

Pierre and Paul Mallet, heading for Santa Fe, were probably referring to the yet unnamed Republican when they called it Costes Blanches, or "white hills." The name is justified by the white limestone in the area. Nearby is White Rock Creek, called the Amiable, or "friendly river," by the Mallet brothers. [103]

In 1776 the Kitkehakis broke from the Grand Pawnees on the Platte to follow their chief to the Kansas border. The French are believed to have associated this act by the Pawnees with the rebellion of the British colonies. They supposedly called the Indians the Pahni Republicaine and their village the Pahni Republique.[104] The Spaniards within a year adopted the French name and referred to the tribe as the Nación de la República.[105] In 1785 they called the village the Aldea de la República. In typical French fashion, the river was given the name Fourche de Republicaine. Americans at first used the dual name and called the river the Republican Pawnee Fork. They soon found it simpler to use only one of the names, calling the river Pawnee, as did the Kansa Indians, who called it the Pa-ne-ne-tah, or "Pawnee River."[106]

There has been considerable controversy about the origin and meaning of Topeka. It may have been the name of a Pawnee band. Its original meaning has been obscured by many interpretations. In folklore we are told of an Indian ferryman refusing to cross the Kaw for passengers during a flood because the river was "Too Beega."[107] The most common interpretation of the origin of Topeka associated the name with *pomme de terre*, French for "potato." In eastern Kansas, Spring River, which flows into Missouri, was called the Pomme de Terre.[108] Lewis H. Morgan, who visited Kansas in the 1850's, said that "To-poo-ka" meant "a good place to dig potatoes."[109] Eli Moore, a pioneer on a hunting expedition, said, "Our next camp was at 'To-pe-ka,'" signifying in the Kaw language "a place to find small or wild potatoes."[110] This interpretation was accepted by many, but there was disagreement about what kind of potatoes there might be in an area devoid of potatoes. They were described as being "prairie potatoes," "little potatoes," "wild potatoes," and "mountain potatoes." The so-called potatoes were edible tubers collected in the Topeka area by the Indians.[111]

The Pawnees who lived on the lower Kaw in the Topeka area were called Pitahauerat, a name which was said to mean "eastward" or "downstream." Otoes were said to have called them To-pi-u-ke.[112] But the French called them the Topage Pawhni, also written Tapago Pawnee. In French, *tapage* means "noisy," making the French name "Noisy Pawnee."[113] The Smoky Hill River was listed as Topeka on Major Angus L. Langham's map of 1825.[114]

Several pioneers have been given credit for naming Topeka. Cyrus K. Holliday, promoter of Topeka and the Santa Fe railroad, had used the name in a letter before it was adopted, but he proposed to name the town Webster. Another suggested the name of Mid-Continent because the town was near the geographical center of the United States. But this name was rejected as being too cumbersome. The Reverend S. Y. Lum was not at the town meeting to select a name, but it is possible that he had suggested the name. Frye W. Giles, active in Topeka politics, is generally given credit for presenting the merits of the Topeka name. He wanted a name that was easy to pronounce and easy to spell, and a name that was "novel," "euphonious," and "simple," with an "Indian flavor."[115] Topeka satisfied all these requirements. Seldom has a Kansas town been named with greater care and discrimination. Whether it was Pomme de Terre or Topage, the name was French.

In a tribute to the French *coureurs de bois* and *voyageurs*, Lydia Huntley Sigourney wrote:[116]

> *But their name is on your waters;*
> *Ye may not wash it out.*

CHAPTER XI

ND GORDON GORHAM GOVE GRAINFIELD GRANTVILLE GREAT BEND GREELEY GREEN GREENLEAF

ADDITIONAL FRENCH NAMES

RG GRENOLA GRIDLEY GRINNELL GYPSUM HADDAM HAGGARD HALFORD HALSTEAD HAMILTON HA

AMERICAN INTEREST in French people, politics, and places was based partly on gratitude for French aid during the American Revolution. After that conflict, there were some who thought the United States should make French its official language. This was not done, of course, but French was well represented by place-names in America, even where there were no settlers of French descent. Some of the French names in Kansas, including Bourbon, Paris, and La Fayette, were names which had been used earlier in other states.

The first French outpost in Kansas was Fort de Cavagnial. It was named for the governor of Louisiana, Vaudreuil-Cavagnial, also spelled Cavagnol and Cavagnolle. The fort was built as defense against the Spaniards, but it was also a means of controlling both the Indians and the troublesome French traders. Lewis and Clark discovered its ruins at the site of an old Kaw settlement known as Fort Village.[1]

From New Orleans came the Lacledes and the Chouteaus to found the city of St. Louis. Laclede, Missouri, was named for Pierre Laclede, and the Laclede north of Manhattan, Kansas, was named for that town. Only a church and a school have preserved the name of Laclede in Kansas.[2]

Jean Pierre Chouteau was Laclede's son, but he took his mother's maiden name. The Chouteaus, who intermarried with the Osages, became one of the great families of the French frontier. Pierre Chouteau traded with the Kansa Indians as early as 1796, and the family sent agents up the Kaw River to tap the trade of the interior.[3]

Cyprian Chouteau had a warehouse in what became Kansas Landing, Town of Kansas, City of Kansas, and finally, Kansas City in Missouri. Since Daniel Morgan Boone was the only one there who was not a Frenchman, the community was called "French Colony."[4] Francis Chouteau crossed the Missouri and built his home above the mouth of the Kaw where Bonner Springs, Kansas, is located. One of the Chouteau trading posts had four buildings and the Indians named it "Four Houses."[5] Across the Kansas River from one of the posts is a station still named Chouteau. It has been spelled Choteau to conform to a typical English pronunciation. North of Independence is a stream named Chouteau Creek, named for Lewis Chouteau, who settled in the area.[6]

There was also a Chouteau Trading Post north of Fort Scott. The name was shared with Chouteau's partner, Michael Girard, also written "Giraud," "Gireau," and even "Ierros."[7] But whether it was Chouteau or Girard, the name was too long, and residents called the place Trading Post. In daily conversation the name was shortened to "the Post."

Auguste Pierre Chouteau, the son of Jean Pierre, was a West Point graduate who entered the western fur trade with his relative, Jules De Mun, in 1815. De Mun was from Santo Domingo and had married the "lovely" Isabelle Gratiot, granddaughter of Pierre Laclede and Madam Chouteau.[8] What is today Big Coon Creek near Kinsley was for a time known as De Mun's Creek, also written "Dumun," named for Jules De Mun.[9] Thomas County had a post office named DeMunn in 1887. When Chouteau and De Mun returned from Santa Fe in 1816, they were attacked by a band of Pawnees and took refuge on an island in the Arkansas River henceforth known as Chouteau's Island. The islands of the Arkansas are difficult to identify, but Chouteau's Island was at the Upper Ford, west of Dodge City and across from Indian Mound on the north bank.[10]

Labette, the name of a county, creek, and town, is one of the better-known French names in Kansas. According to the Indian folklore there had been in the vicinity a fearful evil spirit "the like of which they never saw before or since."[11] The French called it *la bête*, the beast. This may be associated with Isaac McCoy's calling the stream "Riviere de Bate," the "river of reptiles."[12] The Indians called the river En-gru-scah-opo, perhaps a description of a white elk, with *scah* meaning "white" and *opo* translated "elk."[13]

There is the story of two Frenchmen returning from a hunt and finding a skunk in their camp. One of them cried out, "*La bête!*" The French called the skunk *enfant de diable*, "child of the devil," as well as *bête puante*, easily simplified to *la bête*. Certainly, the skunk was an unwelcome beast. But naming a creek, a town, and a county for this *bête puante* would not have been popular had the pioneers known what the translation meant.[14]

Fortunately for sensitive souls, there is a better explanation for the origin of the name. A French hunter, trader, and guide by the name of Pierre Le Bête or La Baete came to Kansas before 1840 and settled near a stream which has since been known as Labette Creek.[15] Pierre Chouteau knew him well and recommended him to Washington Irving as a guide for Irving's "Tour of the Prairies." La Bête, a "Cajun" from Canada, married an Osage woman and learned her language. Some said he resembled Napoleon.[16] His name was generally spelled La Bête or Labaete, and occasionally "Billette," but Irving spelled it "Beatte."[17]

Three towns were named Labette, and each one struggled to become a county seat at a time when failure meant death.[18] They all failed. But there is still a railway station named Labette east of Labette Township in Labette County. The Labette Hills were later renamed Bender Mounds for the murderous Bender family.[19]

The station named Penseneau on the Fort Leavenworth and Oregon Trail was named for Paschal Penseneau, a Canadian who had married a Kickapoo woman and settled in Leavenworth County. His name was also spelled Pensoneau and Pensineau, the latter used for Pensineau Spring.[20]

Lewis and Clark came upon a stream in Doniphan County which they called Whipperwill Creek.[21] After the Kickapoo settled there, it was called Kickapoo Creek. Then came Peter Cadue, a Canadian who married a Kickapoo woman and was called "Squaw Pete." His wife learned French while he learned Kickapoo and became an interpreter. After Cadue settled on Kickapoo Creek, the name was changed to Cadue, or Cadew, Creek. The stream was frequently called Peter Creek and Peter's Creek. The Petersburg post office, now Lansing, was named for Peter Cadue.[22]

Louis Vieux lived near the Oregon Trail crossing of the Vermillion, which was then called Vieux Crossing or Ford. Vieux was the French name of a Potawatomi chief. The name was difficult, so he changed it to Young, though *vieux* meant "old." His name was written "Robert L. Young (nee Vieux)."[23] Louisville in Pottawatomie County was named for Louis Vieux.

Madore B. Beaubien had a store at Silver Lake near Topeka, and for him Beaubien Creek was named. François Bourbonnais had a name with the same origin as Bourbon. He lived on Bourbonnais Creek, which Americans, unfamiliar with French, occasionally spelled "Bourbonny."[24]

Among the French Canadians who came to Kansas was Andrew B. Canville. He married Mary Cipriano, three-quarters Osage and one-quarter French. The Canville Trading Post became the Canville post office, which is now deserted, but Canville Creek and Canville Township remain in Neosho County.[25]

South of Garden City is a little town named for William Lewis Sublette. The Sublettes were French Huguenots who had settled in Virginia and moved with the vanguard of the frontier into Kentucky and Missouri. They helped to blaze trails across Kansas, including "Sublette's Trace." Bill Sublette, a Mountain Man, was a partner in the Rocky Mountain Fur Company. The Indians called him "Cut Face."[26]

The streets of the town of Sublette were named for travelers, traders, and trappers, including Henry Inman, William Becknell, Kit Carson, Auguste Chouteau, "Buffalo Bill" Cody, Baptiste Lelande, James Pursely, and Zebulon Pike.[27]

François Xavier Aubrey was a French Canadian who became the talk of town and trail by breaking all speed records between Santa Fe and Independence. Time was important in this period of tedious travel, when the squeaking, creaking, crawling caravans of ox-teams could barely make the Santa Fe trip in one season. Captain Aubrey made two and planned three in one season. He had skeptical critics as well as enthusiastic admirers, and his boast that he could beat his record of eight days on the trail was challenged by a $1,000 bet. He accepted. Before leaving Santa Fe, he had the local newspaper editor run off an "Extra" with an account of his proposed ride, his route, and his time of departure. With this in his pocket he dashed off for Independence, making the distance of nearly eight hundred miles in five days and sixteen hours. "Not one in a hundred thousand," said J. Frank Dobie, "could ride like Aubrey."[28] He earned for himself several flattering titles: "Skimmer of the Plains," "Prairie Telegraph," "Lightening Traveler," "Great Plains Courier," "Little Aubrey," and "Intrepid Aubrey." The Indians called him "White Cloud."[29] He was only five feet two, but he was "made out of rawhide."

Aubrey's tragic death occurred when a critical newspaper article led to a sudden and senseless incident in a saloon. Aubrey, blinded by a glass of liquor thrown into his face, was about to draw his gun when his assailant stabbed and killed him—"in self-defense."

A number of places were named to honor the fleet Frenchman. A fort named Aubrey was established at Aubrey Spring, discovered by Aubrey about four miles east of Syracuse. The fort was near Aubrey's Crossing of the Arkansas on the cut-off of Aubrey's Trail, some distance above the Cimarron Crossing of the Santa Fe Trail. A hill in Kearny County where a wagon train had fought off an Apache and Arapaho raid was called Mount Aubrey.[30] A station east of Fort Aubrey became the town of Aubrey. As a post office, its name was changed to Zamora in 1879, "and that was worse," said one writer.[31] Zamora was a distinctive name of Spanish origin and not necessarily "worse," except that it replaced a name of considerable historical interest. Cram's contemporary map compromised by listing it as "Zamora or Aubrey."[32] Both of these names were replaced by the name of Kendall, probably for the Kendall brothers, local merchants.[33]

South of Kansas City in Johnson County, A. G. Gabbart named a town Aubrey, as he said, "after the famous traveler (Mexican we believe) of that name." The town of Aubrey lost its identity when it merged with a neighbor and became Stilwell, named for a railway conductor.[34] For a time it retained the name of "Old Aubrey." Despite the fame of the Frenchman and the number of places that bore his name—a spring, a fort, a crossing, a trail, a hill, and two towns—nothing remains except Aubrey Township in Johnson County.

Members of the Robidoux family, active in the commerce of Kansas, have left their names on the map from Missouri to California. St. Joseph, Missouri, was named for Joseph Robidoux, who operated a ferry there. In 1841, Michael Robidoux carved his name on the limestone bank of a little stream which flowed into the Black Vermillion. It became Robidoux Creek. The name was forgotten until 1947 when the United States Board of Geographic Names officially restored it. The ford on the old Indian Trail was known as the Robidoux Crossing. It must have been near Vermillion, which has been referred to as "Robidoux or Vermillion."[35] Robidoux Station was near Guitard on the Mormon Trail.[36] The crossing near the present Bigelow was called French Ford.

Eugene Bourassas started a grist mill and a sawmill on Mill Creek near an Indian village in Marshall County. His place was called Bourassas Mills by those who knew French; others called it "Bursaw's Mills."[37] Also in Marshall County was a town named La Grange, named by Mrs. E. F. Jones, a French woman.[38] There had been an earlier La Grange in Morris County.

Elias Boudinot was not French. He was a Cherokee Indian, married to a New England white woman. He took the name of Boudinot to honor a French benefactor whom he admired. A place near Osage Mission was called "Mission at Boudinot on the Neosho."[39]

A Kaskaskia chief in Illinois with the French name of Duquoin was said to be the source of the name of Duquoin in that state. In Harper County, Kansas, the source for the place named Duquoin was probably that Illinois town.[40]

Such distinguished men of the French frontier as Frontenac, La Salle, Marquette, Du Luth, and Dubuque have left their names on the map. Count Frontenac, as governor of New Frence, sent Joliet and Marquette to find a route to the "Sea of California" and to verify the reports of gold mines in Quivira.[41] Frontenac is now the name of a station near Pittsburg, Kansas. From the copper-country town of Marquette, Michigan, came the settlers who changed the Swedish name of Calmar, a town near the Kanopolis dam, to Marquette.[42]

Dubuque, Iowa's oldest town, was named for Julian Dubuque, a French-Canadian who settled in the lead-mining area along the Mississippi. Dubuque, not far from Frontenac in Kansas, was named for the Iowa town.[43] Duluth in Pottawatomie County was named for Duluth, Minnesota, which had been named for Daniel Graysolon Du Luth, a French explorer and companion of La Moth Cadillac, the founder of Detroit.

There is also a Detroit in Kansas. It is a small town east of Abilene. The name in Michigan had been Ville d'Etroit, but it was reduced to Detroit, "the narrows." In Kansas it replaced three earlier names: Lamb's Point, named for William Lamb; Smoky Hill, named for the river; and New Port, a descriptive name.

Governor James M. Harvey sent Stephen G. Marcou and George de Pardonnet to France as agents to promote French immigration to Kansas. But many of the French who came to Kansas were already in the New World. Seven hundred Frenchmen settled in Cloud County. Some came from Kankakee, Illinois, and a few came from France, but most of them came from Canada. Some left their own names on the Kansas map, while others added names of places and people in France.

Some of the places settled by the French were identified by their neighbors as French Creek, French Ridge, and French Valley. For a short time French Valley was the name of a post office in Wabaunsee County. Michael Frachet had a trading post on French Creek in Chase County.[44] John and Mary Cayot and their large family settled on French Ridge in Wabaunsee County. There was also a Frenchman's Ridge in Coffey County,[45] which had the reputation of being "one of the liveliest places in the country."[46] French Valley, however, was named for Isaac L. French, the postmaster.

George Guittard took his French family to Marshall County and started a trading post which became a stage station and a post office. Xavier, one of the sons, could speak English and became a postmaster. The Pony Express was to cross the Black Vermillion at Guittard's Station. Now only Guittard Township is a reminder of the family.[47]

Ernest Valeton de Boissière, a French nobleman, friend of Victor Hugo, and democratic opponent of Louis Napoleon, came to Kansas to organize a co-operative colony as a social and economic experiment. The French community was first called Valeton for the French founder, but the name was later changed to Silkville to advertise its industry. Utopia was not to be found in Silkville, and the experiment failed. Silkville is now a signpost on the highway between Emporia and Ottawa.[48]

Martin Creek in Chase County was named for Peter Martin, who helped Francis Laloge run a trading post at Cottonwood Hole, not far from Durham in Marion County.[49] Collet Creek was named for George Collet, the pioneer who named Middle Creek.[50] Brunot Creek was named for John Brunot, one of the early French settlers in Cottonwood Valley.[51]

Northern Ford County had a French community. Offerle on the Santa Fe, southwest of Kinsley, was named for Laurence Offerle, a Frenchman from Geneseo, Illinois, who surveyed the townsite, opened the first store, and established the post office.[52] The next station west of Offerle is the town of Bellefont, named for the leader of the French settlers.[53]

Louis Lais was better known as "French Louis." His ranch west of Syracuse was called "The Hermitage," and French Louis was known as "The Hermit of Loui Springs." He was a scout, guide, and buffalo hunter, and he captured and sold wild horses. At one time he might have been considered rich, but what the horse thieves did not get, the blizzard of 1886 did. French Louis died a pauper, but he left his name on Loui's Springs.[54]

When Kentucky was still a part of Virginia, one of its counties was named Bourbon because of the aid the Bourbons of France gave the colonies during the American Revolution. A Kansas county was named Bourbon on the recommendation of Colonel Samuel A. Williams, a member of the Bogus Legislature who came from Bourbon County, Kentucky.[55] Thus, Kansas honored the royal French family only indirectly. That Bourbon should have any other reference than to royalty might seem unthinkable in Kansas, and yet there are those whose minds drift to drink. Williams said that the name was "due to the name of the beverage which the party in power drew so largely from for its courage and zeal in pushing its measures in Kansas."[56] This sounds, however, like political palaver.

But the Bourbon family was honored in Kansas by such names as Louisiana, St. Louis, and Louisburg. These names had already been used in America, but they did originally honor the Bourbon kings. Louisiana was named for Louis XIV, also called "Louis Le Grand." A "paper-town" promoted for a place in Douglas County was to be named Louisiana, but it became Salem.[57]

Louisburg in Miami County was first named Lodi. Then its name was changed to St. Louis for the one in Missouri, which had been named to honor Louis IX. The streets of St. Louis, Kansas, were laid out to imitate those of the Missouri town, and the community was frequently referred to as "Little St. Louis." To avoid confusion with the name in Missouri, St. Louis in Kansas deleted the "Saint," sedately added "burgh," and economically deleted the "h."[58]

Massillon, a post office in Sumner County in 1878, could have been named for Massillon, Ohio, but, in any case, it has a French origin. The one in Ohio was named for Jean Baptiste Massillon, a French bishop serving Louis XIV.[59] He was a powerful speaker and opened his funeral oration for the Sun King by declaring, *Dieu seul est grand*, "God alone is great."

Marietta in Saline County in 1874, and the Marietta in Reno County, 1878–87, may be associated with Marietta, Ohio, which was named for Marie Antoinette, wife of Louis XVI. But the Marietta in Marshall County was named for Marietta Mann, wife of T. J. Mann, one of the promoters of the town.[60]

Paris was the proud county seat of Linn County, bordering on Bourbon County. The name might remind one of the gayest city in France, but, like Bourbon, it came from Kentucky. In the county seat war, known as the "Battle of Paris," an armed force made a midnight raid on Paris and carried away the county documents. This *coup d'état* has been called the "death blow to Paris." Another Paris had been planned for Shawnee County but it never developed.[61] A Paris was established in Ness County to compete with Ness City.[62] Lincoln County had a post office named Paris for twenty years. Paris was a popular but impermanent name. Only Paris Township in Linn County survives.

Versailles, site of the famous Bourbon palace, became the name of a town in Osage County. In western Kansas, a stop named Versailles was included on a map of a proposed railway between Garden City and Leoti; it had little chance to survive.[63]

Chantilly, north of Paris, became a name in Kearny County, Kansas. In France it was noted for its royal palace and its race track. Americans, however, associated the name with the battle of Chantilly in Virginia.[64] Aulne is the name of a river, a part of the French canal system, which flows into the Atlantic near Brest. In Kansas it is now a station on the Rock Island railway south of Marion.

Navarre, once a kingdom but now a province divided between France and Spain, gave its name to a town south of Abilene. Peter Wightman named it Navarre for no particular reason, he said, "except that it was a pretty French name." It caused problems, because the settlers on the south side of Main Street wanted the town to be named New Navarre, while the settlers on the north side wanted it called simply Navarre.[65]

Artois in Meade County could have been named for either a place or a person. In France the province of Artois preserves the name of a Belgic tribe called the Atrebates.[66] The Count of Artois, who became Charles X, contributed to its historical importance. Artois in Kansas did not prosper and its only historical importance may be its French name.[67] Meade County also had a place named Artesian City, a name referring to an available source of water and derived from Artois. Like most of its neighbors, both towns soon disappeared.[68]

French political leaders, poets, and other literary men furnished additional names for Kansas. La Fayette, Voltaire, Talleyrand, Victor Hugo, and La Fontaine were among the distinguished men whose names were given to post offices in Kansas.

No Frenchman helping the colonies in their rebellion against England won greater respect and admiration from Americans than the Marquis de La Fayette. John Ledyard, an American explorer, was sufficiently impressed by him to say, "If I find in my travels a mountain as much elevated above other mountains as he is above ordinary men, I will name it Lafayette."[69] Others must have felt as he did, because thirty-seven American towns were named Lafayette before Kansas was open to settlement. La Fayette was the only foreigner to be made an honorary citizen of the United States in the nineteenth century.[70] In Kansas a place was named La Fayette in Doniphan County, and another was named Lafayette in Stevens County. Both have disappeared. La Fayette's full name was Marie Joseph Paul Roch Yves Gelbert Motier, Marquis de La Fayette. Occasionally it was shortened to Fayette, and a town by that name in Illinois provided the name for Fayette in Sedgwick County. The name could also be lengthened. Fayetteville was a town which flourished briefly in Clay County.

Voltaire was the pen name for François Marie Arouet. He was one of those disturbing French intellectuals who challenged the conventional and conservative framework of European traditions and institutions before the French Revolution. His writings were well known in America, but his name was rarely used as a place-name. But in Sherman County, the town of Voltaire was one of the unsuccessful rivals of Goodland for the county seat. It "spent seven years dying," said the local press.[71] The township of Voltaire has kept the name alive. There had earlier been a Voltaire in Rawlins County, but it became McCloud.[72]

Hugoton in Stevens County was named to honor Victor Hugo. His family was of German origin in Lorraine. His godfather's name was Victor Lahorie and his godmother's name was Marie Dessirier, so his name was taken from both—Victor Marie Hugo. He signed the letter of presentation when France gave a gold medal to Mrs. John Brown, wife of the Kansas abolitionist.[73] The town was at first called Hugo, but to avoid confusion with Hugo, Colorado, the name was changed to Hugoton.[74]

Talleyrand, an ambitious bishop and a shrewd politician, served both the Bourbons and the Bonapartes with equal facility. He was unpopular in America after the XYZ affair. Talleyrand is now the name of a township in Wilson County. In Talleyrand Township is a town named La Fontaine, which was the name of a famous French poet. There is the possibility that the name of the town came from a Miami chief named La Fontaine, one of the negotiators of the removal treaty which brought the Miamis from Indiana to Kansas. La Fontaine was a temperate chief in a tribe which was being destroyed and depleted by the white man's whisky.[75] As the name of a post office, La Fontaine became Lafontaine.

Dubois, a French descendant of one of Napoleon's bodyguards, may have influenced the selection of Napoleon as a place-name in Norton County.[76] But by that time, Napoleon III was important enough to have been a possible source for the name. There must have been mixed opinions about the name of Napoleon, because it was soon suggested that it be changed to Melrose. But that name had been pre-empted in Cherokee County. Orleans, the name of Napoleon's royal rivals, was substituted for Napoleon.[77] Nevertheless, Napoleon did have his admirers, and the first white child born in Kansas, the grandson of Daniel Boone, was named Napoleon Boone.[78] Eugenia, the name of the unhappy wife of Napoleon III, was the name of a post office in Rice County. It was later changed to Allegan.

Several names in Kansas were associated with events in Napoleon's spectacular career. To such popular names as Paris and Versailles one may add Marengo, Toulon, Wagram, Austerlitz, Elba, Waterloo, Lodi, and Longwood. These names are reminders of Napoleon's victories, defeats, and exiles. Marengo and Lodi,[79] battles which Napoleon won in northern Italy, gave him prestige, as did the battle of Toulon against the British. Toulon, Kansas, is the name of a station east of Hays. Marengo in Sumner County did not survive, nor did Lodi in Barber County. The Lodi in Miami County became St. Louis. Wagram near Vienna was the site of a bloody battle on the Danube that brought promotions to generals on both sides. The Methodist women in Dickinson County disliked the name of Wagram and changed it to Hope for Hope, Michigan.[80] In Washington County, a place was temporarily name Austerlitz for a battle Napoleon won in 1805.[81]

It was to the Mediterranean island of Elba that Napoleon was first exiled. Twice the name of Elba has been used in Kansas, once in Anderson County and once in Chase County. Both towns were short-lived.[82] Longwood, the name of Napoleon's home in exile on the island of St. Helena, had a brief existence as a name in Miami County.

Wellington defeated Napoleon at Waterloo. The first Waterloo in Kansas was north of Emporia. The name now remains on a township in Lyon County. The second Waterloo, named for Waterloo, Iowa, is near Kingman. When Charles Mullen petitioned for a post office in Iowa, he saw Waterloo in the postal directory and submitted this name because, as he said, it had "the right ring to it."[83] Wellington is a town in Sumner County.

The Franco-Prussian War of 1870 publicized both people and places. Sedan, Metz, and Lorraine became Kansas place-names. The German capture of Sedan marked the end of the war in 1870, and the next year, Sedan became a place-name in Chautauqua County, where there were many German residents.[84] There was a logical German source for the name and yet there are other suggestions. Before Sedan was established, E. K. Parris came to open a store in Howard (now Chautauqua) County. The place had no name but was called "Shoo Fly," the name of a currently popular song. Parris went to Neodesha for printed advertising, and there, John Gilmore, the printer, considered the relative merits of Shoo Fly and Sedan for the town's name. He then supposedly said to Captain Parris, "Of the two names call it Sedan, by all means." The store's posters were printed with Sedan in large letters.[85]

According to another account, Thomas Scurr, hauling a wagonload of lumber for his store, saw a picture of Sedan in a current magazine. As he came over a hill, he is supposed to have said: "Why, this village looks just like this picture, let's call it Sedan."[86] To this we may add an account from local folklore. The man named Dan ran the sawmill and was popular in the community. After chores were done, it was common for his friends to say that they were going to "see Dan," and that is how the town came to be named Sedan.[87] In spite of all the local accounts and fancy tales, the name of Sedan most likely came from France.[88]

Metz was the name given to a town east of Sedan in 1874. In Lorraine, the European town of Metz is also east of Sedan. It may be more German than French but the name has a Celtic origin as Matrici, the name of a Belgic people. The Romans called it Mediomatrica which was shortened to Mettis and easily changed to Metz.[89] Metz was publicized during the Franco-Prussian War as the place where General Bazaine was defeated.

Marshal Achille François Bazaine was the general who had successfully evacuated the French army from Mexico during the Maximilian intervention. Despite his fame, he was defeated by Bismarck's army. It is possible that the creek and town name Bazine in Ness County were named for the French general, with only a slight variation in spelling.[90]

Dunkirk, most famous as the battleground for the gateway to France, is an English name for "church on the dunes." In French it is Dunquer-que. In Kansas, Dunkirk is a town near Pittsburg, named by settlers who came from Dunkirk, New York.[91]

One of the many descriptive terms used in both French and English was "beautiful." In English it might be "fair" and in French, "belle." Two places could be given the same descriptive name, Fairview and Bellevue. Kansas had places named Bellemont, Belle Springs, Belle Grove, Bellefont, Belle Plaine, Belle Prairie, Belle Meade, Belleville, and Bellevue. These were subject to variations in spelling and distortion. Bellevue in Sumner County lost an "e" and became Bellvu. Then it became Belleview and later Marengo. In Jackson County the name was spelled Bellevue; in Pottawatomie County, it is spelled Belvue. Belle Prairie in Rush County disappeared, but the name remains on Belle Prairie Township. The abbreviated form of Belpre, "beautiful prairie," is the name of a station in Belpre Township in Edwards County. Not far from Belpre is Bellefont.[92]

Bellemont and Beaumont are popular French names. A scenic bluff across the river from St. Joseph, Missouri, was first named Belle Mount and then Bellemont. Then the town was renamed Whitehead for its promoters, J. H. and J. R. Whitehead. Because of its steep and slippery climb from the Missouri, Bellemont became known as the "Mountain of Misery."[93]

For a short time there was a Belmont in Woodson County. In Rooks County, there was another Belmont. The only Belmont to survive was the one in Kingman County, supposedly named for the Pennsylvania town.[94] The name could also represent the surname of many Americans, including Belmont the railway promoter.

A swell in the "Grand Prairie" of Brown County was named Mount Roy for John Baptiste LeRoy, an interpreter and trader.[95] A Mount Roy post office was established there.

Belle Plaine in Belle Plaine Township, Sumner County, is accurately named. In northwestern Kansas, a Norton County township, located between Prairie Dog Creek and the Solomon, is called Belle Plaine.

Beaumont and Piedmont are towns in the Flint Hills east of Augusta. Beaumont has sufficient beauty in its wooded hills to deserve the name. The rise was high enough to require an extra locomotive for trains to make the grade, justifying its "mont" name.[96] Piedmont, appropriately used for the foothills of the Blue Ridge Mountains, is inappropriate in Kansas where there are no mountains. Piedmont or "foothills" would indicate that the hills were near mountains, just as Piedmont in Italy is at the foot of the Alps.

According to a Dickinson County legend, a bell-cow once came home without her bell. The farmer searched and found the bell near a fine spring. He named the place "Bell Spring." But the Pennsylvania Dutch community gave the name a French turn by changing it to Belle Spring. Then the post office department, thinking it might be confused with Lost Spring, changed the name to Donegal, which was the name of a town and township in Pennsylvania and a place-name in Ireland.[97]

The Bellaire post office in Smith County is a station on the Rock Island, and a suburb northeast of Wichita is now named Bel Aire. Greenwood County has a Belle Grove. When John Worth located a post office on his timber claim in Meade County, he repeated the name of Meade but gave it a French touch by calling it Belle Meade.[98] Bodarc, Butler County, is an abbreviated form of Bois d'arc, the name of the Osage orange or bow-wood from which the Indians made their bows.

Boicourt in Linn County had been named Barnard and Cobb. It was renamed Boicourt for a Frenchman who owned a thousand acres of land north of Fort Scott. It is now a station on the Frisco line.[99]

The Prairie du Chien of Wisconsin is so well known that it would be a likely source for the naming of Prairie Du Chien in Neosho County, Kansas. It has been translated literally as "Prairie of the Dog." The Kansas town was absorbed by Thayer, a place named for Nathaniel Thayer, a Boston railway promoter.[100]

In Grant County a post office was named Gognac. It was also spelled Cognac, which suggests that the name was that of a popular French brandy from the area around Cognac in France. The transition may have been phonetic, and the French connection is logical.[101]

Many French names in Kansas have remained only as phonetic forms and their meanings may have been lost. But few have suffered as much in transition as the Spanish name of the stream in Colorado called El Río de las Animas Perdidas en Purgatorio, "the river of souls lost in Purgatory." In French it became Purgatoire, difficult for Americans who knew no French. They attempted the French and called it the "Picketwire."[102]

There are no sharp linguistic boundaries around Switzerland, although there are distinct linguistic communities. The Swiss spoke the languages of their neighbors—Italian, French, German, and a vernacular called Romansch. Each neighbor has its own name for the country once called Schwyz. In German it was Schweiz; in French, Suisse; in Italian, Swizerra; and in English, the land of the Swiss was Switzerland. One Swiss settlement in Osage County was known as Swissvale.

Most of the Swiss who came to Kansas spoke French. Among the familiar Swiss names widely distributed over Kansas were Bern, Basel,

Geneva, Lucerne, and Neuchatel. A name like Lucerne may be known by its German spelling of Luzern as well as its French form. Kansas used both. Had it been spelled "lucern," one might assume that the name referred to alfalfa. There was once a Lucerne in Rooks County. Lucerne in Sheridan County has also been spelled Luzerne.[103] The Volga-Germans who came from Luzern in Russia may have been responsible for the name of Luzern in western Kansas.[104] It has been suggested that the name came from the word *lucerna*, meaning "lighthouse."[105] Lucerne is probably best known to American school children through the sculpture of the "Lion of Lucerne," a memorial to the Swiss soldiers who died defending Louis XVI and Marie Antoinette.

Helvetia was one of the many towns that boomed and died in Meade County.[106] The place in Finney County where Adrian Sautter kept a store and post office was also called Helvetia.[107] Helvetia is the classical name for Switzerland. It came from Helvetii, the Roman name for a Celtic tribe, and is especially well known to philatelists.

Swiss settlers in Dickinson County who came from the canton of Bern named their village Newbern. The village is gone, but Newbern Township is still there. In Switzerland, Bern is in bear country, and some believe that Bern referred to bear. But this has been questioned, even though the city's shield has the picture of a bear. Bern keeps a tame bear in a cave as a symbol of the city, but the name could have come from Dietrich of Berne, a personal name, or even from a word which means a "bush" or "forest."[108]

Swiss settlers in Dickinson County also named a town New Basel. Its Latin name was Basilia, possibly from Basilus, the name of a Roman who had served in Gaul. Basilia was changed to Basel and Basle. The French silenced the "s" in Basel, rendered it useless, and dropped it; then they silenced the "e" by putting it after the "l" and this made it Bale.[109] Kansas returned to the old pronunciation but spelled the name New Basell and New Basill. The extra "l" was superfluous and the name was changed back to New Basel. A town in Nemaha County was known for eight days by the Irish name of Collins but its name changed to Basel by Swiss settlers from Ohio. The name lasted slightly over a year and then became Bern, retaining its Swiss connection.[110]

Another Swiss settlement in Nemaha County was Neuchatel, French for Newcastle. Its first settler was Amiel E. Bonjour, known as Ami Bonjour, "friend good-day."[111] Neuchatel was in Neuchatel Township.

The town of Banwill, or Bannville, in Comanche County could have been named for the Swiss town of Bannwyl, or Bonneville, which the French called "BonVielle." In Switzerland, it was a beautiful town on the river Aar in the province of Bern.[112] The Ehrsams who settled in

Dickinson County came from Bannwyl in Switzerland, but their community was named New Schwanau, for Schwanau, the "valley of the swans."[113] In Switzerland, Schwanau was an island in Lowerz Lake.

Zurich is a town on the High Plains in Rooks County in the center of a mixed European community. In Switzerland, Zurich is located in a scenic setting of mountains and lakes. Residents of the Kansas town tell about a traveler from Zurich, Switzerland, who expected to see a duplication of the scenic beauty of his home town. The apparently bleak, although not barren, plains of Kansas were quite a disappointment for the man. On Cram's map, the town is listed as "Zurich or Villisca."[114]

Geneva is the name of a town located in Geneva Township northeast of Iola. It is a popular name in the United States, and Illinois alone has three Genevas. In Kansas, Geneva was settled by colonists of the Union Settlement Association from New York and Michigan. Because there is no Geneva, Michigan, it has been assumed that the name came from Geneva, New York.[115] In Kansas it was planned as a religious and educational center, and the Geneva Academy was founded there. This tends to associate it with Jean Jacques Rousseau whose home was in Geneva, Switzerland.[116] The European city has been called "Switzerland's wide window on the world." Genève, as the French called it, may refer to its location on Lake Geneva near the Rhone, or, like Genoa, a "knee."[117] Although unlike Switzerland in its topography, Kansas has had several place-names of Swiss origin.

CHAPTER XII

VER HANSTON HARDTNER HARLAN HARPER HARRIS HARTFORD HARVEYVILLE HAVANA HAVEN HA

NAMES FROM OLD ENGLAND

HAVILAND HAYNE HAYS HAYSVILLE HAZELTON HEALY HEPLER HERINGTON HERNDON HESSTON H

WE MAY NOT think of Kansas and England as having much in common, but W. D. Howells saw a similarity in his travels from Chester to Liverpool "over lonely levels, with a ground swell like that of Kansas plains . . . ."[1] "Only gradually has it stolen over me," said one commentator, "how much England is a matter of names, or how insufficient is the most perfect photograph for conveying its full delights."[2] England's kings and queens, its dukes, counts and their castles, its towns and hamlets, its people and places have all served as sources for naming places in Kansas. Some of the names came directly from England; others had been used widely in America before their adoption in Kansas.

Few Americans realize how much history there is behind the names of their own towns, especially the names that came from England. Washington Irving was critical of those who "deluged" the country with names from the Old World, comparing such names to "cast off clothes of Europe."[3] One who liked the English names said they "please the mind with their home-like sound, and the ear with their easy flow, . . . they have been clipped, condensed, worked over like iron in a rolling-mill, till they have been fitted to the English tongue."[4]

There were many languages and peoples involved in making place-names in Britain: Britanni, Celts, Picts and Scots, Angles, Saxons, and Jutes. There were Nordic names from Norwegians and Danes, Latin names from Romans, and Romance names from the Norman-French. The early chronicles and the Domesday Book show how far we have gone in merging the many languages into modern English.[5] The origin of British place-names is said to be "one of the greatest mysteries of English history."[6] English scholars have, however, done well in their search for these mysterious origins.[7]

The old and difficult forms which came from the varied languages of those who invaded Britain have been conveniently modified and made comprehensible before being transplanted to America. As they emerged from the hodgepodge of many languages, they described the fields and fords; the boroughs, burys, and burghs; or the hams and hamlets, the hills and dales; and the streams and their glens.[8] However, when these names were transplanted, the new site often had nothing in common with the place described where the name was first used.

The terminals of English names are quite generally descriptive. Ham, as a part of a name, referred to the home or homestead. The homestead or village which was surrounded by an enclosure or hedge was called a *wich*, be it spelled *wic, wich, wik*, or *wick*. *Tun* may be related to *dun*, meaning a hill, and it could also refer to a village within an enclosure. These terminals were naturally combined with other names, as in Warwick, frequently joined as one, and often shortened and simplified until the original meaning might be lost. One may not be sure whether it be a person or place that is honored in a place-name. A couplet illustrates the connection:

> *In Ford, in Ham, in Lay and Ton,*
> *The most of English Surnames run.*[9]

English settlers and English names were most heavily concentrated in eastern Kansas, but their names were most conspicuous from Sumner County in the south to Republic County in the north. British influence in Sumner County may be seen from such names as London, Oxford, Kitley, Rolling Green, and Wellington. So many Englishmen settled in Chase County that J. E. House said the county could boast of having "two or three British titles" because "younger sons of British aristocracy were as thick around Cottonwood Falls as were the bass in South Fork."[10]

Albion is one of the oldest names for England, a name popular in poetry. It is moreover a common place-name. England was called Albion by the Greeks and Romans, who may have learned it from the Gauls. The name was used by both Aristotle and Julius Caesar. England was possibly named Albion for its white cliffs of Dover. Albus means "white," and one may associate Albion with albino. In California, the cliffs along Drake's Bay resemble those of Dover, and Drake named California "Nova Albion."

Albion was for a time the name of a post office in Republic County. In 1880 it became the name of a place in Wabaunsee County, but there the name was changed to Pike, replaced later by a post office named Alta Vista. In Harper County, Albion replaced Gourock, a Scotch name.[11] Barton, Republic, and Reno counties have townships named Albion.

Windsor, Westminster, and London, great names in English history, were adopted as Kansas place-names, but none achieved greatness in Kansas. Windsor was made the surname of the royal family of England during World War I to avoid the stigma of its German names. This was a bit of nationalistic nonsense to obscure the blood relationship between the British king and the German kaiser. The kaiser's clever retort was that his favorite English play was "The Merry Wives of Saxe-Coburg."[12] But the name of Windsor had long been famous as the name of the royal residence of England.[13] One interpretation of the name is that it came from *windelsora* which meant "the winding shore," referring to the riparian line of the Thames. It has also been suggested that it meant "the slope or bank with a windlass," supposedly for landing boats.[14]

The first Windsor in Kansas was in Ottawa County. An 1877 map placed it on the left bank of the Saline River, an 1883 map placed it on the right bank, but it survived on neither bank.[15] The Saline River was sufficiently crooked in Ottawa County to fit the English interpretation as the "winding shore." New Windsor replaced the name of Cheyneyville in Cherokee County. The post office named Windsor in Cowley County has also disappeared, but a township there still bears the name of Windsor. The "Winsor" spelling has been used for places in both Cowley and Ottawa counties.

Both Tacitus and Ptolemy knew London, a place which the Romans called Londinium. The name could have come from the Latin *londo* meaning "wild" or "bold."[16] If it had a Celtic origin, it could refer to the pool at the foot of the *dun* or hill where St. Paul's Cathedral is located.[17] The *Wichita Eagle* predicted in 1873 that the London on the Ninnescah in Sumner County would become a town of "considerable importance,"[18] but it disappeared as a town. The name remains on London Township. New London near Nickerson was located on the right bank of the Arkansas River, which was the wrong bank when the railroad was built on the left bank.

Drury reminds one of Drury Lane in London, or, perhaps, even of the Drury Lane Theatre. In Sumner County, Drury is a railway station on a branch of the Santa Fe. Drury seems to be a variation of *druery*, an obsolete form referring to "love" or "friendship." It may also be associated with the word dowry as "a love-token."

Westminster in London is noted for its famous Abbey where so many of England's great lie buried. Among them is T. S. Eliot, an American poet from Missouri. It has been well said that the poets' corner was "set aside for the lords of the English language." The origin of the name was the "Western Monaster," changed to Westmunster and then to Westminster. In Kansas it was the name of a place near Hutchinson where it is now the name of a Reno County township.

Kensington and Athol in Smith County, Kansas, are believed locally to be the names of the wife and daughter of a railroad builder. Kensington was said to be the family name of his wife, and Athol, the name of his daughter.[19] However, these are British place-names, Kensington in

England and Athol in Scotland. Kensington, noted for its gardens, is a London borough near Westminster and Chelsea. As Chenesitun and Kenesitune, it was the "King's Town." Preston, Pratt County, is a familiar surname in Kansas, but it was originally "priest's town" in England.

The town of Oxford on the Missouri River in Johnson County was promoted by a man with the distinguished name of Christopher Columbus Catron. It was settled by Southern sympathizers whose small number exerted an overwhelming political influence at the polls. There were, according to one account, approximately 42 residents in Oxford who turned in 1,628 votes! This gave rise to a contemporary comment in verse:

> *This little old town*
> *Won its way to fame;*
> *And from "stay at home crime," absolution.*
> *Thirty votes for each man*
> *Won the day for the clan,*
> *And for law and the new constitution.*[20]

Most Oxford residents left to join the Confederate Army. The deserted village soon died, but a township retains the Oxford name.

The town of Oxford, east of Wellington, was organized by A. Graff, a merchant from Oswego, Kansas. As an Indian site it had been called Neptawah,[21] and Neppana, as well as Napawalla, and it was the Napawalla Town Company that promoted Oxford. It has been assumed that Oxford was only a descriptive name of a Walnut River ford, as was its English name of Oxnaford. But Graff said that "the river ford had nothing to do with the naming of Oxford." He named Oxford, he said, to honor "the great college of England."[22] The founders hoped to make it an educational center. A local school is also named Oxford as is the township in which Oxford is located.

Oxford and Cambridge are closely associated in the minds of people and the educational world. The Cambridge in Cowley County, Kansas, is only thirty miles from Oxford in Sumner County. Cambridge in Kansas is believed to have been named for Cambridge in England.[23]

The name of Cambridge was said to be simply the "bridge over the Cam River." When the river's name was Granta, the *Anglo Saxon Chronicle* spelled it Grantabryeg with variations. In Roman times a place nearby was called Grantacaester, the "fort on the Granta." The next step backward would give us the Celtic meaning of *cam*, "crooked." But making Cambridge the bridge over the "crooked" river or the "Crooked Ford," said Taylor, is incorrect, since the Granta is "so remarkably straight."[24]

Groton, Haverhill, and Cambridge in England extend northwestward from London in a neighborly row. Groton in Suffolk County had been called Grotena in the Domesday Book. Its source may be *grot*, said to mean "a small particle" such as sand in a stream.[25] The name had also been spelled "Gnoton," and it was as Gnoton that it was first used in Logan County, Kansas. After two months the name was changed to Groton.

Bristol is a name that came from *brycgstow*, the "site of the bridge." It was widely used in England and exceptionally popular in America, where there were twenty-five Bristols, including one in Coffey County, Kansas. The "Bristol Colony" in Gove County came from Bristol, Pennsylvania.[26] The name in Coffey County has a questionable source except for its English origin.

A convenient crossing of a stream was a logical place for the location of a town or fort. The ford could become a part of a name as in Oxford, Hartford, and Bedford, popular names in England. These are also Kansas names. In England, Bedford was the county seat of Bedford-shire. Its name supposedly came from Bedicanford or Bed-an-ford, referring to a military post at the fort. It has also been suggested that it could mean "Prayer Ford."[27] *Bed* does mean prayer or supplication in both Norse and Old English. Bedford was the place where John Bun-yon preached and was imprisoned, and there he wrote *Pilgrim's Progress*. Among the numerous English names in Sumner County was New Bedford, only three miles from the place once named London. It was possibly named for New Bedford, Massachusetts. It was said to be known as "Naw Bone" before it became New Bedford.[28] One may conclude that Naw Bone came from Gnaw Bone, Indiana.

Butler County had a Keighley, the name of a borough near Leeds in Yorkshire, a likely source for the name in Kansas.[29] If the "ley" terminal comes from *hly* or *hli*, which means "shelter," then Keighley could refer to a person living in this shelter. If it were from *leah* it could refer to a "grove" or even a "glade." The three English names on the Frisco line in Butler County are Keighley, Haverhill, and Andover, but the names need not have come from England.

Matfield Green is a name with the charm of Old England. It was named by its first postmaster, David W. Mercer, "fresh from the old country," whose home had been at Five Oaks near Matfield Green, a suburb of London. In using its name, Mercer had transferred a bit of Old England to the cattle country of Kansas.[30] The township using the name dropped the second word and lost its poetic appeal by being shortened to Matfield.

Mercer Creek was named for the same Mercer who named Matfield

Green. He was described as "a very large blonde man with a huge red beard and a schoolgirl complexion." Since he retained his old English custom of wearing a smock, he appeared unconventional to his neighbors, who said that "David Mercer wears his shirt tail outside his pants."[31]

Roman military camps in England attracted traders and settlers, resulting in the growth of villages and towns. The English name of Chester is an outgrowth of *castra* or *ceaster*, Roman names for a military camp or a fort. Even with their Roman terminals, such names as Manchester, Lancaster, Winchester, and Rochester are quite English. These names have been used freely in the United States, and all are or have been Kansas place-names. Lancaster came to Kansas from Pennsylvania and New York, and Winchester came from Virginia.

In England, the town named Chester was the county seat of Cheshire. Both names have the same Roman origin. Chester was the name of a post office which served in Jefferson County for thirty years before it was closed in 1902. Cheshire in Montgomery County was in Ohio Township which may suggest that the name Cheshire came to Kansas from Ohio.

For two years there was a Manchester in Sedgwick County, changed later to Minneha. As the name of Manchester was abandoned in Sedgwick County, it was chosen to replace the name of Keystone in Dickinson County. The latter was said to be named for Manchester, England, whose source was "Manning-ceaster."[32] At one time the manorial rights over Manchester were granted to Sir Thomas West, who became Baron De La Warr, and from that title we acquired the name of Delaware.

Camchester replaced the name of Cameron in Harper County. It is not listed in Ekwall's *Dictionary of Names*, but it has all the earmarks of an English name. *Cam* is an English river name which in Welsh may mean "crooked." One could conclude that Camchester meant "the fort on the crooked river." It could also have been derived from Grantchester since the Granta was changed to Cam.[33]

Another name of a Roman fort in England which was popular in America was Rochester. Before its adoption in Kansas, twenty-eight places were named Rochester in the United States. Best known was Rochester in New York, but that was named for Nathan Rochester, its founder. In Kansas, the name was used in Anderson and Shawnee counties before becoming post office names in Neosho and Kingman counties. In Shawnee County it was the fifth name given to a town competing with Topeka for location of the state capital. It had been Chapman, Delaware City, Whitfield, and Kansopolis before it was Rochester in its dying days.[34] In Neosho County, Rochester ended its postal services in 1872. Rochester was a post office name in Kingman County for two decades, but in 1899 the name was changed to Zenda, a name which had been popularized by Anthony Hope's novel, *The Prisoner of Zenda*.[35]

In England, the name Rochester had a complicated evolution from Durobrivis, "Bridge of the Stronghold," to Hrofi, joined to *caestra* to make the "Roman fort of Hrofi." Then the initial "H" was dropped and the name evolved from Rovecestre and Rouchestre to Rochester.[36] The early adventures of the Pickwick Club took place at Rochester, the boyhood home of Charles Dickens. In Shawnee County, Dover and Rochester were separated by the Kaw River.

The English Durham may also refer to a fort. It was named Dunholm for a hill, which was almost surrounded by the River Wear. There a fort was built as a defense against the Danes. The name has been said to come from *dun*, "hill-ford," and *holm*, "river." A simpler interpretation would be "hill-island."[37] *Holm* refers generally to an island in a river. Durham is in the County of Durham between York and Northumbria. The Venerable Bede, who in the eighth century was writing about the "English People," lies buried in its beautiful Norman cathedral.[38]

In Marion County the trading post of A. A. Moore was given the post office name of Moore's Ranch. After the post office was moved to Marion Center, the ranch was purchased by Albert Crane who named his place "Durham Park Ranch."[39] This name lasted from 1874 to 1887 and was shortened to Durham. Durham Salmon-fly and Bull Durham tobacco were popular trade-names, of course, but the Durham cattle that came from England could better explain the name of Durham Park Ranch, once described as "Pride of the West." Durham is also used as the name for a township in Ottawa County.

Identification of a place by its direction from some point has been used extensively in England. Among such English names in Kansas are Norfolk, Essex, and Norwich. In England the North Folk were distinguished from the South Folk, each having their variations in speech and dress, although both were East Angles. Their names were combined into Norfolk and Suffolk. Norfolk became the name of a town in Ellis County, Kansas, not far from the English colony at Victoria.

The East Saxons gave their name to Essex, the county south of Suffolk in England. In the southwestern corner of Garfield (Finney) County, Kansas, there was an Essex post office which served from 1886 until 1918.

Norwich was an English town located in Norfolk. The "wich" could mean a hamlet with a protecting hedge or wall. If this hamlet were in the north, the name was Norwich.[40] Norwich in Kingman County is near enough to Runnymede to have been settled by remnants of that English colony. However, since the two men who started the Norwich Bank came from Norwich, New York, it has been assumed that they brought not only their money but the name. It has also been suggested that the place was named by a Missouri Pacific official for Norwich in Connecticut, a town called the "Rose of New England." But the Missouri Pacific, in its own book on names, concluded that the town was named Norwich because of its English settlers.[41]

In England, Warwick is located on the Avon some distance above Monmouth. Even in central England it had trouble with the Danes and was conquered by the Normans. The earls of Warwick had such French names as Beaumont and Beauchamp. Among its legendary heroes was Guy of Warwick, an aide to King Aethelstane, who killed the giant Colbrand while fighting the Danes.[42] Of the names mentioned in this paragraph, six have become place-names in Kansas: Warwick, Avon, Monmouth, Beaumont, Guy, and Aethelstane. Although they originated in England, most of them were used elsewhere before they came to Kansas.

Warwick's long name of Waerincgwican was shortened to Warwic and modernized to Warwick as a place-name and surname. In Kansas, Warwick is a town on the Republican River in Republic County. It had earlier been named Talmadge for a railway official, and it has been said that it was named Warwick for another railway official.[43] There were so many English settlers in Republic County that one might justify the assumption that the name came from England.[44] There were, however, three Warwicks in New England before there was a Warwick in Kansas. Also in Republic County was the place named Fenwick. In Old England, *fen* meant a "marsh," so Fenwic would be the *wic* or "dwelling" by the marsh.

On the Thames near London is that significant center of mathematical science named Greenwich. Greenwich, Kansas, may be from Greenwich, Connecticut, the home of the James R. Mead family. James R. Mead lived nearby in Towanda, Kansas. Kansans, however, fail to follow the English pronunciation of "Gren'ich." The name is derived from Grenewic or Greenwic which has been interpreted to mean "green village" or "sunny place."[45] In Greenwich were born such men of note as Dr. Samuel Johnson and Henry VIII, and that incomparable queen, Elizabeth.

> *On Thames banks in silent thought we stood,*
> *Where Greenwich smiles upon the silver flood;*
> *Pleased with the seat that gave Eliza birth,*
> *We kneel and kiss the consecrated earth.*[46]

Pickwick is a rare place-name, but the *Pickwick Papers* of Charles Dickens and the Pickwick Club made it well known. In Greeley County, Pickwick was a post office name in 1887. It lasted only a summer.

The only Rydal listed by Lippincott's *World Gazetteer* (1886) is in Westmoreland County, England. Another guide listed the one in Kansas as the only Rydal outside of England, but the name has been used in Pennsylvania and in Georgia. In the Lake Country of England is Rydal Mount, Rydal Lake, and "the pretty village of Rydal." There lived William Wordsworth, "the poet of the Cumberlands." James Russell Lowell called it "Wordsworthshire."[47] In Kansas, Rydal is located west of Bellville in Republic County. Rydal could mean, according to Ekwall, "land where rye was grown."

Also associated with literature is the name of Lodore. Lodore Falls in the lake country of Cumberland inspired Robert Southey's nursery rhyme in which he asks the question:

> *How does the water*
> *Come down at Lodore?*[48]

He answers in words that imitate sounds, a technique called onomatopoeia. John Wesley Powell liked the name well enough to give it to Lodore Canyon in Moffat County, Colorado.[49] In Kansas, Neosho County had a township named Ladore, a slight change from the original Lodore. Then the place named Fort Roach had its name changed to Ladore. The residents of Ladore moved to Parsons but Ladore is still the township name.

Many names from foreign languages referred to rivers merely as a "river" or "water" as the description of a stream. Such were also the English names of Exe, Avon, Dover, and Leeds. There were numerous English settlers in Clay County, and there we find a place named Exeter. In England, Exeter is a name that is associated with a city, with a county, with dukes, and with earls of old England. The city was once a Roman stronghold called Isca Damnoniorum. *Exe*, like *esk*, meant "water" or "river,"[50] and the name came from the Exeter River.

Avon is such a popular name that it is used in over thirty places. In addition to Avon Downs and nine Avondales in the United States, there are five Avons in the British Isles, and England alone has three rivers named Avon. Avon meant merely "river." Shakespeare and the appeal of a simple name made Avon popular. The name may have a Welsh origin as *afon*, which, like *exe*, meant "water." The Irish called it *abhann*, pronounced "avain." The Avon River flowing southward through Warwickshire is the one called "Shakespeare's Avon." Kansas used the name of Avon for a post office in Coffey County and as a name of a township in Sumner County. Franklin County once had an Avondale, which replaced the name of Everson.[51]

For over thirty years there was a Chepstow in Washington County. In England, Chepstow was a river-port on the Wye called Ceapstow in Old English. It meant simply a "market-place."

Kent is such an old name that it is difficult to determine which of its various interpretations may be correct. Caesar knew the name as Cantium, but its earlier origin may be Celtic. In Welsh the name was most likely *cant* or *canto*, meaning "rim" or "border."[52] Kent borders on the English Channel and its chief port is Dover. The name Kent has twice served as a post office name in Reno County and it still designates a railway station east of Hutchinson.

In England, Bath is the name of a resort town on the Avon River where there were several hot springs. There the pagans had worshiped the sun, so the Romans called it Aquae Solis, where they enjoyed their *batum bathum*.[53] They also called it Aquae Calidae, "hot water." Like Baden in Germany it is best known as Bath. We find Bath used as a personal name in the *Canterbury Tales* in which the naïve "Wife of Bath," without modesty, entertained her companions with a "delightful bit of self-revelation."[54] Queen Elizabeth's frank but unfriendly comment about the town of Bath was: "It stinks!"[55]

The name of Bath has crossed the Atlantic and spread across America to Kansas. What is now Yates Center in Woodson County was first named Bath, then Chellis, and later Kalida. For a few months in 1876, there was a Bath in Norton County.

For nearly a decade, Kingman County had a post office named Brighton. In England, Brighton came from Brihthelmestone, "the stone of Brihthelm." Brihthelm was the name of a bishop. Brighton is a famous seashore resort that once appealed to the aristocracy, and both Queen Victoria and her playboy son, Edward VII, enjoyed it. [56] Now it is described as "Britain's Miami—brash, extravagant, a curious mixture of vulgarity and elegance, sophistication and naïveté . . . ."[57] In Kansas, a place in Kingman County was named Brighton in 1879. Jackson County had a place named New Brighton, possibly from Brighton, Illinois, although there are other Brightons in New England.

Longton in Elk County was first named Elk Rapids, but with Elk City and Elk Falls on either side, the post office department worried about the possibility of mail becoming lost and requested a new name. The name was changed to Longton for the English home town of Herbert Capper, the father of Senator Arthur Capper. In Old English the name had been Langatun, "long village or homestead."

143

Leeds, Liverpool, Halifax, and Hull are all familiar English names. Between Liverpool and Hull lies the town of Leeds in England. The name is associated with a river whose name could have been Lata or possibly Hlyde, meaning "a loud brook." The name of this English industrial town was used in over a dozen places across America before it replaced the name of Squib as a post office in Chautauqua County, Kansas. Leeds is not far from Longton in Elk County.

About half as many places were named Liverpool as Leeds in America. In England the name had reference to the stagnant pool of the harbor and was said to mean "thick water." In Grant County, Kansas, a railway station named Liverpool served intermittently as a post office until 1903.[58]

Birmingham, the second largest city in England, is surrounded by towns whose names have been used as place-names in Kansas. Originally Birmingham probably referred to "Beormund's People."[59] Birmingham in Kansas is located in Jackson County.

A place named Bismarck in Wabaunsee County had its name changed to Halifax in 1885. A century earlier, Halifax was in disfavor because it was in Halifax, Canada, that the English prize-court condemned captured American ships. For a long time, the phrase "Go to Halifax!" was equivalent to telling one, in a refined manner, to go to Hades. In England, however, Halifax was a respectable textile town in Yorkshire, seventeen miles from Leeds. Halifax, England, was said to be the source for Halifax in Kansas.[60] One interpretation of the name is that it came from "holy flax field."

The English influence in Marshall County is seen in such names as Hull and Nottingham. Hull, said the *Marshall County News*, was named by John Nesbitt for the "great manufacturing city in England."[61] Hull is an important river in England with its busy port called Kingston-Upon-Hull. The name is associated with Hoole La which became Hoole. Its earlier forms had been *hulu* and *hule* which could mean a "hut" or "hovel."[62] The name has been associated with Edward I, its founder, and with the history of the Pilgrims. Hull is the name of a railway station in Marshall County, Kansas.

The English origin of the name of Nottingham appears to have been Snotingham. Since Snot was believed to be a personal name, Snotingham meant "the ham of Snot's people," *snot* meaning "wise." The Normans dropped the "S" from "Snotengaham."[63] As Nottingham, it became a place-name in Marshall County, Kansas, in 1857. In 1869 the name was changed to Frankfurt, indicating a growing German influence in the community.[64]

In western Kansas one may find the English names of Studley, Pendennis, and Kingsdown. Between Bucklin and Bloom in Ford County and on the Coronado Trail is a town named Kingsdown. There are those who would associate this name with a poker game, like that of Show Low in Arizona. But it may have a more respectable source. When two Englishmen settled in the area, one is said to have commented: "How beautiful are these prairies." "Indeed," said the other, "they remind me of King's Down."[65] From this conversation the town is said to have received its name. Kingsdown has a descriptive appeal like Matfield Green. The name referred to "the king's dun or hill pasture."[66] Less logical is the suggestion that the name combines the family names of King and Downs.[67]

Studley, a station between Hoxie and Hill City on the Union Pacific railway in Sheridan County, was settled largely by middle-class Englishmen. J. Fenton Pratt constructed his home in Victorian style to please his English bride, and their taste for tea and crumpets gave an English character to the community. The town had first been named Skelton, later changed to Carl. Finally it was renamed by Abraham Pratt for his home in Studley Royal, a park and royal hunting ground in Yorkshire. The name came from studfold, "an enclosure for a stud of horses."[68]

The Lane County post office of Cutts had its name changed to Dupont and then to Pen Dennis. The one who proposed the name must have intended to make it Pendennis, which became its name after two years. The *Britannica World Atlas* listed only one Pendennis in the whole world, and that one was in Kansas. However, a close look at the map of Cornwall will reveal a Pendennis on the south side of the Cornish coast, shown as a castle near Land's End.[69] Better known is Thackeray's novel *Pendennis*, the leading character in which is Arthur Pendennis, a poet. In 1854, Thackeray wrote a novel called *The Newcomes* using the pen name of Pendennis. This was the accepted source for the place-name.[70] *Pen* is Cornish for "head" or "chief."

Distinctively English colonies were concentrated in three Kansas areas: the Runnymede colony in Harper County, the Wakefield Colony in Clay County, and the Victoria colony in Ellis County. Runnymede, Kansas, was promoted by J. S. Turnley as a colony to care for the younger sons of the English and Irish gentry. Turnley, whose name has been written, Ed, Ned, and Francis, was known as "lord of a western paradise."[71] He built a barracks which was called the "Chikaskia Ranch."[72] Runnymede in England is famous as the place where King John signed Magna Carta in 1215. It is a name which symbolizes liberty. The name may have come from the island of Runo in Riga Bay. There are Finns with the name of Runo, and this name may also have a

Scandinavian origin. Runimede or Runnymede has been translated to mean "Council Island" or, more completely, "the meadow in Council Island."

Liberty and license mixed in Runnymede, Kansas. The gay British blades were supposed to become gentlemen farmers, but their drinking, dancing, horse racing, hunting, and riotous revelries gave them the reputation, honestly earned, of being irresponsible playboys. The bubble burst as reality replaced the fanciful promotional literature, called "Turnley's tainted tales." Runnymede was said to have "withered like a flower and died." The town had been moved two miles to be on a railway, but the remnants of Runnymede have since been scattered over Kansas and Oklahoma, leaving little material evidence on either of its sites except for one lone tombstone. The British settlers were also scattered and some of them became respectable and successful citizens in other areas of Kansas.[73]

Horse racing was popular in Runnymede, but it is the town of Derby that most reminds one of this sport of kings. Derby in Sedgwick County was first named El Paso.[74] After some confusion caused by the same name in Texas, and after the town burned in 1879, the Santa Fe Railroad renamed it Derby. Accounts vary greatly regarding the source of the name. That is was named for the derby hat may be questionable. That is was named for a local farmer named Derby is possible. It has been said, however, that it was named by a railway engineer when he saw a group of boys racing their horses to meet the train, reminding him of the English Derby.[75] When the Earl of Derby promoted horse racing for three-year-old Thoroughbreds, he made the name Derby in Derbyshire synonymous with racing, even in Kentucky. The name was originally Danish as Deoraby, a "village with a deer park."[76]

The Reverend Richard Wake and John Wormold, both from Wakefield in Yorkshire, promoted an English colony of seventy English settlers in Clay County. They pictured Kansas as the new "El Dorado." According to the plat book, "Colonel Loomis named the town Wakefield, partly in honor of the president of the company Richard Wake, and partly because Wakefield, England, was the former home of John Wormold, the secretary of the company."[77] Also a member of the Wakefield colony was Lorenzo Gates, and Gatesville in Clay County was named for him.[78]

The Vicar of Wakefield by Oliver Goldsmith was published at Salisbury, and that was once the name of a town in Cherokee County, Kansas. A possible source for the name would be *searu*, meaning "armor," and adding *burh* for "burg," making it Searburh; but this was modernized to Salisbury and pronounced "sawlzbri."

In the neighborhood of the Wakefield colony, there was also a place named Athelstane, also spelled Aethelstane and Athelstan. Athelstane "the Glorious" conquered the Celts and defeated the Danes, and was said to be the first to call himself "King of England." Athelstane was also a character in Scott's *Ivanhoe*. The name meant "the noble stone." R. Hamilton, "who formerly lived in Athelstane Ford, in Scotland," brought the name to Kansas. There was both an Athelstane post office and perplexing frequency."[79]

The Wild Cat post office in Riley County had its name changed to Keats by a railway official who was a great admirer of poet John Keats.

George Grant was a Scottish businessman from London who had made a fortune which he supplemented by cornering the market on black crepe at the time of Prince Albert's death when all of England went into mourning. He came to Ellis County, Kansas, and bought 50,000 acres which he sold at a good profit to younger sons of English noblemen. The settlement was referred to as the "Victoria Colony," and the settlement's town was named Victoria to honor the Queen. Grant built a large town house and a station. He also built a little church, never suspecting that the first service there would be for his funeral. Its chapel was named Saint George to honor Grant. The name of Victoria has also been given to the creek which flows past the town of Victoria and through the township named Victoria. Queen Victoria restored respect for the British monarchy, and her name is associated with the prestige of the British Empire, yet one writer was of the opinion that Victoria was a name "which is repeated on our maps with inconvenient and perplexing frequency."[79]

The English found the life in the West to be "awfully jolly," but they devoted too much time to hilarious living to succeed as farmers or ranchers. Most of them deserted the area and were replaced by German Catholics from Russia who then built a town named Herzog adjoining Victoria. Because of their poverty and struggle for a living, the English called the German community "Hard-scrabble." On Victoria's skyline may be seen the tall towers of the church of Saint Fidelis, which so impressed William Jennings Bryan that he called it "the Cathedral of the Prairies."[80] With the coming of the Germans, occasionally called "Rooshans," new names were introduced, including that of Catherine, empress of Russia. So a pair of queens have given their names to Ellis County communities.

In addition to Victoria, there were other distinguished leaders of Britain whose names became place-names in Kansas. There was Cromwell, who led a civil war against royalty and set up a parliamentary Commonwealth; Wellington, a general who defeated Napoleon; Gladstone, a distinguished prime minister and statesman. Though written Cromwell, the name was pronounced "Crummell." Cromwell's name was Williams and he was related to Roger Williams, but, to inherit some property, he used his mother's name of Cromwell.[81] Ekwall's *Dictionary* gave its meaning as a "winding" or "crooked stream," similar to Windsor. As a place-name, Cromwell spread from eastern states to become the name of a town in Washington County, Kansas.

Citizens of the "City of Wellington," a rival of Sumner City for the county seat, plowed a curving furrow from the Chisholm Trail to Wellington to divert the trade from its rival. The devious tactic won not only the cattle trade but most of the settlers of Sumner City. R. A. Davis, an Englishman who was an ardent admirer of "the Little Duke," is given credit for naming the town of Wellington.[82]

The Gladstone which was located east of Cottonwood Falls in Chase County was in the heart of an English community and is believed to have been named for Queen Victoria's prime minister. Thomas H. Gladstone, a relative of Sir William, was a reporter who wrote a book about the troubles of Kansas in 1857, making the name familiar to Kansans.[83] There was later a Gladstone post office in Rawlins County.

The town of Reece in Greenwood County was named for William Smith Reece, a pioneer Englishman who raised fine horses on his "Burnt Creek Ranch."

In English history one may read about an incident at the time when Mary Tudor became Queen in 1553: "The queen went to the Tower, where the aged duke of Norfolk, the bishop of Winchester, and the dowager-duchess of Somerset welcomed her to the place of captivity."[84] In that one sentence we find three English names, Norfolk, Winchester, and Somerset, each of which became a Kansas place-name.

Denton in Doniphan County was first named Underwood and was later renamed Darwin for Charles Darwin. Settled by the four Denton brothers from England, it was for twelve years called Dentonville. In 1905 the name was shortened to Denton.[85] When it had been Darwin in 1882, the biologist's shocking views on evolution were gaining support.

Bordering on Somerset in southwestern England is the County of Devonshire or Devon. Within the county are the towns of Exeter and Plymouth and a place called Kitley. The source for the name of Devon seems to be a tribe called Defenas or Dyfnaint,[86] known as the "men of Devon." In Bourbon County, Devon was named for Devon, England.[87] Among the many English names in Sumner County was Kitley, another name from Devon. In Old English it was *cȳtan-lēah*, said to mean "kite wood."[88]

West of London is a town named Newbury. This name is a modernization of New Bourg or the New Town. Eventually the name was adopted in Kansas, where it was spelled in three ways. As "Newburg" it was close to the old form; as "Newberry," it was close to the English pronunciation; as "Newbury," a place in Wabaunsee County, it conforms to the name as it is used in England.[89]

To the people of Kansas today, the name of Olney brings to mind the annual pancake race between Olney, England, and Liberal, Kansas. In England there are two Olneys, one of which may have come from *ana leah*, "lonely glade"; the other could mean "Olla's island."[90] Kansas also had two places named Olney, but neither survived. There was one in Rush County from 1874 to 1888. Olney became the third name of a town in Hodgeman County, first called Marena and later Hanston. One might assume that Marena was named for the Aztec "girl friend" of Cortez, but evidence is lacking. Hanston was named for Benjamin Hann, owner of the townsite. When the governor was a Republican, the post office was named Marena; when the governor was a Democrat, it was named Hanston. To end the controversy, the Santa Fe Railroad renamed the town Olney.[91] This did not end the confusion, since the post office retained the name of Hanston.

A post office named Winterset in Russell County was opened three times in a decade. It is now the name of a township. Wintersettle is an Anglo-Saxon word meaning "winter quarters."[92] It had an English association in Kansas by being located on London Creek.

Old English names came to New England and migrated westward. Many of these were adopted in Kansas after they had gained some special prestige in the New World. In some instances, one may not know which was the source of the Kansas name. But in either case, the old English origin has a special interest for its meaning and its evolution.

Kansas Names from the British Isles

CHAPTER XIII

ICKOK HIGHLAND HILL CITY HILLSBORO HILLSDALE HOISINGTON HOLCOM HOLLENBERG HOLTO

SCOTLAND AND SIR WALTER SCOTT

D HOME HOPE HORACE HORTON HOWARD HOWELL HOXIE HOYT HUDSON HUGOTON HUMBOLDT H

THE SCOTS CONTRIBUTED much to Kansas nomenclature. Caledonia, an attractive name found in poetry, was the name by which the Romans knew Scotland, according to Tacitus. Caledonia was the region's accepted name until the Scotia from Ireland invaded the country. Romans spoke of the Caledonians as the "people of the woods." Thus, the assumption may have been made that Caledonia meant "forest." Because Scotland's national emblem portrays a thistle, some have decided that Caledonia meant "thistle." The most logical origin still seems to be *gael dun*, for "Gaels of the Highlands."[1] Someone, probably a Caledonian, liked the name well enough to give the name to a post office in Ottawa County, Kansas.

When the Scotia from Ireland invaded Caledonia in the third century, they may have changed the name to Scotland. Invaders from Gaul called Scuyths or Scythins could also have been the source for the name.[2] One authority suggests that they were called Scotti because they were tattooed.[3] The Wichita Indians were called Pawnee Pique for the same reason. Another interpretation for Scot is that it was a Celtic name meaning "a wanderer" or "a rover," and this fits their early history.[4] It took several centuries before there was sufficient unity among the warring clans to speak of the "King of Scotland."

A number of Scots came with the English to settle in Kansas. Jefferson County, Kansas, had Scottish settlers and there was a post office named Scott Land, later changed to Scotland. Another reference lists it not only as Scotland, but also as Scott.[5]

Before surnames were in general use, it was common to identify a person by naming him for his nationality. There are thousands of people named Scott, and many a Scott was important enough to leave his cognomen as a place-name. Scottsville in Mitchell County was named for a pioneer named Tom Scott.[6] When the town of Le Roy in Coffey County was first settled, the Indians named it "Scott's Town" for John B. Scott, who had proposed naming it Bloomington for his home town in Illinois.[7] Tescott in Ottawa County illustrates the use of initials as well as a surname and nationality, since it was named for T. E. Scott.

A community in Rush County where four Scots had settled became known as "Scotch Flats."[8]

Republic County, noted for its great variety of nationalities, had distinctive colonies of Scandinavians, Czechs, English, and Scots. Some two hundred Scottish immigrants came as a group and were known as the "David Bruce Colony." The colony, according to opinions of their neighbors, was composed entirely of mechanics who were to become farmers, and they were all said to be atheists except for one woman. The post office name for the colony on Rose Creek was Scotch Plains.[9]

In Scotland the name of Albany was applied to the territory north of the Clyde and Forth. There the rulers of the Picts were known as the "Kings of Alban."[10] Albany, the name which meant "a hill or highland,"[11] is generally associated with the dukes of Albany, and among the most important of these was James VI of Scotland, who became James I of England. Even the Duke of York in England was known as the Duke of Albany in Scotland. So New York and Albany in New York were named for the same duke. New Yorkers in Nemaha County, Kansas, established a short-lived town called Albany.[12] New Albany in Wilson County was a name from Indiana.[13]

In the poetic legends of the Gaelic people, we may read about the Caledonian king named Fingal, "tall as a glittering rock." He came to the aid of Erin in its fight against the Lochlin, as the Norsemen were then called, having come from across the waters of the lakes and seas. Fingal's followers were called Feni, from which came the name of the Fenians. Fingal's own name came from Fion na Gael. Ossian's famous epic about Fingal helped to preserve the name for posterity.[14] The name has there been well preserved as Fingal's Fort, Fingal's Grave, Fingal's Seat, and Fingal's Stair. Best known, however, is Fingal's Cave on the small island of Staffa in the Lesser Hebrides, a deserted place preserved for seals, birds, and sightseers. The name has spread as far as to East Tasmania. North Dakota is the only American state to share the name with Kansas. In Rush County, it was the name of a post office until 1910.

Several of the Scottish names in Kansas came from the names of counties or shires in Scotland. There were names from the counties of Ayr, Argyle, and Elgin, Selkirk and Berwick, Midlothian, Moray, and Perth, Lanark and Roxburgh. There were towns bearing the same name as the counties within which they were located.

In Scotland the town of Ayr or Ayer in Ayrshire is at the mouth of the Ayr River. It may have a Scandinavian origin from *eyrr* as the name for a "beach," "spit," or "tongue of land." If it were of Celtic origin, Ayr would mean "slow or gentle," or possibly "bright" or "clear."

Robert Burns, "the Bard of Ayrshire," lived in Ayr County, and his "Twa Brigs" refer to the bridges across the Ayr. There was once an Ayr in Butler County, Kansas, believed to have been named for Ayershire, Scotland,[15] but in Kansas the name was replaced by Potwin in 1885 to honor Charles W. Potwin, a Topeka businessman. Osborne County, devoid of any mountains, had a Mount Ayr which was started as a store by Omar Gregory.[16] One reference listed the name with variations as "Mount Ayer, Ayr, Ayre." As a post office its name was changed from Mount Ayr to Mountayr. A township in Osborne County has retained the name as Mount Ayr. In 1855 there was an Ayersville on the Little Blue on the border of Marshall and Washington counties. The town now named Lindsey in Ottawa County was earlier known as both Ayersburg and Ayersville,[17] named for Seymour Ayers who promoted the county organizations.[18]

Argyle is probably better known for the Scotch plaid colors, especially in hosiery, than it was for the County of Argyle. Those who knew the Scottish clans, however, were familiar with the homeland of the McLeans, the MacDonalds, and the Campbells, all famous in Argyle history. The town of Argyle was once the home of early Scottish kings. The name of Argyle is abbreviated from Airer Gaidheal, and this meant "the district of the Gael." If it came from Earrgaidhel, which is likely, it could be said to mean the "boundary of the Gael" or "the coast of the Gaels." Argyle was the area of early invasion by the Irish called "Scots."[19]

Argyle, the name of a post office in Sumner County, was said to be named for the Duke of Argyle.[20] Additional Scottish influence in Sumner County is seen in the name of Gourock, changed later to New Albion. Oban is the name of a borough in Scotland in the County of Argyle, and for one season, from February to September, it was the name of the town which in 1879 became Assaria in Saline County. *Ob* meant "bay."

Elgin is a name as likely to be associated with Lord Elgin as it is with the County of Elgin in Scotland. It may remind one of the Elgin marbles which had been collected for the British Museum from the ruins left by the Turks after their bombardment of Athens. The name could have come from Elga, "an old poetical name for Ireland" which meant "noble."[21]

In America, the best-known Elgin was the one in Illinois, made famous by the Elgin watch. The name still came from Scotland. The Elgin Town Company promoted West Wichita which was to be named Elgin, but that name was already in use, so the Elgin Company named the town Delano.[22]

It has been suggested that the Elgin in Chautauqua County, Kansas, was named for Lord Elgin,[23] but it could as well have come from Kane County, Illinois, the home of many Kansas pioneers. It was at first only a post office under an oak tree. The town was built by L. P. Getman and its first name was Hudson, but Hudson was destroyed by fire.[24] Elgin was a "pistol packin' cowtown" at the end of the Quarantine Trail, boasting of being the greatest cattle shipping point "in the whole world." The colorful names around Elgin included Shotgun Ridge, Robber's Cave, Outlaw's Corral, and Hell's Bend. The town lacked stability and moved about so much that the railroad was disturbed over its location and names. It was known as "East Elgin," "Old Elgin" and "New Elgin." The railroad used New Elgin, but judiciously chose to call it Central Elgin. New trails and new rails left it deserted but not dead. It still stands on the Oklahoma border with a distinguished Scottish name and a sign that reads: "Elgin, the town too tough to die."[25]

Moray, the name that replaced East Norway in Doniphan County, seems to be another case where a place-name in Scotland became a surname before it again became a place-name in America. Elgin County, Scotland, is now known as Moray and it has been listed with the dual name as "Moray or Elginshire." It is referred to as Moray "among the seaboard men," and is like the Cornish *morva*, "place near the sea."[26] While the county is called Moray, its political leaders have also used the name of Murray, including the Earl of Murray or Moray, half-brother of Queen Mary, who was the regent of Scotland. The County of Moray is on Moray Firth, which is the outlet for Loch Ness at Inverness. Moray is also the name of a vicious but edible eel.

Berwick has twice been a post office name in Kansas. Two years after Berwick in Saline County closed, Berwick was made a post office in Nemaha County, where it served for fifty years. Now it remains as the name of a railway station in a township with the same name. Like the names of other counties in Scotland, Berwick has become a surname,[27] but as a place-name in Kansas it is said to have come from Scotland.

The town of Berwick-upon-Tweed in Berwickshire has played its bloody part in the border battles with England. It has been called the "Debatable Land" and the "Key of the Border." It was listed as a distinct possession of Queen Victoria, who was "Queen of Great Britain, Ireland, Berwick-upon-Tweed and the Dominions Beyond the Sea."[28] The name could be derived from *beorh-wic*, "hill village," or *bere-wic*, referring to a "grange" or "barn."[29] Ekwall interpreted it to mean "corn farm." Berwick, like *beretun*, meant a "grange, or outlying part of an estate." One should give the "r" a good Scottish roll in pronouncing "Berrrrrrrick."[30]

William Alexander Calderhead, the son of an Ohio preacher, came to Kansas in 1868. While there is a Calderhead in Scotland, the Calderhead in Washington County, Kansas, was probably named for the Ohioan, who lived in Marysville and became a Kansas congressman.

David Turner, Sr., of Scotland was the founder of Clyde in Cloud County, not far from Calderhead. A Concordia resident was of the opinion that the name came from Ohio.[31] However, the Glasco newspaper had this to say: "Clyde is the name of a beautiful and picturesque river in Bonnie Scotland, on whose banks David Turner, Sr., whiled away his boyish days; Mr. Turner, therefore, is godfather of the town."[32] The Turner connection between Clyde in Kansas and the Clyde in Scotland seems acceptable. Clyde could possibly have come from *kleu*, meaning "clear," or *clyd*, meaning "warm."[33] The Kansas town had already been known as Oak Creek, Townsdin's Point, and Elk Creek before it became Clyde.

The province next to Ayr was named Lanarkshire. It included the Clyde Valley and the town of Lanark, once the residence of the Scottish kings. It was also the home of Robert Owen. For a few years, Pawnee County had a post office named Lanark. This name, from the ancient Welsh *llanerah*, meant an "enclosure in wood" or an "open space in a forest."[34]

Glasco, also in Cloud County, had its Scottish background, the Glasgow on the Clyde. It was only a "conjecture" to assume that the name meant a "green field."[35] A Scot by the name of John Hillhouse suggested the name of Glasgow for a town in Kansas, which had been known as Dell Ray or Del Ray. H. C. Snyder, the postmaster, sent the name in as "Glasco" for the purpose of simplification.[36] The Glasgow in Shawnee County, spelled as it is in Scotland, had only a brief existence.[37]

Glenloch is typically Scot in appearance. *Glen* may mean a "valley" or more specifically a "narrow valley." To this is added *loch*, the Gaelic word for "lake." Many a loch is found on the map of Scotland. However, the nearest resemblance to Glenloch in Scotland is Glenlochy in West Perthshire. It may be familiar to those who know Scotch distilleries. In Kansas, Glenloch is the name of a town northwest of Garnett in Anderson County.

In Douglas County, the county with a prestigious Scottish name, there was for a few months in 1875 a town named Glen Burn. If we accept the usual interpretation, this name would mean simply the "narrow stream valley" or the "stream in the narrow valley." *Burn*, referring to a stream or brook, is a very common terminal to names in Scotland. Kansas also has a Glen Elder, a Glendale (redundant), a Glenwood, a Glengrouse, and a Glen.

Invermay, like Inverness, has a Scottish character. Invermay is a place in Perthshire and should mean the mouth of the May. The name is translated as "May Water" in Scotland. It is in the midst of the "Birks of Invermay."[38] In Kansas, Invermay was a post office in Atchison County, located between Muscotah and Whiting. It was named by John Andrew, a Scot from Canada.[39] In place of identifying it with the May, Kansans also called it simply "Inver" which meant the mouth.[40]

Dundee could have come from the Gaelic Dun Taw and it was once as simple as "Dunde." *Dun* is generally considered to refer to a "hill," but in Scotland, also a "fort," and Dundee was said to be the "south hill fort."[41] Dun Taw could therefore mean "the fort on the Tay." Because of the town's association with religious issues, it has been called "the Scottish Geneva." In Kansas, Dundee lay to the southwest of Great Bend. It was named by Scottish settlers because "the sand of the Arkansas recalled the sands of the beach of Dundee."[42]

Holy Rood Abbey adjoins Holyrood castle in Edinburgh, the residence of Mary, Queen of Scotland. Kings were born, married, and crowned there. It held much of Scotland's history. The castle still has its colorful and kilted guards with bearskin caps to appeal to the camera-carrying tourist. The Holy Rood once referred to a piece of the cross taken from Jerusalem. The crossed sticks, with the symbol of the cross, became the rod for measuring land in America. A Canadian named Corrigan brought the name to Ellsworth County, Kansas. There the name was spelled Hollyrood, but, according to a local story, a high wind blew one of the letters from the sign on the depot and no one bothered to replace it.[43] After fourteen years, the railroad made the change to Holyrood official.[44] It was also mistakenly put on a map as "Hollywood,"[45] long before Hollywood became famous as a filmland in California.

In Smith County, Kensington and Athol were said to have been named by a railway official for his wife and daughter.[46] Athole, also spelled Atholl, was, however, the name of a place in the hill country north of Perth. Taylor called it a corruption of Athfodla, possibly meaning "the ford of Fodla," and Fodla was, according to legend, the name of one of the seven sons of a Pict named Cruithni. Fodla has also been used as a poetic name for Ireland.[47] If Kansas did not get Athol from Atholl in Scotland, the name could have come from Massachusetts or New York, where it may have been named for Blair Atholl, ruled by the Murray clan. It was believed to mean "pleasant land" to compliment the Perthshire Hills.[48]

Gilfilan is a name that appears to be Irish, has an Old Norse origin, and comes from Scotland. Though known generally as a Scottish surname, it was originally a place-name for a church in Wigtown, southwestern Scotland. Gill came from *gil* which was Old Norse for "ravine," or "narrow valley,"[49] not unlike the meaning of glen. In Kansas, Gilfillan was the name of a post office in Bourbon County, closed in 1902. The founder of the town was Robert S. Gilfillan, a Scot who managed a flagstone quarry, a profitable business before the popular acceptance of cement.[50]

There were several surnames of Scottish origin which became Kansas county names and other place-names. Such were the names of Douglas, Crawford, Grant, Graham, Gray, Jewell, Lyon, McPherson, Morton, and Scott. These names are considered under other categories such as political or military.

Until well into the twentieth century, Americans were avid readers of Sir Walter Scott's novels. His narratives made history palatable for American readers. When the twentieth century diverted the reading public with radio, television, comic strips, and pastime fiction, Scott's novels were considered too long and too remote in time to compete with the fleeting interests and distractions of the present. They are now largely forgotten, but this was not so when Kansas was young and in search of popular place-names. Scott had made Kansans familiar with Scotland.

In the transition from the names in England to those in Scotland, the titles of Scott's novels are especially appropriate. Scott lived near the border, and, to a great extent, his novels dealt with the borderlands but also with knighthood and adventure. *Waverley, Ivanhoe, Kenilworth, Woodstock, The Legend of Montrose, The Heart of Midlothian,* and *The Fair Maid of Perth*—these are reminders of romantic people and historic places. How well these names have been fixed on the minds of Americans may be illustrated by their use as place-names. The title of every novel mentioned here has been a place-name in Kansas. Some of the novels gave us the names of persons, others gave us the names of places.

Scott's first novel, published anonymously, was *Waverly*. The author was referred to as "The Great Unknown." Since no one knew who wrote it, Scott was free to review his own novel, and, judging by its success, he must have given it a favorable review. Thereafter, he published others in a series called "The Waverley Novels." The title was taken from Captain Edward Waverley, a character who was not heroic.

Waverley changed sides in war and failed to marry the woman he loved, Flora McIvor, taking instead "the more commonplace" and more accommodating Rose Bradwardine. As a place-name in America, the spelling of Waverley was changed to Waverly, even where the name was said to be taken from the Waverley novels. The name was widely used and popular.[51]

When Andrew Pearson laid out a new town in Coffey County, Kansas, a special meeting was called to give it a name. Pearson suggested Waverly, "a pretty name" and "one of which he was fond." There was a special reason for his attachment to the name; he was a Hoosier whose home town was named Waverly.[52] There were however, twenty other places named Waverly in the United States and the original source could be the Waverley novels.

Below Berwickshire and Midlothian is the shire called Roxburgh, which also has a relationship with Scott, because it was the setting for his *Lay of the Last Minstrel*. The name should be softened to "Roxbury" in speech, and in Kansas, it is spelled as it is pronounced. Isaac Taylor questioned the interpretation that Roxburgh referred to the "castle on the rock." He suggested that it could have come from a personal name of Rokesburch. It is also possible that the *rox* may have a connection with the Latin *rex* for king, which is *righ* in Gaelic and *roi* in French.[53] The name became popular in New England and spread westward. In Kansas it is the name of a little place in McPherson County. A colony of Ohio settlers came to Roxbury in 1872, and it is believed that they brought the name from Roxbury, Ohio. The place had first been named Bloomingdale and then changed to Colfax before it became Roxbury in 1875.[54]

Kenilworth Castle, which lent its name to the town of Kenilworth in England, became historically important when Queen Elizabeth gave it to her friend, Robert Dudley, Earl of Leicester. Dudley gave Elizabeth and her sumptuous court and four hundred servants a regal reception at Kenilworth Castle. The queen came riding on a white horse, and there, it was said, "you saw the daughter of a hundred kings." It was there also that Scott prepared his sketch about the queen, Dudley, and the tragic life of Dudley's wife.[55] Kenilworth was probably a woman's name from Kenillewurda, Kenilde, or Cynehild.[56] It has been said that "the town is important only for the ruins of its old castle." But the name lives in history and literature, and was used in Kansas. In Kansas, Kenilworth was a town located not far from Bedford in Stafford County. There we have three good English names. An earlier attempt had been made to promote a town to be named Kenilworth fifteen miles above the mouth of the Republican River near Milford.[57] In Kansas, Kenilworth left a fleeting name but no prestigious ruins.

South of Winchester in Jefferson County, Kansas, was the town of Woodstock, also the name of the royal residence in England. Queen Elizabeth was held prisoner there by Queen Mary. Woodstock was later the home of the Duke of Marlborough of the Churchill family and was the site for the duke's castle of Blenheim. The name could mean just "a place in the woods," but it was also known as the "royal forest." The Woodstock in Kansas could have been named for any one of the many Woodstocks in America or for the name of a novel. The popularity of the name was undoubtedly due to the popularity of Scott's novel *Woodstock*.[58]

The use of Perth as a place-name might well be attributed to another of Scott's novels, *The Fair Maid of Perth*. Perth was the name of a town in Perthshire County in southeastern Scotland, a town which is rich in Scottish history. James I was buried there. If Perth is a Celtic word, it could have come from Abertha, which meant "at the mouth of the Tay" or "height over the Tay," describing its location. It has also been translated to mean "oak" or "bush," as well as "bramble."[59] In Kansas, Perth is a town southwest of Wellington in Sumner County.

Lothian was once a large territory south of the Firth of Forth and Edinburgh, and it included several of the shires as they are organized today. It has been called "Ladonia." In the *Saxon Chronicle*, it was "Laodonia," resembling Ladonia, once the name of a post office in Rice County. The Celtic origin of the name was assumed to be Lodens, Nodens, or Llud, the name of a Celtic war-god and of the legendary king of Lodonesia, also called "Loth, King of the Picts."[60]

The large territory called Lothian was partitioned into East Lothian, West Lothian, and Midlothian. Midlothian became a place-name in Harper County, Kansas, but it was written Mid Lothian. After a few years, this name, so full of legend and romance, was changed to the prosaic name of Freeport, supposedly named for a storekeeper named Freeman.[61] Scott combined the names with a hyphen. It was Midlothian in Scotland, Mid-Lothian in *The Heart of Mid-Lothian*, and, rather strangely, Mid Lothian in Kansas.

The seaport of Montrose, thirty miles northeast of Dundee, was made a Kansas name by a railway surveyor who thought the hills in Jewell County resembled those he knew in Scotland.[62] There had earlier been a Montrose in Elk County, but this attractive name was discarded for the more descriptive name of Cave Springs. In Jewell County the procedure was reversed, and the town of Delta had its name changed to Montrose. One might keep in mind Scott's *Legend of Montrose* as a likely source, as the founders of Montrose in Colorado had done.[63] In Scotland, it had a Gaelic origin from *moine t'ross*, referring to the "moor on the peninsula."[64] *Ivanhoe* was said to be Scott's most popular novel but the *Legend of Montrose* was surely the most pathetic.

Scott wrote the Waverley novels at Abbotsford, a town on the Tweed near Edinburgh and Melrose. Melrose was the setting for the novels titled *The Abbot* and *The Monastery*. The east window in the nave of its abbey is beautifully described in Scott's *The Lay of the Last Minstrel*. Melrose was a name of Celtic origin and appears to have come from *maol ros*, meaning the "bare moor."[65] Not far from Melrose, Scott lies buried. In Kansas, Melrose was a place whose ruins might not inspire poetry, but the origin of the name was surely Scotland's Melrose.

To the reading public of the nineteenth century, none of Scott's novels were more familiar than *Ivanhoe*. The name might arouse memories of a romantic period in the time of Richard the Lion-Hearted, but few would think of it as a place-name. Sir Wilfred, the Knight of Ivanhoe, was disinherited by his father, Sir Cedric, because of his love for Rowena, whom his father had betrothed to Athelstane.

Scott found the name of Ivanhoe in a little rhyme which dealt with an incident on a tennis court when Hampden quarrelled with the Black Prince and hit him over the head with his tennis racket. Novelists must choose appropriate and appealing names, and Scott thought that "Ivanhoe" had "an ancient English sound," as it does in this rhyme:

> *Tring, Wing, and Ivanhoe,*
> *For striking of a blow,*
> *Hampden did forego,*
> *And glad he could escape so.*[66]

But who would have thought that a quarrel on a tennis court in old England would stimulate a rhymester to devise a name which eventually became a place-name in Kansas? Only Iowa had previously chosen Ivanhoe as an American place-name. The post office named Ivanhoe in Haskell County lasted until 1905. North of the county border, in Finney County, Ivanhoe is still the name of a township.[67]

Reno County had a Solvay, which is near enough to Solway, the name of a firth in Scotland, to suggest a Scottish origin. Solway could mean "muddy ford," a place the English had called Scot's Ford. But the name for Solvay could have come from Ernest Solvay, a brilliant Belgian who discovered a new process for making soda from salt. Reno County, with its abundance of salt, should honor such a man.[68]

The border towns of Scotland and England were important in Scott's life. Scott attended school at Kelso in the County of Roxburgh, a name changed to its English pronunciation for Roxbury in McPherson County. Kelso could have come from *calkou*, meaning "chalk hill."[69] When written "Chalkheugh," one might suspect that the *heugh* has the same meaning as the Norse *haug*, meaning "hill" or "knoll." In Kansas there was a railway lawyer by the name of David Kelso and Kelso in Kansas was probably named for him.[70]

Kelso in Rawlins County, Kansas, had only a brief existence as the second of the four names given to the town. It was first Prag (1876–79), then Kelso (1879–80), then Danube, associating the name with Prag, and finally in 1881 it became Ludell, a woman's name.[71] In Morris County the name of Kelso was given to a post office the year after the name was replaced in Rawlins County. The Morris County town has a dual name, since the town is named Downing, but the post office is called Kelso.

Scott attended school at Kelso and he was married at "Merrie Carlisle." Carlisle had its somber side, too, for there Mary Queen of Scots was held prisoner. According to a local account, the name of Carlyle in Carlyle Township, Allen County, was chosen when Adda S. Adams inserted a pen-knife into a book at a page where the first name noticed was that of Carlyle. It was also said that it was probably named by "a fan of Thomas Carlyle," the Scottish historian.[72] In Logan County, the name of Carlyle, according to one authority, was "doubtless for the contracting freighter of that name." This Carlyle had its name changed to Oakley, the maiden name of Mrs. Eliza Gardner.[73]

On the Scottish side of the border near Carlisle was a place called Gretna Green, famous for its hasty marriages at the old Toll Bar. Many a marriage was performed by John Paisley, the village blacksmith, who may have forged as strong a bond as any of his competitors.[74] When Scott was married at Carlisle, he was less than ten miles from this convenient marriage market, reminiscent of Reno in Nevada. There was a Gretna parish and the name of Gretna was also used without the Green. *Graetna* may mean "gravel."[75] There is more than one Gretna in America, and Kansas has a Gretna on the Rock Island east of Phillipsburg in Phillips County.

Athol, Montrose, Gretna, and Kelso in Kansas followed the rail lines westward in a row. Farther south, Selkirk is a station in Wichita County which could have been named by settlers from Selkirk, New York.[76] It is, however, a Scottish name. Scott's law studies gave him an opening for public office, with the result that he became sheriff of Selkirkville in Scotland. The Selkirk Hills served as a picturesque backdrop for Scott's home at Abbotsford Castle. Selkirk has also served as an important surname. Originally, however, it came from Scheleschurche. Since the *scheles* or *shiels* referred to "huts," Selkirk was originally "a number of *shiels* or huts in the forest beside which a church had been planted by the Culdees of Old Melrose." The original name looks formidable, but *churche* or *chyrche* is church even though one may call it a kirk. Norsemen pronounced it "chyrkay" or "cheerkeh." The most publicized of the Selkirks was the one who had been left by his sea captain on Juan Fernández Island in the South Pacific and was rescued by Woodes Rogers, a British buccaneer. Selkirk was the inspiration for Daniel Defoe's *Robinson Crusoe*.

As a postscript to Scott, we may refer to that most popular of Scottish poets, Robert Burns. In "Ye Banks and Brae" we become acquainted with "ye flowery banks o'bonnie Doon," and the bonnie name of Bonnie Doon was for a few years a post office name in Ness County. Only in Georgia does one find another "Bonny Doon" in America.

Afton is a name which came from the Afton River or, as it was called in Ayreshire, Scotland, "Afton Water." Ekwall mentions the name merely as recorded in the *Domesday Book* and its source as AEffa's Dun. More important is the poetry of Robert Burns from which came the folk song whose popularity spread the name far beyond the bounds of Scotland. Who in America has not sung or heard the sentimental appeal of Burns in the lines, "Flow Gently, Sweet Afton"?

The name of Afton from that little river in Scotland became eventually the name of a branch of Clear Creek which flows into the Ninnescah in Sedgwick County, Kansas. In the valley of Clear Creek, south of Garden Plain, we may be sure that Afton Creek did "flow gently," as Burns said it should. When Afton Creek was impounded, a lake was created which was then named Lake Afton. There is also a township named Afton; and, in 1874, a post office in Sedgwick County was named Afton. The post office served for twelve years and the postmaster was given a salary of twelve dollars a year.[77] After the name was dropped in Sedgwick County, Afton became the name of a post office in Marshall County.

Few men, if any, have contributed more place-names to Kansas than has Sir Walter Scott, and certainly, no literature has furnished more names than has Scott's writings, except, of course, the Bible.

CHAPTER XIV

WELSH AND IRISH

THE WELSH, because of their modernized and Anglicized names, have not generally been identified by their nationality in American history. Alexander James, in a speech on the "Cymry of '76," called attention to the large number of Welsh who were signers of the Declaration of Independence and who played a prominent role as officers in the American Revolution. Among these were Thomas Jefferson, Samuel and John Adams, Stephen Hopkins, Francis Hopkinson, and many more. The grandparents of George Washington's wife Martha, or "Patsy," as he called her, were Welsh.[1] Among the Welsh who came to Kansas was Governor Lorenzo D. Lewelling, whose name may be associated with the Llewellyn or Llywellyn who was Prince of Wales in the thirteenth century.

Although Cornwall is a part of England, its place-names have a Celtic character. As one writer expressed it:

> By Tre, Ros, Pol, Lan, Caer and Pen,
> You shall know the most cornishmen.[2]

Wales, known also as "Britannia Secunda," was invaded by the Brythons, a Celtic people related to the Gaels. These were all pushed westward by the Romans and the Anglo-Saxons; and from Cornwall to Scotland, they developed Gaelic dialects from their common Celtic language. The complexities and peculiarities of these languages make their names exceedingly difficult to spell and to pronounce. English simplification, while solving some problems, has created new ones by obscuring the source and meaning of the names. One critic, impressed by the poetry and hidden charm of English names, dismissed Welsh nomenclature somewhat callously by saying that it resembled "the noise made by a bellows with a slit in it."[3]

The long and cumbersome spelling of the Cambrian words in the original Cymraeg language have fortunately been simplified into familiar English. For years it was assumed that the longest name on the map was a Welsh name. What could be done with a name such as *Llanfairpwllgwyngyllgogerychwyrndrobwillllantysiliogogogoch?*[4]

163

Without answering this, one should be warned that the New Zealanders have a name of eighty-eight letters,[5] which puts the Cymraeg name, with only fifty-nine, in second place. Familiarity with the language, however, would surely bring out the poetry and charm of Gaelic, whatever the dialect.

The name for Wales is said to have come from the Anglo-Saxon word *walisc*, "land of strangers," or *wealos*, meaning "foreigners." In the earlier Celtic, the Welsh people were called *Cimbri, Kymry*, and *Cymru*, and this meant "land of brothers."[6] One form of the old Celtic name for the country was *Cambroges*, which meant "compatriots." The evolution of these names resulted in Cambria, a name which was popularized by Geoffrey of Monmouth. The name has also been interpreted to mean the "Land of Mountains," and as such, the land of the Cumbrias has been modernized into Cambrian and Cumberland. Because of its rugged terrain, and its Cambrian Mountains, Wales has become known as "the British Tyrol." Saline County, Kansas, has honored the Celtic name for Wales by naming a township Cambria and a town New Cambria.

Cumberland, the land of the Cumbrias, is, however, a much more popular name in America than Cambria. It has been used for almost every kind of geographical feature. Thomas County once had a Cumberland; it could have come from one of the eight counties called Cumberland in the East, from the Cumberland Mountains, or from the Cumberland River as easily as from Wales. There is also Cumberland County in England, which, bordering on Scotland, is more Welsh than English. Thomas County settlers in Kansas, like many others, must have been impressed by the rich rumbling sound of Cumberland. Morgan Powell came from Crickhowell, Wales, and settled on a creek in Republic County, Kansas, which the neighbors named "Welsh Creek." Later it was renamed Spring Creek.

Welsh miners came from Wales and from the eastern United States to work the mines of Kansas. The Welsh Land and Emigration Society of America was organized in New York to promote and to aid the Welsh settlements in Kansas, some of which received Welsh names.

There was no boundary line between the people of England and Wales in the early days of Celtic migrations. Like Cumberland, Monmouth was the Welsh name of a county in England. Monmouth got its name from Aper Mynuy, meaning the "mouth of the Minnow" where it flows into the Wye.[7] The name has been important since the tenth century, when Geoffrey of Monmouth wrote a somewhat fanciful history of Britain.

Monmouth in Kansas is located in the mining area near Pittsburg.

It was at the Battle of Monmouth in New Jersey that Molly Pitcher helped to load and fire artillery, and there too were Washington and Lafayette. The name moved to Illinois, and from that town came Lafayette Manlove, who named Monmouth, Kansas.[8]

Osage County had a town with the Welsh name of Swansea. In both Kansas and Wales, Swansea was in a mining country. In South Wales it was the seaport of Glamorganshire. Swansea, spelled Sweynesse or Sweneshe, was said to come from Sweyn's *ey*, meaning Sweyn's "inlet." Daniel Defoe spelled it "Swanzey." It was a center for numerous foundries and a great shipping point for copper. The coal-mining communities of Kansas attracted many Cambrian coal miners.

Arfon is the name of a fertile section of Wales which was separated from Mona or Anglessey by the Menai Strait.[9] When Welsh settlers came to Osage County, they changed the name of their Swan River post office to Arvonia, although Blackmar spelled it "Arvoni," possibly following frontier phonetics.[10] The township where they settled was also named Arvonia and its Welsh inhabitants were known as Arvonians.[11]

The island of Anglessey, as it was known to Tacitus, lies northwest of Wales. It was a stronghold of the Druids. It had once been named Mona, a name so unusual that it is seldom listed in current gazetteers. It had also been known as Mon Man Cymru, the "Mother of Wales."[12] In Reno County, Kansas, Mona on the Ninnescah served as a post office for twenty-two years.

In Wales, Mona (Anglessey) was connected by a bridge to Bangor on the mainland. There is also a Bangor in Ireland. The word could mean "an enclosure,"[13] or possibly "high circle," which could also be an enclosure. According to another interpretation, it could mean "white choir."[14]

A contributor to *Atlantic Monthly*, who had little sympathy for difficult Welsh names, suggested that there were "downright and firm-footed names like Bangor, upon which you can get a good purchase with the ordinary organs of speech."[15] In Coffey County, Bangor replaced the name of Frederickstown and remained on the map for fifteen years before it was changed to Gridley, for Walter Gridley, a promoter in the Arkansas Valley Town and Land Company. The Bangor schoolhouse has kept the name alive. The Bangor in Miami County is said to be named for the one in Maine.[16]

East of Bangor in Wales is Conway, a name made prominent as the surname of preachers and politicians. In Wales, Conway was also known as Diganhwy and Aberconwy. Conway castle looks the way a storybook castle should look. There is a Conway Springs in Sumner County,

Kansas. The Conway in McPherson County could have been named for any one of several prominent persons named Conway, especially Martin F. Conway, a prominent Kansas politician. It could also have been named for Conway, New Hampshire.

James H. Jenkins, a Welshman, organized a Welsh colony in New York and brought it to Riley County, Kansas. The colony purchased 19,000 acres from the Kansas Pacific Railroad and named their first town Powys for a province in Wales. A shortage of water made them abandon Powys and move to the site which became Bala, where a street was named Powys.[17]

Bala in north-central Wales is located in a scenic area near Bala Lake. The name meant "efflux" or "outlet."[18] In Kansas, Bala was in the Timber Hill country of Riley County.[19] Four generations of the Davis family have served Bala as postmasters.[20] Bala is now a station on the Rock Island between Manhattan and Clay Center in Riley County. There is also a township which bears the name of Bala.

Melvern, a Kansas town located between Ottawa and Emporia in Osage County, has a name of Welsh origin. Its original source was the Malvern names in Worcestershire, England, and its immediate source was possibly the Malvern Hills in Virginia.[21] In England the name is shared by a cluster of seven towns: Malvern, Malvern Wells, Great Malvern, Little Malvern, Malvern Link, West Malvern, and North Malvern, all in the area of Malvern Hill.[22] Its Welsh origin appears to be from *maelfryn*, "bare hill."[23] Adding "hill" to a name that ends with "hill" is redundant, but who but a Welshman would know?

In America the name took on different forms. Arkansas deleted the Hill from its Malvern. New York did also, but added an "e" to make it Malverne. Virginia kept the full name of Malvern Hill. It won fame as the battlefield near Richmond, where, in 1862, General Lee failed to destroy the Army of the Potomac because of its advantageous position on Malvern Hill. In Kansas the name was changed to Melvern. Near there a hill is eroded sufficiently to expose an abundance of cretaceous fossils, and to that extent, the name with its original meaning of "bare" is meaningful, even in Kansas. There also is Melvern township. Two townships in Osage County have preserved names of Welsh origin, Melvern and Arvonia.

Montgomery is a name that appears to be thoroughly Americanized, but it has an international background from the Norman-French, English, Irish, Scottish, and Welsh, which may merit its inclusion here. Originally it was Monte Gomeri. However, Roger de Mongomerie or Montgomery from Germaine-de-Montgomerie in France came to England with William the Conqueror, and there he was made Earl of

Shrewsbury. Eventually a castle and then a county in Wales was named Montgomery, replacing the Welsh name of Sirydd Tre Falkwyn.[24]

Two Montgomeries may be honored by place-names in Kansas. Richard Montgomery, killed at the battle of Quebec, was born in Dublin, Ireland, but he also had ancestors in Scotland. Colonel James Montgomery, who came to Kansas from Ohio, was said to be a nephew of the general.[25] Colonel Montgomery was a zealous antislavery leader in Kansas who served in the Civil War. Some assume that Montgomery County was named for him, but most Kansas historians assert that it was named for General Richard Montgomery.[26] However, the colorful colonel in Kansas could deserve the honor of a Kansas place-name as much as his illustrious uncle. It is enough that both men share the ancestry of a companion of William the Conqueror and the name of Montgomeryshire in Wales.

In Kansas the prestige of the name is retained in Montgomery County. Within the county, there was for a time a Montgomery City, competing with Independence for the county seat. As a post office it was called merely Montgomery, and even that is now but a memory. It was the Montgomery Town Company which started the town of Montgomery which became Trading Post in Linn County.[27]

Invaders of the British Isles came in great waves, each new wave disturbing the sites and settlements of those who came before them. Relentlessly, the Romans, Angles, and Saxons pushed the Gaelic peoples westward. One may appreciate the difficulty of fixing the name of a place or people by recalling that Ireland was once called "Scotia" before the Scots and the name moved to Scotland. Also in reverse was the use of the term Gaelic, which was more generally applied to the Scottish Highlanders than to the language and culture of the Irish. One writer, referring to "Scott," put it this way: "Originally meaning an Irishman and later a Gaul from Scotland."[28] The Brythons or Britons were related to the Kymryc of Wales, and there was no boundary line between them.

Associated with the name of Ireland and Erin are such names as Erse and Eri, referring to a branch of the Celts. The Romans knew Ireland as Hibernia, a name which is much like Caledonia in its poetic appeal. The Roman name is supposed to be a modification of such Celtic forms as Iverna and Ierna from which we eventually derived Erin. From Eire or Eri came Iralanda, Yrland, and Ireland. The name was originally believed to mean "back" or "behind," and this was also said to mean "to the west" or the "island in the west." One might even find a relationship between Hibernia and Hesperus, the Greek name for the west, especially since the name was also said to mean "the land of the setting sun."[29]

The poetic name for Ireland was said to be Elga, which is very much like the place once named Elgo in Republic County. McCathron, the postmaster of Elgo, changed the name to Norway,[30] but the Irish influence may have been present before the coming of the Norwegians.

Evidence of the Irish in Kansas is seen in their personal names and Irish place-names. The Irish formed a considerable part of the migration to the Middle West. Their names are found along the railways they helped to build and on the sites they settled. As a nationality, they were distinctive, and their settlements were identified by such names as Irish Creek and Irish Valley. Nolan and Sullivan became railway stations.

Among the early Irish immigrants was Patrick Doyle, who settled south of Florence and for whom Doyle Creek, Doyle Township, and the Doyle post office in Marion County were named.[31] The Doyles were among the most successful settlers in the area.

The area around Boston in Howard County, now Chautauqua, was known as "Old Ireland." Brown County in the north has an Irish Valley, and Bourbon County in the south had an Irish Branch, occasionally called Irish Valley.[32] In keeping with such names as Dutch Flats and Scotch Flats, Meade County had its Irish Flats.[33] Its post office was Byers. The name of Irish Creek, flowing into the Verdigris in Montgomery County, identified its settlers. In a similar manner, Irish Creek in Marshall County was said to be named for its immigrants from Ireland.[34]

Among the pioneers who settled on Ianthe Creek in the Anderson-Franklin County area were people whose names were Doolin, Collins, McEvoy, McMann, and McGrath. The highest hill in the area was called Emerald Hill and the local post office was named Emerald to identify the settlers from the Emerald Isle,[35] as Ireland was called in the poem "Erin" by Dr. William Drennan. Sure and the church at Emerald was called St. Patricks and there St. Patrick's Day is celebrated with gusto. Its altar was donated by that man with the fine Irish voice, Bing Crosby.

Erin was the name of a town in Washington County. The name of its first postmaster, Francis McNulty, suggests an Irish connection. But in 1872 the name was changed to Pursley.

Irish counties generally have a city by the same name, and one may not always know which of the two serves as the source for the name in America. Among the county and town names in Ireland which are place-names in Kansas are Longford, Waterford, Dublin, and Donegal. Other county names which are as likely to be surnames as place-names are Mayo, Antrim, and Tyrone.

In early Kansas history there were several men with the name of Mayo. One of these, Charles Mayo, was a census taker in 1858 and a representative to the Free-State Legislature under the Topeka constitution. In Ireland, Mayo was the name of a monastery, a town, and a county. The place has been called Magh-eo, meaning the "plain of the yew tree."[36] Mayo in Kansas was a post office in Comanche County.

In North Ireland or Ulster are the counties of Antrim and Tyrone. Antrim is believed to mean "one tribe" or "one habitation," according to the *Encyclopedia Americana*. The town of Antrim is located fourteen miles northwest of Belfast. In Kansas, Antrim was in the southern part of Stafford County. President Arthur's parents came from Antrim in Ireland. Antrim was also the surname of a free-state politician in early Kansas history.

Tyrone was the name of a county in northern Ireland. Its Gaelic name was *Tir Eoghan*, "the territory of Owen." It was once the principality of the O'Neills. Tyrone in Seward County, Kansas, had at first been named Oak City. The town moved across the border into Oklahoma where it kept its Irish name, said to have come from Tyrone, Ireland.[37]

Waterford County is on the southern coast of Ireland. The town of Waterford is on the Suir River. In ancient times it was called Cuan-na-groith, "haven of the sun." Waterford was also once the name of a post office in Stevens County, Kansas.

A short distance west of Waterford in Ireland is a town in Tipperary County named Clonmel. The name came from *cluain mealla*, meaning "vale of honey." In Sedgwick County, Kansas, Clonmel is a little station on the Santa Fe, southwest of Wichita, first settled by a man named Wall, who came from Clonmel, Ireland.

South of the county of Donegal is a county named Longford with a town named Longford. In Ireland, the long ford was across the river Camlin. In Clay County, Kansas, the Irish settlers had enough influence to change the name of Chapman to Longford as a reminder of their Irish homeland.[38]

Donegal is the name of a county in northwestern Ireland, and Donegal is its seaport at the head of Donegal Bay. In early times it was called Tyrconnell and Tir-conaill. It has also been called both the "Country of Connell" and the "O'Donnell's Country."[39] In Dickinson County, Kansas, Donegal, named for Donegal, Pennsylvania, replaced the name of Belle Springs. The name became popular from a song about the "hills of Donegal." Donegal was also an Irish surname, as was, no doubt, Odell, the source for the Odell in Harper County and Odell in Sheridan County.[40] But Lippincott's *Gazetteer* in 1853 listed no Odell in the

United States.[41] From *Tyrconnell* one might also get O'Connell, the name of the Air Force Base near Wichita. The place had once been named Connell for J. M. Connell, a Santa Fe agent.[42]

Athy was a market town in Ireland. The name was an abbreviation of Athlegar, "the western port." In Grant County, Kansas, it became the name of a post office.

Two of the best-known towns of Ireland are Dublin and Belfast. Dublin is the capital of the Irish Republic, and Belfast is the capital of North Ireland or Ulster. Dublin, rich in Irish lore, was known as the "second capital of Britain." The name evolved from Dhu-b-linn and Dublana to Dublin, and it meant "the black pool" or "dark pool."[43] Its Gaelic name is Baile Atha Cliath. In Kansas, the Dublin in Sumner County was changed to Zyba, possibly a coined name.

Belfast, which calls itself the "Athens of Ireland," is in Belfast County of North Ireland. Its early Celtic name was Bela Fearsad or Belfeirsde, modernized to Belfast. The Celtic names have been interpreted to mean "mouth of the ford" or "ford of the sand-bank." Its popular but questionable interpretation is "beautiful harbour."[44] In Gray County, Kansas, Belfast was on the Arkansas River west of Cimarron. If one accepts its meaning of "ford on the sandbank," then it would be appropriate for the Kansas town.

Oaks have been a popular source for place-names, and, like Holyoke, Derry is associated with oaks. Derry could mean "a place of oaks" or "thick woods."[45] When a London company was given the place called Derry, it became Londonderry, although it is locally called just "Derry." Derry was the Irish name of an Ulster community in New Hampshire which became Manchester.[46] Kansas had its Derry in Greenwood County; it was a station on the Frisco Railway. Cram's map (1883) called it "Derby," but the post office name was Derry.[47]

Avoca is the name of an Irish stream and mountain glen south of Dublin. The name was made popular by Thomas Moore who sang of the beauty of the "vale of Avoca" in his *Irish Melodies*. In Kansas it was first used as the name of a place in Chase County. Later it was the post office name for a town in the western part of Jackson County, serving from 1871 until 1907. It was a Celtic name meaning "meeting of the water."

Emmett in Pottawatomie County is the name of a township and a town. It was named by Irish settlers to honor Robert Emmett, the son of an Irish rebel whose oratorical appeal helped to unite the Irish in opposition to English rule. Not all of the townspeople were happy about the name, and some preferred naming the town Saxon for a rich local rancher.[48] There was little reason for the Irish to like the name of Saxon, and Emmett won.

Shannon in Kansas is a place-name taken from Irish surnames. It is also famous for the phrase "where the river Shannon flows." There were many other Irish place-names which came from surnames of men whose fame rests on their influence or service in America. Such are the names of Ryan, Riley, Moran, and Kelley, all named for railroad men. Finally, a list of Irish place-names from Irish surnames would include McCracken, McFarland, McCune, McGee, McLouth, and McPherson. These came largely from Scotch names which were in common use in North Ireland.

CHAPTER XV

DEUTSCH AND THE DUTCH

INDIAN REMOVAL, passage of the Homestead Act, and railroad expansion aided the rapid migration of Europeans to the empty spaces of the West. Nearly one hundred thousand Germans came to Kansas in the last half of the nineteenth century.[1] H. L. Mencken did not think there were many German place-names in the United States, but in Kansas the German influence on place-names is conspicuous[2] and historically important. "*Name ist Schall und Rauch*," said Goethe in *Faust*. But there is much more to be said for a name than "sound and smoke," since there is personality, prestige, sentimental attachment, and historical significance in almost every name.

For many years, German immigrants to Kansas outnumbered those from any other European country.[3] Over twenty thousand Germans, both Protestant and Catholic, came from southern Russia, where they had once been given land and exemption from military service by Catherine the Great, herself of German origin. Mennonites from Russia settled mostly in the Marion-McPherson-Newton area. The Roman Catholic Germans, also known as the "Volga-Germans," settled in western Kansas, with Ellis County as their center. Whatever their source might be, they brought with them place-names from Russia and Germany, and the latter could include both Dutch and Swiss names. Some Frenchmen, remnants of Napoleon's army, also lived with the Germans in Russia and joined the German migrants to Kansas.

The founder of the Mennonites was Simon Menno, a well-educated Dutch leader whose persecuted followers fled in search of peace and security, first to Russia and later to the United States. When the Russians threatened to cancel their concessions in 1871, the Mennonites sought a new asylum in Canada and the United States where they were promised tolerance, freedom of worship, exemption from military service, and land. Kansas became one of the great centers of Mennonite settlement, promoted largely by agents of the Santa Fe Railroad. Two communities in Kansas have been named Menno, one southeast of Marion and the other southeast of Syracuse. The name remains now only on a township in Marion County, where the first Menno was once located.[4]

When the Mennonites emigrated to Russia, they were met by Czar Alexander who "wished them well." Because of this incident they named their new center Alexanderwohl.[5] It was to Alexanderwohl in Russia that C. B. Schmidt, immigration agent for the Santa Fe, went to promote Mennonite migration to Kansas. The sentimental attachment which the Mennonites had for Alexanderwohl and the Czar for whom it was named is indicated by their use of Alexander's name for three of their community centers south of Hillsboro: Alexanderwohl, New Alexanderwohl, and Alexanderfeld.[6] Now a large Mennonite church north of Newton preserves the name of Alexanderwohl.

The first of the Mennonites in the area followed the European custom of settling in village groups, "each of which was given a characteristic name either brought from Russia or found here."[7] Among these names were Rosenfeld, "the field of roses," Blumenthal, "valley of flowers," Rosenort, "place of roses," and Gruenfeld, "the green field." To these may be added Hochfeld, "the high field," Ebenfeld, the "flat field," and Wiedefeld, "the willow field."[8] Molotoshna was the Russian province from which most of the Mennonites came, and many of these Mennonite names, said C. Henry Smith, were "familiar Molotoshna names."[9] When the Germans began building homes on their own farms, many of the village names disappeared unless they were preserved for the name of a school or church.

One of the "most pretentious" of the villages was Gnadenau which may be translated as "Grace Meadow" or "Valley of Mercy." The German *aue* could mean "meadow," "valley," or possibly "field." Others containing the religious word for grace were Gnadenfeld, Gnadenthal, and Gnadenberg. There was also a Hofnungsau as an expression of "hope," and to these may be added Hofnungsthal and Hofnungsfeld.[10]

The names of respected leaders also became place-names, such as Buhler, Yoder, Hess, and Trousdale. Buhler was named for Elder Bernard Buhler, leader of a group of Mennonites who established the Hebron Mennonite Church northeast of Hutchinson.[11] South of Hutchinson is the little railroad station of Yoder, which was named for Ely M. Yoder, its first postmaster, who had offered free land for the station on the condition that the town were named for him. Yoder of the Pennsylvania Amish, also called the "Hook and Eye Dutch," had come to Kansas in a covered wagon from Belleville, Pennsylvania.[12] Having married a non-Mennonite, he tried to keep his religious affiliation a secret, says Wiebe, except for saving a long-tailed coat and his "barn-door trousers."[13] Yet the Yoders have been active workers in their church and the Yoder school is full of young Yoders.

Hesston, northwest of Newton, was named for one of its founders, Abraham Hess. He was an influential supporter of Hesston College to which he donated eighty acres and a team of mules. Students called him "Uncle Abe Hess."[14]

To Peabody, which some Germans spelled "Pibude," came new Mennonite arrivals who gave brotherly aid to a new community. The settlement honestly earned the name of Brudenthal, "Valley of the Brothers." According to another interpretation, Brudenthal was named for three brothers "whose farms joined the place."[15]

Near McPherson were four neighbors whose first name was Christian: Christian Krehbiel, Christian Stucky, Christian Hirschler, and Christian Voran. Three of them had farms adjoining at one corner, and on Krehbiel's corner they organized a town and named it Christian.[16]

Near Alexanderwohl, north of Newton, which some spelled "Nuden," is Goessel. It was named for a sea captain who had transported many of the Mennonites across the Atlantic and whose ship sank at sea on his return voyage. He rescued the passengers but heroically went down with his ship.[17]

The Mennonites also chose place-names directly from Germany, such as Marienburg and Elbing. Marienburg had been the town "where our parents and grandparents lived" before they left for Russia, said Wiebe. Sentiment gave rise to the name but it did not save the town.[18] A Mennonite settlement east of Newton had a choice between naming its town Regier, after one of its successful families, or Elbing, for a Baltic town in Prussia. It chose Elbing. This European town had been so commercially important that an English company had been known as the "Eastland Company or Merchants of Elbing."[19]

From the Volga River Valley came a large German Catholic group known as "Russian-Germans." Although they preferred to be called "Volga-Germans," their American neighbors generally called them Russian or "Rooshans." Even after a hundred years in Russia, they had preserved their German nationality and had given German names to their Russian towns—names which they later brought to Kansas.

One of their towns in Russia was named Katharinenstadt to honor the Empress; in Kansas they honored her by naming a town Catherine. She, too, was of German origin, as was Queen Victoria for whom the nearby town of Victoria was named. Victoria's mother was of the Saxe-Coburg family.

It was in Herzog, Russia, that three thousand Germans met to consider migrating to America; and Herzog, near Victoria in Ellis County, was named for that Russian city. Herzog in Germany had once meant a leader of a clan, but it later became a title of nobility, equivalent to a duke. When the English abandoned Victoria, the Germans of Herzog took over, but the twin cities used the name of Victoria. At Herzog settlers built the Saint Fidelis church which William Jennings Bryan called the "Cathedral of the Prairies."[20] This community of hard-working but poor Germans was dubbed "Hardtack" by the English settlers.[21]

Other church-centered communities were the towns Loretta and Antonio. Loretta is associated with the name of a famous chapel near Ancona in northern Italy, which had been dedicated to the Virgin of Loretto. In Kansas it was an offshoot of Pfeifer. Antonio was the patron saint of the Russian town of Munjour from which came a number of German settlers, and both names were given to neighboring towns in Ellis County.[22]

South of Hays, snuggled close to the Smoky Hill, lies Schoenchen, a town whose German name came from Russia. It was known to the Russians as Paninskoje. Some of the settlers who came from Neu-Obermonjour wished to name the town San Antonio or Antonio for their patron saint. The two groups then compromised by naming their town Schoenchen and their church Saint Anthony.[23] Schoenchen means the "little beautiful one," or, more affectionately, as one writer put it, "Darling Little Beautiful."[24] In Kansas the pronunciation of Schoenchen has been Americanized to "Schengen."

A neighbor of Schoenchen, across the Rush County line, is Liebenthal, "valley of love," a name which also came from Russia. It was the first settlement in the area.[25] As a post office it had first been named Liebenthal, then Howe, then Lippard, and finally Liebenthal. Two names in Rush County were similar to the Schoenchen and Liebenthal names. There was a Lieblichdorp, which became Pleasantdale.[26] Since Lieblichdorp meant a "lovely place" it is not far different from Pleasantdale. But Schoendahl, the name of a Russo-Germany colony, could better serve as the origin for Pleasantdale, the present name of a Rush County township.[27]

Southeast of Hays is the little town of Pfeifer. Two other names had been recommended: Kamenka, for a Russian town on a mountainside, and Holy Cross, with its religious connotation. Pfeifer, also a name that came from Russia, was finally accepted. It means "piper" or "flute player" and is not a difficult name for Germans, but in Kansas it has become "Pei-fur." Names of the churches have been important in these towns, but the one in Pfeifer was nicknamed the "Two-Cent Church," since it was financed by parishioners who contributed two cents for each bushel of their crop yield for its construction.[28]

Two priests left their names on the Ellis County map. A church-centered community north of Herzog and Victoria was named Emmeram for its Capuchin priest, the Reverend Father Emmeram.[29] The Reverend Hyacinth Epp acquired the land for the "Cathedral of Prairies" at Herzog,[30] and his name of Hyacinth was given to a place in northern Ellis County, which had been named Bantam until 1910. There was nothing German in the Greek name of Hyacinth except for its association with the German named Epp.

Munjour, also written "Munjor" and "Monjour," was the name which the Germans had given to another German settlement on the Volga. Because one town was built above the other, it was named Ober-Monjour, "upper Monjour," and when a new one was established, it naturally became New-Obermonjour. New Upper Munjour in Ellis County began simply as Munjour. The American influence may be seen on Cram's map for 1883 where the name was actually shown as "Over-Muncha," and such was its post office name for nearly five months. A local paper gave it the French name of "Monsieur."[31] If Monjour seems to have a French appearance, one might recall that a few of Napoleon's soldiers remained in Russia with the Germans who were already there.[32] A strong Russian influence may be seen in such street names as Moscow, Petersburg, Volga, and Don.[33]

Milberger in Russell County was originally Muhlberger, in keeping with the spelling of the name of the Russo-German family for whom the town was named.[34] Had it been Muelberger or Mulberger, it would have been on its way to the English Milberger.

Twenty-six families from Ellis County moved to Wichita County and established the town of Marienthal. It is supposed to have had the name of Pfannenstiel also, a cumbersome name for Americans, but not as cumbersome as its Russian name of Tonkoschurowka. Pfannenstiel was a common family name.[35]

In addition to the Volga-Germans and the Mennonites, there were many other Germans who migrated from eastern states or directly from Germany and whose scattered settlements were in some way or another identified with their German nationality. There were two Germanias in Kansas, one in Sedgwick County where it was a post office northwest of Wichita, and another near Ellenwood in Barton County. First Smith County and then Brown County had post offices named Germantown.[36]

When Peter Schulte arrived in New York from Germany, he was so broke that he had to telegraph his sister in Kansas for a railway ticket. Like so many of his countrymen, he worked hard and saved enough money to buy a farm. Then he bought a one-third interest in a town southwest of Wichita which was named Schulte in his honor.[37]

The national suspicion and hatred of anything German during World War I led many states to substitute new names for German place-names. Germantown in Brown County was changed to Mercier to "honor a Belgian Catholic Cardinal persecuted by the Germans."[38]

It was a common practice to speak of the Germans as "Dutch," a term more correctly applied to the people of The Netherlands. In Cowley County a post office by the name of Lone Tree changed its name to Little Dutch, probably named for Dutch Creek.

William Sherman, a victim of John Brown and his band at the Potawatomie Massacre, lived with his brother Henry at the ford of the Pottawatomie. The ford was called "Dutch Henry's Crossing," using Henry's name rather than William's because only Henry could speak English. The post office gave it the family name of Shermanville. During the Civil War the name was changed to Lane which honored James H. Lane, that excitable senator from Kansas.[39]

In western Kansas, Sherman County had a place named Rhine. It was located near Little Beaver Creek, which had little resemblance to the Rhine in Germany except that it did "flow" or "run," which was the meaning of Rhhenus, or Rhine.

More Germans came to Kansas from Hanover than from any other German state. Gerat Henry Hollenberg, a restless Hanoverian adventurer, had been to Australia, to South America, and to California with the Forty-Niners before he returned to Kansas in 1858. Even in Kansas he moved about in search of the best river site for dealing with the west-bound travelers. His Cottonwood Ranch on Cottonwood Creek became the Cottonwood Station for the Pony Express. Hollenberg is known as the "founder of Hanover and the Father of Washington County."[40] Both a town and township were named for Hollenberg, but Hollenberg township was later divided and renamed Highland and Franklin. Hollenberg died on his way back to Hanover, Germany, where he had hoped to recruit new settlers.[41] In Germany the name of Hanover came from *hanovere*, which meant "high shore," or from *hohenufer*, a "high bank," referring to the high banks or cliffs above the river Leine.[42] Munden in Republic County was named for the Hanoverian town of Munden.

If one were to travel through the counties of Marshall, Washington, and Republic, one could pass through Frankfort, Herkimer, Bremen, Hanover, Hollenberg, and Munden. Marshall County also had a post office with the genuine German name of Stolzenbach. It has been suggested that Frankfort in Kansas was named for Frank Schmidt, who had purchased the townsite and built its first house. It has also been said that it was named by Jacob Weisbach for Frankfurt, Germany, his home town.[43] The local press accepted the opinion that it was named for Frank Schmidt.[44]

In Kansas, Bremen is located between Hanover and Herkimer. It was founded by Henry Brenneke, "an agressive and industrious" German from Hanover who had married a woman from Bremen. "We have reason to believe," said the *Marysville Advocate*, "that he called it Bremen for his home in Germany."[45] Even its architecture is influenced by its namesake.[46] The name may mean "by the seashore."[47]

Olpe, south of Emporia, was named for a Westphalian town. It had been known as Eagle Creek Station. It was later named Bitler Town for Gilbert Bitler, owner of the townsite. It has erroneously been written "Bittertown." When Auguste Flusche promoted the town on the north side of the tracks, he named it Olpe to please his German neighbors from Westphalia.[48]

Westphalia in Anderson County was first named Thomas. After two weeks it became Cornell, named for one of its promoters, S. P. Cornell.[49] To avoid duplication of Cornell, the name was changed to Westphalia, after a German state originally called Westfalen, with reference to a "tiller of the soil."[50] From Westphalia, Germany, came the Flusche brothers, Carl and Emil, and they settled in Westphalia, Iowa, before moving to Kansas. They evidently contributed to the naming of Westphalia, Kansas. All three places where they lived preserved their Westphalian connections.[51]

Waldeck, which means "forest corner," was once the name of a ruling family. It has also been used for the name of towns in Austria and Bavaria and on the Eder in Germany. Waldeck in Marion County is a little railway station.

In 1880 there were 1,696 Bavarians in Kansas.[52] Bavaria in Germany, bordering on Switzerland, Austria, and Czechoslovakia, shares the beautiful scenery of its neighbors. The name came from the Baiuwarii, a tribe that came from the border state of Bohemia. Bavaria in Kansas replaced the name of Honek, named for Ernest Hohneck, its postmaster. It was in a German community west of Salina, attractively located yet lacking the grandeur of Bavaria in Europe.

There is a Dresden in Decatur County, a Stuttgart in Phillips County, and a Hamburg in Pawnee County. Dresden in Saxony may have come from *dresen*, meaning "at the ferry." Even its Slavonic name of Trasi is associated with "ferry."[53] Four times the name was given to towns in Kansas. Smith County had a Dresden post office from 1871 to 1877. Dresden in Kingman County retained the name of Dresden on a township. A German community in Sheridan County also promoted a town named Dresden but with no lasting result.[54] Decatur County has both a Dresden railway station and a Dresden Township. German perseverance finally succeeded.

Stuttgart is like the English name Studley, meaning a "stud-yard." It is nestled in the hills along the Neckar River in Bad-Württemberg. In Kansas, Stuttgart is located on Deer Creek in Phillips County about fifty miles from Studley.[55]

Hamburg is a name that goes back to the time when Charlemagne built a fortress in the Hamme, which referred to "a forest," although it could also refer to a meadow enclosed by a hedge or forest.[56] The Hamburg in Reno County had its name changed to Buhler for Bernard Buhler, an elder in the Mennonite church.[57] There was another Hamburgh in Allen County, also spelled Hamburg, located six miles from Humboldt. It could have been named for its first postmaster whose name was W. B. Hamm.[58] Another Hamburg was located below Larned on the Santa Fe Railway.

Politically prominent in Europe but of only passing interest in Kansas were Berlin, Vienna, and Weimar City. The first Berlin in Kansas was in Riley County. In Bourbon County, a second Berlin replaced the names of Timber Hill and Sprattsville, the latter named for W. W. Spratt. Placing the name Berlin in a county with the French name of Bourbon was possible in the American melting pot. Templin in Wabaunsee County had first been named Berlin. Clay Center had a Berlin and a town to be named Berlin was chartered for Sedgwick County.[59] The source for this name appears to be Slavic rather than German, the word meaning "pool" or "uncultivated ground" or "a shelter."[60]

There was a Vienna in Pottawatomie County, connected by a highway to Frankfurt in Marshall County. In Austria it was called Wien and its name could have resulted from the invasion of the Wends. People liked Vienna, "the Paris of the Danube," and for the sophisticated, it aroused a feeling of *gemütlicheit*. In Kansas, Vienna served as a post office for over twenty years, but it had no distinction and died leaving its name on a township.

Weimar City in Leavenworth County was settled by Germans in 1857.[61] It had little in common with Weimar, the "German Athens" and the home of Goethe, except in its name.

Quite different was the town of Welda in Germany, which was so unimportant that the *Encyclopaedia Britannica Atlas* did not list it, but it did list the Welda in Anderson County, Kansas, said to be named for the one in Germany. In Kansas, Welda is located in Welda Township, where there was a German colony from St. Louis.[62]

The Roman bath was a significant social institution, not only in ancient Rome, but also in the conquered provinces. Both Bath in England and Baden in Germany had their Roman baths. The German Baden was distinguished by its duplicated name. Baden-Baden means merely that Baden is in the province of Baden. Kansas had a Bath from England and a Baden from Germany. Douglas County, with its Big Springs and its Willow Springs, should also be entitled to a Baden, with or without its Romans; and from 1883 until 1886, Baden was the name of a Kansas post office.

A few famous personal names from Germany, such as Bismarck and Humboldt, were put on the Kansas map. The town of Bismarck, also spelled Bismark, was a post office in Wabaunsee County named for the Iron Chancellor of Germany. The name was later changed to Halifax, because mail intended for Bismarck went to Bismarck Grove.[63] Bismarck Grove, near Lawrence, was a popular place promoted by the Kansas Pacific Railway for political rallies and picnics. Lincoln County once had a Bismark, but it did not become a post office.[64] Northeast of Dodge City is the town of Windhorst, honoring the German leader of the Catholic Center party, which opposed Bismarck. Settled by Germans from Cincinnati, it was located on "Windhorst Hill."[65]

Alexander von Humboldt, the German philosopher, scientist, and geographer, has twin towns honoring him in Kansas. They are in Humboldt Township in Allen County. The reason for having two Humboldts is that the Katy and the Santa Fe almost merge at this place and each has a Humboldt station with the town sandwiched between.[66] Humboldt, said one writer, was "laid out by Germans and Americans on the Neosho River with streets parallel to the river; the cross streets are: Uhland, Herder, Schiller, Tritschler, Goethe, Robert Blum, Wieland, Jean Paul Lenau Strassen."[67] One should keep in mind that street names like city names do change. In Geary County, there is a Humboldt Creek. Germans in Hartford, Connecticut, organized a town company for which a group from Lawrence selected a location. The Reverend Serenbentz suggested that it be named Humboldt. There was also an attempt to establish another Humboldt on the Little Nemaha.[68]

The town named Flush, northwest of Manhattan, illustrates the simplification and Americanization of German names. The town was originally named Rock Creek, then changed to Floersch for Michael Floersch, a Hessian who lived among Bavarian neighbors. The simplification of Floersch to Flush was done by a decree of the Post Office Department.[69]

Of lesser importance but of local interest are such names as Brenner and Ast. South of Troy in Doniphan County is the railway station of Brenner, named for Adam Brenner, head of a German pioneer family from the Palatinate.[70]

The German pioneers of St. Marks in Sedgwick County encouraged their German friends to settle in the area. By the time the newcomers arrived, the best land had been taken. They were warned against settling on the "worthless" land in the Red Jaw Valley in the south-eastern corner of Reno County. The land was cheap, and having little choice, the Germans, together with one Irishman, settled there. Their post office was named Ast for John Ast, who had the shortest name in the community. The post office department "suggested the American Ost for the German Ast." *Ast* meant "branch" or "bough" or possibly "knot." *Ost* could also be a German word, meaning, however, "east" or "orient"; in Norse it meant "cheese." The Red Jaw Valley was named for its red soil. The place was also called "The Valley of Jehoshaphat," a valley where the last judgment was to take place for the doomed settlers.[71] Then they struck oil!

Among the Swiss and Swedes of Riley County, there was a German named August Winkler, "a Saxon from St. Louis." There Winkler's Mill became the town named Winkler.[72]

There were many Germans and German names in Washington and Marshall counties. Roemer's Creek was named for William, Frederick, and Phillip Roemer. It was first known as Raemer's Creek post office and later became Reamer Creek or Reamer's Creek.[73] It became thoroughly German again when the post office was renamed Herkimer.

The Herkimer family came from the Palatinate in Germany and settled on German Flats in the Mohawk Valley of New York. The head of the family was Johan Host Herkimer; the Johan Host was changed to John Jost[74] in English. Jost's son Nicholas, a famous general in the American Revolution, was killed in 1777 at the Battle of Oriskany. Forty years later, Herkimer County was named in New York to honor the general. Kansas took the name from New York. When its proposed name of Bryan for "Billy" Bryan, a railway conductor, was rejected, Adam Keller proposed the name of Herkimer.[75] In New York, the name is well known to gem collectors who refer to the clear quartz crystals in the area as "Herkimer Diamonds."

Fulda was a German abbey promoted by Saint Boniface on the Fulda River in Hesse. In Chautauqua County, Kansas, the Fulda name was changed to Wauneta.[76]

The Timken family that settled in Dickinson and Rush County, Kansas, came from Mannheim, Germany. Henry, one of the six brothers, sold land to the railroad and bought stock in the company on condition that the station on his land would be named Timken. From this mid-Kansas community, not far from the Walter Chrysler home, came the

Timkens who developed the Timken buggy spring and built the big Timken Roller Bearing Company.[77]

The town of Albert in Barton County was named for its first storekeeper, Albert Kreisinger. The Germans who settled in the area were known as the "Albert Germans."

The German who could precede his name with a "von" was a man of distinction since it meant that he had a title. If a man were entitled to the honor, it would be discourteous not to use it. Comanche County, Kansas, had a place named Von, tempting one to ask, Von whom or what? It was named for B. S. Von Schriltz, the postmaster.

One might well conclude the German names with a post office in Sherman County which was named Klink. The post office was closed in 1897, but Klink has recently become a well-known name from a television show called "Hogan's Heroes" in which a Colonel Klink was a leading character.

From The Netherlands, the Germanic Nederland or "lowlands," came the "Dutch," a term occasionally applied to Germans, especially in Pennsylvania, where their language became a delightful mixture of English and German called "Pennsylvania Dutch." Holland was the nucleus of The Netherlands and its name has been freely used for the whole country. There was both a Netherland and a Holland in Kansas. In Reno County a post office which served with the name of Netherland for ten years had its name changed in 1884 to Lerado.[78] The Holland name, used for a creek, a town, and a township in Dickinson County, came from Michigan.[79]

Netherlanders from the neighborhood of Rotterdam who settled in the Osborne and Smith County area named their Kansas town Rotterdam for the great Dutch seaport and dam on the River Rotte.[80] After Rotterdam post office was closed, a new one opened in Smith County named Dispatch, since that was the place, it is said, from which the mail was dispatched.

In the southern part of Norton County there was a great mixture of nationalities, but the Dutch influence was sufficient to have a town named Almelo for an industrial town in The Netherlands. Almelo's first community center had been "a stockade or fort" named New Elm, but also New Elam.[81] When a town was started around the stockade, it was named Almelo, but it did not flourish. The Catholic congregation then chose an ideal spot for its church overlooking the North Fork of the Solomon and this became the site for New Almelo. For a time the post office remained on a farm a few miles away.[82]

As Dutch settlers moved into Phillips County from Nebraska, they gave their post office the name of Luctor, which meant "I struggle,"

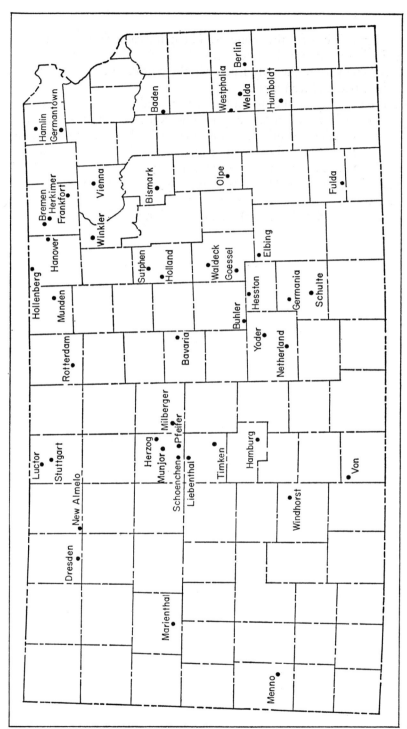

German names in Kansas

and a struggle it was for the pioneers. The name came from the emblem of the Zoeland Province in The Netherlands.[83] This town had the distinction then of being the only Luctor in the world. Even its postmaster, Van Diest, had a Dutch name.

A Dutch colony in Dickinson County named its community center Zutphen for a famous fort and city in The Netherlands. It is a descriptive name meaning "south fen" or "marsh."[84] Its spelling has been changed to Sutphen, and this, according to the Abilene press, was so named for W. J. Sutphen who started the town as Sutphen's Mill.[85] The name is nevertheless Dutch and one may assume that Sutphen came from Zutphen. Even when spelled with a "z" it missed being the last Kansas town listed in the alphabet, a distinction won by Zyba.

CHAPTER XVI

SCANDINAVIAN NAMES IN KANSAS

A LARGE NUMBER of Scandinavian immigrants came to America in the post–Civil War period; a few had come earlier, especially to Illinois and Wisconsin, and from there they came to Kansas. They were propelled by the lack of land in Scandinavia and attracted by its abundance in America. Enthusiastic railroad builders who were pushing their speculative lines into the wide open spaces of the Midwest promoted immigration. The promise of cheap land in a country that was dedicated to freedom made a tremendous appeal to these liberty-loving and land-hungry people. The call to come to Kansas was answered by thousands of Scandinavians whose place-names serve as linguistic links between the Old World and the New.

Scandinavian is a term used to describe residents of Sweden, Norway, and Denmark. The term has been extended to include those Finns who have a Swedish culture. It evolved from Skane, the name for Sweden, or from the French Skaney, the name given to some islands south of Sweden. Another source may have been *skadino*, meaning "dark," the north being the "land of darkness."[1] Later it became Scandia or Scandian, first applied to a province, then to the tip of the Scandinavian peninsula, and finally to the whole peninsula and to Denmark. Most Americans made little effort to distinguish one Scandinavian from the other, and in Kansas, where three-fourths of the Scandinavians were Swedes, the English-speaking settlers generally lumped all Scandinavians together as "Swedes."

Typical of the tradition to name a new home to honor the old was the naming of New Scandinavia in Republic County. The settlement of Swedes in this area was promoted by the Scandinavian Agricultural Society of Chicago. Some wrote the name "Skandinavia" but the official name of their town was New Scandinavia.[2] The name was eventually shortened at both ends; first the New was deleted and then the railroad abbreviated the name to Scandia. The name was foreign and seemed so strange that one writer suggested that it was probably the name of a Sioux Indian chief.[3]

Swedeland, the name of a Morris County railway station, has been replaced. The Swedes wanted it named New Chicago. Finally it was agreed to name it White City for a Katy railway official.[4] Swede Center was a community centered around a church in the Chanute area where a Swede by the name of Ahlquist founded "a settlement of his countrymen from Dalarne."[5]

McPherson County was organized in the Swedish town named Sweadahl, also written Sweadal, Swedal, and Sveadahl, and slightly Anglicized to Sweadale. Svea rike, the "land of the Sveas," became Sverige in Swedish and Sweden in English.[6] One interpretation of Svea is that it meant "we" or "ourselves."[7]

In Sweden there is a county and an island of Gotland, located south of Stockholm in the Baltic. The name could refer to the "land of the Gotar," or, in reference to the island where Goths settled, the "land of the Goths."[8] When Swedish settlers wished to advertise the advantages of their locality for future settlers, they described it as a place with *nytt godt land*, meaning "new good land," and from this, it has been assumed, they named New Gottland. Several of the Swedish pioneers came from Vestergotland, or West Gotland, and New Gottland in Kansas could logically be a reminder of their Gotland home in Sweden.[9]

The province of Smolan or Smoland in Sweden, meaning "little land" or "small land," was the origin of the name for the Smolan post office, now a railway station southwest of Salina. Dropping the "d" made little difference in the pronunciation. Several Swedish settlers in Kansas came from Smoland in Sweden.[10]

A short distance southwest of Smolan on the Missouri Pacific is Falun, a place named by a Swedish pioneer who came from Falun or Fahlun in the province of Dalecarlia in Sweden.[11] Falun moved to the railroad and became known as Falun Station while the post office kept the name of Falun. When the post office moved to the station, the dual name was no longer necessary.

Farland, the "distant land," was the name of a post office southwest of McPherson. The name remains today only on a little lake called Lake Farland located south of Lake Inman.

When Peter Carlson settled on a stream below Mariadahl in Riley County in 1857, it became known as Swede Creek, as did also the township through which it ran. The source of Swede Creek is in Marshall County and there its name was given to the Swede Creek post office. So Carlson, the Swede, was the source for the name of a stream, a township, and a post office.[12] When the Germans settled there, they became known paradoxically as the "Swede Creek Germans." John P. Swenson settled on a creek south of the Smoky Hill in Dickinson

County which became known as Swenson's Creek.[13] In Neosho County a Swedish settlement was named Swede Center.[14]

One of the earliest Swedish pioneers in Kansas was John A. Johnson, who came from Galesburg, Illinois, in 1855. He settled on the Big Blue in Riley County. The first Swedish church in Kansas was built on his farm. Johnson's mother Maria was the first to be buried in its cemetery, and it was for her that the town in the valley of the Blue was named Mariadahl.[15]

Olsburgh on the east side of the Blue in Pottawatomie County was originally "Olesburgh" but it has now lost the "e" from Ole and the "h" from burgh. Its first postmaster, O. Fragerberg, who was born in Sweden, had been postmaster at Mariadahl. It is tempting to assume that "O" Fragerberg was "Ole" Fragerberg until we discover that Fragerberg's name was Oscar. Olsburg was probably named for Ole Thrulson.[16] Ole, a name replacing Middletown in Jefferson County in 1860, also had a likely Scandinavian connection.[17]

Near Salina a Swedish church named Assaria served as a nucleus for the town, which was named for the church. To the Swedish pioneers the church was a bond of union. The church named Assaria gave them confidence amid the confusions of a strange land. The name meant, "In God is our help." Assaria is derived from *Azariah*, a Hebrew term meaning "Yaweh helps," Yaweh being the name from which we get Jehovah.[18]

By 1890 there were ninety-seven Swedes in Logan County, and Page City was nicknamed "Swede Town."[19] In Logan County they changed the name of Boas to Calmar as a reminder of the Swedish province of Kalmar. There was once a Calmar or Kalmar in McPherson County, too. There the name was changed to Marquette, for the town in Michigan. Kalmar, Sweden, was important as the place where in 1397 the three Scandinavian countries were united under one king.

In Wallace County, on the western border, there was once a Stockholm. In Sweden, Stockholm was on an island with a good harbor and from this it got its name of "the island city." *Stock* came from Stack, meaning "inlet," and *holm* from *holmia*, meaning "island."[20] Stockholm in Kansas did not survive, yet the name which commemorates the capital of Sweden is still the name of the township in the southwestern corner of the county.

Galva in Illinois was named by Olaf Johnson for Gefle or Gavle, his home in Sweden. The name refers to the gables of a building. In Kansas, Galva is in the Swedish community of McPherson County and was named by Mrs. J. E. Doyle for her home in Illinois.[21]

There is no community in Kansas better known for its Swedish culture than the town of Lindsborg in McPherson County. It might well be classified as the cultural capital of Swedish America. One of the most popular stories about the importance of Lindsborg concerns the Swedish immigrant who landed in New York, looked at the tall buildings with astonished admiration, and said: "If this is New York, *what* must Lindsborg be!"

There were many Swedish residents whose names began with "Lind," and there was some question as to which Lind should be honored in naming the town. The rivals for the name were Lindgren, Lind, and Lindey.[22] It was suggested that the use of the "Lind" together with "burg" meaning "city" or "a fortified place" or even a "castle," would honor all of them, whether there were two, three, five, or more, as has been suggested. Emory Lindquist said there was a "sizable" number of Linds and he named the following five for whom the town was named: Lindell, Lindh, Lindgren, Lindey, and Lindberg.[23] Carl Swansson gave the same list of names except Lindahl for Lindell and Lind for Lindh. Lindahl was the editor of *Augustana*, the Lutheran college paper from Rock Island. He had provided financial aid for the founding of Bethany College at Lindsborg.[24] When first settled in 1869, the town was called Linsborg, but as a post office it became Lindsborg.[25] One writer in 1893 suggested that by 1993 the name would be "Lynnsbury."[26] However one may wish to spell the name, Lindsborg was more than the castle or fortress of the five Swedes whose names began with Lind; it was "Little Sweden."

The town of Lund near Oberlin was begun by the Oberlin Co-operative Exchange in 1900 and settled largely by Swedes. Lund means a "little forest park," or "grove," and it logically got its name from Lund in Sweden, a town of great historical fame.[27]

Many Swedes came from Swedona, Illinois, and settled among the Scandinavians in Allen County, where they established the town of Savonburg, the only town in the world to have this name.[28] The assumption that the name came from the Earl of Savonburg may be challenged since Burke's *Peerage* lists no such name. Swedona was a place-name in Sumner County, replacing the name of Belinda. It was probably named for an Illinois town.

Finally, to honor the contemporary Oscar II, king of Sweden, the Swedish name of Oberg in Clay County was changed to Oscar in 1899.

There were 1,838 Danes in Kansas by 1880. Scattered though they were, many had settled in Lincoln County. Among the Danes who lived on Spillman Creek were Lorentz Christensen and Eskild Lawritzen. There they named their town Denmark in memory of their homeland.[29] Taylor has interpreted Denmark to mean "forest of the Danes."[30] It could equally well mean "the plain of the Danes."[31]

In Norse mythology, Odin's heaven was called Valhalla, or Valholl, "the hall of the dead," where the heroes enjoyed battles and banquets. In Gove County there was once a Valhalla; but like the discredited gods of old, Valhalla is but a memory.

Odin and Odense are small memorials in memory of the great pagan god who supposedly gave to the Northmen their science and Runic writing. Our name of Wednesday came from Woden or Odin. Odin is the name of an isolated little village in Barton County. It has been suggested that the name came from Odin, Illinois. However, Henry Odin was once a postmaster and storekeeper at the place called Odin.[32] Odense in Denmark, meaning "Oden's Island," was said to be founded by Odin. It has a special distinction as the home of Hans Christian Anderson. In Kansas, Odense is located east of Chanute in Neosho County, logically located in a large Danish community not far from Elsinore in Allen County.

Hertha, "Mother Earth" or the goddess of fertility and the earth, was the mother of Thor, and he was the son of Odin. Like Odin, Hertha also became a Kansas place-name in Neosho County.[33] Hertha is south of Erie and Odense is north of Erie.

Hecla is the name of an Icelandic volcano noted for its frequent eruptions. It was called Hekla Fjoll or Heklufjall, meaning "hill of the hood," or "mountain with a hood," the hood being the mushroom smoke over the volcano, which resembled a knitted hood.[34] Hecla in Kansas is a railway station near Garnett in Anderson County.

Rice County has the unusual name of Galt. That it is a Scandinavian word meaning "hard soil," as suggested, may be questioned. It is a Scandinavian word meaning a "hog" or "boar."

The distinguished name of Elsinore in Elsinore Township was located southeast of Iola in Allen County. The town was kept alive and saved its name by being moved a short distance to become a station on the Missouri Pacific Railroad. Elsinore, called Helsinger or Helsinosore in Danish, was Shakespeare's setting for the tragedy of Hamlet. The tragedy that overtook Elsinore in Kansas was the failure to dot an "i" which changed the "in" to "m." Gray's map of Kansas in 1881 still called it Elsinore. The distinguished Danish name of Elsinore, "the point near the town of Helsing,"[35] became meaningless as Elsmore.[36] Even the township had to decide to be or not to be Elsinore, and, with the vacillation and weakness of a Hamlet, it, too, accepted the change; it is now just plain Elsmore.

Norwegian nationalism was strong in the nineteenth century, and Norwegians, like other Europeans, kept a sentimental tie with the motherland by using Norwegian place-names in America. Ole Bull, the colorful violinst from Norway, demonstrated his nationalism in his music. In Pennsylvania, Oleana was named for Ole Bull, himself; New Bergen for his home town; New Norway for his nation; and Valhalla for the pagan heaven of the Vikings.[37]

As there was a Denmark for the Danes in Kansas, so there was a Norway for the Norwegians. Norway came from such earlier names as Norweg or Norwegum, referring to the "Northern Way" of the Vikings.[38] A town founded in Doniphan County by six Norwegians, three of them named Nelson, was named Norway. It was settled by "Norskes," said the local newspaper, referring to the Norwegians in their own language. There were, however, ninety Danes there, and only eighty Norwegians.[39] The town named Norway became East Norway. If East Norway had to be identified by direction, then there must have been another Norway in Kansas. There was. Any confusion from the repetition of the name should have ended when the name of East Norway was changed to the Scotch name of Morey.[40]

The second Norway was in Republic County, located south of Scandia in Norway township. J. G. McCathron, the postmaster, named it for the ten Norwegians who lived in the community. The place had earlier been named Elgo by Gus Nelson, who promoted the town. It would seem that Norway replaced the name of Elgo, since the deed said it was the "original townsite of Elgo."[41] Isaac O. Savage, county historian, has given us an unusual interpretation when he said that "Elgo and Norway are identical; Norway being the common, and Elgo the scientific name."[42] According to another, Elga, with a change of its final vowel, was the poetical name for Ireland.[43]

The bridge across the Republican River in Norway Township was known as the Norway Bridge. When the state legislature designated new roads in 1871, it provided for one to cross the Verdigris at "Norwegian Ford" in Greenwood County.[44] This county had so many Norwegian settlers that one community was known as "Little Norway." There was a town named Christiana, which could have come from Christiania, formerly the name of the capital of Norway, named in 1624 for its founder Christian IV of Denmark. It replaced Opsolo, or Opsloe, which had been destroyed by fire. In 1925 its name was changed to Oslo. Christiana did not last long in Kansas.

Lapland spreads from northern Norway to Sweden, Finland, and Russia along the Arctic circle. The Swedes had named these northern people Lapps, meaning "nomads." Lapland in Greenwood County is an isolated hamlet whose post office was closed in 1906.

Vinland was the name which Leif Ericson gave to North America when he led a Viking colony from Greenland to the mainland. It was occasionally referred to as "Wine Land." Vinland in Kansas was a place in Douglas County which served as a post office for eighty-six years. It is still a station on the Santa Fe south of Lawrence.

Volland in Wabaunsee County resembles Vollan, the name of a town in Norway, but it could be a personal name. North of Scandia is the town of Sherdahl. Although originally a descriptive name, the town was named for Swen Sherdahl, a pioneer who had donated land for a railway station on his farm. Not far away was the Sherdahl Bridge, which was washed away in 1900.[45]

The invasion of the British Isles by the Vikings left a number of Norse names in Scotland, Ireland, England, and Wales. One might refer to such examples as Derby and Runnymede, and even Denver. Such names are intellectual links with a dim past.

CHAPTER XVII

NAMES FROM SLAVIC SOURCES

PROMINENT AMONG THE SLAVIC PEOPLES along the border of the Germanic states were the Bohemians and Moravians, who were long governed by the Austro-Hungarian Empire. In order to include the three main linguistic groups in the Empire, a place should have been made for the Bohemians or Moravians as representatives of the Slavs. With the end of World War I, the land of the Bohemians and their neighbors was recognized by the United States and England as Czechoslovakia. As a result, after 1918, Bohemians were called Czechs, but they were still known by their earlier name when they came to colonize Kansas.

The Bohemian name came from Boihaemum or Bo-heim, as the Germans used it, meaning "home of the Boii."[1] Many Bohemians came to Kansas as organized colonists. The largest of these colonies came from Chicago in 1876, bringing new names to Kansas.[2] When an American complained about the difficulty of Bohemian or Czech names, his Czech companion asked: "You think 'Machasushetts' is easy?"[3] The Czech place-names in Kansas have, fortunately, been relatively simple.

Prague, the capital of Bohemia, has been called the "Austrian Rome" and the "Moravian Mecca." One writer found its origin in *prah*, meaning "threshold;"[4] others have suggested that it meant a "clearing."[5] The Bohemians in Rawlins County preserved their connection with the homeland by naming a Kansas town Prag. With the transitory populations in the West, it was difficult to preserve community loyalty. Names were changed with shifting populations. The name of Prag was changed in 1879 to Kelso, a Scottish name. But the next year the Slavic influence exerted itself again and the name was changed to Danube, though the town near Beaver Creek had little in common with the Blue Danube. Only from August, 1880, until the following May did the name last, and then it was changed to Ludell. This was said to be the name of a postmaster's daughter whose name was Louella, a name which the post office rejected and changed to Ludell.[6] Thus died the name of the Danube for a postmaster's devotion to his daughter.

Not far from Prague in Bohemia is the town of Pilsen, as famous for its beer as Milwaukee is. The popularity of the name was enhanced by the light opera *The Prince of Pilsen*. The first Pilsen in the United States was evidently in Marion County, Kansas. Its settlers were Bohemians from Iowa.[7]

The town of Olmütz in eastern Bohemia was spelled with its German umlaut, but the Bohemian name was Olomouc and Holomauc. The name is possibly a corruption of Julii Mons, from the name of its founder, Emperor Julius Maximus.[8] In Kansas the town of Olmitz had its name Americanized as one would change Muller to Miller. Miller was the name of the first postmaster of Olmitz. Forty-seven immigrants from Moravia in the Austro-Hungarian Empire settled Olmitz in Barton County.[9]

In 1876 a large number of Bohemians came from Chicago in search of a home in Kansas. Some settled in what became Palacky Township in Ellsworth County.[10] Polaki, referring to the Polish people, originally meant "dwellers on the plains."[11] Palacky resembles Polock, a name used by Shakespeare and a colloquialism frequently used for Polish settlers in America, not necessarily in a derogatory sense. Americans were frequently indifferent to minor national distinctions, like those between Swedes and Norwegians, Czechs and Poles. Palacky was also the name given to the local post office which served until 1905, but it is the township that retains the name.

Also from Moravia were John and Francis Marak who were among the Czech settlers in Brown County, Kansas. Their store became the post office and it was named Marak. Bypassed by the Missouri Pacific Railroad, Marak eventually disappeared.[12]

In Trego County in western Kansas, Bohemian settlers dug a well, found good water, and named the place Voda, which meant "water."[13]

In approaching the Slavic countries from the Germanies via the Danube, one finds several sources for Kansas place-names. The Danube starts in the Black Forest above Ulm, flows past Vienna, separates Buda and Pesth in Hungary, comes to the Yugoslavian border at Belgrade, and then goes on to become the border of the province of Plevna in Bulgaria. All of these names have been place-names in Kansas, including the name of Danube itself, a name which varies in spelling with the language of each country it crosses. In German it is Donau; in Slovakian, Dunaj; in Hungarian, Duna; in Serbo-Croatian, Dunav; and in Rumanian, Dunarea. In Latin it was Danubius, which could well be the form from which the English created the name of Danube. The *da* merely meant "water."

In Hungary, Budapesth was once two towns separated by the Danube. Buda was on the right bank and Pesth on the left. Bridges have united these two into one great city, and their names are now combined. Buda, a Slavonic name, could mean "huts," and Pesth, an "oven" or "grotto."[14] The union of the names has been broken in Kansas, with Buda in Ness County and Pesth in Rawlins County. Buda replaced the name of Newby in 1882 and lasted fifteen years.[15] Like its neighboring post offices, Buda disappeared.

One spokesman at a Bohemian meeting to name a town in Rawlins County mentioned names as prestigious in the eastern United States as Budapest was in Hungary. Then he said: "Far be it from me to propose that we call our little community by that great name. But I would suggest that we cut the name in two and call our settlement by the name of Pest." He was perhaps unaware of its English meaning, but not so the Post Office Department. It rejected Pest and substituted the name of Herndon, for Lincoln's law partner.[16]

The Hungarians of the Austro-Hungarian Empire were not Slavs; they were Finno-Ugrian, situated between Slavic and Germanic peoples. Louis Kossuth, a dedicated Hungarian nationalist, visited the United States in 1851 to win support for the liberation of his people from Austrian domination. He was called "the Noble Magyar." Kossuth's revolutionary movement aroused tremendous popular interest but did not prompt American intervention. He departed, as Thomas A. Bailey said, "a sadder and wiser man, leaving behind him Kossuth beards, Kossuth hats, Kossuth overcoats, and even Kossuth County, Iowa."[17] Ten places in the United States were named Kossuth within five years of his visit. In Kansas, three counties—Linn, Butler, and Pottawatomie—had towns named Kossuth. None survived, and only the one in Linn County became a post office.[18]

Down the Danube in Yugoslavia is a city named Belgrade, which the Slavs called Beograd, meaning "white fortress." One may suggest that the post office named Bellegarde in Pottawatomie County was a Kansas corruption of Belgrade. Coffey County came nearer to the Slavic name when it named a post office Bellgrade.

As we move down the Danube from Budapesth and Belgrade, we reach the borders of Bulgaria, where, on the south side of the river is a place named Pleven, earlier known as Plevna. There in 1877 the Russians under General Skobelof won a strategic battle over the Turks and liberated Bulgaria. In the same year the name was given to a town west of Hutchinson on the Santa Fe Railway in Reno County.

Chase County had a place named Poland competing with North Cottonwood Falls and Bazaar for the county seat. Poland lost and died.[19] Poland was the English form of the German name Pohlen, and it came from the Slavic descriptive name for "plains." Poleska or Poliska was the name for one of the several sites which became Manhattan.[20]

Additional Polish interest is seen in the promotion of a town six miles east of Manhattan. It was to be named Kosciusko to honor Thaddeus Kosciusko, the Polish general who fought for the colonies in the American Revolution.[21] It has been said, however, that he was less interested in the ideals of the Revolution than he was in escaping from his "unrequited passion" for the daughter of a Lithuanian marshal. This would not be unreasonable, but the conclusion may not be fair. According to one report, he was planning to elope when her father's retainers kicked him out. Perhaps America should thank the Polish girl for his military services in the American Revolution. He was popular in America, and Washington admired him. His name has been a popular place-name, not as difficult to spell as the name of his birthplace, Mereczowszczyno.

Beyond Lithuania is the Gulf of Riga with a name that may be of Slavic or possibly Old Norse origin. As Riga it was said to mean a "ridge of sand." As Rig-o, this ridge would be on an island, and in Old Norse it could mean "hill island."[22] Like Voda, Riga in Kansas is located on the Union Pacific in Trego County. It was named by the Volga-Germans who moved westward from Ellis County into Trego.

Arcona, listed also as Arkona, is a promontory on the island of Rugen in the Baltic. Kansas adopted the name, spelling it Arcona in Jewell County and Arkona in Sheridan County.

Alma in Wabaunsee County could have come from Germany or Switzerland, yet some say that it came from the Crimea. The case for German origin rests on the fact that it was settled by Germans from St. Louis. The townsite was selected by Gottlieb Zwanziger, who could have been either German or Swiss.[23] If Alma were a German name, it probably came from *alm*, meaning a "pasture-land on the mountainside." Possibly more appealing is the Swiss meaning, "a high open place, frequented by herdsmen and lovers." Alma in Kansas is believed, however, to have come from Alma in the Crimea, the name of a stream made famous by a battle in which the western allies defeated the Russians during the Crimean War. It has been suggested that veterans of the Crimean War who settled in Wabaunsee County named the town of Alma.[24] According to Isaac Taylor, the name is of Tartar origin and means "apple tree."[25]

A name such as Moscow could commemorate the best known city in Russia, once called "The Holy Mother of the Russians," or it could arouse emotional hostility as a symbol of the Communist world and the Cold War. The Russians called it Moskva, the name of a stream.

The name may have a Finnic origin from *musk*, "to wash clothes," or the Slavic word *mokschow*, "wet."[26] After the Civil War, friendship between Russia and the United States was considered normal, and at this time Alaska, labeled by critics as "Seward's Icebox," was purchased. The first Moscow in Kansas was located northeast of Winfield.[27] The Moscow in Marion County was a Mennonite community, named to honor the country which had once given the sect asylum. The Moscow in Stevens County may have had no connection with Russia. No Russians have lived in Moscow, Kansas, says Edith Campbell Thompson, a local historian, who insists that the Russian thistle is the only Russian influence in the area. According to her, the name should have been "Mosco," for a Colorado pioneer. But a clerk, evidently thinking the name was incomplete, added the "w" to make it Moscow.[28]

Odessa, with its obviously Russian source, has a classical origin in Homer's *Odyssey*. It became a post office in Jewell County, transformed into its Russian dress.[29] There, too, is Odessa Township.

In Russia, a river named the Neva flows into Lake Ladoga in the Gulf of Finland. A railway junction west of Strong City was once named Neva. In Republic County, the place with the Russian name of Neva was changed to Agenda before it became a post office. The Neva limestone identifies a geological stratum in Kansas. Both Wisconsin and Tennessee have towns named Neva.

Among the strange names in Kansas is Kimeo, the name of a town and township in the southern part of Washington County. A similar name, with the interchange in vowels, is Kemio, the name of a Finnish island and town in the Gulf of Bothni. This would place it near the Neva. Kimeo in Kansas could well be a corruption of Kemio, which may be a Finnic rather than Slavic name.

Aral was the name of a small post office in Butler County; it was also the name of the fourth largest inland sea in the world. The name has a Kirghiz origin, *aral denghiz*, meaning "sea of islands."[30]

Having reached that part of Russia which is partly Oriental, we may pass through the gates of Gog and Magog, which supposedly closed Asia from Europe, and find exotic names for the map of Kansas from the Near, Middle, and Far East.

CHAPTER XVIII

ER MANHATTAN MANKATO MANTER MAPLE HILL MAPLETON MARION MARQUETTE MARYSVILLE M

ORIENT AND AFRICA

REEN MAYETTA MAYFIELD MAYLINE McALLASTER McCRACKEN McCUNE McDONALD McFARLAND

FAR REMOVED THOUGH their origins may be, names from Asia and Africa are scattered over the American map. Of those adopted as Kansas place-names, most appear to have been used elsewhere and brought to Kansas by residents who merely wished to memorialize the home town in another state. Medina and Canton from Ohio are good examples, but there were others. The popular interest in an event, such as the Zulu War, could have been the cause for the adoption of some names.

When Mohammed fled from Mecca, he took refuge in Medina which then became known as Medinet-al-Nabi, the "city of the prophet." Medina was a simple and attractive name and used quite widely as a place-name. In Spain, it became a popular family name. Both Mecca and Medina were used as place-names in Ohio. Mecca was considered to be "the end of the trail" for Connecticut immigrants. Mecca had already become an Ohio place-name, so the one south of Cleveland changed its name to Medina. It was said to be named for the town of Medina in New York.[1] In Jefferson County, Kansas, the town of Perryville was renamed Medina at the suggestion of John Speer, because Medina, Ohio, was the home town of its settlers.[2] One of the promoters of Medina was Jerome Kunkel, who moved his town of Rising Sun to the new site.[3]

Also in Arabia was the ancient town of Petrea, whose history goes back to the time of Ashurbanipal. The town was literally carved out of solid rock and it is still one of the marvels of the world. It was logically named Sela, meaning "rock." The Greeks changed its name to Petrea or Petra, which preserved its original meaning. In 1857 a town company was incorporated to establish a town named Petrea in Kansas.[4] It had nothing in common with the ancient Petrea and was certainly not as durable.

After the Romans conquered Petrea, its flourishing caravan trade was diverted to the Palmyrene oasis. Hadrian restored Palmyra and renamed it Hadrian Palmyra. The name meant "the place of the palms." It had earlier been called Tadmor, as it is again today. In Douglas

County, a Kansas town was named Palmyra. It had no palms, but the brilliant fall colors of the oak and the sugar maple may be seen there. Palmyra was absorbed by Baldwin City and "moved to the university section" of Baker University. Palmyra Township has retained the ancient name. Baldwin City was named for John Baldwin, a man from Berea, Ohio.[5] In 1876 a post office in Butler County was named Palmyra, and it lasted for a quarter of a century.

The most famous queen of Palmyra was Zenobia. Before her defeat by the Romans, her empire extended to Asia Minor and Egypt. The military success of her husband has been attributed to her wisdom. There was a post office called Zenobia in Scott County. There are at least four other Palmyras in the United States, but no place in the world had at that time another Zenobia, according to Lippincott's *Gazetteer* (1866).

Among the fascinating tales of *The Arabian Nights* was the story about Aladdin and his magic lamp and ring. Aladdin became the name of a post office in Douglas County. It was a most unique place-name, but Aladdin, Kansas, must have lost its genie for it survived only six years.

Syria not only had place-names such as Palmyra, Aleppo, and Antioch adopted as Kansas place-names; but Syria itself became the name of a post office in Lincoln County.[6] The name has been associated with the city of Assur on the Tigris and with Asshur, the Syrian god. The name was supposed to refer to "water bank." Polybius made it known to the West and someone interested in ancient history must have introduced it to Kansas.[7]

Few names from the Persian Empire are better known than the name of that great cosmopolitan city of Baghdad. As a Persian name it meant "the gift of God." Another has called it the "garden of Dad," with Dad meaning a monk.[8] With the deletion of the "h," Bagdad was for a short time the name of a post office in Coffey County.

Well known in ancient history are the wars between the Medes and the Persians. Media, the land of the Medes or Madai, was the name of a town in Douglas County which had earlier been named Prairie City. The name could have come from media as means of communication, but with names like Syria and Cyrus in Kansas, it is as logical to assume an Oriental source.

The Midians have been described as "troublesome neighbors of the Israelites till Gideon's victory over them." When the Midian Shrine Band of Wichita played at the dedication of a new oil town west of El Dorado, the place was named Midian on the suggestion of the band leader.[9]

Cyrus the Great was the competent king who in the sixth century B.C. created the Persian Empire. Someone on the high plains of western Kansas must have admired him to have named a Trego County post office Cyrus. The town had earlier been named Williamsville. It was an admirer of Cyrus in Ohio who combined "Bu" for beautiful, with "Cyrus" and named a town Bucyrus. This Ohio name was adopted in Miami County, Kansas.[10]

India, of course, was well known, yet it is somewhat surprising to see place-names such as India, Delhi, and Calcutta in Kansas. India is now a railway station south of Lawrence. The name probably came from the Sanskrit *sindhu,* meaning "river," referring most likely to the Indus River. Calcutta, the source for our cloth called calico, is a modern city of mixed civilizations and with a strong British influence. Both Calcutta and Delhi have been capitals of India, Calcutta being the earlier one. Calcutta was sufficiently interesting to have its name adopted for a post office not far from India in Douglas County.

Delhi, the new capital of India promoted by King George V of England, was also made a Kansas place-name. The source of the name was *dahili,* a Persian word meaning "entrance."[11] Delhi was located in the southwestern corner of Osborne County where it survived into the twentieth century, although its post office was closed in 1894.

The special interest in India may be difficult to identify, but the name of Madura, an Indian town and province, was brought to Kansas by William Todd, an English missionary who had served there. Madura was a post office in the English community in Clay County. It was only two miles from Wakefield, and its life was brief. A church in Wakefield was also named Madura.[12]

Agra in India is famous for its Taj Mahal, which was built for the love of a woman. The Agra in Phillips County is believed by some to have been named for a woman,[13] but India would be a most attractive source for the name.

Kismet is a strange name in Kansas. Its Turkish use as *gismat* would mean to "divide," but an Arabic interpretation would make it mean "destiny" or "fate," as a place of Moslem religion. In Seward County, the local residents of Kismet say that it was named by the railroad builders who had some difficulty in crossing the Cimarron River. The river was a "divide." But the railroad had a "destiny" and the road builders built the tracks down one side at an angle and crossed a bridge and up at an angle on the other side. They frequently took only half a train across at a time.[14] Now a new elevated bridge takes the train directly across. Kansas was the only state in the United States "destined" to have a town named Kismet.

Also associated with religion is the name Nirvana. It refers to a final freedom from panic and a complete release from outside reality. This interesting phase of Hinduism was the source for the name of Nirvana City, a town promoted by Judge N. K. McCall in Meade County. J. M. Byers, for whom the Byer's post office was named, moved his store to the "city," which never became a post office—or a "city" either. It had too few citizens to survive,[15] and so it disappeared. One reference lists it as "Nirvana, vacated in 1891."[16]

Portugal, the country that pioneered the route around Africa to the Orient, established colonies in both continents. It was from Portugal that Americans took the Oriental names of Formosa and Canton and the African name of Angola. Although Kansas named its Canton from Ohio, the name came originally from China where it had been Quang Tong, conveniently changed to Canton by the Portuguese. It is said to mean "the wide East."[17]

The town of Formoso in Jewell County was earlier called Omio, supposedly an Indian expression with no more meaning than the white man's "Oh me, oh my." Whatever its meaning, when the railway came to Omio in 1885, the name was changed to Formoso. This is both the name of a town and province in Argentina and the Portuguese name for Ilha Formosa, "the beautiful isle."[18] As the Portuguese were impressed by the beauty of the coast of Formosa, now Taiwan, so the pioneers in Jewell County were impressed by the beauty of the valley which they named Formoso.[19]

Also in the far Pacific was the famous Philippine city of Manila, well known in the Spanish world. Admiral George Dewey spread its fame to the rest of the world when he defeated the Spanish fleet in Manila Bay in 1898. The city surrendered to the United States in August of that year, and four months later a post office in Ford County was named Manila. Fame is fickle and the Manila post office lasted less than two months.

From Egypt came such place-names as Cairo and Memphis. Cairo in the Nile Delta became the capital of Egypt. Of the many Cairos in the United States, one of the most important was in the delta region of the Ohio River in Illinois. The Cairo in Pratt County, Kansas, replaced the name of Irene and is believed to have been named for the one in Illinois. The name came from El Kahir, Arabic for "the victorious."[20]

Memphis in Egypt came from *ma-m-phtah*, "the place of Ptah," and Ptah was "the architect of the Universe." Memphis in Bourbon County, Kansas, was named for the one in Tennessee because it was supposed to be its railway terminal. The towns of Wheeling on the Missouri side and Appleton in Kansas merged to make Memphis.[21]

Egypt was adopted as a post office name in Harvey County. It was a Greek word of uncertain origin and named for the land called Kem, meaning "black," which referred to the black soil of the delta.[22] According to Lippincott's *Gazetteer* (1853), there had already been seven places named Egypt in America before Egypt was named in Kansas.

Also from Africa came such names as Utica and Carthage, popularized by the histories of the Roman Empire. Kuka and Kong came from the British and French empires in Africa. From South Africa we have the names of Angola and Zulu.

When Portugal extended her rule over an African area south of the Congo, she named it Angola. Its source was Donga-Angola or Ngola, Bantu or Congolese names for the Kingdom of Ndonga, ruled by Ngola, the founder of a native dynasty.[23] The Portuguese form of the name was popular, and five towns in as many states were named Angola, the most important one being Angola, Indiana. Any one of these could have been the source for the one in Labette County, Kansas.

The Zulu War may also have aroused an interest in Africa. This was an uprising of a Bantu tribe in which the natives tried to resist the British and Dutch domination. The Zulu War started in 1879 and in that year a post office in Rice County was named Zulu. Chronologically, at least, there was a close connection between the two events.

A good example of outlandish names, technically correct if they came from Africa, are Kuka and Kong. Kuka was a post office in Thomas County, and Kong was a post office in Coffey County. In Africa, Kuka was a Mohammedan state under British control in the Sudan. The British headquarters were in the town of Kuka.

The name of Kong must also have come from Africa where it is the name of a province under French rule which was merged with the Ivory Coast. But Kong, also spelled Koung, was the name of a Chinese statesman who negotiated a treaty with the French and British in 1860. It may be that the Kansas town got its Kong name from a place rather than from a person.

Together with the discussion on African names, it may be convenient to conclude with names associated with the emancipated Africans in Kansas. The "Exodusters" or "Exodites" were freed Negroes from the South, who were encouraged by promoters of varying standards to migrate to Kansas as the "Promised Land." W. R. Hill promised a lot and five dollars to each Negro who settled in a Graham County community. The Negroes came by the hundreds, six hundred to Graham County alone.

The best-known and most successful of the Black settlements was the one named Nicodemus in Graham County. There is, of course, a Bible character named Nicodemus, but the one for whom the town was named was an escaped Negro slave. Nicodemus in Kansas was a name of much greater importance than is indicated by the denigrating assumption of Washington Irving, who said that "a man might sink under the insignificance of his name" and be absolutely "Nicodemised into nothing."[24] To be sure, pioneers did have trouble with the name, and one suggested that it came from "Nigger Demos."[25] But Nicodemus was a meaningful and appropriate name, although it was commonly distorted to "Demus."

When the Nicodemus colony had trouble, W. R. Hill, the promoter, was threatened by both the Negroes and those who opposed them. At one time, Hill hid behind the skirts and shawl of a woman; another time, he hid in a wagon of hay. He survived to become a successful land speculator, and Hill City was named for him.[26]

One of the most active promoters of the Black migration to Kansas was Benjamin Singleton, the "Black Moses." "Pap" Singleton, as he was called, was an escaped slave who offered to lead the former slaves to "the Promised Land." He helped settle Nicodemus and chose Cherokee County for the site of one of his colonies. There the community center was named Singleton in recognition of his leadership.[27] It is now Baxter Springs.

A Negro colony in Hodgeman County was named Morton City for Governor Oliver P. Morton of Indiana, for whom Morton County was also named.[28] He was a forceful politician who opposed the Kansas-Nebraska Bill and ardently supported the amendment to give the franchise to the Negro.

General O. O. Howard, chief of the Freedman's Bureau, was another who worked for the welfare of the emancipated Negro.[29] Not only were the county of Howard (Elk and Chautauqua) and the town of Howard named for him, but so was Howard University, the Negro University in Washington, D.C.

Most of the Exodusters were poorly trained and had trouble fitting into the new competitive system. A few illustrations may serve to show that some did have the ability to succeed. One was George Washington Carver of Ness County, the scientist who produced hundreds of products from the lowly peanut. Another was Lorenzo Fuller, a popular and successful musician from Nicodemus. E.P. McCabe of Nicodemus was the first Negro to be elected to a state office in a northern state; he was elected state auditor of Kansas.[30]

Many of the black immigrants drifted into the fringe of the larger cities, where their communities were given descriptive nicknames. Negro communities along the tracks in Kansas City, Kansas, were called

"Rattlebone Flats," "Rattlebone Hollow," "Mississippi Town," and "Juniper Bottoms," also called "Juniko." The Exoduster community in Topeka was called "Tennessee Town."[31] A Negro colony north of Topeka was called Redmondsville and the one south of town was called "Mud Town." Parsons also had its Negro suburb called "Mudtown," occasionally called "Scuffletown." The two Mudtown names came from the muddy streets where there were no pavements. Some of these suburbs, both in Kansas City and in Topeka, have been changed into attractive residence sections.[32]

CHAPTER XIX

GREEK PLACE-NAMES IN KANSAS

CLASSICAL LITERATURE was the fundamental material for education in colonial America. A friend of John Winthrop thought it would be difficult for "one broughte up amonge boockes and learned men to lyve in a barbarous place where is no learnynge and less cyvillytie." The immigrants solved this by bringing to their "wilderness libraries" books of "Homer, Plutarch, Pliny, Virgil, Seneca, Ovid, Horace, and other Greeks and Romans."[1]

A hundred years ago it was not unusual for Americans, even on the frontier, to have some knowledge of Greek and Latin. The legends of the gods and the characters from Greek literature were familiar not only to college graduates but also to those who had only an elementary education. When plans were being made for an academy at Monica and a college at Palmyra, now Baker University, Theodosius Botkin (notice his given name) recalled that "In either community there were men and women who could discuss Euclid, translate Caesar, read Homer, or call the stars by their names . . . ."[2]

Washington Irving thought it was evidence of "shallow affectation of scholarship" to adopt classical names on the frontier. "The whole catalogue of ancient worthies," said Irving, "is shaken out from the back of Lampiere's Classical Dictionary, and a wide range of wild country sprinkled over with the names of heroes, poets, and sages of antiquity, jumbled into the most whimsical juxtaposition."[3] But Irving could not halt the westward migration of these classical names. The "juxtaposition" of Siouan and Greek to make names like Kanopolis could have been more disturbing than humorous.

Kansas got most of its classical names from those which had already been used as place-names in other states. In some cases, the citizens of a town with a classical name in Kansas, associated the name only with its American source and not with its Greek or Roman origin. The name-givers certainly did reflect their own education or specialized interest in the choice of names; and when one would choose a classical name, another would criticize the choice.

Referring to names in New York, one writer said indignantly that they had been "wantonly imposed on the map" by "a hollow-eyed classicist in the land office at Albany."[4] Whether or not this was true, New York had such historically famous names as Attica, Carthage, Cato, Cicero, Hector, Palmyra, Rome, Syracuse, Troy, Utica, and Virgil. What becomes significant about these names is that Kansas has adopted every one of them, though not necessarily from New York. Nor were they chosen by "hollow-eyed classicists." In Kansas there were those who were sufficiently familiar with Greek and Roman history and literature to choose classical names for the towns they were building.

The map of Kansas is dotted with the names of the mythical gods and goddesses of Mount Olympus, names from the places and characters in the Homeric poems, and such familiar place-names as Arcadia, Argonia, Corinth, Sparta, Athens, and Attica. These names date back two thousand years or more.

The Greek letters may also take on a special meaning, as Alpha and Beta combine to form our "alphabet." Alpha means the first and Omega the last. A woman was said to have named her baby Alpha Omega, as a declaration that it was her first and last. Alpha became a place-name in McPherson County. Beta was skipped, but Jewell County had a place named Delta, later changed to Montrose.

The story of classical Greek place-names might better start with the gods. The Greek gods lived on Mount Olympus, an impressive peak on the border of Macedon. Olympus, meaning "to shine," was the source for the name of Olympia, the site of the Olympic games.[5] Though Olympia became important as the state capital of Washington, Olympia in Pratt County, Kansas, had its name changed to Natrona,[6] also a classical name and a symbol for "carbonate of soda."[7]

Among the gods and goddesses were such distinguished characters as Milo, Halcyone, and Hyacinth, Griffin, Cadmus, and his daughter Ino, Ianthe and Iona, and also Atlanta and Athena. All of these attest to the popularity of Greek mythology in American place-names.

Milo had many of the qualities of Paul Bunyan, the legendary strong man of American woodsmen. Each had an ox which he was able to carry, but Milo killed his ox and ate him in a day.[8] As one might expect, Milo was one of the most consistent winners at the Greek Olympics. In Kansas, Milo was located in Lincoln County, but there one might associate Milo with corn.

Cadmus was, according to legend, the inventor of the Greek alphabet. He was the brother of Europa and he married Harmonia, whose name was a place-name in Linn County. In Kansas, the town of Cadmus was in northern Linn County. So Cadmus and Harmonia, man and wife, god and goddess, found a place together in the same county.

The daughter of Cadmus was Ino. After a tragic life, she threw herself and a son into the ocean. They then became marine deities, always ready to rescue mariners in distress. One of those they rescued was Odysseus. In Kansas, Ino was a town in Osage County whose post office was closed in 1910.

Atlanta is a name with a tradition which goes back to Greek mythology. According to Homer and others, Atlas was one of the Titans who made war on Zeus. For this he was punished and made to hold up the heavens. He was the father of the Pleiades. Atlantis was a female descendant of Atlas. Atlas has become the name for a collection or book of maps. The name was applied to the Atlas Mountains in North Africa which were also believed to support the heavens. Then there was the so-called lost continent of Atlantis in the unknown sea of the Atlantic.

The Shawnees, of course, knew nothing about the god Atlantis; they called the Atlantic Ocean "Stinking Lake." Their legends were as challenging as the Greek, and they said that the earth was held up by a turtle, to which an inquisitive but impolite white man asked: "Who holds up the turtle?" The Indians replied, "White man asks heap fool question." Atlanta, Georgia, was the intermediary site between the Greek god and Atlanta in Kansas.[9]

Ocena or Oceana had something in common with the Atlantic. Oceanus was a Titan, the son of Heaven and Earth and the father of all the river gods—and a number of naughty nymphs. The ancient geographers, described Oceanus as a mighty stream which encircled the world, but it later became the Atlantic Ocean. Remote though this may be in time and space, it nevertheless found a place on the Kansas map. Ocena, also written Oceana, was a promising town in Atchison County. In the words of the county historian, "Ocena, besides having the most musical name, is one of the most beautiful places in Kansas." In Michigan it is a county name. Neither its "musical" name nor its "beautiful" site saved it. "Ocena was killed by Pardee," a rival town, said the *Freedman's Champion*.[10]

In Anderson County, a little stream north of Garnett was named Ianthe. According to Greek mythology, Ianthe was the beautiful daughter of Oceanus and Tethys and the playmate of Persephone. Dr. George W. Cooper laid out "a town on Ianthe Creek and called it Kansas City, afterwards known as Ianthe." The town was not much more than a dream. It had only one log cabin, which was moved four times to establish four different claims.[11]

Aeolia was the god of the winds, and Aeolia in Greece was the "island of the winds." We may recall here that the Indian name for Kansas came from the ceremonials to the spirits of the south wind. In Douglas County, Aeolia was either introduced or copied by Governor Stanton who named his home "Mount Aeolia" for a hill not far from Mount Oread. It has also been listed among the "Extinct Geographical Locations" of Kansas.[12]

Halcyone, daughter of Aeolus, was so grieved when her husband drowned that she threw herself into the sea where she was changed into a kingfisher, and one species of the bird still bears the scientific name of *Alayon*. According to the story, Halcyone's floating nest was capable of calming the sea during the "seven Halcyone days." This calming of the storm-tossed sea has brought about "peaceful tranquility." In western Kansas, a post office in Wichita County was named Halcyone, probably having in mind less the thought of a goddess than of "tranquility."

Among the gods and goddesses associated with the heavenly bodies and whose names graced the map of Kansas were Aurora, Orion, and Hesperus. Aurora, also listed as Eos, rose into the heavens with her chariot to announce the dawn and the rising sun. As Goddess of the Dawn and of Love, she was described as "rosy-fingered and saffron-robed." The town of Aurora near Salina was founded by French Canadians.[13] The Aurora in Jewell County lasted about a decade. Aurora was changed to Lexington in Clark County.[14] Aurora replaced the name of Penfield in Osage County and the name of St. Peter in Cloud County. The only Aurora to survive in Kansas was the Aurora station in Aurora township of Cloud County.

Orion, the handsome son of Neptune, or Poseidon, got into trouble over a woman and was blinded. When Orion ran after the Pleiades, the ladies tried to escape and Zeus turned them into stars. According to the *Odyssey*, Orion married Aurora. After being killed by a jealous rival, he, too, was placed among the stars.[15] The Orion in Gove County, Kansas, may not have been a bright star, but it is still on the map.

Some would include Arion as the "poetical name" of the evening star, but Arion might better be associated with the poet and musician from Greek mythology. To avoid being killed by sailors, Arion threw himself overboard and was saved by a dolphin which had been charmed by his music. Arion was twice the name of a post office in Cloud County.

Hesper, the abbreviated form for Hesperus, also refers to a star since it is associated with Venus, the evening star in the West. Vesper is the Latin name for Hesperus and has the same association with the evening star in that it announces the time for the vesper services. Hesper was a

Douglas County post office from 1868 until 1900, and Hesperia was once a voting center in Madison County.[16] Vesper is now the name of a town in Lincoln County.

Several Greek names which expressed emotions or descriptions have been used as place-names. In Greenwood County, Philadelphia, meaning "brotherly love," was a contestant for county seat. This name was introduced to Pennsylvania by William Penn and was a likely source for the name in Kansas. Johnson County, Kansas, had a place called just Phila, meaning "love," but love did not keep it alive. Adelphi, also associated with "brother," was proposed as a name for Arkansas City. Delphi, the site of Apollo's oracle in Greece, was the name of a place in Ottawa County. People wonder why dolphins are so friendly with human beings; the answer is given by Apollo, who took the shape of a dolphin and guided sailors.

Delphi was the chief shrine of Apollo where one could consult the oracle regarding the future. Ohio copied the name of Delphi from New York where there was a place named Delphos. The one in Ottawa County, Kansas, was Delphos. Levy Yockey, who came from Delphos in Ohio, named Delphos in Ottawa County. He was its first post-master.[17]

Also from Ohio came the Greek name of Xenia, proposed by a preacher who knew Greek.[18] It was occasionally spelled Zenia, as it was pronounced. Xenia meant "hospitality," referring especially to the hospitality of Athena at her Spartan sanctuary. In Ohio it was the home of Preston B. Plumb, a Kansas politician, publisher, and promoter.

In Woodson County, Kansas, a townsite owned by H. T. Chellis was first named Bath, probably from England, and then Chellis. The place was renamed Kalida by H. T. Davidson who had purchased the townsite. Kalida was a name which came from Ohio, but it was a Greek name meaning "beautiful." The name of the town was later changed to Yates Center for Abner Yates, a local landowner.[19]

Kalvesta is located in the panhandle of Finney County. It has been described as of Greek origin but with a Latin ending. *Kalos* meant "good," or possibly "beautiful," like Kalida, and *vesta* referred to the Roman goddess of the hearth as a symbol of a home, and from this we could conclude that Kalvesta meant simply a "good home." But it has also been romantically interpreted to mean "the beautiful and pure of the prairie."[20]

Osma is a Greek word for a plant which was identified by its odor. It is not generally a word used alone, and if it were terminated by an "n," it would be the name of a Turkish dynasty. But Osma, a place-name in Phillips County, is primarily an indication of someone's knowledge of Greek.

High places were logically given descriptive names such as Summit or even Alta Vista. In spite of the confusion it may have caused, Summit was used for several sites. A convenient way of repeating a name without causing confusion was to use the name in a foreign language. One could use Zenith for "summit" as was done for a station in Stafford County west of Sylvia.

As linguists know, there is much Greek in our English, but those who selected the Greek names of Akron and Acme for our summits may not have been aware of their Greek origin. The first Akron was in Douglas County and the next one in Dickinson County. In Cowley County, Akron replaced the name of Little Dutch. There Akron is not on a summit but in the lowlands of the Walnut Valley. The name was likely borrowed from Akron, Ohio. Acme, once a name in Dickinson County, southwest of Abilene, is another Greek word for "summit," "top," or the "highest point." The hills east of Salina are quite conspicuous and as such they could correctly be named Kipp, meaning in Greek, "a sharp-pointed hill." Southeast of Salina, Kipp is the name of a railway station. It is also a surname.

The town of Zeandale, east of Manhattan, is a combination of the Greek *zea*, meaning "grain," "corn," or "spelt," and the English "dale." Zeandale could therefore be "corndale," indicative of its agricultural nature. J. H. Pillsbury, who settled in Zeandale Bottoms in 1855, proposed the name for the town in the rich lowlands of the Kaw Valley.[21]

When Archimedes discovered a method to determine the purity of gold in King Hiero's crown, he is said to have shouted, *"Eureka!"* meaning, "I have found it!" As a word, Eureka has been made to fit the discovery of any satisfactory site. The name had been suggested for the town which became Arcadia. There was once a Eureka some thirty miles west of Atchison on the central Colorado route.[22] In 1854 a Pennsylvania colony promoted a town in Osage County which was named Eureka. But "Ureka," as some spelled it, was not a success, and most of the settlers "left in disgust."[23]

Peter D. Ridenour and Frank Hunt joined M. L. Ashmore and Edwin Tucker to search for a suitable townsite. When they saw "the beautiful rolling prairies of Greenwood County, covered with the rich, bluestem grass, the clear water which tumbled over the rock bottoms in rapids," they were said to have shouted, almost in concert, "Eureka!" Barton, Mitchell, Greenwood, Kingman, and Cheyenne counties have townships named Eureka. These may illustrate imitation more than inspiration.[24]

The *Iliad* and the *Odyssey* were not only "required reading" for Greek students, they were also memorized and recited. Nineteenth-century American students of Greek civilization were familiar with the events, places, and the names of the characters in the Homeric poems. Several of the Kansas place-names are the same as the ones preserved for us by Homer. One should not conclude that these names, although the same, came directly from the *Iliad* or the *Odyssey*, since many of them did not. With this warning, we may, however, list them and discuss them because of their association and as examples of names which have endured for over two thousand years. In the meantime, many of the names have taken on new characteristics and new meanings.

Among the familiar place-names from the *Iliad* and *Odyssey* in Kansas are Argos and Argonia, Attica and Athens, Troy and Mount Ida, Delphos and Ionia. Other place-names may be reminders of the characters in the Homeric poems, including the name of Homer. Kansas had its Ulysses, its Paris and Helen, its Achilles and Hector and Ianthe. Some of these name have become personal names and the immediate source for place-names in Kansas. Nevertheless, they have a Greek origin and an interesting association with the people and places of the *Iliad* and the *Odyssey*.

Homer was probably an Ionian, and both Homer and Ionia are place-names in Kansas. Homer is the name of a station east of Russell in Russell County. Lippincott's *Gazetteer of the United States* (1853), listed a dozen Homers, but Gannett refers to the one in New York and "sixteen other places."[25] The one in Kansas was said to be named by a Union Pacific official who came from Homer, New York.[26]

Ionia referred not only to the Islands but also the Ionian Sea, and the Greeks were once called Ionians. The Ionia in Jewell County, Kansas, was named by three Baxter brothers who came there from Ionia in Michigan,[27] and the source for the name in Michigan was the Greek name.[28] Jewell County also had an Ionian township, and nearby are the townships named Odessa and Athens.

How a name may bring different reminders to different people was well illustrated by a cartoon in *Look*,[29] which pictured two old ladies leaving a theater that had shown the movie based on James Joyce's novel *Ulysses*. One of them, disturbed and confused, said to the other, "Goodness, I thought it was going to be about the one who sailed a boat." Even the Ulysses in Kansas did not refer to "the one who sailed a boat"; it referred to Ulysses S. Grant. Lisbon, the Portuguese name which has twice been a place-name in Kansas, was, according to mythology, founded by Ulysses and named Ulyosippo for its founder.[30]

Homer's *Odyssey* is a sequel to the *Iliad* that relates the adventures of

Odysseus from the end of the Trojan War to the return to his home in Attica. Odysseus was transformed from its Latin Ulixes to the English Ulysses, and as such it has become a fairly popular personal name and an occasional place-name. There was one in New York and another in Pennsylvania, but Gannett listed only the one in Kansas. There was first a Ulysses in Mitchell County which lasted but a few months. The Ulysses in Clark County lasted less than a year before it was replaced by Lexington a few miles away. The Ulysses in Grant County was taken from President Grant's first name. The town and township named Odessa in Jewell County got its name from the Russian form for Odysseus which Kathryn II had used in the naming of Odessa.[31]

When Odysseus departed for the Trojan War, he left a trusted countryman named Mentor in charge of his household and the education of his son Telemachus. Mentor has come to mean a faithful advisor or an educator. In Kansas, Mentor is a station south of Salina. It is believed to be named for Mentor, Ohio,[32] the home of President Garfield.

Even *Iliad*, the name of the epic, is the evolution of another name for Troy. It was Ilias in Greek and it dealt with Ilion, and that was the name of Troy. Rawlins County once had a place named Ilion. According to mythology, Iliona was the daughter of Priam and Hecuba.

When the handsome prince named Paris abducted the Grecian beauty named Helen, his romantic adventure brought on the Trojan War. Helen, also called Helene, is said to be the eponym of Hellenes, a broad term for the Greeks. Helen was already the wife of Menelaus when she was abducted, but Paris was so handsome that some have suggested that she was secretly thrilled by the adventure.

Helen, Paris, and Troy have all been Kansas place-names, and Troy still is. Helen and Paris have taken on new meanings, since Helen was the name of a contemporary woman in Kansas, and Paris was named for Paris, Kentucky, which had borrowed it from Paris, France.[33] In France, Paris came from the Roman name of a tribe called Parisii.[34] The first place named Helen in Kansas was in Sedgwick County and the second was in Meade County. Likewise, Paris has been twice used as a place-name in Kansas, first in Linn County and then in Lincoln County.

From Sparta and Argolis came the Greeks to besiege Troy and to rescue Helen. And behind Troy stood Mount Ida, a backdrop for the dramatic struggle over the possession of a woman. In spite of their admiration for Helen, said to be "the most beautiful woman of the world," the Trojans did not want war. Yet under the leadership of Hector, they fought bravely with the aid of Aphrodite. Athena was on the side of the Greeks from Argos. When the terrified Trojans fled, Hector, brother of Paris, had to meet alone "the handsomest and bravest of all the Greeks," Achilles. Three times Achilles chased Hector around the city of Troy before he caught him and killed him.

Achilles is the name of a little place southeast of Atwood in Rawlins County. It was at first a post office located in a dugout and run by Armstead Morris, who named it for his father, Achilles Morris.[35] The first town named Hector was in Johnson County and when its post office was closed, Hector became the first post office in Greeley County. It was soon surrounded by rival towns: Horace, Tribune, and Greeley Center. Greeley Center and Tribune tried to "gobble up" Hector.[36] The town of Hector did not survive the rivalry, and died, as did Hector, the defender of Troy. Then the name was revived in Johnson County. It lasted a decade. Hector is a fairly popular personal name in Spanish America, but the Hector in Greeley County was said to be named for Greeley's dog.[37]

Second to Achilles in bravery was Ajax, but he was defeated by Ulysses and committed suicide. Ajax is the name of a little place in Cherokee County.

Troy is the most popular of all the ancient place-names in America. Before the coming of the Romans, London was called "Troyovant, or New Troy."[38] In Kansas the name of Troy was first suggested for a town in Anderson County.[39] Doniphan and Reno counties had townships named Troy.

The town company promoting the seat of Doniphan County agreed to let the proprietress of their boardinghouse name the town. She suggested Saltillo, the name of a Mexican town associated with Doniphan's expedition. The name puzzled the members of the town company who admitted that they were poor spellers, and they feared that the town would be called "Sal" or "Sally." Then each member suggested his home-town name as a solution. Finally, James R. Whitehead, the county clerk, spoke up and said: "It does not seem possible for you men to agree upon a name and I wish that you would let me name the town." To this they did agree. "As I shall have to write the name of the new town a good many thousand times," said the clerk, "I will call it Troy, a name having but four letters, and after the ancient city of Troy."[40]

The name of Troy was also proposed for a town in Anderson County in 1857,[41] but that was the year the town in Doniphan County was named. Troy Township in Reno County was named by Zeno Tharp, whose first name may be associated with a Greek philosopher of Athens. It may be that his classical name aroused his interest in Greece and made him an admirer of "beautiful Troy."[42]

Mount Ida near Garnett in Anderson County reminds one of the summit near Troy. In Asia Minor it was associated with the "nymph Ida." In Kansas the name was given to a town by Broomhill for his daughter Ida after his proposed name of Oneida had been rejected.

To counteract the propensity to repeat the word city in names, one could substitute the Greek word *polis*, meaning "city" and the root for the word "politics." Americans have used it as a terminal of a name. So we have the Sioux Indian and Greek name of Minneapolis, which Kansas did not create but borrowed. But Kansas did create such fancy names as Centropolis, Kansasopolis, Kansopolis, and Kanopolis, and each town expected to become the great "City of Kansas" or "Kansas City." Originally the promoters of Kanopolis had planned to call it Centropolis, since Ellsworth County was near the center of Kansas. Kanopolis is a small village, but its name has become well known with the building of Kanopolis Dam on the Smoky Hill River, creating Kanopolis Lake.

A little town on the Missouri border was once called State Line, but as a post office, it was Stevenstown. Then it took on the Greek name of Osopolis which, within the year (1877), was shortened to Opolis.[43] The town wanted distinction, said one writer, and changed its name to Opolis "for the reason of its being a rare and odd name,"[44] and rare and odd it is. It has a Greek companion name in the neighboring town of Arcadia.

North of the Peleponnesus in Greece was Attica with its famous city of Athens, whose cultural achievement makes it one of the most distinguished cities in the history of mankind. The town of Attica in Harper County is not far from Argonia. The town was promoted by the railroad and the name was suggested by Richard Botkin of Harper County.[45] Attica in Greece was the "synonym for great culture," and even the rural town of Attica in Kansas has become an exciting center for creative art, stimulated and directed by Pat Riley, a Wichita artist. The Attica in Ellsworth County, one of the most illustrious of Greek names, was changed to Bosland, a most prosaic name for "Cowtown."

Athens is but a little railway station west of Iola in Woodson County. Athens in Jewell County did not survive, although its name remains on the township. Intellectual centers all over the world like to assume the title of being the Athens of their state or community. Lawrence, the seat of the state university, has been called the "Athens of Kansas." The name for the city of Athens came from the shrine of the Greek goddess Athena. Most of our states have honored Athens by using its name, hoping, no doubt, to bask in the reflected glory of a great city.

The greatest philosopher and teacher in Athens was Plato and his best-known work is his *Republic*. For a few years there was also a town named Plato in Decatur County. At that time only Ohio and Illinois had places named Plato.

Sparta, a rival of Athens in the Peleponnesus, was one of the most militant of Greek cities. In Sparta, Odysseus was victorious in a foot race which won him Penelope for his wife. Spartan today denotes a brave person who lives a simple life under a harsh discipline. In McPherson County, Kansas, Sparta was only a peaceful post office which had outserved its usefulness by 1902.

In New Hampshire a company called the "Laconia Adventurers" must have been associated with the Greek place named Laconia, which was ruled by Sparta.[46] For a summer season in 1888, there was also a Laconia in Meade County, Kansas. Its origin was Greece, but it could have come from Indiana. Laconia is the source for the word "laconic," to be sparing in speech or concise.

Greek civilization which contributed so much to the civilizations of the world also contributed names of people and places scattered all over the map of the United States. Although writers like Washington Irving were critical of the process, the adoption of these place-names serves as an index of the keys illustrating man's effort to become civilized, an effort which is a continuing process and an endless struggle.[47]

CHAPTER XX

MONTROSE MONUMENT MORAN MOREHEAD MORGANVILLE MORLAND MORRILL MORROWVILLE M(

ITALY AND THE ROMAN EMPIRE

UND CITY MOUNDRIDGE MOUND VALLEY MOUNT HOPE MULBERRY MULLINVILLE MULVANE MUND

THERE WERE MORE GREEK THAN ROMAN NAMES in Kansas and even among the Roman names, a few had Greek origins. Rome, Venice, Milan, and Turin are Kansas place-names. The town now named Neosho Rapids in Lyon County was once named Italia because a pioneer on a sunny day compared the blue sky of Kansas to that of Italy. Italy got its name from the Itali, a tribe located south of Rome. Italia was also called Florence, a name that should remind one of the art and architectural greatness of Italy, unless it reminds one of a woman, as does the Florence in Marion County.

Referring to Rome, one critic said the name had been "absurdly given to more than twenty insignificant places in the United States."[1] In Kansas this prestigious name was given to three places. One miniscule Rome remains. The first ephemeral Rome was in Franklin County. Near Hays in Ellis County, Rome was promoted by the Lull brothers of Salina and backed by "Buffalo Bill" Cody. Cody's name had promotional value in the real estate business and Rome was a lusty boom town. No one seemed to know why the town was named Rome, but there must have been a vision of greatness when it was founded in 1867. Rome became one of those exciting centers for English social life and frontier speculation. Its residents were known to boast that ancient Rome was "not built in a day," but Ellis County's Rome was. The railroad missed it by a mile, but a deadly epidemic of cholera did not. The town "oozed away." Having spent their money in riotous living in Rome, the sporty Englishmen departed. While Rome in Italy is known as the "Eternal City," Rome in western Kansas became the "Ephemeral City."[2]

In Sumner County, Rome had ambitions to become the county seat, and it was for a time larger than Wellington. Today it is only a little station on the Santa Fe. The original Rome in Italy was possibly named Groma, referring to the four roads crossing at the forum.[3]

The name Guelph is reminiscent of the twelfth-century rivalry between the Guelphs and Ghibellines, or the pope and the emperor. Frederick Barbarosa was opposed to the Guelphs of Rome. The name appears to have been Welf or Hwelp, which in English would refer to a puppy—dog or wolf. Canadians from the industrial town of Guelph in Ontario brought the name to Sumner County. In Canada it was said to have been named "in complement to the Royal Family whose baptismal name was Guelph."[4] The town of Guelph led a precarious existence in Sumner County. It was made a post office four times before its services were terminated completely in 1902.[5]

Few towns have had more confusion concerning their names than Ravanna. Rivals of the original settlers promoted Ravanna in Garfield County, and the name of the county was as fleeting or transient as the name of the town. Even though Ravanna never moved, it was in four counties: Buffalo, Hodgeman, Garfield, and Finney. The town was first named Mason for Seamon Mason, a local pioneer.

Among the town promoters was John Bull, a Canadian who bore the symbolic name of England, and an aggressive Bull he was. The town's name soon became Bull City, although it was generally called "Bull's Town." That name disturbed the Victorian sensibilities of the women in the community, and some preferred to called it "Gentleman's Cow Town." The women had the name changed to Cowland, as being "more euphonious,"—or possibly more proper for the prudish.[6] Then the name of Cowland, euphonious or not, came under criticism. The community wanted a name with political appeal preliminary to a bid for the county seat. A resident by the name of James Cross suggested that it be named Ravenna for his home town in Ohio. The Ohio town had been named Tappanville for its founder, but Tappan had been so impressed by Ravenna in Italy that he renamed the town for it.[7] The respectable name of Ravenna had trouble in Kansas because a government clerk misspelled Ravenna as "Ravanna," incorrect and unattractive but nevertheless legal. It has been suggested that for a time only the south side of Main Street was called Ravanna, while the north side retained the name of Cowland.[8] The town might have been a memorial, however small, to historic Ravenna, once a Greek town, briefly the capital of the western Roman Empire, and for a time, the Byzantine capital of Italy.

The leading business in Ravanna was conducted by John Bull and Company—the "Company" being Mrs. Bull. The chief rival for county seat was the town with the challenging name of Eminence. Fearing open conflict with John Bull, Eminence secured the aid of Bat Masterson, frontier marshal from Dodge City, who prevented a gun battle. When the ballots for county seat were first counted, Ravanna won. Eminence challenged the election, some ballots for Ravanna were thrown out, and Eminence was finally and eminently successful. Then the town with the many names faded into oblivion.[9]

Trent is one of those elusive place-names which has two sources from which to choose its origin; there is the river Trent in England, and Trent, the capital of the Italian Tyrol, famous for its Council of Trent. The Trent is considered to be one of the three greatest rivers in England, but Daniel Defoe found the origin of the name most confusing. It could be named Trent, as he said:

> Because of its receiving thirty rivers into it, or because there are thirty several sort of fish in it, or that, like the Tibiscus in Hungary, it is three parts water, and two parts fish; all these the learned and judicious Mr. Camden rejects, as I do for the same reason, namely, because they have no authority for the suggestion.[10]

Lippincott's *Gazetteer* (1853) listed twenty-one Trentons and only one Trent. Kansas has added a second Trent, now a railway station in Neosho County.

Turon in Reno County was to have been named Turin for the Italian town, but the post office department objected to another Turin and changed it to Turon. It had abandoned two earlier descriptive names, Pioneer City and Cottonwood Grove.[11] In Italy the name had been Taurini, which could mean the people of the *tors*, or hills.[12] Since Turin is the capital of the Piedmont, the name fits. Kansas has its Piedmont, too, and the origin may be the Piedmont province in Italy, even though its immediate source could be the foothills or Piedmont of the Blue Ridge Mountains.

Judging by the difficulty Kansas had in spelling Mantua, one may assume that it was not named by an Italian. But it was an Italian name of a post office in Allen County, spelled three ways in three years: Mantan and Mantau, and finally Mantua, the name of an Italian city in Lombardy, spelled Mantova by the Italians. In Italy it was possibly named for Mantu, an Etruscan deity.[13]

Also in northern Italy was the ancient town of Arcola which was important enough to be the name of a battle at the time of Napoleon. In Kansas it has been chosen for a place-name four times. The first Arcola was in Sumner County, and this could be the Arcola post office serving for one year in Cowley County. Fifteen years later, Arcola was a post office in Scott County.[14] It is now a station in Saline County east of the town with the Italian name of Terra Cotta.

The Lodi in Kansas could have as its source the Lodi in Italy or the one in California,[15] or possibly one of the other twenty places named

Lodi in the United States. Some of the Lodi names in America seemingly came from Italy; others were imitations of those already in use. It was Napoleon's victory at Lodi that made the name familiar.

There is a folk story which tells how a popular local resident named Dye was always greeted with "Hello Dye," which sounded like " 'lo Dye," and that, they say, was the source for Lodi. In Kansas there was first a Lodi in Miami County and later a Lodi in Barber County.

Venice, on the west fork of the Ninnescah, was twice a post office in Sedgwick County, but it had little in common with the Venice in Italy, except that Rome, a station in Sumner County, was not far away.[16] In Italy it was called Venezia, named for the Veneti who took refuge on the island where canals were substituted for streets.

Milan has its Italian origin with its name considerably modified since the time it was called Midiolanum, "in the middle of the plain." The terminal, whether *lanum* or *planum*, means "plain."[17] Milan in Italy, the center of fashions, gave rise to the word "milliner" from the Milan merchants who were called "Milaner." In Sumner County, Kansas, there was a Milan post office before there was a town, but when a town was built nearby, Milan moved in with its fitting name for the Kansas plains. It has been said that Milan, Kansas, came from Milan, Italy, but it could have come from Milan, Ohio, the home of Chief Quenemo, who also gave his name to a Kansas town. There were, however, nine other Milans in the country from which to choose. It has also been said to refer to the unrequited love a woman had for a settler by the name of Milan Allen.[18]

Also in northern Italy is Lake Como, and near it, is the town of Como. That Lake Como is "the most beautiful lake in Italy" is a justifiable boast; that it is "the most beautiful lake in the world" may be debatable. It had long been a popular resort of the rich, even before there was a jet set. With its simplicity in spelling and its attractive association, it appealed to Kansas in search of new names. First there was a Como in Anderson County but the name was changed to Northcott. Later a place in Cloud County was named Como.

Modena in Butler County had the name of a province and former duchy in northern Italy and a city west of Ravenna. This name predates the Romans and may be of Etruscan origin. It is also the name of a village in Stark County, Illinois, source for many Kansas pioneers. Modena, New York, took its name from Italy and the name migrated westward.[19]

In 1899, for a summer season, Norton County, Kansas, had a post office named Parma. In Lombardy, Parma was the name of a city and duchy, noted as the battleground between the Austrians and Italians.

Kansas could have taken the name from Italy but there is also a Parma in Ohio. Most of the Italian place-names in Kansas were place-names in northern Italy where the towns had been in the historical limelight.

From Sicily to New York and then to Kansas came the name of Syracuse, a Phoenician port named Syraco, said to mean "it stinks." The name probably came from the Greek *suro*, "salt" or "sour." The name of the Greek town of Panormus was changed to Palermo by the Romans. It originally referred to a good harbor or a haven, sheltered from the wind. Palermo in Doniphan County was started by a riverboat clerk named Mahan. William Palmer, a member of Mahan's wife's family, thought he would give the town "prominence" by naming it Palermo for the noted city in Sicily.[20] Some critics would say that the one in Sicily was noted primarily for its anarchists, its macaroni, and its many fine churches, but it does have prestige.

There was probably little thought of a volcanic eruption when Aetna on the Salt Fork in Barber County was named. Yet Aetna, its namesake in Sicily, was the largest and most explosive volcano in Europe. The name came from the Greek *aithein*, meaning "to burn." No wonder that Vulcan was the god of Aetna. In some places the name is spelled Etna, as it was first used in Maine and in Sicily, although its Latin form is Aetna,[21] as it is spelled in Kansas.

One of the most serious and consistent rivals of Rome was Carthage, a Phoenician city in North Africa. The two Romans who were especially prominent in this conflict were Cato, "the Censor," and Scipio Africanus. Cato was an effective orator, an able statesman, and a successful military man. To him Carthage was a constant threat to Rome, and he closed his senatorial speeches with this dramatic appeal: *Carthago delenda est*, "Carthage must be destroyed!" And Carthage was destroyed, not by Cato's oratory, but by the military success of Scipio, who then won the name of Aemilianus Africanus Scipio. Carthage, Cato, and Scipio all became Kansas place-names.

Carthage was the historic name chosen for a town to be built southeast of Topeka. A town well was dug, but before the pump could be installed, a horse fell into the well. Since the town trustees were unable to rescue the horse, it was buried in the well and the town was buried with it—"and thus perished Carthage," without the cry of Cato.[22] A second Carthage was started as a rival of Meade Center for the county seat. Carthage ran third and died, partly because of official "enumerators" called "manipulators."[23]

Utica, located not far from Carthage in North Africa, was another Phoenician town. Once an ally of Carthage, it later sided in with Rome and became the center of Roman government in Africa. It, too, was finally destroyed, not by Romans but by Moslem Arabs. The name was appropriate for a colony because it meant "to settle" or "to colonize."[24]

In Kansas, Utica is a station north of Ness City on the Missouri Pacific Railway. It was first named Wilberforce, for a man believed to have been an English nobleman. It was probably named for William Wilberforce, an English politician who was an active opponent of the slave trade. Farmers in the area thought Wilberforce was "too long and high-sounding," so they changed it to Utica for the town in New York. Utica, New York, had been named for the city in North Africa by a graduate of Dartmouth College.[25] Utica in Ness County replaced the post office of St. Sophia which had its own location north of Utica.[26]

The names of distinguished Romans were occasionally adopted as personal names in modern times. When these names became place-names their immediate source could be contemporary; yet such names as Scipio, Cato, Flavius, and Agricola are names of distinguished characters in Roman history. So are Virgil, Cicero and Seneca and Cincinnatus. Many of these names disappeared when post offices were discontinued.

There was once a Cato south of Kansas City and there is one now between Fort Scott and Pittsburg. A possible source for the Cato name was Sterling G. Cato, a controversial judge and a proslavery man from Alabama. William Connelley spoke of him as "a willing tool of the Ruffians" and, parenthetically, as "a villain in ermine."[27] It is barely possible that the Cato in Crawford County honored this judge. One might assume that he got his name from Cato, "The Censor."[28] Within a year after the naming of Cato, Kansas, a town in Anderson County was named Scipio by its Indiana settlers.[29]

Virgil is a little town northeast of Eureka in Greenwood County. The name has been widely used, but it is best known as the name of that great Roman poet who wrote the *Aeneid*, a story about the adventures of Aeneas. His Roman name was Publius Vergilius Maro. Virgil, Kansas, is believed to have been named for Virgil in New York.

Cicero was a Roman philosopher, orator, able military man, and a just ruler. He became involved in the tragic rivalry of Caesar, Pompey, and Anthony, and was assassinated in 43 B.C. The Cicero in Kansas is believed to have been named for Cicero, Illinois.[30] In Sumner County, Cicero was not far from Rome and Milan and could feel at home with its Italian neighbors. Seneca, the name of a Roman statesman, was the name of a town in Sumner County; but here is a case where the name of an Iroquois tribe, identical in spelling, was the source for the name. Flavius, a man noted for publishing Roman law and depriving the patricians of their powerful monopoly on legal knowledge, was once the name of a post office southwest of Rush Center.

Like the others, the town named New Cincinnati in Rice County was most likely named for Cincinnati, Ohio. But the Ohio name came from Lucius Quintus Cincinnatus, a Roman patriot who left his small farm to fight for Rome. Although he ruled Rome for a time, he returned to his farm and plow.

Agricola was probably the most important Roman general to rule Britain, or Albion, as the Romans called it. He conquered North Wales and defeated the aggressive Caledonians. Tacitus, the noted Roman biographer, was his son-in-law. He made the name familiar. Agricola's name has occasionally been used as a personal name, notably by Georgius Agricola, whose German name was Georg Bauer. He was known as "the father of mineralogy." Agricola was rarely used as a place-name; Lippincott listed none in 1853. But in Coffey County, Kansas, Agricola replaced the name of Hardpan. It was pronounced with the accent on the third syllable.

Other personal names from Italy which were converted into place-names were Pliny and Galileo. Pliny was the Roman intellectual who wrote that remarkable book on Roman civilization called *Historia Naturalis*. Virginia and South Carolina have had post offices named Pliny, but none is listed by Gannett.[31] In Kansas, Pliny was a post office in Saline County.[32] It was changed to Prescott, but after eight days, the name of Pliny was restored, only to be replaced by Gypsum. Pliny was a worthy name, but like Plato, it had no permanence in Kansas.

Then there was Galileo, the astronomer of a later age who challenged accepted beliefs about the relation of the earth to the universe. Under pressure from the church, he recanted. For two years, Gallileo, with a change of spelling, was the name of a post office in Sheridan County.[33]

There were also Italian place-names honoring such people as Caruso and Verdi. Caruso is a little railway station west of Goodland in Sherman County. The naming of Verdi in Ottawa County has been attributed to the influence of a choral society desiring to honor the great composer.[34] The Verdi on the Verdigris River must have been merely a convenient abbreviation.

In Italy, Cremona was famous for its manufacture of superb violins, especially those by Stradivari. Cremona became a place-name in Neosho County.

Roman deities, like their Greek counterparts, were honored by place-names in Kansas. A post office in Labette County was named Minerva for the Roman goddess called the "Queen of the Arts." She was the goddess of intelligence and wisdom and represented the handicrafts and arts. The first part of her name referred to *mens*, the "mind." Minerva was to the Romans what Athena was to the Greeks.

Vesta was a name coming from the Vestal Virgins who kept the eternal fire burning on the hearth. So Vesta became the Goddess of the Hearth. On a trail south of Dodge City, a post office was named Vesta. There are few places named Vesta in America, and Kansas was in 1885 the only place to have one, except for Indiana. The settlers at Vesta, Kansas, did come from Indiana.[35]

Occasionally the source for a place-name might be merely an evolution of Latin words, as in the case of *valeda* and *belvidere*. According to one reference, *valeda* meant "strong" or "healthy."[36] The name may be related to the Latin meaning "valor" or "defender." Valeda, a place in Labette County, was "strong" enough to survive.

Pomona was the Goddess of Fruit to the Romans. J. H. Wheatston must have been familiar with its meaning when he named his apple orchard Pomona, the name from which the town in Franklin County got its name.[37]

Belvidere was another way of naming a place "fairview" or "beautiful view." One does not become confused by its repetition when a name is used in different languages. In Siouan it was Netawaka; in Spanish, Buena Vista; in French, Bellvue; so why not give Fairview in Italian as Belvidere? It replaced the name of Glick, named for George Washington Glick, first Democratic governor of Kansas. Its location was in the picturesque valley of the Medicine Lodge River, said by local devotees to be the "most scenic area in Kansas."[38]

Devize is a name "which is neither British, Roman, English, or French, but Latin without being Roman." Although Latin, the name came from a castle the Bishop of Salisbury in England called the "castle on the boundaries." The name was transplanted to Canada, and from there Reuben Bisbee came to Norton County. He established a post office in his home and named it Devize.[39] Here is a case where a transferred name is descriptively correct, since it means "the border." It is located on the Kansas-Nebraska border.

Kansas, in the middle of America, might appear to be so far removed from Italy as to be beyond her influence. Yet the stories behind the Italian names give a good sampling from the history of the Roman Empire. Schuyler Colfax, vice-president of the United States in Grant's first term, said that Kansas was "the Italy of the American continent."[40]

CHAPTER XXI

ITAH NARKA NASHVILLE NATOMA NEAL NEODESHA NEOSHO FALLS NEOSHO RAPIDS NESS CITY

BIBLE NAMES IN KANSAS

NEW ALBANY NEW CAMBRIA NEWTON NICKERSON NIOTAZE NORCATUR NORTON NORTONVILLE

LIKE MANY OTHER STATES, Kansas has borrowed abundantly from the Bible and the Bible lands for its place-names. Some of these names have a direct relation with their biblical background, but others are Bible names previously used in other states. Even the Bible got its name from the name of a town, a Phoenician town named Biblos which was noted for its sale of parchment for the making of books. The book of all books was therefore called the Bible.

That elusive place called Paradise may be found in Kansas. When James R. Mead reached the wooded valley of a creek flowing south into the Saline River, he said to hunting companions, according to his own recollections, "Boys, we have got into Paradise at last." It was, of course, a hunter's paradise, which Mead said was "the most beautiful spot" he had ever seen. The valley was for a time known as "Mead's Paradise." The name was given to Paradise Creek, which flows down Paradise Valley.[1]

A town built in Paradise Valley was first named Iva for Iva Marr, the daughter of the farmer who owned the townsite. In 1875 the name became Paradise. There is a Paradise township in Russell County, and in Osborne County, a post office was named West Paradise.[2] Since the town of Lucas had a private park called the Garden of Eden, a *Wichita Eagle* headline referred to "Luray, between Paradise and the Garden of Eden."[3]

Ever since Adam's eating of the apple, Eden has been as elusive as Paradise. When pioneers first came to eastern Kansas, most of them spoke well of it, and one pioneer was so carried away by its appeal that he said: "If the Garden of Eden exceeded this land in beauty or fertility, I pity Adam for having to leave it."[4] Eden had a rather vague geographical identity in the Bible, but in Kansas it was eight miles northwest of Atchison and described as "a pretty and prosperous prairie community" and "a modern Garden of Eden." Another described it as "gently swelling, with rich valleys, and sloping everywhere." This man knew his Eden: "Eden sloped, you remember—'beautiful as the garden of the angels upon the slopes of Eden.' "[5] George Remsburg referred to the area as "a veritable Eden," but he did not know who the first Adam and Eve were there, nor who were the first to raise "cane and corn and kine."[6] Eden is said to mean "place of delight."[7]

Eden in Sumner County was short-lived,[8] but the county still has an Eden Township. Eden Prairie was for ten years the name of a post office in McPherson County. "Welcome to Eden" says a sign on U.S. 81, southeast of McPherson. Sherman, Meade, and Ness counties have had townships named Eden, but only the one in Ness County remains. When the promoters of Garfield County, now Finney, referred to it as an Eden, an unkind editor of the *Garfield County Call* had this to say: "It has been discovered that Western Kansas is the Eden from which grandfather Adam and grandmother Eve were driven for fooling with God's winesaps. The stump of the identical tree under which Mrs. Adam was beguiled is just west of Eminence on the Pawnee in Garfield County."[9]

In Sanskrit, Adam simply meant "man." According to one interpretation, Adam meant "red mud." The Greek name of Adam was taken from the words referring to the four cardinal directions: *Arktos*, north; *Dusis*, west; *Anatole*, east; and *Mesembria*, south. The initials spell ADAM.[10] Since Adam was said to be created from clay taken from the four quarters of the earth, the Greek name would be a logical sequence.

Adams is a short form for Adamson, "the son of Adam." But in the Bible, Adam was, of course, the "first man." The sons of Adam came to Kansas, and in Kingman County there is a place named Adams. In Reno County is an Adams Corner. Adamsville, a station on the border of Sumner and Cowley counties, has also been called "Adam's Town." The place named Adams in Wallace County was named for William Adams, its first postmaster. Adams Peak was a Pottawatomie County post office. The biblical connection of the Rooks County post office named Adamson becomes obvious, since this son of Adam was a preacher and his first name was Moses. By name, at least, these places were associated with the sinner who was driven out of the Garden of Eden.

Eve is a meaningful name, and it has been suggested that one meaning is "talk." When Adam asked Eve what he should call her, she might have replied in the poetic lines of Lessing as translated by Coleridge:

> *"Ah," replied my gentle fair,*
> *"Beloved, what are names but air?*
> *Choose thou whatever suits the line:*
> *Call me Sappho, call me Chloris,*
> *Call me Lalage or Doris,*
> *Only, only call me thine."*[11]

Eve was the name of a post office in Bourbon County where Eve Davis, the mother of the apple-growing governor, Jonathon Davis, was postmistress.[12] It was probably only a coincidence that this Kansas place named Eve was located in an apple orchard. But the apples were not Adam's apples. They were the nationally known Jonathans.

In Cain City, Ellsworth County, we have a reminder of one of the troublesome sons of Adam and Eve, but the Kansas town was named for J. A. Cain, postmaster, who also owned the townsite. It never became a "city," and when it moved to the railroad in Rice County it became just Cain.[13]

Seth was born to Eve when Adam was 130 years old. Eve is said to have named him Seth or Set as one who was appointed by God to serve after Abel had been murdered by his brother Cain.[14] Seth was the name given to a town in Norton County, later changed to Neighborville, the name of a nearby post office, and then to Calvert.[15]

Regional or provincial Bible names were also adopted as Kansas place-names. Levant was a name from the French or Italian *levant* which meant "rising," referring to the rising sun. This word came to mean the East and included, at first, the whole of the Orient. It was later confined to the eastern Mediterranean. Levant came to Thomas County in western Kansas, where it was suggested that it was associated with trade.

Lebanon, a famous area between Israel and Syria, got its name from its snow-covered mountains. It is a Hebraic name derived from Lab hen or Laban, "to be white." Laban, brother of Rebekah and an associate of Jacob, was the name of a place in Mitchell County. The beautiful land of Lebanon was noted for its "Cedars of Lebanon" where Solomon got the timbers for his temple.[16] The first Lebanon in Kansas was located near Fort Scott.[17] A church and its community was called Lebanon in Kingman County. The next one was located in Smith County, once the geographical center of the United States, a distinction it lost when Alaska was admitted to statehood.[18] Lebanon in Kansas was named by Dr. R. B. Ray, its first postmaster, who came from Lebanon, Kentucky.[19]

The Land of Goshen may have been the same as the Land of Rameses. It was the area in lower Egypt occupied by the Israelites before the Exodus. The name seems to have followed them to southern Judah. Goshen, Indiana, has continued its religious character, mainly in its Mennonite publications and its Mennonite college. Kansas settlers in Clay County who came from Goshen, Indiana, evidently brought the name to Goshen Township.[20] Farther west, Graham County had a Goshen post office.

Sinai was a name originally applied to a mountain where God gave the laws to Moses. The Jewish *Encyclopedia* gives Sinai and Horeb as "meaning respectively, 'moon' and 'sun.'" Zondervan's *Dictionary* suggests that Horeb meant "drought" or "desert." In the northwestern corner of Rooks County and near Sugar Mound is an eminence called Mount Horeb. There was a Mount Cenis in Dickinson County which was commonly known as "Mount Sinai." It disappeared when the post office was moved to Upland.[21]

When the Israelites entered Canaan, it was to them "The Promised Land." The name came from the Hebrew *kene' an* or *kana*. It could mean "lowlands" or "the plains." Canaan was in reality the early name for Palestine. "Canaanite" was also said to mean a "trafficker" or "merchant." In Kansas, Canaan was in the northwestern corner of Chase County. The merchants of Canaan, Kansas, did not do well enough to keep the town alive. As a post office, it lasted less than six months.

Canaan was called Palaistine by Herodotus; the Romans spelled it Palestina, which later became Palestine. It originated from the name for the Philistines. In Sumner County, Kansas, a post office was named Palestine. The post office was closed, but the name remained on a railway station and on a township.

Sharon was the name of an undulating plain along the Mediterranean from Joppa to Mount Carmel. It was said to mean "plain" or "level." It has been suggested that the "Rose of Sharon," a flower of the crocus family, was the source for the name of Sharon in Barber County. It seems, however, to have a religious connection, since it was founded by Campbellites.[22] Sharon Springs in Wallace County had first been named Eagle Tail, later changed to honor Sharon Springs in New York.[23]

Samaria, north of the Plains of Sharon, was the name of a province, a hill, and a town. The hill was well fortified and the name may be from the Hebrew word *shomeron*, which meant "watchtower." It was there that Ahab and Jezebel lived a life of "luxury, vice, and paganism." Samaria in Kansas was but a dream and a plan and had been described as "a paper town near Walker Mound" in Montgomery County.

The settlement in Dickinson County which became Abilene was for a time known as Mud Creek or Muddy Creek. There lived Tim Hersey, a prominent pioneer and promoter, jovial, but not much on religion. Mrs. Hersey was a devout woman who read the Bible regularly, both for herself and for her neighbors. Tim explained how his wife chose the name for Abilene. "Yep," he said, "Luke, third chapter—Petrach of Abilene or some such. Well, anyway, Maw lit on it an' I says, let her rip, Abilene she be." Of course, this is the way a pioneer might have told the story, including the substitution of "Petrach" for tetrarch.[24]

According to another version, a visitor was asked to open the Bible, place his finger on a page, and the name nearest to his finger would be accepted as the name of the town, and this was Abilene. The owner of the townsite and promoter of the town was Charles H. Thompson, whose son said that the name was suggested by Findley Patterson from Pennsylvania. Patterson was visiting the elder Thompson about a land deal. This interpretation is less romantic but more logical than most of the stories.[25]

Abilene was a Roman political unit in ancient Syria about nineteen miles northwest of Damascus. The name is associated with *abila* which has been translated to mean a "grassy plain" or a "grassy meadow," or simply "prairie plain." Abilene in Kansas certainly fits this description, and it, too, has been called the "City of the Plains."[26]

Abilene has won distinction as a terminal of Texas cattle drives on the Chisholm Trail and more recently as the home town of the Texas-born military leader and President, Dwight D. Eisenhower. An early visitor is reported to have said: "I never seed such a little town with such a big name."[27] The Bible name was pronounced Abba-lée-nee; Abilene in Texas is pronounced Abil-léene; in Kansas it is pronounced Áb-i-lene.

The Apostle Paul not only preached to the Galatians, he also wrote his Epistles to them. Galatia was in the central part of Asia Minor. The Gauls had invaded that land in the third century B.C., and from these invaders Galatia took its name. In Barton County, Kansas, Galatia is a railway terminal on a branch line of the Santa Fe. It had earlier been called "Dogtrot." Harry Weber named it Galatia for his home town in Illinois.[28]

Antioch, northwest of Damascus, was founded by Seleucus in Syria and named for his father Antiochus. It became one of the great centers of Christianity. If the Apostle Paul could call any place his home, it was "Antioch the beautiful." It was a cosmopolitan city and a favorite residence of the Romans, whose revels gave it a reputation for being wicked. Pliny called it the "queen City of the East."[29] Sixteen towns were given this name to honor Antiochus. It was twice adopted as a place-name in Kansas. The first Antioch was a post office in Osage County, 1883–85, where it replaced the interesting name of Eclipse. In 1893 the name was given to a post office in Miami County, where it remains an isolated little village.

Aleppo was conveniently located on the highway between Antioch and Bagdad. It was there that Abraham came down the mountainside to distribute milk to the poor. The Hebrew word for milk is *halab* or *haleb*, and from this the place was named Aleppo.[30] There was once a church-centered community named Aleppo some twenty miles north-west of Wichita. It was first named St. Mary Aleppo.

Jerusalem, the greatest city in Christendom, is also a Jewish and Moslem shrine. Long before the time of Christ this "capital of the king-dom of God" was called *uru-salim*, or *veru-salim* "the city of salim." *Salim*, which meant "peace," became Salem in English. It is associated with the Jewish greeting of *shalom*, or the Arabic *saalem*, "peace be with you." Both Jerusalem and Salem became place-names in Kansas. Jerusalem was for a short time the name of a post office in Johnson County.

Salem was so popular as a name that it was used in America sixty-one times before Kansas was organized. Kansas may have taken it from Salem, Massachusetts, the second oldest town in New England, or from any one of the other sixty. The name of Salem was substituted for Loui-siana on the Santa Fe line in Douglas County. Later there was a Salem in Jewell County which boomed until the Rock Island missed it by five miles. It served as a post office until 1903, even though it suffered from "droughts, grasshoppers, cyclones, prairie fires and hard times."[31] Swedes from the Galesburg Colonizing Company of Illinois established Salemburg, the "castle of peace," south of Salina.[32]

Few places have more Bible characters associated with it than the ancient city of Hebron, which is located on the road to Beersheba about twenty miles southwest of Jerusalem. The name meant "union" or "association." When it was called the "city of four" or the "fourfold city," the four referred to Abraham, Isaac, Jacob, and Adam. When it was called El Khalil by the Arabs, the name meant "the friend of God," referring to Abraham. While there were many names associated with Hebron, none was more important than Abraham, and it was justifiably known as "Abrahamtown."[33] For about six months Hebron was a post office in Saline County, Kansas. Three times it became a post office in Clay County where it was associated with such biblical names as Tabor and Goshen.

Southwest of Jerusalem is the ancient town of Beersheba. The name means "seven wells" or "well of seven." Both Isaac and Abraham have been credited with digging one or more of these wells. The name came to Kansas when twenty-four Jewish families were led from Ohio by Rabbi Isaac M. Wise and Rabbi Adelhartz to establish a colony in Hodgeman County.[34] They preserved their connection with the ancient kingdom of Judah by naming their town Beersheba.

Carmel was an important name in Palestine, referring to a hilly range, a Mount Carmel, and, not far from Hebron, the town of Carmel. The name meant "garden" or "vineyard." Mount Carmel overlooks the Bay of Acre on the northern border of Sharon. In Kansas, Carmel was the name of a post office which served Cloud County for twenty years.

Modern Bethany is about three miles from Jerusalem. The old towers among its ruins are said to be from the home of Mary and Martha and their brother Lazarus. Bethany has been interpreted to mean the "house of unripe figs," or possibly "dates," but also, "God has helped," and, finally, "the house of God."[35]

There was once a station named Bethany in Osborne County, but with another Bethany in Missouri, the railway changed its name to Portis, for a Missouri Pacific vice-president. Another Bethany in Smith County disappeared. Also to be named Bethany was the college planned by the Episcopal church for the town of Tecumseh. The building did not go beyond the first window sill, but the site south of town is known as "College Hill." Bethany is now the name of a Lutheran college in Lindsborg.

The Bible town of Bethel was located eleven miles from Jerusalem. It has been called Luz, but later it became Beth El, the "house of God." Three times the name of Bethel has been given to towns in Kansas: first in Marion County, then in Republic County, and then near Kansas City. Only the latter survived.

Beth was the same as the Greek Beta, and its origin was a picture of a house. Its meaning continued to be a "house" or "place." Bethlehem, meaning the "house of bread," was a place-name in Kansas only for the Bethlehem school in Republic County.[36]

The road from Jerusalem to Bethlehem led over the Mount of Olives, a ridge dotted with olive trees. The Mount of Olives was the source for Olivet, a name given to a town in Osage County. It was promoted as a center of the Swedenborgian movement and the site for a proposed denominational college.[37] Mount Olivet was once the name of a place in Leavenworth County.

Jericho was famous in the wars between the Canaanites and Israelites, and it was the home of King Herod. Interpretations of the name vary widely. It could mean "a place of fragrance," like the township in Dickinson County named Fragrant Hill. It could also mean the "City of the Moon," and it has been described as the "City of Palm Trees." For nearly two decades there was a Jericho in Gove County. It was moved and rebuilt, but finally, without the blare of trumpets, its walls came down forever.[38]

The town named Joppa southwest of Wichita in Harper County was the name of a well-known port in Palestine. It was the seaport for Jerusalem, which had a Joppa Gate. Joppa was also spelled "Joffa," "Japho," "Jaffa," and "Yafa." It has recently been revised as Tel Aviv-

Yafo, the name of the booming port town of modern Israel. The name meant "beauty," or "shining place," or, possibly, "white."[39]

In the Bible country, Shiloh was about twelve miles north and east of Bethel. It was a political center and a defensive site in Canaan. It was there that Joshua placed the tabernacle to house the covenant known as the Ark. One might note that Shiloh, which commemorates one of the bloodiest battles of the Civil War, was a name which meant "place of peace" or "tranquility."

Shiloh Creek in Bourbon County, Shiloh Township in Neosho County, and the post offices named Shiloh in Ness and Hamilton counties are reminders of the Battle of Shiloh in Tennessee. But one should recognize that it was the religious name of the Shiloh Methodist Church which gave its name to the Shiloh battleground. Shiloh Creek in Kansas was named for "Mount Shiloh of Biblical fame," but it, too, was a battle-ground.[40] The town named Shiloh in western Kansas could as likely be named for the Civil War battle as for the biblical town. Tennessee, by the way, has seven Shilohs, but only one gained notoriety and that was the result of a battle.

Berea, like several other biblical names, has two locations, one in Macedonia near Mount Olympus and another in Palestine near Bethel. The one in Macedonia, where Paul preached, could have been named for its founder, Beroea. Berea in Franklin County, Kansas, was founded by a Presbyterian colony called the "Bereans," a group of dissenters led away from the Calvinists by John Barclay in 1773.[41]

Ever since the days of Solomon, Ophir has been synonymous with gold. In biblical times it was located between Sheba and Havilah in southern Arabia, a port town from which Solomon acquired his luxuries and riches from India. Ophir is also referred to as the name of a man in Genesis, the son of Eber and the ancestor of the Hebrews.[42] There are six towns named Ophir in the United States, all of them in mining states; and there was for a time a seventh in Butler County, Kansas, a county which also had a town named Oro for gold and El Dorado for "The Gilded One."

There were so many Kansas pioneers with the name of Jordan that one may not be able to identify the origin of the post office named Jordan Springs in Reno County. But when an Ohio family came to "A Beautiful Creek with a little Timber," flowing into the Marais de Cygnes, they "named it Jordan."[43] It probably did not resemble the Jordan River in Palestine which "moved madly to its dark and bitter end" in "a helpless race to a hopeless goal in the Dead Sea." Its name came from *hayyarden* which meant "flowing downward" or the "descender."[44] Lincoln County once had a post office named Cedron and it still has a Cedron Township. Cedron, also written "Kidron," was the name of a brook near Jerusalem.

The large number of places bearing the descriptive name of Mount in the Bible lands has a special significance. Palestine, then as now, was a land of tribal conflict and imperial wars. Every area had to be defended and any geographical eminence which would give a natural advantage for defense might be selected as the site for a town and the seat of government for a king or a conqueror. These were natural fortifications strengthened by man-made walls and watchtowers. Even in Kansas we find such familiar names as Mount Sinai, Mount Horeb, Mount Nebo, Mount Tabor, Mount Pisgah, and Mount Gilead. Only occasionally were they appropriately descriptive of a hill or mount, and never of a mountain.

The biblical Mount Tabor was located east of Nazareth and west of the Sea of Galilee. At the foot of the "mountain" was the village of Tabor. It had once been a prominent site for pagan rites but it became more important as the most likely site for Christ's transfiguration. It was the home of Gideon. Tabor in Kansas was the name of a town founded by the Hussites of Bohemia and its people were known as "Taborites." Two towns in Republic County were given the name of Tabor, one called Mount Tabor and the other New Tabor. New Tabor had been previously named Prairie Plain.[45] Clay County also had a town named Tabor. Today the name of Tabor is preserved as the name of Tabor College in Hillsboro, Kansas.

East of the Jordan is a ridge known as Mount Gilead. The name is said to mean "rough," "hard," or "firm." The name of Gilead has also been applied to a person, a clan, and a town. The place is associated with the prophet Elijah and many other biblical characters. Pottawatomie City in Anderson County had its name changed to Mount Gilead. The town declined and its residents moved to Greeley, a town named for Horace Greeley. Samuel Wood, a prominent Kansas politician, had practiced law in Mount Gilead, Illinois, and he might have brought the name to Kansas.

In the Mount Gilead range one may also find Mount Nebo. It gives a grand panoramic view of the lands across the Jordan. It was from Mount Nebo that Moses beheld the Promised Land, according to some. Its name came out of the Babylonian country and dates back to the Sumerian civilization. Nebo was the god of wisdom and the deity who introduced writing, according to Babylonian beliefs. He was worshiped by Babylonian priests who also studied astrology, laying the foundations for the space age. In Rooks County, Kansas, a school district is logically named Nebo, honoring the god of learning. Miami County had a town named Mount Nebo. After its post office was closed in 1871, the name was given to a town in southern Pratt County. Rooks County has a Mt. Horeb.

Across the Jordan from Jericho and not far from Mount Nebo was Mount Pisgah. It, too, is mentioned as the site from which Moses viewed the Promised Land. Since there may be no definitive conclusion regarding these conflicting views, we may simply accept the explanation of an Arab who said as he stood on Mount Pisgah: "Moses, he *look* here"; and pointing at Mount Nebo, he added: "Moses, he *sleep* there," implying that he was buried there.[46] Pisgalis Heights in Riley County got its name from Mount Pisgah in the Holy Land.

Several biblical sites were known as Mizpah, and this is logical since Mizpah meant a "watchtower" or "lookout." The name has been used as the Mizpah of Moab or the Mizpah of Gilead. Clay County, Kansas, with such biblical names as Goshen, Tabor, and Hebron, also had a Mispah. The town was not important and Mizpah failed even to become a post office.

Three Benedictine brothers, Fridelin, Raymond, and Andrew, came as pioneer missionaries to establish a monastery on the Kansas frontier. From Dodge City they drove their trusty team, Mustang and Cody, on the road to Fort Coffee. About six miles from Ashland they chose for their monastic site a high hill which overlooked the grassy valley of the buffalo country. Bishop Funk dubbed the place Bueffel Au, "Buffalo Valley."[47] But the Benedictines gave it a name of distinction; they named it Monte Casino for the famous monastery in Italy where St. Benedict had started the Benedictine order in A.D. 529. There he converted the shrine of Apollo to a Christian monastery. Monte Casino in Kansas was not at a good location and it was soon abandoned.[48]

Cowboys, outwardly irreverent, characterized its religious association by calling it "Mount Jesus." When Captain George A. Custer and Major Henry Inman were marching up its side on a foggy morning, Custer turned to Inman and asked: "What mountain is this?" Inman answered: "Mount Jesus."[49] It has been suggested that this incident was the origin of the name, but it is quite likely that the cowboys were the ones who changed the name of Monte Casino to Mount Jesus.

In addition to biblical place-names and biblical personal names, Kansas also borrowed the names of religious observations and ceremonies, such as Vesper, Angelus, and Sabetha. Vesper is the name of a little town west of Lincoln Center. The town had been called Nemo, an Indian name given the questionable interpretation of a "wooded area." A religious group of Pennsylvania Dutch settlers changed the name to Vesper. The original Greek word was *hesperus*, meaning "to the West." Its association with the evening star or Venus made the late afternoon or evening service a vesper service. Vesper was also a family name, since there was a Mrs. Minnie Vesper who came to Graham County in 1887.[50] Closer to the Greek name was Hesper, the name of a town in Douglas County. It was important enough to have a Friends school called the Hesper Academy.

Angelus is a prayer offered at morning, noon, and night at the ringing of a church bell. The name comes from the first words in the prayer: *Angelus Domini.* For a visual impression it has been popularly associated with "The Angelus" painted by Millet. In Sheridan County, Angelus is a German community where the tall church steeple dominates the landscape.[51]

In the 1850's a pioneer heading for California was forced to stop in northern Kansas because one of his oxen died. The man was somewhat of a religious zealot, according to legend, and since the ox died on the Jewish Sabbath, he called his place Sabetha. Another version suggests that a mule, not an ox, died there. The owner thought so much of the animal, whatever it was, that he put a cross over the grave which read, "Here lies Sabetha." Some settlers thought it was the name of a woman. New Yorkers had named a nearby town Albany Hill for their own capital, but its people soon moved to Sabetha where the stranded California-bound traveler sold his supply of surplus whisky for a good price to thirsty immigrants and parched pioneers.[52] Cloud County had a place named Sunday.

Nimrod has today become synonymous with "hunter." The Nimrod referred to in Genesis was much more than a "mighty hunter before the Lord"; he was the ruler over a Babylonian kingdom and the founder of Nineveh. Nimrod was the name of a town in northeastern Lincoln County, a popular hunting area.

The Gideons, members of the Christian Commercial Men's Association of America, have become well known by placing Bibles in hotel rooms. Gideon is not a common place-name, but there was a Gideon post office in Douglas County, Kansas, from 1883 to 1902. Gideon in the Bible was a great warrior who was also referred to as a "feller" and a "hewer." It was he who defeated the Midianites who came from east of the Jordan. "The Day of Midian" became significant for Israel. Midian is a most unusual place-name, yet there was a Midian near El Dorado in Butler County from 1918 to 1950.

The test given by the Gileadites for the identification of the Ephramites, their enemies, was the manner in which they pronounced *shibboleth.* So this word, which originally meant an "ear of corn," or possibly a "stream" or "flood," came to mean a "test" or "watchword."

The British navy used a similar system for identification of American sailors for impressment. In Kansas, Shibboleth was the name given to a town in Sheridan County. Shibboleth joined Old Sheridan and Hawk-eye to form a new town named Selden for Selden G. Hopkins, member of the town company.[53]

In the Bible story, and in the public mind, Delila and Samson are inseparable. Samson, whose name came from *shamshon*, "Little Son," or from the Hebrew *shemesh*, "Sun," was noted for his tremendous strength. He is reported to have killed one thousand Philistines with the jawbone of an ass. His weakness for women was his undoing. Delila, whose name meant "The Dainty One," seduced this Hercules and enticed him into telling her that the secret of his strength lay in his hair. Then Delila lulled him to sleep and clipped his curly locks, leaving him a weakling. The Philistines blinded him and kept him a prisoner. Later they made a spectacle of him in the public arena and thousands assembled on the roof of the temple to watch. In the meantime, Samson's hair had again grown long. With renewed strength, he tore down the pillars which supported the temple roof, and the spectators fell to their deaths.

Both Delila and Samson became place-names in Kansas. Delila became a place-name in Ellsworth County in 1875, but it served as a post office only six months before its name was changed to Trivoli. This appears as if it should have been Tivoli, an Italian name, but there is also a Trivoli in Illinois. Sampson was a post office in Marion County. This one was named for Sampson Jetmore, the postmaster.

Beulah is a biblical name which meant "married." The Crawford County town named Beulah may have a biblical connection since it was founded by a Methodist Episcopal religious group.[54] The name is used poetically for the land of Israel, and popularized in the song about "Beulah Land."

The story of Og belongs to the stories of men like Samson and David. Og was the interesting name of a short-lived post office in the southern part of Reno County. Many a Bible tale has been told about the legendary giant named Og. He was so tall that he survived the biblical flood, and the waters reached only to his ankles. But there is also a story which suggests that he hung on to a rung on the side of Noah's Ark and that Noah fed him through a porthole. Og fell in love with Abraham's wife, hoping that Abraham would be killed by his enemies. But this did not come to pass. Moses killed Og, and this must have been as brave a deed as that of David's killing Goliath. As the story is told, and a tall one, to be sure, "Moses, 10 ells tall, took a 10 ell ax, leaped 10 ells into the air and hewed at Og's ankles so that the giant died."[55] In the boom of the eighties, Og in Kansas might have expected to become a giant but it did not survive beyond infancy.

Zion is a name which has been used in many ways and with a variety of meanings. It was originally one of the hills near Jerusalem which was conquered by David who there built his citadel and his temple. It has consequently been called the "City of David" as well as "Temple Hill." It is frequently used as a synonym for Jerusalem and called the "Heavenly City." Its origin is vague but it could possibly mean "Citadel."

In Kansas, Mount Zion is still a railway station near Kanopolis in Ellsworth County. Zionville in Grant County was one of the boom towns of western Kansas. Its newspaper, the *Zionville Boomer*, was edited by a thirteen-year-old boy, and it lasted for two issues. Zionville was built on an inflated ego but it soon died.[56]

When several Mormon families settled in Stafford County, they named their community Zion Valley, and this became the name of the first post office in the county. After the settlers argued among themselves, they left. Then, because of the county seat war with Stafford, the name of Zion Valley was changed to St. John to honor the governor

The Devil and his den were not neglected in giving descriptive names to Kansas. There was the Devil's Backbone, Doniphan County; another in Republic County; a Devil's Lookout, Wabaunsee County; Devil's Creek, Washington County; and Devil's Garden. The Devil's Lookout near Alma gives one a beautiful view. Poor Abilene had a hard time living up to its biblical connection; in fact, one area was so full of deviltry that it was segregated from the town and called "The Devil's Addition."[57]

Originally the Devil was not as bad as he has been characterized in modern times. His Latin name was *diabolus* and this meant that he was just one of the deities, but his evil characteristics have been amplified to make him a most frightful devil or deity.[58] His name was well hidden when it was written Jarbolo, a town in Leavenworth County. Jarbolo was a far-fetched phonetic evolution from the Spanish Diablo.

Having mentioned the Devil, we may well include Hell as a place-name. James R. Mead, who named Paradise Valley, also named Hell Creek, a tributary of the Saline. He said that it was "appropriately named from some experiences of myself and other hunters in buffalo days."[59] It was the only creek so named, and one may question the merit of the name. Not so in Kentucky where a stream was named "Hell-for-Certain-Creek," and there was the "Hell-for-Certain-School."[60] Other places were known as Hell's Half Acre in Barber County and Hell's Bend in Chautauqua County.

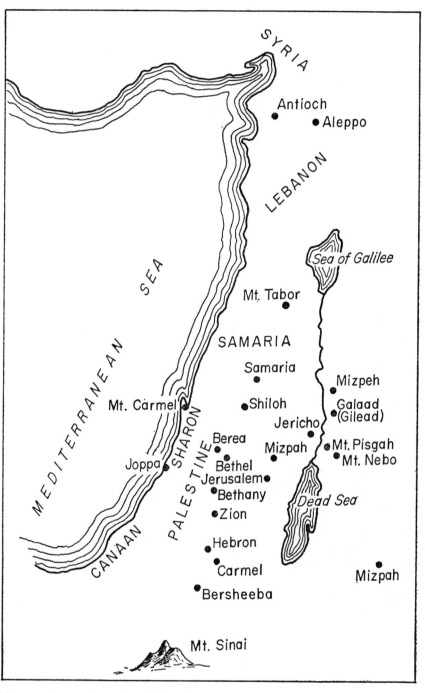

Kansas Names from the Bible

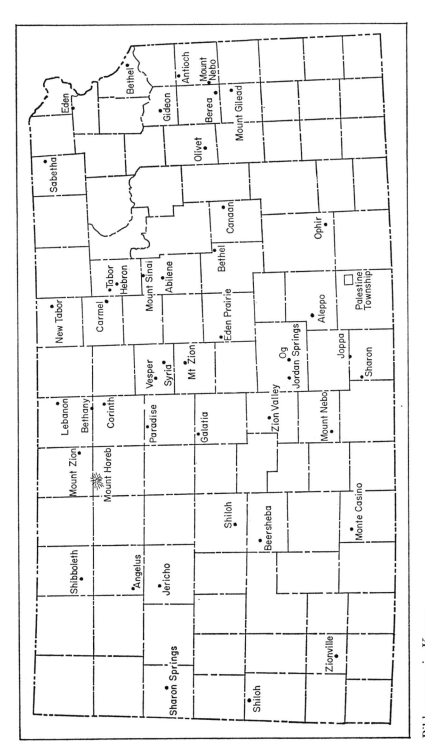

Bible names in Kansas

CHAPTER XXII

OAKHILL OAKLEY OAK VALLEY OBERLIN OFFERLE OGALLAH OGDEN OKETO OLATHE OLIVET OLM

SAINTS

LSBURG ONAGA ONEIDA OPOLIS OSAGE CITY OSAWATOMIE OSBORNE OSKALOOSA OSWEGO OT

A SAINT WAS DESCRIBED in early days as "a good man" or a "pious man," and saints, like preachers, were frequently referred to as "the people of God." Christian martyrs were canonized as saints.

Churches and cathedrals were naturally named for saints, and church names were occasionally used as place-names. Holy Cross, the name of a post office in Pottawatomie County, also had its religious association. After a decade as two words, the name was combined in 1894 as Holycross. The Christian influence on place-names is well illustrated by the use of the names of saints.

There were at least a score of places named for saints in Kansas, eighteen of which became post offices. Ffteen names now remain. When the Vatican deleted several saints as being of doubtful authenticity, some of the names in Kansas may have lost their distinction. There were numerous saints with the same name, and the removal of a particular saint, such as Saint Paul the Hermit, need not detract from the reputation of Saint Paul the Apostle. There might, however, be a logical lament over the loss of Saint Nicholas.

Saint Nicholas was possibly the Bishop of Myra in Asia Minor and the patron saint of Russia. One seldom thinks of him as the patron of pawnbrokers, sailors, and thieves, but that he was. People like to think of him as Santa Claus. His generous reputation is based on the ancient practice of people dressing as bishops and distributing presents. Saint Nicholas, popularly known as "Saint Nick," was the name of a post office in Atchison County, and St. Nicholas is still the name of the community. After its third closing, the post office changed its name to Cummingsville, shortened to Cummings, for William C. Cummings.[1]

The Spanish explorers were generally accompanied by missionaries and their conquests were made in the name of religion. Saints' names were widely used as place-names. The first example of this in Kansas was when Coronado came upon the Arkansas River on the feast day of Saint Peter and Saint Paul, June 29, and named the river El Río de San Pedro y San Pablo. Another Spanish explorer named it El Río Grande de San Francisco to honor his governor, Don Francisco Cuerbas. Peter,

Paul, and Francis were among the most prestigious of the saints, and the name of each became a Kansas place-name. Peter and Paul were widely used for numerous saints, but the most familiar were Peter and Paul, the Disciples.[2]

One may imagine the surprise when a man telephoning the chaplain's office at Buckley Field in Colorado to hear someone answer: "Chaplain's office, Saint Peter speaking." This was not, of course, Saint Peter at the Pearly Gate checking on a passport, but a private whose name was Saint Peter.[3]

There were two Kansas towns named for Saint Peter. The one in Cloud County had its name changed to Aurora. The one in Graham County replaced the name of Hoganville, named for a pioneer. The St. Peter name in Graham County honored a German from Russia whose name was Peter Rome. He had donated the land on which a church was built. The name honored Peter's patron saint and the patron of Rome.[4]

St. Paul was used as a Kansas place-name in both Chautauqua County and Sheridan County before the present St. Paul was named in Neosho County. The one in Neosho County had been known as the Osage Mission and Catholic Mission. When S. J. Gilmore was postmaster, it was also called Gilmore Town. The community wanted a new name but rejected Neona, the name of Chief Little Bear's daughter.[5] The place was finally named St. Paul, supposedly for Father Paul Ponziglione, head of the Indian mission, or possibly for "Saint Paul of the Cross," an eighteenth-century saint who could have been the patron saint of Father Paul.

One of the most popular saints was Francis of Assisi, "The Poor Little Man" who was the inspiration for the Franciscan order. St. Francis City in Marion County was named for Franciscans in Ohio who had aided the Kansas settlers. The name was changed to Burns for a railroad man. St. Francis in Brown County was a good choice to replace the strange name of Buncomb.

There is still a St. Francis in Cheyenne County in the northwestern corner of Kansas. This one was named for a woman, Mrs. A. L. Emerson, whose given name was Frances, and who was known as "Fanny" Phillips. That she was worthy of the saint's name may be seen from a characterization in the local press. Frances Emerson, said the press, had "a strong, religious faith, a well-developed conscience, and an acute sense of obligations to man and God and country . . . ."[6] There were saints with the feminine name of Frances, and yet the town of Emerson chose to use the popular masculine form to honor the popular woman.

Most of the saints were men, even though they may not have been more saintly than women. Most important among the women saints was Mary. As the Virgin Mary, she was given a superior status over the other saints. Among the women saints whose names became place-names in Kansas were Saint Bridgit, Saint Sophia, Saint Theresa, and Saint Clere.

St. Mary's Mission for the Potawatomi Indians was established by Father Christian Hoecken. It is in southeastern Pottawatomie County in the valley of the Kaw. Father Jean-Baptiste Miege and Father Paul Ponziglione, two Jesuits who came from Europe in 1851, expanded the mission as a religious center.[7] Saint Mary's Cathedral, the first in Kansas, was built there, from whence Bishop Miege directed the church activities in six states.[8] After twenty-three years, Mission was dropped from the name and the railroad deleted the final "s." St. Marysville in Miami County had its name changed to Lyons within a year; and in less than a decade, it was changed to Tontzville. Most people had omitted the "Saint" part of the name.

The country around Fairland in Marshall County became the center for an Irish community, and Fairland was renamed St. Bridgit, honoring the saint who ranks next to Saint Patrick in Irish popularity. There, too, is St. Bridgit Township.

The Irish community of Saint Patrick's church in Marshall County was known as "St. Pats." In Marshall County, St. Patrick's was "possibly what was later called St. Joseph's Settlement, St. Joseph's of the Prairie, Irish Creek, and now Lillis."[9] Thomas Francis Lillis was appointed Bishop of Leavenworth in 1905 and later served as coadjutor to the bishop in Kansas City. His parents came from County Clare, Ireland.

Saint Sophia was a martyred saint from Fermo, Italy. For a few years there was a St. Sophia in Ness County, but the name was changed to Utica.

There were several Saint Theresas, and the name was generally written Teresa. The Saint Teresa Convent in Florence, Italy, made the name familiar to those who would use it as a place-name. Wichita County in western Kansas had a post office named St. Theresa for many years. It was named for Theresa, the wife of its founder, Clem Scheve.

Of the many saints named Joseph, the one honored as the patron of the Universal Church is best known. St. Joseph post office in Cloud County, known to the public as "St. Jo," was named by a French priest, Father Louis Mollier.

St. Joe, St. Mark, and St. Leo are little hamlets in south-central Kansas. In the southeastern corner of Reno County, Kansas, is a little place called St. Joe. This name may well refer to Saint Joseph, and, like

Saint Mark, may be the name of a local church. St. Mark was once a post office and is now a church-centered community in Sedgwick County. Of the thirty-one saints called Mark, the best known is the one who followed Saint Peter to Rome, called the disciple of Saint Peter. St. Leo is in Kingman County. Of the twenty-one saints named Leo, three were popes.

More elusive were St. Julian in Clay County, which never became a post office, and St. Leander, the name of a town company which was permitted to establish a town in Johnson County in 1857 but which it seemingly failed to do.

As for St. Louis and Little St. Louis, these names came from St. Louis, Missouri, honoring Louis IX of France. Adding Little to the name was to be a distinguishing feature, but it dropped the Little and then lost its sanctity by becoming simply Louisburg.[10]

A favorite watering hole on the Fort Dodge–Fort Supply military road was given a saintly name when its name of "Little Basin" was changed to St. Jacob's Well. It was one of those remarkable limestone sinks in western Kansas.[11]

Pottawatomie County had three places named for saints, St. Mary's, St. Clere, and St. George. St. Clere may be a variation of Clerus, Clare, or Clara. It was Clare of Assisi who founded the Franciscan order of the Poor Clares. As the patroness of good weather, Saint Clare, if that is the one honored as Clere, should appeal to people anywhere. St. Clere is located in St. Clere Township. Towns were named Clare in Washington County and Clara in Johnson County with no further identification, saintly or otherwise.

When several families left St. Joseph, Missouri (named for Joseph Robidoux), they stopped a short distance east of Manhattan. Mrs. Gillespie, wife of one of the immigrants, refused to go any farther, so they all took homesteads there. Among them were George W. Gillespie, J. George Gillespie, and George Chapman. Then, for the three Georges, the place was named St. George.[12] Saint George, the dragon killer, is the popular English saint. Of the three Georges, George Chapman was said to have been the most saintly.

A traveler in 1860 wrote about a St. Cloud on the left bank of Solomon's Fork.[13] Among the saints there was only one Saint Cloud, the grandson of King Clovis and Saint Clotilde. The name may be derived from Saint Clodoaldus. This name could as likely have come from St. Cloud in Minnesota or St. Cloud, a suburb of Paris in France.

Leoville was first a post office in Barton County, but its name was changed to Nathan. Then a group of German Catholics changed the name of Netherlands to Leoville to honor Pope Leo.[14] There were, of course, several popes named Leo, and three of them were canonized. One of these must have been the source for St. Leo in Kingman County.

One of the most influential of the Catholic orders was the order of Saint Benedict of Nursia. Saint Benedict's Monastery at Monte Casino in Italy served as the inspiration for Benedictine monasteries all over the world. Even in the buffalo country south of Dodge City, Kansas, three Benedictine brothers established a monastery which they named Monte Casino. A Benedictine abbey in Doniphan County was the source for the name of the St. Benedict post office. After it was closed, a place called Wild Cat in Nemaha County had its name changed to St. Benedict.[15] The Benedictine brothers from this abbey in Doniphan County moved to Atchison and there they established Saint Benedict's College. There is a Benedict in Wilson County.

Some of the saint names were from surnames of contemporaries, such as St. John and St. Bernard. The town of St. John in Stafford County was named for Governor John P. St. John, as was St. John County, which later became Logan.

St. Bernard in Franklin County had first been named Centropolis, one of the many towns hoping to become the state capital. It was named St. Bernard for Joab M. Bernard, its first postmaster. Bernard was active in promoting the towns of Buchanan, Missouri City, and Centropolis. The name lasted only a few years before it was changed to Minneola and later back to its first name of Centropolis.[16]

There is a town named Xavier in Leavenworth County. The name goes back to Father Francisco de Xavier, a Jesuit missionary, and a saint who has also been called the "Apostle of the Indies." The name came from his mother's castle of Xavier or Xavero, located at the foot of the Pyrenees in the kingdom of Navarre. In Kansas it is the site of Saint Mary College for women. There was Sister Xavier Ross for whom it is said to be named.[17]

What does one do with a name like Igo, thrice a post office in Rooks County and later the name of a school? In the first place, the name was most likely Iago. This is, of course, the Spanish for James, as we see in Santiago for Saint James, and Saint James was the patron of Spain. This opens the way for Igo to be, at least, associated with saints. After hearing the story of Igo in California, however, one need not come to any final decision. There, a Chinaman, tired of laundry business, went into gold mining. When he struck it rich, a white miner, assuming that wealth was destined only for the white man, pulled a gun on the lucky Chinaman and ordered him to get out. The now unlucky Chinaman raised his arms and said, "I go, I go." So the place was named Igo.

The spunky Chinaman went prospecting again and again he was

lucky. But this time, when the white man came and told him to get out, the Chinaman, having greater understanding of the white man's civilization, pulled his own gun and said, "Oh no, you go!" So the place was named Ono. Both Igo and Ono are in Shasta County, California.

As for the Igo post office in Rooks County, it was closed three times. One may assume that, each time, the postmaster reluctantly said, "I go!"

CHAPTER XXIII

PREACHERS

NOT ALL PREACHERS are saints, but definitions indicate that the two can be placed in the same category. A preacher, like a saint, is assumed to be a "pious man." Preachers were prominent in the pioneer period of Kansas, and they deserved the recognition they were given when their names were used as place-names. The Bogus Legislature was prone to name counties for sympathetic politicians, but they also named counties for two sympathetic preachers, Rev. Thomas Johnson and Rev. David Lykens. Both Johnson and Lykens worked diligently as missionaries to the Indians and both became politicians. Johnson County retained its name, but Lykens was unacceptable to free-state legislators who replaced it with Miami.

Preachers were concerned about the issues of the day and some of them were involved in politics. They were not as successful as politicians in getting their names accepted as place-names, but a fair sprinkling of preachers' names may be found on the Kansas map. It was Henry Ward Beecher, a distinguished Boston preacher, who said, "There is no monument under heaven on which I would rather have my name inscribed than on the goodly state of Kansas."

Beecher was greatly concerned about the struggle in Kansas and he became especially well known after the rifles sent to the free-state men were labeled "Beecher Bibles." A Connecticut colony that settled near Wabaunsee was known as the Beecher Bible and Rifle Company, and there is still the Beecher Bible and Rifle Church.[1] The town named Beecher in Brown County may well have honored the famous preacher,[2] but Camp Beecher at the site of Wichita was named for his nephew, Lieutenant Fred Beecher.

Place-names were also chosen from the Beecher family writings. The town of Norwood in Franklin County was named for Beecher's novel entitled *Norwood*.[3] This was not a great novel. Edwin Perry Whipple, a literary critic, said it was made up from the "fag-ends of his sermons and lectures."[4] Because of the Beecher association, however, the name of Norwood had some distinction and popular interest.

The place named Topsy in Lincoln County could have been named for Topsy in Harriet Beecher Stowe's *Uncle Tom's Cabin*. Having no further information on the source of the name, one may assume that, like Topsy in the story, Topsy in Kansas "just grew."

Leaders of great religious movements have had devoted followers who would preserve their identities in place-names. This was true of the Mennonites and of Martin Luther and John Wesley. Religious groups like the Quakers also left their names on the map.

Quaker is a popularized nickname for a religious group called the Society of Friends. It may have come from the warning of George Fox to "tremble at the word of the Lord," or from the members' trembling with religious emotion. The Quaker label, formerly used individually, is no longer considered derogatory. We may associate Quakers with preachers, because any member of the society could preach when the spirit moved him.

A Quaker settlement in Cherokee County was the source for the post office name of Quakervale, also written Quaker Vale, Quaker Valley, Quakerville, and just Quaker. It seems now to have been renamed Quaker Spur. It all started with a Quaker meetinghouse.[5] Quaker Point in Jewell County was changed to North Branch. Quaker City has been used as a name in both Coffey County and in Reno County, but neither survived.

Individual Quakers also left their names on the Kansas map. One of these was Mrs. Laura S. Haviland, a distinguished humanitarian, whose name was given to Haviland in Kiowa County.[6]

Henry Harvey, a Quaker missionary to the Shawnee Indians, may be included among the preachers. Harvey was appointed by President Zachary Taylor and came to Johnson County in 1840. He was an Ohio man and returned to that state to write a *History of the Shawnee Indians*. Later, he returned to Kansas, became a county commissioner of Wabaunsee County, and was active in free-state politics. After the grasshopper raid, he went again to Ohio to solicit aid, and there he died. Harveyville on Dragoon Creek in Wabaunsee County was named for him.[7]

The name Luther looms large in history, both as the leader of the Reformation and the founder of a church that bears his name. In Kansas the first post office named Luther was in the Mennonite area of Marion County. A few years after this post office was closed, Luther became a place-name in Washington County near the German communities of Hanover and Hollenberg.

One of the greatest preachers of all time was John Wesley, founder of Methodism. He preached to workers and the wealthy in England and the colonies. He is reported to have preached 42,000 sermons.

Kansas Wesleyan University at Salina was named for him, and a station south of Salina, once a post office, was named Wesleyan.

Collyer and Quinter in western Kansas were named for preachers. Collyer, a Trego County town, was named for Rev. Robert Collyer, who came to Kansas with a Chicago colony.[8] A little farther west is the place named for the Rev. James Quinter of Pennsylvania. He was an elder in the Dunkard or Baptist Brethren Church. The town had been named Familton, but the Post Office Department thought it looked too much like Hamilton, so the name was changed to Quinter.[9] The new name was chosen because of the many Brethren living in the area.[10]

Kalloch, north of Independence, was named for Isaac S. Kalloch by Governor Robinson.[11] Ottawa was founded by Kalloch and C. C. Hutchinson, both Baptists. Both preached in the Baptist church in Ottawa. Kalloch was versatile and capable, but he was also independent and outspoken. Dismissed from one college and graduated from another, he was an eloquent orator, an ardent free-state man, a politician, hotelkeeper, railroad president, journalist, and preacher. In Ottawa he was the editor of *Western Home Journal.* He was also restless. Born in Maine, he preached in Boston and New York, was twice a preacher and politician in Kansas, became the mayor of San Francisco, and died in Washington.[12]

Like Kalloch, C. C. Hutchinson has been characterized as "a shrewd preacher." As Indian agent, he was active in the management of the Ottawa lands and his fees were high. He wrote an account of the *Resources of Kansas* which was so good that the legislature ordered five hundred copies. When the Santa Fe marked its westward route, Hutchinson followed the surveyors' stakes to a site which he chose for a town. He built the first house there and named the place Hutchinson, indicative of a justifiable ego.[13]

One of the most militant of ministers and one of the bravest was Pardee Butler. He came to live in Atchison, a proslavery stronghold. When he refused to sign a proslavery resolution, a man asked him if he had a pistol. He did not, so the man gave him a pistol and told him, with an appropriate oath, "I'll blow you through . . . in an instant." The rest of the gang proposed to hang the preacher. The hemp was brought, but a spectator from Missouri insisted that this "scoundrel" should be handled according to law. The mob agreed and put Pardee on a makeshift raft with several posters. One read: "Cargo insured, unavoidable dangers of the Missourians and the Missouri excepted." Pardee used the posters for a sail. The mob threatened to hang him if he ever came back. He did come back, but this time he was tarred and feathered. Yet Pardee Butler was one of the stirring speakers at the Fourth of July celebration at Topeka in 1856. Such characters deserve to be remembered, and for a time there was a town named Pardee in Atchison County. Pardee had preached the first sermon at the townsite of Pardee in a schoolhouse there. The town had been named Ocena for five days before it honored the persecuted preacher.[14]

Helmick, Talmadge, and Hazelton were named for preachers. Helmick, a station west of Council Grove, was named for Rev. J. W. Helmick, who was the pioneer preacher there.[15] Talmadge was a popular name and used both in Woodson and Republic counties. The present Talmadge in Dickinson County was named for DeWitt Talmadge, a preacher for the Methodist Church South.[16] Hazelton, southwest of Anthony in Harper County, was named for Rev. J. D. Hazelton, not for his preaching, but for his donation of a six-hundred-pound bell to a local girls' college. It has also been said that he was the founder of the town.[17]

Haun Creek in Morris County was named for Rev. A. Haun, the first settler in the area.[18] Jacob's Creek in Chase County was named for Gabriel Jacobs, a Dunkard minister. He was buried on Jacob's Mound.[19] Lyle in Decatur County was also said to be named for a preacher.

John L. Baxter was a squatter on a farm near Spring River in Cherokee County. He was classified as a "Universalist Missionary," but critics who disagreed with him called him an "infidel." He was a disagreeable man and difficult to deal with. He was killed in a dispute over land claims. Baxter Springs was named for him. In the records of Cherokee County, his name was given as John H., but his grandson, C. C. Baxter, thought it should have been John L. Baxter.[20]

Baldwin was known as Palmyra until John Baldwin arrived there from Berea, Kentucky, to start a sawmill. Then came Osman Cleander Baker as the first bishop to preside over the Methodist Conference in Kansas. When a college was promoted for Baldwin, Dr. A. T. Still suggested that it be named Baker for the bishop. Baker then gave the college a bell, known as the "10 o'clock Bell" because it was used for curfew.[21]

There are those who believe that Winfield was named for Winfield Scott. It was, but this Scott was a preacher, not a general. C. M. Wood, the first settler in the area, built a stockade on the west side of the Walnut to trade with the Indians. He was on Osage lands and was driven out and his stockade was burned. Woods had, however, selected the site for a town across the river, purchasing the land from Chief Chetopa, for whom the town of Chetopa was named.[22] He promised Mrs. Wood that she could name the town and she chose the lovely name of Legonda, also spelled Lagonda.

Another settler, W. W. Andrews, returned to Leavenworth to bring his family to the new frontier community. As an inducement to get Mrs. Andrews to move west, he promised her that she could name the town. She was a great admirer of Rev. Winfield Scott, pastor of the Baptist church at Leavenworth. Her plan was to raise five hundred dollars for a church, name the town Winfield for the preacher, and then have him come there to be its pastor. When she found that the town was already known as Legonda, she was greatly disappointed. Then she learned that there would be no official name until the settlers voted their approval. The community held an election, and afterwards there was a dance. The ballots were placed in a drawer of a washstand and supposedly locked. Mrs. Andrews is reported to have said, with a twinkle in her eye, that while the people danced, Legonda lost and Winfield won.[23]

White Church was an Indian church in Wyandotte County, built of walnut and painted white. When the white man chose this site for a town, the White Church of the red man was retained as a name. A tornado destroyed the church, but the name remains.[24]

Preachers have been prominent in Kansas, and because of the mixed background of its people, Kansas contains a variety of faiths. Kansas preachers have probably not been any more successful than preachers in other states in affecting behavior, but they have tried. There was once even some support from lawmakers. A devout Kansas legislator introduced a bill to put the Ten Commandments into the Kansas statutes. For better or worse, it failed.

CHAPTER XXIV

PHILLIPSBURG PIERCEVILLE PITTSBURG PLAINS PLAINVILLE PLEASANT GROVE PLEASANTON PL

SECONDHAND NAMES FROM NEW ENGLAND

OMONA PORTIS POTWIN PRAIRIE VIEW PRAIRIE VILLAGE PRATT PRESCOTT PRESTON PRETTY PR

THE MAIN SOURCE for American place-names appears to be place-names already on the map elsewhere. Old names, or "secondhand names," have been chosen from all over the earth—and heaven, too. At least half of the towns in New England were named for places in Old England. Miss Abbie Farwell Brown expressed in poetry the sentimental ties of Old England names in New England:

> Plymouth, Exeter, Bristol,
> Boston, Windsor, Wells,
> Beloved names in England,
> Rang in their hearts like bells.[1]

Every name mentioned in this verse has been transplanted to Kansas, extending the bonds of Old England through New England to Kansas.

The attachment that New England had for old English names was quite similar to the attachment of settlers in Kansas to the names of towns in New England or elsewhere. The "lingering love they had for the land they left behind," said one writer, was kept alive in a name. As a lovelorn swain might carve his sweetheart's name on the bark of a tree, so nostalgia for the home town made men put its name on the map of the state in which they settled. It was done to preserve the feeling for *la patria.*

The naming of New England has been attributed to Captain John Smith. In Kansas, a place on the Wakarusa was listed on the map as the New England settlement. There may have been a tendency to over-emphasize the importance of New England in Kansas, but one must recognize its contribution in making Kansas a free state. Even in 1875, young people were urged "to go to our newer New England, the bright, broad fields of sunny Kansas."[2]

When Victor Murdock wrote a story on New England names, he gave it this headline: "LONG NECKLACE OF NAMES OF NEW ENGLAND ORIGIN STRING ACROSS KANSAS." These, said Murdock, furnished "the key to a biography and the biography furnished the key to some New Englander's abiding faith in the prairies of

Kansas."[3] After the Civil War, New Englanders participated in the great railway boom by furnishing both money and management, and their names became place-names in Kansas. Except for Cyrus K. Holliday, who came from Pennsylvania, most of the financiers and promoters of the Santa Fe Railway came from New England.

Any new town in a neighborhood could be named New Town and commonly condensed to Newton, as was the Newton in New England. When a town was started across the Charles River at the outskirts of Boston, it was named New Town. Then, as a college town, it was renamed Cambridge for Cambridge University in England.[4] Another Newton grew up a short distance farther west. Railroad investors from this Newton named Newton, Kansas.[5]

It is not exclusively an English custom to so name a town, and we find older examples in the Greek Neapolis and the Italian Napoli. A new town could also be identified by using the name of an older town, such as Boston, and calling it New Boston. According to Baughman, thirty-one Kansas post offices were identified by a known name preceded by "New."[6] Seven other places, not identified as post offices, were also identified as "New" something or other.[7] There are now only seven names preceded by New which are left on the Kansas map. So it becomes obvious that most of the towns named New did not become old, yet the town that was vacated in favor of a "New" town was occasionally known as "Old" this or that.

New Bedford in Sumner County, where there are many names from England, may have been transplanted from New Bedford in Massachusetts. It was called "Naw Bone" before it became New Bedford.[8] One might conclude that the Naw Bone came from Gnaw Bone, Indiana, which was later changed to West Point. The inhabitants objected to the change—all eight of them.

Boston and its surrounding communities have left us much that is worthy of remembrance. Many of the events in the area have become indelibly associated with place-names. Among these are Lexington and its minutemen; the battles of Concord and Bunker Hill; Cambridge with its Harvard, Chelsea, Haverhill, and Andover; Newton with its railroad men; and Lawrence, Thayer, and Sumner, fighters for freedom. All of these deserved recognition, and they were remembered, not by monuments but by place-names.

Boston typifies New England, but the name has its origin in Old England. From the name "Botolph's Town" evolved a name that was in England "commonly and corruptly called Boston." It was founded by Saint Botolph, a Saxon, who established a monastery in England in 654. Two centuries later, it was destroyed by the Danes. Originally, Botolph meant "help-ship," a good name for a saint. John Cotton came from Boston in England and it is believed that it was to honor him that the town first named Trimountain was renamed Boston.[9] The Saint Botolph story is well told in the poetic words of Longfellow:

> *St. Botolph's Town! Hither across the plains*
> *And fens of Lincolnshire, in garb austere,*
> *There came a Saxon monk, and founded here*
> *A Priory, pillaged by marauding Danes,*
> *So that there no vestige now remains;*
> *Only a name, that, spoke "loud and clear,*
> *And echoed in another hemisphere,*
> *Survives the sculptured walls and painted panes.*
> *St. Botolph's Town!"* . . . .[10]

That echo in another hemisphere is nothing less than Boston, Massachusetts, which has proudly preserved the source of its name in Saint Botolph's Church and the Saint Botolph Club.[11] The echo was eventually recorded in Kansas.

Boston had prestige and its name was popular. Recently it has been described as "a body of culture surrounded by antique shops"; but its earlier reputation made it known as "the hub of the Universe." New Englanders in Kansas proposed the name of New Boston for the town which was later named Lawrence.[12] When the Boston Association of the Kansas Territory settled at the site which became Manhattan, it planned to name the place Boston or New Boston.[13]

Later, a town in Howard (now Chautauqua) County was named Boston, although some residents had preferred naming it New Boston. It was said, and reasonably enough, that the town was named Boston because the name "sounded pretentious." It would be as reasonable to assume, however, that the choice of name was made by its many Irish residents who came from Boston and to whom the place was known as "Old Ireland."[14] In the county seat controversy, known as the "Boston War," residents of that town organized an "army" and captured Elk Falls, loaded the county records into wagons, and returned in triumph to Boston. Boston won the "war," but politicians soon split Howard County into Elk and Chautauqua. Boston was left on the county border. It had no political future, no railroad, no source of water, and no good reason to survive, and so it faded away.[15]

A fifth and final attempt to give Kansas a town named Boston was made in Butler County. A bedraggled, barefoot man known as "Professor" Barton encouraged a group to settle there. Joining them was "Prince" Gorum Davis Morton, dubbed "Pegleg." Perhaps some called him "Prince Pegleg." He had a magnificent voice and boasted of having sung before the crowned heads of Europe, including Mary, Queen of Scots, unaware that she had lost her head about three centuries earlier.[16] Having lived in Boston, he suggested naming the town Boston or New Boston, but the proposal was rejected. One member of the town company happened to have a map of Boston which showed a suburb named Chelsea. Although Chelsea was not the better part of Boston, the town company accepted it.[17]

London, like Boston, has a suburb named Chelsea. It may mean the island with the gravel pit, or the "landing place for chalk limestone." The second interpretation is supported by Baedeker's *Guide*, which called it a "chalk wharf." In England it was the home of great literary and military men; in Massachusetts, it has the reputation of being the "largest junk and waste material center in the world."

Plymouth, Massachusetts, was named by Charles II, and the name in Kansas was surely associated with that one. In England, the Plym in Plymouth referred to the "plum tree," and Plymouth was at the mouth of the Plym River.

Plymouth, England, could be associated with patriots and pirates like Drake and Hawkins, but to the Pilgrims, Plymouth was the point of departure and the terminus of one of the most momentous migrations in history. Free-state immigrants from Massachusetts who came to Kansas by way of Iowa and Nebraska on Lane's Trail to avoid the southern blockade, chose a town site on the Nemaha-Brown County border and named it Plymouth.[18] Richard Hinton said that he had camped in Kansas in 1865 on Pony Creek, "right in direct route for immigrants to found a town under the name of Plymouth."[19] The first Plymouth in Kansas was abandoned, but a new one became a post office in Lyon County in 1858. Russell County has a township named Plymouth.

Above Plymouth, England, was Plympton, "the town on the Plym."[20] Kansas and Massachusetts were the only states to name towns Plympton. Dickinson County once had a post office named Plympton. The source could be a personal name, since a Lieutenant Colonel Joseph Plympton was commander at Fort Leavenworth in 1850.[21]

While one group of Massachusetts immigrants established Plymouth, a second group moved on and started a town named Lexington.[22] The Battle of Lexington, where the minutemen fired the shot heard around the world, made the name so popular that it was adopted across the continent. Kansas added three to the twenty-three then on the map. The Lexington in Johnson County had its name changed to De Soto. Ben L. Stephens of Kentucky changed the name of Ulysses in Clark

County to Lexington.[23] The one in Kentucky was built where some hunters first heard about the Battle of Lexington.[24]

Lexington, Concord, and Bunker Hill are names that remind one of the first battles of the American Revolution. In Kansas, Concord was in 1868 a post office in Ottawa County. In Massachusetts the name was chosen to emphasize the co-operation of its settlers. The minutemen from Woburn, near Boston, joined their neighbors to fight the British at Lexington. Jackson County once had a Woburn, an English name which, like Windsor, meant a "winding stream," but its Kansas association was most likely the minutemen of Massachusetts. Bunker Hill in Atchison County was promoted by Dr. Charles F. Knob of Boston. In Massachusetts it was at first called Bunker's Hill, named for George Bunker, a constable in Charleston.[25]

Two of the best-known promoters of the New England Emigrant Aid Society were Amos A. Lawrence and Eli Thayer. Much of the inspiration and promotion came from Eli Thayer, who wrote a soul-stirring pamphlet called the "Kansas Crusade." Mount Oread was the name of Thayer's castle, and there, near Worcester, Massachusetts, was his Oread Female Seminary.

Charles Robinson may have named Mount Oread in Kansas.[26] One New Englander at the Lawrence site put up a sign in front of his tent which read "Mt. Oread," and there were others who wished to name the town Mount Oread. The name did remain on the high ridge that gives the University of Kansas its beautiful panoramic view of the valley of the Kaw and the valley of the Wakarusa.[27]

When Lawrence promoters organized a town company for a settlement in Coffey County, they printed an exceptionally attractive lithograph for advertising. It was "one of the prettiest pictures I saw when I came to Kansas," said Orson Kent of Burlington. The town was named Oread. Although it had a log house, it was in reality only a paper town. Some said, "The company made money and the shareholders gained wisdom."[28]

As for the town around Mount Oread, it had several names from which to choose. Excelsior would have have been a meaningful name, and it was used.[29] The first New England immigrants had camped on the Wakarusa, and when they pitched their tents at Mount Oread, "they named the new settlement Wakarusa."[30] Although temporarily known as Mount Oread, New Boston, and as Excelsior, the proslavery element dubbed it "Yankee Town." The city of Worcester, site of Eli Thayer's seminary, offered a library to the Kansas town on condition that it be named Worcester.[31] The frontiersman could easily have spoken of "Wooster" even though its spelling, with an extra syllable, could confuse him.

"Regularly christened" on September 6, 1854, the town was given the name of "Lawrence City" to honor Amos A. Lawrence of Boston, the financial angel of the Emigrant Aid Society.[32] According to the report of the meeting, the name was chosen to honor Lawrence, "both as an individual and officer of the company, and second, because the name sounded well, and he had no bad odor attached to it in any part of the Union."[33] In a letter to Lawrence, Charles Robinson said: "I think I was the first to suggest your name for the city, though I have never urged it at all, as I wished every person to be satisfied in his mind ...."[34] Thus spoke the politician. Incidentally, Mrs. Robinson, whose maiden name was Sara Tappan Doolittle Lawrence, was a relative of Amos Lawrence. Rev. Samuel Y. Lum expressed similar sentiments, saying that the name was not only an honor but that it was also "harmonious to the ear." The town was named Lawrence, he said, "without the hope or expectation of remuneration." But the Lawrence philanthropy continued. Not only did he support a college to be named the "Free State College," now the University of Kansas, but he also bought a fur coat for Robinson. This "Santa Claus," as he was called, deserved the distinction of having a town named in his honor.[35]

Among the Massachusetts names were Andover and Haverhill. Andover in Kansas, on the Sedgwick-Butler County line, had been known as Minneha. The name became well-known when "the Andover Band," four students from the seminary in Andover, came to Kansas to preach, pray, and promote freedom. Kansas got its Andover and Haverhill from Massachusetts, but the names came originally from England.[36] Andover was said to have been named for the river Anton or Ann. As Andovre, it could mean "Anna's Ford."[37] In England, Haverhill is located near Cambridge. It means "hill where oats were grown," or "hill above the haven or harbor."[38] It is not pronounced Hay'vrill in Kansas.

Amherst and Holyoke, two college towns, had their names adopted in Kansas. Amherst, Massachusetts, was named for Lord Jeffrey Amherst, a British officer who helped to conquer the French in Canada and served as colonial governor of Virginia. The name was adopted in Russell County, Kansas, in 1888.

The English source of Holyoke was "Holyoak, Hollyoake, Hollyhock." Behind these names may be the "holy oak" or the "gospel oak" of the Druids.[39] The Holyoke in Massachusetts was, however, named for Edward Holyoke, president of Harvard.[40] In Kansas, Holyoke was a post office in Ellsworth County. At that time, it was the only Holyoke outside of Massachusetts, its logical source.

Chicopee and Merrimac were Indian names for two turbulent streams that served as the source for water power in Massachusetts. Both names have been interpreted to mean "a place of strong current." In Kansas, Chicopee is a quiet town near the Missouri border in Crawford County. When a railroad was built into Marble Falls in Marshall County, a man by the name of Gunn established the town of Merrimac.[41] It survived only six years.

Beverly has been used freely as a boy's name and a girl's name. Kansas had a Beverly in Sedgwick County. Later, a place named Colorado in Mitchell County became Beverly. In Massachusetts, Beverly had been known as "Mackerel Cove on Bass River." This Beverly is said to be the source for the Beverly in Kansas.[42] Its Massachusetts source was England, where Beverly referred to an abundance of beaver.[43]

The name of Arlington came to Virginia when Charles I gave the Earl of Arlington a colonial grant. The town of Arlington and the Arlington National Cemetery are across the Potomac from Washington, D.C. The land was once owned by George Washington and later by Robert E. Lee. In Massachusetts, Arlington is only a few miles from Boston on the route followed by Paul Revere. The Revolutionary War battle of Arlington Heights occurred there. The Arlington in Kansas is only one of twenty-nine in America. The first one in Osborne County had its name changed to Tilden, probably because of political considerations. The Arlington in Reno County was named for the "famous Arlington Heights" in Massachusetts.[44]

Massachusetts also supplied the names of such distinguished politicians as Webster, Sumner, Burlingame, and the less well-known Rantoul and Gardner. Daniel Webster is associated with both New Hampshire, where he was born, and Massachusetts, the state he served so well in the Senate.[45]

The best known of the places named Providence is the one in Rhode Island. This was where Roger Williams took refuge among the Narragansett Indians. He said he named it Providence "because of God's merciful providence . . . ."[46] The naming of Providence in Butler County, Kansas, is more likely for Providence, Rhode Island, than any divine providence, although the latter is possible.

The Haskells and the Sages, first settlers of the town named Dover in Dover Township near Topeka, claim different Dovers as the source of the name. "The Haskells say it was named for Dover, New Hampshire, while the Sages say it was named after Dover, England."[47] The Sage family, said one report, "named the town they helped to build after their dear home in England, Dover, with the sea beating against its chalk cliffs."[48] Jacob Haskell had been called the "godfather" of Dover

255

and he should have had a voice in the choice of a name. But since Sage was its first postmaster, he, too, could claim a special advantage in its naming. Of the five Dovers in New England and over a dozen in the United States, the one in New Hampshire might well share honors with the one in England.[49]

The name of Dover came from Dubris, Dofra, or Dour, and refers to "water" or "stream." In the public mind, however, the name presents an image of "the white cliffs of Dover." As one of the "Cinque Ports" about which Longfellow wrote a poem, it played a dramatic part in the defense of England from its early history to the time when Hitler found this "Gateway to England" closed.

When Newell Colby came to Kansas from Meriden, New Hampshire, he named the town of Meriden in Jefferson County. In old England, the word was originally *myrgendenu*, meaning "pleasant valley." The "pleasant" in Meriden was used in the older sense of being "merry," and this could be pleasant.[50]

Bennington is the name of a town in New Hampshire and a town and county in Vermont. The source for the name was Benning Whitworth, the governor of New Hampshire who promoted the colonization of Vermont.[51] The Battle of Bennington, where General Burgoyne was defeated by General John Stark in 1777, was the turning point in favor of the rebellious colonies. The flag used there was "said to be the oldest 'stars and stripes' in existence." Bennington was also the home of Ethan Allen and of William Lloyd Garrison. The name had distinction, and Bennington in Ottawa County, Kansas, was named for the historically famous Bennington in Vermont.[52]

O. E. Learnard, the "father of Burlington," named it for his home town in Vermont. Burlington on the west side of the Neosho was a deadly rival of Hampden on the east side. Hampden was promoted by settlers from Massachusetts and named for Hampden County in their home state. Burlington "set out to kill" Hampden and succeeded.[53] The name of Hampden Township remains as a reminder of its Massachusetts origin. Settlers from Burlington later crossed the Kansas border and built a town in Colorado which they named Burlington for their Kansas town.

C. C. Hutchinson, who promoted the town of Hutchinson, also laid out the town of Castleton, located south of Hutchinson in Reno County. Having used his own name for his first town, he named the next one for Castleton, Vermont. According to a county history, the town was named to "honor the home of the lady whom C. C. Hutchinson expected to wed, he being a widower . . . ."[54]

Lawrence D. Bailey, judge of the State Supreme Court, was the founder of Lynden in Osage County.[55] It was named for Lynden in Vermont, which in turn had been named for Josiah Lynden, the son of an early landholder.[56]

The story of the origin of the name Haddam is perhaps best told in the words of Senator Morrow: "A party of travelers from one of the Eastern States stopped at a small house where this town now stands. During the evening while all surrounded this settler's hospitable table, one of the travelers noticed a number of . . . 'gray-backs,' scaling the walls of the cabin. He asked the lady of the house if they were not infested with 'gray-backs.' Her reply was: 'Oh No! Not now, but we all had-dem.' " Charles Yoder, who gave this report, closed his letter with a word of caution: "Now I do not vouch for the Senator's statement; however, he can usually be relied on."[57]

Leaving folklore, we have the account of John Ferguson who came from Haddam, Connecticut, and who lived for a short time on Mill Creek before the Indians frightened him away. "I am going back to Kansas," he said, "as soon as those Indians is drove out and its safe to stay there. . . . we had suceeded in geting a post office established within one mile of my house and I suckseeded in getting it named *Haddam*."[58] A local newspaper said, however, that it was named by J. W. Tabor of Haddam, Connecticut.[59] Haddam had first been named Knowles, but in 1885 the town became Haddam City.[60] For a time there were two Haddams, and West Haddam contained the post office until it was moved back to Haddam on the railway.

In England, Hartford's history dates back to Roman times. Both Queen Elizabeth and Queen Mary made it a royal residence. It was there that Prince Henry Plantagenet married Isabel of Castile. Hartford castle was built at the "Fort of the Harts," where the hart or deer had a river crossing.[61] In Lyon County, Kansas, the town of Hartford was settled by Harvey D. Rice and A. K. Hawkes, who named it for their home, Hartford, Connecticut. In Kansas, the town was laid out in the form of an H to conform to the initial of its name.[62] Bridgeport in Saline County was named by Connecticut settlers for Bridgeport, Connecticut.[63]

Wabaunsee's ambition was, according to one pioneer, to become a great city and "the New Haven of the West." Williams, the promoter, declared that "when any of the boys died, if they had been good, they would go to New Haven, Connecticut."[64] But the name New Haven was no guarantee of success. The one in Reno County lasted a decade. Another town in the same county was named just Haven. Originally haven referred to a shelter, especially in connection with a sheltered harbor which gave meaning to a name like Le Havre, the name of a sheltered port in France.

Kennebac in Russell County has an Indian name which came from the Kennebec River in Maine. The name was said to mean "long lake," or, more likely, "long reach," referring to its lower course.[65]

Although Welsh in origin, it is possible that Bangor, Maine, was the source for naming Bangor in Kansas. But Bangor in Coffey County was changed to Gridley for Walter Gridley, a town promoter.

In most cases, the New England names in Kansas were from old England, and their use in Kansas was a good example of the westward migration of names as they followed the frontier. A name acquired new significance each time it moved.

CHAPTER XXV

NEW YORK, NEW JERSEY, AND NEIGHBORS

IF THE NAMES of New England towns were used as place-names in Kansas because of their historic prestige, so were those of towns in New York and neighboring states. When Daniel Webster spoke at the Bunker Hill dedication in 1825, which was attended by Lafayette and other veterans of the American Revolution, he said, "Veterans!! . . . you bring with you marks of honor from Trenton and Monmouth, from Yorktown, Camden, Bennington, and Saratoga."[1] All of those names were later adopted as place-names in Kansas, as were Bunker Hill, the place of the dedication; Webster, the name of the speaker; and Lafayette, the name of the guest of honor.

A colorful list of names traveled halfway across the continent from New York to Kansas. Some were prestigious names from the Old World: Greek and Roman names, German names, and names from England and France. From New York, Kansas adopted the name of Syracuse, a classical Greek name from Sicily. Homer, Virgil, and Cicero are also reminiscent of the classical period. Geneva, a French name from Switzerland; Dunkirk, an English name from France; Selkirk, another "kirk" from Scotland; New Lancaster of Old English vintage; Glenloch, with a Scotch flavor; Herkimer, a name of German origin; and Brooklyn, a Dutch name, were all Kansas names from New York. Personal names such as Corning and Courtland and the college name of Vassar were also transplanted New York names.

Most conspicuous among the names that came to Kansas from New York are Indian names. New York was Iroquois country, and its map is filled with Iroquois names. These strange and seemingly unspellable and unpronounceable names have become simplified and made familiar by use. Along the coast of Lake Ontario are contiguous counties with Iroquois names: Oswego, Oneida, Cayuga, Seneca, Onondaga, Chenango, Tioga, Chemung, and Otsego. Farther west are Genesee and Niagara, Erie, Wyoming, and Chautauqua; and farther east is Saratoga. All of these have become Kansas place-names, but not all came directly from New York. Names such as Tioga and Towanda could have come from either New York or Pennsylvania, and others came from Ohio

259

and Illinois. Manhattan, no doubt, is the best-known New York name in Kansas.

Several pioneers and promoters found the junction of the Blue and the Kaw to be an attractive place for a townsite. Towns were begun on both sides of the river, and each had its own distinctive name. But these were given and lost in rapid succession as new sites replaced old. The first towns were known by such diverse names as Dyer's Town, for a pioneer who ran a ferry across the Blue; Juniata, an Indian name for the Blue Juniata in Pennsylvania; Tauromee, for a popular Wyandotte chief also known as "Hat John;" Parkville, for a town promoter who changed its name to Poliska with a Polish association; Pittsburg, with its Pennsylvania background; and Canton, a small town with an Oriental name from Ohio.

Professor Isaac T. Goodnow came to Kansas to select a site for a colony from New England. From the top of Blue Mount Hill, he looked at what he declared to be "the most beautiful townsite he had ever seen."[2] There he founded a town which was to be named Boston. Then came colonists from Ohio destined for the junction of the Republican and Kaw rivers. Their journey ended near Manhattan when their steamer stuck on a sandbar, and they decided to join the New Englanders at the junction of the Blue. The New Englanders wished to name the community Boston or New Boston; the Ohio settlers wanted Cincinnati or New Cincinnati. Andrew J. Mead, head of the Ohio colony, came from New York. He ended the bickering by suggesting the name of Manhattan.[3] Manhattan is an Algonquian Indian name, but no one seems to know its exact meaning. It has been said that the name originated when a person saw an Indian woman with a "man's hat on." Washington Irving dismissed this as "a stupid joke."[4]

When Henry Hudson was host to the natives on Manhattan Island, the natives imbibed too freely of Hudson's liquor.[5] From this incident, some have concluded that the Indians were named Manachaeteneid, which supposedly meant "drunk." The Indian name has many variations and as many meanings. Perhaps it meant "wolf" or "place of dangerous currents," referring to Hell Gate on the Hudson. More likely, it meant "island hill" or "island village."[6] There may be those who think of Manhattan only as a cocktail, but in Kansas it brings to mind a college town.

Tioga is an Iroquois name popular in Pennsylvania and New York. From the Tioga Valley in New York came Israel Stoddard, who settled in Neosho County, Kansas. He is evidently the one who named Tioga Township, from which the town of Tioga took its name.[7] In its rivalry with its neighbors, it won the railways but lost its name to

Chanute, as did the towns of New Chicago and Alliance. The Tioga name would have been most appropriate at this railway junction, since it means "at the crossing" or "junction."[8]

Chemung was for a short time the name of a place in Franklin County, Kansas. The most likely source for the name seems to be either an Iroquois village, the Chemung River, or Chemung County in New York. Its meaning is uncertain, but one authority suggested that it meant "a log in the water." Others thought this log was a petrified bone or possibly a tusk.[9]

Niagara in Kansas was far removed in every way from the Niagara in New York. It was located in the sand hills southwest of Hugoton in Stevens County, where honeymooners would not be distracted by a waterfall nor disturbed by people. This Iroquois name was spelled Ongniaahra by the French, and it was said to mean "a point of land cut in two," or "bisected bottomland." One name for the Falls was Ongiara cataracts.[10]

When a county seat conflict split Howard County, its southern half acquired the exotic name of Chautauqua. Edward Jaquins, who came from Chautauqua County, New York, proposed the name. Tom E. Thompson thought there would be mighty few people in the county who could either spell or pronounce the name; nor could Jaquins, he opined, had he not come from New York. The Chautauqua circuit had not yet made the name popular when it was adopted for a Kansas county.[11] A town in Chautauqua County was named Chautauqua Springs. When the appeal of the springs as a cure-all declined, the name was shortened to Chautauqua.[12] This Iroquois name with the French spelling had several interpretations. It might refer to a place "where a fish was taken out," or the "place where one was lost," or possibly "bag tied in the middle." The last one was said to be a description of the shape of the lake. Among the French forms for the name was Chadakoin. When it was written "Chatakwa," phonetically French, it was in simple English form.[13]

The Onondagas, who built a long house as a meeting place for the Five Nations, were called Hodenosaunee, "people of the long house."[14] The French spelling of Onontage was easily converted into Onondaga, as the Americans wrote it. When New Yorkers from Onondaga County came to western Kansas, they named their town Syracuse after their New York county seat, but they did not succeed in changing the name of the county from Hamilton to Onondaga.[15] A railway station in Linn County was named Onondaga, however.

Otego in New York is located in a county named Otsego. James Fenimore Cooper lived on the shores of Lake Otsego which he called

"Glimmerglass." In Kansas, the first Otego was in Harper County;[16] the second one is a Rock Island station in Jewell County. The name could be an abbreviation of Otsinoghiyta, the name of an Onondaga chief who signed the Fort Stanwix Treaty of 1768.[17] If Otego is a variation of Otsego, then it could mean "place where meetings are held."[18] Only New York and Kansas have places named Otego.

Oneonta is the county seat of Otsego County in New York. In Kansas it is a place in Cloud County. The name is similar to Oneniote, one of the names from which came Oneida, referring to a large rock standing in the village.[19] It is an Iroquois name but it has been associated with an upper Mississippi culture. The name may have derived from *oneote*, the Mohawk word for "maize," or *onea*, the word for "stone."[20]

Chief White Hair's village in Labette County had been called Naniompa by the Osage, and this meant "the village of the pipe."[21] Chief White Hair was given his name while fighting General St. Clair in the War of 1812. Reaching for a scalp-lock, he found that he had a white wig in his hand. He put the wig on his own head and was then called Paw-Hiu-Skah, "White Hair," a name since simplified to Pahuska, now a well-known place-name in Oklahoma. Chief White Hair's Kansas village was popularly known as Little Town, but when New Yorkers arrived, they changed its name to Oswego.[22] In New York it was said to mean "where the stream widens," which could be its "inlet," but it was also said to mean "flowing out."[23]

Cayuga came a long way to become a place-name in Atchison County, Kansas.[24] If it came from Kwenio-gwen, as suggested, it was said to mean "where the locusts were taken out."[25] It was strange coincidence that Cayuga in Kansas was established in Grasshopper Township where the locusts were not yet "taken out." But New Yorkers may not have been aware of the locust interpretation. There were other possible sources for Cayuga, including Kwe-u-kwe, "where they draw their boats," and Go-yo-goh, which was said to mean "mountain rising from the water."[26]

Famous in history and popular as a resort was Saratoga in New York. It is probably a Mohawk name, and a fitting translation would be "hillside springs."[27] The name came to Kansas from New York and was first used in Kansas by the Saratoga Springs Town Company near Bonner Springs. Then it became the name of a town located east of Pratt near the present fish hatchery. It was begun as a sheep ranch, but as a town it had ambitions to become the county seat, a prize both Iuka and Saratoga later lost to Pratt Center. Saratoga was occasionally called "Togy," and its residents were "Togytes," rivals of the "Ukites" of

Ukia.[28] The people drifted to Pratt, and Saratoga slowly died, leaving its name on a township.

Schoharie, once a county seat candidate of Ness County, was named by a postmaster from Schoharie, New York. It came from an Indian word meaning "driftwood."[29] Schoharie County, New York, may also have been the source for Sharon Springs, a New York settlement in western Kansas.

In addition to the biblical name of Sharon for Sharon Springs, there were several classical names in Kansas which are said to have come from New York. These include Virgil in Greenwood County, Homer in Russell County, and Utica in Ness County.

Among the conspicuous and distinguished names of ancient history is that of Syracuse. The Syracuse in New York is located in a beautiful amphitheater of hills. In Kansas, the first town to be named Syracuse was in Doniphan County, and only a schoolhouse preserved the name.[30] The second Syracuse was a town promoted near West Mound in Wilson County. Since Daniel C. Finn, one of the promoters, was from Syracuse, New York, the place was named in honor of his home town. It has been called a "mythical" place, but it did have "a lone" log cabin.[31] The Syracuse that survived was the one established in Hamilton County and named by settlers from New York.

When a New York colony entered Kansas from the north to avoid the Missouri blockade against free-state immigrants, it stopped in Nemaha County. There, in 1858, it established the town of Albany, named for New York's state capital. When the railroad by-passed Albany for Sabetha, Albany's residents moved to the town on the railway. Only Albany school on Albany Hill remains at the site.[32]

William Osborne, it was said, "lived and died" in Waterville, New York, but he made frequent visits to Atchison, Kansas, where he owned the William Osborne Ferry. He also built the Central Branch Railroad from Atchison to Waterville, named for his New York home. To avoid duplication, the Waterville in Riley County changed its name to Randolph, honoring its first postmaster, Gardner Randolph.[33]

John W. Brown bought a tract of land on the headwaters of the Wakarusa which he described as "the garden of Eden." There he started the town of Brownsville, and so it was called even after new settlers "christened it Auburn" in 1856.[34] It lost the county seat contest to Topeka, a defeat attributed to "a five dollar bill and a jug of whiskey ...."[35] But Auburn and Auburn Township are still on the map.

Oliver Goldsmith popularized the Auburn name in his *Deserted Village*, in which he refers to "Sweet Auburn, loveliest village of the plain." The name came from "eel-burn" or "eel-stream."[36] It was deserted because of the encroachment of the sea. There are three Auburns in New England, one each in New York, Pennsylvania, Iowa, and Missouri, six in the south, and one in each of the states of the Old Northwest. New York got the name directly from the *Deserted Village*, and the Auburn in Kansas is believed to have come from New York.[37] The New York town had been called "Hardenburgh Corners," a difficult name to transfer.

Johnson County once had a Mount Auburn, but according to the *Laws of Kansas*, "the village of Mount Auburn, Conboy, Miller and Goble's addition to Aubrey" was renamed Stilwell. There were several politically prominent pioneers in Kansas named Stillwell, any one of whom could have been the source for the new name.[38]

Medway, the name of a river in England, has become the name of a railway station in Hamilton County, Kansas. There could be a tie between the New York settlers in western Kansas and Medway, New York. Its English origin would indicate the second syllable as having come from *wey* or *wye*, referring to water, so the name could mean the "river with sweet water," possibly from mead, a honey drink.[39]

The first name for Courtland Township in Republic County was Soldier because of the large number of veterans who settled there. Then the name became Courtland, "without apparent good reason," said a county historian. The town of Courtland was also to be named Soldier, but with an eye to the future, residents named it Prospect. Its future was bleak until it moved a mile to the track. Then it took the township name of Courtland.[40] The New York community had been named for Pierre Van Cortlandt, or Cordtland, lieutenant governor and aristocrat of the old school.[41] Also from New York came the name of Corning. The town in Nemaha County was named for Erastus Corning, the railroad magnate.[42]

Vassar is a station on the Missouri Pacific in Osage County. When Matthew Vassar, brewer and philanthropist, endowed a "female" college at Poughkeepsie, New York, it was named for him. In Kansas, Vassar replaced the name of La Mont's Hill.

Fredonia, a coined name based on the word freedom, was once suggested as a name for the United States. The name has been used for many towns and for an ephemeral Texas republic.[43] Arthur Heath suggested the New York name of Fredonia for Kansas. A heated argument followed, but Fredonia won and freedom prevailed.[44]

Brooklyn, the name of the colorful Long Island suburb of New York City, is a Dutch name which was spelled Brucklyn and Breukelyn. It was Americanized and spelled Brooklyn, Brooklin, and Brookline.[45] The cultural character of Brookline, a suburb of Boston, is, however, quite different from the "Boilermaker" town of Brooklyn.[46] When Orville C. Brown of Brooklyn, New York, proposed that name for his town of Brownsville, Baptiste Peoria objected, and the town was given the Indian name of Osawatomie.[47] Linn County had a Brooklyn started by E. O. Brooks.[48] The settlers spoke of "Brooklyn Hill" nearby. Barton County also had its Brooklyn.

Although located in France, Dunkirk is an English name. From Dunkirk in New York came the pioneers who named Dunkirk in Crawford County, Kansas. And Geneva, a French name from Switzerland, also came from New York.[49]

Identification merely by association may lead one into error. When a woman was asked the whereabouts of her son, she said she thought he was in China, since his latest letter was postmarked Sing Sing. Unfortunately for the woman, Sing Sing is famous for its prison in New York, but, happily, she did not know it. Sing Sing in Kansas had no post office and probably no prison. It is listed only among the ghost towns of Sumner County.[50] Its source was Seneca or John Sing Sing, the name of an Indian.

A New York Colony came to Jewell County and established a community center called Excelsior on White Rock Creek.[51] The name was taken from the motto on the coat of arms for New York, the Excelsior State. A post office in Mitchell County was named Excelsior in 1874. Rivals of the Lawrence Town Company also promoted a town to be named Excelsior, but they abandoned it for one hundred shares in the Lawrence Company.[52]

Delaware may be a very small state, but it looms large in business and politics. When Senator Ingalls of Kansas was irked by a senator from Delaware, he ridiculed him as being from the state that had three counties at high tide and five at low tide. But the name of Delaware, with its origin as a personal name, then a place-name, and eventually a name for an Indian tribe, came to Kansas when the tribal name was restored as a place-name.[53]

When Thomas West became governor of Virginia, he was given the title of Lord de la Ware or Warr. His name was the source for naming the Delaware River. The Lenape Indians who lived on the Delaware were consequently called Delawares. Settlers in eastern Kansas had trouble with the French name of Soutrelle which was the French translation of the Indian name for grasshopper. To avoid the use of the French name, Kansans translated it into English, which annoyingly advertised the obnoxious grasshoppers. What a relief it was from the stigma of the names Grasshopper River and Grasshopper Falls when the state legislature changed these names to Delaware River and Valley

Falls. Delaware was also the name of a town which became Secondine, named for a Delaware chief, and for the town of Delaware City in Leavenworth County.[54]

New Jersey was named to honor George Carteret who was born on the Isle of Jersey which he later governed. In the Kansas City area, Jersey Creek was named in 1843 by William Walker, a Wyandot chief and one of the promoters of the first Kansas historical and philosophical society.[55] Trenton, Somerset, Newark, Amboy, Camden, and Passaic are familiar New Jersey names, and all of these names have been on the Kansas map.

Trenton, New Jersey, was named for a politically prominent Philadelphia promoter by the name of Colonel William Trent. He crossed the Delaware and sold lots at a place which became known as Trent's Town.[56] As Trenton, it became historically important when Washington crossed the Delaware, unwisely standing up in a boat, according to a popular painting. He defeated the Hessians whose Christmas revelries at Trenton had left them happy, heedless, and helpless. The first Trenton in Kansas was established in Miami County; a second, in Labette County; a third, in Kingman County; and then, the one that survived replaced the name of Nasby in Saline County.

Somerset, a name of Nordic origin in England, was the name given to a town in Miami County which had been settled by pioneers from New Jersey.[57] In New Jersey, Somerset was the name of a county. The Welsh interpretation of Somerset being "land of summer" is reasonable. Somerset could have been derived from *somer satre* in Norway, where the dairy maids cared for the cattle in the upper grasslands during the *somer* and lived in *setre*.

Perth Amboy in New Jersey is a combination of a Scottish and Indian name. The name Amboy migrated westward to California, where it was used for one of a series of towns to be named in alphabetical order, i.e., Amboy, Bristol, Cadiz, etc.[58] It also became the name of a post office in Rooks County, Kansas. This Indian name came from *embolink* and *emboli* to become Amboy, interpreted to mean "hollow inside" or "like a bowl."[59]

Passaic, best known for its New Jersey association, seems to be the source of the Passaic post office name in Kearny County. It was originally Passajeck, an Algonquian name, interpreted to mean "valley."[60]

Newark in New Jersey was a name taken from England. In Kansas, Newark was for a time a post office in Newark Township.

Camden in New Jersey and Camden in North Carolina were named for the Earl of Camden, who had denounced "taxation without representation" as "sheer snobbery." A dozen states had places named Camden before the Kansas town of Skiddy had its unique name changed to Camden by New Jersey settlers. The residents soon restored the original name.[61]

Pennsylvania names in Kansas are as varied as those from New York. Especially conspicuous were the names that came from the coal regions of Pennsylvania to the coal regions of Kansas. Among these were Pittsburg, Carbondale, Scranton, and Altoona. Also prominent were such Indian names as Juniata, Erie, Wyoming, and Lehigh.

Juniata on the Blue in Kansas was named for the Blue Juniata in Pennsylvania, about which Mrs. Marion Dix Sullivan had written an "enormously popular ditty."[62] It was a Delaware name which has been interpreted to mean "it is long since they were here" or "they stay long." Hewett suggested, however, that the name came from *tyu nan yate*, the Seneca word for "standing stone."[63] The name crossed to the west side of the Blue to become the name of the Juniata Ranch owned by Don D. Casement. His own name was given to the Casement station. The name was next seen as a post office in Lane County in the eighties, but it did not survive beyond that turbulent decade. Again it was revived, and now remains as the name of a station between Salina and Lincoln Center.

When a trading post was established on the shore of a small lake, the lake was jokingly called "Lake Erie." The Erie post was promoted by J. L. Denison of Pennsylvania, which would justify the opinion that it was named for Erie in that state. There was both an Old and New Erie in Neosho County, but Old Erie suffered political defeat, a devastating fire, and final destruction by a tornado.[64] A town in Sedgwick County was temporarily named Erie, and Erie Township retains the name.

Erie is only a part of the full Iroquois name which was spelled Erie-rhonon, with variations. *Erie* meant "cat" and *rhonon* meant "people." The French translated this as La Nation du Chat, "the cat nation." The assumption that it was a bob-tail cat does not agree with the interpretation that it was a long-tailed cat. The latter would identify it with the panther or cougar.[65] Lake Erie was popularly known as the "lake of the cat."

Wyoming is the popular name of ten towns, three counties, and a state. The name came from the Wyoming Valley in Pennsylvania and its Delaware name meant "great plains," or something similar, such as "at the big flats," referring to a wide valley near Wilkes-Barre in eastern Pennsylvania. The Wyoming Massacre in 1778 called attention to the name, but it was most likely Campbell's poem called "Gertrude of Wyoming" which made it familiar.[66]

The first Wyoming in Kansas was shown on a map of 1856 as being northeast of Topeka on Odgen Creek.[67] Then a post office in Clay County was named Wyoming Valley, but later renamed Lima. Wyoming in Marshall County remained a post office into the twentieth century.

Lehigh is in the wheat country of Marion County, but it is only one of the five Pennsylvania coal towns which gave their names to Kansas. Three of them are in the Kansas coal country: Carbondale, Pittsburg, and Scranton. Altoona, also a coal town, is in Wilson County. Pennsylvania has five Carbons and two Carbondales, and it is famous for its Lehigh coal. Lehigh, Kansas, may have been founded by Alden Spear of Boston,[68] but it was most likely settled by Pennsylvanians who chose to give it the "beautiful name of Lehigh."[69] The name was the English version of Lechauwekink, a Delaware name meaning at "the fork of the river."[70] It was shortened to Lechau, which later became Lehigh.

The town of Scranton in Osage County, Kansas, was promoted by the Burlington and Scranton Coal Company and named for Scranton, Pennsylvania,[71] which in turn had been named for Joseph H. Scranton, who built the town and developed the coal business at the Lackawanna Iron Works.[72] In Pennsylvania, the town had a remarkably colorful list of names before it settled for Scranton:

> As an Indian village it was called Capouse. White settlers renamed it Unionville, but local people called it Deep Hollow, sometimes Skunk's Misery. Then it became Slocum Hollow, later Harrison, still later Lackawanna Iron Works, then Scrantonia, and finally the present-day Scranton.[73]

Carbondale in Osage County is also a coal town. In Pennsylvania, Carbondale is located northeast of Scranton, and in Kansas the two towns have relatively similar locations. One might reasonably conclude that Carbondale, like Scranton, was adopted from Pennsylvania, as were Pittsburg and Altoona.

Altoona is a town west of Pittsburg in Wilson County. It had been named Geddesburg, which sounds as if it should have been Gettysburg, pronounced by a person with a bad cold. But Geddesburg it was, and named for John Geddes, one of the town founders. Two Pennsylvanians, Isaac and John Spencer, named it Altoona for their home town. The name seemingly came from the Latin word *altus*, meaning "high."[74]

When George Washington defeated the French at Fort Duquesne and renamed the place "Pitt's-Bourgh"[75] to honor William Pitt, he not only commemorated a British victory over the French but also chose a name which became so popular that it swept across the country all the way to Pittsburg, California. Six times the name was given to Kansas towns; some died, one was never born, others changed their names, and one survived. A Pittsburg was started in Doniphan County, "but the name came to naught." The one proposed for Linn County was only a "paper town." Near Juniata on the Blue, J. W. Garrett promoted a Pittsburg to compete with Manhattan across the river. "Beyond the three houses which compose the town of Pittsburg," said one traveler, "we crossed the Big Blue and reached Manhattan—a flourishing Yankee settlement."[76] In Wilson County, another Pittsburg started with some promise in 1869, but it soon faded away.[77] These may all have been named for the one in Pennsylvania, but Pittsburg in Mitchell County was named for W. A. Pitt, treasurer of the local town company.[78]

A railway town between Joplin and Girard was named Pittsburg because it was in the center of rich coalfields, as was the Pittsburgh in Pennsylvania.[79] Since there already was a Pittsburg in Kansas, this one was named New Pittsburg. When the one in Mitchell County, by request, changed its name to Tipton, New Pittsburg became Pittsburg. Pittsburg Township in Mitchell County changed its name to Pittsburgh.[80] The United States Board of Geographic Names tried but failed to make the Pennsylvania city delete its useless "h," but in Kansas the "h" letter was omitted without federal interference.

The "burg" was deleted from Bloomsburg to become Bloom in Ford County. It was named for Bloomsburg, Pennsylvania.[81]

Overbrook in Osage County is on a ridge separating the waters of the Wakarusa and the Marais des Cygnes. It may, like its neighboring towns of Scranton and Carbondale, have come from Pennsylvania, where both Pittsburgh and Philadelphia have suburbs named Overbrook.

Easton, near Leavenworth, was at first named "Eastin" to honor Lucian J. Eastin, its founder, a proslavery man who was also one of the promoters of the town of Buchanan.[82] He was elected to the first Legislative Council but with questionable legality.[83] Within a year, the name became Easton, the name of Governor Reeder's home town in Pennsylvania.[84]

Near Pittsburg, Kansas, is the town named Girard. Stephen Girard was an ambitious and frugal merchant and shipowner who came from France to Philadelphia to seek his fortune. He was eminently successful and had the reputation of being the richest man in America. Girard, Pennsylvania, was named for him as was Girard College which he established. Girard, Kansas, was named by C. H. Strong, of Girard, Pennsylvania.[85] The tie between the two Girards has been revived as seen in the *Wichita Eagle and Beacon* headline: "Mayor of Girard to Visit Girard."[86]

In Greenwood County, a town named Philadelphia came within

four votes of becoming the county seat. When it failed, Kansas lost her chance of honoring the name of the "city of brotherly love."[87]

Pennsylvania had enough colonial history to have chosen numerous place-names from England. A few of these English names, such as Lancaster, Reading, and Westmoreland, moved on to Kansas. The Roman fort called Lone Caster or Long Caster became Lanchester, and, by the time it came to America, it was Lancaster. Lancaster in Atchison County was named by B. F. Stoner for his home town in Pennsylvania.[88] According to George Remsburg, however, it was named for Lancaster, Pennsylvania, by John W. Smith, said to be its first postmaster.[89] In both states, Lancaster was located in land of scenic beauty but far removed from the Lancaster of England.[90] New Lancaster in Miami County was named by Joseph Carpenter for New Lancaster in New York.[91]

John McMann, also written McManus, head of the Reading Iron Works of Pennsylvania, is said to have made the largest purchase of land "ever made in Kansas on individual account." When the Secretary of the Interior sold the lands of the Sac and Fox Indians in 1864, McMann bought whole townships, and some of these he resold to John Wetherell, a wealthy Quaker from Philadelphia. When Wetherell's wife received a letter telling of his purchase, she wrote in return: "John come home. Thou art going crazy."[92] However, James Fagan, a railroad man, was so impressed by McMann's land speculation that he gave the name of Reading to a station near Emporia to honor McMann's home town in Pennsylvania.[93] In England, Reading was said to have been "spelled in a hundred different ways."[94]

Westmoreland, the name of a county in England where the West Moringas lived, is also the name of a county in Pennsylvania and the seat of Pottawatomie County, Kansas. The one in Kansas was named by John McKimmas, also spelled McKimens, postmaster, for Westmoreland County in Pennsylvania where he had lived.[95]

Four places were named Tyrone in Pennsylvania alone, and one of these, the home town of a man named Watson, was the source for the name of Tyrone in Kansas.[96] Tyrone was a cattle terminal on the Oklahoma border in Seward County. With the coming of the railroad, the town moved across the border to become a railway station. Its remnant in Kansas was for a time known as "Old Tyrone." Donegal and Tyrone, both names from Ireland, came to Kansas from Pennsylvania.

Pennsylvania was known as the Keystone State. Dickinson County had a Keystone which survived a decade, and then, in 1889, became Manchester. Unaware of its Pennsylvania origin, some wrote the name "Key Stone." A post office in Logan County by the name of Elkader had its name changed to Keystone in 1912. Five years later it was changed to Ben Allen, a name which lasted until 1925, and then its first name of Elkader was restored. For a time the place was so small that it had only one building on each side of the "street," both labeled "Post Office."[97] This would be convenient for two-way traffic, but traffic is not a problem at Elkader. Lippincott (1853) listed no such name in the United States, but it did list an El Kader as a town in Iowa. Keystone Township in Scott County saved the name of Keystone in Kansas.

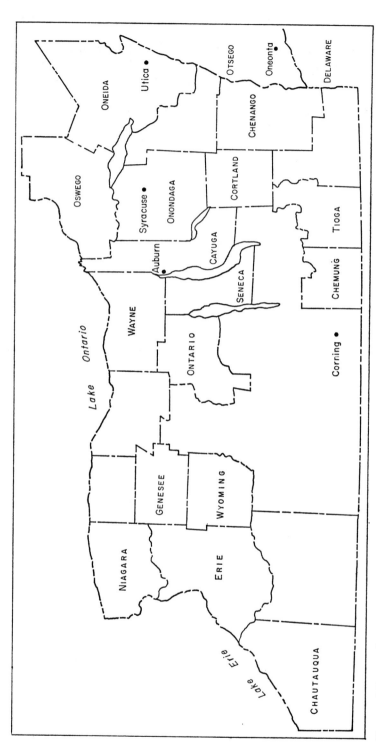

Kansas Names from New York

CHAPTER XXVI

NAMES FROM THE OLD NORTHWEST

AS AMERICANS MIGRATED WESTWARD so did the names of the states and towns from which they came. Kansas received more settlers and more names from the Old Northwest than from any other area in the states. Without detracting from the importance of the contributions from New England, one may still recognize the greater contribution, especially in people, from the Old Northwest, with Illinois and Ohio contributing the most. A sentimental tie with the town from which the settlers came is well expressed in verse:

> But after all is said and done,
> There is not another, there is only one.
> Whether I'm up or whether I'm down,
> All roads lead back to "My Home Town!"[1]

Kansas had more settlers from Ohio than from any other state in 1860.[2] With these settlers came Ohio names and Buckeye influence. The Ohio names came from a great variety of sources and languages; they came from Greece, Rome, Persia, Arabia, and China, and naturally from the native Indians and from England. Delphos, Akron, Kalida, and Xenia have a Greek origin. Cincinnati and Milan have an Italian origin, as does Ravanna, which should have been Ravenna. Columbus, too, is Italian, but we associate him with Spain, and Toledo is Spanish. Clyde came from Scotland and Cheshire came from England. Morris, Chase, Garfield, and Allen counties were named for Ohio politicians. Piqua, Huron, Chillicothe, Seneca, and Ashtabula are Indian names, as is the name of Ohio.

The Ohio name has been given many meanings, depending primarily on the Indian language used as the source. The name came from the river which has been called the "white" river, the "sparkling" river, and, like so many others, the "big" river. Its most popular descriptive name was La Belle Rivière of the French, "the beautiful river," but this may not be a translation.[3]

Ohio was occasionally used as a place-name to identify the source of its settlers. The six counties having townships named Ohio are Morris,

273

Ness, Franklin, Saline, Sedgwick, and Stafford. There was once an Ohio Grove in Ottawa County. Marshall, Smith, and Franklin counties had towns named Ohio City. None of these is on the current map. The one in Franklin County had been named Bowling Green. Some referred to it as "Boling."[4] The first Bowling Green in America was in lower Manhattan. The name migrated westward and could have come to Kansas from any one of six states, but since the one in Kansas was dominated by Kentucky slaveholders, its source was likely Kentucky. Its Ohio settlers changed its name to Ohio City. Then along came a man from Princeton, Illinois, who named it Princeton.[5]

Jacob Augustine, who had moved from Mendota, Illinois, to Tuscarawas County, Ohio, joined C. H. Lebold to promote an Ohio settlement north of Abilene. Another Buckeye colony was organized by Porter Wilson, publisher of the *Tuscarawas Chronicle*. Its community center was the Buckeye Store and the colony gave its name to Buckeye Township.[6] Wilson brought his press to Abilene, where Buckeye Street was another reminder of Ohio.[7] It was recently changed to Eisenhower Street to honor Abilene's most distinguished resident.

In the neighboring county of Ottawa, there is another Buckeye Township, and the county has a Buckeye Creek. An 1867 map made it "Buck Eye Creek." On Johnson's map of 1870, it had changed to "Blue Eye Creek." Commenting on this change, T. H. Scheffer concluded that this was "the work of a susceptible young copy clerk whose thoughts were busy with dimples and lace bonnets." The romance of the name was, however, dissipated as the name of Buckeye was restored.[8] The city-minded settlers of Buckeye Creek in Chase County gave their community of four log cabins the name of Buckeye City. Another Ohio settlement gave its name to Buckeye Township in Ellis County.[9]

Chillicothe was the name of several village sites before the white man established Chillicothe in Ohio. An early form of the name was Chi-la-ka-tha, said to mean a "place where people dwell" or "man made perfect."[10] Phillips County, Kansas, had a Chillicothe with a fairly large Ohio population. The name was later changed to Marvin.

E. L. King brought a colony of destitute veterans from Ashtabula, Ohio, to McPherson County where one community was named Ashtabula and the other King City. The King City post office moved to Elyria, but King City is still the name of its township.

One of the four divisions of the Shawnee was called Piqua, said to mean "dust" or "ashes." Piqua in Ohio was the birthplace of Tecumseh; Piqua, Kansas, was the birthplace of Buster Keaton.[11] George A. Bowles named it for his home in Ohio,[12] and the name was also given to the Piqua Hills in Woodson County.

The Senecas and Hurons were neighboring Iroquois, but they were enemies. A large rock at the Seneca village in New York gave them their name of "the standing stone people."[13] Seneca in Nemaha County, Kansas, was named by Finley Lappin for Seneca, Ohio,[14] which was a bigger town than Seneca, New York.

Lake Huron, where the Hurons had once lived, made their name familiar. The Huron in Atchison County was named by Dr. Amarziah Moore for his home in Huron County, Ohio.[15]

In Jackson County, North Cedar changed its name to Denison for the home town of an Ohio promoter by the name of Tucker.[16] The one in Ohio was named for William Dennison, an Ohio governor.[17] Danville, west of Wellington, was first named Coleville for Mrs. E. J. Cole, who started the town. Then it was changed to Danville, possibly for Mrs. Cole's son Dan, but it could have been named by its Ohio residents who came from Danville, Ohio.[18]

The naming of Circleville in Jackson County, Kansas, was a simple matter. Two men chatting in a blacksmith shop are reported to have decided on a name in this way: "This town has no name," said Mr. Myers to Mr. Cook. "You're from Circleville, Ohio; let's give it that name." "All right," answered Cook, "We'll do it."[19] It was done. One may question the interpretation that it was named Circleville, as someone suggested, because it was "circling around the prairie in search of a location."[20] In Ohio, Circleville was named for a circular Indian mound.[21]

Like Circleville, Crestline was a descriptive name. It was mistakenly believed for a time that it was the highest place in Ohio. Crestline in Cherokee County, Kansas, was named by Henry Wiggins, its first postmaster, for the Ohio town.[22] In Kansas, it is in the lowest part of the state.

The first Dayton in Kansas was only a station in Labette County with a large sign to divert speculators who might compete with the promoters of Parsons.[23] The Dayton in Bourbon County served as a post office from 1858 until 1887. The Dayton in Dickinson County was in an Ohio settlement, as was the New Dayton in Marshall County. All four Daytons in Kansas seemingly came from Dayton, Ohio, which had been named for Jonathan Dayton, a land speculator.[24]

Two coined names in Ohio, Bucyrus and Elyria, were brought to Kansas by Ohio settlers. Bucyrus was made by combining "Bu" for beautiful with Cyrus, the name of a Persian king.[25] Abraham Ely added the last part of Maria, his wife's name, to his own and named his town Elyria. Naming Elyria, Kansas, has been attributed to A. G. Smith of Elyria, Ohio.[26]

In addition to the Canton at the Manhattan site, there were four other Cantons in Kansas. The one that survived in McPherson County had first been given the Polish name of Ostrog. It then became Canton, possibly named for the one in Ohio. The one in Anderson County died when Garnett became the county seat. Johnson's map of 1870 showed one in Linn County, and Cowley County once had a post office named New Canton. A few of the Cantons in America have assumed that they were so named because they were located at a point of the earth directly opposite from Canton, China, but that point is somewhere in South America.

Mentor, the Ohio home town of President Garfield, was named for Hiram Mentor, a pioneer.[27] In 1881, the year Garfield was assassinated, it became the name of a station south of Salina.

Cincinnati in Ohio was first called Columbia and then was given the fancy name of Losantiville, a name made from syllables suggesting "the town opposite the mouth of the Licking." Governor Arthur St. Clair disliked the name and changed it to Cincinnati for the Society of Cincinnatus organized by the officers of the American Revolution. There was trouble over choosing between "i" or "a," as the ending of the name.[28] But it did not matter, it was spelled with the "i" terminal but frequently pronounced as if it had an "a" terminal. Cincinnati may have been annoyed by its nickname of "Pigtown." Kansas ignored the class distinction of the Society of Cincinnatus as well as the nickname when it promoted Cincinnati in Doniphan County which was just "a name and a dream."[29] There was another Cincinnati in Leavenworth County in 1857.[30] The Cincinnati members of the Ohio colony, who joined the Bostonians to build the town of Manhattan, had high hopes of naming the town New Cincinnati.[31] For nearly a decade there was a New Cincinnati in Rice County. Cincinnati in Grant County was surveyed and platted by J. W. Dapport as a competitor for the county seat. "Cincinatti, or Hog Town, more properly speaking, will never amount to anything as a candidate for county seat," said the *Ulysses Tribune*.[32] It joined Tilden in the fight but lost.

Mecca in Ohio was considered to be the end of the trail for Connecticut immigrants. To avoid duplication, the name was later changed to Medina for a town in New York.[33] It would, however, have been appropriate to associate the name with Mecca, as the city from which Mahomet fled to Medina, the Moslem capital of Arabia. The name came from Arabia to New York, then to Ohio, and eventually to Kansas. John Speer proposed Medina as a name for a Kansas railway station between Lawrence and Topeka in Jefferson County.[34]

Quakers from Wilmington, North Carolina, settled in Clinton County, Ohio, and named their town Wilmington.[35] When Clinton County colonizers came to Kansas, they settled in Wabaunsee County and named their town and township Wilmington.[36]

William Penn Montgomery, a Pennsylvanian, as one might suspect with a name like that, settled in Decatur County in 1874. He sponsored a town and named it Westfield for the New York town where he had attended college. After Montgomery left to become editor of the *Hays City Sentinel*,[37] Westfield was renamed Sappa for Sappa Creek, a Siouan word meaning "black." When John A. Rodehaver of Ohio became postmaster at Sappa, he renamed the town Oberlin for the Ohio town which had been named for John Frederick Oberlin, an Alsatian preacher.[38]

Of the five Mansfields in the United States listed by Gannett, each one came from the name of a different man.[39] Kansas had three towns named Mansfield, one in Linn County, a second one in Wabaunsee County, and one in Finney County. The last is said to be named for the one in Ohio, originally named for Colonel Jared Mansfield, United States surveyor general.[40]

Although Ravanna has a Roman origin as Ravenna, its immediate source in Kansas was Ravenna, Ohio. It has been named Mason, Bull's Town, and Cowland. Then came James Cross from Ohio, who solved the controversial name-problem by suggesting that the name be changed to Ravenna, his home town.[41] A clerical error made it Ravanna.

If one followed the alphabetical sequence for names from Ohio, one could skip Y and refer to the name of Xenia, also spelled Zenia, and thereby conclude the alphabet. Zenia had a Greek origin but Kansas got her Xenia from Ohio, the home town of William D. Howells. It must also have had another name in Kansas, since Elliot Coues, in editing Pike's Journals, said that Pike camped in the "vicinity of Xenia, Zenia, or Hay" on a branch of the Little Osage in Bourbon County.[42]

Kansas had the tenth Bunker Hill in the country. In Montgomery County, Bunker Hill was named for Frank Bunker, known as a "vivacious and witty" man who lived on the highest point in the area. A town was started as "Bunker's Addition," and, after Bunker built a station there, the railroad was called "Bunker's Plug."[43] The name was lost when Independence absorbed the community.[44] The Bunker Hill in Russell County was settled by people from Ohio, where there is both a Bunker Hill and a Bunkerhill. In Kansas, both names were used.[45]

Samuel N. Wood, who was born in Mount Gilead, Ohio, and who came to Kansas from Marion County, Ohio, was the legislator who named Chase County and renamed Marion County. He was a champion of Salmon P. Chase of Ohio for the presidency of the United States, and to honor him, he named Chase County. Mount Gilead in Kansas could have a connection with Wood's birthplace.

Since Marion County had first been named by the Bogus Legislature for General Francis Marion, the "Swamp Fox" of South Carolina, one may wonder why its name should have been restored from a different source. "I happen to know," said Wood, "that Marion County was named in honor of my native county, Marion in Ohio." In support of his case, he added: "I introduced the bill making and naming the county, and I am confident I never thought of our Revolutionary hero in connection with the name."[46] But the source for the name in Ohio was General Marion.[47]

A. A. Moore, better known as "Lank" Moore, ran a trading post on the Cottonwood Crossing of the Santa Fe Trail. His place became a post office known as Moore's Ranch. After the decline of the Santa Fe Trail, a new town was started by W. H. Billings, George Griffith, and William Shreve, and they, according to the local press, "named it Marion Centre after the city of Marion, Ohio."[48]

The five townships named Marion in as many counties in Kansas were most likely named directly or indirectly for General Marion, although Ohio could be the intermediate source. The Marion Township in Bourbon County is said to have been named for General Marion, the Revolutionary hero.[49] The town named Marion in Douglas County had its name changed to Globe but retained the name of Marion for the township. The Marion in Phillips County soon joined the roster of ghost towns.

We may combine the influence of Ohio and Indiana in the town named Colony in Anderson County, since a joint colony from these two states settled there and simply named its town Colony.[50]

Ohio was especially important in the history of Kansas as the Ohio names in Kansas suggest. Much of the westward migration was, however, a short move from state to state. Herb Shriner, the Hoosier comedian, said: "I was born in Ohio, but moved to Indiana as soon as I heard about it."

Indiana, which lies between Ohio and Illinois, did not contribute as many names to Kansas as its neighbors. Kansas did have, however, both an Indiana and an Indianapolis. When Kansas adopted such names as Muncie, it did not take the name from Indiana but from the Munsee Indians, who had been living in Kansas.

The name of Indiana was only a slight modification of Indian. It was most likely introduced by a real estate company in Pennsylvania which gave this name to some land acquired from the Indians at the Fort Stanwix Treaty of 1768.[51] For a short time there was an Indiana City in Osage County, promoted by Kentuckians. Frames for the four houses which constituted the town were hauled in from Louisville.[52] Indianapolis was a coined name with "Indian" referring to the state and with a Greek terminal of *polis*, meaning "city." Indianapolis was the name of a post office in what is now Miami County, discontinued twice before it died.

New Albany and Waverly were both Scottish names from Indiana. The New Albany in Kansas was settled by pioneers from New Albany, Indiana, a town across the river from Louisville.[53] Like Albany, Waverly had a Scotch origin. There were numerous Waverlys on the map before the Hoosiers brought the name to Coffey County, Kansas.[54]

Scipio is a classical name which commemorates a fighting family from Rome. Four places in Indiana were named Scipio, and settlers from one of these, known as "Yankees from Indiana," promoted the town of Scipio north of Garnett in Anderson County.[55]

One of the most prominent stockholders of the town company which built Goodland in western Kansas came from Goodland, Indiana.[56] Promoters hoped to capitalize on the name for its implication that Goodland was where the land was good. It has been assumed that its propaganda appeal was "deliberate."[57] Writing to his sister, Leslie Snow said: "It is probably a misnomer."[58] The land is good but it is occasionally dry. Goodland once hired a rainmaker to make sure it could live up to its name. The rainmaker was remarkably successful except for the fact that his torrential rains hit the Nebraska border and did so much damage that Nebraska is reported to have sued him. But Goodland is nevertheless a flourishing town. By its success, it has obliterated such rival towns as Sherman Center, Itasca, Voltaire, and Eustis.[59]

The name of Elkhart in Indiana came from an island which, according to Indian legend, was shaped like the heart of an elk. The source for the Elkhart name in Morton County, Kansas, is believed to be the one in Indiana.[60] Morton County was named for an Indiana governor, Oliver H. P. Throck Morton.[61]

Avilla seems to be a strange name for Kansas. It had a possible source from Ávila in Spain, but a more logical source was Avilla, Indiana. Avilla in Comanche County is in Avilla Township. Italy, too, has such a name.

A name with a stronger association with Indiana is the Wabash in Gray County, Kansas. La Salle wrote it Ouabachi. The name could be of Sioux origin since the Kansas and the Quapaws once lived "On the Banks of the Wabash." It could also have come from *wa-ba-shi-ki*, a Miami word meaning "bright white," or, at least, "white."[62]

Amo was for a short time a place-name in Miami County, Kansas. It is a rare name but Indiana had an Amo. The connection with Kansas may be vague. Yet we know that Horace Greeley Tarbert in Republic County married Lucinda Harlan who came from Amo, Indiana.[63] In the early days, the postmark on a letter was written in longhand. The postmaster in Morrisville, Indiana, found this name to be annoyingly long. While studying Latin, his daughter found a shorter name—it was simply *amo*, "I love,"[64] and Amo replaced Morrisville. We may assume that the name came to Kansas from Amo, Indiana, but the life of Amo in Kansas was brief, 1877–79.

So many settlers came to Kansas from Indiana, Iowa, and Illinois that Kansas was called "the state of the three I's." By 1880, Illinois had more settlers in Kansas than any other state,[65] and it surpassed all the others as a source for Kansas place-names. Most of the names from Illinois were of Old English origin, a few were Indian names with French or English spelling, familiar Spanish names as Peru, Lima, and Havana, and such French names as LaHarpe, LeRoy and Fayette. The Scandinavians from Illinois brought the names of Galesburg, Galva, and possibly, Odin.

Illinois is an Algonquian name which the French spelled Illiniwek and Illini. The name was said to mean "men," or "men of men," with the implication that they were better than other men.[66] Four townships and three creeks in Kansas were named Illinois. Creeks named Illinois were streams flowing into Cross Creek in Jackson County, into the Nemaha in Nemaha County, and into a branch of Mill Creek in Wabaunsee County. The Neosho was also called Illinois.

Mount Hope in Sedgwick County, Kansas, "belies its title," since there is no semblance of a "mount" in the fertile lowlands of the Arkansas Valley. Mount Hope was first the name of a schoolhouse where voters met to name their town. Several names had been proposed, but according to one account, "Mount Hope won after the sponsor sent his wife and another woman on mule-back—both on the same mule—to solicit absentee votes."[67] Mount Hope in McLean County, Illinois, is the township from which came several Illinois settlers to Kansas. The name may be found, however, in six other states. It is deservedly more popular than Forlorn Hope in Louisiana.

Highland, overlooking the Missouri River in northeastern Kansas, is appropriately descriptive even though the name came from Illinois. A Swiss from Highland, Illinois, named it Highland in order to appeal to the Swiss settlers in his home town[68] to come to Kansas.

By coincidence, two Kansas town promoters came from towns named Centralia, one in Illinois and the other in Pennsylvania. It was therefore a simple matter to agree to name their new town Centralia in Nemaha

County. Although most of its residents came from Illinois, both states shared equal honors in the name. It has also been assumed that it was named Centralia for being in the center of Home Township.[69]

The town of Stark, east of Chanute, was once called Grant Center because it was located in the center of Grant Township in Neosho County. Frank Leighton, postmaster, renamed it for Stark County, Illinois, where he was born. There it had been named for John Stark who fought at Bunker Hill and was a general at the Battle of Bennington. New Hampshire's motto was taken from Stark's words, "Live free or die."[70] Dorrance in Stark County, source for many Kansas settlers, being the only Dorrance listed in Lippincott's *Gazetteer* (1866) could have been the source for Dorrance in Russell County. It was first spelled Dorrence, but after ten years, the town's people must have concluded that the name was spelled incorrectly.

In Bourbon County, the railroad named a town Osage, but because of "the confusion with Osage City, Oswego, Osawkie, etc.," Charles Mitchell renamed it Fulton for Fulton County, Illinois, where he was reared.[71] It has been suggested that the new name was to honor a popular neighborhood doctor.[72] Fulton County, Illinois, has a town named Farmington, and from there came settlers who named Farmington in Atchison County, Kansas.[73] After that place disappeared, another Farmington was established in Reno County.

Litchfield in Crawford County has been described as "a coal town in every sense."[74] It was first named Edwin for Colonel Edwin Brown. Its new name came from Litchfield, Illinois, where it had been named for E. B. Litchfield, one of the town promoters.[75] Litchfield probably got his name from the historic town of Litchfield, England, where its people spoke "the purest English," according to the respected opinion of Samuel Johnson, whose home it was.[76] In Kansas, Litchfield is logically on Carbon Creek, keeping up its relationship with coal. The railroad called it "Litchfield Junction."[77]

The Galena Mining and Smelting Company laid out the town of Galena in the lead-mining region of eastern Kansas. To stress its association with its mining industry, it was suggested that it be named Cornwall, but the final choice was to name it for Galena, Illinois.[78]

Monmouth, a town west of Pittsburg in Crawford County, has a name which is famous in both England and America. James Fitzroy, the Duke of Monmouth, also called the "Protestant Duke," gave the name lasting fame. Monmouth means that it was at the mouth of the Monnow River in England. Also famous was the Revolutionary Battle of Monmouth in New Jersey where Molly Pitcher helped to load and fire the artillery. However, credit for naming the town of Monmouth,

Kansas, has been given to its founder, L. Manlove, who named it for Monmouth, Illinois, where it had been named for the Battle of Monmouth.[79]

Viola, Illinois, is located between Monmouth and Moline. James Grimsley of Viola in Sedgwick County said that the name was first given to the township and then to the town in Kansas. Viola had also been a temporary name of places in Elk and Ellis counties.

J. F. Chapman and associates from Moline, Illinois, were the founders of Moline in Elk County, Kansas. Anyone familiar with the manufacture of farm implements in the latter part of the nineteenth century would know the importance of the Moline plow or the Moline wagon from Moline, Illinois.[80]

In addition to the Galesburg colony in Nemaha County, there were others from Galesburg, Illinois, who settled in Kansas. In Neosho County there was a town named Rose Hill for Squire Rose. After this town merged with Neosho Valley, Galesburg replaced both names. Squire Rose became Galesburg's first postmaster.[81]

A trading post in Bourbon County was named Rockford for Rockford, Illinois. The name fits the description since it was located near "a beautiful valley with precipitous sides," known as "Rockford Valley."[82]

When General H. C. Bull and Lyman T. Earl promoted a town in Osborne County, they flipped a nickel to see who should name it. The General won, and, unabashed, he named it Bull City.[83] Bull, a Wisconsin man, was its first postmaster. Mrs. Bull wrote a lot of letters to give the post office enough business to remain open. In an effort to control an obstreperous elk which he had kept as a "pet," Bull and two companions were gored to death. Mrs. Bull then became the postmistress.

Some Illinois residents who disliked the name of Bull City signed a petition, said to have had many false signatures, requesting that the name be replaced by the name of Alton for Alton, Illinois.[84] The name came originally from one of several Altons in England, and one was noted for its "celebrated Alton Ales."[85] Alton had also been a temporary place-name in both Atchison and Sumner counties.

Other Illinois names in Kansas are Urbana, Havana, Odin, and Matoon. In Kansas, Urbana was first used as a name in Linn County but it has survived only in Neosho County. When W. W. Moore settled near Baker's Ford in Nemaha County, his place was called Moorestown.[86] Then it became known as Urbana. Illinois Creek in the same county would indicate an Illinois settlement, but Urbana was only an election center and more rural than urban. The Urbana in Illinois was named for the one in Ohio.

There is a Havana in Montgomery County and once there was also a Matoon in Wyandotte County. These are believed to have come from Illinois,[87] as is Broughton in Clay County. Duncan, Illinois, named for a Massachusetts congressman, may be the source for Duncan in Miami County, Kansas.

New Salem in Cowley County and Cairo in Pratt County take one back to biblical times, but they are both Illinois towns whose names were brought to Kansas. The settlers at New Salem in Cowley County, Kansas, came from Illinois.[88] Cairo in Illinois is in the rich delta land of the Ohio and the Mississippi; in Kansas, Cairo is in Pratt County.

Fayette in Illinois was named to honor Lafayette, that great French friend of the United States. The Fayette in Sedgwick County, Kansas, was in an Illinois settlement and the name could have come with the settlers. LeRoy, founded by John B. Scott, was first named Bloomington for Scott's home town in Illinois.[89] The Indians called it "Scott's Town." Since there was another Bloomington in Kansas, it was changed to LeRoy, the name of a McLean County, Illinois, town and former home of some of the LeRoy settlers.[90]

LeRoy has something in common with Delavan's past since Delavan had been known as Rex. Like LeRoy, or *Le Roi*, Rex means "the king." The founder of the town might have preserved the name of Rex and thereby honored himself, since his own name was Kingman. But Henry Kingman changed Rex to Delavan, naming it for his Illinois home,[91] which had been named for E. C. Delavan, a temperance worker of Albany, New York.[92]

The town of Princeton, south of Ottawa, also has a name with a royal origin, having been named in New Jersey for King William IV, Prince of Orange and Nassau.[93] E. M. Peck, a farmer from Illinois, had his immigrant car billed for Ottawa, but it was attached to a work-train on a siding which had no name. To complete his billing, it had to have a name, so Peck named it Princeton for his home town which in turn had been named for Princeton, New Jersey.[94] Its nearest post office was Ohio City which was soon moved to the railroad and then it became Princeton.

Gannett lists only one place named Lena, and that one is in Illinois. Its original source was the Lena in Ossian's story of *Fingal*, where the Irish fought Lochlin, the Northman, on "Lena's dusky heath."[95] Kansas had a Lena Valley in Lyon County. In Republic County the place named Lena was settled by people who came in three covered wagons from Lena, Illinois, bringing the name with them.[96]

When Chicago became a place-name in Kansas, there was probably no thought of its Indian origin. It was, however, a Sac and Fox name for what Carl Sandburg characterized as "the river of the wild onion." The name could have come from the wild onion, garlic, or skunkweed. A popular interpretation would make it mean "the place of the skunk." This, said an authority on Algonquian names, was simply a "proliferation of nonsense."[97]

Town promoters in Kansas who wished to give their town the reputation of a boom town could do no better than to name it Chicago. In the railroad rivalry over the town which became Chanute, three of the five towns which were merged were named for Chicago. They were Chicago, Chicago Junction, and New Chicago. There was another New Chicago on Coal Creek east of Emporia, but it had only a brief existence. The name of the town was associated with Chicago Mound, and this name was then transferred to the local school as the Chicago Mound School.[98] A post office named Chicago in Sheridan County lasted about seven years.

Chicago was not a lasting name in Kansas but its suburb of Englewood is a name in Clark County for a town started by Colonel C. D. Perry of Englewood, Illinois. It was Perry, aided by some Wichita "capitalists," who built the Bucklin to Dodge City railroad. Chicago hunters in western Kansas witnessed the boom of the eighties and promoted the town of Englewood to be the "Chicago of the West." The town advertised itself as the "Star of the Western Empire." Travelers were, however, warned to avoid Englewood because it was known as "Horse-thief Town."[99] As Englewood in Illinois is near the sand dunes of Lake Michigan, so Englewood in Kansas has its back to the sand hills of southwestern Kansas.

The Geneseo River in New York has an Iroquois name which means "shining valley."[100] This popular name was also used for the name of a county and a city in New York, and a town in Illinois. In Kansas, Geneseo, in the heart of the Quivira country in Rice County, was named by Major E. C. Modderwell of Geneseo, Illinois. The Little River in Kansas may not compare favorably with the "shining valley" of the Iroquois in New York but it did appeal to the Quivira Indians of Kansas. Geneseo had two railway stations, one called "Old Ben" and the other, "Old Tom."[101] Otis in Rush County was said to be named for the son of Major Modderwell.

Other Indian names such as Mendota and Oneida also came from Illinois. Mendota is an Indian word meaning "the meeting place" or "the junction." In Kansas, Mendota is located at the junction of the Labette and Little Labette creeks. The name was said to be borrowed from "a thriving little city" in Illinois.[102]

Shinntown in Nemaha County was named for its founder, Colonel Cyrus Shinn. The Colonel and his associates came originally from

Oneida, Illinois, and so they agreed to change the name of their town from Shinntown to the more appealing name of Oneida,[103] originally an Iroquois name from New York.

Although of Italian origin, Belvidere is a name that came to Kansas from Illinois. It has a meaning similar to Belvue, Buena Vista, and Fairview. So we have the name in Italian, Spanish, French, and English. Belvidere in Kiowa County once had two locations, Belvidere Junction on the railway and nearby Belvidere post office.

The American name of Aurora, Greek though it may be in origin, came from an Iroquois town in New York called Deawendote, "constant dawn."[104] New Yorkers brought the Aurora name to Illinois. If Aurora means the dawn, then dawn has come to Kansas four times. Aurora in Coffey County was promoted by two agents of a land company in Aurora, Illinois. These agents left Lawrence with a wagonload of supplies including a jug of whisky. At their camp on Turquoise Creek in Coffey County, near Eclipse, they ran out of whisky. There was little other inducement to penetrate any farther into a dry country, so they returned to Illinois with "a flattering report" of the townsite they had selected. But the town never got beyond the dawn. For a time it was known merely as "Dixon's Lone House." There is now an Aurora in Aurora Township in Cloud County, also said to be named for the one in Illinois. Aurora should remind one of Wabaunsee, the county named for a Potawatomi chief whose name meant the "Dawn of Day."[105]

From Michigan came the name of Michigan Valley, a town south of Topeka on the Missouri Pacific. The railroad has dispensed with the "Valley" and its station is known as Michigan but for postal service it is still known as Michigan Valley.[106]

Hope and Holland were names of Dutch communities in Michigan and both names are found as centers of Michigan settlers in Dickinson County. The Methodist Ladies Aid Society of Wagram disliked the name of their town and proposed to change it to Hope. The railroad objected to that but the women won and Hope it is.[107] The Michigan name of Holland has been used for Holland Creek, Holland Township, and the town of Holland, leaving no doubt about the influence of the Michigan Dutch in Dickinson County.

South Haven in Sumner County was once called "Shoo Fly City." The author of a book on *Shoo Fly City* confessed that she lacked evidence as to the origin of the name, but she would "guess" that "it derived its name from Shoo Fly Creek." This is, of course, an acceptable guess. The East, West, and Middle Shoo Fly flows southward past the "city." Campers on a creek who had just heard of a popular song called "Shoo

Fly" named the creek. There was also a reference to a Shoo Fly Trail passing through Caldwell and Hunewell to the Southwest.[108] The song contains the following lines:

Shoo, fly, don't bother me,
For I belong to somebody.[109]

Several pioneers from Michigan who settled in the area donated land for a town. They then applied to Washington for a post office with the name of Shoo Fly City. The name was rejected. "Everyone in Shoo Fly City liked the name," but Washington wanted a more "dignified name."[110] The Dye brothers, who had come from South Haven, Michigan, proposed the name of South Haven, which was accepted and the "dignity" of a name was preserved.[111]

Coldwater in Comanche County was at first called "Cold Springs"; the Mexicans called it El Frio; and others, Cavalry Creek. The "clear and sparkling water" of Cavalry Creek is said to have reminded some settlers of the cold water of Michigan, so they supposedly gave it the name of Coldwater, also written "Cold Water."[112] But it was C. D. Bickford of Coldwater, Michigan, who selected the townsite and he is given credit for naming it in memory of his Michigan home.[113]

Lansing, Michigan, got its name from New York, and Lansing, Kansas, is said to be named for the one in Michigan.[114] But the credit has also been given to James W. Lansing, said to be the founder of the town. He was the hospital steward there in 1874. The place was known for a decade as Petersburgh, although it was commonly called "Penitentiary" before the name was changed to Lansing in 1875.[115]

H. S. Bacon from Michigan, while visiting his brother in Rice County, heard about a good mill site on the Smoky Hill. He found it, bought it, and there he built his flour mill in 1874. It was named Marquette "for the city on Lake Superior, Michigan, from which we came to Kansas," said Bacon. So Marquette, the first to put the Kansas name on the map, had his own name perpetuated there.[116] Another French name from Michigan was Detroit, on the Smoky Hill east of Abilene.

Kalamazoo, meaning the "boiling pot," was an Indian name given to some bubbling springs on the Kalamazoo River in Michigan. There was a Kalamazoo post office in Kingman County which lasted only a year. This one was followed by a Kalamazoo in Sedgwick County lasting about four years. A New Yorker who owned the townsite renamed it Anness for Anne S. Wilson, his wife. In 1886 there was a third place named Kalamazoo in Decatur County.

Many towns are named for people and some people have been named for towns. A story has been told about a Chicago baseball player who was known as "Cap" Anson. His real name was Adrian Constantine Anson. At the age of six, he asked his mother why it was that he had such strange names when his brothers had such popular names as John, George, and Robert. His mother told him that she had been born in Adrian, Michigan, and that his father had been born in Constantine, so they named him for their birthplaces. That night, as the little boy knelt by his bed, he thanked the good Lord that his mother was not born in Ypsilanti and his father in Kalamazoo.[117]

Anson in Sumner County was named in 1887, and "Cap" Anson, the baseball player, could have inspired the name. He was home run champion in 1879, 1881, 1887, and 1888. It has been suggested, however, that Anson was named for Anson Wallace, a pioneer.[118]

Mrs. James Hall in Norton County wished to have a town named for her home in Alma, Michigan. She was too late, for eastern Kansas already had a place named Alma. Then she is supposed to have coined a name that could still be a reminder of Alma; she named the town Almena.[119] Since there is an Almena in Wisconsin and another in Michigan, the name may not have been coined. With this suggestion, we may next turn to Wisconsin.

Especially well known among the Wisconsin names in Kansas were Milwaukee, La Crosse, and Beloit. People automatically associate the name of Milwaukee with the state of Wisconsin, or one may even think of it as the source for the beer that made Milwaukee famous. It is a descriptive Indian name for a place where the huckleberries grew well along a stream which the Algonquian called Milioke or Miliaki. *Milo* meant "good" and *aki* meant "land," so Milwaukee was "good land" or "good earth."[120] The name came to Butler County, Kansas, as New Milwaukee.[121] The Milwaukee in the eastern part of Stafford County was started later but lasted no longer.

Also well known in Wisconsin is the name of La Crosse. Since it was on the Mississippi, one might assume that the name referred to the crossing of the river, but it was originally the French name given to an Indian ball game.[122] In Rush County, Kansas, La Crosse was the center of a Wisconsin community named by D. A. Stubbs from La Crosse.[123]

The name of Beloit originated in Wisconsin, where it was coined to resemble Detroit, and it rhymes. In Mitchell County, Kansas, it replaced the descriptive name of Willow Springs, or Sacred Springs, as the Indians called it. Timothy F. Hersey and Aaron A. Bell, two Beloit, Wisconsin, pioneers, were responsible for changing Willow Springs to Beloit.[124] Hersey lived in Maine, Illinois, and Wisconsin before bringing the Beloit name to Kansas.

The town of Hudson, between Pratt and Great Bend, got its Wisconsin name because Mr. Uptegraph had donated the land for the town-site on condition that he be granted the privilege to name it. Under the circumstances he might have given it his own name, as some would, but he named the place for his home town of Hudson, Wisconsin.[125]

Prairie du Chien, "prairie of the dog," is a well-known Wisconsin town on the Mississippi. When used as a place-name in Neosho County, Kansas, it could have had the Wisconsin name as its source. In Kansas, Prairie du Chien was primarily an Indian trading post run by George Shepard before it was replaced by a neighboring town named Thayer.[126]

The town now named Penokee in Graham County was first named Reford, a name that was easily confused with Rexford. According to the local press, a railroad representative and a postmaster searched the atlas for a new name and they chose the name of Penokee from the Penokee Mountains in northern Wisconsin, where there is also a Peno-kee Gap on the Bay of Ashland.[127] Local residents have their own earthy interpretation of this Indian name. They say it was named by an Indian chief when a station master refused to give him the key to the men's restroom. As a post office it was listed as Gettysburgh until 1889, when the name was changed to Penokee.

When an appeal was made in Wisconsin for more free-state settlers for Kansas, Edward D. Holton, a wealthy merchant and banker from Milwaukee, sponsored a well-organized company of settlers. The leader of the colony was Edmund G. Ross, a journalist who won distinction and political ruin when he cast the deciding vote against the impeach-ment of President Johnson. While the Wisconsin pioneers waited for a flooded stream to subside, they chose a townsite and, "at the suggestion of Mr. Ross, the town . . . was named Holton in honor of the patron of the expedition."[128] Holton is now the county seat of Jackson County.

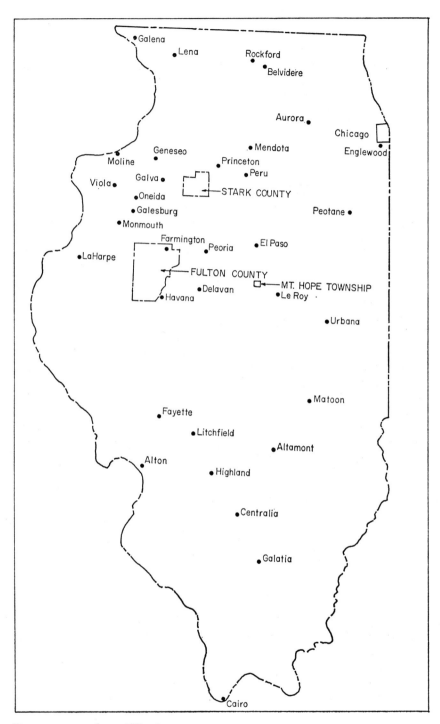

Kansas names from Illinois

CHAPTER XXVII

OENCHEN SCOTT CITY SCOTTSVILLE SCRANTON SEDAN SEDGWICK SELDEN SENECA SEVERANCE

MIDWEST AND WESTWARD

WARD SHARON SHARON SPRINGS SHAWNEE SILICA SILVER LAKE SIMPSON SITKA SMITH CENTER

STATES THAT WERE SETTLED contemporary with Kansas naturally contributed fewer names than did the older states in the East. Yet most of the trans-Mississippi states served as a source for a number of place-names, including the names of the states. Montana, Arizona, Oregon, Nevada, and California are names which may have been chosen for their appeal or to identify the source of their settlers. Among the people who tried their fortunes in the West, there were a few who returned, and these occasionally brought back a western name which was adopted as a Kansas place-name.

Nebraska had many place-names in common with Kansas, generally from the same source. Omaha, the largest city in Nebraska, was the name for one of the smallest towns in Kansas. In Kearny County, Kansas, Omaha was called "a farmer's town."[1] It was, of course, the Indian name of a Siouan tribe related to the Kansas and Osages. It has been interpreted to mean "upstream people."

In 1879, "an epidemic of western fever broke out in Iowa." In the following decade, Iowa settlers came to Kansas and their names followed the frontier all the way to its western border. The name Iowa was most likely derived from the Dakota Sioux Indians. The French spelled it many ways, including Aiaouez. Americans tried to follow the phonetics of the French and made it first Ayuwais and then Ioway. Lewis and Clark spelled it "Ayauwais"; Schoolcraft, "Aiowais." Not only was "Ioway" the accepted prouniciation but it was also the accepted spelling. When S. M. Irvin and William Hamilton published a grammar at their Iowa mission, they named it *An Ioway Grammar*.[2] When the Iowa Indians were called Pahodja or Pahucha, whatever its spelling, the name was said to mean "dusty noses," "dusty heads," or "snow heads." It was supposedly the name given them by the Osages when the Iowas departed during a snowfall.[3] Iowa has also been translated to mean the "sleepy ones."[4]

Iowa Point in Doniphan County was referred to by Major Clifton Wharton in 1844 as "Jeffrey's or Iowa Point."[5] It was named for the Iowa Indians and not the state. Iowa Creek is not far from Iowa Point, and "the Point," as it was called, is in Iowa Township. The place named Iowa in Ness County lost its life in a struggle with Ness City, as did also Sidney, named for an Iowa town.[6] An attempt was made to build an Iowa City near Pittsburg in Crawford County. The post office named Iowaville in Sedgwick County served until 1902. Both Rooks and Sherman counties have townships named Iowa. Except for Iowa Point, these names indicate the presence of Iowa settlers.

The Iowa people were probably as well known by their nickname of Hawkeye as by their Iowa name. The Hawkeye name was proposed by the editor of the *Patriot* in order to give the Iowa people an identity by a nickname like the Badgers of Wisconsin and the Suckers of Illinois. The early settlers of Illinois were lead miners, and, like suckers, they came upstream in the spring and returned downstream in the fall. The Hawkeye name was that of an Indian chief. An Iowa settlement in Thomas County was called "Old Hawkeye."[7] The Hawkeye post office in Decatur County combined with the towns of Shiboleth and Old Sheridan and moved to town on the railroad named Selden for Selden G. Hopkins, a member of the town company.[8]

When James Fitzimmons and Jesse Newell came to Kansas from Oskaloosa, Iowa, they established Newell's Mill near Lawrence. When it was given a post office, Fitzimmons, the postmaster, named it Oskaloosa for his home town. According to a popular but questionable story, the name came from "Oska," a chief, and "Loosa," his squaw. It was also said to be the name of Osceola's wife, interpreted to mean "the last of the beautiful."[9] Oskaloosa has the earmarks of a Creek or Seminole name. It resembles Okaloosa, a name in Florida said to mean "black water." It has been suggested that Oskaloosa came from *ishki*, "mother," and *lusa*, "black." One of Osceola's wives, a beautiful one, had some Negro blood, but her name was Che-cho-ter, "Morning Dawn."[10]

As a well-known chief of the Prairie Sioux, as the Iowas were called, White Cloud II came to Kansas, and Kansas adopted both his Indian name of Maw-hee-ohe-kaw or Mahaska, and its English translation of White Cloud.[11] He and his charming wife, Strutting Pigeon, visited Europe in 1845. The town of White Cloud is in northeastern Kansas and Mahaska is the name of a town in Washington County.

Thomas Bowen, an ordained minister from Ottumwa, Iowa, settled on the site which became Ottumwa in Coffey County, Kansas. Bowen was not only a preacher but a politician. Ottumwa is an Indian name which may mean the "place of the lone chief," but more likely, "rapids" or "tumbling waters."[12]

Ames, Page City, and Springdale were all Iowa names. In Cloud County there is an Ames which was named for Ames, Iowa, and the

Iowa town was named for Oakes Ames, an official of the Union Pacific Railroad.[13] West of Oakley in Logan County is the little Union Pacific station whose name was changed from Boaz to Page City. The name was given to the town by settlers who came from Page County, Iowa, where it had been named for John Page, a casualty in the Mexican War.[14] Springdale near Leavenworth was named by a group of Quaker pioneers from Springdale, Iowa.[15] Jewell County had another Springdale, an "imaginary town" between White Rock and East Buffalo. Imaginary or not, it had a name and it cast twenty-four votes for county seat. It lost and was "never heard from again," said a county historian.[16]

Westphalia and Waterloo were two well-known European names which were transferred to Kansas from Iowa. Westphalia, with its German origin, was the name of a town in Anderson County, Kansas, which replaced the name of Cornell. The name was chosen by the Flusche brothers who came from Westphalia, Iowa,[17] to name Westphalia, Kansas.

Traer and Villisca were place-names which were not listed by Lippincott's *Gazetteer* (1853), yet both of these names are Iowa names and found also in Kansas. Villisca in Rooks County was named for "the pleasant southwestern Iowa city of Villisca," said J. Riseley of Stockton.[18] Pioneers from Traer, Iowa, settled and named the town of Traer on Beaver Creek in Decatur County.

Clarendon has been a widely used place-name from England to Iowa. The one in Barton County, Kansas, is said to have come from Iowa,[19] and it is not likely that the residents of either town were concerned about the historical activities of the Earl of Clarendon.

Leon, east of Augusta, was located near Tong's Watermill but was "first christened Noble." Since Noble had already been used as a name in Kansas, it was changed to Leon for the Leon in Iowa. It has been suggested that, "in the minds of its projectors," there was also a thought of the "far-famed Ponce de Leon," but this seemed far-fetched.[20]

Independence in Montgomery County, Kansas, may have been given this name from the independent action of a town company that deserted one town to start another.[21] But another suggestion is that it was named Independence by Dr. R. W. Wright who came from Independence, Iowa.[22]

Minnesota is well provided with Indian place-names, mostly Siouan names but with a few Chippewa. Most of the Minnesota names in Kansas are of Indian origin. Names such as Winona and Minnehaha were made popular by Longfellow, as was the name of Hiawatha.

Mankato and Itasca were Minnesota names, as was the hybrid name of Minneapolis. One Minnesota name in Kansas which was not an Indian name was Windom.

Mankato was a Siouan name meaning "blue earth," and in Minnesota, Mankato was located on the Blue Earth River. The Monecato River in Kansas was correctly called the "Blue Earth River"[23] by early explorers. Had Kansas kept the Indian name, it would have been Monecato or Mankato. The Mankato in Kansas came not, however, from its own Blue Earth River. It was named by pioneers from Mankato, Minnesota, who settled in Jewell County.

Captain A. D. Pierce from Minneapolis, Minnesota, with fond memories of that city's beautiful river setting, gave the name to a town in Ottawa County.[24] It is located where Salt Creek and Pipe Creek join the Solomon. It has been said that these streams suggested "the name Minneapolis, the City of Waters." The name is, however, a strange combination of *minne*, a Sioux word meaning "water" and *polis*, a Greek word meaning "city."[25] It had been called Ayersburg for Seymour Ayers, who had a cabin on nearby Lindsey Creek.[26]

Lake Itasca is the source of the Mississippi River. The Chippewas called it Omushkos which meant "doe." The French translated this and called it Lac La Biche. Schoolcraft, who knew this country and the Chippewas, used the duel name of "La Biche or Itasca Lake." One interpretation of the name Itasca is that it was a coined word. Schoolcraft had, according to this interpretation, taken the last part of *veritas*, "true" and the first part of *caput*, "head," and joined them to make Itasca. It has also been suggested that Itasca was the name of an Indian girl.[27] This Minnesota name was for a time the name of a town in Sherman County, Kansas, a competitor for the county seat which it lost to Goodland. Itasca called itself the "Queen City of the West." It was not.

A community on the border of Sedgwick County was known as Minneha before its name was changed to Midland, back to Minneha, then to Cloud or Cloud City, and finally to Andover.[28] The little white country school named Minneha has now grown with the boom at Beechcraft and it is now the name of a large and busy elementary school. The border township where the first Minneha started is also called Minneha.

Minneha looks like Minnehaha and it evidently has the same Siouan meaning. The name in Kansas may well have come from Minnehaha in Minnesota. The Minnesota name meant "water"and "falls" or "cascade," and in Minneapolis, the name is given to a waterfall with the

293

English word "falls" added, making it mean "Falls-Water-Falls-Falls."[29] When Longfellow used this name for his heroine in *Hiawatha* he introduced a popular interpretation with poetic license:

> *And he named her for the river,*
> *From the waterfall he named her,*
> *Minnehaha, Laughing Water.*

It must have been the "haha" at the end that gave Longfellow the idea of "Laughing."

Colorado veterans who settled in Lincoln County "baffle description," said the county historian, but they were the source for naming the town of Colorado. After serving fifteen years, the Colorado name was changed to Beverley, which is located in Colorado Township.[30]

The nearest Kansas came to using the name of Utah was Ute, the name of a place in Sheridan County. The Ute Indians were Shoshonean Indians who lived in Colorado and Utah. The logical source for the name of Provo in Greenwood County was Provo, Utah, the "garden city" and the location of Brigham Young University. Provo had been named for Étienne Provot, a French-Canadian in the service of William Ashley.[31]

Montana was used as a name for a gold-mining site in the Pikes Peak area while it was still in Kansas. Because of its final letter "a," suggesting the feminine, someone came to the questionable conclusion that it was feminine for mountain. In Spanish, however, *montaña* does mean mountain. The naming of Montana Territory was done on the suggestion of Governor Denver of Kansas.[32]

Like the rest of the mountain states, Montana had its gold rush. When Samuel Short left Missouri for the gold fields of Montana, he was detained in southeastern Kansas by malaria. The next year he was detained by a flood. In 1861, Stand Watie, the Cherokee chief, confiscated his water bucket, his shoes, and his college diploma. Having lost his shoes and his sheepskin, he was so discouraged that he gave up the mining venture and settled in Labette County. There he proposed the name of "Montana City" for a new town. Then he could still write back to the folks in Missouri with a Montana postmark. The railway bypassed the town, and Montana was too close to Parsons to survive;[33] but the Montana name was left on a township. Although devoid of mountains, Jewell County has a Montana Creek and a Montana Township.

Walla Walla, from the French Oualla Oualla, meaning "little river," was the name of an Indian tribe in eastern Washington State. Patrick Gass on the Lewis and Clark expedition played it by ear and wrote it "Wala-Waltz."[34] It has been said that the second Walla was an echo and also that Walla Walla was a town that was named twice.[35] That it was an echo may be justified by the repetition of the name in Kansas. The Montague family, having visited Washington Territory, liked the name so much that it gave the name of Walla Walla to a town near Junction City. It was made a post office in 1874, the name came back in 1878, and it was restored again in 1894, like a third echo. Only a schoolhouse has retained the Walla Walla name.[36] Walula, a name with the same source, became temporarily the name of a place in Crawford County; and Wallua, with a change of spelling, was the name of a suburb of Wyandotte City.

Oregon was an American destination and dream before California's gold diverted the fanatical Forty-Niners. Oregon was twice a post office in Jefferson County, but it was terminated in 1885. The name may have its source in a river called the Ouaricon which Marquette followed to the Mississippi. From this, it has also been known as "the River of the West."[37]

Those who risked the overland route in the gold rush to California found Kansas fairly attractive, especially by comparison to the desert land they had crossed farther west. Many of the prospectors failed to strike it rich, and for that reason and others, they headed back home in the East. Robert Louis Stevenson, on his way to California in 1873, "remarked with surprise how at every big station they met packed emigrant trains running eastward."[38] This return migration had been going on for some time, and Kansas caught many an immigrant on the rebound, including such distinguished men as Governor Charles Robinson. Forty-Niners who failed in the West found in Kansas a new frontier. California had a volatile population and its exotic place-names became quite familiar. The publicity of these names and the people who returned to Kansas contributed to their adoption as Kansas place-names.

Today the name of California means many things to many people. Early in the sixteenth century, García de Montalvo wrote a romantic thriller called *The Adventures of Esplandian*, which described a fabulously rich island, inhabited by gorgeous women and no men. The queen who ruled this island was Califia and her name was said to be the source for the California name. Cortez described from hearsay such a Utopian island, and, never a man to neglect the women, he headed for the northwest in search of this "Terrestrial Paradise." What he found was the desolation of Baja California.[39] Three hundred years later, California's gold and the Forty-Niner's gold fever put the California name on everybody's lips.

A voting precinct on the California Trail west of Joplin was called

Calafornia [*sic*]. In 1879 the name of California was given to a post office north of Dighton in Lane County. After three years it was changed to Lucretia. But the California name is still the name of a township in Coffey County where it had been adopted by promoters of a "paper town."[40]

Monterey was for a decade a post office in Riley County.[41] The two most famous cities with this name are in Mexico and in California. In Mexico it is spelled Monterrey, but in California it is Monterey, as it is in Kansas. Both the Mexican and the California name honored the same man, Gaspar de Zúñiga, Conde de Monterey, Viceroy of New Spain. In California, Monterey was first called Bahia de los Pinos, "bay of pines." When Sebastián Vizcaino anchored in the beautiful bay, he renamed it Monterey. The name would logically mean the "king's woods."[42] It was the "most beautiful meeting . . . of land and water in the world," said Robert Louis Stevenson.

While exploring the West, John C. Frémont bought a large parcel of land in California and named it the Mariposa Ranch. During the litigation over its ownership, whereby Frémont made a million, the Mariposa name, which meant "butterfly," was given a lot of publicity. When Preston B. Plumb and two associates started a town about a mile from the present Salina, they named it Mariposa, probably for Frémont's ranch. The town grew to "one log house above ground and a well underground," and then, in 1857, it was deserted.[43] "The name sounds very nicely, and why it was not named Plumbville, or Pierce-town, or Huntersburg" for the three promoters "is yet a mystery," said Andreas.[44]

Benicia is a Spanish name from California which has twice been used in Kansas, first in Shawnee County and then in Douglas County. At neither place did the name survive.[45] In California, Benicia was located on land which General Mariano Vallejo donated for a town on condition that it be named for his wife Francisca. When Yerba Buena became San Francisco, the proposed town of Francisca changed its name to Benecia, also one of the given names of Señora Vallejo.[46]

Prominent among the place-names of California were many Indian names. Coloma, Colusa, Modoc, and Inyo are California Indian names, all of which became place-names in Kansas. Coloma was an exciting mining town at Sutter's Mill where the gold rush was started. An old print listed it as "Calluma Valley," and it is said to mean "beautiful vale."[47] Coloma was a Woodson County post office from 1865 to 1902.

Colusa, also known as Colusi, is an Indian name for a ranch in California which became the name of a town and county.[48] Colusa in

Kansas served twice as a post office in Gray County before it was discontinued in 1913.

The Modokni or Moatokni division of the Klamath Indians became known as the Modocs, a name which meant "southerner."[49] John P. St. John, later to become governor of Kansas, was a soldier in the stirring Modoc War. He was wounded and he carried an arrowhead in his body not as a medal but as a constant reminder of his Indian-fighting days. Yet when some Modocs came through Kansas on their way to a reservation, Scarface Charlie, their chief, had a friendly visit with Governor St. John.[50] The first Modoc in Kansas was a place in Jewell County; the second one is still on the map in Scott County.

California named its Inyo Mountains and its Inyo County for the Inyo Indians. The name was said by Chief George to mean "dwelling place of a great spirit." Death Valley, surrounded by its rugged mountains, would be the kind of setting that would inspire such a name.[51] In Harper County, Kansas, a place named Inyo lacked sufficient spirit to survive.[52]

Yuba City and Yuba County were well-known names during the California gold rush. The name came from a native group living in the Feather River area. General Frémont referred to Yuba as a village.[53] In Kansas, Yuba was a post office in Russell County which lasted but six months.

Yuma was named for a local Indian tribe which lived on both the California and the Arizona side of the Colorado River.[54] It was natural, therefore, that the natives should be named Yuma, meaning "son of the river."[55] The Yumas had once closed the Spanish land route to California, restricting its colonization and leaving California weak enough to be conquered by the United States. The Gadsden Purchase, which provided a land strip for a railway route in southern Arizona, moved the boundary south from the Yuma River and advertised the Yuma crossing. In Cloud County, Kansas, Yuma served several times as a post office and it is still the name of a railway station.[56]

Associated with the Golden Gate is that magnetic city of San Francisco. In search of brevity, tourists called it "Frisco," a term which was offensive to the proud, if not saintly, San Franciscans. Western Kansas chose Frisco as a post office name in Morton County. There it had to compete with Richfield, Taloga, and Sunset for survival. With 780 legal residents, Frisco cast 1,488 votes for county seat, fifteen more than Richfield, and yet it lost. Frisco, said Victor Murdock, was "as dead as Nineveh."[57] It was continued as a post office named Morton, named for the county.

Associated with Frisco is the world-famous entrance to the Bay of

San Francisco which General Frémont named the Golden Gate. He had the vision to see that there could be a golden flow of goods from the Orient entering through this Golden Gate. Frémont used the Greek name of Chrysopylae, which meant "golden gate," but his companion Preuss used the combination of "Chrysopylae or Golden Gate," so that the Americans would know its meaning.[58] For a brief time there was a Golden Gate in Chautauqua County, 1872–76. More appropriately named was the Golden Gate in Arapahoe County, a Kansas county, now in Colorado, named in 1860, shortly after the Colorado gold rush started.

The Nevada name came most likely from the Sierra Nevada Range on the California border. Three post offices were named Nevada in Kansas, one in Douglas County, a second in Arapahoe County (now in Colorado), and a third in Ness County. It is a simple name. *Neve* meant "snow" and *nevada* meant "snowfall" or "snow-covered." Ness County had a post office named Nevada and still has a Nevada Township. Since Nevada post office in Douglas County was named before Nevada was a state, we may assume that it came from the Sierra Nevada, the "snowy range" of California.

Arizona got its name from a Papago village called Arizonac. It was also called El Rancho de Arizona, referring to a place of "little waters."[59] Before Augusta was named in Butler County, Kansas, the place had been promoted with the name of Arizonia.[60] A paper town planned for Doniphan County in 1856 was given the name of Arizona, although it was also listed with the fancy terminal of Arizonia.[61] An Arizona was also shown in Breckinridge County (Lyon) on a Kansas map for 1859, but no Arizona in Kansas attained the prestige of having a post office.

Kansas had its Santa Fe, and the Santa Fe trade also made Taos a familiar name. Kit Carson made his home in Taos. This was the name of the village of the Tewas. Its other name, Yahlahaimubahutulbo, "red willow," would never have been adopted in Kansas. Although Indian in origin, Taos, as the Spaniards used it, was short and simple. In 1883 it became a post office name in Marshall County.

Sitka in Clark County created a bond between Alaska and Kansas. The town was built around the store of R. B. Pratt, who supposedly came from Sitka. It is believed that Pratt named the town on a very cold day.[62] In Alaska, Sitka was called the "Paris of the Pacific."

With such names as Sitka from Alaska and Key West from Florida, and other names from Maine to California, Kansas reflects an association through its place-names. The repetition of these names may show a lack of originality, but it illustrates the migration of names. Among all of these names, Indian names and names from England were the most popular.

CHAPTER XXVIII

NAMES FROM THE SOUTHERN STATES

KANSAS WAS UNDER DOMINATION of Southerners and slaveholders when it was first organized. Most of its counties in the eastern one-third of the territory were given names of people from the South. There was such a strong emotional feeling associated with these names that the victory of the North in Kansas polls and on the battlefield brought about the replacement of some county names of a southern flavor with names which were more palatable to the people of the victorious North. But not all southern names were replaced; moreover, southern names were occasionally chosen as place-names even after the Civil War.

The first Territorial Legislature of Kansas included in its county names the names of such prominent men from Virginia as Governor Wise and Senator Hunter.[1] We may also recall that the counties of Washington and Jefferson bore the names of Virginians of an earlier and less controversial vintage. Johnson County was also named for a Virginian. No regional politics were involved in naming Riley County and Scott County, although Riley and Scott were both Virginians.

The town of Winchester in Jefferson County, Kansas, started as a hotel on the military freight road. It was suggested that it be named Savannah. That, too, would be a southern name; and even though it has now become associated with prairies, or an open space in the woods, it was originally associated with the name of the Shawanoe or Shawnee Indians, meaning "southerner."[2] A post office in Pottawatomie County was named Savannah in 1867. But Alvin Best, who chose the Jefferson County townsite, proposed to name it for his home town in Winchester, Virginia. "He being the oldest man in the settlement," it was said, "his wishes were cheerfully acceded to by the others."[3] Winchester is a name that has migrated from England to America and from coast to coast. The one in Kansas is only one of thirty in the United States.[4] Winchester in England was historically famous at the time of Canute the Dane, of William the Conqueror, and of King Arthur and his knights.[5] It was a Roman name for a military camp.

Although French, Chantilly was a name that came to Kansas as a memorial of a Civil War battle in Virginia where General Philip Kearny was killed. During the boom in western Kansas, Chantilly, pronounced "Chantilla," was the largest of four towns competing for the county seat; at one time it defeated Lakin 216 to 51, but today, Lakin is the county seat.[6]

Both the Carolinas contributed place-names to Kansas. The Carolina colonies were named for King Charles II from his Latin name of Carolus.[7] In Doniphan County a place incorporated in 1857 was named Carolina.[8]

One of the most unusual names to come to Kansas from the South was Buncomb from Buncombe County, North Carolina. Asheville, in "The Land of the Sky," was its county seat. Originally the name came from Edward Buncombe, a North Carolina colonel in the American Revolution who won distinction at the Battle of the Brandywine. He lived in lonely splendor on his vast estate. A sign over his mansion read: "WELCOME ALL, TO BUNCOMBE HALL."[9] Buncomb was the name of a post office in Brown County, but the name, associated with "bunk," was not popular and was changed to the more respectable name of St. Francis.

Guilford was for several years the name of a post office in Wilson County. In 1886 the post office was moved to Benedict, but there is still a Guilford station south of Benedict. There is a Guilford in England, one in Connecticut, and one in North Carolina. Guilford, as a name, became well known from the famous battle in the American Revolution when General Nathanael Greene defeated General Cornwallis at Guilford Courthouse in North Carolina. In England the name was Guildford, probably where the guild collected tolls at a ford.[10] There is now a new connection with the name, since Paul Getty, modestly referred to as a millionaire, lives at Guilford Castle in England.[11]

Palmetto, a neighbor of Marysville in Marshall County, was settled by pioneers from South Carolina, the "Palmetto State." These settlers had come from Atchison to build a town at the ford where the government road crossed the Blue and where Frank Marshall built his ferry. For a time the ford was called the "Palmetto Crossing."[12] The community, composed of eighty-four members, was referred to as the "Palmetto Colony." There was local friction according to one headline in the *Marysville Advocate*, which read: "Knives sharpened and guns loaded when Carolinians founded Palmetto."[13] The town was important enough to be the terminal of the Elwood and Palmetto Railroad. Immediately after the election of Lincoln, the Carolinians left to join the Confederates. Their influence was ended and what was left of Palmetto moved to Marysville.[14]

Baltimore was the name which replaced Omnia in Cowley County. It was named for George Calvert who had served his king well and who was given the title of Baron of Baltimore in the Kingdom of Ireland. Later he was given a title to Newfoundland. He complained of the cold there and was given a southern colony which he named Maryland for Henrietta Maria, the wife of Charles I. The Baltimore name came from Ireland, fortunately simplified from *baile-an-tighe-mhoir*, which meant "town of the great house," referring to the Castle O'Driscoll.[15] But Baltimore in Kansas was replaced by Atlanta.

Atlanta, Georgia, was located at a site the Indians called "Standing Peach Tree," a name preserved in the famous Peach Tree Street of Atlanta. The Georgia railroad which headed for a terminal at the Atlantic was simply called "Terminous." Impressed by a visit from former Governor Wilson Lumpkin, the legislature named the town Marthasville for Martha Lumpkin, the governor's daughter. Unhappy with this name, Richard Peters of the Georgia railroad asked his superior for a better one. The boss rose to the occasion and suggested Atlanta, "feminine," he said, "for Atlantic." Peters liked the name and put Atlanta on a handbill, and, legal or not, it stuck.[16]

Although Greek in origin, Atlanta became a Kansas place-name. The first Atlanta was near Independence in Montgomery County where it shared its name with another listed as "Rutland or Atlanta." Neither the town nor the name survived, although Rutland is still the name of the township.

In Rice County a trading post was combined with the Atlanta Hotel and there a town company established the town of Atlanta. The railroad missed it by a mile, but Lyons, a mile farther north, was on the railroad and so Atlanta was deserted. Lyons was named for Truman J. Lyon who owned the townsite. The place was called "Lyon's town," and then the apostrophe was dropped.[17]

In Cowley County, where a railroad bypassed the town of Baltimore, the Darlington family started a new town by the track. They permitted a young lady by the name of Mary Moore to choose its name. She chose Atlanta, primarily because she liked it, and because it, like Baltimore, was southern.[18]

Roanoke is a name that may stir one's memory of Sir Walter Raleigh's lost colony, the Roanoke River, the Civil War battle there, or just the Virginia town. It is a name with an Indian source which may mean "the place of white shells."[19] In Kansas, Roanoke was a lonely post office south of the Sandy Arroyo Creek in Stanton County.

Among the many railway promotion schemes in Kansas was the one to run a railway from Kansas City to Memphis. The road followed the border and came to Appleton below Fort Scott, where it stopped. Several names for the terminal were rejected before it was concluded that if the railroad could not go to Memphis, Memphis might come to the railroad. After all, Memphis was a part of the railroad name, so Memphis, the name of a town in Tennessee, replaced the name of Appleton as the terminal in Kansas. Memphis in Kansas has been settled largely by southerners. As business declined, the name seemed no longer significant and a change was proposed. The choice may have been made in the railway station or the village store where the name of the Garland stove was selected to replace the name of Memphis.[20]

Nashville, Tennessee, was likely named for General Francis Nash, who was struck and killed by a cannon ball in a battle against General Howe. He was a North Carolinian, yet the place best known for his name is in Tennessee. There a town named Nashborough was later changed to Nashville.[21] This name was a likely source for the Nashville in Kansas. There was first a Nashville in Coffey County. After its demise, there was another Nashville in Kingman County, said to be named by a John Brown from Nashville, Tennessee. It had been named "Old Bross" before it was moved to the railroad as Nashville.

The Kentucky influence was strong in Kansas. The Lecompton Constitutional Convention had more delegates born in Kentucky than in any other state.[22] Most of the Kentucky names in Kansas were names of the home town from which Kentuckians came. Kentuck Creek in McPherson County was named for a Kentucky trapper who had settled there.[23] Kentucky Township in Jefferson County suggests the presence of Kentucky settlers. Foreign names such as Paris and Lebanon had taken on the characteristics of Kentucky before their adoption as Kansas place-names. Lexington, with its New England background, had a Kentucky source in Kansas. Garnett in Anderson County was named for W. A. Garnett, a wealthy man of Louisville, Kentucky. He was a member of the town company in Louisville which selected the Garnett townsite.

The Hurst post office was located on the William D. Hurst ranch north of Caldwell. When the railway was built, the post office moved to the tracks. Then came a company of promoters from Corbin, Kentucky, and there they built their town and named it Corbin.[24]

The first Ashland in Kansas was in Davis County, and Davis County was named for Jefferson Davis, a Kentuckian. With the change of county boundaries, Ashland won only three votes for county seat, ending its need for existence. Ashland is still the name of a township in Riley County.[25]

Several Kentuckians in Winfield, Kansas, organized a company to promote a town in Clark County. J. B. Nipp, sheriff of Cowley County, named it Ashland for Henry Clay's home, but Nipp was from Ashland, no doubt a factor in his choice of the name. Ashland had earlier been a post office named Klaine for N. B. Klaine, the postmaster. It was also known as "Baker's Store." The store and post office were moved a short distance to Clark City,[26] which was first identified by a barn on the bank of Bear Creek and called "Bank Barn." Later two soldiers killed by the Indians were buried there and so it became known as "Soldiers' Grave," a name it kept until the founding of Ashland in 1884.[27] Ashland took over the people and post offices of its neighbors.

Lebanon, the land of the snow-covered mountains, has given its name to at least twenty sites before it came from Kentucky to Kansas. The Lebanon that survived in Kansas is located in Smith County. There were settlers in Kansas from Lebanon, Connecticut, and from Lebanon, New Hampshire; but Lebanon, Kansas was named by Dr. R. B. Ray of Lebanon, Kentucky.[28] The post office was moved from its first location in order to be on the railroad, so there was for a time an Old Lebanon as well as a New Lebanon.[29]

It was not the romance of France that brought Paris to Kansas; it was the sentiment of southerners from Paris, Kentucky. Paris in Linn County was named for the former home of James H. Barlow, a Kentucky lawyer. The "fire-eating southerners" of Paris abandoned the place when they went to war, and Paris, Kansas, is no more.[30] A Paris had also been promoted in Shawnee County, but it was too close to Topeka to survive.

The influence of Missouri was not as great as one might expect, except for the five Kansas counties named for Missouri men: Colonel Doniphan, General Marshall, Senators Atchison, Linn, and Joseph C. Anderson. Missouri's name was tried in Kansas and there was a place called Missouri Farm in Doniphan County, a Missouri City in Johnson County, and, equally short-lived, a post office named Missouri Flat in Sumner County.

Louisburg, Miami County, near the Missouri border, was first named Saint Louis for Saint Louis, Missouri. For identification it was generally called "Little Saint Louis," but this was not official. Eventually, to avoid "confounding the new town with Saint Louis, Missouri," the Katy railroad recommended in 1870 that it be renamed Louisburgh. It has now dropped the "h." According to George Stewart, Saint Louis was more likely named for Louis IX than for Louis XIV,[31] the Sun King, who was not a saintly king.

Pierre LaClede was the Frenchman who, together with Chouteau, established Saint Louis, naming it for the king of France. LaClede,

Kansas, was located on the central part of Pottawatomie County. Lucas in Russell County is a name which came from Lucas Place in Saint Louis. The railroad had used the name of Elbon for a time but accepted the change to Lucas Place, later reduced to Lucas for brevity.[32] Kansas adopted the name of Saint Louis, the name of the founder of Saint Louis, and a place within Saint Louis.

In the southwestern corner of Kansas, Morton County has a town named Rolla. According to one account, the name had been Reit, named for a pioneer, but an error by the post office department made it Rolla.[33] It is now spelled like Rolla in Missouri, which was the phonetic spelling by southerners for Raleigh, North Carolina, its source.[34] Rolla Township in Morton County followed the same spelling.

Spring Hill is a townsite with a magnificent setting south of Olathe in Johnson County. "It devolved upon me," James B. Honey said, "to give it a name, which duty I fulfilled, calling it Spring Hill after one of the most beautiful places I have ever seen," Spring Hill, a suburb of Mobile, Alabama. It is noted for its comely groves, gardens, and flowers. Honey would make Spring Hill in Kansas as beautiful as Spring Hill, Alabama.[35]

Iuka is the name of a Chickasaw chief who lies buried in the town square of Iuka in Tishomingo County, Mississippi. During the Civil War, General Sterling Price, who had been the greatest Confederate threat to Kansas, was stationed at Iuka when General Grant was organizing his army in Tennessee. Iuka is on the border of that great battle area of Shiloh and Corinth. Iuka in Kansas is located in Iuka Township in the north-central part of Pratt County. Since most of its settlers came from Iowa, it had been assumed that the name possibly came from Iowa, which once had an Iuka, now named Tama.[36] The name may have been chosen by a Mrs. Dunn of Iowa. According to the local account, the choice of a name was to be made by having each suggestion written on a slip of paper and placed in a hat. The first one to be drawn out was to be the name of the town. Iuka was the name proposed by a veteran of the Battle of Iuka, and it was his choice that was drawn from the hat.[37]

Iuka was an ambitious town before Pratt won the county seat in a typical and, some say, unethical county seat war. There was a meeting to be held at Cullison to decide on the railway route and bonds for the railway. The winning of the railroad could be decisive in choosing the county seat. No delegate came from Iuka. It is the opinion of old-timers at Iuka that Pratt residents got the Iuka delegates drunk and, by this strategy, won.[38]

Jefferson Buford, a Georgian, brought a colony of southerners to

Kansas in 1856. Some of his followers were from South Carolina and Alabama, but most of them came from Georgia, and their Kansas community was called New Georgia. Because of their coming, a Kansas resident warned, "we shall have to look to our locks and our hen coops."[39] The friction between the southern and northern faction was so great that New Georgia became Fort Georgia. It was destroyed by John Brown's followers.[40] Georgia City in Crawford County was, however, said to be named for A. J. Georgia of Pittsburg.[41]

Buford's band made Cofachiqui near Iola its headquarters. Cofachiqui got its name from a Creek princess or "chieftainess" and a Creek village on the Savannah River. It was said to mean "dogwood tree." Princess Cofachiqui cast a spell over the dashing De Soto and gave him a "rope of pearls." He courted her and made her his captive, but she escaped from the romantic Spaniard with the aid of one of De Soto's slaves.[42]

This provocative name, or "mellifluous" name, as it has been called, could have given color to the Kansas map. Local residents simplified this seemingly difficult name by calling it "Coffeechee." The town was unable to compete with Iola, named for another woman,[43] and was abandoned.

For a short time Kansas had a Key West in Coffey County. It was named by a sailor who had spent some unhappy days in Key West, Florida. He disliked the place and was equally unhappy in Kansas, saying that his town was as "desolate as Key West, Florida." The name was meaningless in Kansas, except for the sailor's association, and the Americans had already made the Spanish name meaningless in Florida. The name evolved from Cayo Hueso, meaning "Bone Key," but the Americans did not translate the name. Instead they tried to Anglicize the sound of the Spanish name and this made it Key West. The Kansas Key West might better have kept its original name of Queen City, except for its failure to survive, irrespective of its odious or regal name.[44] Cram's map in 1883 gave it as "Key West or Queen City." Tampa is the name of a station in Marion County. The only other Tampa of note is the one in Florida. It is supposed to be an Indian name. Gannett has suggested that it came from *itimpi*, said to mean "close to it" or "near it."[45] But James C. Simpson, in a more recent study, considers its meaning unknown. Yet Tampa Bay in Tampa, Florida, must have been the source for the name in Kansas.[46]

Texas had its influence on Kansas, as Abilene well knows and as other terminals of the Texas cattle trails learned. Rush County has a Lone Star Township which was once half of Pioneer Township. The Lone Star Township was said to be named by a cowboy from Texas.[47] In addition to the township named Lone Star, Sumner County once had a Lone Star post office, and, after its passing, the name of Lone Star replaced the name of Bond in Douglas County.

Indianola, an ambitious town near Topeka, was given its name by Colonel Fontleroy who had once been stationed at Indianola, Texas. In its brief and turbulent history it was called the "hot spot" for soldiers and officers from Fort Leavenworth. It had ambitions to become the capital of Kansas, but when Topeka won, it declined and finally disappeared.[48] There is also an Indianola Creek in Butler County and there was once the Indianola post office, replacing one named Smithfield.[49] One may now see the name on an overpass on the turnpike as Indianola Road in Butler County.

Seguin in Sheridan County was, according to local folklore, a name that came from a section foreman named Quinn. Whenever anyone asked for a job—or a drink—the suggestion was to "See Quinn." Sequin may be the name of a coin or a spangle, but in Texas, Sequin was named for Colonel Jean Sequin, a Mexican officer.[50] Changing Sequin to Seguin would not be difficult.

The South was the source for most of the county names when the proslavery partisans dominated the first Territorial Legislature of Kansas, as we shall see in the next chapter.

The region contributed many names of distinction to Kansas. Sumner County opened a post office named Dixie in 1873, a name that stands as a symbol of the South.

CHAPTER XXIX

BOGUS LEGISLATURE

AS SOON AS KANSAS WAS OPEN to settlement under the provisions for squatter sovereignty in 1854, each side in the slavery issue promoted settlements in sympathy with its own partisan views. David R. Atchison urged Missourians to do their duty and save Kansas for slavery at the ballot-box. Benjamin Stringfellow, also from Missouri, implied that it was no crime to kill abolitionists. Northern supporters of the free-state settlers supported their partisans by sending them Sharp's rifles, labeled "Beecher's Bibles." They objected to being called abolitionists. Strongly motivated, these "sovereign squats" resorted to force in support of their respective policies. The territory became known as "Bleeding Kansas."[1]

Residents of Missouri came to vote in Kansas as crusaders for a cause, a fee, or a jug of whisky, each according to his own principle and price. Fictitious names were used and fraudulent figures were given for the election returns. McGee (Cherokee) County, with twenty families, turned in 1,200 votes without even holding an election.[2] Poll books indicated that votes had been cast by Henry Ward Beecher, James Buchanan, Horace Greeley, and William H. Seward, quite contrary to their political convictions.[3] But it mattered not. The proslavery faction dominated the polls and the first legislature moved the territorial capital from Pawnee City, near Fort Riley, to Shawnee Mission, where it was easily accessible to its Missouri representatives. The first legislative body of Kansas, dominated by proslavery elements, many from Missouri, was dubbed the "Bogus Legislature."

The political and social leanings of the legislators determined the choice of names for the first thirty-five counties in Kansas. There may have been little partisanship in choosing names such as Washington, Madison, and Jefferson,[4] all Virginians, and Marion, a South Carolinian. Wise County was named for a contemporary governor of Virginia, and Hunter, for a Virginia senator. Johnson County was named for a missionary from Virginia, and Woodson County for a Virginia politician. McGee, Coffey, Wilson, Richardson, Breckinridge, and Davis were men with a Kentucky background, and Bourbon was the name of a Kentucky county. Doniphan, Linn, Atchison, Marshall, and Anderson were Missouri men. No other area furnished as many names for the first Kansas counties as did the states of Virginia, Kentucky, and Missouri. Most of these names represented men of distinction.

Doniphan County, named for Colonel Alexander W. Doniphan, was the first Kansas county to be named. According to tradition, a Doniphan ancestor was a Spaniard who had come to England during the time of Ferdinand and Isabella. His Spanish name of Don Afonso was corrupted into Doniphan.[5] Colonel Doniphan, born in Kentucky of a Virginia family, continued the westward migration into Missouri. He organized a Missouri regiment for the Mexican War. Although he enlisted as a private, he was a natural leader and was soon elected colonel and commander. "My men are rough and ready," he said, and, being hunters from Missouri, they could hit a squirrel in the eye at a hundred paces.[6] As for the marksmanship of the Mexican soldier, we may judge the rumored instructions of an American officer to his men: "If you see a Mexican aim at you, stand still!" Doniphan enhanced his reputation by bringing back from Mexico a cannon as a souvenir. He named it "Old Sacramento," but in Kansas it was named "Old Kickapoo" and was said to have fired "the first shots both for and against slavery in the United States."[7] With his Kentucky-Missouri background, Doniphan, the "Soldier Statesman," was a proslavery man, yet a member of a peace commission in Washington to avert civil war. He was a distinguished man about whom Lincoln made the comment, "You are the only man I ever met who, in appearance, came up to any previous expectations."[8]

When the Bogus Legislature named Marion County, it was to honor General Francis Marion, a South Carolinian and a hero in the American Revolution. Marion's success as a raider against the British and his escapes into the swamps gave him his nickname of the "Swamp Fox."[9] In 1790 he participated in the making of the South Carolina constitution, and he served two terms in the state senate. Marion County was at first only a narrow strip a hundred miles long which reached to the Oklahoma border. It disappeared in 1857. When the county was revived in 1860, it had the same name, but this time the name had a new source, Marion County, Ohio, also named to honor the general.[10] The Marion community now considers General Marion as the original source of its name rather than the Ohio home of Sam Wood.

The national leader of the proslavery movement in Kansas was Senator David R. Atchison of Missouri,[11] and for him Atchison County was named. Atchison was a forceful and confident man who rode roughshod over opposition. He weighed over two hundred pounds but he was only half as big as his brother, "who tipped the scale at four hundred pounds." Born in Frogtown,[12] Kentucky, he boasted that he was the "biggest frog in the puddle, sir." He has been described as "a man of commanding presence," and "a stump orator of no mean order."[13] His parents had named him David Rice for a Presbyterian minister, hoping that he would follow in the minister's footsteps, but he chose law and politics for his career. He attended school with Jefferson Davis.

When Senator Lewis F. Linn died in office in 1843, Atchison succeeded him. He became acting vice-president when William R. King, the vice-president, died. While presiding over the Senate, Atchison signed the act for the territorial organization of Kansas. On a legal technicality, which is debatable, he became "President for a day," since March 4 came on a Sunday in 1849 and General Taylor did not take office until Monday.[14] The battle between Thomas Hart Benton, "Mr. Senator," and Atchison in 1854 resulted in a draw, and for two years Missouri had only one senator. Atchison returned to western Missouri and devoted his energies to making Kansas a slave state and to "abolishing abolition."

Atchison responded to acting Governor Woodson's appeal to lead an army of "good citizens" against Lawrence. "When I saw you last," said Governor Geary, "you were acting as Vice President of the Nation and president of the most distinguished body of men in the world, the Senate of the United States." Then he added: "It is with sorrow and pain that I see you now, leading on to a civil and disastrous war an army of men, with uncontrollable passions and determined upon wholesale slaughter and destruction."[15] Yet for this man, Atchison County and the city of Atchison were named.

The town of Atchison was promoted by Dr. John H. Stringfellow and settled largely by Missourians. It came near being called Oldham for Lee Oldham,[16] but Stringfellow insisted on naming it Atchison for his partner in the campaign to control Kansas politics. Later, Samuel C. Pomeroy, as agent of the Emigrant Aid Society, was successful in purchasing one half of the Atchison townsite. The committee in charge wished to change the name of Atchison to something of "less evil" memory. First they suggested Wilmot for David Wilmot of Pennsylvania, who sponsored the Wilmot Proviso for the exclusion of slavery from the territory acquired from Mexico. Then the name of Pomeroy was proposed, but nothing came of either proposal.[17] Strangely, too, the numerous replacements of county names which honored the proslavery element did not touch Atchison County.

Two counties, Leavenworth and Riley, were named for military forts, and these in turn had been named for military men without any regional connotation. Colonel Henry Leavenworth was a Connecticut Yankee and Major Bennett C. Riley was a Virginian.

It was said of the members of the First Territorial Legislature that "They had a penchant for honoring themselves and immortalizing their names by calling counties and towns for themselves."[18] Among the counties named for legislators were Johnson, Lykens, Coffey, Marshall, Richardson, Anderson, and McGee. Colonel Coffey, General Richardson, and General Marshall were Missouri military men; Johnson and Lykens were missionaries to the Indians; and Anderson and McGee were Missouri representatives in Kansas politics.

Johnson County was named for Rev. Thomas Johnson, a Virginian and a slaveowner, who came to Kansas in 1829. When he visited Washington in 1853, the *Washington Post* referred to him as "a noble speciman of a western man."[19] He established the Methodist Shawnee Mission, now called Mission, and served it with distinction for a quarter of a century. As head of the mission, he worked with vision and vigor to give the Indians the best of the white man's civilization, as he saw it. He established a training school and an experimental farm, a gristmill and a sawmill, a blacksmith shop, a carpenter shop, and a shoe shop. He carried bluegrass seed in his saddlebag which he scattered as he rode along, just like Johnny Appleseed. All this he did for one hundred dollars a year. Indians called him "Big Chief." As president of the territorial council, he became one of the leaders of the Bogus Legislature. Although sympathetic with the South and with slavery, he could not condone secession. During the war, he remained loyal to the Union. In 1865 he was killed in the doorway of his home by an assassin, possibly a member of the Quantrill band, who considered him to be a deserter.[20]

Johnson in Stanton County was named for Colonel Alexander Soule Johnson, one of the twelve children of Rev. Thomas Johnson.[21] At the age of twenty-three, he was the youngest representative in the Bogus Legislature. When the war started, he joined the Union and was lieutenant colonel in the Thirteenth Infantry of the Kansas Militia. For a time he was the land commissioner for the Fort Scott and Gulf Railroad and later for the Santa Fe. He was married twice, and his second wife had the interesting name of Zippie.[22] Johnson was not honored by a place-name because he was in the Bogus Legislature but most likely for his public service in Topeka or his work for the railroads.

David Lykens, a nephew of Thomas Johnson, was born in Indiana and came to Kansas as a missionary to the Weas, Piankeshaws, Peorias, and Kaskaskias.[23] His mission was at Peoria, and Peoria later became the county seat of the county named Lykens. He was elected to the Bogus Legislature and he served as a member of the Lecompton Constitutional Convention. The opposition to men with southern sympathies was so strong in 1861 that Lykens' name was replaced by the neutral name of Miami for the county where the Miami Indians had once lived.[24] Lykens Creek, a branch of the Shunganunga, was named for Rev. Johnston Lykens, son-in-law of Isaac McCoy[25] and the founder of the Shawnee Baptist Mission near Johnson's Methodist Mission.

South of Lykens County, now Miami, is Linn County, named for Dr. Lewis F. Linn, senator from Missouri. Linn was born in Kentucky but moved to St. Genevieve in Missouri to practice medicine and politics. He was an admirer of Andrew Jackson, "the hero of his heart's warmest admiration," and he was a supporter of Senator Benton's policy of Manifest Destiny. He also sponsored the Platte Purchase from the Indians which gave the northeastern corner of Kansas to Missouri before there was a Kansas. His personal charm may explain the statement that "he had political opponents in the Senate, but not one enemy."[26] This may also help to explain why Kansas did not change the name of Linn County.

Francis J. Marshall, better known officially as General Marshall and as "Frank" by his friends, was born in Virginia, where he attended William and Mary College. He moved to Missouri where he was so stirred by the migrations of the Forty-Niners that he decided to seek his fortune, not in the gold fields of California, but by building a much-needed ferry across the Big Blue in northern Kansas. His ferry was on the California Trail, the Overland Route, and the Military Road. There he set up a station named Marysville for his wife, Mary Williams.[27]

Marshall was elected to the Bogus Legislature where he participated in the creation of Kansas counties. He carved out one for himself, with his station in the center to make it the seat of Marshall County. He also was a brigadier general of Kansas Militia and a candidate for governor under the Lecompton Constitution. According to one who knew him, "Frank Marshall was a long-headed man (for a democrat) and was an important factor in Buchanan's administration, as far as Kansas was concerned."[28]

The Bogus Legislature did not name any county for any of the territorial governors, except for Daniel Woodson who once served as acting governor. At the age of thirty, Woodson was appointed the first secretary of Kansas Territory by President Franklin Pierce. It was Woodson who commissioned the officers, all southern sympathizers, for the state militia which had been recruited by Governor Shannon to crush the free-state movement at Topeka. As a Virginian, he was called "a willing tool of the slave power." A critic described him as "a man with sufficient education to be dangerous."[29] Yet he was a modest man, "genial, kind, and courteous." His later life was devoted to journalism and farming, and he served twelve years as city clerk of Coffeyville.[30]

It has been suggested that Woodson County was named for Governor Silas Woodson of Missouri. Senator John Martin stated categorically: "The county was named in honor of Honorable Daniel Woodson," and "Governor Silas Woodson was not even thought of in connection with the naming of the county."[31] The post office named Woodson in Marshall County the year that Woodson came to Kansas lasted only a few months.

Coffey County, "carved out by the infamous legislature of 1855," was named for Colonel Asbury M. Coffey, a native of Kentucky but a resident of Missouri when he was elected to the First Territorial Council of Kansas. He was on the Committee of Three to draw up a code of laws for Kansas, a task that was simplified by using the Missouri code which legalized slavery. While serving in the legislature, he had been for the preservation of the Union in spite of being a strong proslavery man. Governor Shannon said he was "a prudent, discreet man." Coffey resigned in 1857, and when war broke out, he became a colonel in the Confederate army.[32]

The name of Coffey County has occasionally been spelled "Coffee." William A. Phillips spelled Colonel Coffey's name "Coffee."[33] The association with coffee was natural when the name was heard and not read. The Nazi radio during World War II is said to have followed the report on a flood at Coffeyville by stating that the coffee plantations had been flooded and the coffee crop ruined.[34] When a columnist in a Los Angeles paper reported that Coffeyville was considering a change in its name, he suggested that it be changed to "Sanka."[35] So far Coffeyville has been too alert to sacrifice its name for the sleepy sound of Sanka.

Since Coffey County was named for Colonel A. M. Coffey, it was assumed that he was also the source for the name of Coffeyville.[36] But there were several Coffeys in Kansas, and it is more likely that Coffeyville was named for James A. Coffey, the first settler, Indian trader, and first postmaster in the town.[37] James A. Coffey, also called Colonel Coffey, established a trading post at the Coffeyville site to trade with the Black Bob band of Osages.[38] Using the title of colonel for both Coffeys was confusing, and the confusion was compounded when a reference was made to Coffeyville being built by John L. Coffey.[39] Since A. M. Coffey, a Miami County resident, was said to have joined the Confederate army,[40] he would probably not have been made postmaster of the town of Coffeyville. It is reasonable to believe that James A. Coffey was the one for whom Coffeyville was named.

Colonel James A. Coffey laid the foundation for Coffeyville by starting a trading post at an Osage camp called "Talley Springs." He must have had a real hunger for music, because he had a grand piano hauled from Kansas City to his trading post. Because of the "selfishness" of the Talley Springs settlement, the railroad stopped short of Colonel Coffey's post. Octave Chanute surveyed and platted a town just north of Talley Springs, also called "Old Coffeyville," to which he gave the cumbersome name of "Railroad Addition of Coffeyville." Having the railroad, the "Addition" won. It was modestly known as the "Village of Coffeyville" and then Coffeyville.[41]

Not only did Old Coffeyville disappear, but so did a number of neighboring towns: Claymore, or Clymore, Westralia, Talley Springs, and Parker. Claymore, also written Clermont, was named for an Osage chief; Westralia had reference to a trail to the West; Talley Springs was named for Tal-lee or Chief Kahantunka, who was a member of Clymore's band; and Parker was the name of a pioneer town promoter. As a cattle terminal, Old Coffeyville was called "Cow-Town," and its most popular street, especially for the cowboys, was "Red Hot Street."[42]

Anderson County was named for Joseph C. Anderson, whose home was in Missouri. His Missouri neighbors helped to elect him to the Bogus Legislature as a representative from the Fort Scott district. He was enough of a leader to serve as the speaker pro tem of the Territorial House.[43] Anderson participated in the promotion of the towns of Chaumiere and Cofachiqui.[44]

Before Lincoln's fame made his name a worthy memorial to be recorded on the Kansas map, Davis County had already honored the name of Jefferson Davis. "Jeff" Davis was Kentucky-born but he represented Mississippi in Congress. He was a West Point graduate and was appointed secretary of war under President Pierce. As a young lieutenant at Fort Crawford, Wisconsin, he followed that old rule to success: "Marry the boss's daughter." He married and ran away with Sarah Knox Taylor, daughter of Colonel Zachary Taylor, his commanding officer. Sarah died six years after their happy marriage. Davis later married the daughter of a southern plantation owner, a devoted and militant defender of Davis.

Davis was a southern aristocrat, called a "scrub aristocrat" by his critics. He was well read and full of opinions supported by strong convictions. Sam Houston said that Davis was "ambitious as Lucifer and cold as a lizard."[45] On January 21, 1861, a week before Kansas was voted into the Union as a state, Senator Davis walked out of Congress, soon to become president and commander-in-chief of the Confederacy. He was belligerent and vindictive and wished he were in the army instead of the presidency. His walk-out probably helped the cause of freedom in Kansas. Davis County was eventually changed to Geary.

Hunter County was a big county and included the present Cowley County and much of Butler. It was named for Robert Mercer Taliaferro Hunter, a senator from Virginia who had changed from a Whig to a State-Rights Democrat. He backed Calhoun for the presidency in the 1840's, but by 1859, he was a presidential candidate himself. With the coming of the war, Hunter joined Jeff Davis and Toombs as the "Southern Triumvirate."[46] In 1870, Hunter County's name was changed to Cowley.

The Bogus Legislature of 1855 named Breckinridge County for John Cabell Breckinridge, a distinguished politician from Kentucky. Breckinridge did not join his fellow Kentuckians in the war with Mexico, but it was he who gave the memorial address for those killed at Buena Vista and brought back for burial in Kentucky soil. The audience of twenty thousand stimulated his oratorical performance to its highest pitch. He was so carried away by his own patriotic appeal that "he talked himself into the army." So he went to Mexico, too late, however, to win fame in that war. He also gave the funeral oration for Clay, and, in a sense, he became the successor of Clay as spokesman of Kentucky politics. When Breckinridge County was named, he was only a Kentucky representative in Congress but he later became vice-president under Buchanan. Then he ran for the presidency against both Douglas and Lincoln, and lost. He was appointed the Confederate secretary of war by President Davis.

Madison County had been divided between Breckinridge and Greenwood. During the administration of Governor Denver, the legislature proposed that the name of Cawhola be substituted for Breckinridge. The change was not approved by the governor.[47] In 1862 the name Breckinridge was replaced by Lyon, honoring General Nathaniel Lyon.[48]

South of Davis County, now Geary, a county was named for Henry A. Wise, governor of Virginia, characterized as a "rabid pro-slaveryite."[49] After Robert E. Lee and "Jeb" Stuart had captured John Brown, it was Governor Wise who "hung John Brown" and sent his "soul a marching on." Yet Governor Wise spoke of Brown as being "a man of clear head, of courage, fortitude, and simple ingenuousness," but also a "fanatic."[50] The hanging of John Brown was one of his last official acts as governor, and this took place while Lincoln was campaigning in

Kansas. It is not surprising that Wise was an "odious" name which was soon erased from the map of Kansas. Part of Wise County was reorganized as Morris County and named for Senator Thomas Morris, a Bible-quoting senator and crusader from Ohio.

Allen County, south of Anderson, was named for William Allen, a Democratic senator from Ohio.[51] He has been described as a man of "large stature and commanding presence." He was left an orphan in North Carolina, spent his early life in Virginia, and he hiked to Ohio where he became a law partner of Colonel King, the son of Rufus King. He won a seat in the House of Representatives as a Democrat in a Republican stronghold. Perhaps his crowning achievement was to marry the daughter of the man he had defeated by one vote. He is said to have originated the war-cry of "Fifty-four Forty or Fight," but he was not a distinguished senator. In 1873 he was elected governor, and he had enough personal appeal to be considered as a possible candidate for the presidency. The political reason for giving his name to a Kansas county may have been that he could see no sense in the free-soil point of view. He was anti-war and anti-Lincoln.[52]

Calhoun County, now Jackson, was named for John Calhoun, first surveyor-general of Kansas. There were those who believed, mistakenly, that it was named for John C. Calhoun, the fiery statesman from South Carolina. When he was a surveyor in Illinois, Calhoun's assistant was Abraham Lincoln. He was born in New England, but his sympathies were with the South, and he served as the chairman of the Lecompton Constitutional Convention.[53] His views may be appreciated from his comments to the "law-and-order" meeting at Leavenworth: "I would rather be a painted slave over in Missouri, or a serf to the Czar of Russia, than have the abolitionists in power."[54] His name was anathema to the free-state men of Kansas and so the name of the county was changed to Jackson to honor the man who had challenged the greater Calhoun. The embryonic county seat also took its name from the surveyor-general, but that name, too, was wiped from the map.[55]

Butler County was named for Andrew Pickins Butler, a South Carolina senator. As a State-Rights Democrat, he was held in high regard by the Bogus Legislature. Butler County was the largest county in the state. It was called "The State of Butler," and El Dorado was its capital. The county changed its shape and its size five times, but it is still the largest county in Kansas.[56] Though it honored a southern, slave-state senator, Butler County kept its name.

What is now Cherokee County was first named for Mobillon W. McGee. Although born in Kentucky, McGee spent most of his early life in Missouri. Like a lot of other Missouri residents, he insisted on the right to vote wherever he "happened to be" on election day. He not only voted in Kansas but he was elected to the first Kansas Territorial Legislature. He was among the men who proposed to modify the eastern boundary of Kansas by following the Big Blue from the border to its terminal, thereby placing Kansas City, Missouri, and Westport within Kansas. This would make McGee of Westport a bona fide resident of Kansas. Missouri was willing to accept the change. A delegate was sent to Washington to complete the arrangements, but there he fell in love with a lady and took her to Europe. The result was that Kansas City remained a Missouri town, as did Westport, the home of McGee.[57] *Cherchez la femme!* For the love of a woman or the passion of a politician, Kansas City remains divided between two states, with a rampant river as an irresponsible boundary line. McGee later settled on a claim near Burlingame and promoted the hamlet known as One Hundred and Ten on 110-Mile Creek for the Kansas capital. It received one vote, probably McGee's. In 1867, McGee County had its name changed to the Indian name of Cherokee, since that had been Cherokee land.

Indian agents were generally politicians whose appointments were politically motivated. Among those who were important enough politically to have their names become county place-names were A. M. Coffey, Andrew J. Dorn, Hiero T. Wilson, William Godfrey, William P. Richardson, and Alfred B. Greenwood. Of all these names, only three remain—Coffey, Wilson, and Greenwood.

The county west of McGee (Cherokee) County was named Dorn for Major Andrew Jackson Dorn, a popular man who had been appointed Indian agent at the Neosho Agency by President Buchanan. After recruiting Cherokees for the Confederates, he gave up his office as an agent to become a quartermaster in the Confederate army. Though he was popular, "his name was a continual reminder of the aroma surrounding the Bogus Legislature, so the legislature of 1861 did not lose any time in wiping the name from the map."[58] The name of Dorn County was changed to Neosho, a neutral Indian name of the Neosho River.

Godfrey County, originally spelled Godfroy, the fourth county along the southern border, was named for William Godfrey, or as one writer said, for "Bill Godfrey who was a noted trader among the Indians."[59] His trading post was in Allen County. Bourbon County had a town named Godfrey. Politics may account for the change of the county name to Seward, the first of two counties to be named for William H. Seward. It later became Howard County, which in turn was divided into two counties named Elk and Chautauqua.[60]

Wilson County in 1855 included what is now both Wilson and

Montgomery counties. It was named for Colonel Hiero T. Wilson, described as "a noble speciman, physically, of the old Kentucky stock," and "a thorough gentleman." He was the first white settler at Fort Scott where he was a successful Indian trader and later an army sutler. He served as postmaster at Fort Scott and as a delegate to the Lecompton Constitutional Convention.[61] The Osages called him "Big White Chief," and he could speak not only their language but also Cherokee and Creek.

Wabaunsee County was first named Richardson for General William P. Richardson, member of the First Legislative Council of Kansas. He served as an Indian agent for the Iowas, Sacs, and Foxes as early as 1842. In spite of being a proslavery Kentucky man, he was willing to defend Governor Geary against the unfair attacks by his own party. One writer referred to Richardson as a "gentleman of learning and social brilliancy."[62] He was a major general with southern sympathies in command of the northern division of the Kansas Militia, also called the "bogus militia."[63] In a letter to Governor Shannon, Richardson spoke of free-state people as the "outlaws of Lawrence," and he told the governor that "those lawless men" would have to surrender their Sharp's rifles in order to preserve "peace and tranquility."[64] The governor urged him to assemble a large force at Lecompton to pacify Lawrence.[65] He was also directed to stop "Lane's Army" coming into Kansas by way of Nebraska. Richardson died in 1857; two years later the name of Richardson County was changed to Wabaunsee, the name of a Potawatomi chief which meant the "Dawn of Day." This removed another Kentucky name from the Kansas map.

Greenwood County was named for Alfred B. Greenwood, who came to Kansas as United States Indian commissioner. He dealt with the Kaw Indians at Council Grove and with the Indians at the Sac and Fox Agency, also called the Greenwood Agency. His hasty and secret negotiations to deprive the Kaw of their lands have been called a "swindle." The 500,000 acres owned by the Sac and Foxes were to be disposed of "for their benefit."[66] In spite of the criticisms of Greenwood's negotiations, his name was given to a county in 1855.[67] There his name remains even though he represented Arkansas in the Confederate Legislature during the Civil War.

There is a Greenwood Township in Franklin County, and there Thomas Connelley promoted a town at the Indian agency which he named Greenwood in honor of the Indian commissioner. There was another Greenwood in Brown County. Mitchell was elected mayor, but his town-lot titles were not good, so the residents rode him out on a rail. In a meeting to discuss a proposed railroad, a farmer from Virginia is reported to have said: "Mr. President, ladies and gentlemen; I reckon if this heah railroad comes it'll run right squah threw me. But I say, let huh come. I thank you fo' yo' kind attention. I've no mo' to say." But "The Fifth Standard Parallel Railroad" was not built and Greenwood City survived only four years.[68] A railway, a name, and a "city" were all lost.

Two counties, Weller and Broderick, were named for prominent politicians from California. John B. Weller was a veteran of the Mexican War; he had enlisted as a private and came out as a colonel. President Polk appointed him to the commission to settle the boundary between the United States and Mexico. In this settlement, Kansas acquired its southwestern corner, the area west of Dodge City and south of the Arkansas. Buchanan appointed Weller minister to Mexico and Lincoln recalled him. Weller was a roaming politician who served first as senator from Ohio and later he succeeded Frémont as senator from California. Weller was a popular politician and a good debater and had "warmly espoused" the Kansas-Nebraska Bill. His wife was a niece of Senator Benton of Missouri and a cousin of Frémont's wife, Jessie. But his name was also a reminder of the slave-holding domination of Kansas in 1855 and the name of Weller County was changed to Osage by the legislature of 1859.[69] David C. Broderick defeated Weller as senator from California, and in 1857, a Kansas county, now in Colorado, was named Broderick.[70]

There is considerable controversy over the origin of the name for Brown County, and a change in the spelling of the name has added to the confusion. There were three Browns as contenders for the honor: Orville H. Browne, member of the Bogus Legislature; Albert G. Brown, United States senator from Mississippi; and "Old" John Brown, the antislavery crusader. Best known of all the Browns in the state was John Brown, and some residents of Brown County would like to think that the county was named for him.[71] But we can be sure that the members of the Bogus Legislature would not have named it for such an implacable enemy. The place where the sons of John Brown settled in Miami County had no post office name, but "they called their location Brownsville."[72]

Alfred Gray, secretary of the State Board of Agriculture, was of the opinion that Brown County was named for Senator Brown from Mississippi. This opinion was supported by John Martin of Topeka,[73] and others have accepted this view without question.[74] A good reason for rejecting the senator's name is that the name of the county was for some time spelled "Browne," as spelled by Orville H. Browne, a prominent member of the territorial legislature. Dr. J. H. Stringfellow of Missouri said that the county was named for Orville Browne, whom he characterized as "a very brilliant and eccentric" member of the Kansas House. Waterson of Marysville and Halderman of Leavenworth, both contemporaries, support the opinion of Stringfellow, as does Edmund N. Morrill, the historian of Brown County.[75]

Like the rest of the members of the First Territorial Legislature, O. H. Browne was "very desirous" of having a county named for him. One writer said that "O. H. would not have had the 'e' left off his name for a fortune."[76] When the name of Browne County was changed to Brown after 1857, it was said to be a clerical error. Morrill suggested that some think that the "e" was stricken off so as to honor "Old John Brown."[77] Dropping an "e" from the name has not been unusual in Kansas; it was done to the name of Clark(e) County and to the name of Kearn(e)y County.

The Bogus Legislature adopted only two Indian names for county names, Nemaha and Shawnee. Nemaha, a Siouan name, has been translated as "river of the Mahas," and "stream of the Omahas."[78] At the time of Long's expedition, it was also said to mean the "river of cultivation." Nemaha is a simple name, but members of the Lewis and Clark expedition made it very complex; one spelled it "grands-mo-haugh."[79] George Duffield, who traveled in the valley, spelled it "Nimehah" one day; "Nimekah" the next day; "Nimahah" on the third day; and "Nemahah" on the fourth, which was within one "h" of its present name.[80]

The Shawnee Indians were Algonquins who were closely related to the Delawares. They had been driven from their eastern homes by the Iroquois and by the white man. Tecumseh was their most noted chief. Shawnee has been spelled in a variety of ways from "Shawunogi" to "Shawun" and the popular French form of Chaouanon to Shawanoe and Shawnee. It meant "southerner" since this tribe had settled in the south where the Savannah River and the Swanee River still bear variations of the Shawnee name.[81] The name was first suggested by Thomas Johnson for the county now named Johnson.[82] The first Shawnees settled there in 1828. The name was then given to the county within which Kansas later established its capital. The name had already been used for the Shawnee Mission and two Shawnee Creeks. There were Shawnee Townships on both sides of the Kaw, and there was a Shawnee Township in Cherokee County, possibly named for the Shawnee Trail.

With the proslavery element belongs the name of Colonel James Chiles, chairman of a Missouri organization to protect the slave-holding rights of southerners. H. W. Chiles ran the Western Hotel, later named Gillis House, in Kansas City. Chiles in Miami County was probably named for one of these two.[83]

Under the "laws" of the Bogus Legislature, there were those who assumed that they were justified in having "open season" on antislavery spokesmen. Barber and Phillips counties were not named by the Bogus Legislature, but resulted from the assassination of Barber and Phillips, who had dared to voice their convictions against the unlawful acts of the "law and order" faction. These men were among the martyrs in the fight for a free state.

Thomas W. Barber, an Ohio man, came to defend Lawrence against a proslavery raid. He and two companions on their way home were stopped by armed horsemen who ordered them to surrender. Barber refused, rode on, was shot, rode a bit farther, fell off his horse, and died. His body was brought to Lawrence, where the free-state people concluded that non-resistance was no longer possible. Then Colonel William A. Phillips' comment was, "The war has begun."[84] Two men shot at Barber, but it is not known which one killed him. This may not matter, since both claimed the "credit for killing the damned abolitionist." One of them, James N. Burns, was later a member of Congress from Missouri.[85] News of the murder spread rapidly, and John Whittier was so disturbed that he wrote a poem called "The Burial of Barber."[86] For security, several of the men who attended the funeral as mourners came disguised as women in long dresses and big bonnets.[87]

James H. Lane suggested that a monument be erected to Barber. The name of Barber County is the martyr's memorial. It was often spelled "Barbour," and some even spelled it "Barbor." Remsburg's comment was that English spelling was "a system entirely beyond the comprehension of the average Kansas legislator." Another said that "somebody, out of an exceedingly wise head, determined that the spelling should be Barbour, and it stood in this form until 1883, when the Legislature enacted that henceforth the county should bear the name originally given it."[88]

William Phillips was a lawyer in Leavenworth who had signed a protest against a fraudulent election, the one that elected the Bogus Legislature. But a protest would identify a man as an opponent of the proslavery people in power. Phillips had also befriended Cole McCrae, who had reputedly killed a proslavery squatter. Stringfellow, friend of Atchison and spokesman for the extremists from Missouri, proposed to have all abolitionists purged, warning them to leave immediately or they would "leave for eternity." When Phillips refused to leave, he was seized, one side of his head was shaved, and he was "stripped of his clothes, tarred and feathered, ridden on a rail for a mile and a half, and a negro auctioneer went through the mockery of selling him for a dollar." This sordid act was greeted with exaltation and unparalleled joy, said the *Leavenworth Herald*. The "Sovereign Squats" from Missouri then killed Phillips in his home.[89]

One might naturally assume that Phillipsburg in Phillips County was named for the same man for whom the county was named. But in this case, the town was named for William Addison Phillips, a lawyer and journalist who was a reporter for Greeley's *New York Tribune*.

The partisanship shown in the selection of the names for the first thirty-five counties was too obvious to go unchallenged. Eleven counties had their names changed. The first to be challenged were Richardson, Wise, and Calhoun. Rather strangely, the name of Davis County was one of the last to be changed, partly because of other political issues and ambitions which might divide the legislators. Marshall, Doniphan, Atchison, Butler, Brown, and Coffey, although named for proslavery sympathizers, remained on the map, as did Linn, Allen, and Greenwood. The names of Leavenworth, a "Connecticut Yankee," and Franklin from Philadelphia were nonpartisan names.

After Kansas was admitted to the Union as a free state, there was occasion for jubilations and celebrations. Old "Kickapoo," the cannon which Doniphan had captured in Mexico, was placed in the esplanade at Atchison and loaded with the "Bogus statutes" and fired into Missouri, or "as far in that direction as gunpowder would carry them."[90] So ended the partisan work of the Bogus Legislature, and for years to come, the state legislatures busied themselves with the replacement of obnoxious names, worthy in themselves, but incompatible to victors in the War Between the States.

CHAPTER XXX

KANSAS STATE OFFICIALS

WE HAVE SEEN HOW the Bogus Legislature gave a proslavery slant to its political actions. New England and the Old Northwest counteracted this with all the political pressure they could muster. There were high-minded and able leaders among them, but on both sides there were frontier characters described by one Kansas historian as "hirelings, adventurers, blatherskites, fanatics, reformers, philanthropists, patriots."[1] These were among the people who contributed to the choice of place-names in one way or another.

Ten governors served Territorial Kansas in seven years. When Governor Medary was getting his first shave from Sam, a Negro barber, the governor proposed paying by the month. "If you please, mass'r," said Sam, "I prefer to have you pay by de shave, dese gub'ners goes away so mighty sudden!"[2] In spite of dishonorable dismissals and narrow escapes, all of the governors but one left their names on the Kansas map. Anderson County preserved the name of three of these troubled governors: Reeder, Shannon, and Walker. Only Samuel Medary, whose family name had once been Madeira, failed to secure a place for his name in Kansas.

The first territorial governor of Kansas was Andrew H. Reeder, a "Philadelphia gentleman." Reeder made the seal for Kansas with the motto, *Populi voce nata*, "born by the voice of the people." It became a more appealing phrase than "squatter sovereignty."[3] A Kansas historian described Reeder as "a mild, easy, rhetorical, admirable man, of good intellectual parts, . . . and an enthusiastic advocate of popular sovereignty."[4] His efforts to be fair ended in failure. "This infernal scroundrel will have to be hemped yet," said the men from Missouri. Reeder was sufficiently familiar with the frontier colloquialism to know that being "hemped" meant being hanged, so he fled, disguised as a deck-hand on a Missouri River steamer.[5]

Towns have been named Reeder in four counties: Anderson, Kiowa, Graham, and Saline. But these may not all have been named for the governor. The one in Kiowa County was called "Reeder City." Kiowa County still has a Reeder Township. Reeder in Reeder Township in

Anderson County was most likely named for the governor. The life of the town was almost as short as was the term of the governor.

In Anderson County, the Cedar Bluff post office had its name changed to Shannon to honor Wilson Shannon, the second territorial governor of Kansas.[6] Ely Moore described Shannon as "an ex-congressman, twice governor, minister to a foreign court, a profound lawyer, a wit, and an honest man." But with all his wit, experience, and legal training, he was unable to govern Kansas.[7] Unlike Reeder, Shannon decided to ally himself with the Missouri group and he openly condemned the free-state men.[8] His critics said that he was prejudiced, partial, and proslavery. Forced to make peace with the Free-State Party at Lawrence, he gave a speech, interrupted by numerous hiccoughs from too many toasts. If they only knew "Old Wilson," he proclaimed, they would realize that he was "a hell of a nice fellow!" Although Shannon supported the Bogus Legislature, the "Law and Order Party," there was little law and order in the land. Having compromised with Robinson and Lane, Wilson lost the support of his own party, and, like Reeder, fled for his life. "Had Shannon possessed the wisdom of Solomon and the courage of Caesar," said one commentator, "he could not have successfully administered the affairs of Kansas. . . ."[9]

The town of Shannon in Anderson County was the county seat for a year, but it lost this advantage to Garnett.[10] The Shannon in Atchison County is near the site of the old Seven-Mile-House in Shannon Township. Shannon Township in Pottawatomie County was also named for the governor.[11]

The effort to change the name of Davis County to Lincoln failed, as did the attempt to name it Webster. In a letter to Sam Wood, F. N. Blake wrote: "You have my thanks for introducing a bill to change the name of 'Davis' County. I hope you may be successful . . . . You asked me for a name in place of 'Davis,' and I gave you 'Webster . . .'." That this change was not then approved was due to the delicate questions about the location of the capital and the university. This contest in the hot political tinderbox overshadowed the issue over the change of a county name.

Some objected to renaming Davis County because it would cause confusion in the changing of all the records. There were also some who would bury the hatchet and avoid stirring up new hostilities over a war which had been a tragedy for so many. But John K. Wright, a war veteran in the legislature, carried an implacable hatred for Jefferson Davis, and in a dramatic speech, in which he reviewed nearly all the battles of the war, he advocated change. Among the proposed names were Lincoln, Webster, Lyon, and Coronado—all worthy names. Then it was suggested that the choice should be left to the majority of the people, but this was not to be.[12] In 1889 the name of Davis County was changed to honor Governor John W. Geary. It was a good choice and an appropriate recognition of a competent veteran of two wars who was a successful administrator in California and Pennsylvania, even though he failed in Kansas.

Geary gave up school teaching as a profession, thinking it had no future. After the Mexican War, he was appointed postmaster and elected alcalde (mayor) of San Francisco, where Geary Street honors his memory.[13] During the Civil War he was a highly respected officer in the Army of the Potomac. After the war he was military governor of Savannah, Georgia. He was later a two-term governor of Pennsylvania, his home state. When he came to Kansas to rule that unruly territory, he met Governor Shannon fleeing for his life. Maligned and persecuted, he found safety only in flight under cover of darkness; or, as one writer said, like Reeder, he "flew the coop."[14]

George W. Martin was justifiably proud of having proposed Geary's name as a substitute for the name of Davis County.[15] A year after Governor Geary arrived, a place in Doniphan County was named Geary City in his honor.[16] With the name of Geary, it served as a post office until 1905. Of all the territorial governors, Geary was the only one to have his name given to a county.

Fredrick P. Stanton was born in the District of Columbia, but he made Memphis, Tennessee, his home. Stanton represented Tennessee in Congress for several terms. In 1857 he was appointed Secretary of Kansas Territory and he became acting governor before Walker's arrival. He supported Walker in obtaining recognition for the free-state voters and in rejecting the fraudulent elections on the border. He also called for an extra session of the first free-state legislature, after which the antislavery people of Kansas respected him;[17] then Buchanan recalled him.

The governor was honored when a town near Paola in Miami County was named Stanton. A second town was named Stanton in Riley County, but to avoid duplication, it had to choose a new name. On the suggestion of A. S. Edgerton, the postmaster, it was given the delightful name of May Day.[18] Three counties, Miami, Linn, and Ottawa, have townships named Stanton. Although the names are the same, Stanton County and Stanton Township in western Kansas were named for Edwin McMaster Stanton of Lincoln's cabinet.

Robert J. Walker was the fourth territorial governor and the third to have a place named in his honor in Anderson County. The town named Greeley was changed to Walker because some of the Anderson

County citizens did not like Greeley's politics. Later, when the political hostility subsided, Greeley's name was restored. A local township has, however, retained the name of Walker.

Governor Walker was a Pennsylvanian, as were also Reeder and Geary. Among his other distinctions, Walker had married a granddaughter of Benjamin Franklin. He was successful in marriage, politics, and business, and he hoped that his governorship in Kansas might be a steppingstone to the presidency, discounting the fact that Kansas had the reputation of being the "graveyard of governors." Walker wanted fair elections by bona fide residents of Kansas; when this failed, he too failed.[19]

The most successful, the most impressive, and the most popular of the territorial governors was James W. Denver. Like Woodson, the acting governor, he was a Virginian by birth. He was an able military man who was an officer in both the Mexican War and in the Civil War. Before coming to Kansas, he had lived in Missouri and California.[20] It was Denver who turned the tide against the proslavery domination in Kansas by recognizing the free-state electors and officers.

Colorado was then a part of Kansas, and the "Gold Fields of Western Kansas" attracted many prospectors. A Colorado town company was organized in Lecompton which laid the foundation for a town on Cherry Creek. Numerous names were suggested for the town with its beautiful mountain backdrop. Major William Gilpin expected it to become one of the great world cities and proposed to name it "Cosmopolis." The committee of twelve of the Lecompton company had so many names proposed that it could agree on none. Among the names suggested were El Dorado, Eureka, Excelsior, Marshall, Jefferson, Columbia, Mineral, and Mountain City. It was first called Mountain City and then the name was changed to Saint Charles.[21] At each camp on their way home, the committee voted on names without agreement. Then, according to Ely Moore, when they were near home, they were feasting on venison, buffalo meat, and turkey, when the door opened—

> and there, in all his physical and mental magnificence, stood the governor. We all rose from our seats as he uncovered, greeting him most heartily,—for we loved the grand old man. Intuitively, the sight and occasion suggested to me "Denver" as a fitting name for our city. The motion was made and a vote taken, which received unanimous support.[22]

Any other account, said Moore, is "pure fiction." There *is* another account, however, and according to this one, a group of Kansas claim-jumpers in what was then the Saint Charles area renamed the place

Denver in order to get legal approval for their illegal actions. "What man, they reasoned, would send a posse to evict citizens who had just been thoughtful enough to name their town for him?"[23]

Charles Robinson, first state governor of Kansas, played a large part in the formation of the state, but only a small town and Robinson Township in Brown County honor his name on the map. The town had been known as Lickskillet, a local appellation to fit the practice of "an old trapper who allegedly put his dirty dishes outside for his dog to lick clean."[24] Robinson came from a family which represented the Old New England traditions. He was a doctor by profession but an adventuresome pioneer by preference. Like many others in the East, his interest in the Far West was aroused by the glamour of the gold rush to California, when thousands of "normal" Americans became greedy gold-seekers and acted just like the "greedy" Spaniards in Mexico three hundred years earlier. His fortitude and ingenuity were given the most severe tests during the turbulent territorial days of Kansas. His home in Lawrence was burned and he was imprisoned, but he survived. As a land speculator, he promoted a town to be named Oread, and another named Quindaro,[25] and he owned the townsite of Robinson.

Crawford County and the town of Crawfordville were named for Colonel Samuel Johnson Crawford, third governor of Kansas. He was an Indiana lawyer by profession, a military man by circumstances, and a politician by experience and popularity. When Crawford came to Kansas in 1859, he settled at Garnett. He was said to be a cavalry officer of "extraordinary ability," and rose to the rank of colonel in the Civil War. In the border battle of Pleasanton, he participated in the capture of Generals Marmaduke and Cabell.[26] In the Battle of Wilson's Creek, so deadly to many Kansas soldiers, he served under General Lyon. In 1864, while still in the service, he was elected governor. He resigned near the end of his second term to lead a military expedition against the Indians. His troops camped on the Little River in 1868, where a soldier gave his address as "Camp Crawford, Wichita City."[27]

Crawford County was created out of a bit of Bourbon County and a large segment of Cherokee County, while Crawford was still governor. Crawford made Crawfordville its temporary county seat, a place which had been previously named Four Mile Creek for a Delaware chief named Four Mile.[28] After Girard became the county seat, the name of Crawfordville was shortened to Crawford, and then it disappeared, except for an "Old Cottonwood" and a "Town Well." Another Crawford was later established on the northern border of Rice County.[29] Crawford Seminary, also named for the governor, was at the place which became Baxter Springs.

327

Towns were not generally named for lieutenant governors, but when Governor Crawford resigned in 1868, Nehemiah Green became governor. Green was not only a politician but also a Methodist minister. He offered a church bell to the first town to be given his name, and when a Clay County town was named Green, its Methodist church received the promised bell.[30]

James Madison Harvey was the fifth governor of Kansas. He came from Virginia, lived for a time in Illinois, and came to Kansas with an ox team. In Riley County, Kansas, he was elected captain of a company called the "Mudsills."[31] His experiences were not unlike those of Crawford, he having served as an officer in the Civil War, a state legislator and two terms as governor. He also completed the unexpired term of Alexander Caldwell as United States senator.[32]

Parts were taken from Butler, McPherson, and Sedgwick counties to make Harvey County. The promoters of the county named it for the governor to get his political support for their own political plans.[33] Harvey County has a Harvey Township, as do also Cowley County and Smith County, and there is a Harvey Creek flowing into Gypsum Creek in Saline County. Harveyville in Wabaunsee County was, however, named for Henry Harvey, identified as "a Shawnee Indian missionary."[34]

Hoyt in Jackson County was named for George H. Hoyt, a lawyer from Athol, Massachusetts, who defended John Brown at Harper's Ferry. He served as lieutenant colonel of the Fifteenth Kansas during the Civil War. In Kansas he became editor of the *Leavenworth Conservative* and served as attorney general in Governor Harvey's administration.[35]

The town of Eskridge, north of Emporia, was named for Charles V. Eskridge, an Emporia journalist and politician. When Eskridge came to Kansas in 1855 he had the name "KANSAS" painted on the sides of his covered wagon. In 1869 he was elected lieutenant-governor under Governor Harvey. He served in both houses of the Kansas Legislature. Colonel Ephraim Sanford allowed Eskridge to buy the first lot in his town for five hundred dollars and then agreed to give the town his name.[36] Colonel Eskridge prospered in Kansas, but the lot he bought in Eskridge was sold for taxes.

When Harper County was organized, Governor George Tobey Anthony was given the authority to locate the county seat. The reward for his choice was to have the town named Anthony.[37] Governor Anthony was a Quaker farm boy from New York who came to Kansas in 1865. In spite of his Quaker background, he served so successfully in the Union army that he was brevetted major for special service at

Appomattox. As president of the Agricultural Board, Anthony helped to prepare an attractive exhibit of Kansas products for the centennial celebration in Philadelphia in 1876. In that year he was also elected governor. As publisher of the *Kansas Farmer*, he was able to educate the farmers to the need for "diversified farming, economy in management, improvement in livestock, and higher regard for home and social life." In a eulogy for Anthony, P. I. Bonebrake said: "A combination of honors so varied, so responsible, held within a period of thirty years, is without precedent in the history of the state . . . ."[38]

John St. John was a Hoosier of Huguenot stock. When he was nineteen, he piloted an ox-team across the country to California. He did not become rich as a gold miner but he matured as a man and he spent some money wisely for old law books which he studied in his cabin at night. Before leaving California, he enlisted to fight the Indians in the Modoc War.

Colonel St. John led an Illinois regiment in the Civil War, and after the war settled in Olathe, Kansas.[39] In 1878 the Republicans had three strong candidates competing for the governorship: George T. Anthony, John A. Martin, and John P. St. John. St. John was last on the first ballot, but he was first on the seventeenth ballot. He was a successful two-term governor but lost the third nomination because of the "third term bogey." It was as an uncompromising crusader against liquor that he became a national figure. Women, not yet voting in 1884, presented to the Republican party a twenty-thousand-name petition to include prohibition in its platform. The reported action of the Republicans was to "kick it under the table." Miss Frances E. Willard and her WCTU followers then turned to the champion of prohibition in Kansas and chose John P. St. John as their candidate. St. John lost, but he split the New York vote which defeated Blaine, "the magnetic man from Maine," and gave victory to a somewhat unknown, "Ugly-Honest man," Grover Cleveland.[40]

The first town to be named St. John was in Allen County in eastern Kansas. Since it was incorporated in 1860, it probably had no connection with the governor. The St. John in Decatur County was, however, named for him. As his popularity waned, so did the interest in his name, and St. John changed its name to Hooker.[41] It was St. John in Stafford County which finally perpetuated the governor's name. The town had once been the center of a Mormon community named Zion Valley, but the Mormons had quarreled and deserted the place. The town company which rebuilt the town in 1879 named it St. John in order to win the governor's support for the county seat, and sure enough, St. John won.[42]

In western Kansas a county had been named St. John to honor the governor. His prohibition activities and his presidential ambitions stirred up so much hostility that "the legislature took away the honor accorded St. John and gave it to General John A. Logan." So St. John County became Logan County. Logan was the vice-presidential candidate who was defeated with Blaine.[43]

George W. Glick came to Kansas in 1858 and held several offices, including a judgeship, before he became the first Democratic governor of Kansas. He also represented Kansas at both the Chicago World's Fair and the one at St. Louis. The year after he became governor, a post office was named Glick in Kiowa County. Located in an area of scenic beauty, Glick changed its name to Belvidere.[44]

Edmund Needham Morrill was one of the last Kansas governors to have a town named in his honor. He had a long and distinguished service as a territorial legislator, soldier, businessman, state senator, and member of Congress. In 1894 he became governor of Kansas[45] and sponsored a bill for the aid of war veterans.[46] The town named Morrill in Brown County was founded by T. J. Elliot, who named it for his friend, Governor Morrill of Hiawatha. A township also bears his name. Morrill was originally from Maine, as was Hannibal Hamlin, Lincoln's vice-president, for whom the next town east of Morrill was named.

William Corydon Edwards was an aggressive frontier promoter. He was active in Hutchinson, Solomon City, Kinsley, Larned, and St. Paul, primarily in the lumber business. The Edwards family had extensive landholdings south of Kinsley. When the northern part of Kiowa County was under the jurisdiction of Edwards County, it was called "Edwards' Ranch." Edwards served as Kansas' secretary of state in 1895.[47] When Henry Flick went to Topeka to promote the county organization, he is said to have asked what Edwards would do if the county were named in his honor. He evidently did what was necessary when he paid Flick's expenses to Topeka, since the county, organized in 1874, was named Edwards.[48]

Finney County in western Kansas was one of those troubled counties that had its boundaries changed, its name changed, and its county seat changed. In 1873 there was no Finney County, but Sequoyah and Buffalo were approximately where Finney is today. Finney County was organized and named in 1883, and it included the administration of Kearny, Grant, Sequoyah, Gray, Arapahoe, Kansas, Stevens, Clark, and Meade. Then the boom of the eighties led to the settlement of these dependent counties, and Finney County was by 1887 reduced to its present proportions, except for its panhandle which was then Garfield County. The names of Sequoyah, Arapahoe, Kansas, and Buffalo disappeared. Finney County was named for David Wesley Finney, lieu-tenant-governor of Kansas from 1881 to 1885. Finney was a Hoosier and a Civil War veteran who came to Kansas in 1866. He was a merchant and miller who liked politics and served in the Kansas Legislature for several terms. He was lieutenant-governor when Finney County was organized.[49]

Also associated with a governor was the town of Baileyville. N. Bailey was the father of Governor Willis J. Bailey and the two built the town of Baileyville at a place once called "Haytown" in Nemaha County. When Theodore Roosevelt visited Topeka in 1903, he was received by Bailey, a one-term Republican governor.[50]

The two men who first represented Kansas in the United States Senate were James H. Lane and Samuel C. Pomeroy. Of the two, Lane was the most dramatic, the most fiery, and the most effective. Pomeroy left his name on one town; Lane's name was used for two towns, a trail, a spring, a fort, a university, and a county.

Lane was born in Kentucky but started his political career in Indiana. Although he had enlisted as a private in the Mexican War, he was soon elected colonel. After serving as lieutenant-governor and congressman in Indiana, he came to Kansas as the most outspoken leader of the Free-State party. He battled the Border Ruffians and won. When the Missouri gateway to Kansas was blocked, he led immigrants into Kansas by way of Iowa and Nebraska on a route which became known as "Lane's Trail."[51]

When the Civil War opened, Lane organized a "Frontier Guard" of Kansas volunteers and moved into the White House as the personal guard of Lincoln. The dramatic defense of the President by Kansas troops but Lane in the limelight, a place he seldom shunned. According to one estimate, Lane gave the impression of being "a combination of Don Quixote and Daniel Boone."[52] As a leader of the Free-State party in Kansas, Lane was a logical choice for senator. "He is just the man for the times," said Daniel Anthony. "The Free-State Boys *love* him—the National Democrats *hate* him and the Missouri and Border Ruffians generally *fear* him."[53] The sharp-tongued Ingalls, proud of his own oratory, said of him: "His oratory was voluble and incessant, without logic, learning, rhetoric, or grace." One New York journalist called him "Uncouth and unscrupulous, zealous without convictions, pungent, fiery, magnetic . . . ."[54] In Kansas he spoke with the "oracular rhapsodies of a prophet," and he has been called the "Cicero of the United States Senate." "In politics, he was king," said D. W. Wilder.[55]

Lane has been described as being "tall, lean, lanky, swarthy, and hungry looking," like Cassius. He wore a bearskin coat and a calfskin vest. His long and unruly hair, his piercing dark eyes, and his oratorical outbursts gave him the characteristics of a crusading demagogue. But his services for the cause of freedom have been called "imperishable." Folks who knew him well called him a "queer Jim." He was the kind who would be lost without a crusading cause. After his dramatic career, his troubled mind gave way to depression, and James Lane, that distinguished character from Kansas, that "vessel of wrath," committed suicide.[56] "The grim chieftain" has, however, found a place on the map of Kansas.

Lanesfield in Johnson County was named for James H. Lane. McCamish, a rival town, declined as Lanesfield grew, but when the railroad skipped both towns, the people of Lanesfield moved to Edgerton.[57] In Franklin County there was a post office named Shermansville, named for Henry Sherman. In 1857, "at the suggestion of one disgruntled matron," said Van Gundy, "Shermansville was changed to Lane."[58] In Lecompton, once a proslavery stronghold, the foundation for the building of the proposed state Capitol was used for a college which was named Lane University for James H. Lane.[59] After the institution died, the building was occupied by an undertaker.

Finally, the most important memorial to Lane is Lane County, so named in 1873 when twenty-two counties were put on the map. When prosperity failed to materialize, the poverty-stricken settlers were described in a popular poem on Lane County:

> *"My name is Frank Bolar, 'n ole bachelor I am,*
> *I'm keeping ole bach on an elegant plan.*
> *You'll find me out West in the County of Lane,*
> *Starving to death on a government claim."*
>
> CHORUS:
> *"But hurrah for Lane County, the land of the free,*
> *The home of the grasshopper, bedbug, and flea,*
> *I'll sing loud her praises and boast of her fame,*
> *While starving to death on my government claim."*[60]

When the boom collapsed, farms and towns were deserted, and Frank Bolar returned to Missouri to get himself a wife, and "to live on corn dodgers the rest of his life."

Samuel Clark Pomeroy was born in Massachusetts. He had been a teacher and a merchant in New York before coming to Kansas as an agent of the New England Emigrant Aid Society. He became mayor of Atchison by the toss of a coin, and his name was second choice, after Wilmot, for the renaming of Atchison, which never occurred.

During the 1860 drought, he was appointed agent for the distribution of aid to the stricken farmers of Kansas. Much of the aid was in seed corn and his initials, S. C., were used to dub him "Seed Corn" Pomeroy.[61] He was a big, baby-faced politician, and Daniel Wilder gave him the descriptive name of "Pom the Pious." After two terms as United States senator, he was so anxious to be elected to a third term, that he was duped into a situation which indicated the use of a bribe; and this destroyed him politically. A critic called him "a statesman who believed in loyalty, religion and subsidy, especially subsidy,"[62] and he was occasionally called "Subsidy Pom." Certainly, one of the most redeeming acts of Senator Pomeroy was his bill in Congress, in 1871, for the creation of Yellowstone Park,[63] a superb gift to the American people. The town of Pomeroy, northeast of Kansas City, still bears his name.

John James Ingalls was Pomeroy's successor. Both Ingalls and Lane won reputations as great orators, and if Lane was "King," then Ingalls was "the emperor in the realm of speaking." Lane was a spontaneous and natural orator; Ingalls was a polished and poetic speaker. Ingalls could, on occasion, demolish a political opponent with a withering and devastating tongue. The *London Chronicle* spoke of his "clap-trap eloquence." "As a user of sarcasm," said one writer, "he had no equal."[64] Ingalls, a New England egotist, came to Kansas because of the appeal made by a romantic lithograph. He participated in the making of the Wyandotte Constitution. He also chose the motto for Kansas: *Ad astra per aspera*, "To the stars through difficulties." As United States senator he was the pride of Kansas, irrespective of his accomplishments. He failed to keep in touch with the desperate needs of the midwestern farmer and to acknowledge the Populist protests and was consequently defeated.[65]

There had been an Ingalls post office in Lincoln County, also called Ingalls Station, but there the name was changed to Bayne.[66] In western Kansas a post office was named Soule for Asa T. Soule, a wealthy New York financier who was promoting the Eureka Irrigation Canal Company. But Soule saw political advantage in having the town renamed Ingalls. So Ingalls, the senator from eastern Kansas, had his name given to a little town in western Kansas.[67]

Alexander Caldwell, a successful businessman from Pennsylvania, followed Edmund G. Ross as senator from Kansas. In Atchison he organized a company which profitably transported army supplies. He also built railroads and was vice-president and president of two railroad companies. He served as United States senator from 1871 to 1873, but since he "did not like the job," he resigned. The year in which he became senator, Caldwell, Kansas, a border town on the Chisholm Trail, was named for him.[68]

Twice the name of Plumb has been used as a post office name in Kansas, first in Lyon County, the home of Preston B. Plumb, and later, in Chase County. There were for a short time a Plumb Station in Jackson County and Plumb Creek post office in Phillips County. Preston Pierce Plumb from Ohio had a versatile career. He was one of the promoters of Emporia, where he edited the *Kanzas News*. After the Civil War, he practiced law. As a businessman, he was interested in coal mining, manufacturing, and banking. He served in the United States Senate from 1877 until his death in 1891. Plumb was a highly respected citizen, soldier, and statesman.[69]

There is a Conway in McPherson County and a Conway Springs in Sumner County. The Conway part of the name was said to come from Conway Township. Conway Springs, formerly Cranmer Springs, is said to have been named by Hiram Cranmer for Moncure D. Conway, an author he admired. George Martin was told by W. Davis, postmaster, that Conway was named for a "public man" by that name.[70] The most important Conway in Kansas politics was Martin F. Conway, elected to the Bogus Legislature, where he refused to serve because other free-state members had been denied their seats.[71] He became a Kansas representative to Congress and he served as United States consul to Marsailles in France. Conway lived in Washington, where he became so bitter about Pomeroy's politics that he attempted to assassinate him.[72] He was, fortunately for Pomeroy, a poor shot.

Best known of the early judges in Kansas were Samuel D. Lecompte and Samuel A. Kingman. These two Sams gave their names to Kansas towns, and Samuel Kingman was also honored by the name of a county. Samuel Dexter Lecompte of Maryland was appointed chief justice of Kansas Territory by President Pierce and was known as a "Pierce Democrat." He was a popular and pliant tool of the Proslavery party. Free-state suspects were left to rot in jail; proslavery prisoners, summarily dismissed. These conditions shocked Governor Geary. Lecompte's negligence has been explained as follows: "The chief justice adjourned the spring term of his court to plant potatoes, the summer term to hoe potatoes, the fall term to dig potatoes, and the winter term to sell potatoes."[73] What was considered a good sense of humor by his supporters was considered a "frivolous mind" by Governor Reeder, who continued his estimate of "his honor," as a man with "little ability, less integrity, great perversity, and indolence, and limited knowledge of the law, who, having neither property, practice, nor reputation at home," was appointed chief justice of Kansas Territory.[74] After the war, Lecompte was conveniently converted to the dominant Republican party. He then practiced law in Leavenworth, served a term as probate judge, and one term as representative in the Kansas House.

Judge Lecompte was the president of a new town company which took over the townsite of Bald Eagle and Douglas. Associated with him was Woodson, the territorial secretary, Mr. Simmons of Indiana, and Daniel Boone, grandson of Boone of Kentucky. To honor the judge, the town was named Lecompton. The town once had the "more distinguished name of Douglas," but no other town in the world has the distinction of being named Lecompton. The first legislature chose Lecompton as the future capital of Kansas. Several towns had made a bid for the capital, including towns with such names as Kickapoo, Kansopolis, and One Hundred and Ten.

Thomas Ewing, the first chief justice of Kansas, came from a politically prominent family. His father had served as secretary of the treasury in William H. Harrison's administration. In Kansas, Thomas Ewing was a law partner of William Tecumseh Sherman. The town of Ewing may well have been named for this distinguished politician. Ewingsport in Marshall County was named for the judge, but it had to share its name with Vliets. The railroad had asked for a shorter name than Ewingsport and a local farmer named Vliets had such a name.[75]

Samuel A. Kingman illustrates the westward migration in his moves from Massachusetts to Kentucky, to Iowa, and finally to Kansas, where he became chief justice of the state supreme court. He has been called "The best of the old generation of lawyers" and "The John Marshall of Kansas." He became president of the Kansas Bar Association as well as the first president of the Kansas State Historical Society to which he contributed its first books. Less dignified, yet evidence of his popularity, was his membership in the Kansas Ananias Society.[76]

The site of Kingman was on the Ninnescah crossing of the Hutchinson–Medicine Lodge Trail. There Norman Ingraham located his house, which he had hauled from Reno County. He hoped the place would become a city and he named it Sherman. There stood the town of Sherman with one shack and one cottonwood tree, waiting to become a city. J. H. Fical and his brother started a new town at Sherman in 1874 and named it Kingman. The county, the town, and a township were all named for Samuel A. Kingman. Only Sherman Street remains to remind one of the town's first name. Even the first hotel had its name changed from "The Sherman House" to the "Kingman House." In 1878, Samuel A. Kingman gave the Fourth of July oration at Kingman.[77] "Our state history has no nobler name," said D. W. Wilder, than Kingman's, and "it will live with the life of the State."[78]

Horton in Brown County, Harlan in Smith County, and Saffordville in Chase County were also named for Kansas judges. Albert Howell Horton followed Kingman as chief justice. He was a New Yorker and a "drop-out" from the University of Michigan Law School. After having passed the bar examination in New York, he came to Kansas, where he served in both houses of the Kansas Legislature. As a judge in Brown County, he was more interested in broad principles of law and equity than in legal technicalities.[79] For September 23, 1886, the *Annals of Kansas* reported: "A new town on the Rock Island in Brown County was named Horton in honor of Albert H. Horton, Chief Justice of the Supreme Court."[80]

In Chase County, Saffordville was named for Jacob Safford, a Vermonter who was educated in Oberlin, Ohio, practiced law in Nebraska, and served as supreme court justice in Kansas.[81]

Harlan Station is in Harlan Township in Smith County.[82] It was named for Judge John C. Harlan, characterized as a "respected citizen." Harlan's son-in-law, Dan Kelley, wrote the music for *Home on the Range*, and, according to the local press, Harlan Brothers' Orchestra was the first to play it.[83]

Bayneville, a post office in Sedgwick County which served for fifty years, was named for Judge Bayne of Anthony, whose importance was largely due to his success in obtaining a right-of-way for the Missouri Pacific Railroad from Wichita to Kiowa.[84]

William A. Calderhead, a Civil War veteran, practiced law at Marysville. After holding several local offices, he served for twelve years as representative to Congress from the Fifth District. Calderhead in Washington County was most likely named for this highly respected congressman.

Samuel Medary, a "born agitator," poet, and politician from Ohio was responsible for changing the name of Wise County by substituting the name of Morris for his good friend, Senator Thomas Morris of Ohio. Morris had been a vice-presidential candidate on the Liberty ticket in 1844. Slavery was to him a "moral evil" and a "national calamity." His crusades, appealing to Medary, won him a place-name on a Kansas county.[85]

McFarland, a town in Wabaunsee County, had been started by a farmer named Fairfield who named it Fairfield. But there was another Fairfield in Russell County, so Mr. Fairfield of Wabaunsee County took a bag of beans to Russell to get the name of the other Fairfield changed to Hawley. The beans did the trick, whatever it was, and the name of the town was changed to Hawley and later to Lael. Mr. Fairfield finally recommended that his town be named McFarland to honor his friend Judge J. N. McFarland of Topeka, a member of the town company.[86]

Alfred A. Mullin followed the railway stakes to locate a town on the Wichita and Western Railway. With lumber and groceries purchased at Kinsley, he opened a store in Kiowa County; and there, according to a local headline, "A. A. Mullin starts a town." And the town was named Mullinville for Judge Mullin, the promoter.[87]

South of Buffalo County, there was once a county named Foote, named for Andrew Hull Foote, a United States naval officer. In the reorganization and the naming of counties in the west, Foote County became Gray County, renamed for Alfred Gray, a teacher and lawyer from New York who came to Quindaro, Kansas, in 1857.[88] Grant called Gray to Vicksburg during the war, but Gray resigned because of ill health.[89] As secretary of the Kansas Board of Agriculture, he was noted for his superior reports. He was also the secretary of the Kansas Commission to the Centennial Exposition in Philadelphia in 1876. The grasshopper raid on Kansas had put one-third of its population on relief, and many a discouraged pioneer left the state. The Philadelphia exhibit was so well done that it stimulated a new wave of migration to Kansas.[90] Gray was highly respected, and the state legislature voted to set up a monument for him in Topeka. His best-known monument was probably the naming of Gray County.

What had once been Arapahoe County, which disappeared in Finney County, was restored as Haskell County in 1887. It was named for Dudley C. Haskell, a highly respected politician whose family came from Vermont. Haskell has been described as a man of "gigantic stature, and brilliant in intellect."[91] The Kansas gold fever got him, and in 1858 he went prospecting near Pikes Peak. After serving in the Civil War, he returned to Kansas to go into business in Lawrence. He served several terms in the Kansas Legislature before going to Washington as congressman from Kansas. The Prohibition party wanted him to run for governor in 1874, but he refused the nomination. Had he run, however, he might have received more than the 110 votes given to the Prohibition candidate.[92]

It was for Haskell's interest in and support of Indian education that Haskell Indian Institute in Lawrence was named in 1890. Haskell's name is probably better known for its association with Haskell Institute than for his name on a Kansas county. A striking feature of Haskell County is that it is "the most level of all the 105 counties of Kansas."[93] The town named Haskell in Anderson County, also named for Dudley

337

Haskell, was replaced by a town named Bush City.[94] Colonel L. L. Bush of Pennsylvania had invested in the townsite, hence its name.[95]

William Hillary Smallwood, born in Kentucky, came to Kansas and served in the Civil War as captain of Company G, First Regiment of Kansas Colored Volunteers. He was elected to the Kansas legislature and was a two-term secretary of state. Two western post offices were named for him, one in Comanche County and the other in Ness County, both now called "Phantom Towns."[96]

The town named Buena Vista in Barton County was renamed Hoisington when it was bought by a town company which included Andrew J. Hoisington. He served as a recorder of land claims in Garden City, president of the Hoisington State Bank, and a member of the Board of Regents for the Kansas State Agricultural College.[97] Betty Hoisington was the first woman to be commissioned a general in the United States Army.

Dunlap, located between Emporia and Council Grove, was named for Joseph Dunlap, its founder. He was both an Indian trader and Indian agent among the Kaws. With a shrewd eye for business, he also shipped precious walnut logs from Kansas to Europe.[98]

Other towns named for state legislators were Corliss in Johnson County, named for J. E. Corliss, and Frizell in Pawnee County, named for Senator Edward E. Frizell. Corliss was a restless adventurer who had rambled from Vermont to Indiana, to Wisconsin, and to California, before returning to settle in Kansas, where he became chairman of the Board of Supervisors of Atchison County.[99]

Frizell bought the land west of Larned where Sage, named for Frank Sage, was located. With a change of ownership, the name was changed to Frizell. Not only was Frizell a state senator but he also served as president of the Kansas Board of Agriculture and as superintendent of the State Hospital at Larned.[100] The name is still closely associated with the Fort Larned Museum.

State legislators may generally be listed with political officials even though they had other interests. Among these we may include Hewins and Willis. Hewins in Chautauqua County was likely named for Edwin M. Hewins, who had been active in the county seat fight which split Howard County into Elk and Chautauqua. He was also a member of the Kansas legislature and was appointed captain of militia by Governor Crawford.[101] He owned a large ranch which extended from Hewins almost to Cedar Vale.

A man with similiar experience was Martin Cleveland Willis, who came to Kansas from Tennessee in 1855. He was a captain in the Kansas Nineteenth Regiment during the Civil War. He served two terms in the state legislature and for him was named the town of Willis in Brown County.[102]

James R. Hallowell's Quaker ancestors came to Pennsylvania with William Penn. The family made several moves, and James served in the Civil War with Indiana Zouaves under Lew Wallace. In Kansas he was active in the promotion of both Columbus and Galena. Politics appealed to him and he served in both houses of the Kansas legislature. In 1890, while living in Wichita, he ran for Congress against Jerry Simpson. Hallowell was the candidate who was described as a wealthy silk-stocking man, while his opponent, by contrast, became "Sockless Jerry Simpson." Simpson won. Hallowell's name was given to a town west of Columbus.[103]

Morrowville, located between Haddam and Washington, was seemingly named for James Calvin Morrow of Haddam. He was a legislator and active citizen. As a station, the place had first been named Morrow. This caused no end of confusion when a person asked for a ticket to Morrow, especially if he wanted it today. The station agent could question his purpose of getting today what he wanted tomorrow, while the customer continued to request a ticket to Morrow while insisting on going today to Morrow. It has been assumed that the railroad had the name changed to avoid further confusion, but it seems as if the name was changed to Morrowville by the post office before the station changed its name from Morrow.[104]

Robert M. Wright is a typical representative of the frontier spirit. He was born in Maryland but crossed the plains to Denver with an ox-team. He was an Indian fighter, buffalo hunter, and contractor, and served in the state legislature four times. As a post trader, he knew Dodge City very well, and he wrote a book, *Dodge City, the Cowboy Capital*, published in 1913. He was well known and popular and was appointed to the Forestry and Irrigation Commission in 1899. A town in Ford County was named Wright to honor "Bob" Wright.[105]

Business success may not be sufficient to earn one a place-name on the map, but by being elected mayor, a person becomes a public figure. The Albright family of Cowley County were interested in ranching, banking, and real estate. The town of Albright, west of Winfield, was named for P. H. Albright, mayor of Winfield.[106]

To conclude with security, we may now list the names of law officers, M. E. Larkin, William B. Rhodes, and Oscar G. Lee. Larkin has been referred to as "one of the best sheriffs Atchison County ever had."[107] He also served in the state legislature and was henceforth known as the "Honorable" Mr. Larkin. For him was named Larkin in Jackson County, later changed to Larkinburg. Normally, names were changed to make them shorter, but not so for Larkin.

The name of Wilroads, created from the name of William B. Rhodes, marshal of Dodge City, illustrates the trend towards condensation.[108] Most early marshals of Dodge City won fame or notoriety, but Marshal Rhodes was the only one for whom a town was named. Leawood likewise had a change in spelling to make it a "little more euphonious." The Johnson County town was named for Oscar G. Lee, a retired policeman who made some wise investments in real estate.[109]

In spite of the political failures of the territorial governors of Kansas, all but one got his name on the map, and two of them, Woodson and Geary, supplied their names to counties. Five state governors left their names on the map, and four of these—Crawford, Harvey, Anthony, and St. John—became county names. Finney County was named for a lieutenant-governor. Two counties were named for judges of the state supreme court, as were four towns. State representatives left fewer names than did representatives in the territorial legislature. Congressmen Haskell and Calderhead, and five United States senators—Pomeroy, Ingalls, Caldwell, Plumb, and Conway—left their names on the map. Other names came from lesser officials in several categories.

CHAPTER XXXI

VILLE WESKAN WESTMORELAND WESTPHALIA WETMORE WHEATON WHITE CITY WHITE CLOUD W

LINCOLN AND HIS ASSOCIATES

WICHITA WILLIAMSBURG WILLIAMSTOWN WILMORE WILSON WINCHESTER WINFIELD WINONA W

GEORGE WASHINGTON'S NAME was the most popular choice among political place-names in the United States, but Abraham Lincoln's name ran a close second. Lincoln's name was used most extensively in the trans-Mississippi West, since that was the area settled and named after Lincoln won fame. Counties named Lincoln in the Old South, such as those in North Carolina, Georgia, and Tennessee, were probably named for General Benjamin Lincoln of the American Revolution,[1] or possibly for Lincoln, a well-known cathedral town in England.

One of the twenty-two counties in the United States named Lincoln is in Kansas. Lincoln was much concerned about the issues and battles of Bleeding Kansas. After the sack of Lawrence, he had lectured in Bloomington, Illinois, on the plight of Kansas. He came to Kansas in December, 1859, and gave speeches at Atchison, Elwood, Troy, Doniphan, and Leavenworth. He spoke well of Kansas. To Greeley's alleged advice "Go West, young man," Lincoln made the more specific choice: "If I went west, I think I would go to Kansas."[2] His political speeches were received with partisan prejudice, mostly in his favor. Seward seemed, however, to be the popular candidate in Kansas. John A. Martin, editor of the *Atchison Champion*, was so completely sold on Seward that he refused to print Lincoln's speech. Samuel C. Pomeroy, in introducing Lincoln, who was to speak on "Issues of the Day," pretended that he could not even remember his name. Yet this speech, given on the day that John Brown was executed, was to become nationally famous as the Cooper Institute speech. At Leavenworth, the *Weekly Herald*, a Democratic paper, said of it: "We have seldom heard one where more spurious argument, cunning sophistry, and flimsy evasions, were mingled together, and made to work out all right—no doubt to the satisfaction of his audience."[3] In contrast, the editor of the Republican *Leavenworth Register* called Lincoln's speech "the ablest address ever delivered on the soil of Kansas."[4] At Troy, a Kentucky critic who was called on to answer Lincoln admitted that his speech was one of the greatest he had ever heard. Then he added: "While I dissent utterly

341

from the doctrines of this address, and shall endeavour to refute some of them, candor compels me to say that it is the most able—the most logical—speech I have ever listened to."[5]

Lincoln was not yet a presidential candidate when he spoke in Kansas, but it was there that his political ideas took shape and it was there that his host, Judge Delahay, while waving his carving knife at dinner, is reported to have said, "Gentlemen, I tell you, Mr. Lincoln will be our next president."[6]

Lincoln's physical appearance is also associated with Kansas. According to accepted belief, it was a little Kansas girl, Grace Bedell, who, with the candor and curiosity of a child, asked the smooth-shaven Abe why he did not grow whiskers. Unable to give a satisfactory answer to the child, who later became Mrs. Billings of Delphos, Lincoln soon began to grow the beard by which he has since been identified.[7]

When Kansas became a state, it was Lincoln, on his way to Washington for his inauguration on Washington's Birthday in 1861, who first raised the new flag over Independence Hall in Philadelphia which included the thirty-fourth star for Kansas.[8]

Serious efforts to replace the name of Davis County were considered in February, 1864. The legislature was asked to change the name to Webster or to Lincoln. "Lincoln," said one representative, "has become the name for freedom and union, as that of Davis has become the name for *slavery, treason,* and *disunion.*"[9] Neither Webster nor Lincoln was accepted then, and five years elapsed before the name was changed, and then it became Geary in honor of John W. Geary.[10]

Kansas did honor the late President by naming Lincoln County. Rocky Hill in Lincoln County wished to become the county seat and changed its name to Abram, hoping that its association with the name of Lincoln would win it popular support. For a time it was also called Abraham, but it soon reverted back to the shorter name with scarcely a perceptible loss of a syllable. The Kansas press frequently spelled Lincoln's first name Abram.[11] Having failed to become the county seat, Abram again became Rocky Hill. It was too close to its rival, Lincoln Centre, to survive, and "Fate decided that it should die," said Andreas, "and it died."[12] At first the county seat of Lincoln County was called Lincoln Centre, stressing its central location. For a time it was called Lincoln, then it resumed its full name changing the "Centre" to Center, yet Lincoln Center is generally just Lincoln.[13]

Nemaha County had a Lincoln post office as early as 1861 and it "bid fair to outstrip Seneca as the county-seat." Losing the contest, it closed in 1868. In 1872, Lincolnville, named to honor "the martyr President," was established north of Marion on the Herington road.[14] Fort Lincoln, named by James Lane, became a part of the border defense system of Fort Scott during the Civil War. The town of Fulton has replaced the town of Lincoln and its temporary name of Osaga.

What is now Washburn College was once named Lincoln College "out of respect and love for him who was then the chief Magistrate of the Nation, Abraham Lincoln." The name was changed to Washburn after Ichabod Washburn gave a generous grant to the college, not that they loved Lincoln less nor Washburn more, but Ichabod's money was essential. Those who planned Monumental College for Lawrence decided to merge with Lincoln College of Topeka and so the name was for a time Lincoln Monumental College.[15]

The popularity of Lincoln and Lincoln's name in Kansas is further proved by the thirty-one townships bearing the Lincoln name. Next in popularity, as indicated by township names, was Grant, who trailed Lincoln by two. Ulysses is located in Lincoln Township of Grant County.

Seward, like Lincoln, became much concerned over the slavery issue and the constitutional conflicts in Kansas. Kansas, "the Cinderella of the Union," Seward declared optimistically, would "live and survive the persecution." Seward was the presidential choice of A. C. Wilder, Kansas delegate to the Republican Convention at Chicago. In September of 1860, he was given enthusiastic receptions at Atchison and Leavenworth, and he spoke to a large gathering in Lawrence, where he said: "Men will come up to Kansas as they go up to Jerusalem. This shall be a sacred city."[16] Seward considered himself far superior to Lincoln, and, as secretary of state, he thought he would have to lead Lincoln by the hand and guide this "Yokel from Illinois."

Seward was one of the most ardent advocates of Kansas statehood in 1861. In that year Kansas changed the name of Godfrey County to Seward County. But in 1867, during the first great wave of postwar county organization and reorganization, Seward's name was replaced by that of Howard, honoring General Oliver O. Howard.

It was rare for a man to have a second application of his name to a county, but Seward did. In 1873 his name was given to a county between Meade and Stevens. It was only a name, and for a time it was extended over the two counties to the west, Kansas and Stevens. Finally, when neighboring counties were organized, Seward County took shape.[17] It had a Seward Township. Stafford County had a post office named Seward in Seward Township. For a time there was a place named Seward east of Hamlin in Brown County.

John Breckinridge served as vice-president under Buchanan and was a rival of Lincoln for the presidency. His name was given to a

Kansas county by the Bogus Legislature. It is interesting to note that Breckinridge was used for a county name instead of Buchanan. As the secretary of war in the Confederacy, his was not an acceptable name and was replaced by the name of a war hero, General Nathaniel Lyon.

Among the other associates of Lincoln whose names were given to Kansas towns were William H. Herndon, his law partner, and Hannibal Hamlin, his vice-president. The name of Pest or Pesth, from Budapest, was first proposed for the town of Herndon in Rawlins County. The Post Office Department rejected the name, probably worried over its meaning if it were Pest and its spelling and pronunciation if it were Pesth. With patriotic loyalty, the community then suggested Lincoln, but this name had already been pre-empted. The choice of the Post Office Department was Herndon, the name of the lawyer who helped to get Lincoln nominated.[18]

William Herndon was born in Kentucky but his parents moved into Illinois when he was two years old. In Jacksonville he attended Illinois College. His father, still a Kentuckian at heart, was worried for fear that his son would be "contaminated by the Abolition sentiment which prevailed at the institution," and withdrew him. It was too late. For a time young Herndon clerked in a store; later he read law with Logan and Lincoln. He left the declining Whig party and joined the party of Lincoln.[19]

Hamlin in Brown County was named for Hannibal Hamlin of Maine, Lincoln's vice-president. It was probably Edmund N. Morrill, also from Maine, who proposed Hamlin's name for Brown County. Hamlin is only a small town in Kansas, but there it stands to jog the memory of those who fail to remember vice-presidents.[20]

Hamlin was a Democrat but an ardent opponent of the extension of slavery. He had been a farmer, school teacher, lawyer, congressman, governor, and senator before he became vice-president. He served Lincoln well as a friendly and shrewd adviser. Much was made of the names of the candidates during the campaign. One newspaper noticed that the name of Hamlin could be made up from the "last syllable of Abraham Lincoln's first name and the first syllable of his last name . . . that is, 'Abra (Hamlin) coln.'" The *Daily Chicago Herald* ridiculed the Lincoln-Hamlin devotion to the descendants of Ham and said that it "seemed apparent in the fact that in 'Abra*ham Ham*lin' the Republican Party begins and ends 'with its index finger pointing to the colored race.'"[21]

It was Stephen A. Douglas who placed the name of Kansas indelibly on the minds of men. The Kansas-Nebraska Bill which he supported was proposed as a means of opening the West to transcontinental railroads, but it became involved in the slavery controversy by opening Kansas and Nebraska to popular sovereignty. The bill aroused such a political storm that it split the Democratic party, destroyed the Whig party, gave birth to the Republican party, and brought Lincoln back into politics. Lincoln led the Republican party to victory, the only time in the history of the country that a third party has won a national election.

Douglas was one of the most distinguished spokesmen of the Democratic party, and as such he had the presidential bug. As a northerner from Illinois, he courted the South by his tirades against the "nigger-worshippers." After one of his political tirades, Seward walked home with Douglas, and, knowing of his "notorious" ambition to become president, Seward said to him: "Douglas, no man will ever be president of the United States who spells negro with two g's."[22] But Breckinridge and Buchanan deprived Douglas of the Southern support.

Douglas, too, came to Kansas, and he once gave a speech from the balcony of the Planter's House in Leavenworth. He was an eloquent speaker and a formidable debater. The Lincoln-Douglas debates have linked together the names of Lincoln and Douglas almost as closely as "Adam and Eve" and "ham 'n eggs." The long and lanky Lincoln, who looked like a cross between a "windmill and a derrick," was quite a contrast to the chubby and dwarflike Douglas, who was occasionally called a "Steam-engine in Breeches" but was better known as "The Little Giant." Lincoln's careful reasoning, common sense, and consistency matched the oratorical eloquence of Douglas, and Lincoln earned the title of "The Giant Killer."

Douglas had occasion soon to rise above political name-calling. When he heard that Buchanan was about to support the proslavery Lecompton Constitution of Kansas, Douglas took a firm stand against the President and his party. In 1859 he rose from his sick-bed to make an "impassioned appeal . . . for fair dealing in Kansas." After Breckinridge had taken the Southern Democrats away from him and Lincoln had been elected, Douglas gave his full support to Lincoln. He held Lincoln's hat at the inauguration, and he and his charming wife, a relative of Dolly Madison, were among the first to call at the White House.

The most conspicuous memorial to Douglas in Kansas was the naming of Douglas County. Efforts to name towns for Douglas were less successful. Leavenworth, which started as "New Town," came near being called Douglas.[23] Colton's map of 1855 shows a Douglas in Douglas County. It was composed of "a cabin or two and a saw-mill, with a slab on the river bank, marked in knock-kneed letters, 'Douglas.' "[24] This was a marker for a steamboat stop. The territorial capital was "permanently" located at Lecompton, "as the town of Douglas was renamed."[25] On his way from Lawrence to Council Grove, Governor Reeder, in trouble over investments in the proposed capital at Pawnee, bought a lot for $250 in "Douglas City," but he would as soon, it was said, "think of building a city on a crocodile's back."[26]

The town named Douglass, located south of Augusta, was named not for the politically famous Douglas but for a Butler County farmer, Captain Joseph W. Douglass, a native of New York, who owned the land on which he started the town and where he served as postmaster.[27]

In 1847, long before Stephen A. Douglas promoted the Kansas-Nebraska Bill, a New York senator by the name of Daniel S. Dickinson had introduced a resolution advocating popular sovereignty in new territories. During the war, he supported the Union, but he was not a supporter of Seward. Dickinson was one of the candidates for the nomination for vice-president at the time that Andrew Johnson was selected in 1864. For this man, Dickinson County was named.[28]

When the Kansas-Nebraska Bill of 1854 permitted the "sovereign squats" of Kansas to determine whether Kansas was to be free or slave, the nation was given not a compromise but a conflict. "The law," says the biographer of Sumner, "transferred the struggle from the halls of Congress to the plains of Kansas, and made them the battlefield on which the contest was to be won or lost."[29] But the battle which was started in Kansas was the cause of a most dramatic conflict in the halls of Congress. New England was stirred by the determination of the slaveholders from Missouri to direct the destiny of Kansas.

Charles Sumner, dignified and self-righteous senator from Massachusetts, slowly and carefully prepared a speech against slavery which he "intended to be the most thorough phillipic ever uttered in a legislative body." The conflict in Kansas gave him his topic and his title. "The Crime against Kansas," as this speech was called, was an oratorical achievement seldom equaled on the floor of the Senate. Sumner aimed his attack on two of the defenders of slavery, Senator Douglas of Illinois and Senator Andrew Pickens Butler of South Carolina, comparing them to Sancho Panza and Don Quixote, defending a deplorable institution of the past which had neither a moral nor a political defense. The speech was inflammatory and provocative, and each section of the country stood by its regional spokesmen. Whittier and Longfellow spoke well of Sumner's speech. Southerners, including Butler, were equally eloquent in condemning it.

Neither the spoken word nor the written word was enough. Preston S. Brooks, a relative of Senator Butler and a representative from South Carolina, was aroused over Sumner's speech. He entered the Senate room where Sumner had remained alone to write letters, charged him with libel, and began beating Sumner over the head with his gutta-percha cane. The cane broke, and Sumner fell unconscious to the floor.[30]

Brooks then resigned only to be re-elected by an overwhelming vote. His ardent admirers gave him a ceremonial banquet and presented him with a gold-headed new cane to replace the one he had broken over Sumner's head. Sumner, too, was re-elected to the Senate, but his recovery was so slow that he was unable to serve for two years. His health could not be replaced like a broken cane, but friends solicited contributions to serve as a testimonial of their support for the senator. When people raised funds to help pay for his heavy doctor's bill, Sumner sent them a telegram which said: "Whatever Massachusetts can give, let it be given to suffering Kansas."[31]

When Sumner's name was proposed for a county, a most unusual protest was made. Not opposition but admiration was the cause of the protest. It was an "insult to his greatness," said his admirers, to use his name for "a treeless and trackless portion of the Great American Desert."[32]

Sumner City in Sumner County, named for the county, was a competitor for the county seat, a contest it lost to a town named Meridian. Then it too disappeared, defeated by Wellington.[33] There is a Sumnerville in Ottawa County. It was said to be "the only Sumnerville in the United States," though there are nineteen places called Sumner. All apparently "named to honor the eminent statesman, Charles Sumner."[34]

Atchison for a time was surpassed by a neighboring town called "Old Sumner." According to one account, "this town was not named for Charles Sumner, as is generally supposed, but for his brother, George Sumner, one of the original stockholders." Sumner's advertising had such a colorful description on its beautifully illustrated lithograph that it made John J. Ingalls choose Sumner as his Kansas home. If a name does not sell a town, a picture might.[35] This brochure was described as "that chromatic triumph of lithographic mendacity." It was not the deceitful advertising that destroyed Sumner but a Kansas cyclone.[36]

Andrew Pickens Butler was the senator from South Carolina for whom Butler County was named.[37] That Republican Kansas should continue to honor a State-Rights Democrat seemed inconceivable to an interested person from California. He thought the county was named for Ben Butler. In his letter to the *Wichita Beacon*, he had this to say: "I believe Butler County was named for a Civil War general by the name of Ben Butler. How do you account for a rock-ribbed Republican State . . . naming its biggest county for a rebel and a Democrat?" Bliss

Isely, on the *Wichita Beacon* staff, explained that Senator Butler, a colleague of Calhoun, was the kind of statesman which the territorial legislature would "delight to honor." Ben Butler from Massachusetts was an opportunistic general in the Civil War, nicknamed "fuzzbuzz." It was perhaps due to the mistaken assumption that the county was named for Ben Butler, the Union general, that the name remained unchallenged.[38] Now two counties, Sumner and Butler, honoring opposing senators, stand corner to corner on friendly terms, but Sumner County is farther south than Butler County.

Chase County was named by Sam Wood, representative from Cottonwood Falls. Wood, an Ohio man, was an admirer of Salmon Portland Chase, "whom he was always trying to nominate for the presidency."[39] Governor Chase, like Seward, was a rival of Lincoln for the presidential nomination. His senatorial term lasted only two days when it was interrupted by the Civil War. As the victorious presidential candidate, Lincoln honored both of his rivals, Seward and Chase, by appointing them to his cabinet. Chase became his secretary of the treasury, a post he held until 1864. Then he became a presidential candidate, opposing Lincoln and supported by Senator Pomeroy of Kansas.[40] After the war, he was made chief justice of the Supreme Court. He presided at the impeachment trial of President Johnson.

Chase was known as the "attorney-general of fugitive slaves" and he has been said to have been "preeminently the champion of anti-slavery" in the United States. He was "sanctimonious" and impelled by a "burning self-centered ambition," said Bruce Catton.[41] He was an ardent spokesman for the free-soilers of Kansas and urged other governors to give aid to Kansas. The rare occasion when one may see a $10,000 bill will give one an opportunity to see there the dour mien of Chase. But his name is familiar and, as a friend of Kansas, his name is deservedly fixed on a Kansas county. To make room for Chase County, Wise County was pushed upward and later had its name changed to Morris for another Ohio senator.[42]

Stanton is the name of a county located next to Grant on the Colorado border. It was named for Edwin McMaster Stanton, attorney general under Buchanan, who served as Lincoln's secretary of war with questionable loyalty. Stanton Township in Linn County may also have been named for the cabinet officer.[43] Stanton has been called Lincoln's "grand old Secretary of War,"[44] but Catton described him as a "pudgy, bustling figure" who was "prone to disastrous impulses when the going got tough." His "talent for savage criticism" was freely invoked, even against Lincoln whom he once called "the original gorilla."[45] He was a self-centered, opportunistic, and ambitious man, but also an able man. It was for his administrative ability that Lincoln tolerated him.

President Johnson tried to dismiss this obstructionist holdover from Lincoln's cabinet. Stanton challenged the President, refused to resign, and locked himself in his office. Johnson tried unsuccessfully to replace him with Grant, then Sherman, and finally General Thomas, but he failed.[46] Congress then impeached the President, who was saved from dismissal by one vote, and that vote was cast by Senator Edwin Ross of Kansas, who had succeeded Senator Lane by appointment after Lane's suicide in 1866.[47]

In Phillips County there was a small town called Big Bend, named for the bend of the Republican River as it enters Kansas. Dr. Chapman, a Kansas physician, changed its name to Speed to honor James Speed,[48] the attorney general in Lincoln's cabinet and a Union man from Kentucky. It was Speed who carried the official report of Lincoln's death to Vice-President Johnson. He also worked on the legal problems of amnesty and provisional government in the South.[49] Senator Sumner spoke well of him, which probably meant that Speed was closer to the Radical Republicans than he was to President Johnson. Speed also left the lame duck cabinet in protest over Johnson's policy of moderation. Later he became professor of law at the University of Louisville.

Another politician who was considered for a place in Lincoln's cabinet was Schuyler Colfax of New York and Indiana. Lincoln liked him but did not accept the recommendation to make him postmaster general. As the running mate of Grant, he was elected vice-president in 1868. Since he was called "Smiler" Colfax, he must have had political affability. Like so many other politicians, he accepted stock in the corrupt Crédit Mobilier to finance railroads, and this ruined him politically. His later years were devoted to lectures on temperance.[50]

Like his contemporaries, Colfax was interested in Kansas. In 1856, as a representative from Indiana, he gave a forceful speech against the use of troops in Kansas. He also had some progressive ideas on Negro suffrage. In 1865 he traveled across Kansas in a mail coach. He was well known, and several place-names in Kansas have given him recognition. Cloud County, Marion County, and Wilson County had townships named Colfax. In McPherson County his name was used jointly with another as "Roxbury or Colfax,"[51] but in the contest for survival, Roxbury won. The year after Colfax took office as vice-president, a post office was named Colfax in Chautauqua County. Dr. George A. Brown, one of the promoters of Independence in Montgomery County, first named the town Colfax.[52]

Stevens County was named for Thaddeus Stevens, who was born

in Vermont and educated at Dartmouth. Unlike Stanton, who had never held an elective office, Stevens served many years in Congress as a representative from Pennsylvania. Slavery, he thought, was an evil institution which should be abolished. He gave his full support to Lincoln's Emancipation Proclamation and to the Fourteenth Amendment. After the war he was an active supporter of the Freedman's Bureau, headed by General O. O. Howard. Irreconcilably opposed to the moderate policy of Andrew Johnson, he prepared the arguments for the President's impeachment. As a final demonstration of his belief in equality, he asked to be buried in a cemetery open to Negroes as well as whites.

Stevens County was next to the last one of the southern tier of counties in the west. The last one, located in the southwestern corner, is Morton County. It once proudly bore the name of Kansas, but it had a name before it had a political organization strong enough to retain its name.

When the corner county was organized, it was named Morton for Oliver Hazard Perry Throck Morton, governor of Indiana. The few settlers who had once lived in Kansas County were disappointed not to have the Kansas name restored. Morton, the man with the five names, had inherited an abbreviated name himself. His father's surname had been Throckmorton, but after a quarrel with his brother, he dropped the "Throck" from his name and became just Morton. His son resumed the name of Throck, but only as his fourth given name.[53] It was his interest in Kansas and his full support of the Union in the Civil War which earned for him a place-name in Kansas. He had been expelled from the Democratic party for his refusal to support the Kansas-Nebraska Bill. He then joined the People's party on his way into the Republican party. The Indiana legislature had been cool towards the Civil War and critical of Morton's financial support for the Union. Partially paralyzed, Morton walked with the aid of two canes, and critics called him "The Devil on Two Sticks."

Kansas gave full recognition to the politicians involved in the conflict over slavery and the Civil War, especially to those associated with Lincoln. Back of these place-names in Kansas is the story of petty politics and superior statesmanship. The Civil War was a bloody conflict, glorified for its heroes on both sides, yet a tragic example of senseless slaughter when rebellion is substituted for reason. Equally prominent to the political during this great drama is the story of the military. To the men in the military, Kansas gave recognition equal to the men in politics. The emphasis was, of course, on the names of men who were the victors.

CHAPTER XXXII

PRESIDENTS AND THEIR ASSOCIATES

MEN HAVE GIVEN THEIR OWN NAMES to places in various ways: they have bought the privilege, they have gambled for it, and they have bargained for it. But men who have won fame, especially in our national history, have earned the right to be remembered. Washington Irving was of the opinion that engineers and surveyors were prone to choose names to glorify their political patrons. "But woe unto us," he said, if the man in power had an "unpopular or disagreeable name."[1] An interesting escape from this predicament may be seen when a community honoring a man whose name was Albert Jefferson Broadbent chose his middle name as a place-name. But who would think of Broadbent when they saw the name of Jefferson?

From the Atlantic to the Pacific, Americans have chosen the names of presidents and their associates as place-names. Among these, no name has been used more extensively than that of George Washington. The nation's capital bears his name; a West Coast state honors his name; all together, 450 places have been named in his honor,[2] nineteen in Kansas alone. Although intended as a mark of respect, the repetitious use of his name is also confusing.

We may not have had a Washington except for the unpredictable vagaries of the Potomac and the sudden love for a woman. *The Sea Horse of London*, a ship returning to England with a cargo of tobacco, became stuck on a sandbar in the Potomac. Before it was released, John Washington, a ship's officer, met Ann Pope, the daughter of a rich plantation owner. John married the girl, and her father gave them seven hundred acres of land which made a Virginian and an American out of George Washington's grandfather.[3] Once again, *cherchez la femme*.

The first place in the nation to be named in honor of Washington was Washington County in what was then the "illegitimate" state of Franklin, now a county in eastern Tennessee. The first Washington in Kansas was a place located south of Lawrence. There Washington Creek post office was on Washington Creek. Connelley's map of Douglas County showed a Washington on the Santa Fe Trail, a place which could boast of its good food and and its big stone fireplace, neither of which kept it alive. The place was renamed Marion in 1858 and Globe in 1881, names which have also disappeared except for Marion Township. Another Washington was started on the Kaw, but it was too close to Tecumseh to survive. Washington on One Hundred and Ten Mile Creek in Osage County also disappeared.[4]

Only about one-third of eastern Kansas was organized into counties and named by the legislature of 1855. A line was then drawn westward through the center of the territory and the area south of this line, from Marion County to the southern and western Kansas border, was named Washington. Thirty-five counties were carved out of Washington County. The legislature organized the present Washington County out of Washington Township in Marshall County.[5] Washington County, Kansas, was only one of thirty-two counties named Washington in the nation. The county seat is also named Washington, but it was for a time known as Washington Center, later changed to Washington City, and finally the "City" was deleted as being superfluous.[6] In the meantime, Washington's name was given to ten townships, a number far surpassed by the names of Lincoln and Grant.

The Washington influence may also be seen in the efforts made to put both Valley Forge and Mount Vernon on the Kansas map. Such names are familiar and have reputations which give them distinction. Valley Forge was the name of a Smith County post office, which was closed in 1876, a year short of a century after Washington's wintry camp in Valley Forge of Pennsylvania. In Kansas the town had been named Smithville, shortened to Smith before the name was changed to Valley Forge.[7]

Mount Vernon, originally named by Lawrence Washington for his friend, Admiral Vernon of the British navy, has been used four times as a place-name in Kansas. Mount Vernon replaced the name of Landondale on Mosquito Creek in Doniphan County. There was another Mount Vernon in Franklin County. The Mount Vernon in Chautauqua County was just outside Washington Township.[8] Mount Vernon in Kingman County is on the Reno County line.[9]

Alexander Hamilton has been remembered as one of that brilliant group of thinkers and doers who started the United States on its remarkable course of success. Hamilton was born of distinguished parents whose marriage has been questioned on technicalities. He was industrious, ambitious, and a voracious reader. His desire for a good education brought him from his West Indian home to New York where he studied at King's College, now Columbia. At the age of seventeen he spoke effectively in defense of the colonial cause against the

British. At the age of eighteen, he was a brilliant pamphleteer. His views were effectively presented in *The Federalist* papers. It was he who laid the foundation for the fiscal policy of the government. Hamilton became involved in the dispute between Aaron Burr and Jefferson, both of whom he disliked. This culminated in a sporty but stupid duel on the "field of honor," ending Hamilton's brilliant career at the age of forty-seven.

Hamilton County was named in 1873, when New Yorkers came to settle there. They suggested changing the name of the county to Onondaga, but it remained Hamilton. The New Yorkers should have been satisfied to preserve the name of one of their most distinguished statesmen.[10] Several towns were named Hamilton, and one survived. There was a Hamilton in Crawford County and another in Riley County. The town named Hamilton in Cloud County had its name changed to Clyde.[11] Hamilton was also on the list of names proposed for Wichita. The Hamilton that survived is a station on the Santa Fe in Greenwood County and Ellis County has a Hamilton Township.

Jefferson deserves a place-name in Kansas for the good reason that he bought it as a part of Louisiana. As one writer puts it, Jefferson County "was given the name of that farseeing President who profited by the misfortunes of the European monarch, Napoleon Bonaparte, in securing for America . . . the tremendous golden treasure first known as Louisiana."[12] Before Jefferson County was named, Colonel Tibbs suggested that it be named Soutrelle, the French translation of an Indian name which meant "grasshopper." When the committee agreed to name the county Jefferson, the Colonel, who had "strenuously contended" for Soutrelle, accepted defeat gracefully and "furnished the beverage accustomed for notable occasions."[13]

There was once a Jefferson City on the north side of the Kaw, now a part of North Lawrence. There was also a Jefferson in Republic County where there is now a Jefferson Township. The present town of Jefferson, south of Independence, honors Jefferson only indirectly, since it was named for Albert Jefferson Broadbent, an honor granted as much because he had a distinguished middle name as for his ownership of the site of the town. Cowley County once had a Jeffersonville, but there the name was first changed to Lazette and later to Cambridge. Monticello, the name of Jefferson's home in Virginia, was appropriately given to a town in Jefferson County. The town did not survive, but there is now a Monticello in Monticello Township near Kansas City in Johnson County. Eight Kansas townships were named Jefferson.

Benjamin Franklin, called "the American Socrates," was one of the truly great men of America. Kansas could have a special respect for him since he signed a petition to abolish the slave trade and slavery as early as 1790. Had he succeeded, Kansas need not have started the Civil War. Franklin was a practical philosopher, a diplomat of distinction, and a witty companion. In France, the men respected him, the women loved him. He had been called "the most complete representative of his time."[14]

Proof of his popularity may be found in the number of places named Franklin. Lippincott's *Gazetteer* (1853) listed 120 places named Franklin in America before there was a Franklin in Kansas. Of the twenty-three counties named Franklin, all but two were named for Ben.[15] There is the possibility that a few of the many towns named Franklin were named for other Franklins living in Kansas, including a Benjamin J. Franklin.

Franklin County, named for the First Territorial Legislature, was one of the very few counties then named for one who was not a southerner. There is a Franklin Township in Franklin County and there are eight other Franklin townships. Douglas County also had a town named Franklin. In the battle between the free-state fighters and the proslavery faction led by Colonel Titus, Franklin was fortified and boasted of the possession of a cannon. There, in 1856, was fought the "Battle of Franklin." This Franklin is no more.[16] Ness County has a Franklin Township and also a town named Franklinville. There is still a station named Franklin north of Pittsburg in Crawford County.

James Madison, often referred to as the "father of the Constitution," was the third Virginian to become president. In Kansas, a county, a creek, a town, and a township were named in his honor. But when county boundaries changed, Madison County was lost. Madison Creek was named "in honor of the Fourth President of the United States," and Madison Township in Riley County was named for the creek.[17] The town of Madison is in Madison Township in what was Madison County, now a part of Greenwood County. It had been moved and rebuilt to be on the railroad, and "Young Madison," it was said, was the child of "Old Madison." The town at the railway junction was for a time called Madison Junction. So "Little Jemmy," as he was called, is still honored in Kansas.

Monrovia in Africa was named for President Monroe. He was interested in the resettlement of free Negroes in Africa, and their liberation was memorialized in their country's name of Liberia. Monrovia, Kansas, is west of Atchison and one may well associate the name with the movement to liberate the slaves in Kansas. The town was named by S. J. H. Snyder, owner of the townsite. He named the town for a mission in the "far east," said Remsburg, but this would more likely be Monrovia in Africa.[18] Monroe in Lincoln County, northwest of Salina, served as a post office for fifteen years. Anderson County has a Monroe Township. The name of Monroe is so popular that it has been used to name 133 counties, towns, and other places in the United States.

Although Calhoun County was not named for John C. Calhoun, the senator, it was no wonder that the residents of Kansas would believe it was named for him. The very name of Calhoun "smacks" of treason said the free-state people; and to replace this politically unpopular name, the legislature chose the name of Jackson. It was Andrew Jackson who had opposed Calhoun's theory of nullification, and who, "by the Eternal," would have "Nation" spelled with a capital "N."[19]

Andrew Jackson was a strong-willed and determined man, and his critics referred to him as "King Andrew I," but he was better known as "President of the people." He was a man with a limited education, but he was trained in law and experienced in war, and his presidency became known as "Jacksonian Democracy." His greatest connection with the history of Kansas was his part in the removal of the Indians from the East to give them a "permanent home" in Kansas.

"Old Hickory," as he was called, was so popular that it took eleven columns to list the number of places named Jackson and Jacksonville in Lippincott's *Gazetteer*. Twenty-four counties have been named for Jackson, one more than those named for Lincoln, but Jackson had the advantage of becoming famous earlier. Twelve Kansas townships also bear his name.

There was once a Jackson in Linn County and a later one in Decatur County. The first one served twice as a post office and the one in Decatur County lasted but a decade. There was once a Jacksonburg in Smith County. Neosho County had a Jacksonville, named for the one in Illinois, and after it failed to survive, the name was given to a town in Jefferson County.[20]

The people in Jackson County were history-conscious. Names of the townships in Jackson County honor five other presidents: Washington, Jefferson, Lincoln, Grant, and Garfield. To these were added the famous names of Douglas and Franklin.[21] But Republic County also honored the same presidents, except for Garfield, in naming its townships.

Jackson's successor, Martin Van Buren, was a Dutchman from New York. His critics called him the "Flying Dutchman" and the "Red Fox from Kinderhook." As a clever and compromising politician, he was also known as the "Little Magician." He was against slavery and was a strong supporter of Lincoln. These views should have endeared him

355

to Kansas. Yet Van Buren in Graham County, the only place to use his name, is now listed as one of the extinct places in Kansas.[22] Kinderhook is, however, the name of a geological stratum of the Mississippian system in Kansas.

Contemporary with great men like Jackson, Webster, and Calhoun was the equally competent Henry Clay, known as "Harry of the West" and "The Great Compromiser." Born in Virginia, he represented Kentucky in Congress. When the election of 1824 was thrown into Congress, Clay supported John Quincy Adams over Jackson and became known as the "President Maker." Those who opposed this political deal referred to it as the union between the "Blackleg and the Puritan."

Many Kentuckians settled in Kansas. Clay County, the third county west of Jackson County, was named for Henry Clay and its county seat was named Clay Centre. In Davis County (now Geary), a number of Kentucky settlers "who were great admirers of Clay" decided to honor his memory by giving "the name of his late residence to the township and the city which they attempted to build." Ashland was the name of his home in Lexington, and Ashland in Davis County became the county seat, a political plum it lost to Junction City in 1860. Ashland Township was made a part of Riley County when the county boundaries were changed.[23] Several Kentuckians in Winfield organized a company to promote a town in Clark County, which they named Ashland, supposedly for Clay's "Old Kentucky Home."

The names of three senators from Massachusetts, Webster, Rantoul, and Burlingame, became place-names in Kansas. Daniel Webster, the rugged man with the leonine appearance, was occasionally called "Black Daniel." He was born in New Hampshire and educated at Dartmouth but served as a senator from Massachusetts. His oratorical ability was supported by a sharp intellect. In a speech on the West, Webster spoke of that "vast and worthless area," appropriately occupied by savages and prairie dogs.

One Kansas town after another was given the name of Webster, and one survived. Holliday proposed Webster as a name for Topeka. Webster was also proposed as a substitute for the name of Davis County. There was a Webster City across the river from Wabaunsee which had been settled by New Englanders. As the result of a flood in 1903, "it was buried in the sand."[24] Another Webster City was for a short time located in Butler County.[25] Webster in Rooks County was named for Daniel Webster and its optimistic promoters expected it to become as famous as he. The town was in the valley of the Smoky Hill and its site was submerged when Webster dam was built. The remnant of the town was moved to higher ground.[26]

Robert Rantoul was appointed to fill the unexpired senatorial term of Daniel Webster. He was a humanitarian liberal who advocated greater support for public education. He was opposed to the extension of slavery. Mrs. C. C. Cutler, whose name is on a Franklin County township, was so impressed by a speech he delivered that she asked to have a local railway station named Rantoul.[27]

The town of Gardner near Olathe was said to have been named for Henry J. Gardner, governor of Massachusetts, rather than for O. B. Gardner, member of the local town company and a justice of the peace.[28] Governor Gardner was elected on the Know-Nothing ticket in 1854, the year Kansas was opened to settlement. His name was then in the limelight but his reputation was neither great nor lasting. A Kansas guide said that Gardner was named for "Governor O. B. Gardner of Massachusetts." This would appear to give credit to both Gardners, using the title of "Governor" for one person and the initials "O. B." for the other.[29] There seems to be no obvious reason for having named the town for the governor except that he was in office when Sumner fought for Kansas. Gardner was located at the fork of a most famous road, with one sign reading, "Road to Oregon," and the other, "Road to Santa Fe."

Agents of the American Settlement Company of New York found, they thought, an ideal place to establish a colony east of Council Grove, and they named it Council City. It achieved the status of a post office, but it did not flourish. Burlingame on Switzler's Crossing of Switzler's Creek replaced it. Switzler was a pioneer whose name was used by the Santa Fe travelers for the crossing and the creek. When Green mentions Switzler's, he adds, "now Burlingame."[30]

Anson Burlingame, although born in New York, served as a distinguished senator from Massachusetts. Negotiating the Burlingame Treaty made him a friend of China and a national figure. The Kansas Free-State party loved him after his scathing attack on Preston Brooks. Burlingame came to Topeka in 1859 and gave "a rattling old abolition speech." He also visited the town which now bears his name and where he was a guest of Philip C. Schuyler, a New Yorker who was the founder of Burlingame.[31]

The eight presidents between Jackson and Lincoln had little to recommend them for place-names in Kansas except for the dignity of their office. Van Buren, Benjamin Harrison, Tyler, Polk, Taylor, Fillmore, Pierce, and Buchanan were almost completely ignored except for the temporary place-names of Van Buren, Buchanan, and Pierce, possibly named for the presidents. There was once a Filmore in Line County, but no Fillmore. There was a Pierce in Brown County in 1888, but that place, also called Pierce Junction, was named for George Pierce, a pioneer. There was no place named Polk.

There was a place called "Buchanan Town" in Saline County promoted by Southern sympathizers and named the year that James Buchanan became president. It has been "inferred" that the name was "derived from the president."[32] Lucien J. Eastin, one of the founders of Buchanan, was a proslavery member of the Lecompton Constitutional Convention and probably a political backer of Buchanan. Buchanan was on the losing side when he gave his support to the Lecompton Constitution. During the drought which brought desolation to Kansas in 1860, Buchanan donated the first hundred dollars for its relief. Yet no Kansas town nor township bears his name today.

West Wichita was once named Delano for Columbus Delano, secretary of the interior in Grant's administration.[33] The exploitation of the Indians by the Indian agents at that time was so vicious that it aroused public indignation. In 1875, Delano found it expedient to resign. Delano's name, originally French as de La Noye and as a family name of the Roosevelts,[34] was dropped as the name of a town, but Delano Township and the Delano Town Hall have preserved the name.

Politicians in the public eye always had a chance of receiving place-name recognition; such were the names of Tilden, Hayes, Garfield, and Cleveland. The boom of the 1880's in western Kansas opened the field for honoring such contemporaries, if not with a county name, at least with a town or post office name.

In the presidential election of 1876, Samuel J. Tilden won the most popular votes, but Rutherford B. Hayes had the majority of the electoral votes. Questions were raised about the legality of the election. Both men were popular candidates, and Tilden had two towns named for him; yet both names were replaced. The town of Arlington in Osborne County had its name changed to Tilden, but this was soon changed to Bloomington. The Tilden name remains on the township.[35] In Grant County, where several places were named for their political appeal, the towns of Surprise and Cincinnati combined under the new name of Tilden to compete with Ulysses for county seat. Then Tilden was changed to Appomattox, synonymous with victory, and still it lost.

Rutherford B. Hayes, the former governor of Ohio, passed through Kansas on his return from a tour of the West. General Sherman, who traveled with him, drew more attention than the president. The low point of the president's visit took place in Hutchinson, where Reno

County has a township named Hayes. While there, Hayes shook hands with a citizen who "regarded Hayes from head to foot with drunken gravity, scratched his head," and said: "By G—— stranger, you seem to have the advantage of me. Seems to me that I ought to know your face, but durned if I can remember your name at all."[36]

President Hayes attended the Two-County Fair in Woodson County[37] in 1879. He may have deserved better, but no Kansas town bears his name. However, the counties of Clay, Franklin, McPherson, Mitchell, Reno, and Stafford, all have townships named Hayes. A local newspaper said that Hayes Township in Clay County was named while President Hayes was still in good standing with the Republican party.[38]

James A. Garfield was nominated on the thirty-sixth ballot and elected president in 1880 at the beginning of the boom in western Kansas. He had the political advantage of having been born in a log cabin and he rose from "Canal Boy to President," illustrating, like Lincoln, the realization of the democratic dream. Garfield achieved the rank of major general during the Civil War, and he took part in the battles of Shiloh and Chickamauga. On his way to give a commencement address in 1881, he was assassinated by a disappointed office-seeker. Garfield may not have been well known by the ranchers of the West. A report that Garfield was shot raised the question: "What brand did he run?" The laconic comment of one cowboy was, "another poor devil killed over a cow."[39]

In western Kansas a county was named Garfield in 1887. It was made primarily out of what had been Buffalo Country. Since it lacked one and one-half square miles of being legal, its rivals dubbed it an "illegitimate child," and Garfield County became Garfield Township in the panhandle of Finney County. There, too, was a town named Garfield.[40] One of several names suggested for the town named Eminence was Mentor for Garfield's home town.[41] The Garfield that survived is located southwest of Larned in Pawnee County. As a railroad town it was called Camp Criley but it was renamed Garfield by Ohio settlers and veterans who came from Garfield's home district. In appreciation for having a town named in his honor, Garfield donated a bell to the town's new Congregational church.[42] The fourteen Kansas townships named Garfield served as a tribute to a martyred president. The one in Morris County was attributed to the influence of Ohio settlers. The main building of Friend's University in Wichita was first built for Garfield University.

A post office in Hodgeman County was named Arthur in 1878, two years before Chester A. Arthur was nominated to the ticket with General Garfield. Arthur may not yet have been important enough to deserve the honor of a place-name in Kansas, but he did become important when he succeeded to the presidency after Garfield's assassination. Because of its association, it may be of interest that Antrim, the Irish home town of Arthur's grandfather, was made the name of a Kansas post office in Stafford County the same year that Arthur was named. Windom, the name of Arthur's secretary of the treasury, did become a Kansas place-name.

William Windom, a Quaker lawyer from Ohio, became a senator from Minnesota, where he is honored by a town named Windom. In McPherson County, Kansas, a post office named Laura was too much like Larned, so its name was changed to Hallville, and then, in 1884, to Windom.[43] As chairman of the committee to consider transportation routes to the Pacific, Windom must have been well known in Kansas, which had been opened to settlement in order to promote transcontinental railways. Windom was also known for his work on a committee to investigate the migration of Negroes from the South,[44] and this was of special concern to Kansas.

Lamar in Ottawa County was also named for a politician far removed from Kansas. It was named for Lucius Quintus Cincinnatus Lamar. It is believed that the choice of his historic name was due to "the eccentricities of an uncle."[45] How does one live up to a name like that? Lucius (Quintus Cincinnatus Lamar) lived up to the prestige of the name by becoming a forceful and effective orator, a distinguished senator from Mississippi, and a respected justice of the Supreme Court. The Lamar surname, with the Spanish appearance, is believed to be that of a Huguenot family which came to Maryland in the eighteenth century. In 1872, when he was elected to the Senate from Mississippi, he gave a eulogy for Charles Sumner, so effective that it brought tears to the eyes of northern senators. This was a great step toward conciliation between North and South. This was also the year that Lamar was named in Kansas, honoring a most worthy senator from the South.[46]

Benjamin Harrison, twenty-third president of the United States, grandson of the ninth president, served one term between the two terms of Grover Cleveland. Of the seven Kansas townships named Harrison, those in the west would most likely be named for Benjamin Harrison. Both a post office and a township were named Harrison in Jewell County. The post office was named in 1877, however, several years before Harrison became president.

The small town of Cleveland in Kingman County is a reminder of a large town in Ohio. It was named Cleveland in 1880 before Grover Cleveland became a national figure, so the place was likely named for the Ohio town which had been named for Moses Cleveland. However,

Cleveland's middle name, Grover, used in preference to his first name, Stephen, was said to be the source for the name of a town located between Lawrence and Topeka in Douglas County. Grover became a post office in the year that Cleveland became president so that the timing was right for recognition. Ottawa County had a post office named Grover from 1870 to 1885. Cleveland's father was a minister in Caldwell, New Jersey, and he named his son for another local minister, Stephen Grover.[47]

The Hutchinson, Oklahoma & Gulf Railroad, also known as HOG, passed through Cleveland, Kansas. Having another Cleveland in Oklahoma, the HOG railroad asked to have the name of Cleveland, Kansas, changed to Carvel. The citizens protested, but the railroad nevertheless made the change. So this place, with twenty residents, has two names, Cleveland post office and Carvel railroad station.[48] Six townships bear Cleveland's name.

One of the most able and active Republicans in the post–Civil War period was James G. Blaine of Maine. His support of Presidents Garfield and Harrison brought him two appointments as secretary of state. As the Republican presidential candidate, he ran against Cleveland and lost. He visited Topeka in 1882.[49] A town was named Blaine in Pottawatomie County in 1874 when Blaine was Speaker of the House. A town promoted in 1880 in Decatur County was named Blaine when Blaine was a senator from Maine.[50] Six townships in as many counties are also named Blaine. Even though he lost the chance to become president, his was a name that was as well known as that of any of the contemporary presidents except Grant.

Almost as well known was Senator Roscoe Conkling of New York, a conservative rival of Blaine for the Republican nomination for president. He had been a member of the senatorial "triumvirate" which dominated the Republican party and supported Grant for a third term. Roscoe Township in Reno County was named for Roscoe Conkling.[51] During Conkling's last senatorial term, a post office in Graham County was named Roscoe.

When President William McKinley was assassinated in 1901, Theodore Roosevelt became president. Having worn glasses while ranching in North Dakota, he was called "Four Eyes." As president, he was called "That Cowboy in the White House." He had been active in inciting the war with Spain and he led the Rough Riders in Cuba, which won him wide publicity. His injunction to "speak softly" but "carry a big stick" became a quotable policy. He also gave the Japanese a good object lesson on the value of a strong navy, an idea that culminated in Pearl Harbor and the American participation in World War II.

As spokesman of the Progressive party, he gave a speech in Osawatomie, Kansas, in 1912. Kansas was, according to an admirer, "a rampant Roosevelt state."[52] Both Theodore Roosevelt and his secretary of war, William Howard Taft, were sufficiently popular in Kansas to have post offices given their names. Roosevelt was a post office in Graham County, 1901–1905.

Taft was less dramatic and less addicted to histrionic demonstrations than Roosevelt. Anxious to return to political power, Roosevelt challenged Taft and split the Republican party by heading a "progressive" wing called the Bull Moose party. Taft lost the presidency and the Republicans lost to the Democrats under Woodrow Wilson. But Taft, a well-informed and able statesman, regained prestige as chief justice of the Supreme Court. The post office named Taft in Scott County coincided with Taft's administration, 1909–13.

The permanence of a name was more often determined by the success of the town than the prominence of the politician. Both Roosevelt and Taft were men as deserving of recognition as most politicians and statesmen, and here we use the term "statesmen" to mean "a politician after he is dead."

CHAPTER XXXIII

LMENA ALTAMONT ALTA VISTA ALTON ALTOONA AMERICUS ANDALE ANTHONY ARCADIA ARGONIA

THE FOURTH ESTATE

CITY ARLINGTON ARMA ASHERVILLE ASHLAND ASSARIA ATCHISON ATHOL ATLANTA ATTICA ATW

EASTERN EDITORS FOUND that the stirring events in the squabble over squatter sovereignty in Kansas made good copy, and the reports of their correspondents not only informed but also inflamed the reading public. Horace Greeley, William Addison Phillips, James Gorden Bennett, James Redpath, Murat Halstead, and others kept the world informed about the Kansas conflict. Thomas H. Gladstone came all the way from London to make England aware of the colorful events in Kansas. The publicity given to the problems of Kansas by the world press made Daniel Webster Wilder conclude that Kansas was "the child of the newspapers."[1] Public opinion became polarized as a result of the press, and the conflict over Kansas became a national issue. It is no wonder that one could write a convincing article on the "Pens that made Kansas Free."[2]

Local editors were unrestrained in their vindictive attacks on one another. This editorial practice became particularly vitriolic when the issue was over the choice of the county seat. The editorial comments on state and national affairs were not always judicious, but they left no doubt about the opinions of the editors, right or wrong. The editors were rough partisans in a partisan epoch. Editors of the pioneer press were labeled "Pistol-Packin' Pencil Pushers."[3] But Kansas is also noted for its distinguished journalists. Most journalists had a penchant for politics, either by manipulating public opinion or by political participation. Both national and local journalists left their names on the Kansas map.

In a report on Kansas politics, made to the Kansas State Historical Society, Richard J. Hinton said that, during the early epoch, "it was fortunate indeed that the New York *Tribune* was in the upward glory of its wisdom and power." And, he said, "it was the nation's best fortune that Horace Greeley was then its editor—the editor supreme of that monumental epoch."[4] This was, of course, not a universal opinion, since Greeley was a controversial figure. Under the laws of the Bogus Legislature, a person could be "imprisoned at hard labor ... for reading the *New York Tribune*."[5]

Greeley, greatly concerned over the issues in Kansas, wanted a

Kansas "untainted by the pestiferous blight of slavery."[6] He was called a conservative. That title scarcely fits, since he was also the champion of all sorts of reform programs, and some, at that time, were considered radical. Greeley was an individualist, independent in his thinking. This independence showed in his dress and appearance. He "shaved his face, but allowed his whiskers to flourish in the suburbs."[7] Highly partisan in his politics, he ran for the presidency against Grant in 1872 and lost. Two weeks later, he died.

Greeley's first visit to Kansas was an experience on his overland journey to the West Coast. When Josiah B. Grinnell, the founder of Grinnell, Iowa, asked Greeley for advice about his future, Greeley is credited with the suggestion which became a slogan: "Go West, young man, go west and grow up with the country." The origin of this, like so many quotations of the great, has been challenged, and some would give credit to a man from Indiana, but it would be difficult to deprive Greeley of this catchy slogan.[8]

One reason for Greeley's visit to Kansas was to promote the Republican party, even though he did not like Lincoln. The delegates to the Republican convention at Osawatomie were afraid to let him speak, for fear that he might aggravate or polarize, rather than placate the opposing factions. Greeley did speak at Osawatomie before he left. He said he liked Kansas but not its mud, rain, and politicians. He returned to Kansas to give a lecture at Lawrence in 1870.[9] He has been rightly called "a friend of Kansas."

A town in Anderson County was named Greeley in 1857, even before Greeley came to Kansas. There the name caused considerable controversy during the hectic period of territorial politics. Governor Walker did not like Greeley's brand of politics, and even his name on a town was not to be tolerated. So the town named Greeley had its name changed to Walker. Territorial governors had a fleeting fame which flickered and faded out after their hasty departures. So Walker was changed to Mount Gilead, a borrowed Biblical name. In 1861 the name was changed back to Greeley. The town had first been called Pottawatomie City, then changed four times, twice for Greeley, the name which was finally restored.[10]

Greeley County, named for Horace Greeley, completed the organization of Kansas counties from border to border, all 105 of them. There we find a concentration of Greeley names: Greeley Center; Horace; Tribune, for his newspaper; and Hector, said to be named for his dog. Each one was a competitor for the county seat.[11]

Greeley's first name had been chosen by his mother because she liked it and because it had been the name of a member of the family. Even this simple name, with its classical background, was simplified to "Hod." The first town west of Tribune was named Horace.

Before the town of Tribune was named for Greeley's New York paper, it was "called by the poetical name of Cappaqua."[12] It has been suggested that even Cappaqua was the name of a newspaper.[13]

Hector was the first post office in the county but was soon fighting for its very existence. Each of its rivals, said the *Wallace County Register*,[14] was "trying to gobble the four or five little shanties that have mustered under the proud title of 'Hector.'" It was concluded that "It's the name they are after." A headline in the *Hector Echo* declared the town to be "The Biggest Boomer of the Booming Southwest." But Hector didn't boom, it died. Its remaining inhabitants moved to Tribune, four miles to the south.[15]

Saline and Sedgwick counties have townships named Greeley, and Concordia has a Greeley Street. There is a Greeley County in Nebraska, too, to fit the contemporary interest, and Colorado has a college town named Greeley. But it was Kansas that gave Greeley the greatest recognition in place-names.

Whitelaw, named for Whitelaw Reid, Greeley's successor at the *New York Tribune*, had also been a rival for the county seat of Greeley County. West of Tribune, towns by the name of Reid, for Whitelaw Reid, and Astor, across the tracks, fought for their lives, and Astor won. But the Rand McNally Map of 1888 listed both as "Reid Sta. or Astor P. O." Reid, whose Scottish grandparents came from Tyrone, Ireland, started his newspaper career in Xenia, Ohio. He signed his articles "Agate." Greeley liked him and made him managing editor of the *Tribune*. He was able, ambitious, and self-confident—and he married well. Six place-names in Greeley County were associated with men of the *New York Tribune*.

Halstead in Harvey County was named for Murat Halstead of Ohio, characterized as "a brilliant war correspondent" during the Civil War. He was editor and part owner of the *Cincinnati Commercial*. The hanging of John Brown, which he witnessed, aroused his interest in Kansas. He has been described as "vigorous and forceful as a journalist, but was naive and garrulous as a historian." H. D. Allbright, who laid out the town of Halstead, was a great admirer of the journalist. The Halstead Hotel was given his first name of Murat, a name which one tends to associate with Napoleon's family.[16]

What is now Potter in Atchison County was once named Bennett Springs, a station on the "Pollywog" railroad, a branch of the Santa Fe. Henry C. Squires, a banker, named it for James Gordon Bennett in order to appeal for eastern money.[17] Bennett was a Scottish immigrant who was the founder of the New York *Herald*. He put a lot of zest into his newspaper and aroused considerable criticism. One critic referred to him as an "obscure foreign vagabond." He had been exceedingly poor, and he was a foreigner, but he was not "obscure." It was Bennett who sent Henry M. Stanley to Africa to find Livingstone.

Stanley did find Livingstone—and guessed who he was. He came to Kansas during the Indian disturbances in 1867, and he was a correspondent with General Hancock at Fort Hays and at Fort Larned. He was a reporter at the Medicine Lodge Peace Conference for the St. Louis *Daily Missouri Democrat*. His impressions of Kansas were included in his book, *My World Travels and Adventures in America and Asia*. Although born in Wales, he came to America at the age of eighteen. His name was John Rowland until he was adopted by Henry Morton Stanley, a rich merchant of New Orleans, whose name he took.[18] Stanley in Johnson County is said to be named for this globe-trotting journalist,[19] and Stafford County has a post office named Livingston.

William Addison Phillips was the journalist for whom the town of Phillipsburg in Phillips County was named. He was appointed on the staff of the *New York Tribune* by Greeley and he wrote forceful articles and editorials about the Kansas struggle over slavery. It was said of him that "his flaming pen and burning words fired the hearts of millions all over the United States."[20] During the Civil War, Colonel Phillips led an Indian regiment. After the war, he served Kansas in the House of Representatives. He was well informed, versatile, and "a superb conversationalist."[21] His spacious home on a hill had a beautiful view of Salina, the town he had built.

Another New York journalist to have his name on the map was James Bonner, editor of the *New York Ledger*. A town on the Kaw had been named Tiblow for Henry Tiblow, an Indian who ran a ferry across the Kaw. In 1886 the name was changed to Bonner Springs for the journalist, "not for sentiment, but for what at that time were considered sound business reasons."[22] Bonner was a famous horseman, and we may recall here that Dexter was named for one of his race horses.

Hezekiah Niles was the publisher of the *Niles' Weekly Register*, a current affairs periodical that kept the public informed on political events. It was founded in Baltimore in 1811 and later published in Washington, D.C. It is likely that some of the towns named Niles in New York, Ohio, Indiana, and Michigan honored Hezekiah Niles. Niles in Ottawa County, Kansas, may have transferred the name from another state but the honor goes to Hezekiah.[23]

Pawnee County had a place called Brown's Grove, named for Dr.

Gallatin Brown on whose homestead the town was built. In conversation, the place was known by its initials as "B. G." When its residents moved to the railroad, the Santa Fe named the new town Burdett for Robert J. Burdette, with a deletion of the final vowel.[24] Burdette was an artist, lecturer, and humorist. As the publisher of the Burlington, Iowa, *Hawkeye*, he became known as "Burdette the Hawkeye Man."[25]

James Redpath came to Kansas in 1856 with the immigrants who came by way of Lane's Trail to avoid the proslavery blockade. He became an enthusiastic defender of the free-state movement and an ardent supporter of John Brown. He also wrote a *Life of John Brown*. As a reporter, he sent stirring reports on Kansas to the *New York Tribune*, the Chicago *Tribune*, and to the St. Louis *Democrat*. He also edited the *Crusader of Freedom* in Doniphan. He was characterized as "erratic, . . . fearless, and truthful." On the question of slavery, "he was a compound of glycerine and guncotton."[26] Redpath was an able lecturer and he started the first lyceum bureau in the United States in 1868.[27] The town of Plowboy was renamed Redpath as a post office to honor this crusading journalist.

Captain Jacob V. Admire of Indiana was one of the founders of Admire City, now Admire, in Lyon County. He was postmaster in North Topeka and there he purchased the North Topeka *Times*. He later lived in Osage City where he became the owner of the Osage City *Free Press*. Admire, an active Republican in Kansas, spent his last years in Kingfisher, Oklahoma.[28]

Colonel Samuel Newitt Wood had so many interests that it is difficult to classify him with any one. He was a journalist, politician, and a war veteran. Wood was born in Ohio of Quaker parentage and, as a participant in the Civil War, may be classified as a "Fighting Quaker." He served four terms in the state legislature, representing Chase County or the Western District.[29] He was described as "somewhat addicted to journalism," and it was probably journalism that got him into politics. He established the *Kansas Press* in Council Grove and he was once editor of the *State Journal of Topeka*. He was a man of action, independent, and occasionally rash. He got involved in the county seat war in Stevens County where he was killed. As one writer said, "He led a turbulent life and met a violent death."[30]

It was Sam Wood who named Chase County for his political friend, Salmon P. Chase of Ohio; and as representative from Chase County, he revived the name of Marion County. Woodsdale in Stevens County, which he promoted, was named for him.[31] Now there is only a Woods left, a terminal of a branch railway, but not at the Woodsdale location.

Wilder, a small town south of Kansas City, was named for Daniel

Webster Wilder. One might surmise, correctly, from the "Daniel Webster" in his name that he had come from Massachusetts. Wilder studied law but spent most of his time as a newspaper editor. In Kansas he was first the editor of the *Free Press*. For a time he published it in Missouri where his Republicanism lost him his freedom to publish the *Free Press*; he also lost the press. Then he published the *Leavenworth Conservative*, a radical paper. After a short stint in Rochester, New York, he returned to Kansas and published the Fort Scott *Monitor*. He is especially remembered for his publication of that storehouse of information, the *Annals of Kansas*.[32]

Ocheltree in Johnson County was named for William A. Ocheltree, foreman of the Olathe *Herald*.

Rossville, northwest of Topeka, was named for William Wallace Ross, an eminently successful man. He was born in Ohio, moved to Indiana, became a journalist in Wisconsin, and came to Kansas in 1855. He continued as a journalist in Topeka together with his brother Edmund G. Ross and John Speer. His brother Edmund was the senator who cast the deciding vote against the impeachment of President Andrew Johnson, called "the most Heroic Act in American History."[33] William W. Ross, Indian agent for the Potawatomis, once served as mayor of Topeka. He was a delegate to the Republican Convention in Chicago when Lincoln was nominated.[34] Rossville is on Cross Creek which the Indians called Metsapa, meaning "a cross" for the way in which it enters the Kaw.[35] There was located the Cross Creek Agency and the town across the creek was called Edna, which changed its name to Rossville, also the name of the township.[36]

Among the local men of the press whose names were given to Kansas towns, we have Benjamin Bird, J. R. Colby, and L. J. Eastin. Bird City in the northwestern corner of Kansas was named for Benjamin Bird, the editor of the Bird City *Times*.[37] Colby in Thomas County was named for J. R. Colby, who published the first newspaper in the county.[38]

Lucien J. Eastin, a Kentuckian who had long been in the newspaper business in Missouri, set up a press under an oak tree and published the *Weekly Herald* in Leavenworth. Eastin, which was named for him, was changed to Easton as a reminder of Governor Reeder's home town in Pennsylvania. Eastin had its "i" knocked out, said the local press. Eastin was also a partner in the founding of Buchanan in Saline County and Sonora in Lyon County; neither one survived.

Kansas is famous for its influential journalists and among them were the Murdocks. Three members of the same family, Marshall M. Murdock, Roland P. Murdock, and Thomas Benton Murdock, were successful newspapermen who helped to promote the welfare of Kansas. Thomas Benton Murdock contributed to the training and success of William Allen White, the "Sage of Emporia." Originally Virginians, the Murdocks left the South and slavery behind them, and when they came to Kansas in 1856, they were on the side of freedom. All three served in the Civil War. Marshall, better known as "Marsh" or "Colonel" Murdock, fought under General Curtis on the Kansas border against General Price. He served six terms in the Kansas legislature and later served in the United States Senate.

Thomas Benton Murdock, the founder and editor of the *Walnut Valley Times* in El Dorado, also served in the Kansas legislature.[39] He was "a born leader . . . esteemed and admired," but not without enemies, says Rolla Clymer, editor of the *El Dorado Times*. For him was named the town of Murdock in Butler County, a place designated as a post office three times before it disappeared in 1902. It was located in Murdock Township. Thomas Benton Murdock was commonly known by his middle name of Benton, and the town of Benton in Benton Township was also named for him. Most of the towns named Benton in the United States were named for Thomas Hart Benton, "Mr. Senator" from Missouri, but not Benton in Butler County, Kansas.

The little station named Murdock on the Santa Fe, east of Kingman, was named for Colonel Marsh Murdock, best known as the owner and editor of the *Wichita Eagle*. To distinguish it from Murdock in Butler County, it was at first known as New Murdock, but when the first Murdock disappeared, the "New" was dropped. Colonel Murdock was the one who named Wichita County.[40] The post office named Marshall in Sedgwick County was also named for "Marsh" Murdock.[41] It was absorbed by Cheney.

Irving County was carved out of Hunter County in 1860. But the boundaries of the border counties were still uncertain, and most of Irving County was added to Butler County in 1864 when Butler was extended to the Oklahoma border.

Irving County was named for Washington Irving, who may be considered among the journalists, since that is how he began his literary career. He wrote articles for Peter Irving's *Morning Chronicle* and was a contributor to *The Corrector*. He was also for a year the editor of the *Analectic Magazine*. His writings on Spain brought him fame. In America he wrote not only on New York but also on the West. His *Tour on the Prairies* was based on his travels in Indian Territory, and this should have warranted the use of his name on a Kansas county. Decatur, for whom a Kansas county was named, was his close friend, and Labette, for whom Labette County is named, was his guide. Irving's name is preserved in Marshall County, where the town of Irving was organized on the day that Irving died, November 28, 1859.[42]

Contemporary with Irving was Nathaniel Hawthorne, one of America's great novelists. His early publications appeared in periodicals. He also held political office under President Pierce. But he is best known for his novels, especially *The Scarlet Letter* and *The House of the Seven Gables*. Hawthorne in Atchison County was named for this distinguished writer.[43]

One should explain that Lake City was not named for a lake—nor is it a "city." It was named for Reuben Lake, described as "a unique character," who published its first newspaper, *The Kansas Prairie Dog*. Having served as sheriff of Barber County, he knew what was going on.[44]

M. M. Lewis, editor of *The Valley Republican* (*The Kinsley Graphic*), was described as an "accomplished journalist." Lewis in Edwards County was said to have been named for a Virginia family, and the most likely one was M. M. Lewis,[45] a journalist who turned to law and real estate.

Although none of the newspapers mentioned in this chapter included the popular name of "gazette," which means newspaper, Cowley County had a place named Gazette. It was a rare place-name and not even Lippincott's gazetteers list such a name. It seems to have become Lazette.[46]

We have seen how literary men such as Sir Walter Scott and Robert Burns contributed interesting names which became Kansas place-names. Goldsmith and Dickens gave us Auburn and Pickwick. Robert Southey gave us Ladore, and Thackeray gave us Pendennis. Some of the New York names in Kansas were associated with James Fenimore Cooper. Several Indian names came from Longfellow's *Hiawatha*. Ramona was the name of a novel, as was also Zenda. An especially good source for Kansas place-names was Homer, the Greek poet.

CHAPTER XXXIV

POLITICAL NOMENCLATURE

LIKE SO MANY OTHER STATES, Kansas has several place-names with political implications. In addition to political men, there were political actions and political ideals to be recognized and honored. A most logical name to come first would be Independence.

Lewis and Clark were the first to use Independence Day as a source for place-names in Kansas. Passing a stream on July 4, 1804, they honored the occasion by naming it Fourth of July Creek. It is now White Clay Creek. They camped on the next stream where they celebrated Independence Day and they named the stream Independence Creek. Their celebration consisted of firing a fieldpiece and issuing of "an extra gill of whiskey" to each man.[1]

Sumner County must have had the "Spirit of '76" in mind when a township was named Seventy-Six. Also in Sumner County was a place named Centennial, although it did not become a post office until 1878. This may have been a couple of years late, but even the Fourth of July was celebrated for something which happened on the second of July.

If Independence in Montgomery County were named for Independence, Iowa, and it may well have been, it would be associated with the independence of the United States, since the Iowa town was founded on July 4 (1847) and was obviously named to commemorate Independence Day.[2]

According to a county historian, however, a town company from Oswego, Kansas, "brought the name Independence with them, all ready to apply to their county seat that was to be."[3] The company had broken away from the town company of Montgomery City.

The first year tested the fortitude and independence of its residents. They lacked lumber and the settlers were forced to use hay for roofing, so the Indians called the town Pasha-tse-towa, "Hay-house-town." Food was evidently available, according to an enterprising merchant who advertised: "Bred and Pize for Saile."[4]

In order to compete with Independence, Montgomery City and Verdigris City combined and adopted the challenging name of Liberty. Not far from Independence is Jefferson, and those names should be

371

associated. Equally pertinent may be their nearness to Liberty and Radical City. It took seventeen years for Radical City to outgrow its youthful radicalism, and then it changed its name to Ritchie in 1887 and to Larimer in 1890. Montgomery County also had places named Freedom and Union. And in addition to Jefferson, the names of Lincoln and Grant are included.

Republic County, with its Republican City, was named for the Republican River whose name came from the Republican Pawnees. Not until one gets back to the Republican Pawnee Indians does one realize that the name does not refer to the Republican party. The name is, however, political, and is credited to the French who saw in the rebellion of these Pawnees from the Pawnees on the Platte, a similarity to the rebellion in the American Revolution.

Banner is a name that connotes some sort of leadership, or "the foremost." This was the common use for the name of five townships and two post offices in Kansas. The first Banner post office in Kansas was in Banner Township in Dickinson County, where there was also a Banner Creek. The post office had been named Groomer. According to one account, "Groomer was a somewhat distasteful name, and this was a Banner Republican locality," so Groomer was changed to Banner,[5] and then Banner was changed to Elmo. The place named Banner in Trego County may have only stressed its prominence, but that did not keep it alive.

Republic County, whose very name is political, has a place named New Liberty in Liberty Township. Reno County had a Mount Liberty and Osborne County had a Liberty Center. The first use of Liberty as a place-name in America was Liberty Hill in South Carolina, named for a battle during the American Revolution.[6] Kansans stressed their belief in liberty by naming nineteen townships Liberty.

Freedom goes well with Liberty, but it was used as a post office name only in Butler County where Freedom was in Freedom Township. Ellis, Phillips, and Republic counties also had townships named Freedom.

Liberal has many meanings but is most commonly used as a political term, frequently distorted by politicians who give it a partisan slant. A reactionary would speak of a liberal as being a radical. It may well refer to a person who is generous and that is the way in which it was used when the town of Liberal in Seward County was named. There a pioneer generously let thirsty travelers have free water. The travelers said that this was "mighty liberal" of him, and so the place became known as "the liberal well." When a town was built at the well, it was consequently named Liberal, as was the township in which it was located.[7]

An interesting illustration of how a name may be inspired was the change of a name in Republic County. There a town named Neva, the name of a river in Russia, was moved to the tracks to become a station on the Rock Island Railroad. At the town meeting, the chairman asked what was on the agenda. According to one member, the agenda included the question of a new name for the town. They took action and named it Agenda.[8]

Equally political are such names as Government Siding, Federal, Bureau, and Caucus. Government supplies for Camp Criley to build Fort Larned must have been unloaded at Government Siding. Federal was the name of a post office in Hamilton County. These names go well together since it was Hamilton who wrote some of the most convincing articles on federalism in *The Federalist*. There was a Bureau in Logan County which one might assume had a political connotation as the source for bureaucrats. But Bureau did not have enough bureaucrats to keep the name from being changed to McCallaster. Norton County, which organized a posse to drive out the man who had promoted their county, had a place named Caucus.

Believe it or not, Buncomb belongs to the category of political names. The name of Buncomb in Brown County, Kansas, came from Buncombe County in North Carolina. The representative in Congress from Buncombe County was noted for his long and tedious speeches which were described as "empty claptrap oratory." When criticized by his colleagues, he explained that he was speaking only to his constituents in Buncombe County. Such political speeches were then labeled Buncombe, which became the source for such words as "bunk" and "debunk."[9]

Fiat also has a political meaning as by "decree" or "authority." It has been used in connection with the acceptance of paper money by law. One may not know its purpose, however, when it was used as the name of a place in Elk County. For sixteen years it had authority as a post office.

The political philosophy of the name-givers shows a wide range of interest with emphasis on "Liberty and Union." The influence of the Civil War was obvious. Twenty counties contained townships named Union. Union could be in restraint of liberty, but both had their sentimental appeal. Most of the places named Union were surely associated with the preservation of the Union in the Civil War, but there were also local influences, and a few were named before the war.

Uniontown at the river crossing west of Topeka was the name of a Kaw trading post. The Indians had asked for an agency or post on both sides of the river but they were given only the one named Uniontown on the south side. Immigrants called it "Union Village" and "Union-ville." It was there that a meeting was held in 1852 to promote the territorial organization of what was to become Kansas.[10] The town declined after the cholera epidemic and was later burned and deserted.

Uniontown in Wyandotte County was a post office in 1851, opened for the Wyandotte Indians. In 1856 there was a Union Town in Shawnee County. Twin Groves in Republic County had its name changed to Union Valley. A few years later there was a Union Valley in Lincoln County. At the turn of the century, there was a Uniondale in Clay County. Union City was the headquarters of an Ohio colony south of Lyons in Rice County.

In Bourbon County, the settlement of Union soldiers on the Marmaton resulted in the changing of the name of Hell's Bend to Union Bend, and of changing the name of Turkey Creek post office to Uniontown.[11]

Post offices named Union were established in the counties of Chase, Smith, and Osage. Norton County had a West Union, changed to Densmore. In Chase County, Union was probably named for the junction of Diamond Creek with the Cottonwood. There must not have been much else to unite, since the postmaster's compensation in 1863 was forty-nine cents. But the economy improved and the postmaster earned eleven dollars in 1871.[12]

In the words of Senator Ingalls, "Kansas is the navel of the nation." In geographical rather than physiological terms, it was the center of the United States and was known as the Central State before the admission of Alaska threw it off center. It is still the center of the contiguous states and is called the center of the "Lower 48." It is also the geodetic center of North America.

Names indicated an interest in being in the center of the state. Rice County had a place named Kansas Centre and Barton County had a State Centre. They were both quite near to the center of the state. Osborne County had a Grand Centre and that was near the geodetic center of North America. Centropolis in Franklin County was far from the center of the state, but it was not far from the center of population when it changed its name from Minneola to Centropolis for political appeal when it became a candidate for state capital. Land speculators in the legislature expected to make a fortune if it were made the capital.[13]

The Old English spelling of Centre, as used by Chaucer, was widely used in Kansas, but most of these have been changed to Center. Lyon County still has a Centre Township and it once had a Kanzas Center Township, now named Waterloo.[14] One Kansas commentator considered it rather snobbish to use the English form of the word, and "Centre" has now gone the way of "theatre."

The greatest incentive for the use of Center in a name was by the towns which were candidates for county seat. Some of these "towns" had only one building and a few were only paper towns. Nothing seemed to be more important to most towns than the coveted prize of a county seat. The present decline of the small towns has proved them right. The loss of a county seat contest meant almost instant death to the defeated towns; others have only suffered a gradual decline in old age. No wonder that the town promoters chose names which included the word center, since only by being centrally located could they hope to win.

The promotion of Smith County and Smith Center illustrates the problem and the procedure. L. T. Reese, the promoter, said that he had been "advised by older heads to take a homestead in the exact center of the county with the aim of making it the county seat." He was far short of the six hundred residents required for the organization of the county. A friend, we assume, advised him to list the names of all the people he knew in the East as "bona fide" residents. This was done and it worked. The town on Reese's farm was named Smith Center, and it became the county seat.[15] Not all counties were organized in this manner, but there was much skulduggery and irregularity in the creation of several Kansas counties.

Twenty-eight of the 105 counties in Kansas had towns which combined the name of the county with Center. Two towns added a third optimistic word, Marion Center City and Lincoln Center City. Marion Center City has deleted both terminals. Lincoln Center is still accepted although "local usage favors Lincoln a thousand to one." The tax rolls refer to Lincoln City.[16]

A number of towns dropped the Center part of the name as being unnecessary after winning the county seat. Some names disappeared when towns lost. These included Sherman Center, which lost to Goodland; Jewell Center, which lost to Mankato; Cherokee Center, which lost to Columbus; and Rooks Center, which lost to Stockton. Garfield Center and Madison Center even lost their counties, but there is still a Garfield and a Madison.

Center could be used as a complete name by itself, but it was more often used as a part of a double, descriptive word. In this way it could be a part of a name at either end. The most common use of Center as a name was for naming townships; there were twenty-eight Center townships. These were generally associated with county seat politics, but not all were in the center of the county. The Centre in Howard County became Center in Chautauqua County and disappeared, as did Center in Sedgwick County and the one in Crawford County. Dickinson

County once had a place named Center in Center Township. Center in Stafford County got one vote for county seat, but that kept St. John from getting a majority in the first election.[17]

As the first word in a name we find Center used in such names as Center Hill, Centre Mound, Centre Ridge, and Center Grove. Used as the terminal of a name were Prairie Center, Mission Center, Ohio Center, Valley Center, Coal Center, Gas Center, and Buffalo Center. Elk County had a Union Centre which was not in a center and it had little to unite. Fort Riley was first known as Camp Center. Center was also used with personal names such as Ida Center and Lewis Center, both in Republic County. There were other variations of the Center name such as Centralia in Nemaha County, which also had a Central City and a Centerville Township. Centralia in Cherokee County was promoted to become the county seat. It failed even to become a post office. Linn County had a Centerville Station in Centerville Township. Anderson County also had a Central City. Cloud County had a place named Centerburgh. Five towns in as many counties were named Centerville.

The bid for political preferment by adopting the name of Geographical Center was not successful. Geographical Center in Center Township of Wilson County was also known as just "Center" and as "Section 35."[18] Geographical Center in Linn County was only a name when a petition was signed to make it the county seat. In Neosho County, Geographical Center won a county seat election, even against a town named Centerville, as the "permanent county seat." But Erie changed "permanent" to temporary and took over.[19]

In spite of the importance of Center as a name, the hopes and ambitions of the name-givers did not keep the Center towns alive. Those that were named to win the county seat contest either won and lived or lost and died. Those that lived had little or no need for the addition of Center to their names. The places named Center are now primarily historical records, including the Kansas center of the United States, now advertised as the "Historical Geographical Center of U. S. A.," or the center of the "Lower 48."

CHAPTER XXXV

GENERALS AND COUNTY NAMES

THE MILITARY and the political professions mingle to an extent in what President Eisenhower called the "Military-Industrial Complex." In many cases, top military men move into the presidency after a successful war. It has been said that, early in the Civil War, army officers feared that the fighting would be over "before they could distinguish themselves sufficiently to go to Congress on the strength of their military careers." They were justified in anticipating political success by looking at the careers of Washington, Jackson, Harrison, and Taylor; and "they desired to make war a means of political glory."[1] The war lasted long enough to permit the military to win sufficient prestige, not only for political preferment, but also to be honored by place-names, especially in Kansas, "the Soldier State."

The conflict which sparked the Civil War began in Kansas. The preliminary battles of "Bleeding Kansas," the rivalries between the Border Ruffians and Jayhawkers, and the oratorical outbursts like those of Senators Sumner and Butler stirred the nation into a tragic conflict in which rebellion replaced reason. Born in the time of strife, Kansas furnished more than its quota for military service in the Civil War. Wars make heroes, and heroes' names become place-names. The names of Kansas counties stand as a long memorial list of those who served.

Alternating waves of special interest and political partisanship characterized the naming of Kansas counties. Under the Bogus Legislature, most of the names represented the South and proslavery advocates. After the Civil War, names were chosen to honor the winners. Three important military names remained from the county names chosen in 1855—Leavenworth, Doniphan, and Riley. Of the others which could be included in the military, Coffey County kept its name, Marion was restored, but Richardson was replaced. Eastern county names could be changed but western Kansas was wide open for a first choice, not precluding, however, some changes. The biggest wave of veteran influence was shown in the naming of new counties in 1873. Rawlins, Sheridan, Thomas, Sherman, Meade, Scott, Kearny, and Grant[2] were all named for generals.

377

When the Kansas-Missouri border was supposed to become the "permanent" boundary between the white man and the red man, a line of forts was planned to separate the two. Henry Leavenworth, who had built Fort Snelling, was sent to the Kansas border to establish a fort on the Missouri side. He chose the Kansas side as having a better site. There, in 1827, he established Cantonment Leavenworth. The name was changed to Fort Leavenworth in 1832, even before it was fully fortified.[3] The post office continued to call it Cantonment Leavenworth until 1841. Fort Leavenworth had the reputation of being "the most important military post ever established by the government in the West."[4] Its first role was to keep the white man out of the Indian country; its second role was to protect the white man who entered the Indian country. "It's a nice place," said Horace Greeley, "with many excellent people about it," but too expensive.[5]

Henry Leavenworth served with General Scott in the War of 1812. He set up a military school at Jefferson Barracks in St. Louis to modernize military training. Although rated as a competent military man, there were those who thought that he knew little about Indians. He led a campaign against "them rascally Rees" in 1823, and it was said that his "appalling ignorance of the Indians made a slapstick comedy of the Aricara campaign."[6] His trouble was caused in part by white traders who gave him little co-operation.[7] In 1834, after exploring the West with Colonel Henry Dodge, he became ill with a fever and died, not knowing that four days earlier, he had been promoted to brigadier general. In 1902 Leavenworth's body was brought from New York and given a ceremonial burial at Fort Leavenworth.[8]

Leavenworth County and the city of Leavenworth were named for the fort. Ever since Roman times, or earlier, it was natural for people to settle around a fort. They worked as sutlers or vendors of commodities and services which catered to the needs or desires of the soldiers. At the fort Hiram Rich had a soldier's rendezvous which was named "Bedlam."[9] The community which grew up around Fort Leavenworth was at first called "Squatter City," and this was before the squatters had permission to settle there. As the community grew, it became known as "New Town."[10] A gristmill which formed the nucleus of a settlement in East Leavenworth was known as "Slabtown."[11]

When Kansas was legally opened for settlement, Missouri friends of Senator Atchison rushed across the river to select a choice townsite. They saw the advantage of being near Fort Leavenworth. Judge L. D. Bird and Oliver Diefendorf were so happy about the outcome of the "Douglas Kansas-Nebraska Bill," as they called it, that they "favored naming the town Douglas." Mr. Moore, another member of the town company, "urged the name of Leavenworth, after Fort Leavenworth." He thought the name was so popular that it would "greatly assist in the sale of lots and invite settlers from all parts of the country."[12] And this it did, but some were free-staters who were later driven out. It is worthy of note, however, that, like the name of Kansas City, this name was chosen for its real estate appeal.

A new fort was built on the Indian frontier below Fort Leavenworth in 1842. Spencer, the secretary of war, first called it Camp Scott and then Fort Scott, honoring General Winfield Scott even before he became a hero in the Mexican War. The fort was abandoned in 1853, one year before Kansas was opened to settlement. By that time, Fort Riley had been established well within the Indian Territory, and Fort Scott was no longer essential.

Winfield Scott was a Virginian. He was a big man, weighing over two hundred pounds and standing one inch taller than Lincoln. Scott was concerned about detail and noted for his gaudy uniforms and was consequently called "Old Fuss and Feathers." He studied law but gave it up for the army, which he found so inefficient that he returned to law. In the War of 1812 he was captured, threatened by Indians, wounded by an explosion, had two horses shot from under him, and was wounded again; but when it was all over, he was a hero and a dedicated military man. He was involved in the Black Hawk War and the Seminole War and was in command of the expedition which removed the Cherokees to Indian Territory. Although he did his best to alleviate the Indians' misery, their journey was known as the Trail of Tears. He won his greatest fame as commander of American troops in the war with Mexico.

Scott was a man with strong convictions and self-assurance, and his greatest ambition was to become president. After all, Zachary Taylor made it. Scott ran on the Whig ticket in 1852 and was roundly defeated by Franklin Pierce, a less conspicuous general in the Mexican War. When the friction over slavery led to fighting in Kansas, someone suggested that General Scott be sent there to pacify the people. Horace Greeley objected. "To send him there," he said, "to obey the instructions of Jeff Davis [secretary of war] and enforce the acts of the bogus, tyrannical Legislature would be to lacerate his feelings, tarnish his proud fame and probably hasten his descent to the tomb."[13]

Scott has been called the "Patron of Lee"—and as a Virginian he should be—and the "Protector of Lincoln," who was in need of protection. The rumors of riots and plots to assassinate Lincoln aroused Scott to say that "any man who attempted by force or unparliamentary disorder to obstruct or interfere with the lawful count of the electoral vote . . . should be lashed to the muzzle of a twelve-pounder and fired out of a window of the Capitol. I would manure the hills of Arlington with the fragments of his body, were he a Senator or chief magistrate of my native State!"[14] He did, however, discount any chance for a successful riot while he was in command in Washington. His military command during the Civil War was more honorary than functional, and, as Catton said: "He was now barely more than a great reputation bearing up a showy uniform."[15]

Scott County in western Kansas was named to honor Winfield Scott. Fort Scott honors his name in eastern Kansas. Scott City took its name from Scott County. Scottsville in Mitchell County is named for Tom Scott, a pioneer. Winfield in Cowley County was named for a man named Winfield Scott, a popular preacher.[16] There is a Scott Township in Scott County. There are four others elsewhere in Kansas.

Fort Riley ranks next to Fort Leavenworth in importance. The place was first known as Camp Center and as Fort Centre, supposedly because it was assumed to be near the center of the United States.[17] The fort was promoted by Colonel Fontleroy and built in 1853 by Major Edmund Ogden near the junction of the Republican Fork of the Smoky Hill River. Judging by the many descriptions of the beauty of the country, one might be tempted to conclude that the site was chosen as much for its scenic attractions as for its strategic importance. It was the home of the famous Seventh Cavalry and has been called the "cradle of cavalry."

Fort Riley was named for Bennet C. Riley, a Virginian. Riley's first service in Kansas was on Cow Island with Captain Martin in 1818. He followed Colonel Leavenworth as commandant at Fort Leavenworth. The Santa Fe trade meant money for the Missourians and the Missouri legislature gave Riley a sword for leading the first military escort on the trail. Riley was with General Scott at the Battle of Cerro Gordo in Mexico and was there promoted to brigadier general. After the war, he was sent to California and was the territory's last governor.[18] He died in 1853, the year that the fort was given his name.

The name of the fort was sufficiently popular to have given its name to a county, two towns, and a creek. Riley County, named for the fort, had several changes made in its boundaries. It has the most irregular boundary of any county in Kansas.

When Jefferson Davis, as secretary of war, extended the Fort Riley Reservation, he "killed" Pawnee City, which was built to become the capital of Kansas, and "the demise of Pawnee caused the birth of Riley City."[19] Little communities were competing for the soldier trade of Fort Riley, and in addition to Riley City, there was a West Point, also called "Whiskey Point." When a flood on the Kaw left Riley City on an island, it was popularly known as "Island City."[20] Riley City changed its post office to West Point. The name was used again north of Fort Riley and named Riley Centre so as not to be confused with the former Riley City. The present town of Riley is now a railway station and no longer a "Centre."

When the lower part of Wilson County was made into a new county in 1867, it was named Montgomery, said to be named for a hero of the American Revolution as well as for a champion of the free-state cause in Kansas. The most likely source is General Richard Montgomery, who died at the Battle of Quebec in 1775.[21] He was born in Ireland and served with the British, but his marriage to the daughter of Robert Livingstone of New York made him an "American." He gave up his position in the British army to support the cause of the colonies and this cost him his life. Eighteen states have counties named Montgomery, one more than Marion, but only sixteen were named for the general.[22]

There were those who believed that Montgomery County was named for Colonel James Montgomery of Kansas. He believed it himself. He was sufficiently prominent to deserve such an honor, and moreover, he was said to be a relative or "remote cousin" of the Montgomery who died on the Plains of Abraham. The colonel was born in Ohio, taught school in Kentucky, became a preacher, and finally settled on a farm in Linn County, Kansas. He was an outspoken abolitionist, and when John Brown was captured at Harper's Ferry, Montgomery planned to organize a band to rescue him. He predicted correctly: "You can count on the fingers of one hand all the years that slavery has left."[23]

Montgomery City, using the name of the county, had an attractive location on the Verdigris, but rivalry between settlers from Oswego, Kansas, and the town company made the newcomers move on to found the town named Independence. As the town of Independence flourished, Montgomery City declined.[24]

Of the thirty-five counties named in 1867, twenty-four were for the military, and four of these were named for generals: McPherson, Sedgwick, Rice, and Reno. These four had been killed in the war, and most of the other Civil War names chosen in 1867 were from war casualties. One may wonder why such men as Grant, Sherman, Sheridan, and Logan were not honored in this list. They were still alive and they were still in the public eye, Grant and Logan as politicans, and Sheridan and Sherman as Indian fighters. Yet the legislature did not wait for these men to die before giving them recognition in 1873.[25]

Except for the name of Lincoln, no name was more important in Kansas than that of Grant. There was considerable discussion and several suggestions for the naming of Grant when he was born at Point Pleasant, Ohio, in 1822. His mother wished to name him Albert in honor of Albert Gallatin, the Swiss who had served the United States so well. Grandfather Simpson suggested the name of Hiram because he liked it. Having recently read Fenelon's *Telemachus*, his grandmother had been so impressed by the description of Ulysses given by Mentor that she would have him named Ulysses, and this was done. So his name was Hiram Ulysses Grant. His father called him by his middle name, and for brevity, Ulysses became "Lysses" or simply "Lys."[26]

When Grant was leaving for West Point, a clerk initialed his trunk HUG. The implication disturbed him. "The boys will plague me about it," he said to his brother. He might have become known by this acronym. At the hotel, he registered as "U. H. Grant." In his report to the adjutant general, he signed his name in full as Ulysses Hiram Grant.[27] When he was recommended for West Point by a friend of the family, his middle name was given as Simpson, his brother's given name and his mother's family name. The notification of his appointment from Washington gave his name as Ulysses Simpson Grant.[28]

Schoolboys and journalists showed a lot of ingenuity and had a lot of fun in giving fancy interpretations for the "U. S." in Grant's name. The initials were said to mean "United States" Grant, "Uncle Sam" Grant, "Unconditional Surrender" Grant, "Union Safeguard" Grant, and so on, with endless variety.[29] The "Uncle" was deleted from the Uncle Sam nickname, and he was consequently called "Sam" Grant. In spite of his popularity after the war, political partisanship colored some of the current comments about Grant. A Leavenworth paper called him "Sidney Napoleon Simpson." One headline raised the question: "IS SIMPSON A SOT?"[30] There were those who dared to substitute "Useless" for Ulysses.

Grant was a lieutenant at Jefferson Barracks when the Mexican War began. He was with General Zachery Taylor at Camargo and Palo Alto. These names became Kansas place-names. Taylor's battle at Buena Vista gave Kansas another name. Lieutenant Grant was transferred to General Scott's army, and he was at the Battle of Cerro Gordo, also to become a Kansas place-name. Camargo is in Smith County, Cerro Gordo, in Jewell County, and Buena Vista was renamed Hoisington in Barton County.

After the war, while serving at Jefferson Barracks, Grant courted Julia Dent, the eldest daughter of Colonel Frederick Dent, whose home was called "White Haven." The war with Mexico hurried their engagement but delayed their marriage.[31] Grant returned to Missouri, married Julia, and began farming the eighty acres of land given to him by his

father-in-law. The name of his home, "Hardscrabble," was indicative
of his problems. His farming was a failure and so were his efforts to
get permanent and paying employment in St. Louis. He moved into his
brother-in-law's home which was called "Wish-ton-Wish," an Indian
name for the prairie dog. He served in the army on the West Coast but
found army life so monotonous and unrewarding that he resigned.

When the Civil War erupted, he was clerking in his father's leather
store. Being a West Point graduate, he applied for a command in three
states. Governor Yates of Illinois, wishing to replace an incompetent
colonel, accepted him. After Grant's great success, the proud governor
of Illinois said: "God gave him to the country and I signed his first
command."[32]

There was much controversy over Grant's early leadership and,
except for Sherman's encouragement, Grant would have resigned
before the Battle of Shiloh. The rumors and recriminations against
Grant gave him the reputation of being a disobedient officer, incompetent commander, and a drunkard. When these rumors were brought to
President Lincoln's attention, his laconic comment was, "He fights!"[33]

Kansas had many reasons for remembering Grant; after all, he won
the war that Kansas started. Kansas soldiers were not always sympathetic
to Grant. Whenever foraging became an issue, the Jayhawkers were
generally blamed. They could not escape the connotation of the name.
In one raid, the Seventh Kansas got less than its share of loot but it got
all the blame. They were "Jayhawkers." Grant ordered a two-dollar
deduction from their pay to compensate civilians for the raid. "Tell
Grant to go to Hell," was the message they sent back. When other
regiments marched past Grant sitting on his porch, they saluted and
shouted; the Seventh Kansas silently looked skyward.[34]

Grant was a visitor at Fort Leavenworth on July 16, 1868. There he
met his distinguished colleagues Sherman and Sheridan, and at Fort
Wallace he met Custer.[35] Topeka celebrated his birthday in 1885 at a
time when Grant was near death. Laredo Taft's bronze statue of Grant
was erected at Fort Leavenworth in 1889.[36] Kansas place-names gave
him additional recognition.

Grant County was named but not organized as one of the new
counties in western Kansas in 1873. Ten years later it disappeared when
several counties were reshuffled and eight others lost their identity.
When the town of Ulysses was established, it was then in Hamilton
County. Not until Grant County was revived in the boom of 1887 did
the town and the name of Ulysses return to their association with
General Grant.[37]

Lincoln County has a Grant Township and when Mitchell County was a part of Lincoln County, it had a post office named Ulysses. In 1885 Clark County had a place named Ulysses but that name was changed to Lexington in 1886, the year when Ulysses became a post office in Grant County. While the remote source of Ulysses is a Homeric character, it is likely that these may be associated with Ulysses S. Grant as place-names.

Competing with Ulysses for the county seat of Grant County was a town named Surprise.[38] A split in the Surprise Town Company led to the settlement of a new town called the "Peoples Town." The name was democratic but not popular, so the name was changed to Cincinnati. In order to compete with Ulysses, Surprise and Cincinnati—only two miles apart—united and adopted the new name of Tilden, a name that had political importance but only partisan support. So a search was made for a fourth and winning name. General Sheridan suggested the name of Appomattox, a reminder of Grant's victory over Lee.[39] In spite of its new name, Appomattox lost to Ulysses. Then Ulysses suffered from a heavy bonded debt and the emigration of many of its people to the Cherokee Outlet. In 1909, its residents "put wheels under their town" and moved it to an unmortgaged site a few miles away. Ulysses, once called the "Garden of the Gods" by its boosters, became known as "Old Ulysses," now marked only by its cemetery, which might hopefully be called the "Garden of the Gods." The new town became New Ulysses, a booming town in what was once the Dust Bowl.[40]

Townships named Grant, twenty-nine in all, may be found all over Kansas. Only Lincoln, with thirty-one, had more. Four post offices in as many counties have been named Grant. A place named Grantville east of Topeka was named for the general. A station named Grant is located northwest of Lincoln Center. In Chautauqua County, the reason given for naming Grant Creek was that most of the patents for land in the neighborhood were signed by President Grant.[41]

In Grant's home in Galena, Illinois, hangs a picture of three of the most distinguished generals of the Union army—Grant, Sherman, and Sheridan. Grant should also have had a picture of General McPherson, whom he coupled with Sherman as the officer most responsible for his own success. Next to Grant, the best-known general was William T. Sherman, a West Point man. His middle name was Tecumseh, honoring the name of a Shawnee chief who was one of the greatest Indian heroes in American history. Yet it was the white man's general with Tecumseh's name who was assigned the task of crushing Indian resistance in Kansas. Sherman's Indian name was so popular that he was known as "Old Tecumseh."

384

Sherman was an Ohio man who, after his father's death, was brought up by Thomas Ewing, a distinguished senator and cabinet member. Sherman later married Ewing's daughter, and in Kansas he formed a law partnership with Thomas Ewing, Jr. Before the Civil War, Sherman lived in Kansas on a farm in Soldier Township that he managed for eastern relatives; and in Leavenworth, he practiced law.

It was Sherman's steady rise to leadership during the Civil War that gave him prestige, capped by that dramatic march from "Atlanta to the Sea," bringing glory to the North but tragedy to the South. The campaign was of his own design, and it was with reluctance that General Grant gave his approval. But Grant knew the man and trusted him. Thomas, Logan, and McPherson were generals under Sherman's command, and all four left their names on Kansas counties.[42]

After the war, Grant sent Sherman, then a lieutenant general, to direct the military against the Indians on the frontier. Sherman had little sympathy with the Indian cause; Indians were "enemies." He traveled across Kansas in 1868, the year that Grant was elected president. He was also with President Hayes on a train which stopped at Dodge City. Hayes refused to appear before the exuberant cowboys, but Sherman did appear, partly to appease them, introducing himself as "Uncle Billy Sherman."[43]

Another Kansas connection of General Sherman's was his close association with and admiration for "Mother Bickerdyke." Where Sherman's troops fought, wounded, and killed, Mrs. Bickerdyke, like Clara Barton, brought healing medicine, food, shelter, and comfort. When she commanded, generals obeyed. Sherman and others of high rank visited her in Salina, Kansas. While it is a credit to Kansas to have named a county in honor of Clara Barton, one may regret that no county was named for "Mother Bickerdyke."[44]

When Sherman came to Kansas to supervise the defense of the frontier, he discouraged settlers from going to western Kansas. Yet it was western Kansas that honored him with a county name. The battle for the county seat of Sherman County was characterized by bribery and other irregularities. Itasca and Voltaire gave up their names and joined to form a new town which they named Sherman Center, hoping that the name would win votes in the county seat contest. Its chief rival at first was Eustis, named for P. S. Eustis, one of its promoters. It was said that the people of the town that lost would start "a great roller skate parade across the prairies" to the town that won. It meant "death to the loser." It spite of its name and the man it honored, Sherman Center lost and Goodland won. It was then only a matter of time until all the other names, Itasca, Voltaire, Eustis, and Sherman Center, disappeared. The only towns now left in Sherman County are those along the railway and highway.[45]

Sherman's name remains on a township in Sherman County, but strangely enough, it is called Shermanville. The Sherman Township in Anderson County is most likely named for Henry Sherman, for whom "Dutch Henry's Crossing" was named, as was Shermanville in Franklin County. In Cherokee County there is a Sherman post office, but the station is called Sherman City; these could more likely have been named for the general.[46]

General Sheridan was even more active in Kansas than Sherman, his commander. Phillip Henry Sheridan was born in New York of Irish parents, but like Sherman, he grew up in Ohio and was a West Point graduate. "Little Phil," as he was called, was a man with a magnetic personality who had rather strong likes and dislikes. He rose rapidly in rank as his military ability was recognized. His fame was assured when his inspired Army of the Cumberland captured Missionary Ridge in the Battle of Chattanooga. Grant was pleased with his victory, yet irked that it had been won without his orders.[47]

Sheridan, stationed in Texas and Louisiana, was uncompromising towards the South after the war. He clashed with President Johnson, who got rid of him by sending him to Fort Leavenworth. There he could be kept busy fighting Indians. He worked closely with Governor Crawford, and it was Sheridan who in 1868 sent the Nineteenth Cavalry to Camp Beecher, now Wichita.[48] He also returned General Custer to active duty after his court-martial. Sheridan and Custer were the chief hosts for the Grand Duke Alexis of Russia when he came out to hunt in the West.[49] Grant thought so highly of Sheridan that he made him a lieutenant general in 1871; this irked both Thomas and Meade.[50]

For this dashing cavalry officer, Sheridan County was named. A temporary terminal of the Kansas and Pacific Railroad in Wallace (now Logan) County was named Sheridan Station. Some called the town the "Phil Sheridan Station," others called it "Sheridan City."[51]

The Post Office Department changed the name of Sheridan in Sheridan County to Phil Sheridan so as not to be confused with Sheridan in Greenwood County. There had already been a Sheridan in Lyon County which temporarily replaced the name of Americus. Sheridan was also proposed as a name for Wichita but the name had been preempted in Greenwood County. In Sheridan County the mail went to Phil Sheridan, but the public, both in speech and in print, omitted "Phil." Sherman was the typical "End-of-Track" town and accumulated the rough element of the portable towns which it replaced. On payday, Sheridan thought the "Irish mob" reminded him of Stonewall

Jackson's "ragged battalians."[52] Phil Sheridan did not long remain a post office nor did Sheridan City become a city. But the name was popular and seven townships were named Sheridan in honor of "Little Phil." Five Civil War leaders were honored in the township names in Ottawa County: Lincoln, Stanton, Logan, Sherman, and Sheridan.

George Henry Thomas was a West Point man, and, although he came from Virginia, he was a Union general. He showed his loyalty and ability in defending Chickamauga, a heroic defense which won him the nickname of "the Rock of Chickamauga."[53] While in Tennessee, his hesitation to attack General Hood worried the administration at Washington, and some thought his hesitation was due to his sympathy for the South. Grant sent General Logan to check, but in the meantime, Thomas crushed Hood's army at Nashville and secured Tennessee for the Union. He was later with Sherman, Sheridan, and McPherson in the Atlanta campaign. The First Kansas Battery was with General Thomas at Nashville, and this association may have contributed to the naming of Thomas County.[54] His troops referred to him affectionately as "Pop Thomas." On each side of Thomas County are names of four distinguished generals: Sherman, Sheridan, Rawlins, and Logan.

James Birdseye McPherson from Ohio was a West Point man who was graduated at the head of his class, which included Sheridan and Hood. McPherson, for whom McPherson County was named, was a curly-bearded and handsome man, tall and graceful, and with a pleasing manner. He was popular with both his subordinates and his superiors. McPherson was an engineer on Grant's staff and was promoted to command the Army of the Tennessee, "the whiplash of the army." He was associated with Sherman at Atlanta, where Hood's Confederates penetrated the Union army. There McPherson was killed on July 22, 1864, by the men who were led by a West Point classmate.

This was a triple tragedy, or worse: it was a tragedy for his family, a tragedy for his commander and his country, and a tragedy for the Baltimore lady to whom he was engaged. His fiancee's family were fanatical supporters of the South, and one member reported McPherson's death as the "most wonderful news." Sherman's grief aroused this angry attack at those who had brought on the war: "The loss of a thousand men such as Davis and Yancey and Toombs and Floyd and Beechers and Greeleys and Lovejoys, would not atone for that of McPherson."[55]

The Union veterans carried this devotion to Kansas when they named McPherson County. The town of McPherson was on McPherson Flats and there was established McPherson City, although its Salina town promoters called it McPherson Center. Having won the county seat, it dropped the "Center" from its name.[56] An equestrian statue of McPherson is located in the courthouse square of McPherson.

John Alexander Logan, the "untutored civilian," became one of the great generals of the Civil War. He had neither military training, nor did he go to school until he was fourteen. He did, however, attend Shiloh College. He studied law at the University of Louisville, and he got military experience in the Mexican War. That he was a fighting man is indicated by the fact that he took part in the Battle of Bull Run, "unattached and unenlisted." During the war he advanced rapidly, and when McPherson was killed, it was General Logan who was given command of the Army of the Tennessee. General Sherman, West Point trained, did not fully trust Logan, the "political general."[57] Yet Logan's men trusted him. When Logan rode before his troops with his black hat in his hand and his long black hair flowing in the wind, his soldiers shouted, "Black Jack!"[58]

Herndon and Lincoln had studied law with Logan, who had represented Illinois in Congress before the war. After the war, Logan became commander-in-chief of the Grand Army of the Republic, and it was he who started, except for its southern precedent, the custom of decorating the military graves on Memorial Day. As a Douglas Democrat before the war, he found it easy to switch to the Republican party. He was prominent, popular, and outspoken; his speeches have been described as "spread eagle oratory." He was a vice-presidential candidate with Blaine, a ticket that lost because St. John, a Kansas Prohibition candidate, split the New York vote. This makes it doubly interesting that the western county named St. John had its name changed to Logan.[59]

General Logan once gave a political speech in Atchison and later he came to Coffey County with President Hayes to attend the "2-County Fair." The town of Monument was believed by some to have been named for the memorial tower built to honor Logan, but Monument had already been named for the Monument Rocks on Castle Rock Creek. It was first a stage station and later moved to become a railway station as Monument Siding.[60] Logansport in Logan County disappeared after Russell Springs replaced it as the county seat.[61] Union veterans in Phillips County named their town Logan to honor their commander.

Pond Creek Station was named for Captain James Burton Pond, who had served on the Smoky Hill route of the Butterfield Dispatch. Pond was born in New York, served with Wisconsin volunteers, and then came to Kansas where he printed the *Herald of Freedom*. The

Pond Creek Station was ambitious and adopted the name of Pond City. When the railway bypassed it, the soldiers and citizens of Pond City moved to Fort Wallace, about two miles away.[62]

In 1868 two new counties, Gove and Wallace, were extended to the Colorado border along the Kansas Pacific line. The name of Wallace had already been used for Fort Wallace; then it was given to Wallace County. The fort was named to honor General William Harvey Lamb Wallace, who fought the Confederates at the Hornet's Nest near Shiloh where General Albert Sidney Johnston was killed.[63] Wallace died in 1862 from wounds received at Shiloh. He should not be confused with General "Lew" Wallace, also of Shiloh, who outlived the war and who won fame from his historical novels, especially *Ben Hur*.[64]

One would assume that the town of Wallace in Wallace County was named for the same Wallace. But the local press declares that the town of Wallace was named for a railroad superintendent by the name of George Wallace who died in the neighboring town of Sheridan in 1869.[65]

Rawlins County is in the cluster of western counties named for Civil War generals. John A. Rawlins, was, like General Logan, a lawyer from Illinois. He was a trusted adviser of Lincoln, and he was the "dedicated, consumptive little chief of staff" who squelched the wild rumors concerning Grant, not that he would tolerate liquor.[66] One writer described him as "a teetotaler who was punctual, precise, and abstemious to the verge of fanaticism." He had a convincing "no."[67] He has been described as having a good mind, a retentive memory, a high sense of justice, and tireless energy. In the words of Grant, he was the "most nearly indispensible officer of his staff." Grant respected this "peppery little General" and made him his secretary of war.[68]

Howard County was named for Oliver Otis Howard, who had been made a general in the Mexican War and who had participated in most of the major battles of the Civil War. He was born in Maine and he attended Bowdoin College before he went to West Point to teach mathematics. He lost his right arm in the Peninsular campaign and was henceforth known as the "One-armed General." As a man of high ideals, he was also called the "Christian Soldier." But Catton characterized him as a "prim sobersides of a New Englander who seemed excessively pious and straight-laced."[69] Howard's appearance was unusual in that he was clean-shaven; for this he could have been characterized as a nonconformist.

After the war, Howard was appointed head of the Freedman's Bureau to aid the Negroes in their transition from slavery to citizenship. He was too trustful to recognize the corruption which crept into the bureau. But his devoted work for the Negroes was recognized, and Howard University in Washington, D.C., which he promoted, has preserved his name better than the ephemeral county name in Kansas.

Howard County was named in 1867 during the first big expansion of counties in central Kansas after the Civil War. The county had previously been named Godfrey and then Seward. The change was made when Seward was negotiating for Alaska, the state that moved the geographical center of the United States out of Kansas. Howard County lost its identity when a county seat conflict split the county into Elk and Chautauqua, making a total of five names for the county. Howard, for a time listed as Howard City, remains as the county seat of Elk County.[70]

Southwestern Kansas has a county named Meade, named for General George Gordon Meade, the commanding officer at the Battle of Gettysburg who failed to follow up his advantage. He was later at the Battle of Antietam, called the "bloodiest twelve hours in United States history."[71] He was with Grant to meet Lee at Appomattox. Meade was "a tall, thin man, rather dyspeptic . . . lacking in cordiality" and "disliked by his subordinates," said Charles A. Dana, assistant secretary of war under Lincoln. This is partially confirmed by Catton, who described him as "a tall, grizzled man with a fine hawk's nose and a perfectly terrible temper, which would lash out furiously at any officer who failed to do his job." Catton also called him "a damned goggle-eyed old snapping turtle," but a good commander, "wholly admirable as a man" and "a solid and conscientious soldier."[72]

One should be cautious about criticizing Meade. After the Battle of the Wilderness, a report was printed that Meade had counseled retreat at a time when he had been confident of victory and had no other plan. The reporter who had written the story was arrested, placed on a horse, and placards tacked on his back which read, "Libeler of the Press."[73]

Skidmore, named for Miss Skidmore, a resident of Meade County, changed its name to Meade Center. Another Skidmore was later located in Cherokee County. It is a rare name, but New York has a Skidmore College. Meade Center won the county seat over its rivals because of its location, water supply, and the weakness of its rivals.[74] It changed its name to Belle Meade, losing its French look when local settlers wrote it "Bell" Meade, and losing its "Belle" when it was again changed to Meade Center.[75] The legislature dropped the "Center" in 1889[76] because the Rock Island said it was superfluous.

Peketon County, covering the whole of southwestern Kansas, had its name changed to Marion and was later carved into thirty-four counties. Finally, when it was cut down to size, one unit was named Rice for Brigadier General Samuel Allen Rice of Iowa. Rice had been a steamboat pilot on the Ohio, saved his money to get an education, studied law, and, at the age of twenty-eight, became attorney general of Iowa. With the coming of the Civil War, he received command of a regiment of Iowa volunteers. He had never seen a book on tactics, yet he had good discipline, won the support of his men with "courtesy and kindness," and earned the admiration of his superiors by his "cool heroism in battle." He was wounded at the Battle of Jenkins Ferry in 1864 and died soon afterwards. Colonel Crawford, later governor of Kansas, was also at that battle, and he may have been responsible for suggesting the name for Rice County.[77]

Since Rice County was short of citizens for a county organization, a man was sent to the crossing of the Little River to register all the transient freighters, including each member of the freighters' families, without regard for age or sex. According to the story, they were still short, so they added the name of every mule, and there were six mules to each wagon. With this padded roster, Rice County was organized.[78]

Next to Rice County is Reno County, named for General Jesse Lee Reno, another West Point graduate who was a casualty in the Civil War. Reno was with Scott at Cerro Gordo and at Chapultepec, and there he was promoted for gallantry in action. His contact with Kansas came when he was in command of the arsenal at Fort Leavenworth in 1861. At South Mountain, Maryland, when Reno thought the Confederates had left, he allowed his men to stack arms for a "coffee break." Suddenly there was a surprise attack by the Confederates, and Reno was shot out of his saddle. This "capable soldier," as Catton described him, was killed in September, 1862. Some of Reno's soldiers settled in Kansas and served in the legislature which named Reno County.[79]

Reno's name is an English simplification of his original French name of Renault. The town of Reno, Nevada, was named for the same general, but Kansas has the only county in the United States to bear his name. Hutchinson is in Reno Township. According to George Remsburg, Reno village and township in Leavenworth County were named for General Marcus A. Reno of the Seventh Cavalry,[80] who was at the Battle of the Little Big Horn.

Philip Kearny was born in New York but made his home in New Jersey. His father wished him to become a preacher, but he studied law and he chose the military profession as the one that appealed to him the most. He was sufficiently wealthy to have passed up any profession. In 1837 he came to Leavenworth as a lieutenant in charge of dragoon recruits. His uncle, Stephen Watts Kearny, was in command of the post.[81]

Nothing appealed to Kearny as much as the prospect of leading a dashing cavalry charge. He served in the French cavalry in both Algiers and in Italy before he got his big chance in Mexico. He crossed Kansas with Doniphan on his way to help Taylor at Monterey. When Scott requested additional forces from Taylor, he specifically named Kearny and his cavalry. Kearny, said Scott, was "the bravest man I ever knew, and a perfect soldier."[82] At Churubusco, Kearny led the kind of cavalry charge he had dreamed of, and there he lost his left arm. He had once told a servant: "Never lose an arm; it makes it hard to put on gloves." When Kearny visited General Howard in the hospital, they shook hands, and Howard suggested that they should buy their gloves together, for Howard's left hand and Kearny's right.[83]

The loss of an arm did not end Kearny's military career; like Howard, he was just another one-armed general. He was fighting at Chantilly in Virginia one night when he was caught in an overwhelming thunderstorm and it was impossible to distinguish friend from foe. Then, said Catton, Phil Kearny, "galloping through the dark wood with the lightening gleaming on the wet leaves, his sword in his hand and bridle reins held in his teeth, rode smack into a line of Confederate infantry and was shot to death." And with that, another general's name was provided for a county in the Soldier State.[84]

Kearny took part in the battles at Malvern Hill and Chantilly, and both of these names became Kansas place-names. In Kearny County, the community center for cowboys and pioneers was called "Chantilla," named for the battle where Kearny was killed.[85] Chantilly was as appropriate in Kearny County as was Appomattox in Grant County, but neither name survived, nor did Kearny post office in Kearny County.

Kearny's name has frequently been spelled with an extra "e" as in the name of the town of Kearney and Kearney County and as it is in Nebraska. The Kansas legislature in 1889 passed an act to correct the spelling of Kearney "so as to conform to the spelling of the name of General Phil Kearny of New Jersey, in whose honor the county was named."[86]

Sedgwick County was named for Major General John Sedgwick, who was born in Cornwall Hollow, Connecticut. He taught school for two years and then entered West Point. He fought the Seminoles in Florida and helped Scott to bring the Cherokees to the Indian Territory. In the Mexican War he participated in most of the major battles and won promotions at both Churubusco and Chapultepec.

Major Sedgwick served in Kansas as early as 1855. "Jeb" Stuart, the

Confederate general, was one of his companions when he was in command of expeditions to pacify the Indians and to drive white trespassers out of the Indian reservations.[87] In September, 1857, Governor Walker ordered Major Sedgwick to send companies of his cavalry to the eastern Kansas towns of Richmond, Cayltonville, Palermo, and Atchison. The orders looked like an alert for a fearful invasion from the Missourians, but all this military hullabaloo was to police the county elections.[88]

In the critical year of 1856, the army was under the domination of Jefferson Davis, secretary of war, and Governor Shannon in Kansas. Sedgwick's sympathy for the free-state victims may be seen in his diluting of a directive for their arrest. "Dear Captain," he wrote, "I am coming down today with 600 men, six pieces of artillery and a United States Marshal to arrest you Sam Tappan, General Lane, and Sam Wood. I shall reach and surround Lawrence at about two o'clock P.M. You fellows had better get into the bush, and stay there till I am gone. Yours fraternally, Sedgwick."[89]

Then came the Civil War, and General Sedgwick was wounded at Antietam. He was hospitalized twice. He hated hospitals so much that he is reported to have said, lightly, we assume, that if he ever got hit again, he hoped the bullet would finish him off. "Uncle John got his wish at Spottsylvania," said Catton. Another of his light statements, if he were quoted correctly, was that the Confederate sharpshooters couldn't hit an elephant. This was, of course, army talk. While inspecting the lines in the Battle of the Wilderness, he got beyond the point of safety and was struck in the forehead by the bullet of a sharpshooter and instantly killed. This was on May 9, 1864, when he was fifty-one.[90]

Sedgwick was a highly-respected man and one of Grant's most trusted generals. According to Charles A. Dana's estimate: "He was a very solid man; no flummery about him; you could always tell where he was to be found, and in a battle that was apt to be where the hardest fighting was. He was not an ardent, impetuous man, like Hancock, but was steady and sure."[91] Catton called him "cool and unruffled" and able to use an army "as it was meant to be."[92]

Like Sedgwick County, Sedgwick City was named for the general. The town was laid out by William Finn, Wichita's first school teacher. The "city" was first established in Sedgwick County, but a tier of townships in the northern part of the county was added to Harvey County, and this automatically moved Sedgwick City out of Sedgwick County. As an early competitor of Wichita it might justify the inclusion of "City" in its name, but as a small town, it is now only Sedgwick in the township of Sedgwick.[93]

General Sedgwick has been honored by several memorials: an expensive monument in his home town in Connecticut; a bronze statue at West Point; a portrait in Plainfield, New Jersey; an equestrian statue at Gettysburg; and place-names in Kansas and neighboring states.

Like Sedgwick, Nathaniel Lyon was born in Connecticut. He was "fiery" and "fanatic" in his attack on slavery.[94] His life in Kansas, dominated by Missouri, was not an easy one. When Captain Lyon was in command of Fort Riley in 1860, Weichselbaum, a rustler, described him as "a little fellow" who was "a terrible growler" and a "hard nut" but both "smart and honorable."[95] With a name like Nathaniel, one is likely to have it abbreviated or substituted for, and so the general was called "Joe."

General Lyon decided to challenge a superior force of Confederates at Wilson's Creek, a few miles south of Springfield, Missouri. He fought to save Missouri for the Union, but his troops were outnumbered by about four to one, and his repeated and frantic appeals to General Frémont for more soldiers were ignored. Frémont's comment was, "If Lyon fights he will do so on his own responsibility." The failure of Frémont to furnish the necessary troops caused Albert Greene, an admirer of Lyon, to say that Frémont was an "absolutely selfish and insanely jealous" man.[96] In the battle of Wilson's Creek, Lyon's beautiful, dapple-gray horse was shot from under him and Lyon was wounded. Lyon borrowed another horse and directed his poorly equipped and poorly supported troops in a heroic battle on "Bloody Hill," only to be shot down again and killed. He died on August 10, 1862, leading Kansas and Iowa regiments.

The name of Lyon had been suggested as a substitute for the name of Davis County. But it was Breckinridge County that was renamed Lyon, exchanging the name of a Union general for that of a Confederate general.[97]

When Nathaniel Lyon was a captain in the Kansas army, he had surveyed some land southwest of Fort Riley. There Captain McClure, a companion of the general's at Wilson's Creek, chose a site for his homestead because of Lyon's "glowing description of the valley." "I named it Lyon Creek," said McClure. The Indians called it Watunga.[98] Upstream on Lyon Creek in Dickinson County, a town was founded on a "healthy and beautiful" site above the creek and named Lyon City. That name is now gone and the name nearest to the site is Woodbine, possibly named for a popular song in the Civil War.[99] In Cloud County, a county named for another of Lyon's associates, a township was named Lyon to honor the general,[100] and the recruiting camp at Fort Leavenworth was called Camp Lyon.

Nineteen counties had already been named for generals, and there were enough Civil War veterans for naming a score more for military men of lesser rank. Other participants in the Battle of Wilson's Creek for whom counties were named were Sam Crawford, Caleb Pratt, W. F. Cloud, and Avra P. Russell.

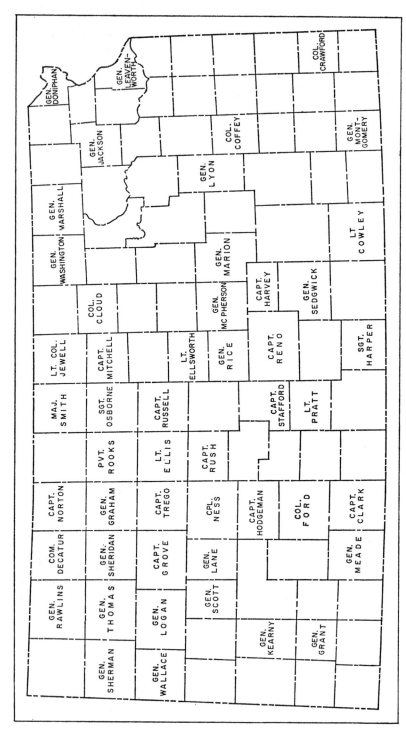

Military names for Kansas counties

CHAPTER XXXVI

PRIVATE ROOKS AND MEN OF RANK

NEXT IN NUMBER to the names of generals for county names were the names of captains. Three counties were named for colonels; one for a major; and four for lieutenants. It was natural for the names of captains to outnumber the names of colonels and majors, since the recruiting was generally done in company units, and captains were in closer contact with their men than were those of higher rank.

A few counties were named for non-commissioned officers. Marion, Harper, and Osborne were named for sergeants, and Ness County was named for a corporal. That left John C. Rooks as the only private for whom a county was named. When soldiers in World War I found that the better restaurants and American women were "for officers only," they decided that the next war should be "for officers only." But it was natural that the officers should be better known than the expendable men who fought and died with little personal recognition. The Civil War press probably did not have an Ernie Pyle or a Bill Mauldin to inform the public of the problems and heroics of the enlisted men.

The three colonels for whom Kansas counties were named were Colonel William F. Cloud, Colonel James H. Ford, and Lieutenant Colonel Lewis R. Jewell. Ford County was named for James H. Ford who had been captain of the Second Colorado Cavalry.[1] For a time he was made a brevet major general of volunteers during the Civil War, but he continued to be known as a colonel. When the Plains Indians combined to resist the white man's advance, the solution was left to the military. Colonel Ford was put in command of the troops in the Dodge City area. When a commission investigating the Indian troubles concluded that "the blame was on our side," it ordered Colonel Ford to suspend military operations, although General Grenville M. Dodge favored a decisive blow by the military.[2] General Dodge directed Ford to build Fort Dodge. This association with the community resulted in his name being given to Ford County.

Because it was near an easy ford of the Arkansas River, possibly where Coronado crossed the river, it has been assumed that the town of Ford was named for the river ford. But Ford in Ford Township was named for the county and indirectly for Colonel Ford. It had first been named Ryanville for Pat Ryan, a local rancher.[3]

The Jewell family came from Massachusetts, moved to Ohio, and then to St. Louis before coming to Kansas. After a fruitless venture with the Forty-Niners, Lewis Jewell returned to Kansas and settled in Crawford County near Arcadia, a town which was founded by a member of the Jewell family.[4] Colonel Jewell was described as a well-built man "with a voice clear down to his boots."[5] When the Civil War broke out, he personally recruited four companies for the Sixth Kansas Cavalry, mostly from Bourbon County.[6] When General Price threatened Fort Scott, General Lane was so scared that he ordered the place burned as part of "a scorched earth" policy. Colonel Jewell refused; he recruited men, boys, and possibly women for defense, and he bluffed Price by painting logs to look like cannon.[7] Jewell was a lieutenant colonel when he fought his tragic battle at Cane Hill, Arkansas, in 1862. There he charged blindly and recklessly into Marmaduke's Confederates and "Fighting Jo" Shelby's cavalry. He was wounded and a horse shot from under him, but he continued to command on foot until he was shot again and killed. Jo Shelby, who knew him well, called Jewell "the bravest man he ever met in battle."[8]

When Samuel A. Manlove represented Fort Scott in the legislature in 1867, he proposed the name of Colonel Jewell for Jewell County.[9] Jewell's name was also given to a fort and two towns. Jewell City was built on the site of a sod fort at the forks of Buffalo Creek. Scarbrough's store, built in a day, gave it a fair start, but it was not in the center of the county. Another town was organized in Centre Township, and it took the name of Jewell Centre. When Minnesota settlers came to Jewell Centre, H. R. Hill had the name changed to that of his Minnesota home town of Mankato. After Mankato became the county seat, Jewell City shortened its name to Jewell.[10]

The county with one of the most controversial names is Cloud County. The county was first called Shirley and mistakenly printed "Shelby" in the Act of 1865.[11] But was Shirley a Puritan governor of colonial Massachusetts or a popular Leavenworth girl who was anything but a Puritan? D. L. Chandler, a territorial representative, said that he had named the county for William Shirley, a governor of Massachusetts, his home state. Shirley was not a popular governor, and there was no good reason for using his name for a Kansas county. However, if the name did come from the "lady" of Leavenworth, the respectable reputation of Kansas could best be saved by changing the county's name.

The first name proposed as a substitute for Shirley was that of Sherman for John Sherman of Ohio, brother of General Sherman. Then

Mr. Rupe proposed the name of Cloud for Colonel William F. Cloud, "idol of the cavalry," whom he described as "one of the bravest and noblest of the state's heroes." General Harvey and Dr. Thomas Lindsay, backed by the governor and, "despite the evil machinations of Wood," carried the bill through the Senate. They were happy to get the "odious" name of Shirley from the county map of Kansas. Only Shirley Township remains now as a reminder of the first name given to Cloud County.[12]

The war activities of Colonel Cloud were primarily in the border area. He was with General Lyon at Wilson's Creek and with Crawford and Jewell at Cane Hill. He defeated the Texas "bowie knife" regiment near Van Buren, Arkansas, and with cavalry and artillery he captured Confederates fleeing on ferry boats below Fort Smith. Colonel Crawford described Cloud as "a nervous, vain, and courageous" man, long-haired like Custer, but he respected him.[13]

With a name like Smith, and there were many Smiths in the army, one would need one or more distinctive given names for identity. Whether Smith County was named for James Nelson Smith or Nathan Smith may still be debatable, but Adams of the Kansas Historical Society accepted the name of James Nelson Smith.[14] The Kansas Historical Society Index to its *Collections* gives it as "Nathan (not Mathew)." As commander of the Second Colorado Cavalry, Smith held the rank of major.[15] He was described as "a gallant Union officer who died at the head of his men in a desperate charge on the Confederates at the battle of the Blue which was fought near Kansas City, Missouri, October 21, 1864."[16] L. T. Reese, a Smith County pioneer, is said to have organized the county by the fraudulent use of names of acquaintances in the East.

The family of Avra Russell was said to have connections all the way back to Olaf, king of Rerick, in the sixth century, and to Hugh, who served William the Conqueror. Avra's great-grandfather was one of the promoters of Yale College. Avra was born in New York. His personality is supposed to have been a combination of "the red-headed blood-thirsty Scandinavian and the gentle, scholarly Congregational ministers." Perhaps it is better to say that he was "lovable and sunny hearted, with quick, impetuous nature."[17] In Illinois, he fell in love with a girl whom he planned to marry after the war. That happy event never took place.

Russell raised a company of infantry and is generally referred to as captain of the Second Kansas, but in the Adjutant's *Report* in Kansas, he was said to have received his commission as a major.[18] His youngest brother Oscar, better known as "Doc," lived in the South when the war broke out. He joined the Confederates and became General Hindman's aide. In the battle with Hindman's army at Prairie Grove, Avra lived in dread of fighting his own brother. Hindman, knowing the situation, sent "Doc" away on a special duty. But Avra had a premonition of death, and when the battle started he was wounded on the first volley. Five days later, on December 12, 1862, he died. His brother was then permitted to cross the lines to see what the war had done to his family.[19] Avra Russell's sword now hangs in the state museum at Topeka. The name of Russell County stands as a memorial to one more of the many casualties of that great American tragedy.

The town of Russell, which also bears his name, had previously been named Fossil Station and then Fossil. From this point westward, Kansas has one of the richest fossil beds in the United States, and its marvelous fossil specimens are found in the museums of the world. Now the street in Russell along U.S. Highway 281 continues the name of Fossil, as does the little lake south of town.

Clark County was named for Charles F. Clarke of Junction City, captain of the Sixth Kansas Cavalry, Company F. He later served as assistant adjutant general at Memphis where he died on December 10, 1862, two days before Russell died. Clarke had a distinguishing vowel at the end of his name, but this was dropped from the county name by an act of the legislature. Some spelled it Clark from the beginning,[20] yet Cram's map still listed it as Clarke in 1883. Clark City was naturally named for the county. It had replaced Klaine, a post office named for N. B. Klaine, a newspaperman and postmaster at Dodge City. When Clark City settlers were offered free lots in Ashland, they readily moved, which explains their preference for "portable" dwellings.[21]

Graham County was named for John L. Graham, captain of the Eighth Kansas Infantry. The early maps also show a town named Graham; its post office name was changed to Whitfield, and then both names disappeared. In 1858, Graham had been a township clerk in Nemaha County. In the Civil War he was in that tough battle along the Chickamauga Creek near Chattanooga in September, 1863. The Confederates had the advantage since they held the high ridges. As Catton said: "They were up in the balconies and all of the Federals were down in the orchestra pit."[22] Grant, Sherman, and Thomas were there, as was Sheridan and many more of the great names of the Civil War; and there Captain Graham was killed before the battle was over.

Captain Edgar P. Trego, for whom Trego County was named, was also in the Eighth Kansas Infantry. He came to Kansas from Preemption, Illinois. His cousin, Joseph H. Trego, enlisted with Charles R. Jennison, known for his command of "Jennison's Jayhawkers."[23] Governor John A. Martin knew Captain Trego at Chickamauga and described him as "a soldier without fear and without reproach." At that famous battle, Captain Trego lost half of his men. After a light supper that evening he asked for permission to take a small squad to look for his wounded. His request was approved, he saluted and left; and while on this humanitarian mission, he ran into an enemy squad and was killed. His body was later found and buried there among twenty thousand of his comrades.[24] Now his name on a Kansas county is surrounded by four counties which bear the names of Civil War participants: Graham, Ellis, Gove, and Ness.

There was a town named Trego about ten miles southwest of WaKeeney in Trego County. But while WaKeeney was being built, the workers were living in a dugout at "Trego Station," about a mile west of the town.[25] Farther south is Trego Center, now only the center of a church community. One post office was called Tregola. A stream flowing into the Saline is named Trego Creek.

Hodgeman County, north of Ford, was named for Captain Amos Hodgeman of the famous Seventh Kansas Cavalry. Some are of the opinion that Hodgeman's name was spelled "Hodgman" and that the legislature inserted the "e," possibly through error, as the name of the county. Yet the Hodgeman spelling is not uncommon.[26] Hodgeman came from Massachusetts and worked as a carpenter in Leavenworth, Kansas. Shortly after joining Company F of the Seventh, he met and married a barmaid in Leavenworth, starting a happy marriage which was soon to end in tragedy. Kitty Hodgeman joined her husband at Corinth, Mississippi, not far from Shiloh, and was content to look after his quarters and to enjoy his companionship. "They were very fond of each other, and that was enough," said one who knew them. Then, in October, 1863, Captain Hodgeman was killed. The mourning widow, with a flag of truce, was able to secure the body for burial. Later she served as a nurse in a Cincinnati hospital. She was pleasant and patient but weak, and soon she died. "Poor Kitty Hodgeman!" it was said, was one who deserved to be "enskied and sainted."[27]

Hodgeman Center was in Center Township, but it lost its post office to Jetmore, which was more centrally located and became the county seat. A post office named Hodgeman in the northern part of the county lasted well into the twentieth century.

Mitchell County was named for William D. Mitchell, and not for General Robert B. Mitchell, although there was an association between the two. General Mitchell had the young private of the Second Kansas Cavalry appointed clerk to the adjutant. Private Mitchell was transferred to the Second Kentucky Cavalry where he was promoted to captain. His outfit was attached to Sherman's army on its march from Atlanta to Fayetteville, North Carolina. Captain Mitchell led an attack to recapture two lost guns and was shot through the heart at Monroe's Cross Roads, North Carolina, shortly before the end of war. "Dear Willie Mitchell," said a friend of his mother, "so bright and loving and beloved," lost his life at the age of twenty-four.[28] Mitchell's family came from Massachusetts in 1855 and settled on Seven Mile Creek near Ogden. It was William's father, Daniel who surveyed the townsite for Junction City, and it was there that William enlisted in 1861.

Alexander Rush, captain of Company H of the Second Kansas Colored Infantry, was the source for the name of Rush County. His company served under Colonel Crawford at the battle of Jenkin's Ferry, also written Jenkins' Ferry and Jenkyns Ferry, with or without apostrophes. The Confederates had orders to take no prisoners, and Crawford referred to the order as the "Black Flag" order of piracy. There in Arkansas, Captain Rush was killed on April 3, 1864.[29]

Rush Center had once been a trading post on Walnut Creek which grew into a town named Walnut City. It was centrally located, changed its name to Rush Centre, and became the temporary county seat with a rival at LaCrosse. When the Pawnee County boundary was pushed northward to help Larned, Rush Center in Center Township was no longer in the center of the county. The county seat "see-sawed" between the two so often that it became known as the "court house on wheels." Rush Centre changed its name to Rushcenter and then back to Rush Center, but LaCrosse became the county seat.[30]

The county of Stafford was named in 1867 in memory of Captain Lewis Stafford. The county came near being obliterated by ambitious counties on the border, but the state supreme court came to its rescue. Lewis Stafford was one of the first to build a home in Holton. He was clerk of the probate court in Calhoun County, now Jackson, and he was also clerk of the Board of Supervisors. He served in the First Kansas Infantry where he was promoted to captain. Like many others, he suffered in the infamous Andersonville prison. Stafford was killed at Young's Point in Louisiana.[31] The town of Stafford was at first known simply as "Vicker's Sod Hotel." This was not the kind of name that would make it a county seat, so it took the name of Stafford, the war hero, hoping thereby to win. Stafford was damaged by a Kansas cyclone and defeated by St. John in the county seat contest.[32]

There were two deserving officers named Ellsworth for whom Ellsworth County could have been named. The first was Colonel Ephraim Elmer Ellsworth, who was killed by General Jackson while attempting to pull down a rebel flag at Alexandria. He was called "the first victim of the rebellion."[33] But the fort was most likely named for Lieutenant Allen Ellsworth, who built it. Colonel Inman said that the town was named for the county, which had been named for the fort, which was in turn "named for Lieutenant Allen Ellsworth."[34] In his own words, Allen Ellsworth had this to say: "I was mustered in as Second Lieutenant, Company H, Seventh Iowa Cavalry, July 13, 1863, at Davenport, Iowa. I was in service in Kansas and I was the man who established Fort Ellsworth, in June, 1864. I was stationed there with about forty men and built that block-house." General Curtis inspected the fort in July of that year, and "at Fort Larned, while on dress parade, he officially read the name of Fort Ellsworth."[35]

Having first been built in the bottomlands and ravaged by floods, Fort Ellsworth was moved to higher ground near Kanopolis in 1866. General Hancock, in command of the Western Division, was said to have named it Fort Harker for Brigadier General Charles G. Harker, who was killed at Kennesaw Mountain in 1864.[36] The fort boasted of having been host to more famous generals than any fort in the United States, a boast that might well be challenged by Fort Leavenworth. Among the generals visiting Fort Harker were Grant, Sherman, Sheridan, Howard, and Custer, all of whose names became Kansas place-names.

Grenville L. Gove, for whom Gove County is named, enlisted in the army as a private but was commissioned as a captain before the end of the war. Gove had the reputation of having the best-drilled company in the Eleventh Kansas. When his Company G drilled, others watched. He must have been known by his middle name since an army companion knew him as "Lew" Gove, not recalling, however, whether his name was "Louis or Lewis." Gove died from a brain fever at Olathe in 1864. Settlers from Davenport, Iowa, laid out the town of Gove City, now Gove, which was centrally located and served as county seat.[37]

Cowley County was carved out of Hunter County and named in 1867 for Lieutenant Mathew Cowley, who had volunteered to serve in the Ninth Kansas Cavalry. In October, 1864, near the end of the war, he died at Little Rock. According to one account, he was "loved and respected by every member of the company."[38] The respect his comrades had for Cowley was shown when they were serving in the state legislature and named Cowley County in his memory.

The casualties at the Battle of Jenkins' Ferry in Arkansas furnished such names as Russell, Rooks, and Ellis for Kansas counties. George Ellis was an Irishman from Pennsylvania who came to Olathe and enlisted in a Kansas company for ninety days. After he re-enlisted, he became a second lieutenant in the Twelfth Kansas Infantry. Between enlistments, he married Amalia Pardee of Paola. Ellis was in the Eldridge House in Lawrence when Quantrill's raiders attacked it. There he was burned out of the hotel: next he was burned out of a barn after fighting off his attackers with a pitchfork. While the guerrilla band took off for a "whisky-break," Ellis escaped. Later at Jenkins' Ferry, ill and poorly equipped, he was killed on April 30, 1864. Three years later, Ellis County was named for him.[39] On Big Creek, a railway pump station became the town of Ellis. There lived a man from Ellis' own military unit, a railway engineer by the name of Henry W. Chrysler, father of Walter P. Chrysler, who has also made a name for himself.

Pratt County was named for Caleb S. Pratt, a pioneer active in Kansas politics during territorial days, who became a member of the Lawrence militia called the "Stubbs." In an effort to acquire the cannon named Old Sacramento, young Pratt volunteered to set fire to the house where it was kept. The attempt was made in moonlight and Caleb, wearing white pants, was easily seen and fired upon. He was for a time auditor of Douglas County and a commissioner of the penitentiary. Pratt was a second lieutenant in the Second Kansas Cavalry and served with General Lyon at the Battle of Wilson's Creek, where both were killed; they left their names on Kansas counties. Pratt has been described simply as a "brave lieutenant."[40]

Iuka and Saratoga, with their Indian names, were established before Pratt, but Pratt had the advantage of being centrally located. It was first called Anderson and then became Pratt Center. It won the county seat contest but was accused of manipulation and multiplication of votes. Delegates were to meet at Cullison to determine the railroad route and to vote bonds. The Iuka delegates did not show up, and "It is contended to this day by old-timers of Iuka that Pratt interests got the Iuka men drunk so they could not reach Cullison." Fair or not, drunk or sober, Pratt won the railroad and the county seat. Or, in their own nomenclature, the "Prattites" won over the "Togytes" and the "Ukites."[41]

In 1885 the Center was dropped from the name, but the public continued to use the term and dropped Pratt, the legal name. The town even had names for its local hills. The one on the east side was called "Battle Hill" by the school children, but this was changed to "Sun Rise Heights." The hill on the west side was called "Quality Hill." On the county border, first in Pratt County, but now in Stafford County, New York settlers from Onondaga had a town named Prattsburg.[42]

Two sergeants, Marion Harper and Vincent B. Osborne, left their names on Kansas counties. Harper enlisted as a private in 1861 and rose to the rank of sergeant in Company E of the Second Kansas Cavalry, commanded by Captain Samuel Crawford. Although fatally wounded at Waldron, Arkansas, on December 30, 1863, he demonstrated both fortitude and a love of fun on his deathbed. "Being a merry man," it was said, "and of a sporting disposition, when brought in wounded, he proposed to wager a man that in so many hours he would be dead . . . . The bet was taken, and Marion Harper won."[43]

Harper County was organized in 1873 by using names from the Cincinnati directory and the names on a few buffalo skulls to make up its deficiency in population.[44] It was fraudulently organized but was given Sergeant Harper's honorable name. Waldron, the name of the Arkansas town where Harper was wounded, also became the name of a town in Harper County. Yet the town may have been named for Howard B. Waldron, who owned the townsite. The town now named Harper was settled by pioneers from Iowa and named Cora City, probably for Cora, Iowa. Its change of name has been explained as follows: "The gender of the infant, not suiting all parties, underwent a metamorphosis and now answers to the name of Harper City."[45] The town of Harper was named for the county.

Osborne County was named for Vincent B. Osborne of Massachusetts, another sergeant in the Second Kansas Cavalry. He had been wounded in the leg at the Battle of Wilson's Creek. Like Lyon, he continued to fight after he was wounded, and when the battle was over, he used his gun as a crutch. A bullet was extracted from his leg at a St. Louis hospital, and after recovering, Osborne joined the Second Kansas Cavalry. When Lee surrendered and Jeff Davis was captured, a number of troops were sent from Fort Smith to Little Rock to be mustered out. On the way, the steamer *Anna Jacobs* was attacked by Confederate artillery. The pilot steered the boat to land near Jay's Ford and all the men fled for safety except Sergeants Osborne and Edwards, who grabbed a cable to anchor the boat to a tree rather than let it drift to the Confederates. A shell burst near them and Osborne lost a leg—his good one—and Edwards lost an arm, but they saved the boat.[46]

As his captain, Samuel Crawford knew Osborne and respected him; and, as his governor, he recommended to Stanton, secretary of war, that Osborne be appointed as sutler at Fort Harker. After reading about his bravery, Stanton wrote: "He is my man." Osborne next settled at Ellsworth where he practiced law and served on a committee to organize Ellsworth County. Osborne accomplished much for a man who died at the age of forty.[47]

The town of Osborne was settled by a Pennsylvania colony and its post office was first named Penn. As a candidate for the county seat, a position it won after several elections, it was renamed Osborne City, later reduced to Osborne.

Norton County was named for Orloff Norton, captain of the Fifteenth Kansas Cavalry. It had first been named Oro. Because Orloff Norton was known as "Ora" and "Oro," it has been assumed that Oro County got its name from the first name of Norton. But Oro was named in 1859 when miners were heading for the "Kansas gold fields" in Colorado. They had gold on their minds and *oro* meant "gold." Some of the prospectors even stopped to pan for gold in Kansas. They were excited by the yellow glint of fool's gold, which is not to say that there was no gold in the alluvial sands of Colorado with which Kansas is surfaced.[48] Orloff Norton was not yet a hero when Oro was named. When the county name was changed to Norton in 1867, he deserved recognition. Captain Norton was killed in 1865 at Cane Hill, Arkansas, in the same battle in which Colonel Lewis R. Jewell was killed. The naming of Norton County was proposed in 1867 by Preston B. Plumb, speaker of the house in the state legislature.[49]

At the time of the organization of Norton County, "a long, lanky specimen of the genus homo made his appearance . . . and introduced himself as Col. N. H. Billings." Inman said that he was "one of the brightest and wittiest of men." He was also referred to as the "fiery untamed Demosthenes of Norton County." He "possessed a fair degree of education, some legal lore, a deal of egotism, and some degree of cunning," said another who knew him.[50]

Billings, one of the founders of Jewell City, was in 1870 elected surveyor of Jewell County. In 1873 he was the representative from the hundredth district in the Kansas legislature and there he promoted the organization of Norton County. There were only 75 legal residents in the county, yet the petition for its organization bore 636 signatures. The county had been named Norton since 1867, but, according to one historian, the legislature named it Billings "as a matter of sport, and to please the overweaning vanity of the Honorable member from the county."[51] Inman suggested that Billings managed to have the name of Norton changed to Billings in two lines hidden in another bill. Becoming aware of the hostile reaction to the name of Billings, the legislature changed the name back to Norton within a year.[52]

Norton County settlers had planned to set aside a section of land for the county seat, but when the new town was established, it was discovered that Billings and his partner, Coleman, owned the site. More annoying was the notice that the town which was to be named Norton was given on the governor's proclamation as "Billingsville." Billings was its first postmaster. The "Colonel" had scored again. He pretended, however, that he was unaware of the governor's plan to name the county seat in his honor. He had already lost the support of the settlers by his ego and arrogance and by exploiting them as a "locator."

Billings' nickname of "Uncle Josh" might indicate a friendly familiarity, yet to many he was considered a "menace in the community." Being aware of frontier justice, Billings of Billingsville in Billings County fled from the county of his own creation. The settlers ignored the governor's name of Billingsville, the county commission rejected it, and a new town, which became both the post office and county seat, was named Norton Center, now Norton.[53] It had also been named Reedtown, named for Shelby Reed, who promoted the town for county seat. Dr. Briggs, owner of the town's only store, preferred the name of Norton Center.[54]

Ness County was named for Corporal Noah V. Ness of the Seventh Kansas Cavalry. Corporal Ness died from wounds he suffered at the Battle of Abbeyville in Mississippi in August, 1864. The most unusual fact regarding the name of Ness is that it honored the only corporal of all the military men to be honored by county names.[55]

Ness County was organized and named in 1867 when it was far short of the 600 residents legally required. The governor "disorganized" it in 1874. In the meantime, Smallwood became its county seat, named for William H. Smallwood, Kansas secretary of state. Naming the town Smallwood was likely a political move at a time when the representative from the county had received 250 votes in a county with a total population of no more than 140 persons—men, women, and children. "Getting out the vote" must have been rewarding in those pioneer days of freedom.[56]

Ness City replaced Smallwood as county seat, but not before it made several changes in its name. The town was surveyed by Richard Dighton whose name was given to the county seat of Lane County. Ness City had first been a post office named Iowa. Then it became Ness, named for the county. Next it was changed to Schoharie, an Indian name for a creek and a county in New York. Finally it became the county seat which gave it an ambition and a distinction which resulted in its change of name to Ness City.[57] Not all of these names were on the same site.

Kansas had its artillery, infantry, and cavalry from which to choose its place-names, but it had no navy. For a navy name, it reached back into history for the "most romantic and brilliant figure in the naval annals of our country" and named a county Decatur. Stephen Decatur was born of French and Irish ancestry in a Maryland town with the interesting name of Sinepuxent. Decatur took part in three wars but won fame from a daring attack and a surprising victory over the Barbary pirates of Tripoli in his "ramshackle boat." Unscathed in war and safe from a previous duel, he was killed in a duel with Commodore James Barron in 1820. He is especially famous for a phrase which has caused no end of debate: "My country! In her intercourse with foreign nations may she always be in the right; but our country, right or wrong."[58]

There were several men by the name of Foote in Kansas, but Foote County, later Gray County, was "probably" named for Andrew Hull Foote,[59] commander of the gunboats on the Tennessee. The commodore boldly attacked Fort Henry on the Tennessee, and though his boats were frequently hit, the cannon balls dropped off the iron sides like hail. The fort was captured, and this prepared the way for the capture of Fort Donelson, where Foote was wounded and walked around on crutches.[60] Back at Cairo, when the Presbyterian pastor failed to appear, Commodore Foote gave the sermon. Foote Township in Gray County is all that remains to honor the commodore's name in what had been Foote County.

In the survey of military names for Kansas counties, we have now come to the bottom of the list. Rooks County was named for a private, the one and only private to be so honored. John C. Rooks enlisted in the Eleventh Kansas Cavalary on September 1, 1862, and died at Fayetteville on December 11, a few days after the battle of Prairie Grove, where Captain Russell also lost his life. His military service was brief, only one hundred days, yet long enough for him to pay the supreme price and to earn as a memorial a place-name on the Kansas map. His name was given to Rooks County in 1867 at the same time that a score of county names honored soldiers of a higher rank.[61]

Rooks Centre was by its very name a contender for the county seat. Two factors contributed to its defeat: Rooks Centre was not quite in the center of the county, and it was on the south side of the Solomon River when the railroad chose a route on the north side. Stockton, or "Stocktown," as it was then called, became the county seat.[62] Rooks Centre lost its name before it lost its existence. As a post office, it became Woodston in 1886, after a pioneer by the name of Charles C. Woods.[63]

CHAPTER XXXVII

THE SOLDIER STATE

FORTY-NINE KANSAS COUNTIES were named for military men. To be sure, some of these men had other interests, yet their military service was generally the reason for their recognition. But even forty-nine counties could not honor all the heroes and worthy men in the military service, so their names were also given to post offices, towns, cities, and streams, and, of course, to forts.

Not only did personal names become Kansas place-names, but so did a number of names referring to war and peace. To West Point, Military City, and Militia Hill, one may add Soldier, Dragoon, Cavalry, Captain, and Defiance, Advance, and Victory, and that jingoistic name of Jingo itself. Equally militant may be the names of battles in Kansas, whether Indian battles or the battles over Bleeding Kansas. Lincoln County had its Battle Creek, Morton County had its Battleax, and Osborne County had a Kill Creek post office and a Kill Creek Township, and Barton County has a Blood Creek. Battle Corners in southeastern Kansas was named by Noble L. Prentis.[1]

When Charles N. Gould lived near Hardscrabble school in Pratt County, he referred to a school district called West Point "because it was a sort of military academy." That is to say, the patrons indulged in an old-fashioned "knock-down and drag-out on every possible occasion."[2] Both Riley County and Rush County had places named West Point. Since the one in Riley County was an outlet for the soldiers at Fort Riley, the military connection seems obvious, even though the name was used facetiously. Possibly more pertinent was its name of Whiskey Point. Because of the heavy concentration of troops at Fort Riley during World War I, a new post office there was named Military City.

The place named Conquest in Kearny County could refer to conquest over nature or anything else. Woodson County had a place named Defiance. Victor, frequently used as a personal name, was the name of a post office in Osborne County, and it is now a place in Mitchell County. Victory Junction in Leavenworth County is obviously a war memorial. It has been suggested that Protection was given

409

its name when two places named Redoubt were established to protect the area from the Indians in Clark County.[3]

The most unusual of these military names was Jingo. The implication of the name is well illustrated in the chorus of a music-hall song:

We don't want to fight,
But, by Jingo, if we do,
We've got the ships,
We've got the men,
We've got the money, too.

This readiness to fight was expressed in the expletive "By Jingo!" and from this evolved the word "jingoism."[4] It was used in the Spanish-American War but may well describe the militant view of the so-called "Warhawks" of any war. Murray's *English Dictionary* considered it an expression of a "blatant patriot."

Perhaps the naming of Jingo in Miami County was a bit more moderate. Failing to come to an agreement on the naming of a town, one man spoke up and said: "By Jingo, we'd better decide upon a name in our next meeting!" Someone reacted to the "By Jingo" and called out: "Why don't we call it Jingo?" The assembly agreed and the name was adopted.[5] The Jingo post office was closed in 1902. The United States was at peace.

Victors like to recall the names of battles which they have won. Such names as Vicksburg and Guilford, Shiloh, Corinth, Iuka, and Appomattox have a familiar ring.[6] These have all been place-names in Kansas. Gettysburgh and Bull Run are, however, local names. Famous though the name may be, Gettysburgh in Kansas was named for Joseph Gettys, the local postmaster.[7] The one in Pennsylvania was named for James Gettys.[8] In Graham County, Kansas, Gettysburgh was changed to Penokee, the Indian name for the Penokee Range in Wisconsin.[9] In Kansas the township kept the Gettysburg name without the "h."

Bull Run in Kansas was named for Bull Creek, but when a battle took place there, bloodless, though it was, it became known as the "Battle of Bull Run."[10] Vicksburg in Jewell County, reminiscent of Grant's first real success, had its named changed to Randall, honoring Edward Randall, the original owner.[11]

The stream called Big Soldier which flows through Jackson County and is joined by Little Soldier in Shawnee County flows into the Kaw near Topeka. The "Conda River," said one writer, "is well known under the more prosaic appelation of Soldier Creek."[12] Conda had reference to the many-headed water serpent called simply Hydra. The stream was also called the "Black Soldier" and the "Black Warrior."[13]

The Indians were familiar with its English name and called it Ne-so-ja, the *Ne* for water or creek, and "so-ja," sufficiently like soldier to be understood.[14] According to one account, it got its name when soldiers found a store of illicit whisky and dumped it into the river. To some, this may seem incredible. Soldiers coming from Fort Leavenworth frequently camped on the stream, and that may be a better reason for its name. Major Langham camped there with a small contingent of troops as early as 1826. The name of Soldier Creek, said John McCoy, "was adopted afterwards in honor of the flag that proudly waved over the Major's shanty, and of the warlike aspect of the camp."[15]

Near the source of Soldier Creek in Jackson County is a town which was named Soldier City, now called Soldier, in Soldier Township. Shawnee County has another Soldier Township. Soldier Township in Greeley County got its name when veterans from Illinois established a "Soldier Colony" there. Now the Soldier has been deleted and it is called just Colony. Johnson in Stanton County was settled by veterans and named Veteran.[16] The town named Glick was replaced by Soldier Creek post office in Comanche County.

West of Soldier Creek flows Cavalry Creek. Before Coldwater got its name from Michigan, the place was called Cavalry. A hill called Magnesia Mound near Marion Center was the place where settlers assembled to organize a militia, and so it became Militia Mound.[17] A place where soldiers were stationed on Mine Creek in Linn County was known as both Rocky Ford and Military.[18] One of the ridges near Coronado Heights in Saline County was given the descriptive name of Soldier Cap Mound. A creek flowing into the Marmaton in Bourbon County was called "Grand Soldo" by Italian missionaries.[19] Captain Creek, entering the Kaw at the Johnson-Douglas County border, seems to imply military rank, but it could have been named for Captain Sam, a Sac and Fox chief.[20]

Cad was the name of a place in Smith County, abandoned, however, after a few months. Cad is said to be an abbreviated form for cadet, originally applied in England to a man hanging around sports. Its present meaning is less complimentary.

One might assume that the town named Ensign in Gray County also referred to military rank, but this one was named for G. L. Ensign, who established the town. Like its neighbor, Montezuma, it has had its rise and fall, or as one said, its "boom," "dormancy" and "normalcy." Its street names, if not its town name, reflect the military with the names of Zarah, Larned, Dodge, and Leavenworth.[21]

Vidette in Shawnee County was a name which referred to a mounted sentinel, especially an advanced picket.[22] The word may also be spelled

Vedette, but as the name of the first newspaper in Wichita, it was *Vidette*. A labor organization in the 1880's, when the town was founded, was also called Vidette.

The origin of dragoon is from the figure of a dragon spurting fire which was pictured on the standard carried by these soldiers.[23] It is associated with the use of a short musket by a mounted infantryman. Pike crossed Dragoon Creek on a branch of the Neosho. Dragoon Creek flowing out of Wabaunsee County has a branch named Soldier Creek. Osage County once had a town named Dragoon in Dragoon Township, supposedly named for a soldier who died there.[24]

Zebulon Montgomery Pike, who crossed Kansas from the Osage River to the Republican River, is one of the best known of the early western explorers. His name has been preserved as a place-name from the Atlantic to the Pacific and for the prestigious Pikes Peak. Yet in Kansas his name is near oblivion. Albion in Wabaunsee County was for a short time named Pike before it became Alta Vista. A township in Lyon County still bears the name of Pike. Both of these places are near the route where Pike crossed the Cottonwood and the Neosho Valley on his way toward the Pawnee Republican village.[25] When George Freeman and friends were on a hunt in Dickinson County, they named one stream "Pike Creek" and another "Hard Crossing."[26]

After Pike, the next official to visit Kansas was Major George C. Sibley, Indian agent at Fort Osage, later Fort Sibley, on the Missouri. He crossed eastern Kansas in 1811 and visited the Pawnee on the Platte. He also visited the hunting camp of the Osages near Wichita.[27] He is probably best known for his part in the negotiations for the opening of the Santa Fe Trail in 1825 and for his inspection of the trail with the official surveyor.[28]

A lake which was once a part of the Republican River in Cloud County was named Lake Sibley, as was the post office north of the lake. Sibley had traveled through this area on his way to visit the Pawnees. In 1867 the military set up Fort Sibley there. Not far away was Sibley Butte. Unable to compete with Concordia, the town of Lake Sibley faded away, leaving the Sibley name on a township. There was also a Sibley in Douglas County which the Santa Fe called Sibleyville.[29]

The first Kansas military post was on an island in the Missouri which the French called Isle au Vache, known both as Buffalo Island and as Cow Island. It was supposedly named after Indians had stolen a cow on the Missouri side and left it on the island. The American military post was first named Cantonment Martin for Captain Wyly Martin. When it was reoccupied by Captain George Croghan it became known as Camp Croghan.[30]

The first of a series of western forts on the Arkansas was Fort Mann, said to be located anywhere from three to eight miles west of Dodge City[31] and near the Cimarron Crossing of the Arkansas. Fort Mann was authorized in 1847 and "a certain Daniel P. Mann" was directed to build it.[32] As a wagonmaster, he was called "captain" and he carried freight and mail between Santa Fe and Fort Leavenworth. The fort was called a "prairie prison," and within three years it was abandoned.

Fort Mann was replaced by a new fort in 1850; it was known as the "New Post on the Arkansas" and its nickname was "Fort Expedient."[33] Since Colonel Edwin V. Sumner built it, the fort was also referred to as Fort Sumner, but this was not official. Sumner was the kind of officer who seemed to enjoy a fight, and he paid the supreme penalty while in the Army of the Potomac. The soldiers called him "Old Bull Head" because of a popular story that a musket ball bounced off his head.[34] Fort Sumner's official name was Camp Mackay, having been named for Colonel Aeneas Mackay, a deputy quartermaster general.[35]

In June, 1851, Camp Mackay was renamed Fort Atkinson for Colonel Henry Atkinson, the one for whom Fort Atkinson in Nebraska was named. Colonel Atkinson had been on Stephen F. Long's expedition in 1818–19, and he was once commander of the Western Department with headquarters on Cow Island.[36] One writer described the fort as being "beneath the dignity of the United States, and at the mercy and forebearance of the Indians."[37] It was also at the mercy of rats, snakes, mice, and centipedes. When the eleven cats purchased at Fort Leavenworth failed to conquer the rats, the fort was abandoned. It was built of sod, poles, and brush, and the soldiers called it "Fort Sod" until, with soldier ingenuity for graphic names, it became "Fort Sodom."[38]

The Civil War brought a flurry of defense activity in Kansas, and the Missouri border became a battleground. Not only was Fort Scott reactivated, but the war actually made it necessary to fortify the post. The new forts around Fort Scott were Fort Blair, Fort Henning, and Fort Insley, and about twelve miles north was Fort Lincoln. Fort Blair was named for Charles W. Blair, who was chosen captain of the volunteer company which he had recruited, later referred to as "Blair's Battery." Blair was an Ohio lawyer who settled at Fort Scott in 1859 and became its postmaster in 1867. He was married to Katherine Medary, daughter of Samuel Medary, governor of territorial Kansas in 1859.[39] He was also a general at the Battle of Wilson's Creek where he served with General Lyon.[40]

Fort Henning, built to guard the ammunition store, was named for Major E. Henning, the post commander. After the war, Henning became superintendent of the Fort Scott and Gulf Railroad.[41] Fort Insley was a blockhouse built to guard the hospital and ordnance. It was named for a Captain Insley, most likely Merrit H. Insley, who was stationed there.

Major Edmund A. Ogden, quartermaster, was a veteran of the Black Hawk War, the Seminole War in Florida, and the Mexican War.[42] It was he who laid out the military road from Fort Leavenworth to Fort Laramie.[43] His name was passed over when the name was chosen for Fort Riley, the post he built. The little town of Ogden, called Ogdensburg and Ogdensburg Station, was named for him. It is located east of Fort Riley in Ogden Township. The town of Ogden, said one writer, "caught the debris of Pawnee when that ill-fated town was swept from its moorings by an official cyclone from Washington."[44] For a time it prospered as a land office and as the county seat. During the cholera epidemic in 1855, Major Ogden faithfully served the sick until he too caught the dread disease and died.[45] Fort Riley has honored him with a monument.

Camp Funston, with the Fort Riley Reservation, was one of the important military training centers during World War I. The camp was named for General Frederick Funston, frequently referred to as "Little Fred Funston," "Fighting Fred Funston," and "the Fighting Bantam." Funston was born in Ohio and came to Kansas at the age of two. He taught school at the Stoney Lonesome schoolhouse. He attended the University of Kansas without earning a degree and failed his examination for admission to West Point. He was a quiet and self-sufficient individualist. After serving with a botany expedition in Death Valley in 140-degree temperature, he cooled off on a long government expedition in Alaska. His greatest success was in war, and he served in Cuba even before the sinking of the *Maine*. He helped to capture Aguinaldo in the Philippines; he was at Vera Cruz in 1914; and he was associated with Pershing in his pursuit of Pancho Villa in Mexico. Even though some of the West Point officers resented his popularity, he was a remarkably able military man.[46]

John Charles Frémont became nationally known as the Pathfinder of the West. To be sure, most of these paths were already familiar to mountain men and guides. Frémont's political prominence was due in part to his marriage to Jessie Benton, daughter of Senator Benton of Missouri. Governor Robinson of Kansas was one of the first to propose his name for nomination for the presidency. The party slogan was made to fit Kansas: "Free Soil, Frémont, and Free Kansas." Even with the appealing combination of "Frémont and Jessie," he was defeated by "Buck and Breck," Buchanan and Breckinridge.[47] When Lincoln was nominated, a third party (actually a fourth), nominated Frémont to run against him.[48] Frémont was independent but somewhat inefficient.

Five towns in as many counties in Kansas have been given Frémont's name, and all but one have died. The first one was started near Topeka by a group of claim-jumpers.[49] Eastern settlers in Osage County named their town Fremont but there the name was first changed to Superior and then to Carbondale.[50] Fremont in Lyon County served three times as a post office and then it disappeared. Wabaunsee County once had a Fremont City, which was important enough to have a Fourth of July celebration in 1857.[51]

Beech Grove post office in Graham County had its name changed to Fremont. Since the railroad had another Fremont on its line in Nebraska, it changed the one in Kansas to Kalula. Its residents, possibly thinking they would be called Kalulans, rejected the name. Other names were submitted, but the Union Pacific Railroad chose to name the town Morland, honoring a railroader.[52] A town in McPherson County named Smoky Hill, commonly called "Smoky," had its name changed to Fremont. The local church was named Freemount, said Lindquist, "in conformity with the action of a Synod . . . since it seemed unwise to use Fremont, a political name, for a Christian congregation."[53] The post office continued to call it Fremont, however, until 1932. Road maps have used three forms: Fremont, Freemont, and Freemount. The Kansas legislature in 1856 gave the name of Fremont to a Kansas County which is now in Colorado.

At the close of the Civil War, the Plains Indians began their last big effort to resist the white invasion. Two forts had been abandoned on the upper Arkansas River, but in 1864 and 1865 the military moved in with a number of new forts as defensive posts and as military centers from which to attack. General Grenville M. Dodge authorized the building of Fort Dodge. Among the notable men named Dodge, there were three involved in the naming of the fort and Dodge City: Colonel Henry Dodge, General Grenville M. Dodge, and Colonel Richard I. Dodge.

One might assume that the fort was named for its promoter, General Grenville Dodge. Although known for his distinguished service in the Civil War, he was probably better known as a railroad builder than as a military man. He built over nine thousand miles of railroads. Indians who knew him as a surveyor called him "Long Eyes."[54] It is believed, however, that General Dodge named the fort for Colonel Henry Dodge, his uncle, who had been a lead miner and Indian fighter on the upper Mississippi and a senator from Wisconsin. In 1835 Colonel Dodge was sent on a military expedition to the Rockies, going up the

Platte and returning down the Arkansas River. He is said to have selected the site for a fort on the border of Mexico where the Arkansas
River reached the hundredth meridian.[55] It was near there that Colonel
James H. Ford later chose the site for Fort Dodge.[56] It was not listed,
however, on Colonel Dodge's map.[57] Even though the general named
it for his uncle, the name of the fort may do honor to both.

Its association with the Dodge family and its proximity to Fort Dodge
have led to the assumption that Dodge City was named for the fort.
Like the old Roman forts, Fort Dodge had its camps and camp-fol-
lowers. One camp was there to sell whisky to the soldiers. As the greatest shipping center in the country for buffalo hides and bones, it was
known as "Buffalo City."

The town was started with a few tents and sod houses in 1871. When
the Santa Fe rails reached Fort Dodge the following year, there were
some wooden shacks on Front Street where Colonel Richard I. Dodge,
commander of Fort Dodge, met with a group "on a sultry day in July"
to promote a town. After a "lively discussion" over the naming of the
"infant city," R. M. Wright, president of the town company, proposed
the name of Dodge for Colonel Richard I. Dodge. The vote was unani-
mous with Dodge abstaining.[58]

The life of a cow-town terminal gave Dodge City a bad reputation
and a wide variety of names. It was described as being "The Beautiful
Bibulous Babylon of the Frontier," "Queen of the Cowtowns," and
the "Deadwood of Kansas."[59] It prefers to be known by its own title
of "Queen City" or the "buckle in the Kansas wheat belt." It has long
been characterized as "The Cowboy Capital of the West." Depicting
its bad reputation has made fortunes for those who perform in the
"Westerns" in movies and on television.

In order to protect the route from Fort Dodge to Fort Supply in the
Indian Territory, the military built two forts in Clark County, both
named Redoubt. The one on the south side of the Cimarron was called
the Cimarron Redoubt[60] and South Redoubt. The place had also been
called "Old Fort" and "Red Bluff."[61] Because of a deep part in the
bend of Redoubt Creek, the post office was named Deep Hole. Deep
Hole Creek was later named Clark Creek.[62] A second defense north
of Ashland was called the North Redoubt.[63] Its defensive wall was
built with hundred-pound coffee sacks filled with clay, sand, or gravel.
On their way to seek a site for a mission, Benedictine monks passed this
fort and called it "Fort Coffee" because of its coffee-bag structure.[64]

Fort Larned, called the most important fort on the Santa Fe Trail,
was on the right bank of the Pawnee and near enough to the river to
have an underground passage for water in case of a siege. When Major

Henry Wassels arrived to build a fort there in 1859, the place was called simply "Camp on the Pawnee Fork."[65] And that is what it was. When Fort Larned was being built, the soldier camp across the river was called "Camp Alert."[66] In June, 1860, the post was given the official name of Fort Larned, named for Colonel Benjamin F. Larned, paymaster-general. Elliot Coues, who was there in 1864, said it was a "mean place, built of adobe and logs, with a drunken officer in command."[67] The troops were withdrawn in 1878, but the fort has been reasonably well preserved and remarkably well restored. The town of Larned was named for the fort.

The trailmakers and railmakers demanded government protection against the Indian, who fought desperately to stop the white man's penetration of his hunting ground. When the army was freed from the devastation of the Civil War, it chose a series of sites for camps and forts along the trails. Along the Smoky Hill Trail were established Fort Hays, Fort Monument, Fort Downer, and Fort Wallace, all initiated in 1865.

General Samuel R. Curtis established a fort on the Walnut near Great Bend and named it Fort Zarah for his son, Major H. Zarah Curtis, who had been killed in the Battle of Baxter Springs in 1863.[68] The local post office was also named Zarah. It was an unusual name and fairly simple, but it was occasionally spelled both "Zara" and "Sarah."[69] Johnson County also had a post office named Zara. It was discontinued in 1887, but in 1890 it was revived and spelled Zarah.

Fort Hays at first was called Fort Fletcher for Governor Thomas C. Fletcher of Missouri. It was called both Camp Fletcher and Camp Big Creek.[70] In 1865 a fort was built at the junction of Victoria Creek and Big Creek on a site which, like that of the first Fort Ellsworth, was in the flood area. In 1867 the fort was destroyed by a terrific flood on Big Creek and several soldiers lost their lives.[71]

The name of the fort had earlier been changed by Major General Hancock, whose order of November 17, 1866, read: "The Post being established at Camp Fletcher will be designated Fort Hays, in commemoration of the name and services of the late General Alexander Hays, United States Volunteers, who was killed in the Battle of the Wilderness."[72] Hays had been captain of a Kansas volunteer company and was wounded at the Battle of Jenkins' Ferry.[73] Troops going to Fort Hays established "Camp Sturgis," evidently named for Colonel Samuel D. Sturgis.[74]

After a flood on Big Creek and after the Kansas Pacific cut off the booming town of Rome, a new town was begun to support both the railroad and the fort. It soon drew the population from Rome, riffraff and all; and "New Town," as it was called, tough and rough as any terminal town, took the name of Hays City.[75] It is now a cultured college town, prosperous and peaceful. The fort was abandoned in 1889, but much of it has been restored and is now a popular tourist attraction.

On the Butterfield Trail a new station site was chosen by a surveying company which included Major James P. Downer, a Civil War veteran. A spring near the station was named Downer's Spring, a local creek was called Downer's Creek, so the station was named Downer's Station. A town was established in 1865 and, because of Indian depredations, it was fortified and called Downer's Fort.[76] The Indians massacred all residents but one in 1866 and burned the fort in 1867. It was abandoned in 1868.

The most logical source for the name of Pope in Leavenworth County appears to be General John Pope, the man with the long whiskers. Pope served with Halleck and other distinguished generals in the Army of the Tennessee. Although accepted as a competent commander, he was not popular because of his indulgence in "unseemly profanity and billingsgate."[77] He was in command of the Department of the Missouri after the Civil War and proposed the Little River Conference in 1865 to establish "perpetual peace."[78]

General Alfred Pleasanton and Colonel Thomas Moonlight were both active in the Civil War and both served together against General Price on the Kansas border. After the battle of Chancellorsville, General Hooker made the following introduction to Lincoln: "Mr. President, this is General Pleasanton who saved the army of the Potomac the other night."[79] Pleasanton and Moonlight defeated Price at the Battle of the Blue. Pleasanton brought in his cavalry from Missouri, and if he had not come, said one participant, "Price would have done us up."[80] Kansas City would have been lost. After the Battle of Mine Creek, Pleasanton and General Curtis "wrangled like children," said Colonel Crawford, and it would seem that Pleasanton was more nearly right than Curtis.[81] When the Confederates headed southward, with considerable destruction, they were followed by Blunt, Pleasanton, and Moonlight. Price's army was taken by surprise near Trading Post, where "every little campfire had beefsteaks on spits." They left their steaks in their hurry to escape.[82] Generals Marmaduke and Cabell were captured at a place now named Pleasanton Mound, probably the same as Round Mound. There, too, is the Pleasanton school. General Pleasanton's name was the one chosen by General Plumb and his associates for the town near the battlefield.[83]

Thomas Moonlight was a young Scot who ran away from home at

the age of eleven to come to America. He longed for adventure and he had it: he fought in the Seminole War; he was a soldier in Texas; he joined the Mormon Battalion; and he served at Fort Leavenworth. As lieutenant colonel of the Eleventh Kansas Cavalry, Moonlight gave spirited support for General Pleasanton on the border.[84] After the war, Moonlight held a number of political positions. He was at first a Republican, but in 1886 he was the Democratic candidate for governor. President Cleveland made him governor of Wyoming Territory and in 1893 appointed him minister to Bogota in Colombia.[85] The name of Moonlight in Dickinson County came not from the moon, as one might assume, but from Colonel Moonlight, the competent Scot of Kansas.[86]

James Gillpatrick Blunt was born in Maine and, like Moonlight, ran away from home. He was fourteen. He served in the navy, studied medicine in Ohio, and came to Anderson County, Kansas, in 1856. A significant service was his participation in the Wyandotte Constitutional Convention. During the Civil War, he became a general and was active in the border warfare of Kansas, losing many of his men in the Quantrill massacre at Baxter Springs. Complaints about Blunt's military decisions went all the way up to President Lincoln.[87] Blunt lived in the area where Greeley, Walker, and Blunt were rival community centers in Anderson County. Blunt's Station honored his name.[88]

One of the best-known officers in Kansas was George Armstrong Custer, the colorful colonel of the Seventh Kansas Cavalry. His great-grandfather was a Hessian officer who spelled his name Kuster.[89] Custer attended West Point and was graduated at the foot of his class. He was not studious, but he was a bright boy and independent. He was fond of military status and became a dashing officer, somewhat flamboyant in his dress. He served well in the Civil War but became better known as an Indian fighter after the war. Much of his time was spent at Fort Hays where he was once court-martialed for being absent without leave.[90] He wore his long curly hair to his shoulders, and the Indians called him "Yellow Hair."

Custer destroyed the Cheyenne village on the Washita, rescued two white women, and killed Black Kettle. Black Kettle Creek flowing into the Little Arkansas in Harvey County was named for Black Kettle, the Kiowa chief. It was, however, after the Battle of the Little Big Horn in Montana, where the Indians killed Custer, that Custer's name became familiar to the world. The painting of "Custer's Last Stand," seen in so many saloons, contributed much to the popularity of his name. On July 26, 1876, one month after the Custer massacre, a town in Smith County was named Custer. The counties of Franklin, Decatur, and Mitchell have townships named Custer. Buzzard's Island on Big Creek below Fort Hays, now washed away, was also known as Custer's Island.

Buckner Creek in Hodgeman County was named for Simon Bolivar Buckner. He was born in Kentucky in 1823 when Simón Bolívar was known as the George Washington of South America. Buckner, a West Point graduate, later taught there as assistant professor of geography, history, and ethics. He was in charge of Camp Mackay or Fort Atkinson in 1852.[91] After the Civil War he was elected governor of Kentucky. A town on Buckner Creek was named Buckner. It later became Hodgeman Center, which, in 1880, moved to a town named Jetmore at the end of the railroad line.

Jetmore was named for Colonel Abraham Buckner Jetmore of Topeka, one of the directors of the Kansas Freedman's Relief Association to aid Negroes who were seeking land and asylum in Kansas. The change of name from Buckner to Jetmore was, by coincidence, a change from Jetmore's middle name to his surname.

The Iowa town of Grinnell and Grinnell College were named for Josiah B. Grinnell. Grinnell in Gove County, Kansas, is believed to have been named for an army officer at Fort Hays who was a relative of the Grinnell in Iowa.[92]

The memorial marking the battle on Beecher's Island in the Arickara includes the name of Lieutenant George W. Culver, who was killed there. He was referred to as a "scout," a "trooper," and a "captain." Another memorial to Culver is the town of Culver in Culver Township in Ottawa County.[93]

Ransom in Ness County was first named Ogdensburgh for Captain W. A. Ogden, who promoted the town. After a year, the name was changed to Ransom for General Thomas E. G. Ransom.[94] It was not likely named for the Ransom who had the interesting middle name of Epaphroditus and for whom a street was named in Fort Scott.[95] The Ransomville in Franklin County was said to be named for James H. or "Cap" Ransom, a coal miner, merchant, and postmaster.[96]

Thomas Edward Green Ransom was a man of considerable ability who was scarcely noted by those who wrote about more colorful military men. Catton does not mention him in either *Lincoln's Army* or *Lincoln's Scapegoat General*. In his three-volume *Lincoln Finds a General*, we find only a reference to Confederate General Robert C. Ransom. Yet Thomas Ransom recruited a company, disciplined a regiment, and advanced to command an army corps. He was wounded at Fort Donaldson, he was brilliant at Shiloh, he was successful at Vicksburg, and though wounded and ill in Georgia, he served with Sherman. This courageous and cool general was promoted for gallant service.

Although comparatively unknown, Ransom was described in the *Dictionary of American Biography* as "one of the most capable volunteer soldiers developed in the Civil War."

Major Henry Inman was the son of Henry Inman, the New York artist. He wrote eight books and is probably as well known for his writings, especially about the Santa Fe Trail, as he is for his military service. Yet he had participated with both the Army of the Potomac and the Army of the Tennessee, and he was wounded at Richmond. After the war he was the chief quartermaster for the Western Division at Fort Harker.[97] He left his family in the East and lived alone in a hotel in Topeka. But that need not be the reason for the assumption that he was somewhat eccentric. A lake in McPherson County had first been described to the War Department by Major Inman and was consequently named Lake Inman. A nearby town was named Aiken for a local commissioner, but after the Inman in Stafford County had its name changed to Emerson, Aiken had its name changed to Inman.[98]

The town of Lowemont in Leavenworth County was named for Percival Lowe, author of *Five Years a Dragoon*. He had been a newsboy, a sailor, a soldier, and a Leavenworth politician. As a dragoon, he had campaigned against the Indians all across the Plains.[99] The Lowe in Finney County was said to be named for Thaddeus Lowe.[100]

James L. Parnell, a private in the Thirteenth Kansas infantry, was killed in a skirmish at Hoare Head, Arkansas, on August 14, 1864. He had lived in Atchison County and there the town of Parnell is named in his honor.[101] This is one of the rare occasions when a town was named for a private.

Lawton in Cherokee County was named for General Henry W. Lawton, who was killed during the Philippine insurrection.[102] He was the one for whom Lawton, Oklahoma, was named.[103] The Lawton post office in Kansas was opened on September 7, 1900, shortly after Lawton's death.

Commodore George Dewey won instant glory and promotion for his defeat of the antiquated Spanish squadron at Manila in the Philippines. His forces sustained no casualties. The Dewey name swept the country as a popular place-name. There had already been a Dewey in Washington County, Kansas, changed to Kara in 1896. On August 13, 1898, Dewey captured Manila; on December 15, Edwards County named a post office Dewey. Wichita honored two heroes of the Philippine War by naming streets for both Dewey and Funston.

Jacob Bartles, disgruntled by the actions of the residents of Bartlesville, Oklahoma, the town that bears his name, moved his part of the town across the Caney River. This was at the time of Dewey's victory in Manila. When asked what he would name his new town, Bartle's quick response was said to be: "Hell, call 'er Dewey."[104] Another town also responded to the admiral's victory and asked to be named Dewey. The request was approved with the condition that Dewey be spelled backward as Yewed![105]

The stream that flows from the north into the Smoky Hill between Abilene and Junction City was known to the Kansa Indians as Nish-co-ba, "Deep Water."[106] Americans called it Sycamore Creek.[107] It was later renamed Chapman's Creek for Major Chapman. The post office near its junction was also named Chapman's Creek, shortened to Chapman in 1872.[108] Perhaps it was Chapman's being a soldier that caused the Indians to name the creek Ne-so-ja, meaning "soldier creek,"[109] as they had named Soldier Creek farther east. Three counties, Ottawa, Clay, and Dickinson, have townships named Chapman. Chapman had the first county high school in the United States, promoted by J. H. Canfield, father of Dorothy Canfield Fisher.[110]

Joe Lebo, a freighter who had been a captain in the Tenth Kansas Cavalry, lived on Lebo Creek, and there, now, is the town of Lebo.

Colonel C. D. Wellsford promoted the town of Dowell in Kiowa County and changed its name to Wellsford.

The latest general to contribute his name to a place in Kansas was probably General John J. Pershing, commander of the American Expeditionary Force in World War I. He had also pursued Pancho Villa into Mexico. The general was a descendant of a French Huguenot family by the name of Pfoershing. Pershing is located in Cherokee County,[111] but, like the place named Military, it was too small to find a place on most maps.

After the militant names in the introduction, we may close the chapter on a more peaceful note. In the Soldier State there were also places named Neutral City, Olive Branch, and Peace. The place named Retreat may not have been associated with the military; it was more likely associated with a peaceful refuge or seclusion. Retreat in Hodgeman County lasted only from May to October in 1879.

Neutral City in Cherokee County was named for an agreement with the Cherokees. It is now a station named Neutral.

One might conclude that Olive Branch in Allen County was named by the "doves" in opposition to the jingoists, whatever the issue was. Peace was the name of a Quaker community in Rice County. In 1876, it was changed to Sterling by two young settlers from New York who named it for their father, Sterling Rosan.[112]

CHAPTER XXXVIII

LO, THE POOR INDIAN

THERE WERE APPROXIMATELY two thousand Indian names in Kansas. We have seen how the French helped to translate and preserve Indian names, notably on the waterways. Five county names were taken from Indian river names: Nemaha, Neosho, Osage, Republic, and Pawnee. But there are still a dozen counties named for Indian tribes, and seven of these are named for immigrant tribes; one is named for an Indian chief. Four counties have lost their Indian names: Kansas, Peketon, Otoe, and Sequoyah.[1]

Kansas had three broad sources for Indian names: the resident Indians, the immigrant Indians, and Indian names transferred from other states. Of the first thirty-five counties named by the Bogus Legislature in 1855, three were given Indian names: Nemaha, Shawnee, and Arapahoe. The western part of Kansas, which is now in Colorado, was named Arapahoe County. Nemaha, the River of the Mahas, or "muddy" river, was the name of a stream flowing out of northeastern Kansas into Nebraska. Shawnee introduces the name of the immigrant Indians. Since Kansas was full of Indians, reasonably well adjusted to its ecology, one may wonder why it should have become the dumping ground for more Indians.

Ever since the white man came to America, the Indians have fought a futile battle to resist his relentless advance. The two civilizations clashed, and contact was destructive to both sides. Descriptions of the West by Zebulon M. Pike and Stephen H. Long suggested a solution. The land west of Missouri and the ninetieth meridian, they said, was fit only for Indians and wild animals. The government could end the border wars by putting the Indians on land which the white man did not want. That was the land west of Missouri, carelessly called the Great American Desert. There the Indian could live in peace. A line of forts would separate the two cultures. This little idea grew into the Indian removal policy, and Kansas was to become the peaceful haven for the Indian; there he could live unmolested by the white man forever. The Indian came, not willingly, but he came; and he left his imprint on the Kansas map, even though "forever" lasted only about a quarter of a century.

In order to make room for the eastern Indians, it was necessary to restrict the resident Indians to compartments called reservations. The Kansas and the Osages were assigned to specific areas with boundary lines, placing an artificial restriction on their freedom. Then treaties were made with the eastern Indians to surrender their homelands for new lands in the Indian Territory. Treaties were poorly understood by the Indians but they were forcefully executed. Indian removal was a traumatic experience.[2]

The generic term of Indian, though originally a misnomer, was used to name over a dozen streams and three post offices. Settlers, twice driven from a stream in Elk County, named it Indian Creek, and from that a local post office took its name. Another Indian Creek post office was in Linn County; and, for a summer, Anderson County had an Indian Valley post office.

Out of the east came the Shawnees and the Delawares to settle along the lower Kaw. Then came the Wyandots who wisely bought the Kansas City site from the Delawares. These were followed by Potawatomis and Miamis from the Great Lakes. The Cherokees came from the South to settle in the southeastern corner of Kansas. Except for the Delaware name, all of these names became Kansas county names.

Thomas Johnson of the Shawnee Mission wanted the Shawnee name for the county where he lived. But a legislative committee accepted the request of Hiram J. Strickler of Tecumseh to use that name for the present Shawnee County. Johnson was honored, however, when Johnson County was named for him.[3] In addition, there is the present town of Shawnee.

The Shawnees, relatives of the Delawares, were pushed northward from the Tennessee-Carolina area by the Cherokee. The white man drove them out of Pennsylvania and Mad Anthony Wayne defeated them in Ohio. The War of 1812 deprived them of much of their land. After the Kansa Indians had given up a part of their land, Shawnees were brought to Kansas and settled on the lower Kaw.

The source of the Shawnee name was Shawanogi, or something similar, meaning "southerner." There appears to be a relationship between Shawnee and such southern river names as Suwanee and Savannah. Shawnees once lived on the Savannah River. The suggestion that their name came from *sintagen* and *sewan*, meaning "pungent" or "salt," would fit into their reputation for being great salt eaters. The French called them Chouanon and Chounois. Jotham Meeker's news-

424

paper was called the *Siwinowe Kesibwi*, "Shawnee Sun." Another popular form for the name was Shawanoe.[4]

The greatest of all the Shawnee chiefs was Ticumthe, now written Tecumseh. When he was born, the natives saw a comet that they compared to "a fiery panther flying across the sky." So the mother named the child Tecumseh, interpreted to mean a "shooting star" or, more dramatically, a "leaping panther." Tecumseh grew up to become a great chief. Together with his brother, the Prophet, he tried to organize a solid front of Indian resistance to the white man. This was broken up by the Battle of Tippecanoe. Then came the War of 1812 and Tecumseh was killed. Two colonels have taken credit, if credit there be, for having killed him. The questionable claim of Colonel Johnson has been stated in verse as a political satire:

> *Humpsy Dumpsy,*
> *Colonel Johnson killed Tecumseh.*

The deed, however, has generally been attributed to Colonel William Whitley of Kentucky.[5]

Tecumseh had been known as a "yeller devil" by his white enemies, but later generations have recognized his devoted service to his people. Colonel Thomas Nesbit Stinson, who married Betsy Rogers, a relative of Tecumseh, gave the name to the town near his trading post on the Kaw. Tecumseh came within one vote of becoming the capital of Kansas.[6]

Piqua, the birthplace of Tecumseh in Ohio, was the source for the name of Piqua in Woodson County, Kansas. Also from Ohio came the Shawnee name of Chillicothe in Phillips County and New Chillicothe in Dickinson County.

The Anglicized names of two Indian women, Lenexa and Eudora, have added variety to the Shawnee names. Lenexa in Johnson County was named for the wife of Blackhoof, a Shawnee chief. Eudora in Douglas County was settled by a company of German pioneers from Chicago who bought their land from Paschal Fish, a Shawnee chief. They named their town Eudora for the chief's daughter.[7]

When Dave Dougherty, a Shawnee Indian, was helping Dr. John Barton to find a good townsite in Johnson County, he came upon a "green knoll carpeted with blue and scarlet, verbenas, lacy white blossoms of wild parsnips, and pink-petaled wild roses." Impressed by its beauty, Dougherty exclaimed "o-la-the!" This was the Shawnee word for "beautiful." Barton wanted an Indian name, and so he chose to name the town Olathe.[8]

The names of two Delaware chiefs, Sarcoxie and Tonganoxie, became place-names in Kansas. Sarcoxie, also called Kock-a-towha, ran a ferry across the Kaw at Lawrence. The town of Sarcoxie or Sarcoxie-ville is no more, but the Sarcoxie name is still on a Jefferson County township.[9]

Tonganoxie's name has been spelled Tonqua-Noxie and Tonganox-wha. The chief was big, but the name was said to mean "shorty." The Tonganoxie name in Leavenworth County is used for a town, a township, and a creek.[10]

The Wyandots belonged to the Iroquois linguistic group, but they were not members of the Iroquois confederation. Their Iroquois neighbors treated them shabbily and drove them out of the beautiful and bountiful Georgean Bay area of Lake Huron.

The Wyandot name, as written by the French, varied from Tiononta-tis and Ionontat or Ouendat and Guayandotte. Americans called them "Yendats" and "Wendots" before the name became Wyandot for the tribal name and Wyandotte for the county and city. According to one interpretation, the name meant "calf of the leg." The French called them Nation du Petun, "tobacco nation." They were also known as the "island dwellers."[11]

After they sold their Ohio lands, the Wyandots came to Kansas. They liked the Delaware land so well that they purchased it and started the town of Wyandott which became Wyandotte City. This was within Atchison County until 1859 when Wyandotte County was organized. Indian names were given to four of the county townships: Wyandotte, Shawnee, Delaware, and Quindaro. Two new suburbs were named Quindaro and Armstrong.

Like most of the Wyandots, Silas Armstrong was part white. He was a promoter of Kansas City on his land and a street still bears his name. Kansas City, Missouri, used the Kansas name as Town of Kansas, Kansas, City of Kansas, and finally Kansas City. Across the river, Quindaro, Wyandotte City, Armstrong, and Armourdale combined to form Kansas City, Kansas. Connected by bridges, the two have become Greater Kansas City.[12]

Quindaro, also known as Nancy Guthrie, was a Delaware-Wyandot woman, the wife of Abelard Guthrie, who was a prominent politician among the Wyandots. *Quindaro* meant "woman" in the Wyandot language. It might also mean "daughter of the sun," associated with the hatching of turtle eggs. The town of Quindaro on the hills above Kansas City was promoted by Governor Robinson. Ridiculing the location, one critic said: "They might as well have sought to build a city on the Natural Bridge of Virginia or the Palisades of the Hudson."[13] This critic should see Quindaro and the Palisades today.

When the Huron Indians merged with their relatives, the Wyandots, they lost their identity. The Huron name is supposed to describe their hair-do, which resembled the bristles of a wild boar. This also gave them the name of "shockheads." D. R. Anthony donated the land for Huron in Atchison County and in a letter to the Kansas Historical Society said, "I named the present town Huron." But a letter from George W. Stabler to George Remsburg stated that it was named by Amarziah Moore for his home county in Ohio. The confusion could be attributed partially to the moving of the town from Old Huron to New Huron.[14]

From the Huron area of Canada came the names of Ontario and Toronto. The Toronto name has been interpreted to mean "gateway," a "place of plenty," and "meeting place."[15] The meeting place could be at the gateway. Canadian settlers in Kansas named Toronto in Woodson County. Ontario in Jackson County was named for Lake Ontario which the natives called the "beautiful lake" or the "good lake."[16]

The Potawatomi of the Woods lived in Michigan and Wisconsin; the Potawatomi of the Prairies, the Mascoutin, lived in Illinois and Indiana. The Potawatomis have been called the "fire nation," possibly because they were called the "pipe lighters," based on an old tradition. *Mascoutin* referred to prairies, but the name has been translated as "prairie fire." This would combine the names of both divisions of the Potawatomi.

After several moves, they were assigned land on the Osage River in Kansas where a tributary was called Pottawatomie Creek. Its junction gave rise to the name of Osawatomie. The Mascoutins moved to a new reservation north of the Kaw and east of the Big Blue. There a county was named Pottawatomie. The two-house settlement called Pottawatomie in Coffey County was characterized as a "Phantom town."[17]

On the south side of the Kaw, a county was named Wabaunsee for a Potawatomi chief. *Wabun* could mean east or east wind, and this would be associated with the dawn.[18] Wabaunsee was first only the county seat of Richardson County, named for a member of the Bogus Legislature. The free-state people changed the county name to Wabaunsee. The county also has a Wabaunsee Township and a Wabaunsee Lake.

Shawnee County had a place called Wah Wah Suk, probably from John Wah Wah Suk, a Potawatomi policeman. A post office in Butler County left off the last syllable and named a place Wah Wah.

Onago and Pashqua were Potawatomi personal names. Paul E. Havens of the Kansas Central Railroad scanned the Potawatomi head-rights book in search of a name for a town. He stopped at Onago, changed it to Onaga, and gave the name to a station on the railroad.[19] Promoters who built a town on Chief Pashqua's land took liberties with his name and changed it to Paxico for a station in Wabaunsee County.[20]

Wamego in Pottawatomie County was probably named for George or Henry Wam-me-go, Potawatomi chiefs. The name has been freely interpreted to mean "running water" or "clear of swamps."

Also descriptive is Netawaka, said to mean "fair view" or "grand view," or, possibly "high divide" from which one could get a "grand view."[21] Netawaka in Jackson County, which was started with a tavern, is in Netawaka Township.

The Ottawas were relatives of the Potawatomis and neighbors of the Hurons in the Georgean Bay area. Their name could have come from *adawc* or *o-dah-wan*, which meant "traders." Another source was their Chippewa name of Watawawiniwok, "men of the bulrushes." Their Huron name of Ondatawawat, like the Chippewa name, had within it letters which spelled *atawa*. The name was even shortened to "Tawa."[22] As a place-name in Kansas, it was commonly pronounced "Ottoway" like "Ioway." The Ottawa were settled in Franklin County where the town of Ottawa became the county seat. The town was first established by C. C. Hutchinson near Ottawa Junction in Ottawa Township. Ottawa County was organized and named in 1866.

Each tribe seemed to have a chief whose exploits made him one of the great historical characters. Such a man was Pontiac, chief of the Ottawas. He could see the threat of the British colonials crossing the Alleghenies and entering the lake country in the West after the British victory in the French and Indian War. He was a courageous man with a vision, but his enemies called him cruel and crafty. Francis Parkman found his fascinating story worthy of a book, *The Conspiracy of Pontiac*. Kansas preserved his name for a station east of El Dorado in Butler County.

Among the Algonquian tribes to come to Kansas from the Old Northwest were the Miamis. In a series of treaties, they lost their lands in Ohio and settled in the Marais des Cygnes area of eastern Kansas. Their Chippewa name of Omaumeg meant "people of the peninsula."[23] The English knew them as "Twightwees" from *twanh twanh*, to represent the cry of the crane. The first syllable was dropped from Oumiamis, their French name, to make Miami.

Miami has been a popular place-name.[24] When Kansas decided to replace the name of Lykens County, they chose the name of Miami, since that was the area where the Miamis were settled in Kansas. Way-towns in Linn County had its name changed to Miami, and Reno County has a Miami Township.[25]

With the Miamis came the Peorias and the Weas. The full name of the Weas was Wawiaqtenang or Ouiatinons, meaning, according to Schoolcraft, "place of the curved channel" or "eddy." Miami County has a town named Wea, a township named Wea, and a Wea Creek. Tar pits which exposed the oil in the area were called the Wea Tar Pits.[26]

Peoria is a well-known name in Illinois where a town was named for the Peoria Indians. Some of these Peorias came to Kansas with the Weas and other members of the Illinois Confederation and settled in what is now Peoria Township in Franklin County.

But in Kansas the Peoria and Paola name evidently came from Baptiste Peoria, a brilliant linguist who knew several Indian languages in addition to French and English. The town in Miami County where Baptiste Peoria lived was first called Baptiste Spring. Then it was changed to Paola, which should have been Peoria except for the difficulty the natives had in pronouncing the "r" in Peoria. The name came from *pireouah*, meaning "turkey."[27]

Although they lived in the South, the Cherokees are related to the Iroquois. The name is a variation of Tsalagi, or Tciloki. Its French form was Chiraquis. The name may be of Choctaw or Creek origin. Its meaning, according to some, is a "hole" or "cave" or "hollow tree"; but according to others it means "tobacco people."[28]

The Cherokees were driven from their homes in Georgia and conducted to Kansas by General Winfield Scott on that tragic Trail of Tears. They purchased the east end of the Osage Strip from the Osages and settled in what became McGee County in the southeastern corner of the state. As a resident of Westport, Missouri, McGee had served in the Bogus Legislature, so, in 1866, the legislature replaced the name of McGee with Cherokee. The town of Cherokee City was within the Indian Territory and was consequently destroyed by federal troops. The builders of the present town of Cherokee thought they were in Cherokee County, but this Cherokee is in Crawford County.[29]

One of the great leaders of the Cherokees was Elias Boudinot, editor of the *Cherokee Phoenix*. He was also known as Buck Watie. The Cherokees were split over the removal policy, and Boudinot was the leader of one faction opposed by John Ross. The rivalry was so bitter that Boudinot was assassinated. Boudinot Creek and the Boudinot Mission on the Neosho were named for Elias Boudinot. Eventually, Boudinot Mission, also known as Osage Mission, was changed to St. Paul.[30]

The Cherokees were among the most advanced of the American Indians. The Cherokee with the greatest reputation for learning was George Guess. He became lame from an accident and was called "the lame one." When he worked on the creation of a Cherokee alphabet in his cabin, he had no time to go hunting and carousing with his fellow-tribesmen. His efforts to make "leaves talk" like the printed page of the white man was not understood. As he labored alone, he was ridiculed by his neighbors who shouted at him: "Sequoyah! Possum in a pen! Pig in a poke!" In these slurring remarks, we have the evolution of his name. The oppossum was called *sequoah*, the white man's pig. Being shut up in his cabin like a "pig in a poke," he became known as Sequoyah.[31] Sequoyah County was named in 1873, but when the counties were organized in 1883, Sequoyah was absorbed by Finney County.[32]

Mingo is a Cherokee name which was popularized by James F. Cooper in his *Leatherstocking Tales*. Cooper said it meant "treacherous" or "stealthy." There was once an Iroquois band called Mingo living at the Pittsburgh, Pennsylvania, site.[33] The Mingo Trail did not reach Kansas, but there is a Kansas town named Mingo in Thomas County.

Four western counties were named for the Indians of the High Plains: Arapahoes, Cheyennes, Comanches, and Kiowas. The Arapahoes and Cheyennes were Algonquians who had made a wide swing westward from Minnesota and then southward from the Dakotas and Wyoming. Some Indians called the Arapahoes "blue-sky men," but the Arapahoes said their name meant "our people."[34] The Arapahoes, like the Cheyennes, were divided geographically into two bands, the northern and southern. The southern band moved into the hunting area of the Arkansas valley.

The first Arapahoe County, named in 1855, included all of that part of Colorado which was within Kansas. The name was later given to the Kansas county now named Haskell. Arapahoe County, like its neighbor Sequoyah, was named before it was organized.[35]

The Cheyennes followed the Arapaho route to the High Plains of Kansas. The Sioux called them Sha-hiyena, possibly meaning "those who spoke a strange language." Cheyennes were lavish in the use of red paint for personal decoration, and this gave the Sioux another phrase which could also become Cheyenne. Sha-sha meant "red" and a popular name for the Cheyenne was "red-legs." One writer went so far afield as to make the name "Shy Anne!" Each tribe gave them different names.[36] Early Americans used terms like "Chien" and "Shian," but the Chien was confusing since it was the French word for "dog."

After the Treaty of Medicine Lodge, the Southern Cheyennes chafed under the restrictions of the reservation. One group, under Chief Dull Knife, escaped and headed north across Kansas to return "home." This was patriotism. Pursued by soldiers, the Cheyennes massacred the whites on their way. They fought for a freedom which they had lost, but the military crushed this last break for freedom.[37]

In spite of the bitterness engendered by the military, battles, and the massacres, there was enough respect for these proud Cheyennes to give their name to a Kansas county, appropriately in northwestern Kansas.

Cheyenne Bottoms, a marshy lowland in Barton County, was probably named for a Cheyenne victory over the Pawnees. Blood Creek flowing into Cheyenne Bottoms got its name for the same bloody battle. A Cheyenne raid in Jewell County in 1865 was the source for naming Little Cheyenne Creek. There is another Cheyenne Creek in Montgomery County.[38] Cheyenne Bottoms was also a post office name.

Well known on the western plains of Kansas were the hard-riding Comanches and their associates, the Kiowas. These were Shoshonis and enemies of the Cheyennes and Arapahoes. In fact, the Comanches and Kiowas were enemies of each other until they agreed to stand together against the menace of the white man.

When Sieur de Bourgmont moved up the Smoky Hill to make peace with the Plains Indians in 1724, he referred to the Comanches as Paducas. This could have come from a name like Paduka or Padonka, the Siouan names for the Comanches. There is some support for the opinion that the Paducas and Comanches were not the same. The French called them Tête Pelée, "bald heads." La Harpe, exploring the Red River in 1719, called them "Cumanche." This was the term used later by Lewis and Clark and other explorers, with variations such as "Cumancias" and "Camanche." They were also called Ietans or Jetans. Dr. Say called them "Ietan or Camanch." Iatan became the name of a town near Leavenworth, supposedly named for an Oto chief[39] who earned this name by fighting Comanches. As for the proud Comanches, they spoke of themselves as "the principal people."

The Comanches were superb horsemen and earned the nickname of "knights of the Plains" and "Arabs of the desert." The horse, strayed from the Spanish remudas or stolen, gave the Indians a tremendous advantage in their struggle for food and in their battles with their enemies. Their buffalo lands in western Kansas were worth fighting for, but they lost them.

Kansas chose a county on the Oklahoma border to be named Comanche, honoring these "American Arabs." A town was named Comanche Center, but like most small towns of western Kansas, it soon disappeared. Barton County has a township named Comanche.

The Utes were related to the Shoshoni tribe but were of little importance to the nomenclature of Kansas. Sheridan County once had a place named Ute, and someone suggested that the county itself should have been named Ute. The Bannocks were also Shoshoni and Bannock was a place-name in Edwards County, probably named for a Bannock in the West.

The next county north of Comanche was named Kiowa. The Kiowas were also Plains Indians who had lived in the area west of the Black Hills. They were familiar with the geyser country of "Colter's Hell," as Yellowstone Park was called. Like the Comanches and Cheyennes, they drifted southward, fighting their way between enemies. They were among the last to come to Kansas. They have been called "great horsemen, horse-thieves, horse breeders, and horse traders."[40] They were good fighters and feared by their enemies, who called them "snakes" and "bad hearts." They were called "ropeheads" because of their practice of braiding horse hair into their own to make long braids. The Comanches also called them "scoundrels" before they formed an alliance to fight together. The Dakota Sioux called them the "people of the island butte," and the butte was probably the Devil's Tower in eastern Wyoming. Their name was commonly pronounced "Kioway" by the pioneers.

Kiowa County was organized in 1886, but Kiowa had already been used as a place-name. The first post office to be named Kiowa was in Barton County. In 1865, the site was chosen for Fort Zarah. The next Kiowa was in Barber County, south of Medicine Lodge where the Kiowas attended the peace conference. For a time the post office had a New Kiowa which had moved from Old Kiowa. Kiowa Township was renamed Aetna, but the town of Kiowa was neither in Kiowa Township nor in Kiowa County. Farther west in the Kiowa hunting country was Kiowa Creek flowing into the Mulberry in Ford County.[41]

"The most dreaded warrior on the plains," said James R. Mead, was Satanta, a Kiowa chief.[42] As the eloquent spokesman of the dispossessed Indians at the Medicine Lodge Conference, he was described as the "orator of the plains." Satanta meant "white bear." His name has occasionally been confused with that of his superior chief, Satank, whose name meant "sitting bear." Satanta was once taken by Custer as a hostage and kept in a Texas prison. He was described as "a tall, finely formed man, princely in carriage, on whom a prison garb seemed elegant."[43] Satanta preferred death to prison and jumped to his death from a prison window. The town named Satanta in Haskell County honors the memory of this honest and eloquent spokesman of the Indians.

Another Kiowa chief was Zip-kah-yay, "Big Bow," for whom Big Bow in Stanton County was named.

The Kiowas were accustomed to take medicine baths at the stream they called A-ya-dalda-P'a, "timber-hill river," now called Medicine Lodge River, the source for the name of Medicine Lodge.

The Wichita Indians were Pawnees called Kirikurus. Coronado called them Quiviras, a name abbreviated from Guadalquivir, or "big river." The Spaniards found them living beyond the Big Bend of the Arkansas River, mostly in the Rice County area. The Wichitas migrated southward towards their old homes on the Red River, where they were menaced by the Civil War. By 1863 they were back in Kansas and had returned to the forks of the Big and Little Arkansas. Their village was known as "Wichita Town."[44]

As Pawnees they were called Paniouassaba and Pani Pique. The Paniouassaba may be broken up into three names: *pani*, for the tribe, *ouas* for "bear," and *saba*, like *sapa*, for "black." Thus they became known as the Black Bear Pawnee. The name was also spelled "Pani Wasaba." In the translation, the "bear" part was often omitted, and this shortened the name to Black Pawnee.

Pani Pique was a name given them by the French who were impressed by the tattoos (*pique*) on their bodies. The Pani Pique were the "tatooed Pawnee" or the "painted Pawnee." The French *pique* was distorted by the English, who changed the name to "Pawnee Picts." "Painted Faces" is a translation of Pani Pique and not a translation of Wichita.

If the Wichita name came from Ahors Widtsa-Tow, it would mean "people of the north." If it came from Eujatah, it would be a Little Osage name for the terminal of the Osage Trail at the Little River near Wichita. The most acceptable translation of the Wichita name is "scattered lodges."[45] Wichita might have retained its French spelling of Ouichita, although Auguste P. Chouteau, also French, spelled it "We-che-tah," in 1838.[46]

A score of names were proposed for the town that became Wichita. Henry Vigus wished to name it Sedgwick for General John Sedgwick. Governor Crawford suggested Hamilton for Alexander Hamilton. One man proposed to name it Opi Ela, "elk tooth," for the loveliest Indian woman he had ever seen. But it was mostly likely named by its promoters, Greifenstein, Munger, and Mead, who said that it was already known as "Wichita Town."[47]

Wichita County in western Kansas was named in 1873, the year that Sequoyah and Arapahoe were named. It was Marsh Murdock, editor of the *Wichita Eagle* and a Wichita booster, who named Wichita County, located far from the home of the Wichita Indians.

Closely related to the Wichitas were the Wacos and the Kechis. Kechi was also written Kichai and Keechai. Keechai, as used in Texas, conforms to its pronunciation. It may mean "water turtle" or "going in wet sand," according to Swanton. In Kansas, Kechi is northeast of Wichita.

Waco and Waco Wego are twin towns south of Wichita. Waco, a Caddoan name, was interpreted to mean "river bend in a sandy place." When a Waco restaurateur advertised his chicken dinners, he appealed to the Sunday diners of Wichita with the slogan: "To Waco We go," and this gave the name to Waco Wego. Members of the Waco Home Demonstration Unit objected to its "silly" name and had the Wego deleted in 1957.

The Kickapoos were squeezed out of the Great Lakes area by Indian rivals and aggressive white men. In 1832, after some time in Illinois, the Kickapoos came to Atchison County, Kansas. The spelling of Kickapoo varied widely. Marquette spelled it Kikabous, and another French form was Quicapoo. A simple interpretation of the name was "he moved about" or "wanderers."[48] Kickapoo is a town in Leavenworth County which was sufficiently ambitious at one time to be called Kickapoo City. Its ambitions included making a bid for the state capital. It lost, but Kickapoo, Kansas, could have had alliterative appeal.

Best known among the Kickapoo chiefs in Kansas was Kennekuk, the "Kickapoo Prophet." Kennekuk is said to have come from *kinnikinnick*, the mixture of sumac and bark used by the Indians for tobacco. Catlin spelled it "K'nick K'nick." The town of Kennekuk is in Atchison County near the border of Brown County where the Kickapoos still live.[49]

Other Kickapoo chiefs whose names became place-names were Kapioma and Mashema. Capioma in Capioma Township in Nemaha County was named for Chief Kapioma. Mashema was planned as a town to compete with Kennekuk. It seemingly remained only a plan. The name meant "elk horn." Chief Mashema was at the Battle of Tippecanoe, but he had no outstanding achievement.[50]

Wathena in Doniphan County was named for a third Kickapoo chief. Chief Wathenah's tipi was used for a church, and his place was sold as a site for the town of Wathena, locally called "Wathene."[51] Also in the Kickapoo area of Atchison County was a town with the Kickapoo name of Muscotah, meaning "prairie," or, as some suggest, "prairie fire." The name resembles Mascoutin, referring to the "prairie people."

The Sacs and Foxes, relatives of the Kickapoo, moved from Wisconsin to Illinois and then to Iowa. The Sac were also known as Sauk, as the name was used in places like Sauk Center or Sauk City. Sauk came from Osa Kiwug, which meant "people of the yellow earth." Chief Ozawkie's name came from the same source. "Yellow Leaf" has been given as one translation of the name, but the more acceptable interpretation is "yellow earth."[52] A town in Jefferson County, Kansas, honored the chief by being named Ozawkie.

A rift between the Sacs and the Foxes occurred when Black Hawk wished to return with his band to their home on the Rock River in Illinois. This also caused a rift between Black Hawk and Keokuk. Black Hawk lost the war in which Abraham Lincoln, Jefferson Davis, and Zachary Taylor participated. As a defender of his people, he won fame. Black Hawk's name was originally Black Sparrow Hawk. Even when referred to as "Black Big Chest," the reference was to the hawk. His name in Osborne County was not a long lasting honor.

Keokuk was a shrewd political manipulator, which helped to make him a chief, but he lost his prestige when he did not support the Black Hawk War. He looked severe but he was affable. He loved his liquor and the sport of horse racing. The meaning of his name has been given as "one who moves about alert," much like the meaning of Kickapoo.[53] His name is better known for Keokuk, Iowa, than for the place once named Keokuk in Linn County, Kansas.

Behind the name of Quenemo is a legend about seven Sac women who escaped from the Sioux and returned to their home in the dead of winter. One woman gave birth to a child, and in desperation, she cried, "*Que-ne-mo!*" This was an appeal to her god. Her survival and that of her son was considered so miraculous by her people that they decided to make her son chief. They named him Quenemo.[54] After several generations, the name came to Kansas, where it was spelled "Kenemo" in 1856.[55] George Throckmorton spoke of having a playmate named "Snowflake Kenemy."[56] The town of Quenemo was located at the Sac and Fox Agency in Osage County and evidently named for "Old Joe Quinemo," as one pioneer wrote it.

Tatonka in the Siouan language meant "buck," or possibly "bull." Sitting Bull's Sioux name was Tatanka-Yatanka. A post office near Ellsworth was named Tatonka. *Menoken*, a Sioux word meaning "growing place," was the name of a town near Fool Chief's village in Shawnee County.

Chetopa was an Osage chief whose name was supposed to mean "four houses." According to one account, he had four houses because he had four wives. One can hardly think of a better reason. It is believed, however, that he earned his name by capturing four lodges from the Pawnees,[57] perhaps less romantic but more dramatic. Chetopa is the name of a town in Labette County and the name of three neighboring townships. The stream where Chetopa lived is called Chetopa Creek.

Neodesha is a corruption of the Osage word *ni-o-sho-de*, meaning "muddy water" according to the book with the interesting title of *Cho-O-Nee* or *High Iron*, by Joseph Allen.

Iowa Indian names became Kansas place-names after the tribe crossed the Missouri River into the northeastern corner of Kansas. In that very corner of Kansas is a town named White Cloud, named for James White Cloud, the son of an Iowa chief who was also called White Cloud. The proposal to name the town Mahushka, his Indian name, was rejected. But Mahushka, changed to Mahaska, was later accepted as the name for a town in Jefferson County.[58] The place was named by its Iowa settlers for their home in Mahaska County, Iowa. Other Indian names which were transferred from Iowa to Kansas were Oskaloosa and Ottumwa.

The Otoes were related to the Iowas and were their neighbors in northern Kansas. Oto came possibly from Watota. Some spelled it Otoe, as it was for Otoe County in Kansas. Its neighbors, especially Butler County, absorbed Otoe County. But Arkaketah, an Oto chief, left his name on a town in Marshall County. Pioneers found Arkaketah too difficult and abbreviated it to Oketo. It was located on the California Trail and became known as the "Oketo cutoff." Oketo Township has also kept the name.

One division of the Teton Sioux was called the Oglala. The name was spelled Ogallala in Nebraska but it became Ogallah in Kansas. Pioneers took privileges with the name and some spelled it O'Gallala to make it Irish; the soldiers called it "O Golly." Oglala has been interpreted to mean "to scatter one's own" or "she poured out her own." Ogalla was once a transient railway camp which became Parks Fort; it is now a railway station in Ogalla Township in Trego County.[59]

Sappa, a Sioux word meaning "black" or "dark," is the name of a tributary of the Republican River in northwestern Kansas. For a time Decatur County had a post office named Sappa, later changed to Oberlin. Rawlins County also had a post office named Sappa. Another named Sappaton was changed to Chardon.

Brown County has both a Powhattan and a Hiawatha. Powhatan, the father of Pocahontas, was first a friend and then an enemy of Captain John Smith. The town of Powhattan had first been named Locknane as a stage station. Powhattan Township touches the corner of Hiawatha Township.

Out of songs came such names as Juniata and Shoo Fly, and out of literature came such names as Ramona and Mingo. Marion County once had a place named Ramona. Several place-names were taken from Longfellow's poetic story of *Hiawatha*, including Hiawatha, the name of a town in Brown County. The railway station named Nekoma in Rush County was most likely named for Nekomis, the grandmother of Hiawatha, and Wenonah's mother. Wenonah, spelled differently in most states, became Winona in Logan County, Kansas, where there is also a Winona Township. There had earlier, however, been a place named Wenona in Doniphan County. Wenonah is a name used to denote the first born child, if the child is a woman. It has also been used popularly to mean "little woman."[60]

A considerable number of Indian names came from other states where they had already been simplified in spelling and their meanings lost. It took much time and practice for whites to become accustomed to names like Chautauqua and Sequoyah, but these, like most Indian names, have now developed a feeling of familiarity.

Indian tribes contributing place-Names to Kansas

CHAPTER XXXIX

NAMES FROM THE SANTA FE

R AILROAD PROMOTION and town building went hand in hand. Railway stations were located approximately six to ten miles apart and each required a name. A few towns were already named and on the railway route before the railway was built. Towns that were bypassed were likely to be abandoned or moved bodily to the tracks, name and all. Many post offices lost both function and name when replaced by a railway station. Names which served primarily as records of pioneers, promoters, ephemeral populations, and temporary post offices are now mostly gone. The railways created towns and destroyed them, just as they contributed names and discarded them.

Perhaps the best known of all the railroads in Kansas was the Atchison, Topeka and Santa Fe. The Atchison and Topeka Railroad was chartered in 1859, and in 1863, Santa Fe was added, a name which was and is popularly used for the whole road. It took some time before the frontiersman changed the pronunciation from Santa "Fee" to the Spanish Santa "Fay." That "Santa Fe" was only the middle part of La Villa de la Santa Fe de San Francisco was not common knowledge. And the "Holy Faith" was completely lost by a local settler in Chase County who told a traveler to follow the "Saty fee road."[1] The railroad company suggested the proper pronunciation in its rhyming slogan, "Santa Fe, All the Way."[2] The lonely town of Santa Fe in Haskell County was said to be named for the railroad; but the railroad missed it by several miles, as it had the one in New Mexico. It may well have been named for the Santa Fe Trail, rather than for the railroad.[3]

It may seem strange that the pioneers should have so much difficulty with a simple name like Santa Fe. In choosing names, railroad men were generally careful to avoid "jawbreakers." The names of railway officials represent many nationalities, but they were generally easily understood, no matter how a conductor might call his stations.

Railway officials moved freely from one railway company to another, yet the Santa Fe system serves as a unifying link for listing place-names. These names include presidents, directors, lawyers, stockholders, contractors, and even a section boss.

439

East of Hutchinson is the meaningful name of Way, named for M. E. Way, a railway agent. The descriptive name of Wayside, Montgomery County, was chosen by the Post Office Department over the names of Heloisse and Corn. Putnam south of Newton was named for another railway official.

Holliday near Kansas City was named for Cyrus K. Holliday of Topeka, the founder of the Santa Fe Railroad. The town had originally been named Waseca, a Sioux name meaning "rich" in provisions.[4] Holliday, with his mutton chop whiskers, was a distinguished looking man with ambition to match his vision. He passed up Tecumseh and promoted Topeka as the county seat, state capital, and railway center. He was the first mayor of Topeka and the first president of the Atchison and Topeka Railroad.[5]

The three later presidents of the Santa Fe to be honored by Kansas place-names were Thomas Nickerson, Thomas Jefferson Coolidge, and William Barstow Strong. There were three Nickersons from Boston working for the Santa Fe: H. R. Nickerson, George A. Nickerson, and Thomas Nickerson. H. R. Nickerson was superintendent at Dodge City. George Nickerson was a director and vice-president.[6] But the town of Nickerson in Reno County was most likely named for Thomas Nickerson, who, as president of the Santa Fe, made Nickerson, Kansas, a booming division point.[7] Tom was the one who drove the golden stake which started the railway on to Pueblo. To fit the western atmosphere he put on a cowboy hat and smoked a corncob pipe. He died in Newton Centre, Massachusetts, where Santa Fe stockholders named Newton, Kansas.[8]

The railway builders under Robinson and Criley thought they had reached the Colorado border when they were still four miles short. This endangered their contract. It was almost Christmas, workers were leaving, and there were no more rails and ties. With a superb effort, the road builders gathered enough men and materials to finish the line to the border. The railway camp was called State Line City. John D. Criley, better known as "Pete," was the builder who completed the line to the Colorado border, and there were those who thought that State Line should have been named Criley.[9] When Governor Harvey rode to the end of the line and approved the land grant, "State Line City was rechristened Sargent."[10] The new name honored M. L. Sargent, a freight agent.[11] The necessity for brevity over the new telegraph lines was illustrated by T. J. Anderson of North Topeka who sent a message of one word: "Hunkadora." Sargent's equally succinct answer was in two letters: "O. K."[12]

Sargent was absorbed by a new town which was given the name of

Coolidge for Santa Fe president Thomas Jefferson Coolidge.[13] His given names were those of one United States president, and he was distantly related to Calvin Coolidge, another president.[14]

Cottonwood Falls in Chase County had a suburb on the tracks which was commonly referred to as "Cottonwood City" or just "Cottonwood" and occasionally as "Santa Fe Station."[15] When William B. Strong became general manager in 1881, the Santa Fe Station was named Strong City. Strong had started as a station agent on a railroad in Wisconsin and worked his way up in a truly Horatio Alger, Jr., tradition. He was the one who extended the Santa Fe to the Far West, where his middle name of Barstow became the source for the name of Barstow, California.[16] Strong City and Cottonwood Falls are now known as the "Twin Cities" of Kansas.

Benjamin P. Cheney was another of the Boston directors for whom a Kansas town was named. There were two towns in the community before the coming of the Santa Fe, one named Marshall and the other Bridgeport, located on the Ninnescah crossing about two miles from the town of Cheney and at the present location of the Riverview filling station. Marshall was named for Marsh Murdock of the *Wichita Eagle*. When the Santa Fe came through, the station was named Cheney, and the Marshall residents moved to the railroad.[17]

The name of Cheney became well known when B. P. Cheney, Jr., had a special train rush him from California to Chicago so that he could be with his son, who was seriously ill. He made it in seventy-nine hours and two minutes. The press made such a dramatic story of the incident that Rudyard Kipling wove it into fictional form in *Captains Courageous*. However, the town of Cheney had been named before Cheney's cross-country train record and before his experience was told in a novel.[18]

Peabody in Marion County had originally been named Conesburg for J. E. Cone, a Wisconsin settler who helped to locate the town. Conesburg moved and for a time was known as North Peabody. F. H. Peabody, for whom Peabody was named, was a Boston banker and philanthropist who was on the board of directors of the Santa Fe. He promised to give funds for a public library for Peabody if the town would provide the land.[19]

West of Peabody is the town of Walton which was named for a Santa Fe stockholder and Walton businessman. On the southern border of Marion County is Burns, named for a Santa Fe official.

Other directors of the Santa Fe whose names became place-names were Raymond, Spivey, Sherlock, Sawyer, and Hunnewell. H. H. Hunnewell, who had once been president of the St. Louis and Southwestern Railroad, became a director of the Santa Fe, and for him was named the town of Hunnewell, "a rip-roaring boom town" on the Oklahoma border in Sumner County.[20]

Sherlock, Finney County, was named for Thomas Sherlock, Sr., but his name was replaced by Holcomb.[21] Commenting on the Holcomb name near the scene of the Clutter murder, Truman Capote said of him: "A *hog*-raiser, he was. Made money, and decided the town ought to be called after him. Soon as it was, what did he do? Sold out. Moved to California."[22] Sherlock Township retained the old name of the town.

The oldest town with its original name and once the "wickedest" town in Rice County is Raymond. As a cattle terminal and inspection station it became the roaring rendezvous of cowboys, gamblers, and others seeking easy money and risky entertainment. Both the town and the township were named for Emmaus Raymond, a Santa Fe director.[23]

John and Joab Mulvane were Topeka bankers and promoters, and Joab was also a railroad contractor. For one or both, Mulvane, south of Wichita, was named. Joab's donation to Mulvane was an art museum.

On the Mulvane-Englewood branch of the Santa Fe there is a little station south of Kingman named Spivey for Reuben M. Spivey, a director of the Mulvane extension. Spivey was also the president of the Arkansas Valley Town and Land Company. As a sidelight on names, one might mention that the maiden name of Mrs. Spivey's mother was Missouri Anne Smith, and she came from Smithville, Missouri, a town which was named for her father.[24] There is no telling where the Anne came from. The first girl born in Spivey was named Spivey Belle Treadway.[25]

Westward from Spivey and south of Pratt is Sawyer, named by J. W. Chamberlain for Warren Sawyer, a Santa Fe director.[26] According to the folklore, a loving couple had been kissing, unseen, they hoped, when the conductor loudly called "Sawyer! Sawyer!" The blushing damsel, disturbed by everybody's attention, blurted out: "We don't care if you did; we are planning to get married anyway!" Those were good old days when a kiss was as good as a contract.

West of Sawyer is the station named Coats. The townsite was owned by the railroad and the town was built for the railroad by W. A. Coats, who had also promoted the town of Sawyer. As a gesture of good public relations, he gave a town lot to the first baby born in the town. The railroad honored the promoter by having the town named Coats.[27]

Severy was named for a Santa Fe director; Gordon possibly was also. When the board of directors met in September, 1860, one of the new directors to be elected was Wilson L. Gordon. Gordon, south of

Augusta, was said to have been named for a railroad man.[28] Severy in Woodson County, named for Luther Severy of Emporia, is located on the Santa Fe crossing of the Frisco.

Although now on the Rock Island, Purcell in Doniphan County was named for E. B. Purcell of Manhattan, a Santa Fe official. Morehead in Labette County was named for another official.

One of the most dynamic and dramatic engineers for the Santa Fe was Thomas J. Peters. He would neither "smoke, chew, nor drink," but he was an exacting and forceful engineer "whose profanity when aroused was fearfully sublime."[29] One cannot credit Kansas for these characteristics; Peters was an Ohio man, but from the New England point of view he was a "western man." He was a friend of Marsh Murdock of Wichita, and when Murdock and Mead wanted a railroad from Newton, Peters proposed the plans to the Santa Fe directors. "They said no."[30] James R. Mead asked Peters what it would cost to run a railroad to Wichita. "If your people will organize a local company and vote $200,000 of county bonds," said Peters, "I will build a railroad to Wichita within six months."[31] Peters' friend, Tom Nickerson, was the conductor of the first scheduled train into Wichita.

When the Santa Fe reached the place now named Kinsley, it was named Petersburg for Tom Peters. Kansas already had a Petersburg in Doniphan County, also spelled Petersburgh, named for Peter Cadue. So the Petersburg in Edwards County was changed to Peters, still honoring the railroad builder. Promoters of the town were members of the New England Homestead and Colonization Bureau, and their agent, who was also the land agent for the railroad, was named Peter H. Niles. For him, it was said, the town was named Peter's City.[32] The town was also referred to as "Peter's Point." Adding to the confusion was the suggestion that the town was named for Mrs. Peters, the wife of Tom Peters. Having been named Petersburg, Peters, Peter's City, and Peter's Point, the town ended the confusion by accepting the new name of Kinsley, for E. W. Kinsley, a Boston stockholder. Yet Tom Peters deserves the honor of a place-name and this he now has in the name of Peterton in Osage County.[33]

The settlers of Edwards County came mostly from New England. E. W. Kinsley came to Kinsley in 1878 for a few hours visit in the town that bears his name. "Mr. Kinsley is a true type of the busy, bustling, sociable Bostonian," said the Kinsley *Graphic*.[34]

Alden Spear, a Boston financier, was interested in the Santa Fe. Both his first and last name have been used for names of other Kansas towns. Alden is on the line following the Arkansas valley from Hutchinson to Great Bend. Spearville is in Ford County on the line from Great Bend to Dodge City. The suggestion that Spearville was named for John Speer was denied by John Speer himself in a letter to Zu Adams of the Kansas State Historical Society. Not knowing the origin of the name for Alden, community residents concocted the somewhat far-fetched story that when the rails from Hutchinson and Great Bend met and were joined, someone announced the completion by saying that the work was "All done." From this, supposedly, Alden got its name.[35]

The next station northeast of Kinsley is named Nettleton. Since there was a superintendent of the Santa Fe western line named George Nettleton, one might guess that the town was named for him. He instructed the Santa Fe trainmen to stop to pick up any lone figure, straggler or bum, and give him a lift, with or without fare. No wonder he was known to the Santa Fe people as "Uncle George." He was also competent and succeeded to Tom Peters' position as general manager.[36]

Tom Peters' hiring of Albert Alonzo Robinson was called "one of the best investments the Santa Fe ever made."[37] Robinson, a Vermonter and a Michigan University graduate, had been working for the St. Joseph and Denver City Road before he was hired by Peters. Not until the Santa Fe reached New Mexico did his name get on the map, but Sylvia, the name of his wife, was the name given to a town southwest of Hutchinson.[38]

Goddard, west of Wichita, is a town named for J. F. Goddard, who was vice-president and general manager of the Santa Fe in 1877. He, too, came from Vermont. He was later chairman of the Trunk Line Traffic Association in New York.[39] J. F. Barnard was manager of a branch and for him was named Barnard at the end of the line from Abilene through Minneapolis.[40] Merrick in Lyon County was named for an assistant freight and traffic manager.[41] Morris on the south side of the Kaw above Muncie[42] was named for a superintendent of the Santa Fe.

Among the engineers and contractors who built the Santa Fe Railroad were Edgerton and Ellinwood, who left their names along the road. Before a Johnson County town was named Edgerton in 1871, it had already had three names: Hibbard in 1855, Lanesfield in 1861, and Martinsburgh in 1871. Edgerton, named for a Santa Fe chief engineer, also absorbed the town of McCamish which had been named for its founder and postmaster, Richard D. McCamish.[43]

When John R. Ellinwood was chided by diners in a Topeka hotel about how rapidly the Union Pacific could lay track, the quiet Tom Peters of the Santa Fe is said to have "sworn fluently" and challenged critics by appealing to Ellinwood to prove the Santa Fe's ability to match it. John's quiet answer was "Sure, Tom." It was John Ellinwood, with rank of captain in the Civil War but called "Colonel," who surveyed most of the Santa Fe line across Kansas.[44] His camp was for some time on an island near the present site of Ellinwood east of Great Bend. He was a Vermonter of English origin, a brilliant man "of wit and refinement," but he is said to have suffered from the popular pastime of drink before Kansas came under the prohibitionary influence of Carry Nation.[45]

A contractor on a smaller scale was William Scofield, a farmer. For him was named the town of Williamsburg southwest of Ottawa.[46] Scofield must have had some standing in the community since he was on the committee to welcome the Grand Duke Alexis when he stopped at Topeka in 1872.[47]

On the Santa Fe line from Dodge City to the southwest are the towns of Copeland and Tice. Tice in Haskell County was presumed to be named for the division superintendent at Dodge City.[48] Copeland was named for E. L. Copeland, a secretary-treasurer of the Santa Fe.[49] Another holding the same office was Edward Wilder of Vermont.[50] Wilder in Johnson County was named for this Vermonter,[51] said Corley, but the Santa Fe brochure entitled *Along Your Way* said it was named for D. W. Wilder, the journalist. Gray in Hodgeman County was named for A. D. Gray, an assistant treasurer of the railway company.[52]

Railroad companies had enough legal problems to make their attorneys well known. One of these lawyers was Michael Sutton, for whom Sutton in Kearny County was named.[53] Peck is believed to have been named for George R. Peck, a native of New York.[54] He was general counsel of the Santa Fe and described as "a lawyer of unflinching honesty," an "heir of the Puritans." He had been a lawyer for the Rock Island and later served the Milwaukee Road. The town of Peck is on the Rock Island south of Wichita.

Colonel Abraham Buckner Jetmore, also called Aaron Jetmore, was an attorney for the railroad, and this may have influenced the people who changed the name of Buckner to Jetmore. It has also been suggested that renaming the town Jetmore was a reward for a canceled debt.[55] The Prohibition party put Jetmore on the ticket as a candidate for governor in 1884.[56] He lost in Kansas, which has never been particularly dry, but he was later elected governor of Kentucky. His mother was Irish and his father was German, and one of his daughters had the singular name of Data Nevada.[57]

When Hunt's Station in Chase County was made a post office, it was named Silver Creek by William C. Shaft for his Michigan home. When it was promoted into a town by Joseph L. Crawford in 1882, its name was changed to Crawfordsville. The next year, the town was renamed Clements to honor H. G. Clements, an auditor of the Santa Fe.[58]

Contractors and roadmasters were sufficiently well known to have left their names along the roads which they built. Spencer and Wellsville were named for George W. Spencer and P. L. Wells, contractors.[59] Spencer is located east of Topeka. Wells was a civil engineer and contractor and for him was named the Santa Fe station of Wellsville between Ottawa and Olathe.[60] The Wells in Ottawa County was named for Henry Wells of the Wells Fargo Company.[61] He was the founder of Wells College in Cayuga, New York. The town of Wells had first been named Poe and then Vashti.

Nortonville, near Atchison, was named for T. L. Norton, Jr., who was roadmaster of this region.[62] Sears, a small station west of Dodge City, was named for Thomas Sears, general superintendent of the Missouri division.[63] West of Sears is Howell, which was named for Tom Howell, a section foreman.[64]

The Santa Fe hoped to sell its vast lands in western Kansas to furnish produce for freight, people for passengers, and all for profit. David Long Lakin was hired to dispose of this railway land. Lakin was born in Zanesville, Ohio, and attended Zanesville College. After a stint of teaching in Alabama, he came to Kansas and made his home in Topeka. There he came under the influence of Colonel Holliday and the promoters of the Santa Fe Railroad. He was made a member of the board of directors in 1864 and served as treasurer. As the first land commissioner for the railroad, he had trouble. The land that Lakin had to sell in western Kansas had the reputation of being overrun by stampeding buffalo, vast herds of cattle, and grasshoppers which destroyed whatever the drought might have left. Ill and baffled, he resigned. But west of Garden City the town that started with a water tank, a small depot, and a Fred Harvey Hotel was named Lakin to honor the commissioner.[65]

After Lakin resigned, the job of selling the Santa Fe lands was given to A. E. Touzalin, said to be a "native of Jamaica." He was known as a hustler and it was he who hired C. B. Schmidt to recruit European settlers to purchase railroad lands.[66] For a time there was a Touzalin in Meade County. The name was seemingly French and sufficiently foreign to cause a problem in spelling. One wrote it "Tuzlon,"[67] and the local newspaper spelled it "Tuesland."[68]

Touzalin's successor was Alexander S. Johnson from Topeka, the son of Thomas Johnson of the Shawnee Mission. When Colonel Johnson joined the Santa Fe, Touzalin joined the Burlington, and the two battled for a share of the European immigrants, Touzalin for Nebraska and Johnson for Kansas. At one time, Johnson had fourteen hundred homeseekers in Topeka to be taken on a special train to inspect railroad lands. Passengers could occasionally pick their prospective homes from the car windows. Now the town of Johnson, seat of Stanton County, bears the name of the man who promoted the settlement of western Kansas.[69] The town had at first been named Veteran, then Veteran City, then Johnson City, and finally just Johnson.[70]

Charles W. and Carlos Pierce were officials of the Santa Fe and their names were used for both the town of Pierce and of Pierceville. Their first names show a neat way to use the same name and yet avoid confusion by switching the language from the English Charles to the Spanish Carlos. Pierceville on the Arkansas River east of Garden City was named for Charles and Carlos.[71] One author gives the honor only to Charles, "an official."[72] Pierceville is "the only town in Finney County which has its original name and location." The Indians burned it in 1874 and it remained a ghost town for four years. Later it was revived with its original name.[73]

Chase in Rice County was named for a Santa Fe official and has no connection with the Chase of Chase County. Manter in Stanton County was named for another Santa Fe official, as was Deerfield in Kearny County. There must have been a change in Deerfield's name since it was believed to have come from the name of one Sam Dear.[74]

Farther west, Garden City saw the need for connecting lines running north and south and hoped to become a railway hub. Of the three or four railways planned, the Garden City, Gulf and Northern was the most successful, but the "Gulf" part was only an ambitious dream. Towns on the line running north from Garden City to Scott City are named for the local promoters and builders.

Basil M. McCue from Hastings, Nebraska, was the organizer of the Garden City Western road, and a town on the line, "ideally located," was named McCue. There was a town named McCune in Crawford County, named for Isaac McCune, a pioneer, and the similarity of names could be confusing.[75] After two years, McCue sold the line to the Santa Fe and the town had its name changed to Friend. The next station south of Friend is Tennis, named for B. M. Tennis, general manager of the road.[76] Near Garden City is the town of Gillespie which was named for F. A. Gillespie, a representative of the sugar interests of Garden City and secretary-treasurer of the Garden City Western Railway.[77]

Then there was a Thayer from Boston who helped to finance the building of the Leavenworth, Lawrence and Galveston Railroad, the "Joy Road," and who served on its board of directors. Because several Thayers have been prominent in Kansas history, writers have had difficulty in deciding which Thayer was the one for whom Thayer was named. In a letter to George Martin of the Kansas Historical Society, it was said that the town was named for Thayer, the railroadman. The writer added with caution: "I think his name was Josiah."[78] Another used Octave Chanute for an authority and said that he "supposed" the town was named for Nathaniel Thayer.[79] A writer for the *St. Paul Journal* admitted that there was some question as to whether the name was for Eli Thayer, who promoted the Emigrant Aid Society, or for Nathaniel Thayer, the railroad financier, both "great men." However, the *Journal* concluded that "circumstances of the naming indicate that Nathaniel Thayer was the one for whom the town was named."[80] Nathaniel Thayer was the son of a Boston preacher. He made money as a West Indies merchant and became a banker, railroad financier, and philanthropist. He donated generously to Harvard.

Merriam in Johnson County had first been known as Campbellton, named for David Gee Campbell. As a post office it was named Spring Place, but, attractive though it be, this name lasted but forty-one days. For nearly a decade it was named Glenwood, also an attractive name. In 1881, the name was changed to Merriam. There were several Merriams in Kansas, but there was a G. F. Merriam serving as township clerk in Johnson County in 1858. The town was, according to one account, named for the man who secured the railroad for the town.[81]

As rival rails converged or crossed, towns fought for their existence and for their names. The town now named Chanute resulted from the merging of several towns and the substitution of Chanute for five other names: Alliance, Tioga, Chicago, Chicago Junction, and New Chicago. The terminal of the Katy was named Alliance and the towns might have merged under such a meaningful name. It was named Alliance with a purpose, since Alliance was planned as a solution of the county seat issue and to avoid the uncompromising rivalry of Tioga and New Chicago. But Alliance lost to Erie and Osage Mission.[82]

Tioga was the name of one of the budding rivals located at the northwest corner of New Chicago. The Tioga River crossed the New York–Pennsylvania border and there are several centers named Tioga in the area. Tioga was originally the name of an Iroquois village, meaning "where the river forks" or "at the crossing." In Kansas the township has kept the name of Tioga.[83]

Such names as Chicago and New Chicago, also called Chicago Junction, indicate the ambitions of its sponsors. New Chicago in Kansas had for a short time a more rapid growth than did Chicago, Illinois. Chicago is a name of Indian origin and it apparently refers to the vegetation in the area. The assumption that it meant "skunk" may have come from skunkweed. One of the best authorities suggests that the name referred to "garlic, leek, or onion."[84]

None of the towns would surrender its name to any of the others. The towns agreed, however, that the rivalry over the name should be decided democratically by the ballot. After the fifth ballot, no decision had been made. It was then suggested that all the old names be discarded and that they substitute the name of Chanute. This they accepted, and a worthy name it was. Octavius Chanute, for whom the town was named, was born in Paris, but his parents, Joseph and Elize (De Bonnaire) Chanute, brought him to America when he was still a young child. He began working for the railroad in New York at the age of seventeen and became a remarkably successful engineer. In Kansas he was one of the promoters of the "Border Tier" railroad, later a part of the Santa Fe system. It was the bridge which he built across the Missouri that has been called his "professional masterpiece." He was a man of vision and pioneered in the field of gliders which paved the way for the success of the Wright brothers. He was called "the Father of Aviation" and Chanute Field in Illinois was named in his honor.[85] Chanute was also interested in the location and naming of Coffeyville, the terminal of the Leavenworth, Lawrence and Gulf Railroad.[86]

Morehead, a conductor on the Santa Fe, got his name on the map. Morehead is the name of a station in Neosho County.[87]

The town of Clift in Grant County expected not one but two railroads, hoping that it was located where the Rock Island would cross the Santa Fe. To get into the railroad spirit it changed its name to Conductor. No conductor ever conducted a train to Conductor and it died.[88]

Overland Park near Kansas City was, according to a Santa Fe pamphlet, named by W. B. Strong who built the railroad from Kansas City to Olathe. The Overland name was chosen because the high ridge gave one a view of the Overland Trail. The additions to the town kept the name with variations: Overland Hill, Overland Heights, Overland View, and Overland Place.[89]

The Atchison, Topeka and Santa Fe, best known of all the Kansas railroads, left the largest number of railroad names on the map. With its headquarters in Topeka and its web of tracks across the state, the Santa Fe has earned an important place in Kansas history. The place-names along its rails serve as a roster of its official personnel.

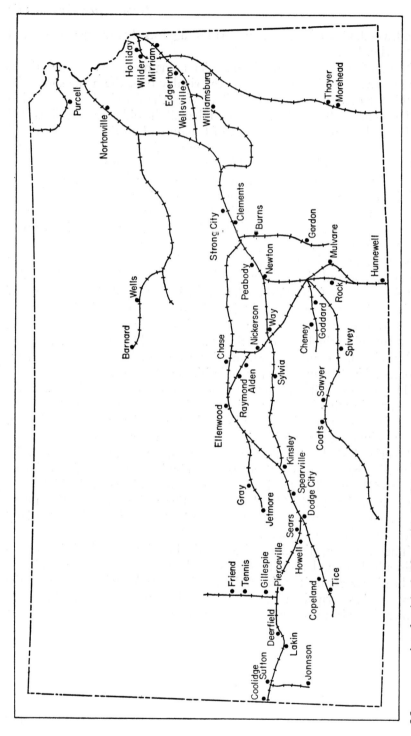

Names associated with the Santa Fe Railroad

CHAPTER XL

RAILROAD ROSTER

ONE OF THE PURPOSES of the Kansas-Nebraska Bill of 1854 was to open the country to transcontinental railways. Government subsidies and eastern money, combined with cutthroat competition and political promotion, led to a wild scramble for land, towns, and terminals. Railways and railway routes covered the state of Kansas like a highly concentrated and complex cobweb. The railroads that succeeded, such as the Santa Fe, the Union Pacific, the Missouri Pacific, the Rock Island, the "Katy," and the "Frisco," were responsible for building and naming a large proportion of Kansas towns.

In 1887 the *Great Bend Tribune* noted that every town in Kansas predicted that it would have "two or three railroads this year; there were 150 'Queen Cities'; 600 towns would double in population; in 450 towns it was impossible to keep up with the construction; 285 towns would become great distributing centers; 585 papers announced their towns would soon be in the midst of the greatest boom ever known, and all towns reported heavy investment by eastern capitalists."[1] One may make allowance for some fancy exaggeration in the use of these figures, but the boom in town building was fantastic. One railroad man boasted that he could organize a town in twenty minutes. The railroads, "the peoples oppressors," would say: " 'let there be a town,' and there is a town."[2]

One should keep in mind that there were towns all over Kansas before the coming of the railroads, even though the railroads did dislocate many and destroy some. There were also trails and stage lines between the towns. Most trails were named for their terminals. The town of Greensburg in Kiowa County is a good example of a place named for a stage-line owner, but the naming did not occur without a little skulduggery.

Jacob Barney of Kentucky was postmaster of a place he named Janesville for his daughter. It was called just Jane as a post office. "Colonel" D. R. Green, a big, self-confident, and ambitious man, ran one of the most efficient stage lines in the state. He owned land adjacent to Jane and he wanted his own town. One night the Jane post office was loaded on a wagon while the postmaster slept, and in the morning it was on a new site named Greensburg.[3] If this sounds fantastic, one may compare it with an experience Colonel Green had with Carry Nation. Seated impressively in a carriage with Carry Nation as a companion, Colonel Green lit a big cigar to point the way. Carry Nation's many causes included a crusade against tobacco. She grabbed the cigar from Green's mouth and threw it away. He stopped the coach, lifted Carry from her seat, and left her on the highway to thumb a ride. One might question the stories about Green, but they seem most appropriate to his personality.[4]

Green's stage line became known as the Cannonball, and he was known as "Cannonball Green." For years, U.S. Highway 54, westward from Wichita, has been known as the "Cannonball." Later, railroads used such names, the "Wabash Cannonball" being the most famous.

Railroad men were more successful than stage-line men in perpetuating their names on the map. Palco on the Union Pacific in Rooks County was said to be named for two railroad workers named Palmer and Coe. It had first been named Cresson for Cresson, Pennsylvania.

North of Palco is a town named Damar. When a tired and disgruntled railway worker was asked to name another town, he is reported to have said, according to local residents: "Dam'er! Call it anything you please." Then the "Dam'er" lost its sting by being changed to Damar. But this story may be challenged, because there was already a Damar south of the station before the rails came through for the "New" Damar on the track. In checking the suggestion that the town was named for a pioneer, one finds that the name nearest to Damar was D. M. Marr, the name of a man who owned land near Plainville.

Near Palco was a post office with the appropriate western name of Wild Horse. The railroad rejected this name and substituted the name of Bogue to honor the engineer of the first Union Pacific train to run through the town.[5] Other engineers to be honored by place-names were Critzer in Linn County and Richter in Franklin County. Richter was the name of a Missouri Pacific engineer.[6] When the Missouri Pacific reached Marvin, west of Kerwin Dam, the name of the town was changed to Glade for another engineer.[7]

Engineers were important in the public eye but so were conductors, who had a closer contact with the public. Stillwell, south of Kansas City, was named for the conductor on the first train to the town on the Missouri Pacific Railroad. Edwardsville, a suburb of Kansas City, was named for John Edwards, general passenger agent on the Union Pacific. It had once been owned by a Delaware Indian chief named Half Moon. Edwards moved to Ellsworth where he served as justice of the peace, a political post of greater importance then than it is now. He was a state senator from Ellis County when the town was named for him.[8]

The names of railway men could also be replaced, as witness the name of A. A. Talmadge, who was an engineer on the Missouri Pacific. Talmadge, north of Yates Center, was changed to Vernon; Talmadge on the Blue, near the Nebraska border, was changed to Warwick, possibly for another railroad man.[9]

Railway companies frequently rewarded farmers for land donations by naming stations for the donors. Boyle in Jefferson County was named for John Boyle who gave land for a station to the Leavenworth, Kansas and Western.[10] The most common donation was forty acres. A. G. Barrett in Marshall County,[11] John C. Richmond in Franklin County, and Thomas Lovewell in Jewell County, each gave forty-acre donations, and for each a town was named.[12]

Thirty miles southwest of Alta Vista lived a rancher by the name of Monroe D. Herington. He had traded a business lot in Bloomington, Illinois, for fourteen hundred acres of land in Dickinson County, Kansas. He named his ranch "Alioth Ranch." When he saw a surveyor marking a railway route with stakes, he is reported to have said: "You mean you are not building this line through Herington?" Wishing to know who was responsible, he was informed that the manager's name was Marcus Low. He joined a Council Grove delegation, uninvited, to call on Low at St. Joseph. According to one account, this is what happened:

> At Kansas City the Council Grove boosters missed the train to St. Joseph, but Herington caught it, and, arriving there, found that Mr. Low had gone to Kansas City, whither he followed him, only to find that he had gone to Topeka. Nothing daunted, Herington kept up the chase and finally found Mr. Low in the lobby of the Copeland Hotel at Topeka. There he promptly approached him, and when Mr. Low asked if he represented a city, a commercial club, or some organization authorized to speak, he responded: "Who—me? Why, yes; I represent the whole works . . . . I am the town, the commercial club, the mayor and the city council. My name is Herington and I come from Herington, Kansas, and we want your road and we are willing to pay for it."

Representing so many facets of his community, Herington could well refer to himself as "we."

According to another version, when Low asked Herington to identify himself, the reply was said to be: "I'm M. D. Herington, and Herington is my town. I own all that land down in that part of Kansas. In fact, I'm the whole thing down there." With his Vandyke beard and western hat, he was impressive. Low was perplexed but pleased.[13] Herington offered a right-of-way, and Low accepted. The town of Herington is now a railroad hub with six lines converging on the town like spokes in a wheel.[14]

Joel Ryan agreed to start a town for a station in Doniphan County provided the railway company would not build another within three miles. However, the town of Severance, named for one of the owners of the townsite, was within the three-mile limit. Ryan built his town, which was named Ryan Station, but popularly called "Ryans." Now it is just Ryan.[15]

Even such appealing names as Pleasant and Fairview gave way to the name of Waldo, honoring an official of the Union Pacific Railway. First the town of Pleasant was renamed Waldo, and later, a part of Fairview Township was named Waldo.[16]

The Indians became quite hostile when they saw the railroads penetrating their homelands. Construction camps were attacked and a number of railway workers were scalped. The first defense was to arm the railroad workers, the next was to call on the cavalry, and the third was to fortify the camps. One such fort was Parks Fort on the Union Pacific. It must have been on wheels since it moved westward from Ellsworth and it finally settled in Gove County. It was named for Thomas Parks, a railroad contractor. The fort may have saved many of Parks' men but it did not save Parks. He and three workers were killed in September, 1867.[17] The name of Parks Fort was later changed to Buffalo Park. This, of course, ignored the original source for the Park part of the name. But the post office has deleted both the fort and the Buffalo by calling it simply Park, vaguely reminiscent of the man who was killed in the war between the railroads and the Indians.

The Union Pacific connects with the Rock Island at Colby, and west of Colby was the town of Hastings, which became Brewster for L. D. Brewster of Illinois, a director of the Rock Island Railway.[18] In a meeting to select directors, Brewster was the tenth and last to be named. A history of the Rock Island does not mention his name again.[19]

Vernier, east of Colby in Thomas County, had its name changed to Halford for a Union Pacific official.

C. C. Furley, a doctor, and O. H. Bentley, a lawyer, promoted branch lines out of Wichita. Furley in the northeastern part of Sedgwick County was named for Dr. Furley, an active promoter of the Omaha, Abilene and Wichita Railroad, later absorbed by the Rock Island. Dr. Furley was an adventurer and was once attracted to California, but he spent most of his life in Wichita.[20]

Wichita's link with Ellsworth was by means of the Kansas, Midland

Railroad, which is now a part of the Frisco line. O. H. Bentley was the secretary-treasurer of the board of directors of the Midland Railroad. Bentley also compiled a two-volume history of Sedgwick County, and for him, the town of Bentley in northern Sedgwick County was named.[21]

Byers, a station on the Wichita and Northwestern Railway in Pratt County, was named for Oliver Philip Byers, a Hoosier who came to Kansas in 1878. Byers worked for five different railway companies and he lived in nine different Kansas towns. His first job was with the Chicago, Kansas and Nebraska Railway. It was Byers who organized the Anthony and Northern, which became the Wichita and Northwestern Line, also called the Wichita Northern.[22]

Financing the railway companies was one of its greatest problems and occasionally involved considerable finagling. Much of it was done by political pull, with or without "conflict of interest." The Central Branch road nearly bypassed Lawrence by four miles because that recently raided city could not raise the $300,000 asked by the railroad to come down to the Kaw. The decision was evidently left to John D. Perry, president of the Exchange Bank of St. Louis, financial promoter, and president of the Eastern Division of the Union Pacific. Senator Lane of Kansas, although ill in Washington, persuaded Perry not to pass up Lawrence. Perry built the road as requested, and a town west of Lawrence was named Perry in appreciation for his aid.[23]

The Loring station near Kansas City is believed to have been named for a railway official. The earlier Loring near Topeka may have been named for a Major Loring.

The Central Branch Railway of the Union Pacific was later absorbed by the Missouri Pacific. Everest, west of Atchison, was named for Colonel Aaron S. Everest, attorney for the Central Branch. The Missouri Pacific does not mention his legal association but gives Everest credit for being a "courageous army officer."[24] Everest represented Atchison County in the state senate.[25] South of Everest is the town of Effingham, named for Effingham H. Nichols, one of the Boston promoters of the Central Branch.[26]

Westward on this line are Wetmore, Goff, Corning, and Greenleaf, all from the names of railroad men. Wetmore was named to honor W. T. Wetmore, vice-president of the Central Branch. The town of Wetmore is now near the springs where Major Wetmore once camped with his troops.[27] Wetmore was also proposed as the name for Brown County.[28] West of Wetmore was Goff, a station named for Edward H. Goff, also an official of the Central Branch.[29] Jamestown, west of

Concordia, was named for James P. Pomeroy, the vice-president of the Central Branch, not for Pomeroy, the politician.[30]

Corning was named for Erastus Corning, a Connecticut Yankee, who became a successful businessman and banker in New York and one of America's great railroad men. He was president of two railroads and served as director of eight. His Kansas interests started through his connections with the Hannibal and St. Joseph Railroad, which in turn promoted the Atchison and Pike's Peak Railroad and then substituted "Pacific" for Pike's Peak as evidence of its growing ambitions. After Lincoln's Cooper Institute address in New York, a polished version of a speech he first gave in Kansas, Corning is reported to have offered Lincoln $10,000 a year to serve as general counsel for the New York Central. Dr. N. B. McKay, postmaster at America City, Nemaha County, was a New York friend of Corning, and the two promoted the town which McKay named Corning. It became "Old Corning" after the name and post office moved to the railroad. The town has also been known as the "step-child of America City." The Corning family, the Corning Glass Works, and the city of Corning are all familiar names in New York.[31]

Before the arrival of the railroad, Greenleaf's nearest post office was called Round Grove. It had been called both Prospect Hill and Hopper. When the railroad missed Round Grove, the postmaster packed up and moved to the station which was named Greenleaf, for A. W. Greenleaf, treasurer of the Central Branch.[32] Nearby Barnes was named for A. S. Barnes, a stockholder.

From Greenleaf one route swings southwest to the Washington-Clay County border. There we find what appears to be one town with two names and three railroads. The town of Vining took the place of a post office named Riverdale which was located in the valley of the Blue. The new name honored a Union Pacific freight agent, E. P. Vining, for favors to the town.[33] A rival railroad town near Vining was called Clifton, so named for a "friendly government surveyor."[34] When the Junction City and Fort Kearney Railroad came up from the south, it missed Vining and Clifton far enough to call its station West Clifton. So the old Clifton naturally became East Clifton. Since that time, East Clifton and West Clifton have merged and are again known as Clifton.[35] The reason for the town's having two names concerns its location on separate railways. If one arrives in town on the Missouri Pacific, he gets to the town named Clifton; if he arrives on the Union Pacific road, he gets to the same town with the name of Vining.

Six years after the Missouri Pacific built its road westward from Fort

Scott, the town of Wilsonville had its name changed to Bronson for Ira Bronson, a Fort Scott attorney.[36] Moran, first called Morantown, was said to be named for the Moran brothers of Chicago. Others say it was named for Daniel Comyan Moran of New York, who had helped to finance the Fort Scott, Wichita and Western.[37]

The Katy crosses the Missouri Pacific at Moran, and on the line south of Moran was the town of Dalton in Neosho County, which changed its name to Kimball, honoring C. H. Kimball, a military man and politician from Parsons and president of the town's first railroad. Kincaid in Anderson County was named for Robert Kincaid, who promoted a branch of the Missouri Pacific.[38] Roper in Wilson County was named for a Missouri Pacific engineer.

The Missouri Pacific Railroad with its many branches has sixteen hundred miles of track in Kansas, tapping towns and tying them together with bands of steel.[39] One of its most successful presidents was Cornelius Kingsland Garrison. He was interested in banking, shipping, and railroads. He was a popular reform mayor of San Francisco in 1853. His shipping interests earned him the title of "Commodore," which would rank him with "Commodore" Vanderbilt. As president of the Missouri Pacific, Garrison had been active in gaining control of the Central Branch of the Union Pacific. His son, Daniel R. Garrison, took over the management of the Missouri Pacific and negotiated its sale to Jay Gould for more than twice the first proposed price. When the railroad reached the Blue River on the border of Pottawatomie County, it came to Garrison and Garrison Crossing, named for C. K. Garrison.[40] The townsite is now flooded by the Tuttle Creek Dam.

Jay Gould's "marriage" to the Missouri Pacific and his "rape of the Katy" illustrate the manipulations of the railroad speculators during the nineteenth century. Several attempts were made to perpetuate the name of this speculator by naming towns in his "honor." The town now named Severy, east of Augusta, had earlier been named Gould as a Frisco station. Then it was moved about a mile to the crossing of the Santa Fe where the Frisco name of Gould gave way to the Santa Fe name of Severy, named for Luther Severy of Emporia.[41]

There was once a Gould City in Rooks County, but this "City" was missed by the railroad and then deserted. Mr. Risely, a Rooks County resident, is of the opinion that it was named not for Jay Gould but for Helen Gould. This could have been Helen Day (Miller) Gould who was the first wife of George Jay Gould, the son of Jay Gould. Jay Gould's first name was actually Jason, and like Jason of the ancient Argonauts, Jason must have sought the golden fleece when he tried to corner the gold market, failing only because of a desperate effort of the federal government to save the financial system of the country by releasing its gold.

The town of Hammond, named for W. O. Hammond, a former superintendent of the Memphis road, is now a station on the Frisco road north of Fort Scott.[42] The next station to the north is Prescott, named for C. H. Prescott, auditor and treasurer of the Fort Scott and Gulf Railroad. Prescott has also been referred to as a colonel and as the surgeon for the railroad company.[43] The town once had the descriptive name of Coal Center, reminding one of the abundance of coal in eastern Kansas.

Also on the Frisco line is the town of Latham in Butler County. It was named for Latham Young, a railroad commissioner from Chicago. It has been suggested that the town was named for Arlie Latham, a baseball player with the St. Louis Browns.[44]

The confusion over the name of Latham was the result of a report in Ripley's "Believe It or Not," which listed towns in Kansas named for the members of the Chicago White Sox. According to another report, the towns were supposedly named by a railway contractor who was a fan of the St. Louis Browns. Arlie Latham played third base with the Browns. Comiskey in Morris County was likely named for Charles Comisky, the White Sox manager. Bushong in Lyon County is believed to have been named for "Doc" Bushong, the catcher. But some of the names listed were on the St. Louis team and others were White Sox of Chicago. Some of the names were not on the Missouri Pacific.[45]

North of Fort Scott is a town named Harding, named for Russell Harding, general superintendent of the road. John A. Post was its first postmaster but he missed the chance of having the post office named "Post."[46] Harding in Bourbon County, though named for a railroad man, has now lost its railroad.

Other towns named for railroad men have also lost their railroads. Such are the towns of Amiot, Fanning, Leonardville, and Havensville. Amiot in Anderson County had been named Mineral Point. The Kansas, Nebraska and Dakota Railroad changed the name to Amiot, supposedly for a railway official.[47] The question of its origin was asked in verse:

> How did we come to be on this spot
> In our dear community of Amiot?

The answer to this question was the coming of the K. N. and D. railroad in 1887:

> Which did its duty 'til times terrific,
> Now its owned by the Missouri Pacific.[48]

458

The town of Fanning in Doniphan County was named for Major Fanning who was an engineer on the Atchison-Nebraska line.[49] It is no longer on a railway. Summerfield is in a similar situation. It is on the Nebraska border in Marshall County. The town was named for Elias Summerfield of Lawrence, an official of the Kansas City, Wyandotte and Northwestern Railroad.[50]

Kelly, called the "walking boss," was the head of a construction crew,[51] and Kelly's camp became the town named Kelly. Piper in Wyandotte County, once a railroad town, was said to be named for a railway official, possibly A. M. Piper, a constable in Johnson County.[52]

Westward from Kansas City are the towns of Havensville and Leonardville. Havensville was named for Paul A. Havens, who was at one time the president of the Lawrence, Kansas and Western. It was first called Havens, but that name had already been used for a post office, so it was changed to Havensville.[53] Stilwell, south of Kansas City, was named for the conductor on one of the first Missouri Pacific trains to the town.

West of the Blue in Riley County is the railway station of Leonardville, named for Leonard T. Smith, president of the Kansas Central. As Havensville had started as Havens, so Leonardville had started as Leonard. The Post Office Department thought Leonard was too easily confused with Larned and changed it to Leonardville.[54] The town was in a Swedish community and the Swedes liked the name, saying it was *vackra namnet*, a "beautiful name," translating it to mean "lion's heart."

Cleburne in northern Riley County was named for John C. Cleburne, a railway superintendent.

Axtell and Beattie in northeastern Kansas illustrate how easily names may be chosen. Jesse Axtell, an official of the Grand Island Line, was sitting before a campfire with his hunting companions, talking about building a town. When asked about a name, one of the hunters is reported to have answered: "Well, here is Dr. Axtell, and everybody likes him so I suggest that we name it Axtell." The first store was started by "Shoestring" Dickinson, but the town, promoted by the St. Joseph Town Company, was named Axtell.[55]

The town named Beattie, also in Marshall County, was named for A. Beattie, the mayor of St. Joseph, who, while visiting the townsite with some railway officials and stockholders, is reported to have said: "I want to give this town my own name, and not any Indian name like these other towns."[56] Bigelow, a station on the Missouri Pacific in Marshall County, was said to be named for General Bigelow, a railway official.[57]

459

Healy in Lane County was named for another Missouri Pacific official, and so was Neal in Greenwood County.

The town of Downs in Osborne County, with a name which sounds very English, was named for Major William F. Downs, the general superintendent and land commissioner of the Western Division of the Missouri Pacific. It was his business to sell land along a strip "100 miles long and 40 miles wide." He also negotiated the land sale in the Kickapoo Reserve, and it was said that he did it with "great care and skill." The town was first named Downsville before being abbreviated to Downs, a shorter name with sufficient distinction.[58]

Bethany, not far from Downs, had its name changed because the Missouri Pacific already had a. Bethany on its line in Missouri. The Post Office Department seldom objected to the repetition of a name when it was in another state, but the railroad found that it could be embarrassing to sell a ticket to a man and then discover that he had been sent to the wrong state. So Bethany in Kansas had its name changed to Portis, the name of the railroad's vice-president. This was done for the "sentiment felt for the Missouri Pacific," said the Missouri Pacific.[59]

H. M. Hoxie of Des Moines, for whom Hoxie in Sheridan County was named, was a close associate of Grenville Dodge and received the contract to build the first hundred miles of the Union Pacific Railroad at $50,000 a mile. Working with Durant, he became involved in the manipulations which led to the Credit Mobilier scandal. Later he became vice-president of the Missouri Pacific and General Manager at the St. Louis office.[60]

William McCracken of New York directed the building of the Missouri Pacific westward from Salina, and it has been assumed that the town of McCracken, west of LaCrosse, was named for him.[61] The town may have been named, however, for J. K. McCracken, who was a pioneer, one of the founders of McCracken, and a relative of Jay Gould. The Missouri Pacific has given the credit to the Kansas pioneer rather than to the New York promoter.[62]

Westward on the line was the town of Brownell, which was named for the attorney for the Memphis and Denver road before it was purchased by the Missouri Pacific.[63]

There were several roads competing for a route to the Indian Territory and their promoters were ambitious to extend their lines to the Gulf, to Mexico, or to the Pacific. One of these lines was called the Border Tier Road, and being promoted by James F. Joy, it was also known as the "Joy Road." It later became a part of the St. Louis and San Francisco, better known as the "Frisco."

A post office by the name of Mathewson on the Frisco line in

Labette County was changed by the railway, since a conductor calling the station made Mathewson sound like Madison, even without the impediment of a cold. So the railway gave it the name of Strauss, after one of its officials.[64] The post office ignored the problem of phonetics and continued to call it Mathewson until the office was closed in 1914.

Competing with Joy were Colonel Robert Smith Stevens and Judge Levi Parsons, New York promoters of the road which later became the Missouri, Kansas, and Texas, called the "Katy." Levi Parsons had visions of a great empire for the Katy, especially if he could get generous land grants by beating Joy to the Indian Territory. His road ran from Junction City to Chetopa. Stevens and Parsons selected the site for a town which they would control. "Here," they said, "we will build a city that will become the metropolis of this whole section of the country."[65]

Stevens and Parsons had trouble with intruders who put in claims for the townsite. In order to distract competition, a dummy station was set up a few miles away and named Dayton, "a big name," and it was to be printed in letters "a yard high." But when the claims were cleared over the Parsons site, the competition ended and the Parsons boom was on. Judge Parsons, president of the Katy, wanted the town to be named Stevens for Bob Stevens, general manager. Others had decided, however, that it should be named Parsons with the addition of "City." Parsons was properly impressed but skeptical about the "City" part. Colonel Stevens showed him how Andrew Pierce, Jr., managing director of the Atlantic and Pacific, had a sign advertising "Pierce City" in "glaring letters," which he expected to outshine Parsons City. Parsons prospered and the neighboring communities, such as Ladore and Dayton ("those cesspools of vice") moved to Parsons "overnight." In spite of its growth, Parsons dropped the "City" from its name.[66] Stevens was not completely forgotten; a street bears his name, and other streets bear the names of the president's financial "angels."

Kincaid, on the Katy in southeastern Anderson County, was named for a railway promoter of the St. Louis and Emporia Railway. He also promoted the town of Kincaid.[67]

In Morris County three towns were named for railroad men: Kelso, White City, and Skiddy. For a time there were two names for the post office of Kelso, the railway station was named Downing, and the post office was named Kelso. The Missouri Pacific and the Katy, both in the Gould system, ran into labor trouble and strikes. Laborers were objecting to the twelve-hour day at the rate of ten to twelve cents an hour and went on strike in 1886. David Kelso, the lawyer for the Missouri Pacific, appealed to Governor Martin for the use of the military against the striking laborers. The governor suggested the use of all civil powers first; if they were defied, then the military could be used. The citizens of Parsons blamed the railroad, starting a long conflict in which Kelso was a participant.[68]

F. C. White, superintendent of the Neosho division of the Katy, was responsible for the construction of the road from Parsons to Fort Scott. For him was named White City at the crossing of the Katy and Rock Island south of Junction City. Other names proposed first were "Swedeland" and "New Chicago." The building of the road was a battle for time in competition with the "Joy men." In order to win, White was instructed to "Bull-whack" the builders of the road.[69]

North of White City on the border of Morris County is a town with the singular name of Skiddy. Francis Skiddy of New York was "donor of that amusing moniker," said Baxter Brown of Herington.[70] Skiddy was a distinctive name and only its uniqueness made it an "amusing moniker." Francis Skiddy, generally called "Frank," was known as "a suave socialite." He controlled the northern extension of the Tebo and Neosho Railroad branch. Francis Skiddy, a heavy shareholder in the Katy, was made president of the Land Grant Railway and Trust Company of New York by Levi Parsons. In his office, Skiddy had a map so large that it nearly covered one wall, and there he and Parsons would take turns in drawing long lines to illustrate the length of the railroads they would build or the extent of their dreams. Skiddy was also president of the proposed Tebo and Neosho railway.[71]

In addition to his support for the railroad, Skiddy had also promised to build a town hall and a library in the new town on the Katy if the town were named for him. So the town was named Skiddy, but Skiddy did not finance the town's public buildings. Since the agreement had been broken, Dr. Adams, a state representative, concluded that the town no longer had an obligation to keep the "amusing moniker." Skiddy was discarded and Camden (for Camden, New Jersey) was substituted. But when the residents of Camden heard that there were already twenty-three Camdens in the United States, they decided to restore the old and unique name of Skiddy. This name they need share with no one. When citizens of Skiddy traveled and met strangers, they were remembered "not by their names but by the name of their town." A letter from Sweden which was addressed to a man at "Skiddy, USA" reached its destination in Kansas.[72]

The railroad companies built or bought feeders for their main lines and extended spur tracks which were named like any other town with the addition of the terminal "Spur." There were names such as Dents Spur in Bourbon County, Dolese Spur in Butler County, Beckley Spur in Woodson County, and several more. Some of these Spurs could be considered descriptive. There was a Quaker Spur in Cherokee County, a Clydesdale Spur in Chautauqua County, a Clover Cliff Spur in Chase County, and in Montgomery County, there was a Tank Farm Spur as well as a Prairie Spur. Cowley County has three stations named Spur: Eschs Spur, Perings Spur, and Hullco Spur.

Occasionally the railroads added "Junction" to a name such as Pierce Junction in Brown County and Sherwin Junction in Cherokee County. "Siding" was also used, such as Nolan Siding, Washington County, Monument Siding in Logan County. Two were identified only by initials: R. O. Siding, Coffey County, and K. X. Siding in Woodson County. There was once a Monotony Siding on the Kansas Pacific near the Colorado border. It ended by having Siding deleted, and Monotony may have been sufficiently descriptive. Many of these names are found only on railroad maps.

Every railroad camp took on the appearance of a little town. The town of Campus in Gove County, said the local resdents, got its name from being a railroad camp. But nameless terminals for the advancing tracks were merely designated as End-of-Tracks or End-o-Track. This was generally where transfer was made from the railroad to the stage coach. On the Union Pacific in western Kansas, End-of-Track had a fixed location for some time and it also served as a military post to defend the terminal.[73] End-of-Track was generally a wild town, especially on payday, and it was given the descriptive name of "Hell on Wheels."[74] Since it was on wheels, a new camp or terminal could retain this unsavory title as it moved westward.

The place named Pauline south of Topeka appears to be named for a woman. The railway station was located on the farm of W. A. Paul, so the railroad company named the place Pauline.[75] As a feminine name it could have been included in the chapter on women's names. The place today is best known, however, as the Forbes Air Force base, named for Major Daniel H. Forbes, Jr., who was killed in a test flight.

CHAPTER XLI

CHERCHEZ LA FEMME

THERE ARE MANY PLACES named for women in Kansas, but in most cases there is less information about the women than about the men whose names were used. Men were in public life, in the army or in politics; and public figures were most often chosen for place-names. The women were housekeepers, they were mothers, wives, or daughters, and only a few left their names on the map. Some women served as postmistresses, called postmasters. The first names of sweethearts made a special appeal to clerks, postmasters, railroaders, and town promoters, and their names, without explanation, became place-names.

Women were essential and appreciated far beyond the publicity they were given. Their names on the map, however, indicates one type of appreciation. For further appreciation, one may always turn to the poets. One had this to say:

> *There is no gift of earth or heaven,*
> *There's not a task to mankind given,*
> *There's not a blessing or a woe,*
> *There's not a life or death, or birth,*
> *That has a feather's weight of worth,*
> *Without a woman in it.*[1]

At one of Governor Medary's dinners, a toast was given to Kansas, "the Eden and the Ophir of the Far West." This was then followed gallantly by a toast to the women of Kansas, "without them our Eden would be a desert, our Ophir valueless."[2]

The legislature of 1867 organized several counties in central Kansas, naming most of them for veterans of the Civil War. Among these, one was named for a woman, Clara Harlow Barton of Massachusetts. Clara Barton had held a job in the Patent Office in Washington, but Buchanan reputedly had her dismissed because of her antislavery sentiments. Miss Barton was the Florence Nightingale of the Civil War, for it was she who started the American Red Cross. She had no rank, no duties, no rights, no job, no compensation, and no authority. But she won the undying devotion of the enlisted men, co-operation from most of the commanding officers, and sympathy and support from the president. Not all accepted her presence. When she appeared on the battlefield–unchaperoned–men were shocked, as were some women. But she followed in the wake of the destructive armies to heal and to help the wounded and to give them comfort and courage. She was a philanthropist who gathered the support of other philanthropists. L. P. Brockett's book on *Woman's Work in the Civil War* was published in 1867, the year in which Barton County was named to honor Clara Barton.[3]

Cloud County was first named Shirley, a name whose source might have been that of Governor Shirley of Massachusetts or the name of a popular dance hall entertainer in Leavenworth. When it was suggested that D. L. Chandler, a representative, had the governor in mind, possibly an afterthought to save the reputation of Kansas, there was immediate repudiation. "Perish the thought," said a commentator, "that the loyal territorial legislature of 1860 ever named a county for such a man." But it was considered equally ridiculous that the county was named for a "notorious Leavenworth dance hall girl."[4]

The legislature accepted the name of Shirley in a "freak of fun," said Colonel Inman, adding that this was "not unusual in such bodies," especially under the leadership of "an able and witty man." Ward Burlingame, reporter for a Leavenworth newspaper, is also credited with suggesting, in jest, the name of Shirley. It was likely Sam Wood, said Dr. Thomas Lindsey, who was "as usual poking his nose into other people's business" who "offered the name of Jane Shirley, of unsavory reputation and fame." Inman gave the credit or blame to N. H. Billings, the man who promoted Norton County.[5] One legislator said he had been born in a town named Shirley. This gave a tone of respectability to the name and a "pretext for the blackguards of the house to leave off Jane."[6] Rumors that the name was that of Jane Shirley, a girl of easy virtue and an eye-lifting reputation, stirred the citizens to action. Mr. Rupe of the *Clyde Herald* assumed that the name was given in a "spirit of levity," but he would not have the name remain as a permanent reflection on the Kansas legislature. The name had best be replaced and forgotten.

Several names were suggested to replace the unsavory name of Shirley. The final choice was the name of a respectable veteran of the Civil War, Colonel William F. Cloud. Shirley was not easily forgotten, although the name could be relegated to an inconspicuous place such as a township name. There is a Shirley Township, innocently named for the county and not the woman, we suppose. The Elm Creek post office had its name changed to Shirley in 1869. It took nearly a decade to have it replaced by the name of Ames, said to be for Ames, Iowa,[7] named for a Union Pacific official.

Among the places named for women, Mariadahl and Oakley represented mothers' names. Maria Johnson for whom Mariadahl in Riley County was named was one of the first mothers to be honored by a Kansas place-name. She was the mother of John A. Johnson, who owned the land on which the Mariadahl Church was built. In the church cemetery, Maria was the first to be buried. This town, settled mostly by Swedes from Galesburg, Illinois, was the first Swedish settlement in Kansas. It included a few Norwegians who were, however, called "Swedes."[8] The suffix *dahl* is the English *dale* or the German *thal*. Marienthal in Wichita County is a name of similar origin.

The town of Oakley in Logan County was first known as Carlisle, also spelled Carlyle.[9] It was changed to Cleveland Station, generally called "Cleveland." There was another Cleveland in Kingman County, so in 1885, the year that Cleveland became president, it was changed again. David D. Hoag, a Kansas City man who was the founder of the town, requested that the town be named for his mother, Eliza Oakley Gardner Hoag. Here were four names from which to choose, and the community chose Oakley.[10]

In Marshall County, A. B. Walker started a town which was known as "Walkersberg." When a town was started nearby, Walker was asked what his mother's name was, and when he answered "Winifred," the community agreed to name the new town Winifred.[11] Also in Marshall County is the town of Carden which was named for Mrs. Attilio Carden.[12]

Railroad officials named numerous stations in Kansas, and among them were names of members of their families. Sylvia, west of Hutchinson, was named for the wife of one Santa Fe official, and Partridge was the maiden name of the wife of another official.[13] Narka in Republic County was named for the daughter of a Rock Island official.[14] A Missouri Pacific official named Aliceville in Coffey County for his daughter. Most of the town of Aliceville blew away in 1903, but the name is still on the station.[15] Vera in Wabaunsee County was named for the daughter of M. A. Low, an attorney for the Rock Island.[16]

The place first called Plum Creek Flats in Ellsworth County had its name changed to Green Garden. For a time it was named Ashmead for an army officer. With the coming of the railroad, the name was changed to Lorraine, being "named for Lorraine Stanley, daughter of a Frisco railroad official of Wichita,"[17] said George Jelinek. Originally the name came from Lotharingia, a border province between France and Germany, whose name came from Lothar I, grandson of Charlemagne.[18] It is, however, a popular girl's name. In Nemaha County, the name indicated man's proclivity for brevity, for there it is spelled Lorain.

When the Santa Fe built a branch westward from Minneapolis, Kansas, the railroaders named the first station Brewer for Miss Thirza Brewer on whose land the station was built. The post office in the neighborhood had been named Penquites for its first postmaster, Nathaniel B. Penquite. The residents of Penquite moved to Brewer, on the tracks, but the post office kept the name of Penquite until it was closed in 1895. Although Miss Brewer changed her name to Mrs. Blades, the station kept her maiden name.[19]

The first post office to be named for a woman was Marysville in Marshall County. Colonel Frank I. Marshall had moved from Missouri to establish a tavern, a town, and a ferry at the crossing of the Blue in northern Kansas. The town that grew up around the tavern was then named Marysville for Marshall's wife, Mary Williams of Missouri. Marshall had "a passion for the name Mary," said one who knew him. Mary was also spoken of as "the first white woman to make Kansas a summer resort."[20]

One could add variety by using the maiden name of a married woman. Senator Pomeroy not only had a town named for himself, but he named Whiting in Jackson County with his wife's maiden name.[21]

The town of Claflin in Barton County was first named Giles City, also written "Guils City," and so named for Stella Giles. She was said to be "an elderly woman" who lived there and who owned stock in a railroad, probably the Missouri Pacific. Then the name was changed to Claflin, the maiden name of Mrs. O. P. Hamilton, whose husband had been active in the founding of the town. Here is a town twice named for women. There had been a Claflin in Bourbon County, too, probably named for Horace Claflin of the Emigrant Aid Society. This Claflin was, however, changed to Mapleton, clearing the way for changing the name of Giles City to Claflin in Barton County.[22]

East of El Dorado in Butler County, a pioneer, casting about for a name for a post office, had "the happy thought of honoring his wife . . . and he called it Rosalia."[23] Then the township was also named Rosalia. With names like Rose and Rosalia already on the map, what would one do with names like Roseila or Rozella, the name of the daughter of a land agent in Pawnee County? Whatever her name, she was honored when a town was named Rozel. The town had first been named Keysville, then changed to Ben Wade, honoring that outspoken rival of Chase from Ohio and that gadfly critic of President Johnson. In 1893 the town was named Rozel.[24]

It took three attempts to find an acceptable name for St. Francis in northwestern Kansas. First it was called Wano. When it moved to the railroad, it was renamed Emerson, for one of the town's founders, Captain A. L. Emerson. Captain Emerson had sailed around the Horn many times, accompanied by his devoted wife. Both the captain and his wife were highly respected in the community. He was described as "a lovable character," and she must have been a "saint." When the Emerson name had to be replaced because there was another in Kansas, the name was changed to St. Francis for the captain's wife, Frances L. Emerson.[25]

Agnes City, named for A. I. Baker's wife,[26] was first a post office in Lyon County and for a time it was important enough to be the county seat. The township in the area is also called Agnes City.

Ada and Bellville were named for postmaster's wives. Jacob B. Lane was postmaster of a new post office in Ottawa County, "and in honor of his wife, Ada, he suggested the name for his cabin which held the soap box which held the few communications received once a week from the outside world."[27] According to a local historian, "On the motion of A. B. Tutton," the town of Bellville was christened in honor of Arabelle, the postmaster's wife.[28] It might have been embarrassing for the rest of the town promoters to question the postmaster's choice—he was also chairman of the town company. For a time the name was spelled Bellville, but the missing "e" was later restored to make it Belleville.[29]

In a leaflet advertising a hobby show at Bazaar in Chase County, it was stated that "the town was named by Martha J. Leonard . . . in memory of a shoppe or bazaar she had owned in Pennsylvania where she had sold pretty fancy work and infant's clothes." In 1876 the name was changed to Mary, which was the name by which Martha was also known. But later, by her own request, be it Mary or Martha, the name was changed back to Bazaar. On the station the name is spelled Bazar, but a block away, the post office spelled it Bazaar.[30] The name has an Arabic origin and refers to a covered market.

Three times the name of Elizabethtown has been given to Kansas communities. When road commissioners were planning a town in Johnson County, they found that every name they proposed for the place had already been used elsewhere. Stumped for a new name, they readily accepted the suggestion of their hostess, Elizabeth Cook, that they use her first name. So they named it Elizabethtown. Isaac Moffatt, who spent a night at Elizabeth Cook's place, made the comment that "Our host,—and hostess fill their pipes, immediately after supper, and join in the conversation of the evening."[31] After its post office was closed in 1883, Elizabethtown, named for the pipe-smoking Yankee woman, lasted another sixteen years.[32]

Elizabethtown in Anderson County was named for Elizabeth Baldwin, daughter of the Rev. David Baldwin. The public called it "Liztown."[33] Elizabethtown in Gove County was near the town of Campus which evidently replaced it. Elizabeth in Marshall County and Elizabeth in Wallace County were both of short duration.

Margaret, the wife of Colonel Sam Wood, participated in the promotion of Cottonwood Falls and it is believed that the town of Margaretta in Chase County was named for her. Lincoln County also had a town named Margaret. Elinor in Chase County was named for Ellinor Hargrove Martin. Mrs. Charles R. Young, a relative of Ellinor's who once lived there, said that no one knows who knocked the "l" out of Ellinor.[34]

When C. N. James moved from Missouri to Kansas, he is reported to have had only ten cents in his pocket. He maintained financial solvency by teaching school for five dollars a month. He gave up this pauper's profession and established a trading post above the junction of the Whitewater and Walnut in Butler County. Twice the place had been the site for ephemeral towns, Fontanella and Arizonia. They were located on Osage land and were discontinued in 1859. When James established his trading post, he also became postmaster. He named his town Augusta for Augusta C. Boynton, the Wisconsin girl he married.[35]

Delia and Calista were named for wives. Delia, a station on the branch line of the Union Pacific in Jackson County, was named for Mrs. Delia Cunningham.[36] A large ranch was owned by a man named Bennet in Kingman County, and on this ranch he built a town he named Calista for his wife.[37]

A pioneer in Rice County named the town of Laura for his wife, Laura McLain. It was found that Laura was occasionally confused with Larned, indicative of poor handwriting, and so the name was changed to Windom.[38]

Jonah F. Colburn, who came to Kansas from Illinois, built the first cabin on a site which was to become Iola in Allen County. A special meeting was called to name the new town. Someone suggested Caledonia, but this was rejected. Then Colburn proposed the name of Elgin for his home town in Illinois. Attractive though they be, it was said that these names did not "catch the ear." The first white woman in the community was Iola Colburn, Jonah's wife. Her name was proposed and accepted unanimously. Iola is of Greek origin, but Mrs. Colburn was given this name for a great aunt who was French.[39] The name was accepted in Colorado because it had "a pretty sound." By winning the county seat contest, Iola destroyed a town with the unusual and distinctive Indian name of Cofachique.

According to legend and the *Kansas Guide*, Leoti was the name of an attractive white girl who had been captured and adopted by an Indian chief. It was said to mean "prairie flower."[40] However, Daniel C. Brandner of the community said that Leoti was named for Mrs. Henry Kebbe. After a conflict with the town of Coronado, the town named Leoti won the county seat, but the name was discontinued for a time because it was too much like Leota of Norton County. For a year it was called Bonasa, but when the Leota post office in Norton County was closed, Congressman Peters requested the restoration of its original name, and in 1887 it became Leoti again.[41]

Governor Samuel J. Crawford was the treasurer of the town company which named Florence in Marion County for his daughter. Florence Crawford married Arthur Capper, who also became the governor of Kansas, so Florence was the daughter of one governor and the wife of another.[42] Florence was the name of the French form of a famous city in northern Italy, interpreted to mean "city of flowers."[43]

The name was so popular in Kansas that two other towns were temporarily named Florence. The one in Allen County lost its post office to Carlyle. Neosho Rapids in Lyon County was called both Florence and Italia. That it was named Florence for the daughter of John Van Gundy has been denied by Van Gundy himself. His daughter was named Sarah Elizabeth, not Florence. Van Gundy seems to have preferred naming the town Florence to either Italia or Neosho Rapids. "I don't know," he said, "who the meddlesome fool was that suggested the change in name."[44]

Many of the daughters for whom towns were named were not personally well known and generally left little information about their names. Daughters' names were expressions of family feelings rather than community interests. A twentieth-century town west of Dighton was named Ellen for Ellen Patterson, the wife of a pioneer. Since there was already an Ellen post office in Osage County, its name was changed to Amy for the daughter of J. R. Brunner, who had once owned the townsite.[45]

The first child born in a new community was occasionally given special recognition. In Doniphan County the first child to be born in a new town was Leona Shock. The town company showed its appreciation by naming their town Leona. The fact that her father, J. W. Shock, was president of the town company could have influenced the choice. Leona later became Mrs. John Miller of Hiawatha.[46] When Layton

White of Barber County got news of the birth of a daughter who was given the name of Isabel, the town he was surveying was consequently named Isabel.[47] Abbeyville in Reno County was named for Abbey McLean, the first child born there.

While on the subject of baby names, one may also consider the folk-lore about a town which got its name from baby talk. In Gray County an attractive girl by the name of Willie Roberta Edwards had some speech difficulty. She pronounced "yes" as if it were "hess." Haskins, a town promoter, called her his "chum" and spoke of her as "Little Miss Hess." To honor her, it is said, the Hess City Town Company named their town Hess. There are still two townships bearing this name, East Hess and West Hess.[48] This is such a familiar German name, however, that a German source would seem more logical. Hesston, for example, was named for Abraham Hess.

Considerable confusion developed around the name of Edna in Labette County. Three families had daughters named Edna in the county, and who would dare say that one Edna was a more deserving source than another? The William Prouty family claimed the honor for their two-year-old daughter, Edna. Later a claim was made for "Little Edna Brink."[49] The daughter of the postmaster, "Little Edna Gregory," would be as logical a candidate for the naming of the town as any other Edna.[50] O'Connell of Oswego accepted Edna Prouty as the source. To avoid duplication, the town named Edna in Shawnee County was later changed to Rossville.

Giving the name of Pearl to a child is a way of expressing a senti-mental feeling for something precious. Pearl Atkinson came to Meade County with a group of Zanesville, Ohio, settlers. She was known as "the fairest and brightest of our jewels." Pearl was not only fair but also frail, and she did not long survive. Her memory was preserved for a short time by the name of the Meade County town of Pearlette, a name recommended by J. T. Copeland.[51] Once there was a Pearl City in Stevens County and there had been a Pearl in Elk County. There still is a Pearl in Dickinson County, named for the youngest daughter of John Taylor who settled on Logan Ridge in 1872.[52]

Mr. C. S. Smith was a tinsmith in Osage County, thus living up to his name. He started a tinshop and Mrs. Smith ran the restaurant. The town company was having a meeting when it was announced that a baby girl had been born to the Smith family. The members were "greatly excited" over the news. The business of the meeting was side-tracked and the town company offered a town lot to the baby for the privilege of naming her. The Smiths accepted, and the town company named the baby "Lyndon" and gave the baby's name to the town.[53]

Others have said, however, that the town was named for Lyndon, Vermont.[54]

When J. W. Wagner, president of a cement company, promoted a town in Allen County, he named it Mildred for his daughter. Mildred is a station on the Katy in the northeastern corner of the county.[55]

Both Mount Helen and Mount Ida were named for daughters. Colonel C. D. Perry named a hill in Clark County for his daughter Helen, enlarging the hill, however, to a mount and making the name Mount Helen.[56] When the E. J. Broomhall family of Anderson County named their town Oneida, there were already two other Oneidas in Kansas. The railroad renamed the place Mount Ida, now Mont Ida, for one of Broomhall's daughters.[57] For a decade, Republic County had an Ida, named for Ida Williams, the daughter of a pioneer.[58]

Several stories have been told about the naming of Lenora in Norton County. Lenora was partially an outgrowth of its merging with Spring City, located about two miles farther west. According to one source, it was named Lenora for the "first little white girl born here." Another said that it was named for the only white woman living on the Solomon west of Kirwin. To add to the confusion, another said that it was named for Lenora Harrison; and still another said that it was for Lenora Hanson, a relative of one of the members of the original town company. The Post Office Department is supposed to have arbitrarily changed the name of the town from Spring City to Lenora. Among all these possibilities, the most likely source for the name was Lenora Hanson.[59]

A different relationship may be illustrated by the name of Mayfield in Sumner County. While the townsite was still a field with wild flowers, the niece of George Hutchison, who owned the townsite, was fond of roaming the country. Her name was May, and before there was a town, the prairies she loved were referred to as "May's field." It was a simple matter to combine this into a name for the town and call it Mayfield. There was, however, a pioneer in Kansas with the surname of Mayfield.[60] Mayetta was a combination of the two names of one person, Mary Henrietta, daughter of the man who established the town.[61]

Anness was a name which replaced Kalamazoo in Sedgwick County. It was made by adding the initial to the given name of Anne S. Wilson and doubling it for pronunciation. Mrs. Wilson was the wife of the New Yorker who owned the land. The Anness station on the Santa Fe has been brought to Wichita as a part of the restored "Cowtown."[62]

Ludell in Rawlins County is a coined name which was changed by the Post Office Department which had rejected the name of Louella. Adding "dell" to "Lu" was seemingly acceptable. It has been said that

Louella was the daughter of William H. Dimick, founder of the town and "first postmaster." This seems to be in error, since the first postmaster was George T. Williams. Another has suggested that Virgil Dimick named the post office for Louella Goodin.[63] She was, of course, somebody's daughter, and her lovely name of Louella became Ludell for a girl named "Lou." Ludell replaced three worthy names: Prag, Kelso, and Danube.

Annelly, Idana, and Minneola were coined names. Annelly in Harvey County was named for Anne and Nelly Bly.[64] Idana in Clay County was named for Ida Howland and Anna Broughton, the wives of the men who promoted the town. The Clark County town of Minneola was named for Mrs. Minnie Davis and Mrs. Ola Watson.[65]

Many a lonely pioneer on the Great Plains carried the name of his lady-love in his heart and perpetuated it by naming a town or post office in her memory. Some ladies had been loved but lost and others loved and left. Some of the romances had flourished and died, as did some of the names they had memorialized. Early maps of Kansas are dotted with girl's names, names which were once significant in the lives of individual Kansans but whose origin may be forgotten. The romance of others may still be recalled.

One of the early railway stations in Doniphan County was named Albers for John Albers, described as "a worthy pioneer" who owned the townsite. When the Post Office Department rejected the name, the local telegraph operator was "permitted to immortalize the name of his sweetheart by having the town and post office named for her." The lady's name was Bendena, described as "a beautiful name, full of sweet vowels, it was well received, and the operator ascended to the top notch of mundane bliss." Such can be the sentimental association with a name. Then, sad to say, "the romance did not end romantically, for the agent married another woman." The town was for a time known by two names, but the other name was not the name of the other woman; it was the old rejected name of Albers Station. Finally Bendena won, now a memorial to a romance that flourished and failed.[66]

A man by the name of Allen is reported to have wandered over the vast plains of Kansas because he had lost the love of a girl named Lura. Even though she had been unfaithful in love, Allen preserved her memory as the name of a town in Russell County. Since it could not have been a pleasant memory, it might better have been erased; instead, it was modified and camouflaged. John Fritts, the postmaster, changed Lura to Luray.[67] The new name was already a well-known name in Virginia.

Between Diamond Springs and Lost Springs on the Santa Fe Trail is a town named Burdick. It had been named Linsdale but was renamed Burdick for the sweetheart of a Santa Fe official.[68]

Thomas Hoops and R. A. Van Winkle established a sawmill in Atchison County which became the nucleus for a town in 1858. Mr. Hoops named the town Arrington in honor of Miss Arrington, a friend, who lived in California. That she was "perhaps his betrothed" was qualified by " I think," in the words of Mary S. Van Winkle, who gave this information to George Remsburg.[69] One author said that Hoops' name was Hooper. Since Mary Van Winkle had the same family name as R. A. Van Winkle, the postmaster, her connection would give merit to her opinion.[70] The name was first spelled Arington and then changed to Arrington.

Several towns were named for women who owned the land for a townsite, women who served as postmistresses, and for women who had other qualifications worthy of recognition. A county historian gave this simple explanation for the naming of Wilsonton in Labette County: "Mrs. Elsa B. Wilson is the proprietor of the town."[71] At the other end of the state, Wilburton in Morton County, at first called Tice, was renamed Wilburton for Mrs. Nellie D. Wilbur, the postmistress, who was admired for her civic service in the community.[72]

Other places named for women postmistresses were Heisler, for Mrs. Nancy Heisler in Phillips County; Densmore, for Elizabeth E. Densmore in Norton County; Fox, for Sue Fox in Kingman County; and Dalrymple in Mitchell County, for Mrs. Adelaide Dalrymple. It is believed that Youngsville in Greeley County was named for Emma C. Young. Wagnerville, a temporary post office in Phillips County, was given its name for Isabel Wagner, postmistress.[73] Latitia in Thomas County was named for Latitia Reed, postmistress.

Three different forms of the same name were used for a town in Wilson County, where Margaret L. Jasper was the postmistress. It was Buffton for a day, then it was Buffington for a week, and finally it settled for Buffville. Should one suggest that the postmistress could not make up her mind?

Haviland in Kiowa County was named for Laura S. Haviland, referred to as "a Michigan Quaker woman."[74] She was born in Canada, married in New York, and lived and worked in Adrian, Michigan. She was a philanthropist, humanitarian, abolitionist, and prohibitionist. Before the Civil War, she was interested in helping slaves to escape to freedom; during the war, she promoted hospitals for soldiers; after the war, she was interested in the education of orphans.[75] Both she and Mrs. Comstock, another crusader, came to Kansas to help the Negroes.[76] The naming of Haviland was suggested by her friends in Indiana,

474

although it is also said that the name was proposed by someone who read a book about her.[77]

The three names of Victoria Claflin Woodhull have all been used as Kansas place-names. As Victoria in Kansas honors the British Queen, one may assume that Victoria Claflin got her name from the same respectable source. But she was no Victorian in a Victorian age. Claflin was the name of her family, which was not noted for respectability, nor was it the source for the name of Claflin in Kansas.

The Claflin girls grew up in the latter half of the nineteenth century to challenge the sanctimonious pretense of men and their double standard of morality. Victoria married a Dr. Woodhull before she was sixteen and concluded that the double standard was not to be a special privilege of men. She later left Woodhull for a more attractive male. She lectured forcefully and effectively on women's rights and carried her crusade into print by publishing the *Woodhull and Claflin's Weekly*. Having a cause, she ran for the presidency on a branch of the People's party in 1872. Commodore Vanderbilt found her charming; Susan B. Anthony and Elizabeth Cady Stanton found her useful; Senator Pomeroy knew her; Harriet and Catherine Beecher, sisters of Henry Ward Beecher, wished to drive her out of New York. She did leave New York, but it was to upgrade her marriages; this time she married a successful English banker. Her critics, and they were numerous, called her "wicked Woodhull." Taking advantage of her reputation, the author of one biography of Woodhull gave it the scurrilous title of *Mrs. Satan*.[78] She was also described as "mad and magnificent." The reason given for the naming of Woodhull in Chase County was that Victoria Woodhull once put Kansas on her itinerary. Woodhull served as a post office for ten years, 1872–82. The name was preserved on the Woodhull School District.[79]

Medora is an attractive name but was not listed by Lippincott in 1853. There is, however, a Medora in the Theodore Roosevelt country of western North Dakota. There it was named for the wife of Marquis de Morès, a Frenchman who came to New York and became interested in promoting the beef business in the western ranch country. Medora was also the name of the wife of Conrad, "The Corsair," in the story written by Lord Byron. It is possible that the former Medora in Barber County and the Medora in Reno County came from the one in Indiana, but, as a woman's name, it has a special interest, whether its origin be of fiction or fact.[80]

A branch of Independence Creek, named by Lewis and Clark, is called Girls Creek. The reason for this, said one writer, concerned "there having been born so many members of the female sex in that locality." Girls Creek was the east fork, so the west fork, in order to be different, was named "Boys Creek." During the skating season, the girls went skating on Girls Creek and the boys skated on Boys Creek, but the two must have skated downstream, since they met at the junction.[81]

With the scarcity of women on the frontier and the economic and social necessity of having a wife, there was little likelihood of a woman's becoming an "old maid," a term then applied to single women over twenty-five. Yet, with the scarcity of women in this category, a stream flowing into the Walnut in Rush County was known as the "Old Maid's Fork," and one of those natural limestone sinks near Sharon Springs was called "Old Maid's Pool."

There was a greater likelihood that places would be named for bachelors. A post office was named Bachelor in McPherson County. On a stream in Labette County lived James H. Fleming, who, unlike some of his neighbors and though no white woman was available, refused to marry an Osage woman. The stream was named Bachelor Creek. Next to Fleming's name on a census report was the notation, "Wants a wife."[82] As a transition from the topic of place-names for women, and without any invidious intent, we may point out that the town named Utopia in Greenwood County is in Bachelor Township.

Incidents, even concerning unidentified women, could also contribute to place-names. Because of legend and conflicting accounts, it has been difficult to distinguish White Woman's Creek from Punished Woman's Creek. Four changes in name have added to the confusion of the latter. White Woman's Creek is located south of Scott City and has the reputation of being the only stream to end in Kansas. It disappears in a sandy sink which has been called White Woman Basin.

The white man's legend tells of a young man who had to cross this stream in order to visit the woman he loved. The creek was shallow and easily crossed, but one night there was a flood and the man drowned. His sweetheart searched for him and found his body washed up on the bank of the creek. Despondent, she threw herself into the creek and drowned also. The stream became known as White Woman's Creek.[83]

According to a story told by a couple of bone-pickers, Punished Woman's Creek got its name when a white woman was captured by Indians and the chief forced her to become "one of his wives." To them a child was born and the chief rejoiced; but when the child died, he accused the mother of having caused its death. The chief punished her so severely that she died. So the place became known as Punished Woman's Creek. Hunters are supposed to have changed this to "White Woman's Creek," thereby confusing the two.[84]

Robert A. Wright, a pioneer from western Kansas, gave another version of the origin of Punished Woman's Creek. Indians, he said, captured a government ambulance and killed all the men but saved the lone woman as a captive. To end her suffering, she hanged herself to a tree on the banks of a little stream. This creek the Indians named White Woman, a name it bears today.[85] One would assume that this referred to the White Woman's Creek south of Scott City except for the writer's statement that it was on this creek that Major Lewis was killed by the Cheyennes. That would be on the Punished Woman's Fork or Beaver Creek.[86]

This is something like the story carried by a Scott City café menu as a temporary pastime for impatient tourists anxious to "gulp, get up, and go!" The story concerns the northward trek of Dull Knife and his Cheyennes. They captured an army wagon, killed the escort, and then captured the young wife of an army officer. She escaped by moonlight, and all the pursuers could see was a "wraith-like" figure in a "swirling mist." She was never again seen alive, but her ghost, they say, may still be seen on a moonlight night. This was also said to be the origin of the name for White Woman's Creek.

Punished Woman's Fork was used interchangeably with Famished Woman's Fork. Then it became known as Beaver Creek.[87] When some pioneers found a ladder along the stream, a most puzzling discovery, they referred to the stream as Ladder Creek. The name became popular and official. Referring to the pursuit of Dull Knife north of Scott City, one writer identified the stream as "Punished Woman's Fork or Famished Woman's Fork, later known as Ladder or Beaver Creek."[88] So, in the case of White Woman's Creek, the creek disappears; and in the case of Punished Woman's Creek, the name disappears.

The Whitewater River which flows toward the Walnut in Butler County has now a name which is popular and descriptive. It seems to imply that the river was named for the milky color of its water which is caused by the lightly colored limestone over which it flows. According to legend, the Whitewater was once called the White Woman River, having been given this name after Indians had slain a white woman and thrown her into the river.[89] Some have taken the crime out of the story and have said that the woman accidentally fell into the river, raising that age-old question: "Was she pushed or did she stumble?" The change of name to Whitewater River has drawn a veil over the crimes of the past and left us a descriptive name which is pleasant and so popular that a town on the west branch of the river has taken the name of Whitewater.

In the account on Indian names we should include two other names which made some reference to women. Big Woman Creek in Leavenworth County was named, not for a woman, but for a Delaware chief.[90] Stranger's Wife Creek which flows into Big Woman Creek has eliminated the "Wife" to become only Stranger's Creek. The name was said to be the translation of its Indian name of Okeetsha, "stranger," or "wandering aimlessly about."[91]

Such names as Quindaro, Eudora, Lenexa, Juniata, Waunita, and Winona show that the names of Indian women, too, were adopted for Kansas place-names.

CHAPTER XLII

ELLIS ELLSWORTH ELMDALE ELMO ELSMORE ELWOOD ELYRIA EMMETT EMPORIA ENGLEWOOD

POTPOURRI

ERPRISE ERIE ESBON ESKRIDGE EUDORA EUREKA EVEREST FAIRVIEW FALL RIVER FLORENCE FOI

KANSAS HAS A WIDE RANGE of nomenclature with sources from all over the world, and Kansans, like the people of Kentucky and Tennessee, had a number of folksy names. One need only consult the maps of the last half of the nineteenth century or Baughman's book on *Kansas Post Offices* for examples of unusual or whimsical names. Even Example was twice used as a place-name in Haskell County. Many a place-name was chosen for its sentimental association. Some names were modifications of words or names, some were combinations, others were chosen on the spur of the moment and based on a suggestion or a situation.

Although most names on the land appear to be commonplace, there were those who made an effort to adopt a name of distinction, a name that was different or pertinent. When a town in Missouri wanted a name that was "peculiar" to its community, the Post Office Department responded favorably and named it Peculiar.

Most of these unusual names have disappeared with the closing of the post offices. Many were chosen in a haphazard manner, including the town named Haphazard in Dickinson County. By contrast, Stafford County had a place named Tidy.

Some promoters were slaves to the conventional and familiar names, but others showed remarkable ingenuity and originality in making names. Starting properly with the young, there was a place named Rock-a-By with the "baby" omitted. Its post office name was Strawn, but its popular name was Rock-a-By.[1] Later, all but the Rock was deleted. A town in Montgomery County seemed modestly to acknowledge its inexperience by accepting the name of Tyro, which means "novice." It had first been named Fawn, but when it took the name of Tyro, it had a name so unusual that Lippincott in 1866 listed no other such name in the whole world. Young America on One Hundred and Ten Creek in Osage County could be a most appropriate name even though Mr. Little, one of its promoters, was over sixty. The town company had fifty-three members, but the town died young.[2]

One may think of novelty as a word that refers to something new or novel. That Novelty should be the name of a town may seem novel, but there it was, a post office in Montgomery County. It was, however, only of short duration, from May to June in 1881, and when the novelty wore off, the town of Novelty disappeared.

Faith, hope, and charity go together, but only Hope and Charity have been Kansas place-names. Charity in Clay County disappeared from the modern Kansas map, but Hope in Dickinson County may still be found on the map. One need not conclude that Kansans have neither faith nor charity. Hope has won new fame as the Kansas home of the Eisenhower family.

There were various ways in which the name of Hope could be used. In Jewell County it was given a sense of direction by being called Westhope. Mount Hope was a name borrowed from Michigan as was also Hope. Hopefield in Labette County was a Presbyterian mission where the building of a school by Dr. Requa was said to be "a project based on hope."[3] But hope must have diminished when the mission was destroyed by a flood on the Neosho in 1826.[4] Not far from Hope in Dickinson County was the post office and church named Good Hope. The Oneida community in Neosho County gave itself the name of Esperanza, the Spanish name for "hope." Its newspaper title was *The Star of Hope*.[5]

Dickinson County, which had so many sentimental names, had a township named Noble, and so did Ellsworth, Marshall, and Norton counties. Leon in Butler County was to be named Noble, but the name was already in use.[6] There is now a station named Noble north of Lyons in Rice County. One might suggest that it was noble to be loyal. One may not think of these words as place-names but they are. In Garfield County, now Finney, a place was named Pattonville for S. Van Patten, the postmaster. The next postmaster changed it to Pansy, and not much later, it was named Loyal.[7]

While in Osage County, James R. Mead said that he had traveled on the Topeka Trail through "Superior, J. M. Winchell's offspring."[8] The place had been called Frémont, then changed to Superior by its New York settlers. Like Burlington, its neighbor, it had been crippled by a tornado, and Superior "never recovered from its blow," said the *People's Herald* of Lynden,[9] probably with an intentional pun.

When an Atchison County community showed its religious spirit by starting a Sunday school, Miss Hattie Dorman was so impressed that she had its post office named Good Intent. With an interest in brevity, it was changed to Goodintent.[10] Pennsylvania is the only other state to have such a name. Atchison County had a place named Good Will. The post office named Free Will in Osborne County implied a greater

480

risk and less responsibility than the Good Will of Atchison County. Freedom was adopted as a name for five townships. In explaining the reason for naming Freedom Township in Bourbon County it was said that there was no particular appeal "except it caught the fancy of the commissioners when they organized it."[11] The post office named Freedom in Butler County did not survive beyond the turn of the century.

Nonpareil is a French word that is generally used to indicate something "unequalled in excellence," or even "nonesuch." This is not unlike Superior. In Reno County, Kansas, a place named Idaville had its name changed to Nonpareil, but perhaps it could not live up to its ambition of being "unequalled." When spelled "Nonpariel" it must have followed frontier phonetics.[12]

One's ego may be associated with pride and a desire for eminence and fame. Ego, Pride, Eminence, and Fame were all Kansas place-names. Ego was a post office in Gray County. Barton County had a Pride. Eminence could, of course, be a geographical term. It was so popular that it was adopted as the name for three post offices. The first Eminence was in Sumner County where it lasted only a few months, contrary to the expectations of those who named the place. Eminence in Smith County lasted a few years. In Finney County, Eminence, which had first been named Creola and then Cuyler, outlasted all of its immediate neighbors, but nothing remains to support its name except longevity. Fame was the name of a post office in Greenwood County. After its post office was closed in 1920 there was nothing more to give it fame and Fame in the Flint Hills faded into oblivion.

The town named Eureka in Greenwood County would indicate that the pioneers had found a Utopia. Not far from Fame was a place named Utopia, that dreamland of perfect contentment depicted by Thomas More's *Utopia*. Fame, Eureka, and Utopia are indicative of the optimism of the pioneers.

There were a number of places in Kansas with names of a romantic aura, such as Romance, Rapture, Desire, Love, Purity, Fidelity, Trust, and Constant. Reno County had a place named Purity and another named Desire. Love was a place of short duration in Miami County. Amo, the Latin for "I love," was also in Miami County. Rapture was a place in Jewell County and Romance was found in Johnson County. Fidelity in Nemaha County lasted twelve years while Amo lasted only two. For a few months there was a Trust in Osage County. Constant in Cowley County had its name changed to Hackney, possibly named for W. P. Hackney, a member of the state legislature.[13]

Jewell County had a town named Amity and Cherokee County had a place named Friendship, both expressing similar feelings. The town named Friend in Finney County was, however, named for a railroad promoter.[14] Neighborville in Norton County was named by Abraham Bieber, its first postmaster.[15]

Kansas had a Concord in Sumner County, Discord in Brown County, a Concordia in Cloud County, and a Bon Accord in Dickinson County. The town of Concordia should have been named "Discordia" according to the *Kansas City Star*. There had been a bitter fight between two rival town companies, one of them at Townsend's Point which became Clyde, and the other at the present site of Concordia, then known as "Hagaman's Town," for its founder. After the final compromise, H. C. Snyder, one of the officials, is supposed to have said: "In view of the Harmony and unanimity prevailing here, I name this future city Concordia."[16] But it has also been suggested that Judge Sturgis named it for his home town in Missouri.[17] The suggestion that it should have been named Discordia seems to be ridiculous until one discovers the name of Discord on the Brown County map. Discord lasted seven years before being changed to Comet.[18] Sumner County had a Concord for over two decades, probably named for its Revolutionary War fame. Kansas was not alone to adopt such names. When a town in New York requested the name of "Discord," the Post Office Department with paternalistic solicitude, named it Concord.

With the same meaning as Concordia, Dickinson County named one of its towns Bon Accord, also written "Bonaccord." This was the name of a community southwest of Abilene which is preserved only by a home demonstration unit.[19] Similar to Bonaccord was the name of Harmony given to a Neosho County Mission. As with Concordia, it was in a way a misnomer. The missionary in charge, Rev. Benton Pixley, quarreled with the Indian agent at St. Louis and with General Atkinson, after which even the Osages asked him to leave. Harmony was a name later revived for a post office in Pawnee County.[20]

Among the many moods expressed in the Kansas place-names was Happy, the name of a town in Graham County. Happy Township is still there. Its first name was Happy Hollow and its postmaster's name was Crank. The Joy in Osborne County was not an expression of joy; it was named for John Joy, an Ohio man who lived on Joy Creek.[21] There is now a Joy on the Rock Island west of Greensburg.

In contrast to Happy Hollow was Hungry Hollow, the name of a stage station in Anderson County.[22] Hunger could probably have been alleviated at Dinner Creek in Coffey County.[23] From the phonetics of the Coffey County name, one might have assumed that it referred to coffee rather than to a man. Then there was the cavalryman who said that after riding fifty miles, he had camped on a branch of "Supper Creek." He must have been influenced by phonetics or hunger when he changed the name of Sappa Creek to "Supper Creek."[24] One may extend the association with food by listing the name of Sauce in Ness County. The names of game animals in Kansas would indicate what one might expect for dinner, seasoned with the numerous names for salt.

Whisky became a place-name for creeks but never for a post office in Kansas, although we may recall that Riley City was also known as Whiskey Point. The word came from the old Gaelic as *wisgebeatha*, "water of life." To the Indians it also meant death. In Atchison County, Whiskey Creek got its "barley-cornic" name, said Remsburg, from a distillery on its banks. It had been known as Alcorn Creek for J. Alcorn and had nothing to do with corn whisky.[25] There was a Whiskey Lake on the Mormon Trail. For this name we cannot blame the Mormons, since they do not even drink coffee. Brewery Creek in Atchison County must have been associated with the same business. A branch of the Pawnee "now rejoices in the name of Guzzler's Gulch" in Ness County, but it does not identify the liquid guzzled.[26]

Riley County also had a place with the unusual name of Alembic. This means a cap of a still, without reference to what might be distilled. But the name was changed to the less disturbing name of Leonardville, "village of the lion heart."

The name for Buttermilk Creek, which flows into Soldier Creek in Leavenworth County, may have been descriptive of its appearance. There was another in western Kansas near Aubrey's Cut-off. The one located south of Coldwater in Comanche County must have had its name changed, since the town named Buttermilk now located there is on Salt Creek.[27]

The use of the term "vegetarian" goes back only to 1842, but among the vegetarians were Socrates and Plato, Saint Francis of Assisi, George Bernard Shaw, and John D. Rockefeller. In Middletown, Connecticut, the vegetarians coined the name of Vegetonia or Vegetaria for their place-name.[28] One of the promoters of the vegetarian colony in Kansas was Henry S. Clubb, an Englishman, who has been identified as "a reporter by trade, a promoter by disposition and an enthusiastic disciple of vegetarianism by conviction and inspiration." In Kansas, the vegetarians would gather in colonies, "away from the contamination of flesh, alcohol, and social vices." One of their towns was planned by the Octagon Settlement Company. There were to be Octagon units of four square miles centering in a town to be called Octagon City. The colony did not flourish. Its utopian dream was wrecked by a harsh, flesh-eating frontier.[29] Its name of Octagon City was changed to Neosho City, but Vegetarian Creek kept its name.

Anatomy Hill, mentioned earlier, was so named because many of its settlers had names which represented parts of the human body. One of Father Dumortier's Irish congregations north of Fort Riley was named Elbow. The Germans called it "Devil's Elbow." Smith County contributed to the anatomy by naming a town Plexus. This may refer to any intertwining network, but refers especially to interlacing blood vessels. When a trapper in Bourbon County was "disabled and delayed by a bunion on his foot," the creek where he stayed was named Bunion Creek.[30] Jackson County contributed a pleasant tone to a place called Tickle Hill.[31] With its springs of curing waters, people came to Kansas for their health. The town in Shawnee County named Hygienic must have had some propaganda value. Richard Dighton came to Kansas for his wife's health. He was a surveyor by profession, and for him, Dighton in Ness County was named.

Rooks, Cloud, and Geary counties have all had towns named Welcome. The Welcome in Rooks County disappeared in 1883, and in the same year, Cloud County got the spirit and named a town Welcome. Two years after its demise, another Welcome was named in Geary County. This one lasted until 1902. Mr. Risely of Stockton suggested that Welcome in Rooks County was "a bit of satire" in an area which was dangerous for snoopers in the days of "strayed cattle and liberated horses."[32] Welcome was not far from Robbers Roost Creek. The stealing of livestock in western Kansas was a lucrative but dangerous occupation during and after the Civil War. Doc Middleton's band of outlaws established one of their exchange centers and hideouts in Rooks County. There a woman in 1871 found her stolen horses tied to a tree, and there a stream is named Robbers Roost Creek. The name was also transferred to Robbers Roost schoolhouse.[33]

In spite of hardships, Kansas pioneers tried to create the impression that Kansas was a pleasant place in which to live. Pleasant was used as a part of a place-name to describe a Dale and a Valley, a Hill and a Ridge, a Spring and a Run, a Green and a Grove, and also a View.

Even the very air received recognition. Lyon County had a post office named Air in 1880. It was discontinued for a week in 1888 and then was reopened. Graham County improved on the name by naming a place Bonair, "good air." The name was French, but in this age of air pollution, Bonair sounds good in any language, as does also Aroma, if one may associate it with Fragrant Hill. When Dickinson County got a post office which had been named Far West in Morris County, it changed the name to Aroma.[34] The name was characterized as "a sweet sounding name."[35] Aroma is in the southern part of the county and the northern part has a township named Fragrant Hill.

In the shimmering light, the Kansas scene frequently produced a mirage with shining lakes, cities, and forests. A place was named Mirage in Rawlins County. As a mirage has a way of losing its reality, so did the town named Mirage. It served as a post office for a decade, and then, like a mirage, it disappeared.

A mirage is as real as an echo, but neither has any solid substance, one deceiving the sight by its vagaries of light and air, the other, by a recurrent sound wave which is but a diminishing repetition of an original sound. An echo is best heard in the mountains, for there the sounds bounce back to the delight of those who enjoy hearing their own voices repeated. There is both an Echo Canyon and an Echo Peak among American place-names. In Kansas, devoid of deep canyons and lofty peaks, there was nevertheless an Echo in Douglas County. Quite fittingly, the Echo post office name was repeated three times, 1874, 1878, and 1894, before it died in 1900.

People react differently to the sound of names. One name was described as a "cute" name. Kansas could improve that only by naming a town Cuter! This name in Barber County gave it no lasting distinction.[36] One may be tempted to question the fact about a name like Cuter until one discovers names like Fact itself.

Only in folklore or legend may one find the explanation for names like Fact. The name seemingly came from a spontaneous suggestion, as is often the case of rare and uncommon names. When it was said in a meeting that the community was in need of a post office, the question was raised: "Is that a fact?" The citizens insisted that it was a "fact," and then someone asked: "Why not call it Fact?" They agreed, and it became a Fact,[37] and it remained a Fact for twenty years. There may be some facts missing from the folklore since the place had earlier been named Carter Creek.[38]

It is easy to move from Fact to Fancy, and each may be challenged for the lack of proof. Wichita County actually had a place named Proof, without information about what it was supposed to prove. Proof was not lasting, and in 1894, it was closed.

The Randolph family which left its name for a town in Riley County was also credited with the naming of Fancy Creek. When looking at its "picturesque panorama," one could well recognize that it was given "a singularly appropriate name."[39] A township was also named Fancy Creek. Since May Day is on Fancy Creek, it may be mentioned that

A. S. Edgerton, the postmaster, in search of a name to replace Stanton, decided in May to name it May Day, and this also became the name of the township.[40]

Riley County also had a town named Lasita. The name supposedly evolved from an exclamation, "What a site," and eventually became Lasita.[41]

A mystic was originally one that was associated with religious rites of the ancient mysteries. It is a rare place-name, yet Mystic was the name of a post office in Sheridan County. There is an explanation for the town named Mystic near Hill City in South Dakota. There a worker on the Burlington road called attention to a mistake by writing the word "mystic" for mistake, which was a serious mistake in spelling. But the mistake was perpetuated when the misspelled word became the name of the town. Regrettably, no such delightful explanation has been encountered for Mystic in Kansas. So it remains with the mysteries as it started.

In McPherson County, neighbors gathered around a pot-bellied stove in a country store waiting for the mail and groping for a name for their post office. If the cuspidors were out of reach, and that would be a considerable distance, it was quite common practice to open the stove door and expectorate into the fire. As Mr. Buckman did this, he slammed the stove door and noticed its trade name of Monitor. That, he said, should be the name of their post office, and Monitor it became.[42]

In Bourbon County, the people of Memphis wanted a new name. The name of Garland, from the Garland stove in the local depot, was accepted as being "unusual, short, and distinctive."[43]

Protection is the name of a town in Comanche County. Its meaning seems obvious. Yet five different reasons have been given to explain the source of this unusual place-name. It has been associated with the protective tariff which was reduced the year the town was founded. Since it was located at the forks of a stream, it was, according to the Indians, protected against tornadoes. This location would also protect it from prairie fires. The town would give the pioneers protection against the cattlemen and lawless cowboys who tried to drive out the farmers and nesters. The name is also said to have come from the "People's Grand Protective Union," a prohibition organization under Governor St. John. Finally, the town had two redoubts in the area and these would protect the people from Indian raids.[44] Any one of the five ways of protection could justify its name, but the last one appears to be as logical as any. Clark County has its Protection, but Shawnee County has Security, generally referred to as Security Spur.

Most of the names expressing feelings or emotions were on the optimistic side, but not all. Troublesome was first the name of a creek and then the name of a post office. Troublesome in Smith County was on a branch of East Beaver Creek but not far from Troublesome Creek which flows into White Rock Creek in Jewell County. It was also listed as "Smith (or Troublesome)." There was another Troublesome Creek in Coffey County.[45] Chavez, now Jarvis, Creek in Rice County was known as Difficult Creek.[46] Equally pertinent was the Indian name of Ni-hi-pa for a creek west of the Big Arkansas and near the Oklahoma border; it was an Osage word which meant "good-for-nothing creek."[47]

Hardscrabble is a name which is quite distinctive but not original in Kansas. Pennsylvania, Kentucky, and California have had places named Hardscrabble. California named its Hardscrabble Creek to describe the hardships in the mining camps.[48] Pratt County, Kansas, had a place named Hardscrabble, a name retained for a rural school. Mitchell County had a creek named Hardscrabble, also spelled Hard Scrabble. This name was used as a frontier name wherever the "scrabble for daily grub was hard."[49] Rush County had a place named Frugal.

The only distinction a name like Tailholt in Greenwood County had was that it was unconventional. Such names seem seldom to be lasting. Tailholt was unable to maintain its grip on its name; it was changed to Quincy, said to be the name of a pioneer.

Names were occasionally coined by combining parts of two names into one. This we have seen was done to make such names as Colwich, Palco, Osawatomie, and Elyria. Names along state borders have been made from combining state names like Texarkana for Texas and Arkansas, and Mexicali and Calexico for Mexico and California. The Kansas-Colorado border inspired such names as Kanorado. Since there were two places with this name, one became Kanado. By placing Colorado first, the name of Colokan was coined. Then a syllable was deleted and the name became Cokan Spur, and in speech the Spur has been dropped. Between Kolokan on the Rock Island and Cokan on the Missouri Pacific is a place named Weskan, known as "a windswept village" in western Kansas. The Kansas name was also combined with Wakarusa to make Kanwaka, once the name of a town in Douglas County and still the name of Kanwaka Township.

The names of Lane County and Ness County were combined to make La Ness, a name with a fine foreign look. Rockwell City in Norton County was named for Mrs. William Rockwell, a shrewd buyer of townsite land. When the Rockwell City moved to the county border, it was renamed Norcatur, a name coined from the combination of Norton and Decatur.[50]

Albert E. Warren and James F. Keeney came from Chicago to

487

participate in the boom of western Kansas. They bought a whole section of land from the Kansas and Pacific Railroad. The town they started near Trego was named Wa-Keeney to honor both Warren and Keeney.[51] The hyphen was later deleted but the capital "K" was retained even after it was combined into one word as WaKeeney. The capital "K" is gradually being belittled to a lower case. Keeney was a natural leader and elected captain of the Trego home guards during the Cheyenne raids under Dull Knife. But Warren was called the county's chief booster.[52]

A partial use of a name may be seen in the make-up of Walsburg, a station in Riley County. The town is on Walnut Creek, so the name was coined from "Wal," the first part of Walnut, and with "burg" as an appendage. An "s" was inserted to make the name "more euphonious."[53]

Like Elyria, the name of Gerlane in Barber County was made up from a husband and wife combination. M. J. Lane, who promoted the town, took the first syllable from Geraldine, his wife's name, added it to his own surname and coined the name of Gerlane.[54]

Ed Harris, a pioneer in Sherman County, honored his son without using his name by adding "son" to his own first name to make Edson.[55] Robert Wilson did better for his son Louis when he named Louisville in Pottawatomie County.[56]

After an argument between Woods, a groceryman, and a rival named Houston, over the naming of a town in Rooks County, they compromised by naming the place Woodston. With only the "ton" from Houston, one may question the comment that "everyone was satisfied."[57]

Likewise, Stanton in Miami County was supposedly named for Captain H. B. Standifer and Senator Thomas H. Benton.[58] But the commonplace "ton" at the end of Stanton gave no real recognition to Benton.

Like Wascott in Wisconsin, made from W. A. Scott, so Tescott in Ottawa County was coined by changing T. E. Scott to Tescott.[59] The town had been called Churchill for the New England mother of one of the town promoters. Scott, called a "progressive" farmer, rejected the proposal to rename the town Scottsville. Left equally vague was Collano in Meade County, believed to be a combination of Collingwood and Gano.

Names could also be coined by adding something descriptive to a name. A farmer near Belleville asked the railroad workers to name a town for his son. One of the railroaders asked the farmer to bring his son to the railroad camp. When he came, his face was covered with tallow and molasses, so the engineer suggested naming the town "Talmo"—and it stuck.[60]

At the junction of U.S. 50 and 75, the crossroad is known as Beto Junction from the initials of its four neighboring towns: Burlington, Emporia, Topeka, and Ottawa.[61] This makes an interesting acronym, but Beto is ignored by most map makers.

Niota in Chautauqua County was near the old site of Jay Hawk and Matanzas. It had the same name as Niota on the Mississippi in Illinois, but Niota was too easily mistaken for Neola, the name of a town in Labette County, so Niota was changed to Newport. But Newport, Kansas, was too much like Newport, Kentucky, when the state names were abbreviated as "Ks" and "Ky." So the confusion was perpetuated. The postmaster found a solution by restoring the name of Niota with the addition of "ze," coining the name of Niotaze. This did give it distinction.[62]

Goss in Harper County was named for Giles M. Goss, who brought an Iowa colony to the community. It was called the "Goss and Glenn colony." Its members also started the town of Harper. Goss was located on the big Goss ranch. The land was bought by Bill Barber, and his comment on the renaming of the place is at least original. "We shook the name of Goss," said he, "so we'll just call the new town Shook."[63]

The methods of choosing the names of Cawker City and Edmond were unique. Cawker and three companions, Huckell, Rice, and Kshinka, established a town, and each wanted his own name for the town. They then agreed to decide the choice by playing a game of poker— some say seven-up—and E. H. Cawker won. Later the town named Cawker added "City."[64]

Mr. Weaver, a merchant in Norton County, would have his place named Weaver, but there was already a Weaver in Kansas. Jack Edmond, described as a "smooth" and "fast-talking salesman," offered Weaver forty sacks of flour if he would name the town for him. The offer was accepted, and Edmond is now the name of the town.[65]

Having started a town in Morton County, the townspeople searched "the cyclopedias, lexicons, and dictionaries to find a name for the new town."[66] One may still wonder where they got the name of Taloga, an Indian name said to mean "Happy Hunting Ground." Residents of Taloga in Oklahoma say it means "beautiful valley."[67] In Kansas the post office was revived using its first name of Taloga, but it was spelled backward and became Agolat.

Punkin Center, which should have been Pumpkin Center for the purists, became Punkincenter. This is a neighborhood name which could be given humorously to any rural gathering place. It has the same connotation as Podunk.[68] As a name of a roadside station in Iowa, Podunk was given national publicity when the place was offered for sale. According to legend, the one in New York got its name from the sound of the water of Bolter Creek splashing over the waterwheel of a mill, "po-dunk, po-dunk, po-dunk." But it was commonly used as a name for a place of no distinction. In Ottawa County a bend in the Solomon River was called Podunk Bend, and when it was fortified after an Indian raid, it was named Fort Solomon but popularly known as "Fort Podunk."[69] Punkincenter is southeast of Hutchinson and no bigger than a Podunk.

Perhaps the craziest name of all was Loco, and that means "crazy" in Spanish. Loco was first a post office name in Haskell County and was sufficiently popular to be revived as a name in Seward County, where there was for a time a Loco Township. Boys herding cattle in this area frequently carried hoes to destroy the noxious locoweed, which was poisonous to stock.[70] This could have been the source for the name. In New Mexico the name was used with a qualifying adjective as Poco Loco, just a "little crazy." Loco was a term used lightly and need have no connection with the place south of Paola once called Asylum.[71]

Running the gamut of names in Kansas from A to Z, one could conclude with Zorro, a romantic name of a post office in Linn County. The name came from the title of Johnston McCulley's novel, *The Mark of Zorro*. The story dealt with a romantic Robin Hood who left his mark by cutting a "Z" on his rivals' foreheads. The story was a natural for the antics of Douglas Fairbanks in a movie.

But the alphabet is better completed with a name like Zyba. This was a coined word from the first two and last two letters of the alphabet, reversed to make Zyba.[72] So Zyba in Sumner County makes a fitting end to place-names in Kansas.

APPENDIX

Postmasters and pioneers for whom additional places were named.

Towns	County	Postmasters and Pioneers
Alexander	Rush	Alexander Harvey, postmaster
Allison	Decatur	Pioneer
Alloway	Sumner	G. A. Alloway, townsite owner
Arkalon	Seward	Arkalon Tenny, father of postmaster
Arnold	Ness	J. G. Arnold, elevator owner
Baker	Brown	C. D. Baker, pioneer
Barnesville	Bourbon	J. and F. Barnes, pioneers
Bartlett	Labette	Robert A. Bartlett, townsite owner
Basehor	Leavenworth	Ephraim and Ruben Basehor, pioneers
Beeler	Ness	Elmer E. Beeler, postmaster
Berryton	Shawnee	George Washington Berry, pioneer
Bigelow	Marshall	George Bigelow, pioneer
Blair	Doniphan	Joel P. Blair, townsite owner
Blairs Station	Doniphan	Joel P. Blair, postmaster
Block	Miami	John Block, pioneer
Bodaville	Riley	William Bode, pioneer
Bolton	Montgomery	Jeff Bolt, rancher
Boyd	Barton	Townsite owner
Burden	Cowley	Robert F. Burden, pioneer
Burt	Woodson	Daniel H. Burt, postmaster
Carlton	Dickinson	Carlton, pioneer blacksmith
Clare	Johnson	Local landowner
Claudell	Smith	Pioneer family
Coleman	Sedgwick	W. C. Coleman, industrialist
Coopersville	Clark	Dr. John Cooper, pioneer
Corwin	Harper	Oscar A. Corwin, postmaster
Covert	Osborne	Covert, pioneer
Coyville	Wilson	Oscar Coy, store owner and postmaster
Craig	Johnson	Landowner
Cravensville	Cherokee	Townsite owner
Cullison	Pratt	James B. Cullison, lawyer
Dearing	Montgomery	Pioneer

Towns	County	Postmasters and Pioneers
Dennis	Labette	Townsite owner
Densmore	Norton	John T. Densmore, town founder
Denton	Doniphan	Moses, John and William Denton, town promoters
Dillon	Dickinson	Dillon brothers, pioneers
Dwight	Morris	Dwight Rathbone, townsite owner
Earlton	Neosho	Earle, pioneer
Englevale	Crawford	Cecil Engle, town promoter
Esbon	Jewell	Ezbon Kellogg, pioneer
Farlington	Crawford	Eugene D. Farley, postmaster
Farlinville	Linn	Alonzo Farlin, pioneer
Fellsburg	Edwards	Fells family, pioneers
Ferguson	Sedgwick	Pioneer
Fostoria	Pottawatomie	Charles W. Foster, pioneer
Fowler	Meade	George Fowler, town promoter
Garnett	Anderson	W. A. Garnett, town promoter
Gaylord	Smith	C. E. Gaylord, pioneer
Goodman	Johnson	Landowner
Goodrich	Linn	John S. Goodrich, postmaster
Gorham	Russell	Gorham, pioneer
Halls Summit	Coffey	Ezra E. Hall, postmaster
Hammond	Bourbon	William Hammond, townsite owner
Hamner	Kingman	Hugh E. Hamner, landowner
Hardtner	Barber	John Hardtner, Illinois doctor
Harris	Anderson	A. A. Harris, townsite owner
Haworth	Republic	Haworth family, pioneers
Haysville	Sedgwick	William W. Hays, postmaster
Hayter	Harper	C. H. Hayter, pioneer
Healy	Lane	O. H. Healey, pioneer
Hedville	Saline	Hed, a pioneer
Heizer	Barton	D. N. Heizer, townsite owner
Hepler	Crawford	Dr. B. F. Hepler, town company
Hiatville	Bourbon	Townsite owner
Hickok	Grant	Frank W. Hickok, pioneer
Hitschman	Barton	Joseph Hitschman, townsite owner
Hoge	Leavenworth	Joseph Hoge, postmaster
Holcomb	Kearny	D. C. Holcomb, pioneer
Hollis	Cloud	Hollis family, pioneers
Hooser	Cowley	George H. Hooser, postmaster
Huscher	Cloud	David Huscher, postmaster
Hymer	Chase	Frank and George Hegwer, pioneers
Idenbro	Labette	Thomas T. Iden, postmaster
Imes	Franklin	Harmon Imes, postmaster

Towns	County	Postmasters and Pioneers
Jennings	Decatur	Warren Jennings, postmaster
Johnstown	McPherson	John Johnson, postmaster
Kackley	Republic	Joe Kackley, townsite owner
Kenneth	Johnson	Local landowner
Kimball	Neosho	Kimball, pioneer
Lasswell	Barber	Allen B. Lasswell, postmaster
Latimer	Morris	Latimer, town promoter
Lawrenceburg	Cloud	L. D. or Frank Lawrence, pioneers
Layton	Chautauqua	Layton brothers, pioneer cattlemen
Lowe	Finney	Thaddeus Lowe, military man
Lowell	Cherokee	Town promoter
Lebo	Coffey	Joe Leabo, pioneer on Leabo Creek
Lewis	Edwards	Lewis family, town promoters
Lindsey	Ottawa	Lindsey, pioneer
McDonald	Rawlins	R. L. McDonald, pioneer rancher
McLains	Harvey	Earnest McLains, banker
McLouth	Jefferson	Amos McLouth, townsite owner
Macksville	Stafford	George Mack, pioneer
Macyville	Cloud	George W. Macy, postmaster
Mantey	Linn	Pioneer
Maywood	Wyandotte	Pioneer storekeeper
Milberger	Russell	Charles Milberger, postmaster
Millard	Barton	Francis Millard, postmaster
Miller	Lyon	Miller brothers, ranchers
Milton	Sumner	J. Milton Broomfield, merchant
Morganville	Clay	Ebenzer Morgan, town promoter
Morris	Wyandotte	Morris Packing Company
Morse	Johnson	Owner of townsite
Mortimer	Labette	Emanuel Mortimer, pioneer
Munden	Republic	John Munden, townsite owner
Naylor	Cherokee	Naylor, pioneer
Newman	Jefferson	H. L. Newman, town promoter
O'Brien	Miami	Perry O'Brien, pioneer
Otis	Rush	Donator of land
Oursler	Marion	N. J. Oursler, postmaster
Padonia	Brown	Jesse Padon, innkeeper
Palmer	Washington	J. Palmer, educator
Parker	Linn	J. W. Parker, postmaster
Parkerville	Morris	C. G. Parker, townsite owner
Pence	Scott	John W. Pence, postmaster
Porterville	Bourbon	Levi G. Porter, postmaster
Purcell	Doniphan	John Purcell, pioneer
Ramsey	Butler	A. C. Ramsey, rancher

493

Towns	County	Postmasters and Pioneers
Randall	Jewell	Townsite owner
Rapp	Osage	Rapp brothers, ranchers
Reager	Norton	William Wesley Reager, pioneer
Reamsville	Smith	David Reams, pioneer
Redfield	Bourbon	Dr. John S. Redfield, physician
Reece	Greenwood	William Smith Reece, pioneer
Rexford	Thomas	Jacob Rexford, pioneer
Richman	Franklin	John C. Richman, pioneer
Ruleton	Sherman	J. E. Rule, merchant
Sallyards	Greenwood	S. G. Sallyards, rancher
Sanford	Pawnee	Sanford Arnold, pioneer and townsite owner
Sayre	Ford	Kaye Sayre, pioneer
Schroyer	Marshall	Peter Schroyer, town promoter
Severance	Doniphan	John Severance, town promoter
Shaffer	Rush	Franklin P. Shaffer, postmaster
Sherwin	Cherokee	Landowner
Shields	Lane	Shields, pioneer
Simpson	Mitchell	Alfred Simpson, grain dealer
Sparks	Doniphan	John Sparks, pioneer
Stickney	Barton	Judson W. Stickney, postmaster
Stippville	Cherokee	F. M. and Sarah J. Stipp, pioneers
Strawn	Coffey	Enos Strawn, pioneer
Stull	Douglas	Silvester Stull, postmaster
Susank	Barton	Susank family, pioneers
Teterville	Greenwood	"Jim" Teter, rancher
Thompsonville	Jefferson	C. L. Thompson, pioneer and mill owner
Thornburg	Smith	Postmaster
Thrall	Greenwood	Pioneer landowner
Thurman	Chase	William Thurman, pioneer
Tisdale	Cowley	Henry Tidsale, pioneer
Treece	Cherokee	J. O. Treece, real estate
Turkville	Ellis	Benjamin M. Turk, postmaster
Tyler's	Brown	John S. Tyler, pioneer
Udall	Cowley	Cornelius Udall, town promoter
Varner	Kingman	David Varner, pioneer
Vaughn	Pawnee	Riggs Vaughn, pioneer
Wagstaff	Miami	W. R. Wagstaff, pioneer
Waldron	Harper	Howard D. Waldron, postmaster
Walker	Elk	J. E. Walker, pioneer
Walker	Ellis	Pioneer
Walton	Harvey	James Walton, merchant
Watson	Shawnee	George H. Watson, postmaster

Towns	*County*	*Postmasters and Pioneers*
Webber	Jewell	Dan Webber, townsite owner
Wellsford	Kiowa	Col. C. D. Wellsford, town promoter
Wheeler	Cheyenne	Pioneer
Williamstown	Jefferson	Charles Williams, postmaster
Willis	Brown	Martin C. Willis, pioneer
Wilmore	Comanche	Thomas Wilmore, pioneer
Wilsey	Morris	John D. Wilsey, pioneer
Wolcott	Wyandotte	Herbert W. Wolcott, pioneer
Womer	Smith	Daniel Womer, pioneer
Zook	Pawnee	John B. Zook, pioneer

NOTES

I

INTRODUCTION

1. Will E. Stokes, *Episodes of Early Days*, 110.
2. Federal Writers' Project, *Kansas, A Guide*, 48.
3. Adolph Roenigh, *Pioneer History of Kansas*, 356.

II

SUN, WATER, AND WEATHER

1. Wayne E. Corley, *County and Community Names in Kansas* (mimeographed, 1962), 72, 82.
2. Robert W. Baughman, *Kansas Post Offices*, 124; "Extinct Geographical Locations," *KHC*, XII, 488.
3. *The Golden Jubilee Anniversary of Thomas County and its Neighbors, 1885–1935*, 26.
4. *Tescott News*, December 26, 1940.
5. Henry Gannett, "A Gazetteer of Kansas," *Bulletin*, U.S. Geological Survey, No. 154, 47.
6. Nathaniel T. Allison, *History of Cherokee County, Kansas, and Representative Citizens*, 46; *Oswego Independent*, July 2, 1954.
7. Joseph B. King, "The Ottawa Indians in Kansas and Oklahoma," Kansas Historical Society *Collections* (listed hereafter as *KHC*) XIII, 373.
8. Albert D. Richardson, *Beyond the Mississippi*, 163.
9. Marion *Record-Review*, September 14, 1944.
10. *Leavenworth Times*, January 24, 1907.
11. Martha B. Caldwell, "Exploring the Solomon River Valley in 1869," *Kansas Historical Quarterly* (listed hereafter as *KHQ*), VI, 72.
12. *Kansas Post Offices, passim.*
13. David V. Wiebe, *They Seek A Country*, 112, 128.
14. "Letters of Julia L. Lovejoy, 1856–1864," *KHQ*, XV, 376.
15. Irene D. Paden, *The Wake of the Prairie Schooner*, 36.
16. Kate L. Gregg, ed., *The Road to Santa Fe*, 36n., 60, 254n.
17. Robert Taft, "The Editors Page," *Transactions*, Kansas Academy of Science, LIII, 302.
18. Stella Drumm, ed., *Down the Santa Fe Trail, Diary of Susan Shelby Magoffin, 1846–1847*, 17; George P. Morehouse, "Diamond Springs, 'Diamond of the Plain,'" *KHC*, XIV, 796.
19. Alice C. Smith, "Through the Eyes of My Father," *KHC*, XVII, 709n.; Alfred T. Andreas and W. G. Cutler, *History of the State of Kansas*, 796. (Alfred Andreas compiled this monumental work with the assistance of W. G. Cutler, Mrs. Cutler, S. S. Prouty, J. C. Hebbard, and others. This work will be referred to hereafter as Andreas, *Kansas*.)
20. Andreas, *Kansas*, 1255; Stanley Vestal, *Old Santa Fe Trail*, 67.

496

21. Clara M. Shields, "The Lyon Creek Settlement," KHC, XIV, 143n.
22. Dodge City *Daily Globe*, January 25, 1933.
23. *Lakin Independent*, August 27, 1948.
24. Nyle H. Miller, *A Survey of Historic Sites and Structures in Kansas*, 25.
25. Frank C. Montgomery, "Fort Wallace and its Relation to the Frontier," *KHC*, XVII, 196–98.
26. Cecil Howes, "Mineral Springs in Kansas," *The Kansas Teacher*, LVII (January, 1949), 38–40; Andreas, *Kansas*, 1221.
27. John J. Mathews, *The Osages: Children of the Middle Waters*, 7, 77.
28. G. E. Patrick, "The Great Spirit Spring," *Transactions*, Kansas Academy of Science, VII, 22–26.
29. Frank W. Blackmar, *Kansas: A Cyclopedia of State History*, I, 748.
30. Andreas, *Kansas*, 1509.
31. *Wichita Beacon*, October 7, 1928.
32. See map in Andreas, *Kansas*, 1014.
33. Victor Murdock, in *Wichita Evening Eagle*, December 28, 1938.
34. *Ibid.*, April 13 and April 27, 1938.
35. Andreas, *Kansas*, 1430.
36. Nyle Miller, "Kansas Boundary Survey," *KHQ*, I, 110 and n.
37. Howes, *Kansas Teacher*, LVII (January, 1949), 38; Louis Johnson Cone, "1265 Western Avenue and the People who lived there," *Bulletin* No. 27, Shawnee County Historical Society (April, 1957), 28.
38. Irene G. Stone, "The Lead and Zinc Field of Kansas," *KHC*, VII, 245.
39. Eugene F. Ware, "The Neutral Lands," *KHC*, VI, 149.
40. *Ibid.*, 245; Miller, *KHQ*, I, 110 and n.; Allison, *Cherokee County*, 35, 152.
41. Paden, *The Wake of the Prairie Schooner*, 51; *Topeka State Journal*, April 13, 1935.
42. Andreas, *Kansas*, 875.
43. Baughman, *Kansas Post Offices*, 121.
44. P. L. Gray, *Gray's Doniphan County History*, 19.
45. *Desert Magazine*, XVII (March, 1954), 18.
46. Ely Moore, Jr., "The Naming of Osawatomie," *KHC*, XII, 345.
47. Conway Springs, Russell Springs, Bonner Springs, and Bennett Springs are discussed under other topics.
48. Edmund N. Morrill, *History and Statistics of Brown County, Kansas*, 17.
49. Harry E. Chrisman, *Lost Trails of the Cimarron*, 157, 234.
50. George P. Morehouse, "History of the Kansa or Kaw Indians," *KHC*, X, 335; Marion *Record-Review*, September 14, 1944; John Rydjord, *Indian Place-Names*, 120.
51. Marion *Record-Review*, September 14, 1944.
52. Oliver Lawson, in Scott City *News-Chronicle*, April 25, 1937.
53. George W. Martin, "The Territorial and Military Combine at Fort Riley," *KHC*, VII, 379; George A. Root, "Ferries in Kansas," *KHQ*, IV, 17.
54. Lew W. Duncan and Charles F. Scott, *History of Allen and Woodson Counties, Kansas*, 610.
55. *Washington County Register*, January 18, 1935.
56. Sedan *Times-Star*, August 14, 1941.
57. Most of the creek names fit into the categories of names discussed in other chapters.
58. *In the Wake of the Prairie Schooner*, 42.
59. Charles R. Green, *Early Days in Kansas*, 100.
60. Roenigh, *Pioneer History*, 82; Andreas, *Kansas*, 1274.
61. Andreas, *Kansas*, 1529.
62. Roenigh, *Pioneer History*, 71.
63. Andreas, *Kansas*, 587.
64. Edna Nyquist, *Pioneer Life and Lore of McPherson County, Kansas*, 78.

65. Bernice C. Shackleton, *Handbook on the Frontier Days of Southeast Kansas*, 92.

66. Kearny County Historical Society, *History of Kearny County, Kansas*, I, 362.

67. J. W. Berryman, "Early Settlement of Southwest Kansas," *KHC*, XVII, 565.

III
HILLS, HIGHLANDS, AND LOWLANDS

1. Ainsworth R. Spofford, "American Historical Nomenclature," American Historical Association, *Annual Report*, 1893, 35.

2. John J. Ingalls, "Blue Grass," *Kansas Magazine*, II, 275.

3. See map in William F. Zornow, *Kansas, A History of the Jayhawk State*, 4; Walter H. Schoewe, "The Geography of Kansas," Kansas Academy of Science, *Transactions*, LI, 253–88.

4. Lecture by Walter Ver Wiebe, late Professor of Geology, Wichita State University.

5. The Gypsum Hills are included in Chapter VII.

6. "The Kansas Prairie or Eight Days in the Plains," *KHQ*, VI, 160 and n.

7. Federal Writers' Project, *Kansas, A Guide to the Sunflower State*, 411; Harry Johnson, *A History of Anderson County, Kansas*, 348.

8. Johnson, *Anderson County*, 347; Andreas, *Kansas*, 1332.

9. L. L. Dyche, "The Puma or American Lion," Kansas Academy of Science, *Transactions*, XIX, 160.

10. For a good account of the Bluestem, see James C. Malin, "An Introduction to the History of the Bluestem-Pasture Region of Kansas," *KHQ*, X, 3–28.

11. Cecil Howes, "Chisholm Trail—1949 Model," *Kansas Teacher*, LVII (May, 1949), 47.

12. John Fisher, "Bluestem Hills,—'Peace on Earth,'" Kansas State Board of Agriculture, *Annual Report*, 1947–48, XLI, 20.

13. See Chapter on "French Name the Rivers."

14. J. W. Beebe, "Notes on Kansas Physiography," Kansas Academy of Science, *Transactions*, XV, 116.

15. Jose Antonio Pichardo, ed. by Charles W. Hackett, *Limits of Louisiana*, III, 190.

16. See map in Andreas, *Kansas*, 1021.

17. Max Greene, *The Kansas Region*, 40.

18. J. T. Willard, "Bluemont," *KHQ*, XIII, 330.

19. See Chapter XXI.

20. Andreas, *Kansas*, 1306.

21. Charles S. Scott, "The Old Road and Pike's Pawnee Village," *KHC*, VII, 317.

22. Charles E. Cory, *Place Names in Bourbon County, Kansas*, 32.

23. Andreas, *Kansas*, 1221; Sedan *Times-Star*, August 14, 1941; *Cedarvale Messenger*, November 18, 1932.

24. *Leavenworth Times*, January 24, 1907.

25. Andreas, *Kansas*, 1060.

26. George Crofutt, *Crofutt's New Overland Tourist and Pacific Coast Guide*.

27. Matt Thomson, *Early History of Wabaunsee County, Kansas*, 143.

28. Margaret Whittemore, *Historic Kansas*, 61.

29. Cory, *Bourbon County*, 29.

30. *Hill City Times*, August 22, 1946; Interview with Francis W. Schruben.

31. Wiebe, *They Seek A Country*, 71; H. H. Fast to G. W. Martin, November 9, 1901, "Names," MS., KSHS.

32. Root, *KHQ*, IV, 154.

33. Andreas, *Kansas*, 825.

34. *Protection Post*, May 9 and 30, 1947; *Clark County Clipper*, September 20, 1934.

35. Greene, *Kanzas*, 43; Root, *KHQ*, III, 21, 289n.

36. Harry E. Ross, *What Price White Rock?*, 15.

37. Whittemore, *Kansas*, 34.
38. Federal Writers' Project, *Kansas, A Guide*, 326.
39. Miller, *Survey of Historic Sites*, 34.
40. "Kansas History in the Press," *KHQ*, V, 333; William B. Bracke, *Wheat Country*, 40.
41. "Governor Denver's Administration," *KHC*, V, 489.
42. Johnson, *Anderson County*, 50–52.
43. Andreas, *Kansas*, 889.
44. Johnson, *Anderson County*, 348.
45. *KHC*, VII, 482.
46. Randall to Reingold, November 14, 1901, "Names," MS., *KSHS*, Topeka.
47. Andreas, *Kansas*, 1108.
48. Darius N. Bowers, *Seventy Years in Norton County, Kansas, 1872–1942*, 7.
49. Whittemore, *Kansas*, 34; Andreas, *Kansas*, 1563.
50. Andreas, *Kansas*, 1115; *KHC*, VII, 476.
51. These are shown on the Johnson map of 1870.
52. Paden, *Wake of the Prairie Schooner*, 30.
53. Joseph Allen, *Cho-O-Nee to High Iron*, 1–23.
54. F. M. Lockard, *The History of the Early Settlement of Norton County, Kansas*, 21.
55. *Tales of the Trail*, 96.
56. *Wichita Evening Eagle*, May 28, 1953.
57. Charles N. Gould, *Covered Wagon Geologist*, 49.
58. Greene, *Kanzas*, 106.
59. Ed Blair, *History of Johnson County, Kansas*, 241.
60. Wynne P. Harrington, *History of Gove County, Kansas*.
61. Evan J. Jenkins, *The Northern Tier; or Life Among the Homestead Settlers*, 175.
62. Andreas, *Kansas*, 987.
63. There are several versions for this name. Rydjord, *Indian Place-Names*, 141–43.
64. Jacob Fowler, ed., *The Journal of Coues*, 22; Elliot Coues, ed., *The Expedition of Zebulon Montgomery Pike*, II, 433.
65. George W. Martin, "Memorial Monuments and Tablets in Kansas," *KHC*, XI, 267.
66. Henry Inman, *Buffalo Jones' Forty Years of Adventure*, 121 and n., and illustration opposite page 123.
67. R. M. Wright, "Personal Reminiscences of Frontier Life in Southwest Kansas," *KHC*, VII, 77.
68. Harrington, *Gove County*, 6; Montgomery, *KHC*, XVII, 192.
69. Elizabeth N. Barr, *A Souvenir History of Lincoln County, Kansas*, 92 and illustration, 9; Theodore H. Scheffer, "Geographical Names in Ottawa County," *KHQ*, III, 236.
70. Greene, *Kanzas*, 143.
71. Federal Writers' Project, *Kansas, A Guide*, 307.
72. Whittemore, *Kansas*, 141–43; *Topeka Capital*, July 21, 1957.
73. Corley, *Names*, 69.
74. Whittemore, *Kansas*, 33.
75. Greene, *Kanzas*, 104; *Leavenworth Times*, January 24, 1907.
76. Bowers, *Norton County*, 69.
77. Nyquist, *Pioneer Life and Lore*, 150.
78. Alberta Pantle, "The Connecticut Kansas Colony," *KHQ*, XXII, 146 and n.; Hugh M. Moore, "Letters of Hugh M. Moore, 1856–1860," *KHQ*, X, 117.
79. *KHQ*, XVI, 217; Andreas, *Kansas*, 904.
80. Joseph Romig, "The Chippewa and Munsee Indians in Franklin County," *KHC*, XI, 314.
81. Bliss Isely, in *Wichita Beacon*, May 5, 1929; W. A. O'Connell, in *Oswego Democrat*, January 29, 1954.

82. John C. Van Gundy, *Reminiscences of Frontier Life on the Upper Neosho in 1855 and 1856*, 41.
83. Sheffield Ingalls, *History of Atchison County, Kansas*, 42.
84. George Remsburg, *Scrapbook*, IV, 96, Kansas State Historical Library (listed hereafter as KSHL).
85. Berryman, *KHC*, XVII, 568.
86. *KHC*, XII, 483; *Oswego Democrat*, January 15, 1954.
87. Mary Miller, *A Pillar of Cloud*, 10; Corley, *Names*, 74, 82.
88. Ross, *What Price White Rock?*, 19.
89. Francis W. Schruben, Stockton, to author, July 25, 1959.
90. Remsburg, *Scrapbook*, I, 157 and III, 44, *KSHL*.
91. Gannett, *Bulletin* 154, U.S. Geological Survey, 178; Baughman, *Kansas Post Offices*, 103.
92. Horace Greeley, *An Overland Journey from New York to San Francisco*, 61.

IV
PRAIRIES AND PRAIRIE FLOWERS

1. Coues, ed., *Pike*, II, 525.
2. Robert R. Hubach, "Walt Whitman in Kansas," *KHQ*, X, 153.
3. *The First Hundred Years of Jefferson County, Kansas, 1855-1955*, frontispiece.
4. Greene, *Kanzas*, 121.
5. Edmund N. Morrill, *History and Statistics of Brown County, Kansas*, 29, 33; *Horton Headlight*, October 29, 1936.
6. Andreas, *Kansas*, 1031.
7. Patrick L. Gray, *Doniphan County History*, II, 101.
8. Andreas, *Kansas*, 640.
9. "Letters of John and Sarah Everett," *KHQ*, VIII, 32.
10. Andreas, *Kansas*, 1531; *People's Herald* (Lynden), April 29, 1948.
11. *Leavenworth Times*, January 24, 1907.
12. *KHC*, V, 443, XII, 474 and 480.
13. *Chase County Historical Sketches*, II, 324.
14. *Hutchinson News*, November 24, 1957.
15. Rydjord, *Indian Place-Names*, 191-93.
16. *Leavenworth Times*, December 2, 1937.
17. Howes, *Kansas Teacher*, LVII (May, 1949), 48.
18. Lew Wallace Duncan, *History of Montgomery County, Kansas*, 86; *Southern Kansas Tribune*, June 18, 1930.
19. Andreas, *Kansas*, 1566.
20. Coues, ed., *Pike*, II, 396n.
21. Milo M. Quaife, ed., *The Journals of Captain Meriwether Lewis and Sergeant John Ordway*, 88n.
22. Corley, *Names*, 73.
23. Andreas, *Kansas*, 1273.
24. *KHC*, XII, 479.
25. Finney County Historical Society, *History of Finney County, Kansas*, I, 16, 98, 204.
26. Leola Howard Blanchard, *Conquest of Southwest Kansas*, 229; *Kansas City Times*, May 31, 1947.
27. Robert Easton and McKenzie Brown, *Lord of Beasts: The Saga of Buffalo Jones*, 30.
28. Cummins Scott, *Reminiscences of the Early Days*, 7.
29. Missouri Pacific, *The Empire*, 94.
30. Victor Murdock, in the *Wichita Evening Eagle*, December 28, 1937.
31. Robert W. Baughman, *Kansas in Maps*, 21.

32. *KHC*, IX, 11.
33. Murdock, in *Wichita Evening Eagle*, December 28, 1937.
34. Mrs. A. L. Slosson, "Personal Observations upon the Flora of Kansas," *Publications*, Kansas Academy of Science, XI, 22.
35. *Wichita Evening Eagle*, December 11, 1959.
36. Arch O'Bryant, "The Bystander," *Wichita Beacon*, January 29, 1968.
37. *KHC*, VIII, 300; Charles Howes, *This Place Called Kansas*, 118.
38. Missouri Pacific, *The Empire*, 141.
39. Grant W. Harrington, *Historic Spots or Mile-stones in the Progress of Wyandotte County, Kansas*, 249.
40. William W. Graves, *History of Neosho County, Kansas*, II, 750; *St. Paul Journal*, June 20, 1948.
41. Volney P. Mooney, *History of Butler County, Kansas*, 207.
42. Robert R. Wilson and Ethel M. Sears, *History of Grant County, Kansas*, 240.
43. Nelson Case, *History of Labette County, Kansas*, 119.
44. LeRoy R. Hafen and Harley M. Fuller, eds., *The Journal of Captain John R. Bell*, in *The Far West and the Rockies*, VI, 220.
45. *Beyond the Mississippi*, 121
46. Scheffer, *KHQ*, III, 243; *Tescott News*, December 26, 1940.
47. Corley, *Names*, 81.
48. Bowers, *Norton County*, 123.

V
TREES

1. William A. Mitchell, *Linn County, Kansas, A History*, 324.
2. For an interesting account of Kansas trees, attractively illustrated by the author, see Whittemore, *Historic Kansas*, 203–16.
3. Stillwell, *The Giant Elm*, 3.
4. Edwin Way Teale, *Journey into Summer*, 274; Margaret E. Whittemore, "Kansas and her Historic Trees," *Trees in Kansas, Report* (1928), Kansas State Board of Agriculture, 12.
5. Greeley, *Overland Journey*, 26, 40.
6. O'Connell in *Oswego Democrat*, January 29, 1954. *The Manhattan Standard* reported the killing of a bear near Timber City in 1868, several years after Timber City post office had been closed, *KHQ*, XII, 329.
7. Kate L. Gregg, ed., *The Road to Santa Fe*, 57 and n.; Greene, *Kanzas*, 114.
8. John Maloy in *Council Grove Cosmos*, March 5, 1886.
9. Whittemore, *Kansas*, 211.
10. Lalla Maloy Brigham, *The Story of Council Grove on the Santa Fe Trail*, 7-8.
11. Works Project Administration, "Park City," Wichita State University Library, M.S.
12. Blair, *Johnson County*, 59; Miller, *Historic Sites*, 30.
13. Cora Dolbee, "The Fourth of July in Early Kansas," *KHQ*, VIII, 131 and n.
14. Andreas, *Kansas*, 1060.
15. Ruth H. Dudley, *Favorite Trees of Desert, Mountain, and Plain*, 82; Fred W. Brinkerhoff, "The Kansas Tour of Lincoln the Candidate," *KHQ*, XIII, 300.
16. Hubach, *KHQ*, X, 151.
17. Anona Shaw Blackburn and Myrtle Strom Cardwell, compilers, *History of Republic County, Kansas*, 79.
18. *KHQ*, X, 102; Ingalls, *Atchison County*, 36.
19. Floyd B. Streeter, *Prairie Trails & Cow Towns*, 42.
20. Corley, *Names*, 23; James L. King, *History of Shawnee County, Kansas and Representative Citizens*, 55.
21. *The Western Advocate*, Mankato, July 25, 1940.

22. Greene, *Kanzas*, 126; Horace Jones, *The Story of Early Rice County*, 74.

23. *Map and Description of the Gold Regions in Western Kansas and Nebraska* (St. Louis, 1858).

24. Robert Taft, "Pictorial Record of the Old West," *KHQ*, XVI, 123.

25. Jones, *Rice County*, 29; W. Julian Fessler, ed., "Captain Nathan Boone's Journal," *Chronicles of Oklahoma*, VII, 78.

26. "Executive Minutes of Governor Geary," *KHC*, IV, 622.

27. Franklin County Historical Society, *Reflections of Franklin County and Chautauqua Days*.

28. O'Connell in *Oswego Democrat*, September 3, 1954.

29. William J. Chapman, "The Wakefield Colony," *KHC*, X, 518.

30. Donald C. Peattie, *A Natural History of Trees*, 180.

31. *Kansas City Times*, May 31, 1947; *Along Your Way* (Santa Fe Railway Brochure), 13.

32. Elizabeth N. Barr, *A Souvenir History of Lincoln County, Kansas*, 79; Andreas, *Kansas*, 1423.

33. Blackburn and Cardwell, eds., *Republic County*, 79.

34. Peattie, *History of Trees*, 427, 493.

35. Andreas, *Kansas*, 1350.

36. "Kansas Historical Notes," *KHQ*, VII, 336; James C. Malin, "J. A. Walker's Early History of Edwards County," *KHQ*, IX, 283.

37. John S. Barnum to the editor of the *Wichita Eagle*, March 25, 1900.

38. Teale, *Journey into Summer*, 244.

39. *KHC*, XVII, 720.

40. Gould, *Covered Wagon Geologist*, 93.

41. Andreas, *Kansas*, 355; James R. Stewart, "The Diary of . . . ," *KHQ*, XVII, 139 and n.; *Wichita Beacon*, August 17, 1954; Greeley, *Overland Journey*, 40.

42. *Washington County Register*, January 11, 1935.

43. *Burr Oak Herald*, April 7, 1960.

44. Andreas, *Kansas*, 941.

45. Quaife, ed., *Sergeant Ordway's Journal*, 94 and n.

46. Chapman, *KHC*, X, 490.

47. Baughman, *Kansas Post Offices*, 22.

48. Andreas, *Kansas*, 1356; *KHC*, XII, 475.

49. Andreas, *Kansas*, 1336, 1338.

50. *Ibid.*, 624.

51. Amy Lathrop, *Tales of Western Kansas*, 60.

52. Andreas, *Kansas*, 912, 1221; Isely in *Wichita Beacon*, May 19, 1929.

53. Lowell Thomas, "The Painful Lesson of the Cedars of Lebanon," *National Wildlife*, VIII, 52.

54. F. W. Albertson, "Studies of Native Red Cedar in West Central Kansas," *Transactions*, Kansas Academy of Science (listed hereafter as *KAS*), XLIII, 85, 94.

55. Frank A. Root and William E. Connelley, *The Overland Stage to California*, 565–66; Andreas, *Kansas*, 942.

56. George A. Root, "Extracts from Diary of Captain Lambert Bowman Wolf," *KHQ*, I, 200 and n.

57. Edwin A. Minninger, *Fantastic Trees*, 8.

58. *Hiawatha Daily World*, January 18, 1934; Andreas, *Kansas*, 1430, 1563.

59. Scheffer, *KHQ*, III, 233.

60. William C. Grimm, *Familiar Trees in America*, 89.

61. *Overland Journey*, 40.

62. Albert Morrall, "Statement and Autobiography," *KHC*, XIV, 134 and n.; Andreas, *Kansas*, 501.

63. William A. Phillips, *The Conquest of Kansas by Missouri and her Allies*, 359.

64. Peattie, *History of Trees*, 256.

65. Ida E. Rath, *Early Ford Country*, 103; Wright, *KHC*, VII, 64.
66. William F. Connelley, "First Provisional Constitution of Kansas," *KHC*, VI, 113n.; Rydjord, *Indian Place-Names*, 279.
67. *KHC*, VII, 481; *Leavenworth Times*, January 24, 1907.
68. Bill Thomas, "Festival King, Ohio," *Travel*, CXXXIII, 38.
69. Elizabeth N. Barr, *Business Directory and History of Wabaunsee County*, 75.
70. Cory, *Geographical Names* (Clippings), 171, *KSHL*; Andreas, *Kansas*, 1097.
71. Whittemore, *Kansas*, 203.
72. Alice Nichols, *Bleeding Kansas*, 167; Corley, *Names*, 45.
73. Lela Barnes, ed., "North Central Kansas in 1887–1889," *KHQ*, XXIX, 383.
74. Andreas, *Kansas*, 1173; C. S. Burch, *Handbook of Elk and Chautauqua Counties, Kansas*, 6.
75. J. C. Leland, "Indian Names in Missouri," *Names*, I, 270.
76. F. H. Barrington, *Kansas Day, Containing a Brief History of Kansas*, 101.
77. *Trees in Kansas*, 1928 Report, 77.
78. Dudley, *Favorite Trees*, 119.
79. *Autobiography*, 65.
80. Peattie, *History of Trees*, 480.
81. Howes, "Herbs, Roots, Amulets and Nostrums," *Kansas Teacher*, LVII (March, 1949), 46.
82. Whittemore, *Kansas*, 203.
83. *KHQ*, VI, 301 and 307.
84. Hafen and Fuller, eds., *Journal of John R. Bell*, VI, 221.
85. Andreas, *Kansas*, 1585.
86. Root, *KHQ*, VI, 144.
87. *KHQ*, VII, 217.
88. Richardson, *Beyond the Mississippi*, 161.
89. Howes in *Kansas City Star*, January 16, 1942; Andreas, *Kansas*, 1054.
90. Greene, *Kanzas*, 118.
91. Taft, *KHQ*, XVI, 370; Coues, ed., *Pike*, II, 401 n.
92. Isely in *Wichita Beacon*, September 9, 1929.
93. Andreas, *Kansas*, 1357 and 1360.
94. Alberta Pantle, "History of the French-speaking Settlement in the Cottonwood Valley," *KHQ*, XIX, 13.
95. Montgomery, *KHC*, XVII, 198.
96. J. D. Graham, "The Cottonwood," *Trees in Kansas*, 1928 Report, 14.

VI
BEES, BIRDS, AND BEASTS

1. Isaac T. Goodnow, "Personal Reminiscences and Kansas Emigration, 1855," *KHC*, IV, 251.
2. Adolph Roenigh, *Pioneer History of Kansas*, 194.
3. Hafen and Fuller, *Journal of John R. Bell*, 247.
4. Isely in *Wichita Beacon*, September 8, 1929.
5. William J. Meredith, "Old Plum Grove Colony in Jefferson County," *KHQ*, VII, 342.
6. George W. Martin, "The First Two Years of Kansas," *KHC*, X, 141 n.
7. Andreas, *Kansas*, 754.
8. *Laws of the State of Kansas, 1875*, 168.
9. See map in Andreas, *Kansas*, 1430.
10. *KHC*, VII, 476.
11. "Reminiscences of Northwest Kansas," *KHC*, VII, 201.
12. Lawrence Pringle, "Why They're Called Wild Turkey," *National Wildlife*, IV, 20.

13. Cory, *Bourbon County*, 22.
14. See Chapter X.
15. Andreas, *Kansas*, 1002.
16. Coues, ed., *Pike*, II, 518n; *KHC*, XI, 598.
17. Charles S. Triplet, "The End of Coronado," *KHC*, XII, 447.
18. Bowers, *Norton County*, 5.
19. Ely Moore, Jr., "The Story of Lecompton," *KHC*, XI, 465.
20. *Idem*, XI, 467.
21. Andreas, *Kansas*, 1386.
22. Gray, *Doniphan County*, 24.
23. Mitchell, *Linn County*, 321.
24. Rydjord, *Indian Place-Names*, 210.
25. Hafen and Fuller, *Journal of John R. Bell*, VI, 219.
26. Quaife, ed., *Journal of Lewis and Ordway*, 93n.
27. See map of Andreas, *Kansas*, 1587.
28. J. R. Mead, "Saline River Country in 1859," *KHC*, IX, 13ff.; George Remsburg, "Geography of Kansas has Many Animal Names," *Leavenworth Times*, October 24, 1935.
29. Richard I. Dodge, *The Plains of the Great West and their Inhabitants*, 118.
30. *Ibid.*, 119–47.
31. Mead, *KHC*, IX, 18; Cf. *Wichita Beacon*, July 14, 1929.
32. Paul King, "The Sportsman's Paradise," *The Aerend*, VII, 103.
33. Streeter, *Prairie Trails*, 196.
34. *Rush County News*, May 19, 1949.
35. To G. W. Martin, November 8, 1901, MS., *Archives, KSHS*.
36. *KHC*, XII, 474.
37. Wayne Gard, *The Great Buffalo Hunt*, 101.
38. James L. Marshall, *Santa Fe—The Railroad that Built an Empire*, 67; *Kansas City Star*, May 12, 1954.
39. Andreas, *Kansas*, 1020.
40. *Nickerson Argosy*, June 25, 1964.
41. Elliot Coues, ed., *Journal of Jacob Fowler*, 19, 21n.
42. C. C. Hutchinson, in *Wichita Eagle*, April 19, 1872.
43. Mead, *KHC*, IX, 13.
44. Wright, *KHC*, VII, 64.
45. Lola Shelton, *Charles Marion Russell, Cowboy, Artist, Friend*, 98.
46. *Beyond the Mississippi*, 163.
47. Stanley Vestal, *Old Santa Fe Trail*, 67.
48. Kearny County Historical Society, *History of Kearny County, Kansas*, 26.
49. Edwin James, *Account of S. H. Long's Expedition*, in R. G. Thwaites, ed., *Early Western Travels*, XIV, 181n.
50. Quaife, ed., *Journal of Lewis and Ordway*, 94.
51. Remsburg, in *Leavenworth Times*, October 24, 1935.
52. Mead, *KHC*, IX, 13; See map in Andreas, *Kansas*, 1283; *Wichita Eagle*, November 9, 1970.
53. Chase County Historical Society, *Historical Sketches*, I, 16.
54. Isaac O. Savage, *A History of Republic County, Kansas*, 39.
55. *KHC*, XII, 472.
56. A. M. Gibson, *The Kickapoos*, 121.
57. *Travels and Works of Captain John Smith* I, 59.
58. Rydjord, *Indian Place-Names*, 240.
59. Coues, ed., *Journal of Jacob Fowler*, 26.
60. Remsburg, in *Leavenworth Times*, October 24, 1935.
61. Bowers, *Norton County*, 5.
62. Louise Barry, ed., "Kansas before 1854: A Revised Annals," *KHQ*, XXX, 71;

LeRoy R. Hafen and Ann W. Hafen, eds., *Rufus B. Sage, His Letters and Papers, 1836–1847*, in *Far West and the Rockies*, II, 297.

63. In his *Gazetteer of Kansas*, Gannett does not list the Otter Creeks in neither Clay nor Norton counties. Cf. *Bulletin* 154, U.S. Geological Survey (1898), 172.

64. *The Wichita Eagle and Beacon*, January 25, 1970, 6D.

65. F. Robert Henderson, *Beaver in Kansas*, 10.

66. Paden, *Prairie Schooner*, 38.

67. Mead, *KHC*, IX, 13.

68. *KHC*, XII, 473.

69. Montgomery, *KHC*, XVII, 272.

70. Scott County *News-Chronicle*, December 8, 1932.

71. Bowers, *Norton County*, 5.

72. *Overland Journey*, 94.

73. Charles C. Howes, *This Place called Kansas*, 51.

74. Bowers, *Norton County*, 1; H. Horton Liliburn, *Fremont's Expeditions Through Kansas, 1842–1854*; Fort Hays Studies, No. 2 (1962), 40.

75. Rufus Gray, *Saints and Sinners*, 52.

76. Cf. map in Andreas, *Kansas*, 683.

77. *The Daily Republican*, Burlington, December 10, 1945.

78. George Remsburg, "Frontier," *Pony Express Courier*, December, 1936.

79. Lyon County, *Coronado Centennial*, Map, 1941.

80. Ida M. Ferris, "The Sauks and Foxes in Franklin and Osage Counties, Kansas," *KHC*, XI, 388.

81. *Horton Headlight*, October 29, 1936.

82. *Fort Scott Tribune*, May 30, 1942.

83. Coues, ed., *Pike*, II, 522.

84. Kirk Meacham, "Home on the Range," *KHQ*, XVII, 313.

85. *Ibid.*, XVII, 321–32.

VII
NATURAL RESOURCES

1. James, *Account of Long's Expedition, 1819–1820*, in Thwaites, ed., *Early Western Travels*, XIV, 174.

2. T. C. Henry, "The Story of a Fenceless Winter-Wheat Field," *KHC*, IX, 505.

3. Francis S. Laing, "German-Russian Settlements in Ellis County, Kansas," *KHC*, XI, 526n.

4. James R. Mead, "The Little Arkansas," *KHC*, X, 9.

5. *Independence Daily Reporter*, April 4, 1958.

6. Laura Lu Tolsted and Ada Swinford, *Kansas Rocks and Minerals*, 32.

7. *A Gazetteer of Kansas, Bulletin* 154, U.S. Geological Survey, 199.

8. L. W. Spring, *Kansas, The Prelude to the War for the Union*, 22; Coues, ed., *Pike*, II, 523.

9. Andreas, *Kansas*, 1014, 1032; Mrs. E. F. Hollibaugh, *Biographical History of Cloud County, Kansas*, 73.

10. Baughman, *Kansas Post Offices*, 27.

11. *KHQ*, IX, 217; Andreas, *Kansas*, 1555.

12. Montgomery, *KHC*, XVII, 192.

13. Scheffer, *KHQ*, III, 234.

14. W. R. Crane, "Geography and detailed Stratigraphy of the Kansas Coal Measures . . . ," *The University Geological Survey of Kansas*, III, 143.

15. Corley, *Names*, 13.

16. Andreas, *Kansas*, 1169; Richard L. Douglas, "A History of Manufacturers in the Kansas District," *KHC*, XI, 167.

17. L. M. Dillman to George Martin, November 17, 1901, "Names," MS, Archives, *KSHS*, Topeka; Andreas, *Kansas*, 1167.

18. Cecil Howes in *Kansas City Star*, December 8, 1941; Stone, *KHC*, VII, 248.
19. Allison, *Cherokee County*, 160; Shackleton, *Handbook of Frontier Days*, 65.
20. G. P. Grimsley, "Gypsum in Kansas," *Kansas Academy of Science*, XV, 122.
21. Erasmus Haworth, "Historic Sketch of the Gypsum, Cement and Plaster Industry in Kansas," *KHC*, VII, 88.
22. Allen County *Scrapbook*, II, 26, 185, *KSHL*, Topeka.
23. Ellis County, *Golden Jubilee Report*, 1926.
24. *Sumner County Press*, Wellington, January 29, 1874.
25. Risely to Schruben, Stockton, August 17 and September 1, 1959.
26. See Chapter on "French Name the Rivers."
27. Gannett, *A Gazetteer of Kansas, Bulletin* 154, 197–99.
28. *Leavenworth Times*, January 24, 1907.
29. Savage, *Republic County*, 36.
30. Andreas, *Kansas*, 1271.
31. The county maps in Andreas, *Kansas*, mark the numerous millsites.
32. Cory, *Bourbon County*, 11.
33. *Atchison Daily Globe*, May 24, 1907.
34. *KHC*, XII, 472.
35. Leslie Fitz, "The Development of the Milling Industry in Kansas," *KHC*, XII, 57.
36. Louise Barry, ed., "Kansas Before 1854: A Revised Annals," *KHQ*, XXIX, 345.
37. Greeley, *Overland Journey*, 61.
38. Coues, ed., *Journal of Jacob Fowler*, 17.
39. The fencepost museum in LaCrosse illustrates the use of limestone.
40. Blackburn and Cardwell, *Republic County*, 182; *Courtland Journal*, June 28 and August 2, 1951.
41. Sister M. Evangeline Thomas, "The Rev. Louis Dumortier, S. J., Itinerant Missionary to Central Kansas, 1859–1867," *KHQ*, XX, 270n; Andreas, *Kansas*, 1274.
42. Evan T. Sage, "Classical Place-Names in America," *American Speech*, IV, 268.
43. The Frederic Remington High School north of El Dorado was named for the artist.
44. Taft, *KHQ*, XVI, 126.
45. For lists of mineral names see *Lawrence Journal-World*, January 18, 1952; and *Meade Globe News*, June 10, 1943.
46. Andreas, *Kansas*, 875.
47. For a report of the oil industry in Kansas, see Douglas, *KHC*, XI, 135, 144.
48. Mooney, *Butler County*, 62.
49. Franklin Bigler, in *Wichita Eagle*, June 24, 1956.
50. *Kingman County Diamond Jubilee Souvenir Historical Program*, 1958.

VIII
ECONOMIC IMPRINT

1. Lillian L. Fitzpatrick, *Nebraska Place-Names*, 34.
2. See Chapter IX.
3. Gould, *Covered Wagon Geologist*, 119.
4. "Brief Summary of the Santa Fe Trail through Kansas," *Eighteenth Biennial Report*, *KSHS*, 113.
5. *Sherman County Herald*, August 19, 1937.
6. Blanchard, *Conquest of Southwest Kansas*, 79–82.
7. Lathrop, *Tales*, 116, 120.
8. Rydjord, *Indian Place-Names*, 63; Andreas, *Kansas*, 531.
9. Corley, *Names*, 74.
10. James McDermitt to Martin, November 8, 1901, MS, *KSHS*.
11. *Rooks County Record*, Stockton, March 14, 1940.
12. George W. Martin, "Memorial Monuments and Tablets in Kansas," *KHC*, XI, 274.

13. Moffat, *KHQ*, VI, 154.
14. Sheridan Ploughe, *History of Reno County, Kansas*, I, 50.
15. Lathrop, *Tales*, 72.
16. George Jelinek, *The Ellsworth Story*.
17. *The Wilson World*, July 22, 1948; F. J. Swehla, "Bohemians in Kansas," *KHC*, XIII, 474.
18. *KHC*, VII, 486; *The Wilson World*, July 15, 1948.
19. Isely in *Wichita Beacon*, June 30, 1929.
20. *KHC*, X, 664.
21. Andreas, *Kansas*, 1273; Jelinek, *Ellsworth Story*, n.p.
22. *Chase County Historical Sketches*, II, 114.
23. Richard W. Lewis, *Early Days History of Home City*, 3.
24. Cf. maps in Andreas, *Kansas*; Kansas Board of Agriculture, *Fifth Biennial Report* (1876), *passim*; *KHC*, XII, 447.
25. Baughman, *Kansas Post Offices*, 43, 59.
26. *Kansas Precancel News*, No. 159, December, 1967.
27. J. J. Lutz, "Methodist Missions among the Indian Tribes in Kansas," *KHC*, IX, 198n; *Kansas City Star*, November 12, 1942.
28. Carley, *Names*, 73.
29. Kittie Dale in *Salina Journal*, April 2, 1964.
30. Howes, *Kansas City Star*, July 17, 1942; Federal Writers' Project, *Kansas, A Guide*, 405.
31. Kos Harris to Bliss Isely, Wichita, n.d., MS, Wichita State University Library.
32. Remsburg, *Scrapbook*, IV, 76.
33. Nyquist, *Pioneer Life*, 89, 102.
34. "It Happened in Kansas," *The Advocate-Democrat*, Marysville, July 10, 1941.
35. Manhattan, *Mercury Chronicle*, December 19, 1948.
36. *Chase County Historical Sketches*, cf. map, I, 14.
37. Larry Roberts in *Wichita Sunday Eagle*, December 13, 1959.
38. *Wichita Evening Eagle*, December 16, 1936.
39. Bowers, *Norton County*, 69.
40. Edward C. Janzen, *Green Garden*, 49.
41. Remsburg, *Scrapbook*, I, 153, KSHL.
42. *Abilene Reflector Chronicle*, June 7 and 8, 1948; Edward G. Nelson, *The Company and the Community*, 183.
43. Nyquist, *Pioneer Life*, 89, 102.
44. Andreas, *Kansas*, 1167.
45. Root, *KHQ*, V, 324.
46. Blackmar and Caldwell, *Republic County*, 295.
47. Harry W. Mollhagen, *In Reminiscence*, 18; Missouri Pacific, *The Empire*, 96.
48. Gould, *Covered Wagon Geologist*, 32.

IX
CASTILIAN NAMES IN KANSAS

1. William D. Overman, *Ohio Town Names*, 32.
2. *The Modern Light*, Columbus, August 16, 1951.
3. Ingalls, *Atchison County*, 42.
4. Andreas, *Kansas*, 896.
5. Van Gundy, *Reminiscences*, 36–38; *KHC*, X, 209, and XVI, 454.
6. Andreas, *Kansas*, 896.
7. *KHC*, XII, 476.
8. See "America" by Marrion Wilcox in *Encyclopedia Americana* (1966); M. S. Beeler, "America—The Story of a Name," *Names*, I, 1–14.
9. Andreas, *Kansas*, 847; *Emporia Times*, August 11, 1949.

10. Everett Dick, "The Long Drive," *KHC*, XVII, 92.

11. John Rydjord, "The Conquistadores Came to Kansas," John Bright, ed., *Kansas, The First Century*, I, 1.

12. David E. Sopher, "Arabic Place-Names in Spain," *Names*, III, 8.

13. George Hammond and Agapito Rey, eds., *Narrative of the Coronado Expedition, Coronado Cuarto Centennial Publications, 1540-1940*, II, 291n; James N. Baskett, "Prehistoric Kansas," *KHC*, XII, 228.

14. Charles W. Hackett, ed., *Pichardo's Treatise on the Limits of Louisiana and Texas*, II, 376.

15. Frederick W. Hodge, ed., *Handbook of American Indians North of Mexico, Bulletin* No. 30, BAE., II, 346; George E. Hyde, *Pawnee Indians*, 64.

16. Martin, *KHC*, VII, 376.

17. Bracke, *Wheat Country*, 15.

18. Charles W. Hackett, "Policy of the Spanish Crown regarding French Encroachments from Louisiana, 1721-1762," George P. Hammond, ed., *New Spain and the West*, I, 137; Rydjord, "French Frontier and the Indian Trade," Bright, ed., *Kansas, The First Century*, I, 34.

19. Hackett, ed., *Pichardo*, II, 232, 386.

20. Charles O. Paullin, *Atlas of the Historical Geography of the United States*, Plate 22 A.

21. Alfred B. Thomas, *After Coronado*, 18, 30.

22. Archer B. Hulbert, *Southwest on the Turquoise Trail*, 51.

23. Carl Irving Wheat, *Mapping the Transmississippi West, 1500-1861*, I, 126, 136.

24. Thomas, *After Coronado*, 65, 73; Hackett, ed., *Pichardo*, II, 40.

25. Rydjord, Bright, ed., *Kansas, The First Century*, I, 38; Barry, ed., *KHQ*, XXVII, 206.

26. Wheat, *Mapping the Transmississippi West*, I, 29, 32n.; Erwin G. Gudde, *California Place Names*, 257.

27. Greene, *Kanzas Region*, 132.

28. Coues, ed., *Pike*, II, 522n.

29. Leroy R. Hafen, *The Overland Mail, 1849-1869*, 71.

30. Coues, ed., *Pike*, II, 438n.

31. Fessler, ed., *Chronicles of Oklahoma*, VII, 91n.; Charles N. Gould, *Oklahoma Place Names*, 23; E. B. D. Beachy in *Kansas City Times*, January 17, 1950.

32. Chrisman, *Lost Trails of the Cimarron*, 15; John F. McDermott, "A Glossary of Mississippi Valley French," *Studies* No. 12 in *Language and Literature*, Washington University (1941), 101.

33. Heinie Schmidt in *Dodge City Journal*, January 8, 1848.

34. H. C. McDougal, "Historical Sketch of Kansas City, Missouri," *KHC*, XI, 582.

35. George P. Morehouse, "Padilla and the Old Monument near Council Grove," *KHC*, X, 472.

36. C. W. Hackett, "New Light on Don Diego de Penalosa . . . ," *Mississippi Valley Historical Review*, VI, 313-35; Henri Folmer, *Franco-Spanish Rivalry in America*, 139.

37. Rydjord, Bright, ed., *Kansas, The First Century*, I, 16-17; John B. Dunbar, "Massacre of the Villasur Expedition by the Pawnees on the Platte, in 1720," *KHC*, XI, 400-406, 417-18.

38. Rydjord, *Kansas, The First Century*, I, 16; Thomas, *After Coronado*, 264, 270.

39. Federal Writers' Project, *Kansas, A Guide*, 401; Helen Ward Rennie, *A Tale of Two Towns, passim*.

40. *KHC*, XII, 463; *Kansas City Journal*, May 5, 1912.

41. *KHQ*, XXV, 371; Ralph Tennal, *History of Nemaha County, Kansas*, 47.

42. See map in Andreas, *Kansas*.

43. *KHC*, XII, 457; India Harris Simmons, "Kendall in Early Days," *KHQ*, VII, 68; Howes, *Kansas City Star*, December 8, 1941.

44. *Chase County Historical Sketches*, I, 29; Overman, *Ohio Town Names*, 133.

45. Blackburn and Cardwell, *Republic County*, 104, 198, 211; Savage, *Republic County*, 187, 226.

46. Anniejane H. Cover, "Some Place Names of Kansas," *Heritage of Kansas*, Publications, Kansas State Teachers College, Emporia, IV, 14.

47. Isaac Taylor, *Names and their Histories*, 102; Washington Irving, *Christopher Columbus, In Works*, (1868), IV, 214.

48. John W. Vandercook, *Caribbee Cruise*, 46–47.

49. Andreas, *Kansas*, 1231; *Peoples Herald*, Lynden, April 29, 1948.

50. Corley, *Names*, 31.

51. Andreas, *Kansas*, 1224; George Stewart, *Names on the Land*, 19.

52. J. C. Leland, *Names*, I, 270; Eloise Lambert and Mario Pei, *The Book of Place-Names*, 12.

53. H. H. Bancroft, *Annals of Early Central America*, 326; Taylor, *Names*, 104.

54. *KHC*, XII, 485; *Sabetha Herald*, October 19, 1938.

55. Hubert Herring, *A History of Latin America*, 145.

56. Andreas, *Kansas*, 1433.

57. Lambert and Pei, *Book of Place-Names*, 104.

58. *Wichita Evening Eagle*, March 4, 1938; United States Board of Geographical Names, *Third Report*, 15.

59. Lathrop, *Tales*, 70.

60. *Sedan Times-Star*, January 3, 1935.

61. Bancroft, *Early Central America*, 486.

62. William H. Prescott, *Conquest of Peru*, II, 28.

63. *KHC*, XII, 481.

64. Gwendolin B. Cobb, "Potosí, A Mining Frontier," in *Greater America*, Adele Ogden and Engel Sluiter, eds., 40.

65. Eugene C. Barker, "The Austin Papers," *Annual Report*, American Historical Association, 1919, Part I, Volume II, 29, 123; Oliver and Betty Roskam and Bryan and Ida Purteet, "Missouri's Official State Mineral and Rock," *Lapidary Journal*, XXII, 632.

66. Andreas, *Kansas*, 1101; Mitchell, *Linn County*, 321.

67. Mooney, *Butler County*, 62.

68. Luis Lara y Pardo, *Diccionario de Geografía, Historia, y Biografía Mexicana*, 945.

69. Gudde, *California Place Names*, 301.

70. *KHC*, XII, 489.

71. Hamlin Garland, "Grant in Mexico," *McClures*, VIII, 366–80.

72. *KHQ*, XX, 288.

73. Marshall S. Hiskey, *History of Derby*, MS., (Derby Public Library), 14; D. B. Emmert, "History of Sedgwick County, Kansas," in John P. Edwards, *Historical Atlas of Sedgwick County*, 11.

74. Henry Gannett, *American Names*, 181.

75. For these and other California names see Chapter on the "Midwest and Westward."

76. W. W. Graves, *History of Neosho County Newspapers*, 24.

77. Blair, *Johnson County*, 177.

78. *Ibid.*, 178.

79. J. S. Bird, ed., *Historical Plat Book of Jackson County*, 11.

80. Wayne A. O'Connell, "Origin of Names," *Oswego Democrat*, January 15, 1954; Andreas, *Kansas*, 1485.

81. *Council Grove Republican*, December 3, 1886; *Business Directory and History of Wabaunsee County*, 52.

82. Andreas, *Kansas*, 963; Stone, *KHC*, VII, 246.

83. *KHC*, XII, 480.

84. Coues, ed., *Pike*, II, 424n., III, 621 n.; Fessler, ed., *Chronicles of Oklahoma*, VII, 61.

85. George Jelinek, *Ninety Years of Ellsworth and Ellsworth County History*.

86. Douglas, *KHC*, XI, 190.
87. Ellis County *Golden Jubilee Report*, 1926.
88. Walt Neibarger, ed., *Sunflower Petals*.
89. *KHC*, XII, 482.
90. Supplement to *Sublette Monitor*, June 12, 1930.
91. *KHQ*, XXIII, 139; A. Theodore Brown, *Frontier Community, Kansas City to 1870*, 56.
92. Taylor, *Names*, 174.
93. *Sedan Times-Star*, August 14, 1941.
94. Baughman, *Kansas Post Offices*, 75; W. F. Thompson, "Peter Robidoux: A Real Kansas Pioneer," *KHC*, XVII, 288.
95. Corley, *Names*, 10.
96. Blanchard, *Conquest*, 94.

X
FRENCH AND INDIAN RIVER NAMES

1. For Marquette's map see *KHC*, X, insert page 80; Andreas, *Kansas*, 46.
2. James O. Dorsey, "Siouan Sociology," *Fifteenth Annual Report*, 1893-94, Bureau of American Ethnology (referred to hereinafter as *BAE*), 231-33; W. J. McGee, "The Siouan Stock," *ibid.*, 157, 189-92.
3. McGee, "The Siouan Stock," *15th Annual Report, BAE*, 162; William E. Connelley, *A Standard History of Kansas and Kansans*, I, 193-205.
4. For a longer list see "This Name 'Kansas,'" *KHQ*, XX, 450; Howes, *Kansas*, 28.
5. George R. Brooks, "George C. Sibley's Journal of a Trip to the Salines, in 1811," Missouri Historical Society, *Bulletin*, XXI, 176.
6. Greene, *Kanzas Region*, 23; Morehouse, *KHC*, X, 327-68; *Kansas City Star*, August 5, 1940.
7. Henry Dodge, "Report on the Expedition of Dragoons, under Colonel Henry Dodge, to the Rocky Mountains in 1835," *American State Papers*, Military Affairs (1861), VI, cf. maps.
8. Walter H. Schoewe, "Political Geographical Aspects of Territorial Kansas," *Territorial Kansas*, University of Kansas Social Science Publications (1954), 14; *Kansas City Times*, December 6, 1951.
9. Cora Dolbee, "First Book on Kansas," *KHQ*, II, 164; Edward E. Hale, *Kanzas and Nebraska*, v.
10. *Junction City Union*, August 6, 1864; Greene, *Kanzas Region*, 139-47; Kittie Dale, "Story of Chetolah," *Salina Journal*, April 12, 1964.
11. George B. Grinnell, "Some Indian Stream Names," *American Anthropologist* (n.s.), XV, 331.
12. James Mooney, "Calendar History of the Kiowa," *17th Annual Report*, 1895-96, *BAE*, Part I, 415, 438; see Huntington's map of 1839, *KHQ*, XVI, opp. 17.
13. Baughman, *Kansas in Maps*, 23, 39.
14. Wheat, *Mapping the Transmississippi West* , I, 129.
15. Hyde, *Pawnee Indians*, opp. 279.
16. Grinnell, "Cheyenne Stream Names," *American Anthropologist* (n.s.), XIII, 18; Hyde, *Pawnee Indians*, 282.
17. *Pike*, II, 423n. In the West Indies, *bucaniers* is the name given to the pirates who smoked their meat, and from which came the word Buccaneer.
18. Coues, ed., *Pike*, II, 404n.
19. Wheat, *Mapping the Transmississippi West*, II, 144.
20. *Beyond the Mississippi*, 34.
21. See Emory K. Lindquist, *Smoky Valley People*; James R. Mead, "Origin of Names of Kansas Streams," Kansas Academy of Science, *Transactions*, XVIII, 215.
22. Remsburg, *Scrapbook, KSHL*, I, 153, II, 28, and IV, 28, 32; Edwin James,

Account of Expedition ... of S. H. Long, in Thwaites, ed., *Early Western Travels*, XIV, 181 n., 187; *Atchison Daily Globe*, May 24, 1907.

23. Cf. maps in Kansas State Board of Agriculture Reports for 1877 and 1887.

24. Virgil J. Vogel, "The Origin and Meaning of 'Missouri,'" *Missouri Historical Society, Bulletin*, XVI, 214; J. T. Link, "The Origin of Place Names of Nebraska," Nebraska Geological Survey, *Bulletin*, VII, 2nd Series, 73.

25. McGee, "The Siouan Stock," *15th Annual Report, BAE*, 162; Francis LaFlesche, *A Dictionary of the Osage Language, BAE, Bulletin*, CIX, 110.

26. Rydjord, *Indian Place-Names*, 43–50; Vogel, Missouri Historical Society, *Bulletin*, XVI, 216.

27. Rydjord, *Indian Place-Names*, 50.

28. Hulbert, *Southwest of the Turquoise Trail*, 31.

29. Hackett, ed., *Pichardo*, III, 570.

30. *Wichita Eagle*, April 12, 1872.

31. *Ibid.*

32. Stewart, *Names on the Land*, 336.

33. *Wichita Eagle*, May 31, 1872.

34. Mathews, *Osages*, 137; Baughman, *Kansas in Maps*, 25.

35. James, *Expedition of S. H. Long*, in Thwaites, ed., *Early Western Travels*.

36. For more detailed information cf. Rydjord, *Indian Place-Names*, 90 ff.

37. D. A. Millington, "History of Cowley County, Kansas," in *The Courier*, Winfield, January 31, 1900.

38. G. E. Patrick, "The Great Spirit Spring," Kansas Academy of Science, *Transactions*, VII, 22; Remsburg, *Scrapbook*, I, 73, *KSHL*, Topeka.

39. Henri Folmer, "The Mallett Expedition of 1739 . . . ," *Colorado Magazine*, XVI, 165.

40. W. R. Chambers, in *Rooks County Record*, March 14, 1940.

41. Scheffer, *KHQ*, III, 231.

42. Folmer, *Colorado Magazine*, XVI, 165, b 23; Herbert E. Bolton, "French Intrusion into New Mexico," ed. by Bolton and H. M. Stephens, *Pacific Ocean in History*, 391 n.

43. Scheffer, *KHQ*, III, 233.

44. *KHC*, VII, 484; Federal Writers' Project, *A Guide to Salina*, 23.

45. Fessler, ed., "Boone's Journal," *Chronicles of Oklahoma*, V, 212.

46. *Kingman County Diamond Jubilee* (1958).

47. A. B. Stubbs, to George Martin, May 23, 1896, MS, Archives, *KSHS*; Fessler, ed., "Boone's Journal," *Chronicles of Oklahoma*, VII, 67 and n.

48. Muriel H. Wright, "Some Geographical Names of French Origin in Oklahoma," *Chronicles of Oklahoma*, VII, 190 n.; Miller, *KHQ*, I, 117 n.

49. Wheat, *Mapping the Transmississippi West*, II, No. 284 and 720.

50. *Ibid.*

51. For additional information on these names see Rydjord, *Indian Place-Names*, Chapter VIII.

52. Grinnell, "Some Indian Stream Names," *American Anthropologist* (n.s.), XV, 331.

53. Mathews, *Osages*, 187, 708.

54. Hulbert, *Southwest on the Turquoise Trail*, 51.

55. See Chapter IX.

56. Mathews, *Osages*, 108; McGee, "The Siouan Indians," *BAE, Fifteenth Annual Report* (1893–94), 192.

57. Mitchell, *Linn County*, 318–20.

58. Shackleton, *Handbook of the Frontier Days*, 76; Mathews, *Osages*, 140, 181.

59. Whittemore, *Historic Kansas*, 147; *Topeka Capital*, July 7, 1950.

60. *Kansas City Star*, April 18, 1946, and December 10, 1949.

61. Wheat, *Mapping the Transmississippi West*, I, 120.

62. Coues, ed., *Pike*, II, 30.

63. Graves, *Neosho County*, I, 30.

64. Root, *KHQ*, IV, 268; Coues, ed., *Jacob Fowler's Journal*, 3, 6, 165.

65. Hafen, ed., *Journal of John R. Bell*, VI, 261n.

66. John F. McDermott, ed., *Tixier's Travels on the Osage Prairies*, 115, 118, 126.

67. Andreas, *Kansas*, 796, 826; Maloy in *Kansas Cosmos*, Council Grove, April 23, 1886.

68. T. F. Morrison, "Osage Treaty of 1865," *KHC*, XVII, 695; Mead, "Origin of Names of Kansas Streams," Kansas Academy of Science, *Transactions*, XVIII, 216.

69. *Osages*, 181 and 298.

70. Duncan, *Neosho County*, 23; Andreas, *Kansas*, 826.

71. Russell Hickman, "The Vegetarian and Octagon Settlement Companies," *KHQ*, II, 380–83.

72. Van Gundy, *Reminiscences*, 33; Flora R. Godsey, "Early Settlement and Raid on the 'Upper Neosho,'" *KHC*, XVI, 455.

73. C. E. Cory, "The Osage Ceded Lands," *KHC*, VIII, 196.

74. S. W. Brewster, "Reverend Father Paul M. Ponziglione," *KHC*, IX, 26.

75. O'Connell in *Oswego Democrat*, September 3, 1954; Tillie K. Newman, *Black Dog Trail*, 116.

76. C. E. Cory to William Gladstone, April 20, 1928, "Names," MS, *Archives, KSHS*.

77. Mathews, *Osages*, 140, 181.

78. Coues, ed., *Pike*, II, 386n.

79. A. L. Van Osdel, *Historic Landmarks*, 343.

80. *Ibid.*; *KHC*, XII, 449n.

81. Coues, ed., *Pike*, II, 386n.; Cory, *Bourbon County*, 10.

82. David E. Ballard, "The First State Legislature, 1861," *KHC*, X, 250; *KHC*, XII, 449n.

83. Coues, ed., *Fowler's Journal*, 3n.; Coues, ed., *Pike*, II, 555n.

84. Mathews, *Osages*, 181.

85. James C. Horton, "Peter A. Ridenour and Harlow W. Baker," *KHC*, X, 599.

86. Wheat, *Mapping the Transmississippi West*, II, No. 315.

87. LeRoy Hafen, ed., *Southwest Historical Series*, IX, 48n.

88. Baughman, *Kansas Post Offices*, 132; *KHC*, XII, 489.

89. Edgar Landsdorf, "The First Survey of the Kansas River," *KHQ*, XVIII, 149.

90. Wheat, *Mapping the Transmississippi West*, I, 158.

91. *Ibid.*, II, Plates 287 and 291.

92. Rydjord, *Indian Place-Names*, 60–62.

93. Grant Foreman, *Indian Removal*, 220.

94. George A. Root and Russell K. Hickman, "Pike's Peak Express Companies," *KHQ*, XIII, 516.

95. Aubrey Diller, "Origin of the Names of Tributaries of the Kansas River," *KHQ*, XXI, 402.

96. Hyde, *Pawnee Indians*, 13; Waldo R. Wedel, "An Introduction to Pawnee Archaeology," *Bulletin* 112, *BAE*, 2–3.

97. Hyde, *Pawnee Indians*, 93, 200; Roenigh, *Pioneer History of Kansas*, 232.

98. Andreas, *Kansas*, 1092.

99. Goodnow, *KHC*, V, 246; "Governor Shannon's Administration," *KHC*, V, 254.

100. Hyde, *Pawnee Indians*, 64; M. R. Gilmore, "Some Indian Place Names in Nebraska," *Publications*, Nebraska State Historical Society, XIX, 134.

101. J. T. Link, "Origin of the Place-Names of Nebraska," in Lillian L. Fitzpatrick, *Nebraska Place-Names*, 183.

102. Mathews, *Osages*, 139.

103. Folmer, *The Colorado Magazine*, XVI, 165n.

104. Gilmore, "Some Indian Place Names," *Publications*, Nebraska State Historical Society, XIX, 134; Hyde, *Pawnee Indians*, 64.

105. J. C. McCoy to F. G. Adams, Chouteau, July 5, 1883, MS, *Archives*, KSHS, Topeka; Barnes, ed., "Journal of Isaac McCoy," *KHQ*, V, 368.
106. Hyde, *Pawnee Indians*, 73, 78; Rydjord, *Indian Place-Names*, 145–47.
107. Frank Haucke, "The Kaw or Kansa Indians," *KHQ*, XX, 49.
108. Leslie A. White, ed., *Lewis Henry Morgan, The Indian Journals, 1859–62*, 68.
109. Barry, ed., "Kansas Before 1854," *KHQ*, XXIX, 543; and XXXI, 150.
110. Ely Moore, "A Buffalo Hunt with the Miamis in 1854," *KHC*, X, 404.
111. William E. Connelley, "Origin of the Name Topeka," *KHC*, XVII, 591 ff.; F. W. Giles, *Thirty Years in Topeka, A Historical Sketch*, 53–54.
112. Isely, *Wichita Beacon*, April 14, 1929.
113. Hyde, *Pawnee Indians*, 63; Connelley, "Origin of the Name Topeka," *KHC*, XVII, 591–93.
114. Cecil Howes, "What About the Name Topeka," *Bulletin* No. 1, Shawnee County Historical Society, 106; King, *Shawnee County*, 133.
115. Giles, *Thirty Years in Topeka*, 51; Cecil Howes, "Ninety Years for the Santa Fe," *Kansas Teacher*, LVIII (September, 1949), 46.
116. Quoted in H. L. Mencken, *The American Language*, 528.

XI
ADDITIONAL FRENCH NAMES

1. Charles E. Hoffman, "Fort de Cavagnial," *KHQ*, XXX, 425ff.; Émile Lauvrière, *Histoire de la Louisiane Francaise, 1673–1939*, 275.
2. Andreas, *Kansas*, 49; *Onaga Herald*, August 21, 1941.
3. Barry, ed., "Kansas before 1854," *KHQ*, XXVII, 529.
4. Charles P. Deatherage, *Early History of Greater Kansas City*, I, 334.
5. F. G. Adams, "Reminiscences of Fredrick Chouteau," *KHC*, VIII, 425; Miller, *Historic Sites*, 64.
6. William R. Bernard, "Westport and the Santa Fe Trade," *KHC*, IX, 558; Andreas, *Kansas*, 1563.
7. Connelley, *Kansas*, I, 210; Shackleton, *Southeast Kansas*, 13; "Explanation of Map," *KHC*, IX, 570.
8. John F. McDermott, ed., *The French in the Mississippi Valley*, 45–47.
9. Otis E. Young, *First Military Escort on the Santa Fe Trail*, 24; Hafen, ed., *Journal of John R. Bell*, VI, 218.
10. *Lakin Independent*, August 9, 1935; Barry, ed., *KHQ*, XXVII, 360, 378.
11. Grant Foreman, "Down the Texas Road," Series No. 2, *Historical Oklahoma*, 16–17.
12. J. F. McDermott, "Isaac McCoy's Second Exploring Trip in 1828," *KHQ*, XIII, 450n.
13. Case, *Labette County*, 31; O'Connell in *Oswego Independent*, October 19, 1951.
14. Andreas, *Kansas*, 1454; Beachy, *Kansas City Times*, January 17, 1950.
15. Andreas, *Kansas*, 1454.
16. Case, *Labette County*, 24; O'Connell in *Oswego Democrat*, July 2, 1954.
17. Washington Irving, *A Tour of the Prairies*, John McDermott, ed., 24n.
18. Case, *Labette County*, 21, 26, 118; O'Connell in *Oswego Independent*, July 2, 1954.
19. Vincent V. Masterson, *The Katy Railroad*, 120.
20. Remsburg, *Scrapbook*, I, 150, KSHL.
21. Quaife, ed., *Journal of Lewis and Ordway*, 93n.
22. Gray, *Doniphan County*, Part II, 23, 44; Remsburg, *Scrapbook*, I, 153, 175, 233, KSHL; J. Neale Carman and Karl S. Pond, "The Replacement of Indian Languages of Kansas by English," Kansas Academy of Science, *Transactions*, L, 146.
23. Shawnee County Historical Society, *Bulletin*, I, 128; William E. Smith, "The Oregon Trail Through Pottawatomie County," *KHC*, XVII, 454.

24. Andreas, *Kansas*, 587; George A. Root, "Reminiscences of William R. Darnell," *KHC*, XVII, 499.

25. Graves, *Neosho County*, I, 125; Andreas, *Kansas*, 826.

26. John E. Sunder, *Bill Sublette, Mountain Man, passim*; Greene, *Kanzas*, 82; *Sublette Monitor*, May 7, 1936; Don Berry, *A Majority of Scoundrels*, 207, 272.

27. *Kansas City Journal*, May 5, 1912; Remsburg, *Scrapbook*, I, 173, *KSHL*.

28. J. Frank Dobie, "The Saga of the Saddle," *Southwestern Review*, XIII, 135; Ralph P. Bieber, ed., "Cooke's Journal of the March of the Mormon Battalion, 1846–1847," *The Southwestern Historical Series*, VII, 61.

29. George D. Brewerton, *Overland With Kit Carson*, 252–58; W. Pride, *The History of Fort Riley*, 48.

30. Bernard B. Smyth, *The Heart of the New Kansas*, 67; *KHC*, XII, 483.

31. Howes in *Kansas City Star*, December 8, 1941; *KHC*, XII, 457; *Lakin Independent*, August 9, 1935.

32. Cf. map in Andreas, *Kansas*.

33. Ida H. Simmons, "Kendall in Early Days," *KHQ*, VII, 68; *KHC*, XII, 457.

34. Blair, *Johnson County*, 167.

35. Barry ed., *KHQ*, XVIII, 159; *Marysville Advocate*, July 2, 1953.

36. *Marshall County News* (Marysville), February 27, 1931.

37. *KHC*, XII, 473.

38. Maynie Shearer Bush and Winifred Shearer, eds., *The Frankfort Story, A History of Frankfort, Kansas*, 147.

39. Duncan, ed., *Neosho and Wilson Counties*, 17, 18.

40. Gannett, *American Names*, 111.

41. Edna Kenton, ed., *Black Gown and Redskins, Adventures and Travels of the Early Jesuit Missionaries in North America*, 334.

42. *KHC*, VII, 481.

43. Corley, *Names*, 21.

44. Pantle, *KHQ*, XIX, 13.

45. J. Neale Carman, "Continental Europeans in Rural Kansas, 1854–1861," in *Territorial Kansas*, University of Kansas Publications in Social Science, 170.

46. *Burlington Daily Republican*, December 10, 1945; George Throckmorton, et al, *First Hand Historical Episodes of Early Coffey County*, 34.

47. Root and Connelley, *Overland*, 197, 518.

48. George A. Huron, "Earnest Valeton Boissiere," *KHC*, VII, 552–64; Whittemore, *Kansas*, III; Bracke, *Wheat Country*, 62.

49. Pantle, *KHQ*, XIX, 23.

50. *Chase County Historical Sketches*, I, 17.

51. Pantle, *KHQ*, XIX, 13, 20; *Ibid.*

52. Andreas, *Kansas*, 1368; Malin, *KHQ*, IX, 259.

53. *Dodge City Journal*, October 22, 1936 and January 8, 1948.

54. Simmons, *KHQ*, VII, 69, and in *History of Kearny County*, I, 36, 58; William F. Chollar, "French Louis," clipping from *Syracuse Journal*.

55. T. F. Robley, *History of Bourbon County*, 43–44; Beachy in *Kansas City Times*, December 6, 1951.

56. Andreas, *Kansas*, 1065; Inman in *Topeka Daily Commonwealth*, January 12, 1886.

57. *KHC*, XII, 482; Andreas, *Kansas*, 310.

58. *An Historical Atlas of Miami County*, 12; Andreas, *Kansas*, 891.

59. Overman, *Ohio Town Names*, 84.

60. *Marshall County News* (Marysville), February 27, 1931.

61. King, *Shawnee County*, 62.

62. Minnie Dubbs Millbrook, *Ness: Western County, Kansas*, 86.

63. Baughman, *Kansas in Maps*, 87.

64. *The Lakin Independent*, August 27, 1948.

514

65. Abilene *Reflector-Chronicle*, November 7, 1946, and April 3, 1956; "Kansas History in the Press," *KHQ*, XV, 216.

66. Taylor, *Names and their Histories*, 52.

67. *KHC*, XII, 472.

68. *Idem.*

69. James Dugan, "The Incredible Adventures of John Ledyard," *Holiday*, XXVIII (October, 1960), 36.

70. In the twentieth century, he shares the honor with Winston Churchill.

71. *Sherman County Herald*, August 22, 1937.

72. Andreas, *Kansas*, 1608.

73. Andre Maurois, *Victor Hugo and his World*, 10–11; "The Annals of Kansas," *KHQ*, XX, 288.

74. Howes in *Kansas City Star*, July 17, 1942.

75. Foreman, *The Last Trek*, 126, 132n.; Corley, *Names*, 39.

76. Lathrop, *Tales of Western Kansas*, 83.

77. *Ibid.*, 83, 117.

78. D. W. Wilder, *Annals of Kansas*, 27.

79. Lodi may have been named for Lodi in California, cf. Gudde, *California Place Names*, 170.

80. Missouri Pacific Lines, *The Empire*, 34; Roenigh, *Pioneer History*, 34.

81. "Dead Towns," MS, III, *KSHS*.

82. Johnson, *Anderson County*, 346; *Chase County Historical Sketches*, I, 26.

83. Henry G. Alsberg, ed., *The Lake States* in *The American Guide*, 637.

84. *Independence Daily Reporter*, April 20, 1958.

85. Adrian Reynolds to George Martin, November 6, 1901, "Names," MS, *KSHS*.

86. *Topeka State Journal*, November 19, 1918.

87. Beachy in *Kansas City Star*, February 23, 1950.

88. Sedan *Times-Star*, August 14, 1941; *KHC*, VII, 484.

89. Taylor, *Names and their Histories*, 193.

90. Corley, *Names*, 8.

91. *Ibid.*, 21.

92. Baughman, *Kansas Post Offices*, 10–11; *Dodge City Journal*, October 22, 1936; *KHC*, XII, 473.

93. Charles M. Clark, *A Trip to Pike's Peak*, 6; R. F. Smith, *Doniphan County, Kansas, History and Directory for 1868–69*, 276, 280; *KHC*, XII, 490.

94. *Kansas Precancel News*, No. 157, August, 1967.

95. *Horton Headlight*, October 29, 1936.

96. John Roe in *Wichita Beacon*, July 11, 1968.

97. Belle Spring was the community center for the Eisenhower family and the General's grandfather lies buried there. Abilene *Reflector-Chronicle*, November 7, 1946.

98. Frank S. Sullivan, *History of Meade County, Kansas*, 40; Louise A. Barry, "Circuit-Riding in Southwest Kansas in 1885," *KHQ*, XII, 384.

99. W. A. Mitchell, "Historic Linn," *KHC*, XVI, 615; and Mitchell, *Linn County*, 322.

100. Shackleton, *Handbook on the Frontier Days*, 107.

101. Rex Lee Schwein, "A County in the Making," *Aerend*, VIII, 18.

102. Stewart, *Names on the Land*, 315.

103. Andreas, *Kansas*, 1520; *KHC*, XII, 482.

104. Laing, *KHC*, XI, 482.

105. Taylor, *Names and their Histories*, 178.

106. Sullivan, *Meade County*, 38.

107. Martha J. Newby Unsell, Finney County Historical Society, *History of Finney County, Kansas*, II, 135.

108. Taylor, *Names and their Histories*, 68.

109. *Ibid.*, 63; Abilene *Reflector-Chronicle*, January 30, 1959.

110. Seneca *Courier-Tribune*, December 15, 1938.
111. Carman, in *Territorial Kansas*, 171; Tennal, *Nemaha County*, 48.
112. Nelson, *The Company and the Community*, 10, 15, 154; *KHC*, XII, 472.
113. Nelson, *The Company and the Community*, 15.
114. Andreas, *Kansas*, frontispiece; Riseley to Schruben, Stockton, August 26, 1959.
115. Andreas, *Kansas*, 680.
116. Allen County *Scrapbook*, II, *KSHL*.
117. Taylor, *Names and their Histories*, 132; cf. Lambert and Pei, *Book of Place Names*, 159.

XII

NAMES FROM OLD ENGLAND

1. *Seven English Cities*, 4.
2. "The Contributor's Club," *Atlantic Monthly*, C, 569–71.
3. Geoffrey Crayon (Washington Irving), "National Nomenclature," *The Works of Washington Irving* (1897), IV, 437.
4. J. L. Sanborn, "American Town Names," *Kansas Magazine*, III (1873), 163, 167.
5. Mark A. Lower, *English Surnames, Essays on Family Nomenclature*, 63.
6. L. G. Pine, *The Story of Surnames*, 43.
7. Encyclopedias and dictionaries and specialized studies have been used as source material for British place-names. The following references have been especially useful: Eilert Ekwall, *The Concise Oxford Dictionary of English Place-Names* (4th ed., Oxford, 1960); and P. H. Reaney, *The Origin of English Place-Names* (London, 1960).
8. R. H. Whitbeck, "Regional Peculiarities in Place Names," *Bulletin of American Geographical Society*, XV, 275.
9. Lower, *English Surnames*, 63.
10. Federal Writers' Project, *Kansas, A Guide*, 392.
11. Andreas, *Kansas*, 368.
12. American Name Society, *Bulletin* No. 14 (April, 1969), 10.
13. Allen Forbes, *Towns of New England and Old England, Ireland and Scotland*, 212–14.
14. Pine, *The Story of Surnames*, 18.
15. Kansas State Board of Agriculture, *Fifth Annual Report*, 1876, 54; Andreas, *Kansas*, frontispiece.
16. Reaney, *Origin of English Place Names*, 71, 79.
17. Taylor, *Names and their Histories*, 176.
18. July 17, 1873.
19. Interview with residents of Smith Center.
20. Blair, *Johnson County*, 171, 181; Andreas, *Kansas*, 644.
21. Whittemore, *Historic Kansas*, 192; Buffington to Martin, January 27, 1901, "Names," MS, *KSHS*; cf. Baughman, *Kansas Post Offices*, 90.
22. A. Graff to *Wichita Beacon*, July 8, 1929, Kansas Collection, Ablah Library, Wichita State University; Bliss Isely, *Wichita Beacon*, July 21, 1929.
23. Corley, *Names*, 12.
24. *Names and their Histories*, 815; Forbes, *Towns of New England and Old*, Part I, 80.
25. Ekwall, *Oxford Dictionary of English Place-Names*, 207.
26. Harrington, *Gove County*, 14.
27. Forbes, *Towns of New England and Old*, Part I, 93–95.
28. Gwendoline and Paul Sanders, *The Sumner County Story*, 99.
29. Corley, *Names*, 37.
30. *Chase County Historical Sketches*, II, 113, 313.
31. *Idem*.
32. Abilene *Reflector-Chronicle*, June 7, 1948; Forbes, *Towns of New England and Old*, 117–22.

33. Taylor, *Names and their Histories*, 82.
34. *KHC*, XII, 486; Cecil Howes, "Ghost Towns of Shawnee County," *Bulletin*, Shawnee County Historical Society, I, 25–31.
35. Corley, *Names*, 82.
36. Reaney, *Origin of English Place-Names*, 80; Ekwall, *Oxford Dictionary of English Place-Names*, 390.
37. Taylor, *Names and their Histories*, 114; Reaney, *Origin of English Place-Names*, 201.
38. E. M. Newman, *Seeing England and Scotland*, 251–54.
39. *Marion County Record*, July 27, 1961.
40. Aethelstane lived in Norwich in the tenth century, and his name came to Kansas, too.
41. *Kingman County Diamond Jubilee*, 1958; Missouri Pacific, *The Empire*, 133; F. J. Cloud to G. W. Martin, November 12, 1901, "Names," MS, *KSHS*.
42. William S. Walsh, *Heroes and Heroines of Fiction, Modern Prose and Poetry*, Part II, 133.
43. Missouri Pacific, *The Empire*, 150.
44. Blackburn and Cardwell, comps., *Republic County*, 83 and *passim*; Forbes, *Towns of New England and Old*, 198–201.
45. Taylor, *Names and their Histories*, 138.
46. Forbes, *Towns of New England and Old*, Part II, 77.
47. Newman, *Seeing England and Scotland*, 261, 267.
48. Robert Southey, *The Complete Poetical Works*, (1869), 175.
49. Frank Dawson, *Place Names in Colorado*, 30.
50. Forbes, *Towns of New England and Old*, Part II, 69–72.
51. *KHC*, XII, 472.
52. Ekwall, *Oxford Dictionary of Place-Names*, 272; Taylor, *Names and their Histories*, 161.
53. Taylor, *Names and their Histories*, 63; See "Bath" in *Encyclopedia Americana*.
54. Walsh, *Heroes and Heroines of Fiction*, Part II, 47.
55. Newman, *Seeing England and Scotland*, 170.
56. Forbes, *Towns of New England and Old*, Part II, 59.
57. J. H. Plumb, "An Oriental Palace," *Horizon*, V, 21.
58. *KHC*, XII, 482.
59. Ekwall, *Oxford Dictionary of Place-Names*, 45.
60. Corley, *Names*, 30.
61. Marysville, February 27, 1931.
62. Ekwall, *Oxford Dictionary of Place-Names*, 249, 256.
63. Reaney, *Origin of English Place-Names*, 199.
64. *Marshall County News* (Marysville), February 27, 1931.
65. Heinie Schmidt, *Ashes of my Campfire, Tales of Old Dodge City*, 30.
66. Ekwall, *Oxford Dictionary of Place-Names*, 277.
67. *Dodge City Journal*, October 22, 1936.
68. *Hays Daily News*, August 2, 1953; *Topeka State Journal*, January 28, 1922; Taylor, *Names and their Histories*, 267.
69. See map in *National Geographic*, CXX, 154.
70. *Topeka Capital*, December 31, 1936.
71. Rebecca Wells Taylor, "Some Lost Towns of Western Kansas," *The Aerend*, VI, 242; Maggie Neff, "History of Old Runnymede," in *Condensed History of the City of Harper, Kansas, 1877–1961*, Ray E. Carr., ed.; Gwendoline and Paul Sanders, *The Harper County Story*, 139.
72. Sanders, *The Harper County Story*, 139.
73. Taylor, *Aerend*, VI, 242; Charles Seton, "Reminiscences of Runnymede," *KHC*, XII, 467–69; Ray E. Carr, ed., *Condensed History of the City of Harper, Kansas, 1877–1961, passim*.

74. See Chapter IX for El Paso; *Derby Reporter*, September 29, 1967.
75. Isely, *Wichita Beacon*, April 4, 1929.
76. Edward Latham, *Dictionary of English Names*; Taylor, *Names and their Histories*, 107.
77. Chapman, *KHC*, X, 488; Whittemore, *Historic Kansas*, 111.
78. Andreas, *Kansas*, 1312–13; Chapman, *KHC*, X, 513.
79. Taylor, *Names and their Histories*, 288.
80. "Bypaths of Kansas History," *KHQ*, VI, 397; Whittemore, *Historic Kansas*, 132.
81. Alexander Jones, *The Cymry of '76*, Appendix, 45.
82. Andreas, *Kansas*, 1496; *Wellington Daily News*, April 2, 1936.
83. Thomas H. Gladstone, *Kansas; or, Squatter Life and Border Warfare in the Far West* (London, 1857).
84. Charles Knight, *The Popular History of England*, I 580.
85. Corley, *Names*, 20.
86. Taylor, *Names and their Histories*, 190; Ekwall, *Oxford Dictionary of Place-Names*, 143.
87. Cory, *Place Names in Bourbon County*, 16.
88. Ekwall, *Oxford Dictionary of Place-Names*, 281.
89. *KHC*, XII, 484.
90. Taylor, *Names and their Histories*, 211.
91. Margaret H. Raser and Ina Rumford, comps., *A History of Hodgeman County*, 12; Corley, *Names*, 31.
92. Taylor, *Names and their Histories*, 262.

XIII
SCOTLAND AND SIR WALTER SCOTT

1. Benjamin Vincent, *Haydn's Dictionary of Dates and Universal Information relating to all Ages and Nations*, 125; S. Augustus Mitchell, *Ancient Geography*, 133.
2. Vincent, *Haydn's Dictionary of Dates*, 125.
3. Taylor, *Names and their Histories*, 253.
4. Rev. James MacKenzie, *Our Country, A History of Scotland for the Young*, 26.
5. *KHC*, XII, 487.
6. Missouri Pacific, *The Empire*, 143.
7. *Ibid.*, 176; Throckmorton in *First Hand Historical Episodes*; *Topeka Capital*, March 27, 1915.
8. WPA, American Guide, MS, Wichita State Library, 10.
9. Ida L. Smith, "National Group Settlement," *Aerend*, VII, 105; Whittemore, *Historic Kansas*, 104.
10. O. D. Von Engeln and Jane McElway Urquhart, *Story Key to Geographical Names*, 70.
11. Taylor, *Names and their Histories*, 41.
12. *Sabetha Herald*, January 28, 1909, and October 19, 1938; Andreas, *Kansas*, 956.
13. *Twentieth Biennial Report*, KSHS, 315.
14. James McPherson, trans., "Preliminary Discourse," *Ossian's Poems* (Boston, 1858), 12, 293; Walsh, *Heroes and Heroines of Fiction*, Part II, 111.
15. *List of Dead Towns and Post Offices*, MS, KSHS, III.
16. *Osborne County Farmer*, December 13, 1934.
17. *KHC*, XII. 483; Greene, *Kanzas*, cf. map.
18. Andreas, *Kansas*, 1425.
19. Taylor, *Names and their Histories*, 51; C. Blackie, *A Dictionary of Place-Names*, 150.
20. *List of Dead Towns and Post Offices*, MS, KSHS, II.
21. Taylor, *Names and their Histories*, 117.
22. *Wichita Eagle* clippings, Ablah Library, Wichita State University.

23. Corley, *Names*, 22.

24. *Wichita Sunday Eagle*, Magazine, January 22, 1956.

25. Anne Rusher, "A Trail through the Wilderness," *Wichita Sunday Eagle*, November 14, 1965; Lucy E. Goodykoontz, Sedan *Times-Star*, August 14, 1941; Independence *Daily Reporter*, June 27, 1965.

26. William C. MacKenzie, *Scottish Place-Names*, 158, 165.

27. *KHC*, XVII, 690. There was at one time a member of the State Board of Regents of the State College at Emporia by the name of W. S. Berwick.

28. Newman, *Seeing England and Scotland*, 357.

29. Taylor, *Names and their Histories*, 68.

30. Thomas Whiteside, "Berwick-upon-Tweed," *Holiday*, VIII (August, 1950), 75–76.

31. J. M. Hageman to G. W. Martin, Concordia, September 20, 1902, "Names," Archives, *KSHS*, Topeka.

32. *Clyde Democrat*, September 15, 1880; *KHC*, VII, 477.

33. Lambert and Pei, *Book of Place-Names*, 7; MacKenzie, *Scottish Place-Names*, 95, 118.

34. Taylor, *Names and their Histories*, 168; *KHC*, XII, 481.

35. MacKenzie, *Scottish Place-Names*, 44.

36. W. A. Hillhouse to G. W. Martin, October 21, 1901, "Names," Archives, *KSHS*, Topeka; Federal Writers' Project, *Kansas, A Guide*, 326; *Kansas City Star*, November 6, 1942.

37. Howes, "Ghost Towns of Shawnee County," *Bulletin*, Shawnee County Historical Society, I, 29.

38. John G. Bartholamew, *Gazetteer of the British Isles*, 368.

39. Remsburg, *Scrapbook*, II, 85, *KSHL*.

40. *KHC*, XII, 480.

41. MacKenzie, *Scottish Place-Names*, 22.

42. Isely, in *Wichita Beacon*, September 1, 1929.

43. Jelinek, *Ellsworth Story*.

44. *Hutchinson News*, March 2, 1958; *Wichita Beacon*, August 18, 1929.

45. Kansas State Board of Agriculture, *Fifth Annual Report, 1876*, cf. map.

46. Interview with resident of Smith Center, Kansas.

47. Taylor, *Names and their Histories*, 54.

48. Forbes, *Towns of New England and Old*, Part II 40–44.

49. Reaney, *Origin of English Place-Names*, 187; C. L'Estrange Ewen, *A Guide to the Origin of British Surnames*, 130.

50. Cory, *Place-Names of Bourbon County*, 26.

51. Stewart, *Names on the Land*, 251, 271.

52. A. J. Rose to George W. Martin, November 13, 1901, "Names," Archives, *KSHS*, Topeka; *Coffey County Clippings*, KSHS, *Topeka*, I, 209.

53. Taylor, *Names and their Histories*, 239.

54. Corley, *Names*, 63; Andreas, *Kansas*, 811.

55. Newman, *Seeing England and Scotland*, 15.

56. Ekwall, *Oxford Dictionary of Place-Names*, 271; Reaney, *Origin of English Place-Names*, 55.

57. Greene, *Kanzas*, 142; *KHC*, XII, 481.

58. Forbes, *Towns of New England and Old*, Part II, 205, 208.

59. Lambert and Pei, *Book of Place Names*, 35; Taylor, *Names and their Histories*, 220.

60. Taylor, *Names and their Histories*, 178; MacKenzie, *Scottish Place-Names*, 165.

61. Corley, *Names*, 26.

62. *Ibid.*, 49.

63. Dawson, *Place Names in Colorado*, 35.

64. Taylor, *Names and their Histories*, 197.

65. Forbes, *Towns of New England and Old*, 171–73; *Encyclopedia Britannica* (14th ed.), XV, 229.

66. Sir Walter Scott, *Ivanhoe*, Introduction; American Names Society, *Bulletin*, No. 3 (July, 1966), 3.
67. "The Annual Meeting," *KHQ*, XVIII, 72.
68. MacKenzie, *Scottish Place Names*, 159.
69. Taylor, *Names and their Histories*, 161; See "Kelso," *Encyclopedia Britannica* (14th ed.).
70. Corley, *Names*, 37; "Roster of Kansas for Fifty Years," *KHC*, VIII, 523.
71. Corley, *Names*, 44.
72. *Iola Register*, March 1, 1957.
73. Montgomery, *KHC*, XVII, 246, 273; Isely, in *Wichita Beacon*, June 11, 1929.
74. Newman, *Seeing England and Scotland*, 257.
75. MacKenzie, *Scottish Place-Names*, 192.
76. Corley, *Names*, 66.
77. D. B. Emmett, "History of Sedgwick County, Kansas," in *Edward's Historical Atlas of Sedgwick County, Kansas*, 9.

XIV
WELSH AND IRISH

1. Jones, *The Cymry of '76*, 5–31.
2. John Betjeman, "The Magic of Cornwall," *Holiday*, XXIX, 53.
3. "Contributor's Club," *Atlantic Monthly*, C, 570.
4. John Shand, "Report from Wales," *Holiday*, IV, 13–14.
5. *New York Times*, July 6, 1958, I, 59; referred to by American Name Society, *Onomastics Bulletin*, No. 2, March, 1966.
6. Richard Llewellyn, "Wales," *Holiday*, IX, 60; Taylor, *Names and their Histories*, 290.
7. Ekwall, *Oxford Dictionary of Place-Names*, 330.
8. Andreas, *Kansas*, 1134; Shackleton, *Handbook on the Frontier Days*, 41.
9. E. G. Bowen, *Wales*, 314.
10. *Kansas, A Cyclopedia*, I, 106.
11. Andreas, *Kansas*, 1550; *People's Herald*, Lynden, July 15, 1948.
12. Bowen, *Wales*, 314.
13. Lambert and Pei, *Book of Place Names*, 48.
14. Taylor, *Names and their Histories*, 60; Llewellyn, "Wales," *Holiday*, IX, 61.
15. "Contributor's Club," *Atlantic Monthly*, C, 569–71.
16. Corley, *Names*, 7, 30.
17. Winifred N. Slagg, *Riley County, Kansas*, 159.
18. *Names*, VIII, 194.
19. Ernest B. Boder, "Kansas, the First Decade of Statehood," in *Kansas: The First Century*, ed. by Bright, I, 216; Slagg, *Riley County*, 160.
20. Andreas, *Kansas*, 1302.
21. Andreas' statement that it was named by Charles Cochran for his home in Malvern Hills, Scotland, must be in error. *Kansas*, 1551.
22. Newman, *Seeing England and Scotland*, 49.
23. Ekwall, *Oxford Dictionary of Place-Names*, 312.
24. Pine, *Story of Surnames*, 34; Taylor, *Names and their Histories*, 197.
25. Mitchell, *Linn County*, 15; *Independence Daily Reporter*, October 28, 1939.
26. Duncan, *Montgomery County*, 55; Charles C. Drake, *Who's Who in Coffeyville, Kansas, and Vicinity*; Andreas, *Kansas*, 1564.
27. Andreas, *Kansas*, 1302.
28. W. O. Hassell, *History through Surnames*, 11.
29. Taylor, *Names and their Histories*, 154; Lambert and Pei, *Book of Place Names*, 28; McPherson, *Ossian's Poems*, 296.
30. Taylor, *Names and their Histories*, 117; Savage, *Republic County*, 168.

31. Thomas, *KHQ*, XX, 257.
32. *Fort Scott Tribune*, May 30, 1942; Cory, *Place Names in Bourbon County*, 9.
33. *Meade Globe-News*, October 17, 1948.
34. Sister Mary Raphaella, Seminar Report, Wichita State University.
35. Johnson, *Anderson County*, 345; Franklin County Historical Society, *Reflections of Franklin County*.
36. Taylor, *Names and their Histories*, 191.
37. George H. Shirk, *Oklahoma Place Names*, 210.
38. Corley, *Names*, 43.
39. See "Donegal" and "Tyrconnell," *Encyclopedia Britannica*; Taylor, *Names and their Histories*, 110; Stewart, *Names on the Land*, 114.
40. *KHC*, XII, 484.
41. Kansas did have residents whose names were G. N. O'Dell, Robert Odell, W. H. Odell, and Solomon Odell. Cf. Index, *KHC*.
42. Marshall, *Santa Fe*, 353.
43. Forbes, *Towns of New England and Old*, Part II, 124–27.
44. *Ibid.*, Part I, 45, 61; Taylor, *Names and their Histories*, 65.
45. Taylor, *Names and their Histories*, 176.
46. Elmer M. Hunt, "American Soldiers and Sailors in the North Ireland Home Towns of New Hampshire," *Historical New Hampshire*, I, 3.
47. Cf. frontispiece map in Andreas, *Kansas*; Baughman, *Kansas Post Offices*, 35.
48. Pottawatomie County Historical Research Committee, *Early History of Pottawatomie County*, n.p.; Corley, *Names*, 23.

XV
DEUTSCH AND THE DUTCH

1. Jacob C. Ruppenthal, "The Germanic Element in Central Kansas," *KHC*, XIII, 513.
2. Mencken, *The American Language*, 32; cf. Walter E. Weidhaus, "German Religious Influence in American Place Names," *American German Review*, XXIII, 32–34.
3. For immigration figures see Carrol D. Clark and Roy L. Roberts, *Peoples of Kansas*, 51.
4. *KHQ*, VI, 221.
5. C. Henry Smith, *The Coming of the Russian Mennonites*, 146.
6. David V. Wiebe, *They Seek a Country*, 69 and map p. 123.
7. *Ibid.*, 145.
8. *Ibid.*
9. *Coming of the Russian Mennonites*, 145.
10. Wiebe, *They Seek a Country*, map p. 123.
11. *Ibid.*, 118.
12. Harley J. Stucky, "The German Element in Kansas," in *Kansas: The First Century*, ed., Bright, I, 332.
13. *They Seek a Country*, 40; Missouri Pacific, *The Empire*, 154.
14. Miller, *A Pillar of Cloud*, 25, 59.
15. Wiebe, *They Seek a Country*, 59; cf. Smith, *Coming of the Russian Mennonites*, 133.
16. *Ibid.*
17. *Wichita Sunday Eagle and Beacon*, March 8, 1964; Wiebe, *They Seek a Country*, 112n.
18. Smith, *Coming of the Russian Mennonites*, 149.
19. Walter Besant, *London*, 197.
20. Andreas, *Kansas*, 1290; Whittemore, *Kansas*, 107; *KHC*, XI, 492.
21. Marjorie Gamet Raish, *Victoria*, Series 3 in Fort Hays College Studies in Language and Literature, 64.

22. *Ellis County Golden Jubilee Report*, August-September, 1926; Laing, *KHC*, XI, 498ff.

23. Laing, *KHC*, XI, 498.

24. Sister Mary Eloise Johannes, "A Study of the Russian-American Settlements in Ellis County, Kansas," *Studies in Sociology*, Catholic University of America, XIV, 27; Ellis County Map, Hays Public Library.

25. *Rush County News*, May 19, 1949.

26. *KHC*, XII, 481.

27. Oliver M. Lippert, *History of Rush County*, MS (WPA), Wichita State University Library.

28. Laing, *KHC*, XI, 490, 515; *Rush County News*, May 19, 1949; Bracke, *Wheat Country*, 69.

29. Laing, *KHC*, XI, 517 and map p. 496; Amy Brungarat Toepfer and Agnes C. Dreiling, *Conquering the Wind*, 198.

30. Toepfer and Dreiling, *Conquering the Wind*, 184.

31. Sister Johannes, *Studies in Sociology*, 20.

32. Laing, *KHC*, XI, 489–528; B. M. Dreiling, *Golden Jubilee of the German-Russian Settlements of Ellis and Rush Counties, Kansas*, in *Ellis County News*, September 1, 1926.

33. Sister Johannes, *Studies in Sociology*, 19.

34. Corley, *Names*, 48.

35. Laing, *KHC*, IX, 490, 498, 502, 517.

36. Andreas, *Kansas*, 1388 and 1405; Smyth, *The Heart of the New Kansas*, 122.

37. O. H. Bentley, ed., *History of Sedgwick County*, II, 872.

38. Corley, *Names*, 47.

39. Andreas, *Kansas*, 620; Franklin County Historical Society, *Reflections*.

40. Andreas, *Kansas*, 1054; *Wichita Eagle and Beacon*, June 11, 1961.

41. Carman, "Continental Europeans," *Territorial Kansas*, 168.

42. Taylor, *Names and their Histories*, 142.

43. Corley, *Names*, 26; Missouri Pacific, *The Empire*, 109.

44. *Marshall County News*, February 27, 1931; *KHC*, VII, 478.

45. July 9, 1953.

46. Federals Writers' Project, *Kansas, A Guide*, 314.

47. Taylor, *Names and their Histories*, 74.

48. Johnson, *Anderson County*, 349; *Emporia Times*, September 1, 1949.

49. Johnson, *Anderson County*, 349.

50. Taylor, *Names and their Histories*, 74.

51. Andreas, *Kansas*, 1333.

52. Ruppenthal, *KHC*, XIII, 516.

53. Taylor, *Names and their Histories*, 112.

54. Mrs. Pearl Toothaker, *The History of Sheridan County*, n.p.

55. Taylor, *Names and their Histories*, 267.

56. *Ibid.*, 41.

57. Wiebe, *They Seek a Country*, 118.

58. Allen County *Scrapbook*, II, 59, *KSHL*.

59. According to Taylor, *Names and their Histories*, there is little agreement as to the meaning of Berlin.

60. Lambert and Pei, *The Book of Place Names*, 50, 67.

61. Root, "Ferries in Kansas," *KHQ*, II, 13.

62. Andreas, *Kansas*, 1321; Corley, *Names*, 78.

63. Thompson, *Wabaunsee County*, 275.

64. *KHC*, XII, 473.

65. *Dodge City Journal*, October 22, 1936 and January 3, 1948; *Spearville News*, January 30, 1936.

66. Andreas, *Kansas*, 669, 671; *Kansas City Times*, October 17, 1914.

67. Ruppenthal, *KHC*, XIII, 514.
68. Nelson, *The Company and the Community*, 82.
69. Carman, *Territorial Kansas*, 184.
70. *Ibid.*, 180.
71. *Wichita Sunday Eagle*, April 15, 1934.
72. Carman, in *Territorial Kansas*, 172.
73. *Ibid.*, 187; Andreas, *Kansas*, 921; Missouri Pacific, *The Empire*, 109.
74. Jost was also the name of a German town in Russia. See Ruppenthal, *KHC*, XIII, 522.
75. *Marshall County News*, February 27, 1931.
76. *Sedan Times-Star*, August 14, 1941.
77. *Rush County News*, May 19, 1949.
78. *KHC*, XII, 484.
79. *Abilene Reflector-Chronicle*, October 30, 1957.
80. *The Beloit Daily Call*, January 23, 1951; Taylor, *Names and their Histories*, 239.
81. Bowers, *Norton County*, 147-48; Baughman, *Kansas Post Offices*, 91.
82. Bowers, *Norton County*, 148.
83. Conrad Vandervelde, "Hollanders in Kansas," *Heritage of Kansas*, VII, 14.
84. *Ibid.*, VII, 9.
85. *Abilene Reflector-Chronicle*, May 30, 1944.

XVI
SCANDINAVIAN NAMES IN KANSAS

1. Taylor, *Names and their Histories*, 251.
2. Ross, *What Price White Rock?* 16; Savage, *Republic County*, 184.
3. Andreas, *Kansas*, 184; *KHC*, VII, 484.
4. *White City Register*, March 14, 1963.
5. P. Lovene, *History of the Swedish Baptist Church of Kansas and Missouri, 1869-1927*, 9.
6. Taylor, *Names and their Histories*, 270.
7. *National Geographic*, CXIII, 456.
8. Taylor, *Names and their Histories*, 136.
9. Lindquist, *Smoky Valley People*, 178; Nyquist, *Pioneer Life and Lore*, 70.
10. Rev. Alfred Bergin, "Swedish Settlements in Central Kansas," *KHC*, XI, 21.
11. Lindquist, *Smoky Valley People*, 176; Missouri Pacific, *The Empire*, 108.
12. Andreas, *Kansas*, 1302; *Manhattan Mercury-Chronicle*, November 21, 1948.
13. Carman, in *Territorial Kansas*, 167, 175; Emory Lindquist, "Swedes in Kansas Before the Civil War," *KHQ*, XIX, 264.
14. Lovene, *History of the Swedish Baptist Church*, 9.
15. Bergin, *KHC*, XI, 19; Whittemore, *Historic Kansas*, 104.
16. William E. Connelley, *History of Kansas Newspapers*, 20th Biennial Report, *KSHS*, 263; Andreas, *Kansas*, 983; *Lawrence Journal-World*, September 2, 1954.
17. *KHC*, XII, 484.
18. *Salina Herald*, October 1, 1881; *KHC*, VII, 475; *Kansas City Times*, May 13, 1947.
19. *Golden Jubilee of Thomas County*, 61; Interview with Emory Lindquist.
20. Taylor, *Names and their Histories*, 265.
21. Nyquist, *Pioneer Life and Lore*, 103; Interview with Dr. Folke Hedblom of Upsala University.
22. *Kansas City Times*, May 13, 1947.
23. *Smoky Valley People*, 147.
24. *Ibid.*, 94; Swansson to Martin, February 7, 1902, "Names," MS, KSHS, Topeka.
25. Emory Lindquist, *The Swedish Pioneer Historical Society*, IX, 118.
26. Lindquist, *Smoky Valley People*, 249.

27. Taylor, *The Aerend*, VI, 227; Blackie, *A Dictionary of Place-Names*, 131.

28. Allen County *Scrapbook*, II, 123, *KSHL*, Topeka; Interview with Mrs. June Bennett, formerly of Savonburg.

29. Thomas P. Christensen, "The Danish Settlements in Kansas," *KHC*, XVII, 301; Barr, *Lincoln County*, 96.

30. *Names and their Histories*, 106.

31. Blackie, *Dictionary of Place-Names*, 134.

32. Corley, *Names*, 54; *Great Bend Daily Tribune*, May 7, 1961.

33. The Hertha was the source for the name of the earth from Eartha. This brings out an association with *jord*, the last part of the author's name, which has evolved from Hertha, Eartha, Jorth to *jord*, meaning earth or land. Ryd-jord would mean a clearing of the land, possibly for someone's homestead. Cf. Gertrude Jobes, *Dictionary of Mythology, Folklore, and Symbols*, II, 887.

34. Taylor, *Names and their Histories*, 144.

35. Blackie, *Dictionary of Place-Names*, 150.

36. Allen County *Scrapbook*, III, 48, *KSHL*.

37. Mortimer Smith, *The Life of Ole Bull*, 118.

38. Taylor, *Names and their Histories*, 209.

39. Carman, *Territorial Kansas*, 174.

40. Gray, *Gray's Doniphan County History*, 51; *The Kansas Chief*, May 5, 1932.

41. Blackburn and Cardwell, *Republic County*, 317; Savage, *Republic County*, 168.

42. *Republic County*, 168.

43. Taylor, *Names and their Histories*, 117.

44. *Laws of the State of Kansas*, 1871, 301.

45. Blackburn and Cardwell, *Republic County*, 158, 163.

XVII
NAMES FROM SLAVIC SOURCES

1. Taylor, *Names and their Histories*, 70.

2. Swehla, *KHC*, XIII, 482.

3. James P. Blair, "Czechoslovakia," *National Geographic*, CXXXIII, 163.

4. J. F. Schulz, *Newest Guide Through Prague*, 26.

5. Lambert and Pei, *The Book of Place Names*, 35.

6. *Citizen Patriot*, Atwood, September 29, 1960.

7. *Wichita Eagle and Beacon*, January 26, 1964.

8. Taylor, *Names and their Histories*, 210.

9. *Hoisington Dispatch*, September 10, 1936.

10. Swehla, *KHC*, XIII, 482, 298.

11. Taylor, *Names and their Histories*, 225.

12. Carman, in *Territorial Kansas*, 172.

13. Corley, *Names*, 76.

14. Taylor, *Names and their Histories*, 77.

15. Millbrook, *Ness: Western County, Kansas*, 286.

16. Alfred Carney, "The Christening of a Kansas Town," *The Aerend*, V, 174.

17. *A Diplomatic History of the American People*, 288.

18. Mitchell, *Linn County*, cf. map; Mooney, *Butler County*, 62; *KHC*, XII, 481.

19. Andreas, *Kansas*, 1357; *KHC*, XII, 485; *Chase County Historical Sketches*, I, 28.

20. Andreas, *Kansas*, 1306; *The Manhattan Tribune-News*, September 2, 1951.

21. *KHC*, XII, 481.

22. Taylor, *Names and their Histories*, 235.

23. *Business Directory and History of Wabaunsee County*, 14–30; Andreas, *Kansas*, 995; Federal Writers' Project, *Kansas, A Guide*, 347.

24. *St. Mary's Star*, January 14, 1943; Gannett, *American Names*, 22; Remsburg, *Scrapbook*, I, 90, KSHL.

25. *Names and their Histories*, 43.
26. *Ibid.*, 198.
27. *KHC*, XII, 483.
28. E. W. Hoch, "All about Marion County," *Marion County Record*, 10; Ollie Thompson on CBS newscast, Wichita, Kansas.
29. *KHC*, XII, 484.
30. See "Aral," *Encyclopedia Britannica.*

XVIII
ORIENT AND AFRICA

1. Overman, *Ohio Town Names*, 85.
2. Allen Crafton, "What's in a Name," *Progress in Kansas*, I, 27; Corley, *Names*, 47.
3. *KHC*, X, 250.
4. *KHC*, XII, 485.
5. Theodosius Botkin, "Among the Sovereign Squats," *KHC*, VII, 425n.
6. *KHC*, XII, 488.
7. Taylor, *Names and their Histories*, 270.
8. See "Baghdad" in *Encyclopedia Americana*; Lambert and Pei, *The Book of Place Names*, 57.
9. Reported by Joel Davis of Towanda.
10. See Chapter XXVI.
11. V. Krishna Chari and Kelsie B. Harder, "Terminal Elements of Place-Names in the Northeastern Sector of Indian Railways," *Names*, XIV, 43.
12. Chapman, *KHC*, X, 497, 505, 521.
13. Interview with banker at Phillipsburg.
14. Interview with Kismet residents.
15. Sullivan, *Meade County*, 33.
16. *KHC*, XII, 484.
17. Taylor, *Names and their Histories*, 83; Stewart, *Names on the Land*, 208.
18. Taylor, *Names and their Histories*, 128.
19. Corley, *Names*, 25.
20. Taylor, *Names and their Histories*, 80.
21. Andreas, *Kansas*, 1093; Taylor, *Names and their Histories*, 192.
22. Taylor, *Names and their Histories*, 116; Lambert and Pei, *Book of Place Names*, 56.
23. David Birmingham, *The Portuguese Conquest of Angola*, 8.
24. Washington Irving, "Crayon Papers," *Works*, I (1819), 69.
25. W. L. Fleming, " 'Pap' Singleton, the Moses of the Colored Exodus," *American Journal of Sociology*, XV, 69.
26. *Hill City Times*, August 22, 1940.
27. Roy Garvin, "Benjamin, or 'Pap' Singleton, and his Followers," *Journal of Negro History*, XXXIII, 7ff.; Federal Writers' Project, *Kansas, A Guide*, 57.
28. *The High Plains Journal*, Dodge City, January 10, 1912.
29. *Wilson County Citizen*, December 23, 1903.
30. Garvin, *Journal of Negro History*, XXXIII, 20.
31. *Kansas City Times*, December 3, 1953; Federal Writers' Project, *Kansas, A Guide*, 210.
32. Garvin, *Journal of Negro History*, XXXIII, 13ff.

XIX
GREEK PLACE-NAMES IN KANSAS

1. National Geographic Society, *America's Historylands*, 117.
2. Botkin, *KHC*, VII, 425.

3. Geoffrey Crayon, "National Nomenclature," *Works of Washington Irving*, IV, 437.

4. Whitbeck, *Bulletin of the American Geographic Society*, XL, 277.

5. Blackie, *Dictionary of Place-Names*, xiv.

6. Blackmar, *Kansas, A Cyclopedia*, II, 389.

7. Sage, *American Speech*, IV, 269; Gannett, *American Names*, 220.

8. Walsh, *Heroes and Heroines*, Part II, 192.

9. See Chapter XXVIII.

10. Pardee was a town named for Pardee Butler, a Free-State preacher. Ingalls, *Atchison County*, 48, 94.

11. Johnson, *Anderson County*, 59, 61, 346.

12. *KHC*, XII, 472; Moore, Jr., *KHC*, XI, 471.

13. *Salina Journal*, December 25, 1949.

14. *Clark County Clipper*, December 6, 1934.

15. Walsh, *Heroes and Heroines*, Part II, 210.

16. *KHC*, XII, 480.

17. *Tescott News*, December 26, 1940; Scheffer, *KHQ*, III, 24.

18. Overman, *Ohio Town Names*, 146.

19. Green, *Early Days in Kansas*, IV, 27; Overman, *Ohio Town Names*, 67; *KHC*, VII, 486; "Kansas History in the Press," *KHQ*, XVIII, 105.

20. Blanchard, *Conquest of Southwest Kansas*, 214; *Kansas Precancel News*, No. 170, October, 1969.

21. Andreas, *Kansas*, 1301; *Manhattan Mercury-Chronicle*, December 19, 1948.

22. Ingalls, *Atchison County*, 171.

23. *People's Herald*, Lynden, May 15, 1948; Andreas, *Kansas*, 1531.

24. Horton, *KHC*, X, 599; Federal Writers' Project, *Kansas, A Guide*, 413.

25. Gannett, *American Names*, 159.

26. Corley, *Names*, 33.

27. Lester Stites, *History of Ionia, Kansas*, 3.

28. Gannett, *American Names*, 165.

29. July 11, 1967.

30. See "Lisbon," *Encyclopedia Britannica*.

31. Taylor, *Names and their Histories*, 210; Lambert and Pei, *Book of Place Names*, 103.

32. Corley, *Names*, 47.

33. *KHC*, XII, 430.

34. Taylor, *Names and their Histories*, 217.

35. *Citizen Patriot*, Atwood, July 2, 1953.

36. *Wallace County Register*, October 9, 1886.

37. Conner Sorensen, "Ghost Towns in Greeley County," MS, term paper, University of Kansas.

38. Llewellyn, "Wales," *Holiday*, IX, 61.

39. *KHC*, XII, 488.

40. *Atchison Daily Globe*, May 24, 1907; Gray, *Gray's Doniphan County History*, 67.

41. *KHC*, XII, 488.

42. Plough, *Reno County*, I, 116.

43. Shackleton, *Handbook on the Frontier Days*, 40.

44. Andreas, *Kansas*, 1131.

45. *Attica Independent*, June 28, 1934; Hoffman to Martin, November 28, 1901, "Names," MS, *KSHL*.

46. Elmer Munson Hunt, "American Soldiers and Sailors . . . in New Hampshire," *Historical New Hampshire*, I, 3; Gannett, *American Names*, 178.

47. For a survey of Greek names see Wilbur Zelinsky, "Classical Town Names in the United States," *The Geographic Review*, LVII, 463–95.

XX
ITALY AND THE ROMAN EMPIRE

1. Taylor, *Names and their Histories*, 238.
2. *The Aerend*, VII, 159–60; VI, 227; *Hutchinson News-Herald*, August 3, 1952.
3. Taylor, *Names and Their Histories*, 238.
4. G. H. Armstrong, *The Origin and Meaning of Place Names in Canada*, 121.
5. Sanders, *Sumner County*, 96; Baughman, *Kansas Post Offices*, 54.
6. F. Claudine Lindner, "History of Garfield County, Kansas," M. S. thesis (University of Wyoming, 1949), 31; Taylor, "Lost Towns," *The Aerend*, VI, 238.
7. Overman, *Ohio Town Names*, 116; Taylor, *The Aerend*, VI, 225–44.
8. *The Wichita Eagle*, June 11, 1961.
9. A good account of the shifting names and changing county seats is found in Blanchard, *Conquest of Southwest Kansas*, 101–105, 188–90, 210–14.
10. Daniel Defoe, *A Travel through England and Wales*, in Everyman's Library, II, 139–40.
11. Cram's map in Andreas, *Kansas*; Plough, *Reno County*, I, 314; Missouri Pacific, *The Empire*, 148.
12. Taylor, *Names and their Histories*, 282.
13. *Ibid.*, 187.
14. *KHC*, XII, 472.
15. Gudde, *California Place Names*, 170.
16. Andreas, *Kansas*, map p. 134.
17. Taylor, *Names and their Histories*, 194; Lambert and Pei, *Book of Place Names*, 35.
18. Andreas, *Kansas*, 1508; Isely, in *Wichita Beacon*, June 23, 1929.
19. Gannett, *American Names*, 211.
20. "Addenda," *KHC*, XI, xiii; Remsburg, *Scrapbook*, I, 153, KSHL.
21. Eric Partridge, *Name into English*, 151.
22. King, *Shawnee County*, 50; Andreas, *Kansas*, 534.
23. Sullivan, *Meade County*, 17; *The Commonwealth*, Meade, October 6, 1885.
24. Von Engeln, *Story Key to Geographical Names*, 69.
25. Missouri Pacific, *The Empire*, 149; Stewart, *Names on the Land*, 187.
26. See Cram's map in Andreas, *Kansas*.
27. *History of Kansas*, I, 546, 560.
28. *Topeka Capital*, December 31, 1936.
29. Johnson, *Anderson County*, 345.
30. Corley, *Names*, 15.
31. *American Names*.
32. *KHC*, XII, 485.
33. Andreas, *Kansas*, 305; *KHC*, XII, 478.
34. Scheffer, *KHQ*, III, 241.
35. *Clark County Clipper*, November 2, 1939.
36. Corley, *Names*, 75.
37. *KHC*, VII, 483.
38. *Kiowa County Clippings*, KSHL.
39. Taylor, *Names and their Histories*, 108; Bowers, *Norton County*, 163.
40. Sister M. Evangeline Thomas, *Footprints on the Frontier*, 107.

XXI
BIBLE NAMES IN KANSAS

1. Mead, *KHC*, IX, 15; Mead, *Transactions, Kansas Academy of Science*, XVIII, 216.
2. A Paradise merchant informed the author that Angel was the name of one of the settlers in Paradise Valley.

3. April 24, 1959.
4. Ralph Hinman, in *The Wichita Beacon*, May 20, 1959.
5. Henry King, "At Kawsmouth Station," Everett Rich, ed., *The Heritage of Kansas*, 104.
6. Remsburg, *Scrapbook*, III, 36, KSHL, Topeka.
7. Lambert and Pei, *Book of Place Names*, 58.
8. *KHC*, XII, 477.
9. F. Claudine Lindner, quoting *The Garfield County Call*, July 8, 1887, in "History of Garfield County," M.S. thesis (University of Wyoming, 1949), 40.
10. E. Cobham Brewer, *The Reader's Handbook*, 7.
11. Noah J. Jacobs, *Naming-day in Eden*, 41.
12. *New York Times*, November 26, 1922, Sec. II, 6.
13. Andreas, *Kansas*, 305, 1276.
14. J. D. Douglas, *The New Bible Dictionary*, 1962.
15. Bowers, *Norton County*, 67.
16. Taylor, *Names and their Histories*, 172; Cecil Hunt, *Talk of the Town*, 73.
17. Green, *Early Days in Kansas*, I, 44; *KHC*, XII, 481.
18. Alaska was so large that the center moved to South Dakota.
19. *KHC*, VII, 480.
20. *The Times*, Clay Center, January 5, 1882.
21. *Abilene Reflector-Chronicle*, January 30, 1957.
22. McNeal to Martin, October 19, 1901, "Names," MS, KSHS, Topeka.
23. *The Western Times*, Sharon Springs, October 24, 1957.
24. Stuart O. Henry, *Conquering our Great American Plains*, 22–23; Roenigh, *Pioneer History of Kansas*, 30.
25. *Kansas City Star*, January 22, 1954; *KHC*, VII, 475.
26. *Kansas City Star*, April 22, 1954; Streeter, *Prairie Trails and Cow Towns*, 105.
27. Henry, *Conquering our Plains*, 108.
28. *Great Bend Daily Tribune*, May 7, 1961.
29. Madeleine S. Miller and J. Lane Miller, *Harper's Bible Dictionary*.
30. See "Aleppo," *The Catholic Encyclopedia* (1907).
31. C. Clyde Myers, "Salem: A Town that Bloomed then Faded," *KHC*, XVII, 384–88; Taylor, *The Aerend*, VI, 231.
32. Corley, *Names*, 65.
33. Merrill C. Tenney, ed., *Zondervan Pictorial Bible Dictionary*; Isaac Landman, ed., *The Universal Jewish Encyclopedia*.
34. A. James Rudin, "Beersheba, Kansas: 'God's Pure Air on Government Land,'" *KHQ*, XXXIV, 282–98.
35. Blackie, *Dictionary of Place-Names*, xxvi.
36. Blackburn and Cardwell, *Republic County*, 105.
37. Andreas, *Kansas*, 1553; *People's Herald*, Lynden, July 15, 1948.
38. Miller and Miller, *Harper's Bible Dictionary*.
39. Lambert and Pei, *Book of Place Names*, 57; Taylor, *Names and their Histories*, 155.
40. T. F. Robley, *History of Bourbon County, Kansas*, 191; Cory, *Bourbon County*, 11.
41. Andreas, *Kansas*, 622.
42. Tenney, ed., *Zondervan Pictorial Bible Dictionary*, 611.
43. Harry J. Harris, "My Story," *KHC*, XV, 555.
44. Tenney, ed., *Zondervan Pictorial Bible Dictionary*, 455.
45. Blackburn and Cardwell, *Republic County*, 134.
46. Miller and Miller, *Harper's Bible Dictionary*; cf. Tenney, ed., *Zondervan Pictorial Bible Dictionary*.
47. *Clark County Clipper*, December 28, 1939; *Wichita Eagle*, July 7, 1939.

48. *Clark County Clipper*, December 28, 1939; Chrisman, *Lost Trails of the Cimarron*, 148.

49. *Clark County Clipper*, November 7, 1955; *High Plains Journal*, Dodge City, November 8, 1951.

50. Interview with Fern Bolte of Vesper, granddaughter of pioneers; *KHQ*, XIX, 405.

51. *Hoxie Sentinel*, November 15, 1957.

52. Bracke, *Wheat Country*, 48; *Sabetha Journal-Leader*, October 26, 1950.

53. Toothaker, *Sheridan County*.

54. Andreas, *Kansas*, 1140; Shackleton, *Handbook on Frontier Days*, 38.

55. See "Og" in Funk and Wagnall's *Standard Dictionary of Folklore, Mythology and Legend*.

56. Wilson and Sears, *Grant County*, 83, 100.

57. Roenigh, *Pioneer History of Kansas*, 36–38.

58. Walsh, *Heroes and Heroines*, Part II, 276.

59. Mead, *Transactions, Kansas Academy of Science*, XVIII, 216.

60. *Life*, XXVII, 64.

XXII
SAINTS

1. Remsburg, *Scrapbook*, I, 245, *KSHL*.

2. A comprehensive list of saints may be found in *The Book of Saints*, compiled by the Benedictine Monks of St. Augustine's Abbey, Ramsgate.

3. Eldon C. Smith, *The Story of Our Names*, 236.

4. *Moreland Monitor*, November 24, 1955; Laing, KHC, XI, 517.

5. Duncan, *Neosho and Wilson Counties*, 51; Rydjord, *Indian Place-Names*, 114.

6. *Bird City Times*, January 21, 1932; *Kansas City Star*, November 6, 1942.

7. J. Neale Carman, "The Bishop East of the Rockies Views his Diocesans, 1851–1853," *KHQ*, XXI, 81.

8. James A. McGonigle, "Missions Among the Indians in Kansas," *KHC*, IX, 155; Anna Heloise Abel, "Indian Reservations in Kansas and the Extinguishment of their Title," *KHC*, VIII, 83n.

9. Peter Beckman, *The Catholic Church on the Kansas Frontier, 1850–1877*, 70; Blackmar, *Kansas, A Cyclopedia*, II, 160.

10. *Andreas*, Kansas, 891.

11. Miller, *Historic Sites*, 11; *Clark County Clipper*, July 13, 1944.

12. *Wamego Reporter*, January 2, 1947.

13. W. Stitt Robinson, "The Kiowa and Comanche Campaign of 1860 . . . ," *KHQ*, XXIII, 390n.

14. Corley, *Names*, 41.

15. Carman, in *Territorial Kansas*, University of Kansas Publications in Social Science (1954), 181.

16. *KHC*, VII, 442.

17. J. Franklin Murray, S. J., "Jesuit Place Names in the United States," *Names*, XVI, 11; Corley, *Names*, 81.

XXIII
PREACHERS

1. Blackmar, *Kansas, A Cyclopedia*, I, 167.

2. *List of Dead Towns*, Archives, MS, *KSHS*, Topeka.

3. Franklin County, *Chautauqua Days*.

4. Charles Wilson Moulton, ed., *The Library of Literary Criticism*, VII, 607.

5. *KHC*, XII, 486; Whittemore, *Historic Kansas*, 121.

6. *Pratt Daily Tribune*, October 4, 1951.

7. Stephen Jackson Spear, "Reminiscences of the Early Settlement of Dragoon Creek, Wabaunsee County," *KHC*, XIII, 348n; *Business Directory and History of Wabaunsee County*, 11, 69.

8. Federal Writers' Project, *Kansas, A Guide*, 365.

9. Harrington, *Gove County*, Chapter xii.

10. *Ibid.*, 23.

11. *Coffeyville Daily Journal*, September 12, 1957; Franklin County, *Chautauqua Days, passim.*

12. Abel, *KHC*, VIII, 79n.

13. Andreas, *Kansas*, 1371; Isely in *Wichita Beacon*, May 5, 1929.

14. *KHC*, I–II, 257; Andreas, *Kansas*, 94, 407; Ingalls, *Atchison County*, 407.

15. *Council Grove Republican*, January 28, 1887.

16. *Abilene Reflector-Chronicle*, June 8, 1948; *KHC*, VII, 169.

17. Missouri Pacific, *The Empire*, 115; *KHC*, VII, 479.

18. Mallory, in *Kansas Cosmos*, April 23, 1886.

19. *Chase County Historical Sketches*, II, 257.

20. Miller, *KHQ*, I, 110n.; Stone, *KHC*, VII, 245; *Joplin Globe*, January 17 and February 7, 1943.

21. Cecil Howes, "Baker Nears a Centennial," *Kansas Teacher*, LVIII (November, 1949), 31; Whittemore, *Historic Kansas*, 142.

22. Andreas, *Kansas*, 1588; Missouri Pacific, *The Empire*, 153.

23. Andreas, *Kansas*, 1589; H. L. Hart, in *Independence Daily Reporter*, April 15, 1954.

24. Lutz, *KHC*, IX, 204.

XXIV
SECONDHAND NAMES FROM NEW ENGLAND

1. Forbes, *Towns of New England and Old*, Part I, 224.

2. Sister Thomas, *Footprints on the Frontier*, 107.

3. *Wichita Evening Eagle*, June 15, 1933; William H. Carruth, "New England in Kansas," *New England Magazine*, XVI, 3–21.

4. Writers' Program, *The Origin of Massachusetts Place Names*, 12.

5. *KHC*, VII, 482.

6. *Kansas Post Offices.*

7. *KHC*, XII, 484.

8. Sanders, *The Sumner County Story*, 99.

9. Stewart, *Names on the Land*, 46.

10. Henry W. Longfellow, *The Poetical Works of Henry Wadsworth Longfellow*, (1881), 834.

11. Forbes, *New England and Old*, Part II, 16–24.

12. *KHC*, XII, 421.

13. Willard, *KHQ*, XIII, 324.

14. Thomas E. Thompson, "Early Days in 'Old Boston,'" *KHC*, XVI, 479–87.

15. Mary A. Neeland, "History of Elk County, Kansas," M.A. thesis (Wichita State University, 1933), 9, 22; Thompson, *KHC*, XVI, 479–87.

16. Mooney, *Butler County*, 103–104.

17. Murdock in *Wichita Evening Eagle*, January 17, 1934; Mooney, *Butler County*, 104.

18. William E. Connelley, "Colonel Richard J. Hinton," *KHC*, VII, 490.

19. Robert Morrow, "Emigration to Kansas in 1856," *KHC*, VIII, 314n.

20. Ekwall, *Oxford Dictionary of English Place-Names*, 369.

21. Jesse A. Hall and Leroy T. Hand, *History of Leavenworth County, Kansas*, 175.

22. Andreas, *Kansas*, 870, 952; Connelley, *KHC*, VII, n.

23. Florence H. Herrick, "Recollections," *Notes on Early Clark County*, III, 49, KSHL.

24. *Ibid.*, II, 49, 73.

25. Writers' Program, *Origin of Massachusetts Place Names*, 14; Gannett, *American Names*, 89; Stewart, *Names on the Land*, 64.

26. Isely, in *Wichita Beacon*, July 21, 1929.

27. Andreas, *Kansas*, 308, 313; Blair, *Johnson County*, 62.

28. Throckmorton, et al, *Coffey County*, 96; KHC, XII, 432.

29. KHC, XII, 477; Dolbee, KHQ, IX, 249.

30. Louise Barry, "The Emigrant Aid Company Parties of 1854," KHQ, XII, 122.

31. John Bright, "Topeka's Year I," *Bulletin*, Shawnee County Historical Society, I, 74.

32. KHC, XII, 421.

33. Andreas, *Kansas*, 313.

34. Spring, *Kansas, The Prelude to the War*, 34.

35. Russell K. Hickman, "Lewis Bodwell," KHQ, XII, 350n.

36. Blackmar, *Kansas, A Cyclopedia*, I, 77.

37. Ekwall, *Oxford Dictionary of English Place-Names*, 10.

38. Von Engeln, *Story Key to Geographical Names*, 57.

39. Reaney, *Origin of English Place-Names*, 52.

40. Gannett, *American Names*, 159.

41. *Marshall County News*, Marysville, February 27, 1931; KHC, XII, 483.

42. Corley, *Names*, 9.

43. Forbes, *Towns in New England and Old*, Part I, 62.

44. Connelley, *History of Kansas Newspapers*, 20th Biennial Report, KSHS, 268.

45. See Chapter on "Presidents and their Associates."

46. Stewart, *Names on the Land*, 53.

47. Lena Baxter Shenck, "History of Dover," *Bulletin* No. 31, Shawnee County Historical Society (December, 1958), 22.

48. *The Topeka Capital*, January 29, 1944.

49. Shenck, *Bulletin* No. 31, Shawnee County Historical Society, 22; King, *Shawnee County*, 46; Andreas, *Kansas*, 593.

50. Stewart, *Names on the Land*, 274; KHC, VII, 481.

51. Gannett, *American Names*, 43.

52. Scheffer, KHQ, III, 239.

53. Throckmorton, et al, *Coffey County*, 82, 98; *Burlington Daily Republican*, December 10, 1945; Andreas, *Kansas*, 653.

54. Ploughe, *Reno County*, I, 113, 312.

55. Charles R. Green, "Historical Work in Osage County," KHC, VIII, 113.

56. KHC, VII, 481; Gannett, *American Names*, 193.

57. Charles W. Yoder to George Martin, December 4, 1901, "Names," MS, Archives, KSHS.

58. KHQ, XII, 345.

59. *Washington County Register*, May 31, 1940.

60. *Laws of the State of Kansas*, 1885, 233.

61. Forbes, *Towns of New England and Old*, 156.

62. Andreas, *Kansas*, 866; R. E. Fuller and Mrs. J. C. McKinny, *The First Hundred Years, A History of the City of Hartford, Kansas, 1857–1957*, 4.

63. Corley, *Names*, 11.

64. S. H. Fairfield, "Getting Married and the Ague," KHC, XI, 611.

65. Stewart, *Names on the Land*, 40.

XXV
NEW YORK, NEW JERSEY, AND NEIGHBORS

1. Daniel Webster, *An Address Delivered at the laying of the Corner Stone of the Bunker Hill Monument*.

2. Goodnow, *KHC*, IV, 247.

3. Andrew J. Mead, "Reminiscences of Kansas," *KHC*, VII, 469.

4. William M. Beauchamp, *Indian Names in New York*, 46.

5. Von Engeln, *Story Keys to Geographical Names*, 67; Rydjord, *Indian Place-Names*, 224.

6. Stewart, *Names on the Land*, 68; Virgil J. Vogel, *Indian Place-Names in Illinois*, 60; "Miscellany," *American Speech*, IX, 154.

7. Shackleton, *Handbook on Frontier Days*, 134–46; Rydjord, *Indian Place-Names*, 263.

8. Amos S. Lapham, "Looking Backward, Early History of Chanute," *KHC*, XVI, 505, 508; Hodge, *Handbook of the American Indians*, II, 755; *Southern Kansas Tribune*, Independence, September 10, 1902.

9. *KHC*, XII, 475; Lewis H. Morgan, *League of the Ho-de-no-sau-nee or Iroquois*, II, 133.

10. J. N. B. Hewitt in Hodge, *Handbook of the American Indians*, II, 68; Rydjord, *Indian Place-Names*, 267.

11. Isely in *Wichita Beacon*, May 19, 1929; H. B. Kelly, "Building the Sedan Court House," *KHC*, IX, 89; *Oswego Independent*, December 19, 1958.

12. *Sedan Times-Star*, *Chautauqua County Scrapbook*, *KSHL*.

13. Beauchamp, *Indian Names in New York*, 13; L. F. Hawley, "The Chadakoin River," *Names*, III, 32.

14. Edna Kenton, ed., *The Indians of North America*, II, 51–52, 315.

15. H. N. Lester, "Colonization of the Upper Arkansas Valley in Kansas," *KHC*, IV, 263.

16. Sanders, *The Harper County Story*, 137.

17. Hodge, *Handbook of the American Indians*, II, 167.

18. Gannett, *American Names*, 234.

19. Hodge, *Handbook of the American Indians*, II, 123.

20. James G. Wilson, "Arent Van Curler and his Journal of 1634–35," American History Association, *Annual Report*, 1895, 100.

21. Newman, *Black Dog Trail*, 62; Graves, *Neosho County*, I, 102.

22. Andreas, *Kansas*, 1466.

23. Gannett, *American Names*, 234.

24. Ingalls, *Atchison County*, 118.

25. Hodge, *Handbook of the American Indians*, I, 223.

26. Kenton, ed., *Indians of North America*, I, 227n.

27. Beauchamp, *Indian Names in New York*, 74; Rydjord, *Indian Place-Names*, 226.

28. Gray, *Saints and Sinners*, 36, 39, 96, 104.

29. Hodge, *Handbook of the American Indians*, II, 488; Millbrook, *Ness: Western County*, 85.

30. Gray, *Doniphan County*, II, 23; Smith, *Doniphan County*, 50.

31. Andreas, *Kansas*, 901; Duncan, *Neosho and Wilson Counties*, 829–30.

32. *Sabetha Herald*, January 28, 1909, and October 19, 1938; Andreas, *Kansas*, 956.

33. Ingalls, *Atchison County*, 191; Andreas, *Kansas*, 1302.

34. Giles, *Thirty Years in Topeka*, 382.

35. Lillian Stone Johnson, "Auburn," *Bulletin 31, Shawnee County Historical Society*, 4–5.

36. Taylor, *Names and their Histories*, 55.

37. Stewart, *Names on the Land*, 270; Corley, *Names*, 7.

38. *Laws of the State of Kansas*, 1889, 260.

39. English Place Name Society, *The Place-Names of Sussex*, VI, Part I, 5; Ekwall, *Oxford Dictionary of English Place-Names*, 320.

40. Savage, *Republic County*, 159.

41. *Courtland Journal*, July 26, 1951; Blackburn and Cardwell, *Republic County*, 281; *The New Era*, Formoso, July 18, 1935.

42. Tennal, *Nemaha County*, 49.
43. Stewart, *Names on the Land*, 173.
44. Missouri Pacific, *The Empire*, 109; *KHC*, VII, 478.
45. Stewart, *Names on the Land*, 70, 111; Lambert and Pei, *Book of Place Names*, 48, 145.
46. "Letters of Julia L. Lovejoy, 1856–1864," *KHQ*, XVI, 196 & n.
47. Moore, Jr., *KHC*, XII, 338.
48. W. A. Mitchell, "Historic Linn," from *La Cygne Weekly Journal*, February 22, 1895, *KHC*, XVI, 609, 619.
49. Corley, *Names*, 28.
50. *KHC*, XII, 487.
51. M. Winsor and James A. Scarbrough, "Jewell County," *KHC*, XVII, 399.
52. R. G. Elliot, "The Big Springs Convention," *KHC*, VIII, 368n.
53. Rydjord, *Indian Place-Names*, 228.
54. *Idem.*
55. George A. Crawford, "The Candle-stick under the Wood-pile," *KHC*, X, 196n.
56. Stewart, *Names on the Land*, 122.
57. Edwards Brothers, *Illustrated Historical Atlas of Miami County*, 12.
58. Gudde, *California Place-Names*, 10.
59. Federal Writers' Project, *Origin of New Jersey Place Names*, 29; Donald E. Becker, *Indian Place Names in New Jersey*, 6.
60. Becker, *Indian Place Names*, 57; *Lakin Independent*, August 27, 1948.
61. Stewart, *Names on the Land*, 155; Andreas, *Kansas*, 809.
62. Sigmund G. Spaeth, *A History of Popular Music in America*, 101.
63. Hodge, *Handbook of the American Indians*, I, 637; Gannett, *American Names*, 171.
64. Duncan, *Neosho and Wilson Counties*, 88; *St. Paul Journal*, July 7, 1949.
65. Kenton, ed., *Indians of North America*, I, 559.
66. Stewart, *Names on the Land*, 311; George E. Shankle, *State Names*, 94.
67. Baughman, *Kansas in Maps*, 52.
68. Andreas, *Kansas*, 1266.
69. Wiebe, *They Seek a Country*, 120n.
70. Hodge, *Handbook of the American Indians*, I, 763; Gannett, *American Names*, 184.
71. Andreas, *Kansas*, 1549.
72. Von Engeln, *Story Keys to Geographical Names*, 73.
73. *National Observer*, July 5, 1965.
74. *KHC*, VII, 475; Von Engeln, *Story Keys to Geographical Names*, 71.
75. National Geographic Society, *America's Historylands*, 175.
76. Richardson, *Beyond the Mississippi*, 161.
77. Smith, *Doniphan County*, 49.
78. Andreas, *Kansas*, 1030; *KHQ*, III, 332.
79. *KHC*, VII, 483.
80. Andreas, *Kansas*, 1030; *Kansas City Times*, April 13, 1954.
81. Corley, *Names*, 9.
82. Crawford, *KHC*, X, 196n.; *KHC*, XII, 474.
83. "Executive Minutes," *KHC*, III, 273.
84. "Kansas History in the Press," *KHQ*, XVI, 220; *Lawrence Journal-World*, September 2, 1954.
85. Andreas, *Kansas*, 1120; Shackleton, *Handbook on the Frontier Days*, 35.
86. August 25, 1968.
87. *The Herald*, Eureka, September 29, 1955.
88. H. O. Whitaker to George Martin, December 7, 1901, "Names," MS, Archives, *KSHS*, Topeka; *KHC*, VII, 480.
89. *Atchison Daily Globe*, August 26, 1910, cf. Baughman, *Kansas Post Offices*, 159.
90. Forbes, *Towns of New England and Old*, Part II, 100.

91. Andreas, *Kansas*, 896.
92. Ferris, *KHC*, XI, 367n.
93. Andreas, *Kansas*, 869; Abel, *KHC*, VIII, 101.
94. Forbes, *Towns of New England and Old*, Part I, 152–55; Taylor, *Names and their Histories*, 232.
95. *St. Mary's Star*, January 14, 1943; *KHC*, VII, 485.
96. Chrisman, *Lost Trails on the Cimarron*, 247.
97. *Ellsworth Messenger*, January 7, 1943.

XXVI
NAMES FROM THE OLD NORTHWEST

1. Alta White, "My Home Town," *The Aerend*, VIII, 235.
2. George W. Martin, "Early Days in Kansas," *KHC*, IX, 130.
3. Archer B. Hulbert, *The Ohio River*, 2–4; R. E. Banta, *The Ohio*, 8.
4. Howes in *Kansas City Star*, December 8, 1941; *Reflections of Franklin County*.
5. *KHC*, XII, 473.
6. Roenigh, *Pioneer History of Kansas*, 34.
7. Joseph G. McCoy, *Historic Sketches of the Cattle Trade of the West and Southwest*, in *Southwestern Historical Series*, edited by Ralph P. Bieber, VIII, 293n.
8. *KHQ*, III, 235.
9. Sister Johannes, *Studies in Sociology*, XIV, 4.
10. Gannett, *American Names*, 80; Overman, *Ohio Town Names*, 27.
11. Buster's father was on a road show with Houdini when his wife took refuge in a Piqua church from a storm, and there the sadfaced comedian was born. Federal Writers' Project, *Kansas, A Guide*, 410.
12. Corley, *Names*, 58.
13. Morgan, *League of the Ho-de-no-san-nee*, I, 6; Leland, *Names*, I, 271.
14. *Seneca Courier-Tribune*, December 15, 1938; Andreas, *Kansas*, 944.
15. Stabler to Remsburg, May 14, 1909, "Names," MS, *KSHS*; Rydjord, *Indian Place-Names*, 272.
16. Corley, *Names*, 20.
17. Overman, *Ohio Town Names*, 38.
18. Sanders, *The Harper County Story*, 132, 135.
19. *Holton Record*, March 14, 1935; Bird, *Jackson County*, 34.
20. *KHC*, VII, 476.
21. Van Osdel, *Historic Landmarks*, 247.
22. Overman, *Ohio Town Names*, 35; Andreas, *Kansas*, 1168.
23. Masterson, *The Katy Railroad*, 96.
24. O'Connell in *Oswego Democrat*, January 29, 1954; Cory, *Place Names in Bourbon County*, 25; Overman, *Ohio Town Names*, 36.
25. Overman, *Ohio Town Names*, 20.
26. *Ibid.*, 43; Corley, *Names*, 23.
27. Overman, *Ohio Town Names*, 86.
28. *Ibid.*, 28.
29. Gray, *Doniphan County*, Part II, 23.
30. *KHC*, XII, 475.
31. Gray, *Doniphan County*, Part II, 23.
32. Wilson and Sears, *Grant County*, 111, 115, 240.
33. Overman, *Ohio Town Names*, 85.
34. Corley, *Names*, 47.
35. Overman, *Ohio Town Names*, 145.
36. Michael J. Broadhead and John D. Unruh, Jr., "Isaiah Harris' 'Minutes of a Trip to Kansas Territory' in 1855," *KHQ*, XXXV, 375.
37. Montgomery, *KHC*, XVII, 256.

38. Andreas, *Kansas*, 1613; Overman, *Ohio Town Names*, 102.
39. *American Names*, 198.
40. Corley, *Names*, 45; Overman, *Ohio Town Names*, 82.
41. Overman, *Ohio Town Names*, 116.
42. Coues, ed., *Pike*, II, 396n; Remsburg, *Scrapbook*, I, 177, KSHL.
43. Duncan, *Montgomery County*, 83, 92.
44. Charles C. Drake, "*Who's Who?*," *A History of Kansas and Montgomery County* . . . , 13.
45. Andreas, *Kansas*, 1284; Corley, *Names*, 11.
46. *Topeka Daily Commonwealth*, June 12, 1875; KHC, VII, 473.
47. Overman, *Ohio Town Names*, 83.
48. *Marion County Record*, July 27, and November 27, 1961.
49. Cory, *Place Names of Bourbon County*, 5.
50. Blackmar, *Kansas, A Cyclopedia*, I, 391.
51. Stewart, *Names on the Land*, 191; Jacob Piatt Dunn, "Indiana Geographical Nomenclature," *Indiana Magazine of History*, VIII, 110.
52. Andreas, *Kansas*, 1531; *People's Herald*, Lynden, April 29, 1948.
53. Connelley, *20th Biennial Report, KSHS*, 315.
54. *KHC*, VII, 485.
55. Johnson, *Anderson County*, 345; Carman, *Territorial Kansas*, 183.
56. *KHC*, VII, 478.
57. "Names," MS, Archives, *KSHS*, Topeka.
58. Barnes, ed., *KHQ*, XXIX, 292.
59. E. E. Blackman, "Sherman County and the H. U. A.," *KHC*, VII, 50, 58.
60. Corley, *Names*, 22.
61. See Chapter XXXI.
62. Hodge, *Handbook of the American Indians*, II, 885.
63. Blackburn and Cardwell, *Republic County*, 47.
64. Dunn, *Indiana Magazine of History*, VIII, 109.
65. Martin, *KHC*, IX, 131.
66. Hodge, *Handbook of the American Indians*, I, 597.
67. Marjorie M. Robeson, *Wichita Sunday Eagle*, August 20, 1961.
68. *Topeka Capital*, July 21, 1957; *Atchison Daily Globe*, May 24, 1907; C. W. Johnson, "Survey of the Northern Boundary Line of Kansas," *KHC*, VII, 321.
69. *Seneca Courier-Tribune*, December 15, 1938; *KHC*, VII, 476.
70. Joseph N. Kane, *The American Counties*, 443; *Saint Paul Journal*, October 6, 1949; Fred M. Caswell, "John Stark," *Historical New Hampshire*, I, 1-6.
71. (Cf. authority), "Names," MS, *KSHS*, Topeka.
72. Cory, *Place Names in Bourbon County*, 18; Andreas, *Kansas*, 1095.
73. Corley, *Names*, 25.
74. Andreas, *Kansas*, 1140.
75. Gannett, *American Names*, 187.
76. Newman, *Seeing England and Scotland*, 52.
77. Shackleton, *Handbook on Frontier Days*, 47; Andreas, *Kansas*, 1140.
78. Andreas, *Kansas*, 1165; *KHC*, VII, 249.
79. Cory, *Place Names in Bourbon County*, 27, 35; Andreas, *Kansas*, 1094; William D. Barge and Normal Caldwell, "Illinois Place-Names," *Journal*, Illinois State Historical Society, XXIX, 257.
80. "Names," MS, Archives, *KSHS*.
81. *St. Paul Journal*, June 20, 1948; Duncan, *Neosho and Wilson Counties*, 75.
82. Andreas, *Kansas*, 1094; Cory, *Place Names in Bourbon County*, 27, 35.
83. *Kansas City Star*, March 9, 1950.
84. Andreas, *Kansas*, 934, 937; "Station Names," *Missouri Pacific Lines Magazine*, XXV, 9.
85. Taylor, *Names and their Histories*, 44.

86. Tennal, *Nemaha County*, 45; Andreas, *Kansas*, 941.
87. Gannett, *American Names*, 308; Corley, *Names*, 11, 31, 54, 79.
88. Corley, *Names*, 52.
89. *Topeka Capital*, March 27, 1915.
90. Missouri Pacific, *The Empire*, 126; Throckmorton, et al, *Coffey County*, 70.
91. "Names," MS, *KSHL*, Topeka; *Kansas Cosmos*, Council Grove, December 18, 1885, and April 16, 1886.
92. Gannett, *American Names*, 103.
93. Federal Writers' Project, *Origin of New Jersey Place-Names*, 31.
94. Barge and Caldwell, *Journal*, Illinois Historical Society, XXIX, 273.
95. Gannett, *American Names*, 184; McPherson, *Ossian's Poems*, 295, 303.
96. Blackburn and Cardwell, *Republic County*, 84; *KHC*, XII, 481.
97. Vogel, *Indian Place-Names in Illinois*, 23; cf. Hodge, *Handbook of the American Indians*, I, 258.
98. Van Gundy, *Reminiscences*, 40.
99. Clark County Historical Society, *Notes on Early Clark County*, I, 43; *Wichita Eagle*, May 13, 1886.
100. Frederick G. Mather, "The River of Gen-nis-he-yo," *Magazine of Western History*, III, 101.
101. *Wichita Evening Eagle*, October 23, 1953; Andreas, *Kansas*, 1302.
102. O'Connell, *Oswego Democrat*, January 15, 1954.
103. "Names," MS, Archives, *KSHL*; *Seneca Courier-Tribune*, December 15, 1938.
104. Barge and Caldwell, *Journal*, Illinois Historical Society, XXIX, 196.
105. Andreas, *Kansas*, 663; D. A. Wiseman, in *The Gridley Light*, July 5, 1934.
106. Andreas, *Kansas*, 1529.
107. Roenigh, *Pioneer History of Kansas*, 34; Missouri Pacific, *The Empire*, 117.
108. Ann J. Failing, *Shoo Fly City*, 15; Sanders, *Sumner County Story*, 62; Root, *KHQ*, V, 26n.
109. S. J. Sackett, "Play-Party Games from Kansas," *Heritage of Kansas*, V, No. 3, 43.
110. Failing, *Shoo Fly City*, 19.
111. *The New Era*, South Haven, August 5, 1937.
112. Barry, ed., *KHQ*, XII, 301.
113. *KHC*, VII, 477; *Coldwater Diamond Jubilee* (1959), 1.
114. Corley, *Names*, 39.
115. *Kansas City Star*, December 8, 1941; *Leavenworth Times*, January 24, 1907.
116. "Names," MS, Archives, *KSHL*; Missouri Pacific, *The Empire*, 128; Nyquist, *Pioneer Life and Lore*, 333; *Marquette Tribune*, April 1, 1937.
117. V. Spencer Goodreds, *Good Stories and How to Tell Them*, 147.
118. Corley, *Names*, 5.
119. Lockard, *Norton County*, 21; Federal Writers' Project, *Kansas, A Guide*, 446; Bowers, *Norton County*, 73.
120. Hodge, *Handbook of the American Indians*, I, 863; Stewart, *Names on the Land*, 86.
121. *KHC*, XII, 483.
122. Von Engeln, *Story Keys to Geographical Names*, 86.
123. *Rush County News*, May 19, 1949.
124. Missouri Pacific, *The Empire*, 93.
125. *Ibid.*, 117.
126. Shackleton, *Handbook of Frontier Days*, 107; Duncan, *Neosho and Wilson Counties*, 72.
127. *Hill City Times*, August 22, 1940; Corley, *Names*, 58; "Ashland, Wisconsin," *Magazine of Western History*, IX, 13.
128. Edward Bumgardner, *Life of Edmund G. Ross*, 29; Richard W. Robbins, "The Life of Sen. Edmund G. Ross of Kansas," *KHQ*, XXXIII, 94-116.

XXVII
MIDWEST AND WESTWARD

1. Kearny County Historical Society, *History of Kearny County*, 101.
2. Andreas, *Kansas*, 472; Lela Barnes, "Notes on the Imprints from Highland," *KHQ*, VIII, 140; John R. Swanton, *The Indian Tribes of North America*, Bulletin, 145, *BAE*, 265.
3. Mathews, *The Osages*, 128; Thomas Donaldson, "The George Catlin Indian Gallery," Smithsonian Institution, *Annual Report, BAE*, II, 1885, 153.
4. Hodge, *Handbook of the American Indians*, I, 612.
5. "The Expedition of Major Clifton Wharton in 1844," *KHC*, XVI, 302; Lewis Henry Morgan, *The Indian Journals*, Leslie A. White, ed., 137.
6. *KHC*, XII, 469; Millbrook, *Ness: Western County*, 85.
7. Thomas County, *Yesterday and Today*, XII, 17.
8. Toothaker, *Sheridan County*.
9. *Oskaloosa Independent*, June 6, 1935; Richardson, *Beyond the Mississippi*, 97.
10. Vogel, *Indian Place-Names in Illinois*, 100; J. Clarence Simpson, *Florida Place-Names of Indian Derivation*, 80, 87; "Tuscalusa" in Hodge, *Handbook of the American Indians*, II, 694; Rydjord, *Indian Place-Names*, 54–56, 296–97.
11. Rydjord, *Indian Place-Names*, 296.
12. Gannett, *American Names*, 234; *The Gridley Light*, April 26, 1934; Throckmorton, et al, *Coffey County*, 94.
13. Corley, *Names*, 5.
14. Bergin, *KHQ*, XI, 33; Kane, *American Counties*, 206.
15. *Leavenworth Times*, January 24, 1907.
16. Winsor and Scarbrough, *KHC*, XVII, 408.
17. Andreas, *Kansas*, 1333; Missouri Pacific, *The Empire*, 151.
18. Letter to Dr. F. W. Schruben, August 20, 1939.
19. Corley, *Names*, 15.
20. Andreas, *Kansas*, 1445.
21. *Southern Kansas Tribune*, Independence, June 18, 1954.
22. *Kansas City Star*, April 19, 1954; Missouri Pacific, *The Empire*, 118.
23. McDermott, ed., *KHQ*, XIII, 443; Langsdorf, *KHQ*, XVIII, 149.
24. Scheffer, *KHQ*, III, 237.
25. Andreas, *Kansas*, 1426.
26. Scheffer, *KHQ*, III, 230, 238.
27. Vogel, *Indian Place-Names in Illinois*, 44–46; Philip P. Mason, ed., *Schoolcraft's Expedition to Lake Itasca*, xix, 97n.
28. Baughman, *Kansas Post Offices*, 4, 64–65.
29. Stewart, *Names on the Land*, 291.
30. Barr, *Lincoln County*, 88.
31. Federal Writers' Project, *Utah, A Guide*, 216.
32. Stewart, *Names on the Land*, 307.
33. O'Connell in *Oswego Democrat*, January 15, 1954; Andreas, *Kansas*, 1482.
34. Quaife, ed., *Journals of Lewis and Ordway*, 347–50.
35. *Wichita Beacon*, November 1, 1968.
36. *Junction City Union*, March 9, 1935; *KHQ*, IV, 220; Hodge, *Handbook of the American Indians*, II, 220.
37. George R. Stewart has made careful study of the name, see "Ouarian Revisited," *Names*, XV, 166–72.
38. Adela E. R. Orpen, *Memories of the Old Emigrant Days in Kansas, 1862–1865*, 3.
39. Stewart, *Names on the Land*, 14; Gudde, *California Place Names*, 46.
40. *The Gridley Light*, July 19, 1934.
41. *KHC*, XII, 483.

42. Gudde, *California Place Names*, 198; Nellie Van de Grift Sanchez, *Spanish and Indian Place Names of California*, 102.

43. John Bigelow, *Memoir of the Life and Public Services of John Charles Fremont*, 379–81; William E. Connelley, "The Lane Trail," *KHC*, XIII, 277–79.

44. *Kansas*, 697.

45. *Ibid.*, 310; *KHC*, XII, 473.

46. Sanchez, *Spanish and Indian Place Names*, 140; Gudde, *California Place Names*, 25.

47. Rydjord, *Indian Place-Names*, 333.

48. Gudde, *California Place Names*, 68.

49. *Ibid.*, 195.

50. I. O. Pickering, "The Administration of John P. St. John," *KHC*, IX, 380; Lela Barnes, ed., "An Editor Looks at Early-Day Kansas," *KHC*, XXVI, 289.

51. Gudde, *California Place Names*, 143.

52. *KHC*, XII, 480.

53. Sanchez, *Spanish and Indian Place Names*, 191.

54. Hodge, *Handbook of the American Indians*, II, 1010.

55. LeRoy R. Hafen, "Colorado Cities," *Colorado Magazine*, IX, 183.

56. *KHC*, XII, 490.

57. *Wichita Eagle*, July 17, 1937; *KHC*, XII, 478.

58. Gudde, *California Place Names*, 116.

59. Frederick W. Lawrence, "The Origin of State Names," *National Geographic Magazine*, XXXVIII, 141.

60. Andreas, *Kansas*, 1439.

61. Gray, *Doniphan County*, 24; *KHC*, XII, 472.

62. *Clark County Clipper*, June 22 and November 2, 1939.

XXVIII
NAMES FROM THE SOUTHERN STATES

1. See Chapter XXIX.

2. Hodge, *Handbook of the American Indians*, II, 530.

3. Andreas, *Kansas*, 517; *Lawrence Journal World*, September 2, 1954.

4. Stewart, *Names on the Land*, cf. map, "Winchester Moves West."

5. Newman (*Seeing England and Scotland*, 164) said that American troops would remember Winchester. After crossing the Atlantic in January, 1918, the American troops with whom the author traveled through Winchester named the town "Camp Starvation" because of the restricted English rations during the war. Out of such experiences, names are made.

6. *The Lakin Independent*, August 27, 1948; Kearny County Historical Society, *History of Kearny County*, 101, 104.

7. Stewart, *Names on the Land*, 42.

8. *KHC*, XII, 475.

9. Jonathan Daniels, "North Carolina," *Holiday*, II, 39.

10. Taylor, *Names and their Histories*, 139.

11. The name of Getty's grandson is indicative of his own interest in music and the interest of the parents in astrology. Paul's grandson was named "Tara Gabriel Galaxy Gramaphone Getty." American Name Society, *Bulletin*, No. 14 (April, 1969), 11.

12. Andreas, *Kansas*, 917.

13. October 15, 1964.

14. Jenkins, *The Northern Tier*, 30; William E. Connelley, "Wild Bill—James Butler Hickok," *KHC*, XVII, 10.

15. Taylor, *Names and their Histories*, 60.

16. Stewart, *Names on the Land*, 256; *Friends* (Chevrolet), October, 1965.

17. *Lyons Daily News*, July 23, 1935; *Wichita Evening Eagle*, September 17, 1935.

18. Andreas, *Kansas*, 757.
19. Stewart, *Names on the Land*, 22.
20. Andreas, *Kansas*, 1065, 1093; Cory, *Place Names of Bourbon County*, 19.
21 Stewart, *Names on the Land*, 199; Gannett suggested that Nashville was named for Abner Nash of North Carolina, *American Names*, 220.
22. Robert W. Johannesen, "The Lecompton Constitutional Convention," *KHQ*, XXIII, 234.
23. Nyquist, *Pioneers*, 154.
24. *Kansas Precancel News*, No. 163 (August, 1968).
25. Andreas, *Kansas*, 1301; "Statement of Theodore Weichselbaum," *KHC*, XI, 563n.
26. *Clark County Clipper*, November 2, 1939.
27. Mrs. Minnie L. Roberts, "Soldiers Grave," *Notes on Early Clark County*, I, 1.
28. Andreas, *Kansas*, 1337; *KHC*, VII, 480.
29. *Smith County Pioneer*, September 26, 1946, and July 19, 1951.
30. *KHC*, XII, 430.
31. *Names on the Land*, 148; *KHC*, VII, 481; Andreas, *Kansas*, 891.
32. "Names," MS, Achives, *KSHL*, Topeka.
33. Corley, *Names*, 62.
34. Gannett, *American Names*, 226.
35. Blair, *Johnson County*, 131–34; *Leavenworth Times*, January 24, 1907.
36. Andreas, *Kansas*, 1267, 1269.
37. *Pratt Daily Tribune*, August 30, 1951; Thomas P. Field, "The Indian Place Names of Kentucky," *Names*, VII, 119, 163.
38. Oliver P. Byers, "Early History of the El Paso Line of the Chicago, Rock Island, and Pacific Railway," *KHC*, XV, 574.
39. "Letters of John and Sarah Everett," *KHQ*, VIII, 143.
40. Rev. Cyrus R. Rice, "Experiences of a Pioneer Missionary," *KHC*, XIII, 310; Oswald Garrison Villard, "Historical Verity," *KHC*, XIII, 425.
41. *KHC*, XII, 419.
42. Theodore Maynard, *De Soto and his Conquistadores*, 176; C. E. Cory, "Slavery in Kansas," *KHC*, VII, 238.
43. Shackleton, *Handbook on Frontier Days*, 74; Moffatt, *KHQ*, VI, 163n.
44. Stewart, *Names on the Land*, 315; C. E. Romany, *Coffey County*, 79; *Burlington Daily Republican*, December 10, 1945.
45. Gannett, *American Names*, 296.
46. Simpson, *Florida Place-Names*, 109; Corley, *Names*, 72.
47. Amercian Guide, W. P. A., MS, Wichita State University Library, 12.
48. Howes in *Kansas City Star*, October 18, 1941; William W. Cone, "Shawnee County Townships," *Bulletin* No. 4, Shawnee County Historical Society, I, 111.
49. Baughman, *Kansas Post Offices*; *KHC*, XII, 429.
50. Gannett, *American Names*, 279.

XXIX
BOGUS LEGISLATURE

1. *Bleeding Kansas* by Alice Nichols is recommended with reservations.
2. *Wichita Eagle*, April 1, 1886.
3. Richardson, *Beyond the Mississippi*, 101.
4. See Chapter XXXII.
5. D. C. Allen, "Builders of the Great American West," *Journal of American History*, IV, 511.
6. Gray, *Doniphan County*, Part II, 13ff.
7. Report from *Kansas City Times*, June 3, 1935; *KHQ*, IV, 328.
8. Allen, *Journal of American History*, IV, 524.

9. Andreas, *Kansas*, 1256.

10. See also Chapter XXVI.

11. W. E. Parrish, *David Rice Atchison of Missouri*, University of Missouri Studies, XXXIV, No. 1, 163–64.

12. The town changed its name to Fayettville after a visit by the Marquis of Lafayette in 1825; later the name was changed to Kirklevington. Parrish, *David R. Atchison*, 1.

13. Springs, *Kansas, The Prelude*, 24.

14. George W. Haynes, "President of the United States for a Single Day," *American Historical Review*, XXX, 308.

15. Nichols, *Bleeding Kansas*, 157; Charles R. Tuttle, *A New Centennial History of the State of Kansas*, 277ff.

16. *Atchison Daily Globe*, April 8, 1920.

17. Russell K. Hickman, "Speculative Activities of the Emigrant Aid Company," *KHQ*, IV, 254.

18. *Topeka Daily Commonwealth*, June 16, 1876.

19. Cora Wellhouse Bullard, "Horticulture in Kansas," *KHC*, VII, 207n; Andreas, *Kansas*, 300.

20. Deatherage, *Greater Kansas City*, I, 665; Cecil Howes, "Indian Missions of Kansas," *Kansas Teacher* (March, 1950), LVIII, 47.

21. Wilder to Martin, December 2, 1901, "Names," MS, Archives, *KSHS*.

22. Lutz, *KHC*, IX, 190n.

23. Blackmar gave Iowa as his birthplace (*Kansas, A Cyclopedia*, II, 195); but it was more likely Indiana, as suggested by Bernice B. Wallace, in *History of Paola, Kansas, 1855–1955*.

24. Andreas, *Kansas*, 875; Connelley, *History of Kansas Newspapers*, 20th Biennial Report, *KSHS*, 239.

25. Lela Barnes, "Journal of Isaac McCoy . . .," *KHQ*, V, 347n.

26. Andreas, *Kansas*, 1101; *Dictionary of American Biography*.

27. Erasmus Haworth, "Historic Sketch of Gypsum, Cement and Plaster Industry in Kansas," *KHC*, VII, 86.

28. F. G. Adams, "General Frank Marshall," *The Agora*, V, 286; Andreas, *Kansas*, 917; Emma E. Forter, *History of Marshall County, Kansas*, 63.

29. Tuttle, *Kansas*, 519.

30. "Documentary History of Kansas," *KHC*, V, 157; George W. Brown, *Reminiscences of Governor R. J. Walker*, 14.

31. Duncan and Scott, *Allen and Woodson Counties*, 579; Andreas, *Kansas*, 1189.

32. "Governor Shannon to the President," *KHC*, IV, 387; Throckmorton, *et al*, *Coffey County*, 95; *Topeka Capital*, March 27, 1915.

33. *Conquest of Kansas*, 71.

34. Report by Francis W. Schruben.

35. *Los Angeles Times*, January 11, 1960.

36. *KHC*, VIII, 477; Andreas, *Kansas*, 574.

37. Baughman, *Kansas Post Offices*, 207; Corley, *Names*, 16.

38. Duncan, *Montgomery County*, 122; *Kansas City Star*, April 25, 1954.

39. H. C. Bergman, Jr., "Coffeyville, Kansas," *Kansas Magazine*, III, January (n.s., 1910), 45.

40. *The Daily Republican*, Burlington, December 10, 1945; Andreas, *Kansas*, 647.

41. *Coffeyville Daily Journal*, September 12, 1957; Bergman, *Kansas Magazine*, III, 45; Drake, *Who's Who*, 21; Missouri Pacific, *The Empire*, 100.

42. Duncan, *Montgomery County*, 111; Andreas, *Kansas*, 574.

43. *KHC*, VII, 472.

44. *KHC*, XII, 475, 476.

45. Carl Sandburg, *Abraham Lincoln: The War Years*, I, 243–47.

46. *Kingman Journal*, March 22, 1935.

47. *Chase County Historical Sketches*, I, 22.

48. Colorado solved the association of Breckinridge with the Confederacy not by changing to a new name, but by changing the spelling to Breckenridge. The change of one vowel was sufficient to show its loyalty to the Union. Muriel Sibell Wolle, *Stampede to Timberline*, 74.
49. John Maloy, in *Council Grove Cosmos*, March 12 and 19, 1886.
50. O. G. Villard, *John Brown, 1800–1859*, 455.
51. *KHC*, VII, 472.
52. Andreas, *Kansas*, 1323; *KHC*, VII, 472.
53. Johannsen, *KHQ*, XXIII, 237–40.
54. Martin, *KHC*, X, 125n.
55. King, *Shawnee County*, 54; Wilbur C. Abbott, *Adventures in Reputation*, 188; James H. Lowell, "Romantic Growth of a Law Court," *KHC*, XV, 590–97.
56. Mooney, *Butler County*, 150; Andreas, *Kansas*, 1430.
57. *KHC*, VIII, 451 n., 489; *Topeka Daily Commonwealth*, January 12, 1886.
58. Duncan, *Neosho and Wilson Counties*, 23; Newman, *Blackdog Trail*, 113, 131; Andreas, *Kansas*, 1453.
59. Blackmar, *Kansas, A Cyclopedia*, I, 761.
60. Helen G. Gill, "The Establishment of Counties in Kansas," *KHC*, VIII, 453–70; *Topeka Daily Commonwealth*, January 12, 1886.
61. Duncan, *Neosho and Wilson Counties*, 818; Beachy, in *Kansas City Times*, December 6, 1951.
62. Moore, Jr., *KHC*, XI, 47.
63. Joel Moody, "The Marais des Cygnes Massacre," *KHC*, XIV, 218.
64. *KHC*, III, 297.
65. William F. Coffin, "Settlement of the Friends in Kansas," *KHC*, VII, 338; Wilder, *Annals of Kansas*, 88.
66. Abel, *KHC*, VIII, 98; Ferris, *KHC*, XI, 367.
67. *KHC*, VII, 473; Andreas, *Kansas*, 621, 799.
68. *Franklin County and Chautauqua Days*, 1961; *KHC*, XII, 451–53; Andreas, *Kansas*, 621.
69. *Topeka Daily Commonwealth*, January 12, 1886; *People's Herald*, Lynden, March 11, 1948.
70. Gill, *KHC*, VIII, 450.
71. Morrill, *Brown County*, 6.
72. *Hiawatha Daily World*, August 31, 1918.
73. Andreas, *Kansas*, 710.
74. Kane, *American Counties*, has perpetuated this opinion, 57.
75. *Brown County*, 7; *KHC*, VII, 472; *Horton Headlight*, November 29, 1936.
76. *Topeka Daily Commonwealth*, June 16, 1876.
77. Morrill, *Brown County*, 4–7.
78. McCoy to Adams, 1883, "Names," MS, *KSHS*.
79. Quaife, ed., *Journal of Lewis and Ordway*, 95 and n.
80. Dick, *KHC*, XVII, 92; Rydjord, *Indian Place-Names*, 71.
81. Mathews, *The Osages*, 110; Joab Spencer, "The Shawnee Indians," *KHC*, X, 384.
82. Inman, in *Topeka Daily Commonwealth*, January 12, 1886.
83. Margaret Whittemore, *One-Way Ticket to Kansas*, 34; Elmer LeRoy Craik, "Southern Interest in Territorial Kansas, 1854–1858," *KHC*, XV, 385.
84. Sara Robinson, "The Wakarusa War," *KHC*, X, 468.
85. S. J. Shively, "The Pottawatomie Massacre," *KHC*, VIII, 185n; Martin, *KHC*, X, 135.
86. Wayne Delavan, "Whittier Promoted Free-Kansas," *The Aerend*, XII, 83.
87. *Lawrence Democrat*, April 23, 1936.
88. Andreas, *Kansas*, 1521; Remsburg, in *Wilson County Citizen*, December 23, 1903.
89. Martin, *KHC*, X, 131; Shively, *KHC*, VIII, 184n.
90. *KHC*, III, 410.

XXX
KANSAS STATE OFFICIALS

1. Spring, *Kansas*, 23.
2. Richardson, *Beyond the Mississippi*, 296.
3. Robert Hay, "The Great Seal of Kansas," *KHC*, VIII, 293.
4. Spring, *Kansas*, 37.
5. Martin, *KHC*, VII, 373.
6. Moffatt, *KHQ*, VI, 159n.
7. Moore, Jr., *KHC*, XI, 469.
8. Charles Gleed, "Samuel Walker," *KHC*, VI, 256.
9. Connelley, *Kansas and Kansans*, I, 412ff.; Gladstone, *Kansas*, 268.
10. Andreas, *Kansas*, 1324; Johnson, *Anderson County*, 256.
11. Remsburg, *Scrapbook*, I, 245 and IV, 35, *KSHL*; *Atchison Daily Globe*, January 4, 1907.
12. *Kingman Journal*, March 22, 1935.
13. Jack L. Kennedy, "'Bloody Old Kansas' Drew Men of History," *Wichita Sunday Eagle*, October 29, 1967.
14. Moore, Jr., *KHC*, XI, 470.
15. Martin, *KHC*, VII, 374–76.
16. Andreas, *Kansas*, 478.
17. *KHC*, V, 159.
18. Andreas, *Kansas*, 1302.
19. *Ibid.*, 1331; Moffatt, *KHQ*, VI, 157; Brown, *Reminiscences of Governor Walker*, 21 n.
20. Blackmar, *Kansas, A Cyclopedia*, I, 508.
21. Edward E. Wynkoop, "Edward Wanshear Wynkoop," *KHC*, XIII, 71 n., 72n.
22. Ely Moore, "The Lecompton Party which located Denver," *KHC*, VII, 449–50.
23. Kenneth Ruth, *Colorado Vacations*.
24. William Koch, in *Kansas State Collegian*, March 2, 1966.
25. Phillips, *Conquest of Kansas*, 15; Remsburg, *Scrapbook*, I, 188, *KSHL*; "Names," MS, *KSHL*, Topeka; *KHC*, VI, 187ff.
26. Edwin C. Manning, "A Kansas Soldier," *KHC*, X, 423n.
27. *KHQ*, XX, 150.
28. Richardson, *Beyond the Mississippi*, 90.
29. Andreas, *Kansas*, 1120; G. Raymond Gaeddert, "First Newspapers in Kansas," *KHQ*, X, 135.
30. Gaeddert, *KHC*, X, 266.
31. Weichselbaum, *KHC*, XI, 570.
32. John S. Dawson, "The Legislature of 1868," *KHC*, X, 266; Van Gundy, *Reminiscences*, 35.
33. Isely in *Wichita Beacon*, August 18, 1929.
34. Corley, *Names*, 31.
35. *Ibid.*, 34; Abel, *KHC*, VIII, 167n.
36. "Names," MS, *KSHS*, Topeka; *St. Mary's Star*, January 14, 1943; *KHQ*, XX, 52.
37. Blackmar, *Kansas, A Cyclopedia*, I, 78.
38. "George T. Anthony," *KHC*, VI, 204.
39. Hay, *KHC*, VIII, 295n.; Remsburg, in *Pony Express Courier*, December, 1936.
40. F. L. Owsley, O. P. Chitwood, and H. C. Nixon, *Short History of the American People*, 227; Pickering, *KHC*, IX, 378ff.
41. *KHC*, XII, 487.
42. Andreas, *Kansas*, 1271; Howes, in *Kansas City Star*, December 8, 1941; *KHC*, XII, 487.
43. *Kansas City Star*, November 21, 1941.
44. Andreas, *Kansas*, 241; Blackmar, *Kansas, A Cyclopedia*, I, 733.

45. Grant W. Harrington, *Annals of Brown County*, 404.
46. It was another Morrill, J. S. Morrill, who won support for the land grant colleges.
47. *Courtland Journal*, November 11, 1954.
48. *Topeka Capital*, June 23, 1900.
49. Gill, *KHC*, VIII, 463, 467, 469; *KHC*, X, 270; *Lakin Independent*, August 27, 1948.
50. *Sabetha Herald*, January 28, 1909; *Courier-Tribune*, Seneca, December 15, 1938 and May 22, 1952.
51. Connelley, *KHC*, XIII, cf. map opposite 276.
52. Richardson, *Beyond the Mississippi*, 151; Edgar Langsdorf, "Jim Lane and the Frontier Guard," *KHQ*, IX, 16.
53. Edgar Langsdorf, ed., "Letters of Daniel R. Anthony, 1857–1862," *KHQ*, XXIV, 19.
54. Richardson, *Beyond the Mississippi*, 44.
55. John Speer, "Incidents of the Pioneer Days," *KHC*, V, 131.
56. *KHC*, XVI, 34; Van Gundy, *Reminiscences*, 35.
57. Andreas, *Kansas*, 644; Federal Writers' Project, *Kansas, A Guide*, 373.
58. *Reminiscences*, 36.
59. Incidentally, the parents of President Eisenhower were students at Lane University and were married at Lecompton. Miller, *Historic Sites*, 16.
60. S. J. Sackett and William E. Koch, eds., *Kansas Folklore*, 146–49; Bill Koch and Mary Koch, "Kansas History and Folklore," *Heritage of Kansas*, V (May, 1961), 10.
61. Thomas A. McNeal, *When Kansas was Young*, 29; Edgar Langsdorf, "S. C. Pomeroy and the New England Emigrant Aid Company, 1854–1858," *KHQ*, VII, 227 et seq.
62. Charles E. Hill, "John James Ingalls," *Kansas Magazine*, IV (August, 1910), 16; Albert Castel, *A Frontier State at War*, 24.
63. Clarence S. Jackson, *Picture Maker of the Old West, William H. Jackson*, 143.
64. Hill, *Kansas Magazine*, IV (August, 1910), 15.
65. *Ibid.*; *KHQ*, IX, 98; Federal Writers' Project, *Kansas, A Guide*, 169; *KHC*, XII, 464.
66. Andreas, *Kansas*, cf. map, 1420.
67. *KHC*, XII, 464.
68. Andreas, *Kansas*, 1502; Isely, in *Wichita Beacon*, May 19, 1929.
69. Andreas, *Kansas*, 859; *KHC*, X, 274.
70. Davis to Martin, December 2, 1901, "Names," MS, *KSHS*; *KHC*, VII, 477; Isely, in *Wichita Beacon*, May 5, 1929; Cover, *Heritage of Kansas*, IV, No. 4, 38.
71. Franklin G. Adams, "The Capitals of Kansas," *KHC*, VIII, 336.
72. Blackmar, *Kansas, A Cyclopedia*, I, 442; Andreas, *Kansas*, 303.
73. Nichols, *Bleeding Kansas*, 160.
74. "Biography of Governor Andrew H. Reeder," *KHC*, III, 203.
75. Bush and Shearer, eds., *The Frankfort Story*, 154; Missouri Pacific, *The Empire*, 149.
76. Samuel A. Kingman, "Reminiscences," *KHC*, VII, 153n.; Edwin A. Austin, "The Supreme Court of the State of Kansas," *KHC*, XIII, 115.
77. Jesse H. Lowe, "The Pioneer History of Kingman," M.A. thesis (Wichita State University, 1933), 6; Missouri Pacific, *The Empire*, 122.
78. *KHC*, IV, 241.
79. Austin, *KHC*, XIII, 912; *Horton Headlight*, November 29, 1936.
80. Kirke Mechem, ed., "Annals of Kansas: 1886," *KHQ*, XX, 176.
81. Austin, *KHC*, XIII, 120.
82. Andreas, *Kansas*, 912; Blackmar, *Kansas, A Cyclopedia*, I, 808.
83. *Smith County Pioneer*, September 26, 1946.
84. "Cities of Sedgwick County," WPA, MS, Wichita State University Library.
85. Maloy, in *Council Grove Cosmos*, March 12 and 19, 1886; *KHC*, VII, 473; *KHC*, XII, 14n.

86. *Business Directory and History of Wabaunsee County*, 82–85.
87. *Mullinville News*, July 9, 1959; D. M. Morris, "Kiowa County," *Kansas Magazine*, IV (November, 1910), 98.
88. Gill, *KHC*, VIII, 461, 463.
89. Ballard, *KHC*, X, 248.
90. George W. Veale, "Coming in and Going out," *KHC*, XI, 10, 11n.
91. McNeal, *When Kansas was Young*, 66.
92. Abel, *KHC*, VIII, 96n.; Clara Francis, "The Coming of Prohibition to Kansas," *KHC*, XV, 210.
93. *Wichita Sunday Eagle*, June 11, 1961; Federal Writers' Project, *Kansas, A Guide*, 228.
94. Johnson, *Anderson County*, 349.
95. Corley, *Names*, 12.
96. Minnie Dubbs Millbrook, "Dr. Samuel Grant Rodger," *KHQ*, XX, 324; *KHC*, XII, 469n.
97. *KHC*, VII, 479; Barry, *KHQ*, XII, 386.
98. *Council Grove Cosmos*, Supplement, January 15, 1886; "Names," MS, *KSHS*.
99. *KHC*, V, 483; *KHC*, X, 245.
100. "Official Roster of Kansas, 1854–1925," *KHC*, XVI, 677, 689, 709; Corley, *Names*, 26.
101. Kelly, *KHC*, IX, 90n.
102. *Horton Headlight*, November 29, 1936; Andreas, *Kansas*, 751; *KHC*, VII, 486.
103. Stone, *KHC*, VII, 251n; Corley, *Names*, 30.
104. Corley, *Names*, 50; Blackmar, *Kansas, A Cyclopedia*, II, 322.
105. Wright, *KHC*, VII, 47n; Connelley, *Biennial Report*, *KSHS*, I–II, 24.
106. *Sedan Times Star, Scrapbook*, 198, *KSHL*; interview with Penrose Albright of Wichita State University.
107. *Leavenworth Times*, January 5, 1912; Andreas, *Kansas*, 1338.
108. Schmidt, in *Dodge City Journal*, October 22, 1936.
109. *Johnson County Herald*, September 8, 1969.

XXXI
LINCOLN AND HIS ASSOCIATES

1. Stewart, *Names on the Land*, 165; Gannett, *American Names*, 187.
2. Murdock, in *Wichita Evening Eagle*, February 12, 1938.
3. *KHQ*, XX, 531.
4. Elizabeth M. Dinsmore, "Genesis in Kansas," *Kansas Magazine*, II (October, 1909), 10.
5. Brinkerhoff, *KHQ*, XIII, 305; Albert Richardson, *The Secret Service*, 315.
6. *KHC*, VII, 536ff.
7. Gray, *Doniphan County*, 65.
8. Deatherage, *Greater Kansas City*, I, 616.
9. F. N. Blake to Sam Wood, "Names," MS, Archives, *KSHS*.
10. Gill, *KHC*, VIII, 458.
11. Murdock, in *Wichita Evening Eagle*, January 17, 1944.
12. *Kansas*, 1423.
13. Lincoln *Sentinel-Republican*, January 15, 1948; *KHQ*, VI, 216.
14. Root and Connelley, *Overland Stage*, 195; *Marion County Record*, July 27, 1961.
15. *Topeka State Journal*, October 30, 1935; Russell K. Hickman, "Lincoln College," *KHQ*, XVIII, 23.
16. George W. Martin, "The Boundary Lines of Kansas," *KHC*, XI, 74; Martha B. Caldwell, "The Eldridge House," *KHQ*, IX, 363.
17. Gill, *KHC*, VIII, 453–69.

18. Alfred Carney, "The Christening of a Kansas Town, Herndon, Kansas," *Aerend*, V, 174.
19. Ida Tarbell, "Lincoln as a Lawyer," *McClure's Magazine*, VII, 174.
20. Harrington, *Annals of Brown County*, 411; Remsburg, *Scrapbook*, I, 188, *KSHL*.
21. Melvin L. Hayes, *Mr. Lincoln runs for President*, 112–13.
22. Quoted from John Bigelow in Charles A. Shriner, *Wit, Wisdom and Foibles*, 565.
23. Abbott, *Adventures*, 183, 186; *Topeka Capital*, July 6, 1956.
24. John Speer, "Told by a Pioneer," Shawnee County Historical Society, *Bulletin*, No. XII, 58.
25. Abbott, *Adventures*, 186.
26. Cora Dolbee, "The Third Book on Kansas," *KHQ*, VIII, 252.
27. Andreas, *Kansas*, 1435, 1443; Mooney, *Butler County*, 115.
28. Andreas, *Kansas*, 684; Peter R. Levin, *Seven by Chance*, 99; Inman, in *Topeka Daily Commonwealth*, January 12, 1886.
29. Moorfield Storey, *Charles Sumner*, 130–40.
30. David Donald, *Charles Sumner and the Coming of the Civil War*, 278ff.
31. Storey, *Charles Sumner*, 155.
32. Albert A. Richards, *History of Sumner County in Edward's Historical Atlas of Sumner County*, 7.
33. Andreas, *Kansas*, 1495.
34. Scheffer, *KHQ*, III, 242.
35. Ingalls, *Atchison County*, 94.
36. *KHC*, XII, 437 and XX, 603.
37. Mooney, *Butler County*, 150.
38. Spring, *Kansas*, 9; Storey, *Charles Sumner*, 130–40; *Wichita Eagle*, May 16, 1954.
39. Clark E. Carr, "Why Lincoln was not Renominated by Acclamation," *The Century Magazine*, LXXIII, 503–506.
40. *The Kansas Cosmos*, Council Grove, March 12, 1886; *Chase County Historical Sketches*, II, 7.
41. *Mr. Lincoln's Army*, 85.
42. Gill, *KHC*, VIII, 452; *Chase County Historical Sketches*, I, 32, II, 7; Andreas, *Kansas*, 1355.
43. Mitchell, *Linn County*, 322.
44. "Names," MS, *KSHS*, Topeka.
45. Ida Tarbell, "Lincoln's Method of Dealing with Men," *McClure's Magazine*, XII, 448–49.
46. Garland, *McClure's Magazine*, VIII, 440.
47. Kennedy, *Profiles of Courage*, 146–71; Catton, *Lincoln's Army*, 11, 86.
48. Missouri Pacific, *The Empire*, 145.
49. Levin, *Seven by Chance*, 110.
50. James Marshall, *Santa Fe Railroad*, 14.
51. Streeter, *Prairie Trails*, 30.
52. *Kansas City Star*, April 19, 1954.
53. *National Cyclopedia of American Biography*, XIII, 271.

XXXII
PRESIDENTS AND THEIR ASSOCIATES

1. Geoffrey Crayon (Washington Irving), "National Nomenclature," *Works*, I, 70.
2. Stewart, *Names on the Land*, 165.
3. Frederic G. Vosburgh, "Shrines of each Patriots Devotion," *National Geographic*, XCV, 65.
4. King, *Shawnee County*, 60; *People's Herald* (Lynden), April 29, 1948.
5. Gill, *KHC*, VIII, 450 map.

6. Andreas, *Kansas*, 1056; Federal Writers' Project, *Kansas, A Guide*, 315.

7. *KHC*, XII, 483; Andreas, *Kansas*, 603.

8. *Ibid.*

9. *Wichita Evening Eagle*, July 27, 1960.

10. Lester, *KHC*, IV, 263.

11. Missouri Pacific, *The Empire*, 100.

12. One might also here note the names of the two Hopewell brothers from Kentucky who were among the first Jefferson County officers: one was named Napoleon Bonaparte Hopewell and the other was James Henry Clay Hopewell. Meredith, *KHQ*, VII, 339.

13. Inman, in *Topeka Daily Commonwealth*, January 12, 1886.

14. W. P. Trent, "Benjamin Franklin," *McClure's Magazine*, VIII, 277.

15. Kane, *American Counties*, 9, 110.

16. "Selections from the Hyatt Manuscripts," *KHC*, I-II, 218–19.

17. Andreas, *Kansas*, 1208.

18. Frank Bishop to George Remsburg, May 26, 1909, "Names," MS, *KSHS*.

19. Andreas, *Kansas*, 1335.

20. *KHC*, XII, 480.

21. Giles, *Thirty Years*, 129.

22. *KHC*, XII, 489.

23. Andreas, *Kansas*, 1301; *KHC*, XI, 563n.

24. Fairfield, *KHC*, XI, 611.

25. Mooney, *Butler County*, 62.

26. Reports from Riseley and F. W. Schruben, Rooks County residents; *Webster Dam Dedication*, Stockton, October 6, 1956.

27. Franklin County Historical Society, *Reflections*.

28. Andreas, *Kansas*, 642; *KHC*, V, 450 and VII, 478.

29. Federal Writers' Project, *Kansas, A Guide*, 373.

30. Green, *Early Days*, 94, 97, 144; *People's Herald* (Lynden), April 3, 1948.

31. *Ibid.*, April 22, 1858 and October 8, 1859; *KHC*, XI, 542n.

32. *Ibid.*, XII, 474; Roenigh, *Pioneer Life*, 228.

33. *Wichita Eagle*, November 18, 1940.

34. National Geographic Society, *America's Historylands*, 68.

35. Andreas, *Kansas*, 938.

36. McNeal, *When Kansas Was Young*, 114.

37. *Wichita Eagle*, August 7, 1963.

38. *The Times* (Clay Center), January 5, 1882.

39. Angie Debo, *The Cowman's Southwest*, 80.

40. N. A. Crawford, "The County that Never was," *Kansas Magazine* (1944), 2; Gill, *KHC*, VIII, 469; Gaeddert, *KHQ*, X, 407.

41. Lindner, "Garfield County," M.A. thesis (University of Wyoming, 1949), 19.

42. Andreas, *Kansas*, 1350; *The Tiller and Toiler* (Larned), October 21, 1955.

43. *KHC*, VII, 486.

44. Pickering, *KHC*, IX, 386n.

45. See "Lamar," *Dictionary of American Biography*.

46. Scheffer, *KHQ*, III, 243.

47. "Names," MS, *KSHL*, Topeka; *KHC*, VII, 479.

48. *Kingman County Diamond Jubilee*, 1958.

49. "Kansas Chronology," *KHC*, XII, 420.

50. *Oberlin Herald*, March 4, 1880; *Journal World* (Lawrence), September 2, 1954.

51. Ploughe, *Reno County*, I, 121.

52. Henry J. Allen, "Roosevelt in Kansas," *Kansas Magazine*, IV (September, 1910), 65–71.

XXXIII
THE FOURTH ESTATE

1. D. W. Wilder, "The Newspapers of Kansas," *KSHS, Transactions*, III, 406.
2. Richard J. Hinton, *KHC*, VI, 371–82.
3. Cecil Howes, "Pistol-Packin' Pencil Pushers," *KHQ*, XIII, 115.
4. Hinton, *KHC*, VI, 371.
5. Howes, *This Place Called Kansas*, 196.
6. Wilder, *KSHS, Transactions*, III, 409.
7. Charles Forrest Moore, *Parade of the Presidents*, 89.
8. Gerald Johnson, *The Lunatic Fringe*, 59.
9. Martha B. Caldwell, "When Horace Greeley Visited Kansas," *KHQ*, IX, 124.
10. Andreas, *Kansas*, 1331; Beachy, in *Kansas City Star*, March 9, 1950.
11. Sorensen, "Ghost Towns," 6–10.
12. Federal Writers Project, *Kansas, A Guide*, 368.
13. *Kansas City Star*, April 9, 1950.
14. October 9, 1886.
15. Sorensen, "Ghost Towns," 6–10.
16. Andreas, *Kansas*, 784; Isely, in *Wichita Beacon*, September 8, 1929.
17. Ingalls, *Atchison County*, 124; Remsburg, *Scrapbook*, IV, 40, *KSHL*.
18. "A British Journalist Reports the Medicine Lodge Peace Councils of 1867,"*KHQ*, XXXIII, 249.
19. J. H. Beach, "Old Fort Hays," *KHC*, XI, 573; *Kansas City Star*, March 9, 1958.
20. T. Dwight Thacher, "Col. William A. Phillips," *KHC*, V, 100–101.
21. William Bishop, "Memorial Discourse," *KHC*, V, 104.
22. *KHC*, VII, 476; William E. Connelley to Martin, March 21, 1919, "Names," MS, *KSHS*.
23. Scheffer, *KHQ*, III, 240.
24. "Progress in Pawnee County, 1872–1952," *Weekly Tiller and Toiler*, 1952.
25. Cf. "Burdette," *National Cyclopedia of American Biography*.
26. Hinton, *KHC*, VI, 377, 378, 381.
27. Abby Huntington, "Dispersion of the Territorial Legislature of 1856," *KHC*, IX, 343; "Kansas Newspaper History," *KHC*, I–II, 177.
28. Eighteenth Biennial Report, *KSHS*, 43; Missouri Pacific, *The Empire*, 88.
29. Blackmar, *Kansas, A Cyclopedia*, I, 312; Henry F. Mason, "County Seat Controversy," *KHQ*, II, 54–64.
30. "The Lane-Jenkins Claim Contest," *KHC*, XVI, 128n.; A. P. Riddle, "The Senate of Kansas," *KSHS, Transactions*, III, 411.
31. Federal Writers' Project, *Kansas, A Guide*, 403.
32. *KHC*, VII, 12; Santa Fe, *Along Your Way*, 10.
33. Kennedy, *Profiles in Courage*, 146; Abel, *KHC*, VIII, 107.
34. A. G. Procter, "First Appearance of Kansas at a National Convention," *KHC*, XI, 13n.
35. Andreas, *Kansas*, 589.
36. Howes, Shawnee County Historical Society, *Bulletin*, I (1946), 29; King, *Shawnee County*, 50.
37. *KHQ*, I, 299.
38. Gaeddert, *KHQ*, X, 393.
39. W. W. Admire, *Admire's Political and Legislative Hand-Book for Kansas*, 382.
40. Rolla A. Clymer, "Thomas Benton Murdock," *KHQ*, XXIII, 248 *et seq*; Mooney, *Butler County*, 178.
41. Emmett, "Sedgwick County" in *Edward's Atlas of Sedgwick County*, 9.
42. Corley, *Names*, 35.
43. *Ibid.*, 32.
44. McNeal, *When Kansas was Young*, 5; *Barber County Clippings*, III, 54, 85.

45. Malin, *KHQ*, IX, 279; Andreas, *Kansas*, 1367.
46. *KHC*, XII, 481.

XXXIV
POLITICAL NOMENCLATURE

1. Dolbee, *KHQ*, VIII, 116.
2. Federal Writers' Project, *Iowa, A Guide to the Hawkeye State*, 452.
3. Duncan, *Montgomery County*, 85.
4. *Ibid.*, 78; *Southern Kansas Tribune* (Independence), June 18, 1930; Andreas, *Kansas*, 1564.
5. *Ibid.*, 1337.
6. Taylor, *Names and their Histories*, 173.
7. *The Liberal News*, May 2, 1935; Chrisman, *Lost Trails*, 155.
8. Blackburn and Cardwell, *Republic County*, 313.
9. Partridge, *Name into Word*, 75; Daniels, *Holiday*, II, 39.
10. James S. Merritt, "Movements for Territorial Organization," *KHC*, I–II, 261.
11. Cory, *Place Names in Bourbon County*, 22, 36.
12. *Chase County Historical Sketches*, I, 29.
13. Pantle, ed., *KHQ*, XXII, 16.
14. Laura M. French, *History of Emporia and Lyon County*, 13.
15. Federal Writers' Project, *Kansas, A Guide*, 318.
16. Andreas, *Kansas*, 1255, 1420; *Lincoln County News*, March 18, 1937.
17. Andreas, *Kansas*, 1271.
18. Duncan, *Neosho and Wilson Counties*, 835.
19. *Ibid.*, 87.

XXXV
GENERALS AND COUNTY NAMES

1. Hamlin Garland, "Grant's First Great Work in the War," *McClure's Magazine*, IX, 722.
2. Gill, *KHC*, VIII, 457.
3. Edward R. De Zurko, "A Report and Remarks on Cantonment Leavenworth," *KHQ*, XV, 358.
4. P. G. Lowe, "Recollections of Fort Riley," *KHC*, VII, 101.
5. *Overland Journey*, 47.
6. Don Barry, *A Majority of Scoundrels*, 25, 243.
7. Van Osdel, *Historic Landmarks*, 113ff.
8. "Addenda," *KHC*, VII, 577.
9. Andreas, *Kansas*, 419.
10. Rev. C. B. Boynton and T. B. Mason, *A Journey through Kansas*, 23.
11. Fitz, *KHC*, XII, 56.
12. *Ibid.*; H. Miles Moore, *Early History of Leavenworth, City and County*, 18–20.
13. Arthur D. H. Smith, *Old Fuss and Feathers*, 355.
14. Bruce Catton, *The Coming Fury*, in *The Centennial History of the Civil War*, I, 224.
15. Bruce Catton, *Lincoln's Army*, 86.
16. Scott County *News-Chronicle*, March 4, 1937; Isely, in *Wichita Beacon*, June 30, 1929.
17. Andreas, *Kansas*, 1300; Lowe, *KHC*, VII, 101.
18. Albe B. Whiting, "Some Western Border Conditions in the 50's and 60's," *KHC*, XII, 1 n.
19. Martin, *KHC*, VII, 373.
20. Andreas, *Kansas*, 1002.
21. *Wilson County Citizen*, July 8, 1875; *KHC*, VII, 473.

22. Kane, *American Counties*, 191.
23. O. E. Morse, "An Attempted Rescue of John Brown," *KHC*, VIII, 220; A. H. Tannar, "Early Days in Kansas," *KHC*, XIV, 233.
24. Andreas, *Kansas*, 1566.
25. Gill, *KHC*, VIII, 456–57.
26. Hamlin Garland, "The Early Life of Ulysses Grant," *McClure's Magazine*, VIII, 129.
27. Similarly the name of David Dwight Eisenhower was changed to Dwight D. Eisenhower, since his mother preferred to call him Dwight, which then became his first name.
28. Hamlin Garland, "Grant at West Point," *McClure's Magazine*, VIII, 200.
29. Eldon C. Smith, *Story of Our Names*, 81.
30. *Leavenworth Daily Commercial*, July 14, 1868.
31. Hamlin Garland, "Grant in the Mexican War," *McClure's Magazine*, VIII, 367.
32. Dorothy B. Goebel and Julius Goebel, Jr., *Generals in the White House*, 81; Garland, *McClure's Magazine*, IX, 610.
33. Bruce Catton, *This Hallowed Ground*, 228.
34. S. M. Fox, "The Story of the Seventh Kansas," *KHC*, VIII, 31.
35. Federal Writers' Project, *Kansas, A Guide*, 368.
36. *Topeka State Journal*, October 30, 1935.
37. Wilson and Sears, *Grant County*, 16, 117.
38. *Ibid.*, 113.
39. *Ibid.*
40. *Ibid.*, 68–70, 87; Mason, *KHQ*, II, 50.
41. *KHQ*, III, 216; *Cedarvale Messenger*, December 20, 1951.
42. Harrison Hannahs, "General Thomas Ewing, Jr.," *KHC*, XII, 281.
43. Howes, in *Kansas City Star*, December 12, 1941; Raymond L. Welty, "The Policing of the Frontier by the Army, 1860–1870," *KHQ*, VII, 246ff.
44. Julia A. Chase, "Mother Bickerdyke," *KHC*, VII, 189–98.
45. Blackman, *KHC*, VIII, 50ff.
46. Andreas, *Kansas*, 603; John C. and Winona Jones, *The Prairie Pioneers*, 13.
47. Catton, *This Hallowed Ground*, 294–97.
48. Hortense Balderston Campbell, "Camp Beecher," *KHQ*, III, 182.
49. James Albert Hadley, "A Royal Buffalo Hunt," *KHC*, X, 564.
50. Clarence E. Macartney, *Grant and his Generals*, 307.
51. Nyle H. Miller and Robert W. Richmond, "Sheridan, a fabled End-of-Track Town on the Union Pacific Railroad, 1868–1869," *KHQ*, XXXIV, 427–31.
52. Randall Parrish, *The Great Plains*, 369.
53. Macartney, *Grant and his Generals*, 1–4.
54. Thomas County, *Yesterday and Today*, II, 21; Theodore Gardner, "The First Kansas Battery," *KHC*, XIV, 280.
55. Catton, *This Hallowed Ground*, 343–45.
56. Andreas, *Kansas*, 813.
57. Goebel, *Generals*, 17; Catton, *Lincoln's Army*, 208.
58. Catton, *This Hallowed Ground*, 345.
59. "The Annals of Kansas: 1887," *KHQ*, XX, 274; George W. Martin, "A Chapter from the Archives," *KHC*, XII, 356n.
60. Remsburg, *Scrapbook*, IV, 44, *KSHL*, Topeka; *KHQ*, VII, 108; Charles R. Wetzel, "Monument Station, Gove County," *KHQ*, XXVI, 250.
61. *KHQ*, XX, 283.
62. Montgomery, *KHC*, XVII, 189; Marvin H. Garfield, "Defense of the Kansas Frontier, 1864–65," *KHQ*, I, 140–52.
63. Macartney, *Grant and his Generals*, 73.
64. Montgomery, *KHC*, XVII, 189n., 194, 200.
65. *The Western Times* (Sharon Springs), November 17, 1955.

549

66. Catton, *This Hallowed Ground*, 228, 316.
67. William E. Woodward, *Meet General Grant*, 206.
68. Rawlins was also a friend of General Grenville M. Dodge, the builder of the Union Pacific. While inspecting the route through the dry country of central Wyoming, they discovered a gushing spring. After quenching his thirst from its cool waters, Rawlins commented on the beauty of the spring. Then General Dodge admired it for a moment and said: "General Rawlins, we will name this spring for you." That is how Rawlins, Wyoming, was named. Jacob R. Perkins, *Trails, Rails, and War*, 153, 214.
69. Catton, *This Hallowed Ground*, 346.
70. Andreas, *Kansas*, 1173.
71. *Life*, January 20, 1961.
72. Catton, *Lincoln's Army*, 116; Catton, *This Hallowed Ground*, 169, 315; Charles A. Dana, "Reminiscences of Men and Events of the Civil War," *McClure's Magazine*, X, 28-30.
73. Dana, *McClure's Magazine*, X, 35.
74. *Topeka Capital*, July 3, 1888.
75. Sullivan, *Meade County*, 26.
76. *Meade Globe-News*, August 1, 1948; Barry, *KHQ*, XII, 384n.
77. Andreas, *Kansas*, 753; Jones, *Rice County*, 118.
78. Jones, *Rice County*, 108.
79. Catton, *Lincoln's Army*, 33, 226, 242; Isely, in *Wichita Beacon*, May 5, 1929.
80. Remsburg, *Scrapbook*, IV, 56, *KSHL*; Hall and Hand, *Leavenworth County*.
81. Barry, ed., *KHQ*, XXIX, 68; Kearny County Historical Society, *History Of Kearny County, Kansas*, 85.
82. *Dictionary of American Biography*.
83. Catton, *Lincoln's Army*, 32.
84. *Ibid.*, 46, 321.
85. *Lakin Independent*, August 27, 1948; Sara E. Madison, "Founding a Town," *KHQ*, VII, 69.
86. *Laws of the State of Kansas, 1889*, 242.
87. Lowe, *KHC*, VII, 112; Robert M. Peck, "Recollections of Early Times in Kansas Territory," *KHC*, VIII, 486n.
88. "Governor Walker's Administration," *KHC*, V, 301-304.
89. Gleed, *KHC*, VI, 249.
90. Catton, *Lincoln's Army*, 291.
91. Dana, *McClure's Magazine*, XI, 28.
92. Catton, *Lincoln's Army*, 212-14.
93. Andreas, *Kansas*, 782; *The Newton Kansan*, August 22, 1922.
94. Jay Monaghan, *Civil War on the Western Border*, 38.
95. Weichselbaum, *KHC*, XI, 568.
96. Albert R. Greene, "On the Battle of Wilson Creek," *KHC*, V, 125; James A. McGonigle, "First Kansas Infantry," *KHC*, XII, 293.
97. When General Fontleroy joined the Confederates, Fort Fontleroy in New Mexico was renamed Fort Lyon for Nathaniel Lyon. Robert W. Frazer, *Forts of the West*, 108.
98. James R. McClure, "Taking the Census," *KHC*, VIII, 231; Shields, *KHC*, XIV, 146.
99. George C. Anderson, "Touring Kansas and Colorado in 1871," *KHQ*, XXII, 382.
100. Hollibaugh, *Cloud County*, 73.

XXXVI
PRIVATE ROOKS AND MEN OF RANK

1. *KHC*, VII, 472.
2. Perkins, *Trails, Rails, and War*, 178.

3. *Dodge City Journal,* October 22, 1936; *Wilson County Citizen,* December 23, 1903.
4. Connelley, *Kansas and Kansans,* III, 1200.
5. Charles E. Cory, "The Sixth Kansas Cavalry," *KHC,* XI, 220.
6. This was also the unit in which Captain Charles F. Clarke served and for whom Clark County was named.
7. Cory, *KHC,* XI, 232.
8. Cory, *KHC,* XI, 217–38; Robley, *Bourbon County,* 171.
9. Robley, *Bourbon County,* 172.
10. Andreas, *Kansas,* 967; *Western Advocate,* Mankato, July 25, 1940.
11. Gill, *KHC,* VIII, 453.
12. Hollibaugh, *Cloud County,* 34.
13. Samuel J. Crawford, *Kansas in the Sixties, passim.*
14. *Wilson County Citizen,* December 23, 1903; "Governor Denver's Administration," *KHC,* V, 507; *KHC,* VII, 474.
15. Andreas, *Kansas,* 908.
16. *Smith County Pioneer,* July 27, 1876, and September 26, 1946.
17. Mrs. Seigniora Russell Laune, "Avra P. Russell," *KHC,* XIV, 84.
18. "Military History of Kansas Regiments," in *Report of Adjutant General of Kansas,* 1861–65, I, 21.
19. *Ibid.,* 84–88; Andreas, *Kansas,* 1286; Crawford, *Kansas, passim.*
20. Blackmar, *Kansas, A Cyclopedia,* I, 356; *Wilson County Citizen,* December 23, 1903; Gill, *KHC,* VIII, 456 and maps.
21. Walden, in *Clark County Clipper,* September 13, 1934, September 20, 1934, and November 2, 1939.
22. Catton, *This Hallowed Ground,* 91–95; *Hill City Times,* August 22, 1940.
23. Edgar Langsdorf, ed., "Letters of Joseph Trego," *KHQ,* XIX, 289n.
24. Memorial address by Governor Martin, in *The Wichita Eagle,* June 1, 1886.
25. Andreas, *Kansas,* 1297.
26. "Forgotten Counties in Kansas," *Progress in Kansas,* I, 25–26; Fox, *KHC,* VIII, 22, 24.
27. Fox, *KHC,* VIII, 22, 25.
28. Mrs. S. B. White, "My First Days in Kansas," *KHC,* XI, 559n.; Martin, *KHC,* VII, 376.
29. Andreas, *Kansas,* 1585; *Rush County News,* LaCrosse, May 19, 1949.
30. Andreas, *Kansas,* 1586.
31. *KHC,* V, 487, 507; Isely, in *Wichita Beacon,* July 21, 1929.
32. Federal Writers' Project, *Kansas, A Guide,* 394.
33. Andreas, *Kansas,* 1274, 1278.
34. *KHC,* VII, 472, 477; Jelinek, *Ellsworth Story,* 2.
35. Andreas, *Kansas,* 1274.
36. Frazer, *Forts of the West,* 53; Jelinek, *Ellsworth Story,* 4.
37. Harrington, *Gove County, passim.*
38. Andreas, *Kansas,* 1587; Mooney, *Butler County,* 71; Gill, *KHC,* VII, 456.
39. Andreas, *Kansas,* 1289; Isely, in *Wichita Beacon,* June 23, 1929; Kittie Dale, *Echoes and Etchings of Early Ellis,* 12–16.
40. Greene, *KHC,* V, 118, 139; *KHC,* I–II, 219.
41. Byers, *KHC,* XV, 574; *Pratt Daily Tribune,* October 31, 1964.
42. Gray, *Pioneer Saints and Sinners,* 52, 88–96.
43. *Topeka Daily Commonwealth,* January 17, 1875; *Wilson County Citizen,* December 23, 1903.
44. Andreas, *Kansas,* 363.
45. Sanders, *Harper County Story,* 101, 144.
46. Manning, *KHC,* X, 425; *Ellsworth Reporter,* March 26, 1953.
47. Joyce Farlow and Louise Barry, eds., "Vincent B. Osborne's Civil War Experiences," *KHQ,* XX, 126; Manning, *KHC,* X, 425.

48. Lathrop, *Tales of Western Kansas*, 16, 23; Bowers, *Norton County*, 16.
49. Lathrop, *Tales of Western Kansas*, 23.
50. Lockard, *Norton County*, 15; Bowers, *Norton County*, 16, 36; Van Gundy, *Reminiscences*, 78.
51. Andreas, *Kansas*, 1062.
52. Winsor and Scarbrough, *KHC*, XVII, 406–409; Inman, in *Topeka Daily Commonwealth*, January 12, 1886.
53. Lockard, *Norton County*, 21.
54. Lathrop, *Tales of Western Kansas*, 24.
55. Millbrook, *Ness: Western County*, 63.
56. *KHC*, XII, 469n.; Andreas, *Kansas*, 1524.
57. Baughman, *Kansas Post Offices*.
58. Andreas, *Kansas*, 1613; Cyrus T. Brady, "Decatur," *McClure's Magazine*, XIV, 62–67.
59. Gill, *KHC*, VIII, 451.
60. Richardson, *The Secret Service*, 213ff.; Catton, *This Hallowed Ground*, 65, 92–95.
61. *Wilson County Citizen*, December 23, 1903; *Rooks County Record*, Stockton, March 14, 1940.
62. Risely to Schruben, Stockton, August 17, 1959.
63. Schruben to Rydjord, Reseda, California, July 25, 1959.

XXXVII
THE SOLDIER STATE

1. Cory, *KHC*, XI, 221.
2. *Covered Wagon Geologist*, 32.
3. Marshall, *Santa Fe*, 88; Horace Jones, *Up from the Sod*, 148.
4. Leopold Wagner, *Names and their Meaning*, 117.
5. Corley, *Names*, 36.
6. Some of these names are considered under other categories. See index.
7. Baughman, *Kansas Post Offices*, 185; Blackmar, *Kansas, A Cyclopedia*, I, 771.
8. Gannett, *American Names*, 136.
9. "Ashland Wisconsin," *Magazine of Western History*, IX, 13.
10. Blair, *Johnson County*, 205; Andreas, *Kansas*, 626.
11. Missouri Pacific, *The Empire*, 139.
12. Fannie E. Cole, "Pioneer Life in Kansas," *KHC*, XII, 354 and n.
13. Barry, ed., *KHQ*, XXIX, 462.
14. John C. McCoy to F. G. Adams, Chouteau, November 3, 1901, "Names," MS, *KSHS*; *Emporia Daily News*, July 23, 1883.
15. Barnes, *KHQ*, V, 352n.
16. *Leavenworth Times*, December 2, 1937.
17. Alexander Case, "Reminiscences," *Journal of American History*, II, 249–54.
18. Mitchell, *Linn County*, 146.
19. Bononcini, *Autobiography*, 78.
20. Ferris, *KHC*, XI, 382.
21. Federal Writers' Project, *Kansas, A Guide*, 401; *Kansas City Journal*, May 5, 1912.
22. Howes, *Bulletin*, Shawnee County Historical Society, I, 30.
23. Albert P. Southwick, *Wisps of Wit and Wisdom*, 255.
24. *People's Herald* (Lyndon), March 11, 1948.
25. For Pike's route, see map, *KHC*, IX, 577.
26. Nelson, *The Company and the Community*, 121.
27. Brooks, Missouri Historical Society, *Bulletin*, XXI, 167–207.
28. Coues, ed., *Pike*, II, 517n.
29. William D. Street, "The Victory of the Plow," *KHC*, IX, 34; *Concordia Blade*, February 1, 1907.

30. George Remsburg, "Isle Au Vache," *KHC*, VIII, 439n.; Phil E. Chappell, "A History of the Missouri River," *KHC*, IX, 277.

31. *Hutchinson News-Herald*, March 23, 1941, quoted in *KHQ*, X, 216; James H. Birch, "The Battle of Coon Creek," *KHC*, X, 409.

32. Taft, ed., *KHQ*, XVI, 348n.

33. Greene, *Kanzas*, 89; *KHC*, XII, 478; Barry, ed., *KHQ*, XXXII, 109; "Early Military Posts, Missions and Camps," *KHC*, I–II, 264.

34. Herbert M. Hart, *Old Forts of the Far West*, 9; Peck, *KHC*, VIII, 485.

35. Blackmar, *Kansas, A Cyclopedia*, I, 656; Root, *KHQ*, I, 199n.

36. Ingalls, *Atchison County*, 33.

37. *KHC*, I–II, 264.

38. Blackmar, *Kansas, A Cyclopedia*, I, 656; Robert Taft, ed., "Kansas, its Forts, Settlements, and Missions, 1854," *New York Tribune*, June 22, 1954.

39. Robley, *Bourbon County*, 140, 166; E. J. Dallas, "Kansas Postal History," *KHC*, I–II, 256.

40. Greene, *KHC*, V, 418.

41. "Names," MS, Archives, *KSHS*.

42. Coues, ed., *Pike*, II, 405.

43. Ingalls, *Atchison County*, 36.

44. James Humphrey, "The Country West of Topeka," *KHC*, IV, 294.

45. Lowe, *KHC*, VII, 101.

46. "Adventurous Career of Frederick Funston," *Current Opinion*, LVI, 427–28.

47. Whittemore, *One-Way Ticket*, 25.

48. Carr, *Century Magazine*, LXXIII, 503–508.

49. George Root, "Chronology of Shawnee County," *Bulletin*, Shawnee County Historical Society, XXXV, 14n.

50. *People's Herald* (Lyndon), April 22, 1948.

51. *The Wabaunsee County News*, July 26, 1896.

52. *Hill City Times*, August 22, 1940.

53. *Smoky Valley People*, 174.

54. Perkins, *Trails, Rails, and War*, 176.

55. Andreas, *Kansas*, 1560; D. M. Morris, "Dodge City, Kansas," *Kansas Magazine*, IV, 89.

56. Henry Schmidt, in *Dodge City Journal*, October 22, 1936 and January 15, 1948.

57. Dodge, *American State Papers, Military Affairs* (1861), VI, 130–46.

58. Dodge City *Daily Globe*, May 20, 1947; Schmidt, in *Dodge City Journal*, October 22, 1936.

59. Stanley Vestal, *Dodge City, Queen of Cow Towns*, 3.

60. *Clark County Clipper*, September 13, 1934 and December 28, 1939.

61. *Protection Post*, May 16, 1947.

62. The author visited the place with an expedition conducted by Ross M. Taylor of Wichita State University. There are interesting remains of the redoubt, and Big Hole is still an accurate description.

63. Rand McNalley, *Map of Kansas*, 1876; Miller, *KHQ*, I, 122n.

64. India Simmons, in *Daily Globe* (Dodge City), March 26, 1937.

65. William E. Unrau, "The History of Fort Larned, Kansas," M.A. thesis (University of Wyoming, 1956), 15.

66. Wright, *KHC*, VII, 49n.; *KHC*, IX, 572.

67. *Pike*, II, 425.

68. Garfield, *KHQ*, I, 142; Wright, *KHC*, VII, 68n.

69. Coues, ed., *Pike*, 425n.

70. Marion M. McDonough, "Quest of Health, Not Wealth, 1871," *Montana: Magazine of Western History*, XIV (January, 1964), 28.

71. Montgomery, *KHC*, XVII, 196; Beach, *KHC*, XI, 571.

72. Beach, *KHC*, XI, 571.

73. Andreas, *Kansas*, 627.
74. Alberta Pantle, ed., "Fort Wallace," *KHC*, XVII, 238.
75. Beach, *KHC*, XI, 571, 575; *KHQ*, XVI, 411.
76. Montgomery, *KHC*, VII, 198; Dodge City *Daily Globe*, August 31, 1935; *KHC*, XVI, 720.
77. Richardson, *The Secret Service*, 251.
78. Frank Doster, "Eleventh Indiana Cavalry in Kansas," *KHC*, XV, 528; Montgomery, *KHC*, XVII, 245; Andreas, *Kansas*, 223.
79. Alfred Pleasanton, "The Successes and Failures at Chancellorsville," *The Century Magazine*, XXXII, 758n.
80. William T. McClure, "The Fourth Kansas Militia in the Price Raid," *KHC*, VIII, 151.
81. Crawford, *Kansas*, 175.
82. Mitchell, *KHC*, XVI, 654; Andreas, *Kansas*, 1107.
83. *KHC*, VII, 483.
84. Mitchell, *KHC*, XVI, 655; Andreas, *Kansas*, 196, 204.
85. Blackmar, *Kansas, A Cyclopedia*, II, 309; Langsdorf, *KHQ*, XIX, 391n.
86. Corley, *Names*, 49; Winsor and Scarbrough, *KHC*, XVII, 407.
87. *KHQ*, IV, 323.
88. Johnson, *Anderson County*, 79–99.
89. "Custer," in *Dictionary of American Biography*.
90. Montgomery, *KHC*, XVII, 212–21.
91. P. G. Lowe, "Kansas, as Seen in the Indian Territory," *KHC*, IV, 363; *KHC*, I–II, 265.
92. Federal Writers' Project, *Kansas, A Guide*, 366; Interview with Grinnell residents.
93. Roenigh, *Pioneer History of Kansas*, 143; Montgomery, *KHC*, XVII, 231.
94. Missouri Pacific, *The Empire*, 139; Corley, *Names*, 61; Barge and Caldwell, *Journal*, Illinois State Historical Society, XXIX, 61.
95. *Daily Tribune and Monitor* (Fort Scott), June 4, 1917.
96. Franklin County Historical Society, *Reflections on Franklin County*; Federal Writers' Project, *Kansas, A Guide*, 391.
97. Hill P. Wilson, "Black Kettle's Last Raid, 1868," *KHC*, VIII, 111; Jelinek, *Ellsworth Story*.
98. Nyquist, *Pioneer Life and Lore*, 77.
99. *Leavenworth Times*, January 24, 1907; Lowe, *KHC*, VII, 101n.
100. Corley, *Names*, 43.
101. Ingalls, *Atchison County*, 121; Remsburg, *Scrapbook*, I, 157, KSHL.
102. Corley, *Names*, 40.
103. Shirk, *Oklahoma Place Names*, 122.
104. Sam Henderson, "Bartles dug deep for Black Gold," *Golden West*, VI, 54.
105. Shirk, *Oklahoma Place Names*, 227.
106. Lela Barnes, ed., "Journal of Isaac McCoy for the Exploring Expedition of 1830," *KHQ*, Vn.
107. Martin, *KHC*, XI, 61.
108. Nelson, *The Company and the Community*, 120.
109. *Emporia Daily News*, July 23, 1883.
110. McDonough, *Montana*, XIV, 27n.
111. Corley, *Names*, 58.
112. *Sterling Bulletin*, November 15, 1901; Jones, *Rice County*, 96.

XXXVIII
LO, THE POOR INDIAN

1. For a more complete study of Indian place-names, see Rydjord, *Indian Place Names*.

2. For a general account, see Foreman, *Indian Removal, passim.*
3. Admire, *Political and Legislative Hand-Book*, 213.
4. Spencer, *KHC*, X, 388.
5. John M. Oskison, *Tecumseh and his Times*, 219; Leland, *Names*, I, 272; Hodge, *Handbook*, II, 714.
6. King, *Shawnee County*, 59.
7. Blackmar, *Kansas, A Cyclopedia*, I, 598.
8. Blair, *Johnson County*, 86; *Johnson County Herald*, September 3, 1969.
9. Barry, *KHQ*, XXXI, 145.
10. Hall and Hand, *Leavenworth County*, 151.
11. Merwin, *KHC*, IX, 79; Hodge, *Handbook*, I, 584.
12. Rydjord, *Indian Place-Names*, 275.
13. Richardson, *Beyond the Mississippi*, 29–33; Andreas, *Kansas*, 1229.
14. "Names," MS, *KSHS.*
15. Leland, *Names*, I, 272.
16. Armstrong, *Place Names in Canada*, 286; Stewart, *Names on the Land*, 82.
17. *Gridley Light*, July 5, 1934.
18. Vogel, *Indian Place Names in Illinois*, 160; Barr, *Wabaunsee County*, 12.
19. *St. Mary's Star*, January 14, 1943; *KHC*, VII, 482.
20. Barr, *Wabaunsee County*, 90.
21. *KHC*, VII, 485; *St. Mary's Star*, January 14, 1943.
22. Swanton, *Indian Tribes of North America*, 244.
23. Hodge, *Handbook*, I, 852.
24. The Miami in Florida came from the name of a local river, the Mayaimi, or "big water."
25. The Illini and Mishigamaw were also related tribes whose names were used in Kansas.
26. Andreas, *Kansas*, 875.
27. Vogel, *Indian Place Names in Illinois*, 108.
28. Swanton, *Indian Tribes of North America*, 215; Lauvrière, *Histoire de la Louisiane Francaise*, 276.
29. Andreas, *Kansas*, 1149.
30. Duncan, *Neosho and Wilson Counties*, 17, 19.
31. Catherine C. Coblentz, *Sequoyah*, 111; Gould, *Oklahoma Place Names*, 56.
32. Gill, *KHC*, VIII, 457, 463.
33. Hodge, *Handbook*, I, 867.
34. *Ibid.*, 72.
35. Gill, *KHC*, VIII, 457, 469.
36. George B. Grinnell, *The Cheyenne Indians*, I, 2; Rydjord, *Indian Place-Names*, 303.
37. The story is told sympathetically in Mari Sandoz, *Cheyenne Autumn.*
38. Andreas, *Kansas*, 1015, 1313, 1563; Howes, *Kansas Teacher*, LVIII (February, 1950), 39.
39. Remsburg, *Scrapbook*, I, 173 and II, 859, *KSHL*; Hafen, ed., *Journal of Bell*, in *Far West and the Rockies*, VI, 224n.
40. Mildred P. Mayhall, *The Kiowas*, 3, 17.
41. Rydjord, *Indian Place-Names*, 311.
42. *The Wichita Beacon*, February 26, 1956.
43. Blackmar, *Kansas, A Cyclopedia*, I, 318.
44. Mead, *KHC*, VIII, 171–77.
45. Rydjord, *Indian Place-Names*, 158ff.
46. Barry, ed., *KHQ*, XXXIII, 378.
47. Mead, *KHC*, VIII, 173; *Wichita Evening Eagle*, March 3, 1933.
48. Hodge, *Handbook*, I, 684; Vogel, *Indian Place Names in Illinois*, 52.
49. Ingalls, *Atchison County*, 29, 191; Vogel, *Indian Place Names in Illinois*, 53.

50. Ingalls, *Atchison County*, 29; *Atchison Daily Globe*, June 13, 1916.
51. *Ibid.*, 106; Andreas, *Kansas*, 410; Remsburg, *Scrapbook*, I, 95, KSHL.
52. Hodge, *Handbook*, II, 471; Swanton, *Indian Tribes of North America*, 256.
53. Hodge, *Handbook*, I, 673.
54. Green, *Early Days in Kansas*, V, 52–68.
55. *KHC*, XII, 481.
56. *Coffey County*, 14.
57. Duncan, *Neosho and Wilson Counties*, 843.
58. Pryor Plank, "The Iowa, Sac and Fox Indian Mission and its Missionaries," *KHC*, X, 323.
59. Hodge, *Handbook*, II, 109; Garfield, *KHQ*, I, 58.
60. See Chapter XXVI in Rydjord, *Indian Place-Names*, 339.

XXXIX
NAMES FROM THE SANTA FE

1. *Chase County Historical Sketches*, II, 260.
2. Marshall, *Santa Fe*, 278–79.
3. *Dodge City Journal*, January 8, 1948.
4. Warren Upham, *Minnesota Geographical Names*, 565.
5. King, *Shawnee County*, 133; Richardson, *Beyond the Mississippi*, 40.
6. Andreas, *Kansas*, 1378.
7. Ploughe, *Reno County*, I, 310; Charles S. Gleed, "The Rehabilitation of the Santa Fe Railway System," *KHC*, XIII, 451; *Nickerson Argosy*, June 4, 1964.
8. Marshall, *Santa Fe*, 79; L. L. Waters, *Steel Trails to Santa Fe*, 114n.
9. Marshall, *Santa Fe*, 57, 61.
10. *Ibid.*; *KHC*, VII, 477.
11. *Ibid.*, XII, 456.
12. Marshall, *Santa Fe*, 45.
13. *History of Kearny County*, 37; *KHC*, VII, 477.
14. Isely, in *Wichita Beacon*, April 21, 1929.
15. *Chase County Historical Sketches*, I, 24, II, 362.
16. Gudde, *California Place Names*, 24.
17. *The Wichita Eagle*, April 1, 1963.
18. Marshall, *Santa Fe*, 279; Waters, *Steel Trails to Santa Fe*, 175.
19. Andreas, *Kansas*, 1260; Santa Fe Railway, *Along Your Way*, 13.
20. *KHC*, VII, 479; Andreas, *Kansas*, 1509.
21. *History of Kearny County*, I, 41.
22. "Annals of Crime: In Cold Blood," *The New Yorker* (September 25, 1965), 154.
23. Andreas, *Kansas*, 761; *Lyons Daily News*, April 12, 1961.
24. "Names," MS, KSHL; Byers, *KHC*, XII, 105n.
25. *Kingman County Diamond Jubilee*, 1958.
26. Marshall, *Santa Fe*, 357.
27. *Pratt Daily Tribune*, July 3 and August 30, 1951; Gray, *Pioneer Saints and Sinners*, 127.
28. Marshall, *Santa Fe*, 349; *Kansas City Star*, March 9, 1950.
29. Rich, ed., *Heritage of Kansas*, 161.
30. Carruth, in the *New England Magazine*, XVI, 16.
31. Mrs. George Whitney, in *Wichita Eagle*, March 4, 1933.
32. Malin, *KHQ*, IX, 271–73.
33. Andreas, *Kansas*, 1546.
34. Malin, *KHC*, IX, 233n.
35. "Names," MS, KSHS; *Spearville News*, January 30, 1936; Marshall, *Santa Fe*, 357.
36. Marshall, *Santa Fe*, 62.

37. *Ibid.*, 56.
38. *Ibid.*, 357.
39. *KHC*, VII, 478; Gleed, *KHC*, XIII, 455.
40. Marshall, *Santa Fe*, 353.
41. *Ibid.*, 356.
42. Andreas, *Kansas*, 644.
43. "Kansas Postal History," *KHC*, I–II, 256; Andreas, *Kansas*, 643; Federal Writers' Project, *Kansas, A Guide*, 373.
44. Marshall, *Santa Fe*, 12, 56, 118; Santa Fe, *Along Your Way*, 14; *KHC*, VII, 477. 477.
45. *Leader* (Ellinwood), March 16, 1944; Smyth, *Heart of the New Kansas*, 119.
46. Corley, *Names*, 80.
47. Hadley, *KHC*, X, 874n.
48. Corley, *Names*, 73.
49. *Dodge City Journal*, June 8, 1948; Andrew Stevenson, Jr., "Many Towns Names in Honor of Santa Fe Men," *The Santa Fe Magazine*, XXIII (August, 1928), 55.
50. *Dodge City Journal*, June 8, 1948; Blair, *Johnson County*, 180.
51. Corley, *Names*, 80.
52. Marshall, *Santa Fe*, 354.
53. *Ibid.*; Corley, *Names*, 71.
54. Carruth, in *New England Magazine*, XVI, 17; Kos Harris to Isely, July 24, 1929, MS, Wichita State University Library.
55. Raser and Rumford, *Hodgeman County*, 5; Federal Writers' Project, *Kansas, A Guide*, 386.
56. Pickering, *KHC*, IX, 385n.
57. Connelley, *Kansas and Kansans*, III, 1695.
58. *Chase County Historical Sketches*, I, 23; Santa Fe, *Along Your Way*, 13.
59. Marshall, *Santa Fe*, 357.
60. Franklin County Historical Society, *Reflections*.
61. Scheffer, *KHQ*, III, 242.
62. Remsburg, *Scrapbook*, I, 245, II, 89, *KSHL*; Marshall, *Santa Fe*, 356.
63. *Dodge City Journal*, January 8, 1948; Marshall, *Santa Fe*, 357.
64. Schmidt, in *Dodge City Journal*, January 8, 1948.
65. Marshall, *Santa Fe*, 81, 83; King, *Shawnee County*, 261–63.
66. Marshall, *Santa Fe*, 81, 83; C. B. Schmidt, "Reminiscences of Foreign Immigration Work for Kansas," *KHC*, IX, 487.
67. William E. Connelley, "Life and Adventures of George E. Brown," *KHC*, XVII, 132.
68. *Meade Globe-News*, August 1, 1948.
69. Marshall, *Santa Fe*, 81–94.
70. *KHC*, XII, 489.
71. *Hutchinson News*, March 9, 1955; *History of Finney County*, II, 149.
72. Marshall, *Santa Fe*, 356.
73. *Kansas Precancel News*, No. 172, February, 1970.
74. Nyquist, *Pioneer History*, 110; *Dodge City Journal*, January 8, 1948.
75. Blanchard, *Conquest of Southwest Kansas*, 326.
76. *News-Chronicle* (Scott City), April 8, 1937.
77. Blanchard, *Conquest of Southwest Kansas*, 327.
78. "Names," MS, Archives, *KSHL*.
79. *Idem.*
80. Shackleton, *Handbook on Frontier Days*, 110; *St. Paul Journal*, April 28, 1949.
81. *KHC*, V, 491; Kendall E. Bailes, *From Hunting Ground to Surburb, a History of Merriam, Kansas*, 17; Corley, *Names*, 47.
82. Lapham, *KHC*, XVI, 505–11.
83. *Ibid.*

84. Vogel, *Indian Place Names in Illinois*, 24.

85. *Kansas City Star*, December 8, 1941; *St. Paul Journal*, August 24, 1933; Duncan, *Neosho and Wilson Counties*, 64–66.

86. Masterson, *Katy Railroad*, 54.

87. Corley, *Names*, 49.

88. Wilson and Sears, *Grant County*, 78; 20th Biennial Report, *KSHS*, 197.

89. Blair, *Johnson County*, 152; *Kansas City Star*, May 8, 1959.

XL
RAILROAD ROSTER

1. *KHQ*, XX, 279.

2. *Miltonvale Record*, September 14, 1933.

3. *Kiowa County Signal*, June 20 and August 13, 1960; *History of Finney County*, II, 102.

4. John Watson, in *Wichita Evening Eagle*, September 13, 1954.

5. *Hill City Times*, September 8, 1949.

6. Franklin County Historical Society, *Reflections*.

7. Missouri Pacific, *The Empire*, 111.

8. Blackmar, *Kansas, A Cyclopedia*, I, 567; Andreas, *Kansas*, 1253.

9. Missouri Pacific, *The Empire*, 149.

10. Corley, *Names*, 10.

11. Andreas, *Kansas*, 927.

12. *Courtland Journal*, June 28, 1951.

13. William E. Hayes, *Iron Road to Empire*, 118–19.

14. *Ibid.*; Byers, *KHC*, XV, 574n.; *Topeka State Journal*, October 30, 1935.

15. Gray, *Doniphan County*, 45.

16. Corley, *Names*, 30, 77.

17. John D. Cruise, "Early Days on the Union Pacific," *KHC*, XI, 548; Kitty Doyle, *Echoes and Etchings of Early Ellis*, 113.

18. *Thomas County Herald*, September 26, 1957; Hayes, *Iron Road to Empire*, 12.

19. Hayes, *Iron Road to Empire*, 12.

20. Anne Jones, "The Medical and Business Career of Dr. Charles Carrol Furley," Seminar report, MS, Wichita State University, 1935; George W. Martin, "John A. Anderson," *KHC*, VIII, 320.

21. Isely, in *Wichita Beacon*, September 8, 1929.

22. Byers, *KHC*, XV, 573; Byers, *KHC*, XII, 99.

23. James C. Horton, "Reminiscences," *KHC*, VIII, 204; Oliver P. Byers, "Railroading in the West," *KHC*, XVII, 340.

24. Missouri Pacific, *The Empire*, 108; Andreas, *Kansas*, 751.

25. Andreas, *Kansas*, 751.

26. *KHC*, VII, 477.

27. Andreas, *Kansas*, 956; *Courier-Tribune* (Seneca), December 15, 1938.

28. A. N. Ruley, *A. N. Ruley's History of Brown County*, 45.

29. *Sabetha Herald*, October 19, 1938; *KHC*, VIII, 478.

30. J. W. Hanson to Martin, December 2, 1901, "Names," MS, Archives, *KSHS*.

31. Andreas, *Kansas*, 962; *KHC*, VII, 477; Tennal, *Nemaha County*, 49.

32. Baughman, *Kansas Post Offices*; Andreas, *Kansas*, 1059.

33. *KHC*, VII, 485; Andreas, *Kansas*, 1061.

34. Missouri Pacific, *The Empire*, 100.

35. "Names," MS, *KSHL*, Topeka.

36. Missouri Pacific, *The Empire*, 95; *KHC*, VII, 476; Cory, *Place Names in Bourbon County*, 16.

37. Missouri Pacific, *The Empire*, 130; "Names," MS, *KSHL*, Topeka; *KHC*, VII, 482.

38. *St. Paul Journal*, September 29, 1949; Shackleton, *Handbook on Frontier Days*, 124; Johnson, *Anderson County*, 350.

39. For a map of the Missouri Pacific Lines, see *KHQ*, XXII, opposite 328.

40. Masterson, *The Katy Railroad*, 108n., 214; A. Bower Sageser, "The Rails Go Westward," in *Kansas, The First Century*, Bright, ed., I, 247.

41. Andreas, *Kansas*, 1210; *KHC*, VII, 484.

42. Remsburg, *Scrapbook*, I, 177, *KSHL*.

43. Andreas, *Kansas*, 1114; *KHC*, VII, 483.

44. *Latham Leader*, April 29, 1937; Corley, *Names*, 40.

45. *Topeka Capital*, September 17, 1948; Report from Lorene Anderson Hawley, *KSHL*; Missouri Pacific, *The Empire*, 96.

46. *KHC*, XII, 449; Missouri Pacific, *The Empire*, 146.

47. Johnson, *Anderson County*, 312, 343.

48. Corley, *Names*, 5.

49. *Atchison Daily Globe*, May 24, 1907.

50. *KHC*, VII, 484.

51. *Seneca Courier-Tribune*, October 5, 1950.

52. Corley, *Names*, 58; *KHC*, V, 499.

53. *KHC*, VII, 479; *St. Mary's Star*, January 14, 1943.

54. *KHC*, VII, 480; Manhattan *Mercury-Chronicle*, October 3, 1948.

55. *KHC*, VII, 475; Andreas, *Kansas*, 931.

56. *Marshall County News*, Marysville, July 14, 1949.

57. *Ibid.*, February 27, 1931.

58. George L. Anderson, "Atchison and the Central Branch Country," *KHQ*, XXVIII, 11; Morrill, *Brown County*, 50; Nelson, *The Company and the Community*, 423n.

59. Missouri Pacific, *The Empire*, 138; Andreas, *Kansas*, 939.

60. *Hoxie Sentinel*, August 15, 1957; Perkins, *Trails, Rails, and War*, 135, 277.

61. *KHC*, VII, 481.

62. *Rush County News*, May 19, 1949; Missouri Pacific, *The Empire*, 129.

63. Missouri Pacific, *The Empire*, 95.

64. Corley, *Names*, 71.

65. Masterson, *The Katy*, 51.

66. *Ibid.*, 88, 96; Andreas, *Kansas*, 1456.

67. Johnson, *Anderson County*, 350.

68. Dorothy Leibengood, "Labor Problems . . . ," *KHQ*, V, 198ff.

69. Isely, in *Wichita Beacon*, September 1, 1929; Masterson, *The Katy*, 84; *White City Register*, March 14, 1963.

70. *Herington Times*, August 3, 1939.

71. Masterson, *The Katy*, 35–37.

72. *Junction City Republican*, June 1, 1944.

73. Garfield, *KHQ*, I, 62.

74. Perkins, *Trails, Rails, and War*, 201.

75. *Kansas City Star*, November 12, 1942.

XLI
CHERCHEZ LA FEMME

1. Quoted by Helen Kimber, "The Progress of Women," *KHC*, VII, 297.

2. Caldwell, *KHQ*, IX, 363.

3. Linus P. Brockett, *Woman's Work in the Civil War*, 111–32; Isely, in *Wichita Beacon*, September 1, 1929.

4. *Clyde Herald*, June 10, 1904; *Topeka Daily Commonwealth*, June 30, 1887; *KHQ*, XXII, 299.

5. *Topeka Daily Commonwealth*, January 12, 1886.

6. *Ibid.*, January 1, 1886; Hollibaugh, *Cloud County*, 31–33.
7. Corley, *Names*, 6.
8. Bergin, *KHQ*, XI, 19; Whittemore, *Kansas*, 104; Manhattan *Mercury-Chronicle*, November 11, 1948.
9. It was most likely named Carlisle for a contract freighter. Montgomery, *KHC*, XVII, 273.
10. *KHC*, VII, 482; *Oakley Graphic*, June 22, 1934.
11. *Marshall County News*, Marysville, gave Walker's name as Isaac, February 27, 1931; cf. Bush and Shearer, *Frankfort Story*, 135.
12. *Marshall County News*, February 27, 1931.
13. Marshall, *Santa Fe*, 356.
14. *KHC*, VII, 482.
15. *Iola Register*, October 9, 1903.
16. *Topeka Daily Capital*, July 30, 1916.
17. *Ellsworth Story*; Mollhagen, *In Reminiscence*, 7, 20.
18. Taylor, *Names and their Histories*, 177.
19. Scheffer, *KHQ*, III, 242.
20. Savage, *Republic County*, 33–35; Haworth, *KHC*, VII, 86.
21. Bird, *Jackson County*, 35; Andreas, *Kansas*, 1337.
22. Missouri Pacific, *The Empire*, 99; Samuel A. Johnson, "The Emigrant Aid Company in Kansas," *KHQ*, I, 434.
23. Mooney, *Butler County*, 211; Jesse P. Stratford, *Butler County's Eighty Years, 1855–1935*, 44.
24. Corley, *Names*, 63; "Progress in Pawnee County," supplement to *The Weekly Tiller and Toiler* (Larned), 1952.
25. *Bird City Times*, January 21, 1932.
26. Andreas, *Kansas*, 871.
27. Scheffer, *KHQ*, III, 242; *Tescott News*, December 26, 1940.
28. Savage, *Republic County*, 175; *KHC*, VII, 475.
29. Gaeddert, *KHQ*, X, 145.
30. *Topeka Capital*, August 16, 1956.
31. Moffatt, *KHQ*, VI, 151.
32. *KHC*, XII, 477; Johnson, *Anderson County*, 218.
33. Johnson, *Anderson County*, 346.
34. Interview with Mrs. Charles Young of Wichita.
35. Mooney, *Butler County*, 95; Andreas, *Kansas*, 1436–39.
36. Corley, *Names*, 20.
37. *Kingman County Diamond Jubilee*, 14.
38. Nyquist, *Pioneer Life and Lore*, 147.
39. Emerson Lynn, "Iola not an Indian Name," *Kansas City Star*, April 28, 1954.
40. Gannett, *American Names*, 185.
41. *KHC*, XII, 442.
42. Andreas, *Kansas*, 1264; James A. Whittey, "Florence, Kansas," *Kansas Magazine*, III (May, 1910), 58.
43. Lambert and Pei, *Book of Place Names*, 34.
44. *Reminiscences*, 35.
45. *News-Chronicle* (Scott City), January 30, 1958.
46. Andreas, *Kansas*, 492; *Hiawatha Daily World*, May 23, 1935.
47. Corley, *Names*, 3, 35.
48. Schmidt, *Ashes of My Campfire*, I, 59–62.
49. O'Connell in *Oswego Democrat*, January 15 and 22, 1954.
50. *KHC*, VII, 477; *Oswego Democrat*, January 15, 1954.
51. Gaeddert, *KHQ*, X, 380; Sullivan, *Meade County*, 18.
52. *Abilene Reflector-Chronicle*, May 30, 1944.
53. *The People's Herald* (Lyndon), March 26, 1953.

54. *KHC*, VII, 481.
55. Allen County *Scrapbook*, II, 28, *KSHL*.
56. *Clark County Clippings*, II, 29.
57. Johnson, *Anderson County*, 348; Andreas, *Kansas*, 1334.
58. Blackburn and Cardwell, *Republic County*, 19, 45; *KHC*, XII, 480.
59. Andreas, *Kansas*, 1064; Bowers, *Norton County*, 141; *Kansas City Star*, November 6, 1942.
60. Corley, *Names*, 46; Franklin B. Sanborn, "Some Notes on the Territorial History of Kansas," *KHC*, XIII, 253n.
61. *Kansas City Star*, November 6, 1942.
62. Grimsley of Viola to *Wichita Beacon*, n.d., MS, Kansas Collection, Wichita State University Library.
63. *Citizen Patriot*, Atwood, September 29, 1960; Andreas, *Kansas*, 1607; Corley, *Names*, 44.
64. Interview with Mrs. Charles Young of Wichita; cf. Mooney, *Butler County*, 175.
65. *Kansas City Star*, November 6, 1942.
66. Gray, *Doniphan County*, 56; *Atchison Daily Globe*, May 24, 1907.
67. *Luray Herald*, August 28, 1952.
68. Corley, *Names*, 12.
69. Remsburg, *Scrapbook*, I, 245, *KSHL*.
70. Andreas, *Kansas*, 414; *Lawrence Journal World*, September 2, 1954.
71. Case, *Labette County*, 121.
72. Corley, *Names*, 80.
73. *Phillips County Review*, Phillipsburg, March 22, 1951.
74. Weston F. Cox, *The Community of Haviland, Kansas*, 1.
75. Ida Tarbell, "The American Woman," *American Magazine*, LXIX, 377.
76. Pickering, *KHC*, IX, 385n.
77. *Pratt Daily Tribune*, October 4, 1951; Cox, *The Community of Haviland*, 1.
78. Johnson, *The Lunatic Fringe*, 81–105; Johanna Johnston, *Mrs. Satan*, 85, 194.
79. *Chase County Historical Sketches*, I, 29 and III, 363.
80. Federal Writers' Project, *North Dakota, a Guide*; Corley, *Names*, 47.
81. Gray, *Doniphan County*, II, 101.
82. O'Connell, in *Oswego Democrat*, July 2, 1954.
83. Beachy, in *Kansas City Times*, January 17, 1950.
84. Oliver S. Lawson, "History of Scott County, Kansas," M.A. thesis, MS, *KSHL*, Topeka, quoting the Scott City *News-Chronicle*, December 8, 1932.
85. Wright, *KHC*, VII, 55.
86. *Ibid.*; Montgomery, *KHC*, XVII, 272.
87. John A. Boyer, Scott City, Kansas, August 25, 1961, to author.
88. Montgomery, *KHC*, XVII, 272; Chaffin, in *News-Chronicle* (Scott City), April 4, 1937.
89. Stratford, *Butler County*, 44; Isely, in *Wichita Beacon*, July 14, 1929.
90. Remsburg, *Scrapbook*, I, 316, *KSHL*.
91. John C. McCoy, "Survey of Kansas Indian Lands," *KHC*, IV, 305; *Atchison Daily Globe*, July 24, 1912.

XLII
POTPOURRI

1. Throckmorton, *et al*, *Coffey County*, 75.
2. Andreas, *Kansas*, 1266.
3. O'Connell, in *Oswego Democrat*, January 29, 1954.
4. *Ibid.*; Rev. Jotham Meeker, "High Waters in Kansas," *KHC*, VIII, 480n.
5. Graves, *Neosho County Newspapers*, 24.
6. Andreas, *Kansas*, 1445.

KANSAS PLACE-NAMES

7. Lindner, "Garfield County," M.A. thesis (MS, University of Wyoming, 1949), 29–30.
8. "Trails of Southern Kansas," *KHC*, V, 92.
9. April 29, 1948.
10. Andreas, *Kansas*, 416; Remsburg, *Scrapbook*, I, 371 and II, 96, *KSHL*.
11. "Geographical Names," *Scrapbook*, 177, *KSHL*.
12. Baughman, *Kansas Post Offices*, 38.
13. Edwin C. Manning, "The Kansas State Senate," *KHC*, IX, 367.
14. Blanchard, *Conquest of Southwest Kansas*, 326.
15. Lockard, *Norton County*, 6.
16. *Journal-World* (Lawrence), May 5, 1954.
17. *Ibid.*; *Concordia Blade*, February 1, 1907; Andreas, *Kansas*, 1016.
18. Morrill, *Brown County*, 29–30.
19. *Reflector-Chronicle* (Abilene), January 30, 1959.
20. Graves, *Neosho County*, I, 54–64.
21. Andreas, *Kansas*, 934.
22. Johnson, *Anderson County*, 347.
23. Andreas, *Kansas*, 646.
24. Louise Barry, ed., "With the First U.S. Cavalry in Indian Country," *KHQ*, XXIV, 411.
25. Remsburg, *Scrapbook*, IV, 55, 75, *KSHL*.
26. Millbrook, *Ness: Western County*, 34.
27. Greene, *Kanzas*, 51.
28. Gerald Carson, "Vegetables for Breakfast . . . and Lunch . . . and Supper," *Natural History*, LXXVII, 18–24, 78–81.
29. Allen County *Scrapbook*, II, 62, *KSHL*; Root, *KHQ*, II, 382.
30. Thomas, *KHQ*, XX, 258; Cory, *Place Names in Bourbon County*, 13.
31. *Horton Record*, April 14, 1935.
32. Risely to Schruben, Stockton, August 17, 1959.
33. W. A. Hill, "Robbers Roost Creek," *The Aerend*, VIII, 45.
34. Baughman, *Kansas Post Offices*.
35. Andreas, *Kansas*, 685.
36. *Barber County Clippings*, III, 54, *KSHL*.
37. Corley, *Names*, 24.
38. Baughman, *Kansas Post Offices*, 42; *Clay Center Dispatch*, January 9, 1951.
39. Andreas, *Kansas*, 1302.
40. *Ibid.*, 1302; *Mercury-Chronicle* (Manhattan), December 12, 1948.
41. Slagg, *Riley County, Kansas*, 184.
42. Nyquist, *Pioneer Life and Lore*, 157.
43. Corley, *Names*, 27.
44. *Protection Post*, January 24 to May 16, 1947; Ida Bare, "Protection: It's Name," in *Protection Post*, January 24 to May 23, 1947; *Diamond Jubilee*, Coldwater, August 30–31, September 1–2, 1959 (pamphlet), 46.
45. "Jewell County," *KHC*, XVII, 389; Andreas, *Kansas*, 908, 946, 966; Ross, *What Price White Rock?*, 2.
46. Jones, *Rice County*, 28.
47. Miller, *KHQ*, I, 116.
48. Gudde, *California Place Names*, 127.
49. *Ibid.*
50. Federal Writers' Project, *Kansas, A Guide*, 321.
51. Andreas, *Kansas*, 1297; *KHC*, XII, 115.
52. Isely, in *Wichita Beacon*, September 1, 1929; *Lawrence Daily Journal*, March 2, 1881.
53. Corley, *Names*, 77.
54. *Barber County Clippings*, III, 54, *KSHL*.

562

55. *Kansas City Star*, March 9, 1950.
56. Root, *KHC*, XVII, 499.
57. Missouri Pacific, *The Empire*, 153.
58. Andreas, *Kansas*, 895.
59. Scheffer, *KHQ*, III, 243; *Kansas City Star*, November 6, 1942.
60. *Topeka Capital*, July 12, 1942.
61. Howes, in *Kansas City Times*, May 31, 1947.
62. Sedan *Times-Star*, August 14, 1941; *Kansas Precancel News*, No. 167, April, 1969.
63. Sanders, *Harper County*, 143.
64. Burl Hunt, "Pioneers with Many Talents," *Golden West*, II, 16; Missouri Pacific, *The Empire*, 97.
65. Missouri Pacific, *The Empire*, 106.
66. T. G. Shillinglaw, "History of Taloga" (Speech delivered September 25, 1887), *KSHL*.
67. Gould, *Oklahoma Place Names*, 67, 107. For a different version see Shirk, *Oklahoma Place Names*, 202.
68. Charles E. Bess, "Miscellany," *American Speech*, X, 80.
69. T. H. Scheffer, "Old Fort Solomon at Lindsay," *KHQ*, XXII, 343.
70. Ralph T. Kersey, *History of Finney County, Kansas*, I, 68.
71. Noble L. Prentis, *A History of Kansas*, cf. map, 315.
72. Link, "Origin of Place-Names of Nebraska," in Bulletin No. 7, *Nebraska Geological Survey* (1933), 65.

BIBLIOGRAPHY

ABBREVIATIONS

BAE, Bureau of American Ethnology
KHC, Kansas State Historical Society
    Transactions and Collections
KHQ, Kansas Historical Quarterly
KSHL, Kansas State Historical Society Library
KSHS, Kansas State Historical Society
WSU, Wichita State University

I. MANUSCRIPTS

Boyer, John A. Letter to author, Scott City, Kansas, August 25, 1961.

Corley, Wayne E. "County and Community Names in Kansas" (mimeographed), Denver, 1962.

Cox, Weston F. "The Community of Haviland, Kansas" (mimeographed), Haviland, 1966.

Harris, Kos. Letter to Bliss Isely, Wichita, July 24, 1929, WSU Library.

Hickey, Marshall S. "History of Derby, Kansas," Derby Public Library.

Jones, Anne. "The Medical and Business Career of Dr. Charles Carrol Furley," Seminar Report, WSU, 1935.

Lawson, Oliver S. "History of Scott County, Kansas," M.A. thesis, Colorado State College, Fort Collins, 1936. Also at KSHL, Topeka.

Lindner, F. Claudine. "History of Garfield County, Kansas," M.A. thesis, University of Wyoming, 1949.

Lowe, Jesse Hamilton. "The Pioneer History of Kingman," M.A. thesis, WSU, 1933.

"Names," MS, KSHS Archives, Topeka.

Neeland, Mary A. "History of Elk County, Kansas," M.A. thesis, WSU, 1933.

Raphaella, Sister Mary. Seminar Report, WSU.

Riseley, Jerry. Letter to Francis W. Schruben, Stockton, Kansas, August 17 and 26 and September 1, 1959.

Schruben, Dr. Francis W. Letter to author, Reseda, California, July 25, 1959 and August 20, 1959.

Sorensen, Conner. "Ghost Towns in Greeley County," term paper, University of Kansas, Lawrence, 1966.

564

Unrau, William E. "The History of Fort Larned, Kansas: Its Relation to the Santa Fe Trail and the Plains Indians," M.A. thesis, University of Wyoming, 1956.
Works Project Administration. "American Guide," WSU Library.

II. GOVERNMENT PUBLICATIONS

Dodge, Henry. "Report on the Expedition of Dragoons, under Colonel Henry Dodge, to the Rocky Mountains in 1835," *American State Papers, Military Affairs*, VI. Washington, 1861.
Dorsey, James O. "Siouan Sociology," *BAE Fifteenth Annual Report* (1893–94). Washington, 1897.
Hodge, Frederick Webb, ed. *Handbook of American Indians North of Mexico, BAE Bulletin* 30. 2 vols. Washington, 1907.
Laws of the State of Kansas. Topeka, 1871–89.
McGee, W. J. "The Siouan Indians," *BAE Fifteenth Annual Report* (1893–94). Washington, 1897.
Miller, Nyle H. *A Survey of Historic Sites and Structures in Kansas*, KSHS. Topeka, 1957.
Mooney, James. "Calendar History of the Kiowa Indians," *BAE Seventeenth Annual Report* (1895–96), Part I. Washington, 1898.
Report of the Adjutant General of the State of Kansas, 1861–65, I. Topeka, 1896.
Simpson, J. Clarence. *Florida Place-Names of Indian Derivation*, Florida Geological Survey, Special Publication No. 1. Tallahassee, 1956.
Spofford, Ainsworth R. "American Historical Nomenclature," American Historical Association, *Annual Report*, 1893. Washington, 1894.
Swanton, John R. *The Indian Tribes of North America, BAE Bulletin* 145. Washington, 1952.
Whittemore, Margaret E. "Kansas and her Historic Trees," *Trees in Kansas, Report of the Kansas State Board of Agriculture*. Topeka, 1928.

III. NEWSPAPERS

A. Kansas Press

Abilene Reflector-Chronicle
Advocate-Democrat (Marysville)
Atchison Daily Globe
Attica Independent
Barber County Clippings
Beloit Daily Globe
Bird City Times
Burlington Daily Republican
Cedarvale Messenger
Citizen Patriot (Atwood)
Clark County Clipper (Ashland)
Clay Center Dispatch
Clyde Democrat
Clyde Herald
Coffey County (clippings), KSHL
Coffeyville Daily Journal
Commonweatlh (Topeka)
Concordia Blade
Council Grove Republican
Courier (Winfield)

Courtland Journal
Daily Tribune (Great Bend)
Daily Tribune and Monitor
 (Fort Scott)
Dodge City Daily Globe
Dodge City Journal
Ellinwood Leader
Ellsworth Messenger
Ellsworth Reporter
Emporia Daily News
Emporia Times
Geographical Names (clippings),
 KSHL
Gridley Light
Hays Daily News
Herald and Greenwood County
 Republican (Eureka)
Herington Times
Hoisington Dispatch
Holton Record
Horton Headlight
Hoxie Sentinel
Hutchinson News Herald
Independence Daily Reporter
Iola Register
Johnson County Herald (Olathe)
Junction City Republican
Junction City Union
Kansas Chief (Troy)
Kansas Cosmos (Council Grove)
Kansas State Collegian
 (Manhattan)
Kingman Journal
Kiowa County (clippings), KSHL
Kiowa County Signal
 (Greensburg)
Lakin Independent
Latham Leader
Lawrence Daily Journal
Lawrence Democrat
Lawrence Journal-World
Leavenworth Daily Commercial
Leavenworth Times
Liberal News
Lincoln County News (Lincoln)

Lincoln Sentinel-Republican
Luray Herald
Lyons Daily News
Manhattan Mercury-Chronicle
Manhattan Tribune-News
Marion County Record (Marion)
Marion Record-Review
Marquette Tribune
Marshall County News
 (Marysville)
Marysville Advocate
Meade Globe-News
Miltonvale Record
Modern Light (Columbus)
Moreland Monitor
Mullinville News
New Era (Formosa)
New Era (South Haven)
Nickerson Argosy
Oakley Graphic
Oberlin Herald
Onaga Herald
Osborne County Farmer
 (Osborne)
Oskaloosa Independent
Oswego Democrat
Oswego Independent
People's Herald (Lyndon)
Phillips County Review
 (Phillipsburg)
Pratt Daily Tribune
Protection Post
Rooks County Record (Stockton)
Rush County News (Rush Center)
Sabetha Herald
Sabetha Journal-Leader
St. Mary's Star
St. Paul Journal
Salina Herald
Salina Journal
Scott City News-Chronicle
Sedan Times-Star
Seneca Courier-Tribune
Sherman County Herald
 (Goodland)

Smith County Pioneer
(Smith Center)
South Kansas Tribune
(Independence)
Spearville News
Sterling Bulletin
Sublette Monitor
Sumner County Press
(Wellington)
Tescott News
Thomas County Herald (Colby)
Times (Clay Center)
Topeka Capital
Topeka Daily Commonwealth
Topeka State Journal
Wabaunsee County News (Alma)

Wallace County Register
(Wallace)
Wamego Reporter
Washington County Register
(Washington)
Weekly Tiller and Toiler (Larned)
Wellington Daily News
Western Advocate (Mankato)
Western Times (Sharon Springs)
White City Register
Wichita Beacon
Wichita Eagle
Wichita Eagle and Beacon
Wichita Evening Eagle
Wilson County Citizen (Fredonia)
Wilson World

B. Non-Kansas Press

Joplin Globe
Kansas City Journal
Kansas City Star
Kansas City Times

Los Angeles Times
National Observer
New York Times
New York Tribune

IV. DIARIES, MEMOIRS, AND ORIGINAL WRITINGS

Bieber, Ralph P., ed. "Cooke's Journal of the March of the Mormon Battalion, 1846–1847," Vol. VII in *Southwest Historical Series*, 12 vols. Glendale, 1931–43.
———. *Historic Sketches of the Cattle Trade of the West and Southwest by Joseph G. McCoy*, Vol. VIII in *Southwest Historical Series*. Glendale, 1940.
Bigelow, John. *Memoir of the Life and Public Services of John Charles Fremont*. New York, 1856.
Bolton, Herbert E. "French Intrusion into New Mexico," *Pacific Ocean in History*, 389–407. Ed. by H. Morse Stephens and H. E. Bolton. New York, 1917.
Brown, George W. *Reminiscences of Governor R. J. Walker; With the True Story of the Rescue of Kansas from Slavery*. Rockford, Ill., 1902.
Coues, Elliot, ed. *The Expedition of Zebulon Montgomery Pike*, 3 vols. New York, 1895.
———. *The Journal of Jacob Fowler*. . . . Minneapolis, 1965.
Defoe, Daniel. *A Travel Through England and Wales*, 2 vols. London and New York, 1928.
Fuller, Harlin M., and LeRoy R. Hafen, eds. *The Journal of Captain John R. Bell*, Vol. VI in LeRoy R. Hafen, ed., *The Far West and the Rockies*, 15 vols. Glendale, 1954–61.

Greeley, Horace. *An Overland Journey from New York to San Francisco.* New York, 1860.

Gregg, Kate L., ed. *The Road to Santa Fe.* Chehalis, Wash., 1952.

Hafen, LeRoy R., and Ann W. Hafen, eds. *Rufus B. Sage, His Letters and Papers, 1836–1847,* Vols. IV and V in *Far West and the Rockies,* 15 vols. Glendale, 1956.

Hammond, George P., and Agapito Rey, eds. *Oñate, Colonizer of New Mexico,* Vol. VI in *Coronado Cuarto Centennial Publications, 1540–1940.* Albuquerque, 1953.

James, Edwin. *Account of an Expedition . . . from Notes of S. H. Long,* Vols. XIV–XVII in R. G. Thwaites, ed., *Early Western Travels, 1748–1846,* 32 vols. Cleveland, 1904–1907.

Kenton, Edna, ed. *Black Gown and Redskins.* London, 1956.

McDermott, John F., ed. *Tixier's Travels in the Osage Prairies.* Norman, 1940.

Mason, Philip P., ed. *Schoolcraft's Expedition to Lake Itasca.* East Lansing, 1958.

Mollhagen, Harry W. *In Reminiscence.* Lorraine, Kansas, 1964.

Morgan, Lewis Henry. *Lewis Henry Morgan: The Indian Journals, 1859–62.* Ed. by Leslie A. White. Ann Arbor, 1959.

Pichardo, Jose Antonio. *Pichardo's Treatise on the Limits of Louisiana and Texas.* Ed. by Charles W. Hackett, 4 vols. Austin, 1931–46.

Quaife, Milo M., ed. *The Journals of Captain Meriwether Lewis and Sergeant John Ordway.* Madison, 1965.

Thwaites, Reuben Gold, ed. *Early Western Travels, 1748–1846,* 32 vols. Cleveland, 1904–1907.

V. PERIODICALS AND PUBLICATIONS OF LEARNED SOCIETIES

Abel, Anna Heloise. "Indian Reservations in Kansas and the Extinguishment of their Title," *KHC,* VIII, 72–109.

Adams, Franklin G. "The Capitals of Kansas," *KHC,* VIII, 331–51.

———. "General Frank Marshall," *The Agora,* V, 286–93.

———. "Reminiscences of Frederick Chouteau," *KHC,* VIII, 423–34.

Albertson, F. W. "Studies of Native Red Cedar in West Central Kansas," Kansas Academy of Science, *Transactions,* XLIII, 85, 94.

Allen, D. C. "Builders of the Great American West," *Journal of American History,* IV (1910), 511–24.

Allen, Henry J. "Roosevelt in Kansas," *Kansas Magazine,* IV (September, 1910), 65–71.

American Speech, "Miscellany," IX, 154.

Anderson, George C. "Touring Kansas and Colorado in 1871," *KHQ,* XXII, 193–220 and 358–85.

Anderson, George L. "Atchison and the Central Branch Country, 1865–1874," *KHQ*, XXVIII, 1–24.
Atlantic Monthly, "Contributor's Club," XLVII, 720–33.
Austin, Edwin A. "The Supreme Court of the State of Kansas," *KHC*, XIII, 95–125.
Ballard, David E. "The First State Legislature, 1861," *KHC*, X, 232–54.
Barge, William D., and Norman Caldwell. "Illinois Place-Names," Illinois State Historical Society, *Journal*, XXIX (October, 1936), 189–311.
Barker, Eugene C. "Austin Papers," American Historical Association *Annual Report*, 1919, Vol. II.
Barnes, Lela, ed. "An Editor looks at Early-Day Kansas," *KHQ*, XXVI, 267–301.
———. "Journal of Isaac McCoy for the Exploring Expedition of 1828," *KHQ*, V, 227–77.
———. "Journal of Isaac McCoy for the Exploring Expedition of 1830," *KHQ*, V, 339–77.
———. "North Central Kansas in 1887–1889," *KHQ*, XXIX, 267–323.
———. "Notes on Imprints from Highland," *KHQ*, VIII, 140–42.
Barry, Louise. "The Emigrant Aid Company Parties of 1854," *KHQ*, XII, 115–55.
———. "The New England Emigrant Aid Company Parties of 1855," *KHQ*, XII, 227–68.
Barry, Louise, ed. "Circuit-Riding in Southwest Kansas in 1885," *KHQ*, XII, 378–89.
———. "Kansas Before 1854: A Revised Annals," *KHQ*, XXVIII–XXXIII.
———. "With the First U.S. Cavalry in Indian Country," *KHQ*, XXIV, 399–425.
Baskett, James N. "Prehistoric Kansas: A Study of the Route of Coronado between the Rio Grande and Missouri," *KHC*, XII, 219–52.
Beach, James H. "Old Fort Hays," *KHC*, XI, 571–81.
Beede, J. W. "Notes on Kansas Physiography," Kansas Academy of Science, *Transactions*, XV, 114–20.
Beeler, M. S. "America—The Story of a Name," *Names*, I, 1–14.
Bergin, Rev. Alfred. "Swedish Settlements in Central Kansas," *KHC*, XI, 19–46.
Bergman, Jr., H. C. "Coffeyville, Kansas," *Kansas Magazine*, III (n.s., January, 1910), 45–49.
Bernard, William R. "Westport and the Santa Fe Trade," *KHC*, IX, 552–65.
Berryman, J. W. "Early Settlement of Southwest Kansas," *KHC*, XVII, 561–70.
Bess, Charles E. "Miscellany," *American Speech*, X, 79–80.
Betjeman, John. "The Magic of Cornwall," *Holiday*, XXIX, 58–63, 135–36.
Birch, James H. "The Battle of Coon Creek," *KHC*, X, 409–13.
Bishop, William. "Memorial Discourse," *KHC*, V, 101–106.

Blackman, E. E. "Sherman County and the H. U. A.," *KHC*, VIII, 50–62.
Blair, James P. "Czechoslovakia," *National Geographic*, CXXXIII, 151–94.
Bonebrake, P. I. "George T. Anthony," *KHC*, VI, 202–206.
Botkin, Theodosius. "Among the Sovereign Squats," *KHC*, VII, 418–41.
Brady, Cyrus T. "Decatur," *McClure's Magazine*, XIV, 62–67.
Brewster, S. W. "The Reverend Father Paul M. Ponziglione," *KHC*, IX, 19–32.
Bright, John. "Topeka's Year I," Shawnee County Historical Society, *Bulletin* No. 1, 74–85.
Brinkerhoff, Fred W. "The Kansas Tour of Lincoln the Candidate," *KHQ*, XIII, 294–307.
Brodhead, Michael J., and John D. Unruh, Jr. "Isaiah Harris' 'Minutes of a Trip to Kansas Territory' in 1855," *KHQ*, XXXV, 373–85.
Brooks, George R. "George C. Sibley's Journal of a Trip to the Salines in 1811," Missouri Historical Society, *Bulletin*, XXI, 167–207.
Bullard, Cora Wellhouse. "Horticulture in Kansas," *KHC*, VII, 206–12.
Byers, Oliver Philip. "Early History of the El Paso Line of the Chicago, Rock Island & Pacific Railway," *KHC*, XV, 573–78.
———. "Personal Recollections of the Terrible Blizzard of 1886," *KHC*, XII, 99–118.
———. "Railroading in the West," *KHC*, XVII, 339–48.
Caldwell, Martha B. "The Eldridge House," *KHQ*, IX, 347–70.
———. "Exploring the Solomon River Valley in 1869," *KHQ*, VI, 60–76.
———. "When Horace Greeley Visited Kansas," *KHQ*, IX, 115–40.
Campbell, Hortense B. "Camp Beecher," *KHQ*, III, 172–85.
Capote, Truman. "Annals of Crime: In Cold Blood," *The New Yorker* (September 25, 1965), 57–166.
Carman, J. Neale. "The Bishop East of the Rockies Views his Diocesans," *KHQ*, XXI, 81–86.
———. "Continental Europeans in Rural Kansas, 1854–1861," in *Territorial Kansas*, University of Kansas Publications, 1954, 164–96.
———. "Critique of Carruth's Articles on Foreign Settlements in Kansas," *KHQ*, XXV, 386–90.
———, and Karl S. Pond. "The Replacement of the Indian Languages of Kansas by English," Kansas Academy of Science, *Transactions* (Summer, 1955), 131–50.
Carney, Alfred. "The Christening of a Kansas town, Herndon, Kansas," *Aerend*, V, 174–75.
Carr, Clark E. "Why Lincoln was not Renominated by Acclamation," *The Century Magazine*, LXXIII, 503–506.
Carruth, William H. "New England in Kansas," *New England Magazine*, XVI, 3–21.
Carson, Gerald. "Vegetables for Breakfast, Lunch, and Supper," *Natural History*, LXXVII, 18–24, 78–81.

Case, Alexander. "Reminiscences," *Journal of American History*, II (1908), 249–54.

Case, Leland D. "Back to the Historic Black Hills," *National Geographic*, CX, 479–509.

Caswell, Fred M. "John Stark, Originator of New Hampshire's State Motto, 'Live Free or Die,' " *Historical New Hampshire*, I (June, 1945), 1–6.

Chapman, William J. "The Wakefield Colony," *KHC*, X, 485–533.

Chappell, Phil E. "A History of the Missouri River," *KHC*, IX, 237–94.

Chari, V. Krishna, and Kelsie B. Harder. "Terminal Elements of Place-Names in the Northeastern Sector of Indian Railways," *Names*, XIV, 43–44.

Chase, Julia A. "Mother Bickerdyke," *KHC*, VII, 189–98.

Christensen, Thomas P. "The Danish Settlements in Kansas," *KHC*, XVII, 300–305.

Clark County Historical Society, *KSHS, Notes on Early Clark County*, I, *passim.*

Clymer, Rolla A. "Thomas Benton Murdock and William Allen White," *KHQ*, XXIII, 248–56.

Coffin, William F. "Settlement of the Friends in Kansas," *KHC*, VII, 322–61.

Cole, Fannie E. "Pioneer Life in Kansas," *KHC*, XII, 353–58.

Cone, Lois Johnson. "1265 Western Avenue and the People who lived there," Shawnee County Historical Society, *Bulletin* No. 27 (April, 1957), 28.

Cone, William W. "Shawnee County Townships," Shawnee County Historical Society, *Bulletin* No. 1 (September–December, 1947), 109–12.

Connelley, William E. "Col. Richard J. Hinton," *KHC*, VII, 486–93.

———. "First Provisional Constitution of Kansas," *KHC*, VI, 97–113.

———. *History of Kansas Newspapers*, Twentieth Biennial Report, *KSHS*. Topeka, 1916.

———. "The Lane Trail," *KHC*, XIII, 268–79.

———. "Life and Adventures of George E. Brown," *KHC*, XVII, 98–134.

———. "Origin of the Name Topeka," *KHC*, XVII, 589–93.

———. "Wild Bill—James Butler Hickok," *KHC*, XVII, 1–27.

Cory, Charles E. "The Osage Ceded Lands," *KHC*, VIII, 187–99.

———. "The Sixth Kansas Cavalry," *KHC*, XI, 217–53.

———. "Slavery in Kansas," *KHC*, VII, 229–42.

Cover, Anniejane H. "Some Place Names of Kansas," *Heritage of Kansas*, Kansas State College, Emporia, IV, No. 4, 5–57.

Crafton, Allen. "What's in a Name," *Progress in Kansas*, I, 27.

Craik, Elmer L. "Southern Interest in Territorial Kansas, 1854–1858," *KHC*, XV, 334–448.

Crane, W. R. "Geography of the Coal Measures . . .," *The University Geological Survey of Kansas*, III, 107–39. Topeka, 1898.

Crawford, George A. "The Candle-Box under the Wood," *KHC*, X, 196–204.
Crawford, N. A. "The County That Never Was," *Kansas Magazine* (1944), 1–7.
Cruise, John D. "Early Days on the Union Pacific," *KHC*, XI, 529–49.
Current Opinion, "Adventurous Career of Frederick Funston," LVI, 427–28.
Dallas, E. J. "Kansas Postal History," *KHC*, I–II, 255–62.
Dana, Charles A. "Reminiscences of Men and Events of the Civil War," *McClure's Magazine*, X, 20–31, and XI, 28–40.
Daniels, Jonathan. "North Carolina," *Holiday*, II (October, 1947), 26–51.
Dawson, John S. "The Legislature of 1868," *KHC*, X, 254–79.
Delavan, Wayne. "Whittier Promoted Free Kansas," *Aerend*, XII, 81–86.
DeZurko, Edward R. "A Report and Remarks on Cantonment Leavenworth," *KHQ*, XV, 353–59.
Dick, Everett. "The Long Drive," *KHC*, XVII, 27–97.
Diller, Aubrey. "Origin of the Names of Tributaries of the Kansas River," *KHQ*, XXI, 401–406.
Dinsmore, Elizabeth M. "Genesis in Kansas," *Kansas Magazine*, II (October, 1909), 7–11.
Dobie, J. Frank. "The Saga of the Saddle," *Southwestern Review*, XIII, 127–48.
Dolbee, Cora. "First Book on Kansas," *KHQ*, II, 139– 81.
———. "The Third Book on Kansas," *KHQ*, VIII, 238–78.
Dolbee, Cora. "The Fourth of July in Early Kansas," *KHQ*, VIII, 115–39.
Donaldson, Thomas. "The George Catlin Indian Gallery," BAE Smithsonian Institution, *Annual Report*, Part V in II, Washington, 1886.
Doster, Frank. "Eleventh Indiana Cavalry in Kansas," *KHC*, XV, 524–29.
Douglas, Richard L. "A History of Manufacturers in the Kansas District," *KHC*, XI, 81–215.
Dugan, James. "The Incredible Adventures of John Ledyard," *Holiday*, XXVIII, 34–46.
Dunbar, John B. "Massacre of the Villasur Expedition by the Pawnees on the Platte, in 1720," *KHC*, XI, 397–423.
Dunn, Jacob P. "Indiana Geographical Nomenclature," *Indiana Magazine of History*, VIII, 109–14.
Dyche, L. L. "The Puma or American Lion," Kansas Academy of Science, *Transactions*, XIX, 160–63.
Elliot, R. G. "Big Springs Convention," *KHC*, VIII, 362–77.
Everett, John and Sarah. "Letters, 1854–1864," *KHQ*, VIII, 3–34, 143–74.
Fairfield, S. H. "Getting Married and the Ague," *KHC*, XI, 609–13.
Farlow, Joyce, and Louise Barry, eds. "Vincent B. Osborne's Civil War Experiences," *KHQ*, XX, 108–33.
Ferris, Ida M. "Sauks and Foxes in Franklin and Osage Counties, Kansas," *KHC*, XI, 333–95.

Fessler, W. Julian, ed. "Captain Nathan Boone's Journal," *Chronicles of Oklahoma*, VII, 58–105.

Field, Thomas P. "The Indian Place Names of Kentucky," *Names*, VII, 154–66.

Fisher, John. "Bluestem Hills–'Peace on Earth,'" Kansas State Board of Agriculture, *Annual Report*, 1947–1948, XLI, 20–24.

Fitz, Leslie A. "The Development of the Milling Industry in Kansas," *KHC*, XII, 53–59.

Fleming, Walter L. " 'Pap' Singleton, the Moses of the Colored Exodus," *American Journal of Sociology*, XV, 61–82.

Flood, James. "The Fall of Rome," *Aerend*, VII, 159–60.

Folmer, Henri. "The Mallet Expedition of 1739 through Nebraska, Kansas, and Colorado to Santa Fe," *Colorado Magazine*, XVI (September, 1939), 1–13.

Fox, S. M. "The Story of the Seventh Kansas," *KHC*, VIII, 13–49.

Frances, Clara. "The Coming of Prohibition to Kansas," *KHC*, XV, 192–227.

Gaeddert, G. Raymond. "First Newspapers in Kansas," *KHQ*, X, 380–411.

Gannett, Henry. "A Gazeteer of Kansas," U.S. Geological Survey, *Bulletin No. 154*. Washington, 1898.

Gardner, Theodore. "The First Kansas Battery," *KHC*, XIV, 235–82.

Garfield, Marvin H. "Defense of the Kansas Frontier," *KHQ*, I, 50–62, 140–52.

Garland, Hamlin. "The Early Life of Ulysses Grant," *McClure's Magazine*, VIII (December, 1896), 125–39.

——. "Grant at West Point," *McClure's Magazine*, VIII (December, 1896), 195–210.

——. "Grant's First Great Work in the War," *McClure's Magazine*, IX (June, 1897), 721–26.

——. "Grant in the Mexican War," *McClure's Magazine*, VIII (December, 1896), 366–80.

Garvin, Roy. "Benjamin, or 'Pap' Singleton, and his Followers," *Journal of Negro History*, XXXIII, 7–23.

Gill, Helen G. "The Establishment of Counties in Kansas," *KHC*, VIII, 449–72.

Gilmore, Melvin R. "Some Indian Place Names in Nebraska," Nebraska State Historical Society, *Publications*, XIX, 130–39.

Gleed, Charles S. "The Rehabilitation of the Santa Fe Railway," *KHC*, XIII, 451–68.

——. "Samuel Walker," *KHC*, VI, 249–74.

Godsey, Flora R. "Early Settlement and Raid on the 'Upper Neosho,'" *KHC*, XVI, 451–63.

Goodnow, Isaac T. "Personal Reminiscences and Kansas Emigration, 1855," *KHC*, IV, 244–53.

Green, Charles R. "Historical Work in Osage County," *KHC*, VIII, 126–33.

Greene, Albert R. "On the Battle of Wilson Creek," *KHC*, V, 116–27.

Grimsley, G. P. "Gypsum in Kansas," Kansas Academy of Science, *Transactions*, XV, 122–27.

Grinnell, George B. "Cheyenne Stream Names," *American Anthropologist* (n.s.), VIII (January–March, 1906), 15–22.

———. "Some Indian Stream Names," *American Anthropologist* (n.s.), XV (April–June, 1913), 327–31.

Hackett, C. W. "New Light on Don Diego de Penalosa: Proof that he never made an Expedition from Santa Fe to Quivira and the Mississippi River in 1662," *Mississippi Valley Historical Review*, VI, 313–35.

Hadley, James A. "A Royal Buffalo Hunt," *KHC*, X, 564–80.

Hafen, LeRoy R. "Colorado Cities—Their Founding and the Origin of their Names," *Colorado Magazine*, IX (September, 1932), 170–83.

Hannahs, Harrison. "General Thomas Ewing, Jr.," *KHC*, XII, 276–82.

Harris, Harry J. "My Story," *KHC*, XV, 553–72.

Haucke, Frank. "The Kaw or Kansa Indians," *KHQ*, XX, 36–60.

Hawley, L. F. "The Chadakoin River," *Names*, III, 32–33.

Haworth, Erasmus. "Historic Sketch of the Gypsum, Cement and Plaster Industry in Kansas," *KHC*, VII, 84–90.

Hay, Robert. "The Great Seal of Kansas," *KHC*, VIII, 289–99.

Haynes, George W. "President of the United States for a Single Day," *American Historical Review*, XXX, 308–10.

Henderson, F. Robert. "Beaver in Kansas," *State Biological Survey and Museum of Natural History*. Topeka, 1960.

Henderson, Sam. "Bartles dug deep for Black Gold," *Golden West*, VI (May, 1970), 33–39, 51–54.

Henry, T. C. "The Story of a Fenceless Winter-wheat Field," *KHC*, IX, 502–506.

Hickman, Russell K. "Lewis Bodwell, Frontier Preacher; The Early Years," *KHQ*, XII, 349–65.

———. "Lincoln College, Forerunner of Washburn University," *KHQ*, XVIII, 20–54.

———. "Speculative Activities of the Emigrant Aid Company," *KHQ*, IV, 235–67.

———. "The Vegetarian and Octagon Settlement Companies," *KHQ*, II, 377–85.

Hill, Charles E. "John James Ingalls," *Kansas Magazine*, IV (August, 1910), 15–17.

Hill, W. A. "Robbers Roost Creek," *Aerend*, VIII, 45–48.

Hinton, Richard J. "Pens that made Kansas Free," *KHC*, VI, 371–82.

Hoffhaus, Charles E. "Fort de Cavagnial," *KHQ*, XXX, 425–54.

Horton, James C. "Peter A. Ridenour and Harlow W. Baker," *KHC*, X, 589–621.

——. "Reminiscences of. . .," *KHC*, VIII, 199–205.
Howes, Cecil. "Baker Nears a Centennial," *Kansas Teacher*, LVIII (November, 1949), 30–32.
——. "Chisholm Trail–1949 Model," *Kansas Teacher*, LVII (May, 1949), 46–48.
——. "Ghost Towns of Shawnee County," Shawnee County Historical Society, *Bulletin*, I (December, 1946), 25–31.
——. "Herbs, Roots, Amulets, and Nostrums," *Kansas Teacher*, LVII (March, 1949), 46–48.
——. "Indian Missions," *Kansas Teacher*, LVIII (March, 1950), 46–48.
——. "Largest Lake in Kansas," *Kansas Teacher*, LVIII (February, 1950), 38–40.
——. "Mineral Springs in Kansas," *Kansas Teacher*, LVII (January, 1949), 38–40.
——. "Ninety Years for the Santa Fe," *Kansas Teacher*, LVIII (September, 1949), 46–48.
——. "Pistol-Packin' Pencil Pushers," *KHQ*, XIII, 115–38.
——. "What about the name, Topeka?," Shawnee County Historical Society, *Bulletin*, I (September–December, 1947), 104–108.
Hubach, Robert R. "Walt Whitman in Kansas," *KHQ*, X, 150–54.
Humphrey, James. "The Country West of Topeka Prior to 1865," *KHC*, IV, 289–97.
Hunt, Burl. "Pioneers with Many Talents," *Golden West*, II, 16–56.
Hunt, Elmer M. "American Soldiers and Sailors in the North Ireland Home Towns of New Hampshire," *Historical New Hampshire* (November, 1944), I, 2–6.
Huntington, Abby. "Dispersion of the Territorial Legislature of 1856," *KHC*, IX, 540–45.
Huron, George A. "Ernest Valeton Boissiere," *KHC*, VII, 552–64.
Ingalls, John J. "Blue Grass," *Kansas Magazine*, II (September 1872), 270–77.
Johannes, Sister Mary Eloise. "A Study of the Russian-American Settlements in Ellis County, Kansas," Catholic University of America, *Studies in Sociology*, XIV. Washington, D.C., 1946.
Johannesen, Robert W. "The Lecompton Constitutional Convention: An Analysis of its Membership," *KHQ*, XXIII, 225–43.
Johnson, C. W. "Survey of the Northern Boundary Line of Kansas," *KHC*, VII, 318–22.
Johnson, Lillian Stone. "Auburn," Shawnee County Historical Society, *Bulletin*, No. 31 (December, 1958), 4–5.
Johnson, Samuel A. "The Emigrant Aid Company in Kansas," *KHQ*, I, 429–41.
Kansas Precancel News, Wichita, Nos. 150–72 (June, 1966–February, 1970).

Kansas State Board of Agriculture, *Fifth Biennial Report*, 1876. Topeka, 1877.
Kansas State Historical Society. "Addenda," *KHC*, VII, 573–80.
——. "The Annals of Kansas: 1887," *KHQ*, XX, 271–97.
——. "The Annual Meeting," *KHQ*, XVIII, 59–76.
——. "Biography of Governor Andrew H. Reeder," *KHC*, III, 197–205.
——. "Brief Summary of the Santa Fe Trail through Kansas," *Eighteenth Biennial Report*.
——. "A British Journalist Reports the Medicine Lodge Peace Councils of 1867," *KHQ*, XXXIII, 249–320.
——. "Bypaths of Kansas History," *KHQ*, VI, 394–403.
——. "Documentary History of Kansas," *KHC*, V, 157–62.
——. "Early Military Posts, Missions and Camps," *KHC*, I–II, 263–70.
——. "Executive Minutes," *KHC*, III, 226–337.
——. "Explanation of Map," *KHC*, IX, 565–78.
——. "Extinct Geographical Locations," *KHC*, XII, 471–90.
——. "Governor Denver's Administration," *KHC*, V, 464–561.
——. "Governor Shannon's Administration," *KHC*, V, 234–64.
——. "Governor Shannon to the President," *KHC*, IV, 386–89.
——. "Governor Walker's Administration," *KHC*, V, 290–464.
——. "Kansas Chronology," *KHC*, XII, 404–26.
——. "Kansas History in the Press," *KHQ*, I, *et seq.*
——. "Kansas Newspaper History," *KHC*, I–II, 164–82.
——. "Official Roster of Kansas, 1854–1925," *KHC*, XVI, 658–745.
——. "Origin of City Names," *KHC*, VII, 475–86.
——. "Origin of County Names," *KHC*, VII, 472–74.
——. "A Roster of Kansas for Fifty Years," *KHC*, VIII, 508–42.
——. "Selections from the Hyatt Manuscripts," *KHC*, I–II, 203–21.
Kearny County Historical Society, *History of Kearny County*, Dodge City, 1964.
Kelly, H. B. "Building the Sedan Court-House," *KHC*, IX, 89–93.
Kimber, Helen. "The Progress of Women," *KHC*, VII, 297–301.
King, Joseph B. "The Ottawa Indians in Kansas and Oklahoma," *KHC*, XIII, 373–78.
King, Paul. "The Sportsman's Paradise," *Aerend*, VII, 102–12.
Kingman, Samuel A. "Reminiscences," *KHC*, VII, 153–55.
Koch, Bill, and Mary Koch. "Kansas History and Folksong," *Heritage of Kansas*, V (May, 1961), No. 2, 6–31.
Laing, Rev. Francis S. "German-Russian Settlements in Ellis County, Kansas," *KHC*, XI, 489–528.
"The Lane-Jenkins Claim Contest," *KHC*, XVI, 21–175.
Langsdorf, Edgar. "First Survey of the Kansas River," *KHQ*, XVIII, 146–58.
——. "Jim Lane and The Frontier Guard," *KHQ*, IX, 13–25.

——. "S. C. Pomeroy and the New England Emigrant Aid Company, 1854–1858," *KHQ*, VII, 227–45.

Langsdorf, Edgar, ed. "Letters of Daniel R. Anthony, 1857–1862," *KHQ*, XXIV, 6–30.

——. "Letters of Joseph Trego," *KHQ*, XIX, 287–309.

Lapham, Amos S. "Looking Backward, Early History of Chanute," *KHC*, XVI, 504–14.

Laune, Mrs. Seigniora Russell. "Avra P. Russell," *KHC*, XIV, 84–89.

Lawrence, Frederick W. "The Origin of State Names," *National Geographic Magazine*, XXXVIII, 105–43.

Leibengood, Dorothy. "Labor Problems in the Second Year of Governor Martin's Administration," *KHQ*, V, 191–207.

Leland, J. C. "Indian Names in Missouri," *Names*, I, 266–73.

Lester, H. N. "Colonization of the Upper Arkansas Valley in Kansas," *KHC*, IV, 262–65.

Life, XXVII (December 26, 1949, and January 20, 1961).

Liliburn, H. Horton. *Fremont's Expeditions Through Kansas, 1842–1854*, Fort Hays Studies, No. 2 (1962).

Lindquist, Emory. "Swedes in Kansas Before the Civil War," *KHQ*, XIX, 254–68.

Link, J. T. "The Origin of Place-Names of Nebraska," Nebraska Geological Survey, *Bulletin* No. 7, Lincoln, 1933.

Llewellyn, Richard. "Wales," *Holiday*, IX, 56–68, 80–93.

"Letters of Julia Louisa Lovejoy, 1856–1864," *KHQ*, XV, 368–403, and XVI, 175–211.

Lowe, Percival G. "Kansas, as Seen in the Indian Territory," KHC, IV, 360–67.

——. "Recollections of Fort Riley," *KHC*, VII, 101–13.

Lowell, James H. "Romantic Growth of a Law Court," *KHC*, XV, 590–97.

Lutz, J. J. "Methodist Missions among the Indian Tribes in Kansas," *KHC*, IX, 160–235.

McClure, James R. "Taking the Census and other Incidents in 1855," *KHC*, VIII, 227–50.

McClure, William T. "The Fourth Kansas Militia in the Price Raid," *KHC*, VIII, 149–51.

McCoy, John C. "Survey of Kansas Indian Lands," *KHC*, IV, 298–311.

McDermott, John F. "Glossary of French," *Language and Literature*, Washington University Studies No. 12. St. Louis, 1941.

——. "Isaac McCoy's Second Exploring Trip in 1828," *KHQ*, XIII, 400–62.

McDougal, H. C. "Historical Sketch of Kansas City, Missouri," *KHC*, XI, 581–89.

McDonough, Marion M. "Quest of Health, not Wealth, 1871," *Montana: Magazine of Western History*, XIV (January, 1964), 25–37.

McGonigle, James A. "First Kansas Infantry in the Battle of Wilson's Creek," *KHC*, XII, 292–95.

———. "Missions Among the Indians in Kansas," *KHC*, IX, 153–59.

Madison, Sara E. "Founding a Town," *KHQ*, VII, 69–71.

Malin, James C. "An Introduction to the History of the Bluestem-Pasture Region of Kansas," *KHQ*, X, 3–28.

———. "J. A. Walker's Early History of Edwards County," *KHQ*, IX, 259–84.

Manning, Edwin C. "A Kansas Soldier," *KHC*, X, 421–28.

———. "The Kansas State Senate of 1865 and 1866," *KHC*, IX, 359–75.

Martin, George W. "The Boundary Lines of Kansas," *KHC*, XI, 53–74.

———. "A Chapter from the Archives," *KHC*, XII, 359–75.

———. "Early Days in Kansas," *KHC*, IX, 126–43.

———. "The First Two Years of Kansas," *KHC*, X, 120–48.

———. "John A. Anderson—A Character Sketch," *KHC*, VIII, 315–29.

———. "Memorial Monuments and Tablets in Kansas," *KHC*, XI, 253–81.

———. "The Territorial and Military Combine at Fort Riley," *KHC*, VII, 361–90.

Mason, Henry F. "County Seat Controversy in Southwestern Kansas," *KHQ*, II, 45–64.

Mather, Frederick G. "The River of Gen-nis-he-yo," *Magazine of Western History*, III (December, 1885), 101–102.

Mead, Andrew J. "Reminiscences of Kansas," *KHC*, VII, 467–70.

Mead, James R. "The Little Arkansas," *KHC*, X, 7–14.

———. "Origin of Names of Kansas Streams," Kansas Academy of Science, *Transactions*, XVIII, 215–16.

———. "Saline River Country in 1859," *KHC*, IX, 8–19.

———. "Trails of Southern Kansas," *KHC*, V, 88–93.

———. "The Wichita Indians in Kansas," *KHC*, VIII, 171–77.

Mechem, Kirke, ed. "The Annals of Kansas: 1886," *KHQ*, XX, 161–82.

———. "Home on the Range," *KHQ*, XVII, 313–39.

Meeker, Rev. Jotham. "High Waters in Kansas," *KHC*, VIII, 472–81.

Meredith, William J. "Old Plum Grove Colony in Jefferson County, 1854–1855," *KHQ*, VII, 339–75.

Merritt, James S. "Movements for Territorial Organization," *KHC*, I–II, 261–63.

Mervin, Ray E. "The Wyandot Indians," *KHC*, IX, 73–88.

Millbrook, Minnie Dubbs. "Dr. Samuel Grant Rodgers, Gentleman from Ness," *KHQ*, XX, 305–49.

Miller, Nyle H. "Kansas Boundary Survey," *KHQ*, I, 104–39.

Miller, Nyle H., and Robert W. Richmond. "Sheridan, a fabled End-of-Track Town on the Union Pacific Railroad, 1868–1869," *KHQ*, XXXIV, 427–42.

Missouri Pacific Lines Magazine, "Station Names," XXV, 9–11.

Mitchell, W. A. "Historic Linn," *KHC*, XVI, 607–57.

Moffatt, Isaac. "The Kansas Prairie, or, Eight Days on the Plains," *KHQ*, VI, 147–74.

Montgomery, Frank C. "Fort Wallace and its Relation to the Frontier," *KHC*, XVII, 189–283.
Moody, Joel. "The Marais des Cygnes Massacre," *KHC*, XIV, 208–23.
Moore, Ely. "A Buffalo Hunt with the Miamis in 1854," *KHC*, X, 402–409.
——. "The Lecompton Party which located Denver," *KHC*, VII, 446–51.
Moore, Ely, Jr. "The Naming of Osawatomie," *KHC*, XII, 338–46.
——. "The Story of Lecompton," *KHC*, XI, 463–80.
Moore, Hugh M. "Letters of Hugh M. Moore, 1856–1860," *KHQ*, X, 115–23.
Morehouse, George P. "Diamond Springs, 'Diamond of the Plain'," *KHC*, XIV, 794–804.
——. "History of the Kansa or Kaw Indians," *KHC*, X, 327–68.
——. "Padilla and the Old Monument near Council Grove," *KHC*, X, 472–79.
Morrall, Dr. Albert. "Statement and Autobiography," *KHC*, XIV, 123–42.
Morris, D. M. "Dodge City, Kansas," *Kansas Magazine*, IV (October, 1910), 89–97.
——. "Kiowa County," *Kansas Magazine*, IV (November, 1910), 95–102.
Morrison, T. F. "Osage Treaty of 1865," *KHC*, XVII, 692–708.
Morrow, Robert. "Emigration to Kansas in 1856," *KHC*, VIII, 302–15.
Morse, O. E. "An Attempted Rescue of John Brown from Charlestown, Virginia, Jail," *KHC*, VIII, 213–26.
Murray, S. J. "Jesuit Place Names in the United States," *Names*, XVI, 6–12.
Myers, C. Clyde. "Salem: A Town that Bloomed then Faded," *KHC*, XVII, 384–88.
Names: Journal of the American Name Society, Vol. VIII, 194.
Pantle, Alberta. "The Connecticut Kansas Colony," *KHQ*, XXII, 138–83.
——. "History of the French-speaking Settlement in the Cottonwood Valley," *KHQ*, XIX, 12–49.
Parrish, William E. *David Rice Atchison of Missouri*, University of Missouri *Studies*, XXXIV, No. 1. Columbia, Mo., 1961.
Patrick, G. E. "The Great Spirit Spring," Kansas Academy of Science, *Transactions*, VII, 22–26.
Peck, Robert M. "Recollections of Early Times in Kansas Territory," *KHC*, VIII, 484–507.
Pickering, I. O. "The Administration of John P. St. John," *KHC*, IX, 378–94.
Plank, Pryor, "The Iowa, Sac, and Fox Indian Mission and its Missionaries," *KHC*, X, 312–25.
Pleasanton, Alfred. "The Successes and Failures at Chancellorsville," *The Century Magazine*, XXXII, 745–61.
Plumb, J. H. "An Oriental Palace," *Horizon*, V, 21–31.
Pony Express Courier, III (December, 1936).
Pringle, Lawrence. "Why They're Called Wild Turkey," *National Wildlife*, IV, 20–22.

Procter, A. G. "First Appearance of Kansas at a National Convention," *KHC*, XI, 12–18.

Progress in Kansas, "Forgotten Counties in Kansas," Kansas State Chamber of Commerce, I (April, 1935), 25–26.

Raish, Marjorie Gamet. "Victoria, the Story of a Kansas Town," *Fort Hays Kansas State College Studies*, XVI, No. 17, Topeka, 1947.

Remsburg, George. "Isle au Vache," *KHC*, VIII, 436–43.

Rice, Rev. Cyrus R. "Experiences of a Pioneer Missionary," *KHC*, XIII, 298–318.

Riddle, A. P. "The Senate of Kansas," *KHC*, III, 410–17.

Robbins, Richard W. "The Life of Senator Edmund G. Ross of Kansas," *KHQ*, XXXIII, 90–117.

Robinson, Sara T. D. "The Wakarusa War," *KHC*, X, 457–71.

Robinson, W. Stitt. "The Kiowa and Comanche Campaign of 1860 as Recorded in the Personal Diary of Lt. J. E. B. Stuart," *KHQ*, XXIII, 382–400.

Romig, Joseph. "The Chippewa and Munsee (or Christian) Indians of Franklin County, Kansas," *KHC*, XI, 314–23.

Root, George A. "Chronology of Shawnee County, 1724–1854," Shawnee County Historical Society, *Bulletin* Nos. 1–36 (December, 1946–July, 1962).

——. "Extracts from Diary of Captain Lambert Bowman Wolf," *KHQ*, I, 195–210.

——. "Ferries in Kansas," *KHQ*, II–VI, *passim*.

——. "Reminiscences of William Darnell," *KHC*, XVII, 479–513.

Root, George A., and Russell K. Hickman. "Pike's Peak Express Companies," *KHQ*, XIII, 485–526.

Roskam, Oliver and Betty, and Bryan and Ida Purteet. "Missouri's Official State Mineral and Rock," *Lapidary Journal*, XXII (August, 1968), 632–33.

Rudin, A. James. "Beersheba, Kansas: 'God's Pure Air on Government Land,'" *KHQ*, XXXIV, 282–98.

Ruppenthal, Jacob C. "The Germanic Element in Central Kansas," *KHC*, XIII, 513–34.

Sackett, S. J. "Play-Party Games from Kansas," *Heritage of Kansas*, V (September, 1961), 5–56.

Sage, Evan T. "Classical Place-Names in America," *American Speech*, IV, 261–71.

Sanborn, Franklin B. "Some Notes on the Territorial History of Kansas," *KHC*, XIII, 249–65.

Sanborn, J. L. "American Town Names," *Kansas Magazine*, III (February, 1873), 158–67.

Scheffer, Theodore H. "Geographical Names in Ottawa County," *KHQ*, III, 227–45.

——. "Old Fort Solomon at Lindsay," *KHQ*, XXII, 342–46.

Schmidt, C. B. "Reminiscences of Foreign Immigration Work for Kansas," *KHC*, IX, 485–97.

Schoewe, Walter H. "The Geography of Kansas," Part I, Kansas Academy of Science, *Transactions*, LI, 253–88.

——. "Political and Geographical Aspects of Territorial Kansas," *Territorial Kansas*, University of Kansas Publications, Lawrence, 1954.

Schwein, Rex L. "A County in the Making," *Aerend*, VIII (Winter, 1937), 17–23.

Scott, Charles S. "The Old Road and Pike's Pawnee Village," *KHC*, VII, 311–17.

Seton, Charles. "Reminiscences of Runnymede," *KHC*, XII, 467–69.

Shand, John. "Report from Wales," *Holiday*, IV, 13–14.

Shenck, Lena Baxter. "History of Dover," Shawnee County Historical Society, *Bulletin* No. 31 (December, 1958), 22–25.

Shields, Mrs. Clara M. Fengel. "The Lyon Creek Settlement," *KHC*, XIV, 143–70.

Shively, S. J. "The Pottawatomie Massacre," *KHC*, VIII, 177–87.

Simmons, India Harris. "Kendall in Early Days," *KHQ*, VII, 67–69.

Slosson, Mrs. A. L. "Personal Observations upon the Flora of Kansas," Kansas Academy of Science, *Publications*, XI, 19–23.

Smith, Alice Strieby. "Through the Eyes of My Father," *KHC*, XVII, 708–18.

Smith, Ida L. "National Group Settlement," *Aerend*, VII (Spring, 1936), 105–12.

Smith, William E. "The Oregon Trail through Pottawatomie County," *KHC*, XVII, 435–464.

Sopher, David E. "Arabic Place Names in Spain," *Names*, III, 8–9.

Spear, Stephen J. "Reminiscences of the Early Settlement of Dragoon Creek, Wabaunsee County," *KHC*, XIII, 345–63.

Speer, John. "Incidents of the Pioneer Days," *KHC*, V, 131–41.

——. "Told by a Pioneer," Shawnee County Historical Society, *Bulletin* No. 12, 55–59.

Spencer, Joab. "The Shawnee Indians," *KHC*, X, 382–96.

Stevenson, Andrew. "Many Towns Named in Honor of Santa Fe Men," *Santa Fe Magazine*, XXII, 55–56.

Stewart, James R. "The Diary of James R. Stewart, Pioneer of Osage County," *KHQ*, XVII, 122–75.

Stone, Irene G. "The Lead and Zinc Field of Kansas," *KHC*, VII, 243–60.

Street, William D. "The Victory of the Plow," *KHC*, IX, 33–43.

Swehla, Francis J. "Bohemians in Central Kansas," *KHC*, XIII, 469–512.

Taft, Robert. "The Editors Page," Kansas Academy of Science, *Transactions*, LIII, 302–304.

——. "Over the Santa Fe Trail through Kansas," *KHQ*, XVI, 337–80.

——. "Pictorial Record of the Old West," *KHQ*, XVI, 113–35.

Tannar, A. H. "Early Days in Kansas," *KHC*, XIV, 224–34.
Tarbell, Ida. "The American Woman," *American Magazine*, LXIX, 363–77.
——. "Lincoln as a Lawyer, *McClure's Magazine*, VII, 171–81.
——. "Lincoln's Method of Dealing with Men," *McClure's Magazine*, XII, 442–54.
Taylor, Rebecca Wells. "Some Lost Towns of Western Kansas," *Aerend*, VI, 225–44.
Thacher, T. Dwight. "Colonel William A. Phillips," *KHC*, V, 100–106.
Thomas, Bill. "Festival King: Ohio," *Travel*, CXXXIII, 36–41.
Thomas County, *Yesterday and Today*, XII (December, 1960).
Thomas, Lowell. "The Painful Lessons of the Cedars of Lebanon," *National Wild Life*, VIII(December–January, 1970), 50–55.
Thomas, Sister M. Evangeline. "The Rev. Louis Dumortier, S. J., Itinerant Missionary to Central Kansas, 1859–1867," *KHQ*, XX, 252–70.
Thompson, Thomas E. "Early Days in 'Old Boston,' " *KHC*, XVI, 479–87.
Thompson, W. F. "Peter Robidoux: A Real Kansas Pioneer," *KHC*, XVII, 282–90.
Trent, W. P. "Benjamin Franklin," *McClure's Magazine*, VIII, 273–77.
Triplet, Charles S. "The End of Coronado," *KHC*, XII, 441–47.
Vandervelde, Conrad. "Hollanders in Kansas," *Heritage of Kansas*, VII (September, 1963), 6–23.
Veale, George W. "Coming in and Going out," *KHC*, XI, 6–12.
Villard, Oswald G. "Historical Verity," *KHC*, XIII, 423–29.
Vosburgh, Frederick G. "Shrines of Each Patriots Devotion," *National Geographic*, XCV (January, 1949), 57–82.
Vogel, Virgil J. "The Origin and Meaning of 'Missouri,' " Missouri Historical Society, *Bulletin*, XVI (April, 1960), 213–23.
Ware, Eugene F. "The Neutral Lands," *KHC*, VI, 147–69.
Wedel, Waldo R. "An Introduction to Pawnee Archaeology," *BAE*, *Bulletin* No. 112, Washington, 1936.
Weichselbaum, Theodore. "Statement of Theodore Weichselbaum," *KHC*, XI, 561–71.
Weidhaas, Walther E. "German Religious Influence in American Place Names," *American German Review*, XXIII (August–September, 1957), 32–34.
Welty, Raymond L. "The Policing of the Frontier by the Army, 1860–1870," *KHQ*, VII, 246–57.
Wetzel, Charles R. "Monument Station, Gove County," *KHQ*, XXVI, 250–54.
Wharton, Major Clifton. "The Expedition of Major Clifton Wharton in 1844," *KHC*, XVI, 272–305.
Whitbeck, R. H. "Regional Peculiarities in Place Names," American Geological Society, *Bulletin*, XLIII, 273–81.
White, Alta. "My Home Town," *Aerend*, No. 4 (Fall, 1937), 235–36.
White, Mrs. S. B. "My First Days in Kansas," *KHC*, XI, 550–60.

Whiteside, Thomas. "Berwick-upon-Tweed," *Holiday*, VIII (August, 1950), 75–78.

Whiting, Albe B. "Some Western Border Conditions in the 50's and 60's," *KHC*, XII, 1–10.

Whittey, James A. "Florence, Kansas," *Kansas Magazine*, III (May, 1910), 58–65.

Winsor, M., and James A. Scarbrough. "Jewell County," *KHC*, XVII, 389–409.

Wright, Muriel H. "Some Geographic Names of French Origin in Oklahoma," *Chronicles of Oklahoma*, VII, 188–93.

Wright, Robert M. "Personal Reminiscences of Frontier Life in Southwest Kansas," *KHC*, VII, 47–83.

Zelinsky, Wilbur. "Classical Town Names in the United States," *The Geographic Review*, LVII, 463–95.

VI. GENERAL WORKS

Abbott, Wilbur C. *Adventures in Reputation*. Cambridge, 1935.

Admire, W. W. *Admire's Political and Legislative Hand-Book for Kansas*. Topeka, 1891.

Allen, Joseph W. *Cho O-Nee to High Iron . . . Neodesha, Wilson County, Kansas*. Neodesha, 1962.

Allison, Nathaniel T. *History of Cherokee County, Kansas, and Representative Citizens*. Chicago, 1904.

Alsberg, Henry G. *The Lake States* in *The American Guide*. New York, 1949.

Andreas, A. T., and W. G. Cutler. *History of the State of Kansas*. Chicago, 1883.

Armstrong, G. H. *The Origin and Meaning of Place Names in Canada*. Toronto, 1930.

Bailes, Kendall E. *From Hunting Ground to Suburb, A History of Merriam, Kansas*. Merriam, 1956.

Bailey, Thomas A. *A Diplomatic History of the American People*. New York, 1942.

Bancroft, Hubert H. *Annals of Early Central America*. New York, 1886.

Banta, Richard F. *The Ohio*. New York, 1949.

Barr, Elizabeth N. *Business Directory and History of Wabaunsee County*. Topeka, 1907.

———. *A Souvenir History of Lincoln County, Kansas*. Topeka, 1908.

Barrington, F. H. *Kansas Day, Containing a Brief History of Kansas*. Topeka, 1892.

Baughman, Robert W. *Kansas in Maps*. Topeka, 1961.

Beauchamp, William M. *Indian Names in New York*. Fayetteville, N.Y., 1893.

Becker, Donald E. *Indian Place-Names in New Jersey*. Cedar Grove, N.J., 1964.

Beckman, Rev. Peter. *The Catholic Church on the Kansas Frontier, 1850–1877*. Washington, D.C., 1943.
Bentley, O. H., ed. *History of Sedgwick County*, 2 vols. Chicago, 1910.
Berry, Don. *A Majority of Scoundrels*. New York, 1961.
Besant, Walter. *London*. London, 1925.
Bird, J. S., ed. *Historical Plat Book of Jackson County*. Chicago, 1881.
Birmingham, David. *The Portuguese Conquest of Angola*. London and New York, 1965.
Blackburn, Anona Shaw, and Myrtle Strom Cardwell, compilers. *History of Republic County*. Belleville, Kans., 1964.
Blair, Ed. *History of Johnson County, Kansas*. Lawrence, 1915.
Blanchard, Leola Howard. *Conquest of Southwest Kansas, A History and Thrilling Stories of Frontier Life in the State of Kansas*. Wichita, 1931.
Boder, Ernest B. "Kansas, The First Decade of Statehood," in *Kansas: The First Century*. Ed. by John D. Bright, 2 vols. New York, 1956.
Bononcini, Father Eugene. *Autobiography*. St. Paul, Kans., 1942.
Bowen, E. G. *Wales*. London, 1965.
Bowers, Darius N. *Seventy Years in Norton County, Kansas, 1872–1942*. Norton, 1942.
Boynton, Rev. C. B., and T. B. Mason. *A Journey through Kansas; with Sketches of Nebraska*. Cincinnati, 1855.
Bracke, William B. *Wheat Country*. New York, 1950.
Brewerton, George D. *Overland with Kit Carson*. New York and Chicago, 1930.
Brigham, Lela Maloy. *The Story of Council Grove on the Santa Fe Trail*. Council Grove, Kans., 1921.
Brockett, Linus Pierpont. *Woman's Work in the Civil War*. Boston, 1867.
Brown, A. Theodore. *Frontier Community, Kansas City to 1870*. Columbia, Mo., 1936.
Bumgardner, Edward. *Life of Edmund G. Ross*. Kansas City, 1949.
Bush, Maynie Shearer, and Winifred Shearer, eds. *The Frankfort Story, A History of Frankfort, Kansas*. N.p., 1967.
Case, Nelson. *History of Labette County, Kansas*. Chicago, 1901.
Castel, Albert. *A Frontier State at War: Kansas, 1861–1865*. Ithaca, 1958.
Catton, Bruce. *The Coming Fury*, Vol. I in *The Centennial History of the Civil War*. Garden City, N.Y., 1961.
———. *Mr. Lincoln's Army*. Garden City, N.Y., 1951.
———. *This Hallowed Ground*. Garden City, N.Y., 1956.
Chase County Historical Society. *Chase County Historical Sketches*, 3 vols. N.p., 1940–1966.
Chrisman, Harry E. *Lost Trails of the Cimarron*. Denver, 1962.
Cory, Charles E. *Place Names of Bourbon County, Kansas*. Fort Scott, 1928.
Clark, Carroll D., and Roy L. Roberts. *Peoples of Kansas: A Demographic and Sociological Study*. Topeka, 1936.
Clark, Charles M. *A Trip to Pike's Peak*. San Jose, 1958.

Coblentz, Catherine C. *Sequoyah.* New York, 1946.
Connelley, William E. *A Standard History of Kansas and Kansans,* 15 vols. Chicago and New York, 1918.
Crawford, Samuel J. *Kansas in the Sixties.* Chicago, 1911.
Crofutt, George A. *Crofutt's New Overland Tourist and Pacific Coast Guard.* Omaha and Denver, 1882.
Dale, Kittie. *Echoes and Etchings of Early Ellis.* Denver, 1964.
Deatherage, Charles P. *Early History of Greater Kansas City.* 2 vols., Kansas City, Mo., 1927.
Debo, Angie. *The Cowman's Southwest: Reminiscences of Oliver Nelson.* Glendale, 1953.
Dodge, Richard I. *The Plains of the Great West and their Inhabitants.* New York, 1959.
Donald, David. *Charles Sumner and the Coming of the Civil War.* New York, 1960.
Drake, Charles C. *Who's Who? A History of Kansas and Montgomery County* .... Coffeyville, 1943.
Dreiling, B. M., compiler. *Golden Jubilee of the German-Russian Settlements of Ellis and Rush Counties, Kansas.* Hays, 1926.
Drumm, Stella, ed. *Down the Santa Fe Trail, Diary of Susan Shelby Magoffin, 1846–1847.* London, 1926.
Dudley, Ruth H. *Favorite Trees of Desert, Mountain, and Plain.* New York, 1963.
Duncan, L. Wallace. *History of Montgomery County, Kansas.* Iola, 1903.
———. *History of Neosho and Wilson Counties, Kansas.* Fort Scott, 1902.
Duncan, L. Wallace, and Charles F. Scott. *History of Allen and Woodson Counties, Kansas.* Iola, 1901.
Easton, Robert, and McKenzie Brown. *Lord of Beasts: The Saga of Buffalo Jones.* Tucson, 1961.
Finney County Historical Society (Ralph T. Kersey, historian), *History of Finney County, Kansas,* 2 vols. Garden City, 1950–54.
Folmer, Henri. *Franco-Spanish Rivalry in North America, 1524–1763.* Glendale, 1953.
Forbes, Allan. *Towns of New England and Old England, Ireland and Scotland.* New York and London, 1921.
Foreman, Grant. *Down the Texas Road.* Norman, 1954.
———. *Indian Removal.* Norman, 1932.
———. *The Last Trek of the Indians.* Chicago, 1946.
Forter, Emma E. *History of Marshall County, Kansas: Its People, Industries, and Institutions.* Indianapolis, 1917.
Frazer, Robert W. *Forts of the West.* Norman, 1965.
French, Laura Margaret. *History of Emporia and Lyon County.* Emporia, 1929.
Fuller, R. E., and Mrs. J. C. McKinny. *The First Hundred Years, A History of the City of Hartford, Kansas, 1857–1957.* Hartford, 1957.

Gard, Wayne. *The Great Buffalo Hunt.* New York, 1959.
Giles, F. W. *Thirty Years in Topeka, A Historical Sketch.* Topeka, 1886.
Gladstone, Thomas H. *Kansas; or, Squatter Life and Border Warfare in the Far West.* London, 1857.
Goebel, Dorothy B., and Julius Goebel, Jr. *Generals in the White House.* New York, 1945.
Golden Jubilee Anniversary of Thomas County and its Neighbors, 1885–1935. N.p., n.d.
Goodreds, V. Spencer. *Good Stories and How to Tell Them.* Minneapolis, 1958.
Gould, Charles N. *Covered Wagon Geologist.* Norman, 1959.
———. *Oklahoma Place Names.* Norman, 1933.
Graves, William W. *History of Neosho County,* 2 vols. St. Paul, Kans., 1949–51.
———. *History of Neosho County Newspapers.* St. Paul, Kans., 1938.
Gray, J. Rufus. *Pioneer Saints and Sinners.* Pratt, Kans., 1968.
Gray, Patrick L. *Gray's Doniphan County History.* Bendena, Kans., 1905.
Green, Charles R. *Early Days in Kansas,* 5 vols. Olathe, 1912–13.
Greene, Max. *The Kanzas Region: Forest, Prairie, Desert, Mountain, Vale, and River.* New York, 1856.
Grimm, William C. *Familiar Trees of America.* New York and London, 1967.
Grinnell, George B. *The Cheyenne Indians: Their History and Ways of Life,* 2 vols. New York, 1962.
Hafen, LeRoy R. *The Overland Mail, 1849–1869.* Cleveland, 1926.
Hale, Edward Everett, *Kanzas and Nebraska.* Boston, 1854.
Hall, Jesse A., and Leroy T. Hand. *History of Leavenworth County, Kansas.* Topeka, 1921.
Harrington, Grant W., compiler. *Annals of Brown County.* Hiawatha, Kans., 1903.
———. *Historic Spots or Mile-Stones in the Progress of Wyandotte County, Kansas.* Merriam, Kans., 1935.
Harrington, Wynne P. *History of Gove County, Kansas.* Gove City, 1920.
Hart, Herbert M. *Old Forts of the Far West.* Seattle, 1965.
Hassall, William O. *History through Surnames.* New York, 1967.
Hayes, Melvin L. *Mr. Lincoln runs for President.* New York, 1960.
Hayes, William E. *Iron Road to Empire: The History of the Rock Island Lines.* New York, 1953.
Henry, Stuart O. *Conquering our Great American Plains.* New York, 1930.
Herring, Hubert. *A History of Latin America.* New York, 1961.
Hollibaugh, Mrs. E. F. *Biographical History of Cloud County, Kansas.* N.p., 1903.
Howells, William D. *Seven English Cities.* New York and London, 1909.
Howes, Charles C. *This Place Called Kansas.* Norman, 1952.

Hulbert, Archer B. *The Ohio River, A Course of Empire.* New York and London, 1906.
———. *Southwest on the Turquoise Trail.* Colorado Springs and Denver, 1933.
Hunt, Cecil. *Talk of the Town, the Place Names in our Language.* Toronto, 1951.
Hyde, George E. *Pawnee Indians.* Denver, 1951.
Ingalls, Sheffield. *History of Atchison County, Kansas.* Lawrence, 1916.
Inman, Henry. *Buffalo Jones' Forty Years of Adventure.* Topeka, 1899.
———.*Tales of the Trail, Short Stories of Western Life.* Topeka, 1917.
Irving, Washington. *National Nomenclature.* Vol. IV, 436–42, in *Works*, 15 vols. New York, 1897.
———. *Christopher Columbus.* Vol. VI, in *Works*, 15 vols. New York, 1897.
———. *A Tour of the Prairies.* Ed. by John F. McDermott. Norman, 1956.
Jackson, Clarence S. *Picture Maker of the Old West, William H. Jackson.* New York, 1947.
Jacobs, Noah Jonathan. *Naming-Day in Eden.* New York, 1958.
Janzen, Edward C. *Green Garden, the Autobiography of Professor Edward Carl Janzen.* Denver, c. 1962.
Jelinek, George. *Ninety Years of Ellsworth and Ellsworth County History.* Ellsworth, 1957.
Jenkins, Evan J. *The Northern Tier; or Life Among the Homestead Settlers.* Topeka, 1880.
Johnson, Harry. *A History of Anderson County, Kansas.* Garnett, Kans., 1936.
Johnson, Gerald W. *The Lunatic Fringe.* New York, 1957.
Johnston, Johanna. *Mrs. Satan; The Incredible Saga of Victoria C. Woodhull.* New York, 1967.
Jones, Alexander. *The Cymry of '76; or Welshmen and their Descendants of the American Revolution.* Baltimore, 1968.
Jones, Horace. *The Story of Early Rice County.* Lyons, Kans., 1959.
———. *Up from the Sod.* Lyons, Kans., 1968.
Jones, John C., and Winoma C. Jones. *The Prairie Pioneers of Western Kansas and Eastern Colorado.* Boulder, 1956.
Kenton, Edna, ed. *The Indians of North America.* 2 vols., New York, 1927.
King, James L. *History of Shawnee County, Kansas, and Representative Citizens.* Chicago, 1905.
Knight, Charles. *The Popular History of England.* 8 vols., New York, 1880.
Lathrop, Amy. *Tales of Western Kansas.* Kansas City, Mo., 1948.
Lauvriére, Émile. *Histoire de la Louisiane Francaise, 1673–1939.* Baton Rouge, 1940.
Levin, Peter R. *Seven by Chance: the Accidental Presidents.* New York, 1948.
Lindquist, Emory K. *Smoky Valley People.* Lindsborg, Kans., 1953.

Lockard, F. M. *The History of the Early Settlement of Norton County, Kansas.* Norton, Kansas, 1894.

Longfellow, Henry W. *The Poetical Works of Henry Wadsworth Longfellow.* Boston, 1881.

Lovene, P. *History of the Swedish Baptist Church of Kansas and Missouri, 1869–1927.* N.p., n.d.

Lower, Mark A. *English Surnames, Essays on Family Nomenclature.* London, 1844.

Macartney, Clarence E. *Grant and his Generals.* New York, 1953.

Mackenzie, Rev. James. *Our Country, A History of Scotland for the Young.* London, 1868.

MacKenzie, William C. *Scottish Place-Names.* London, 1931.

McDermott, John F., ed. *The French in the Mississippi Valley.* Urbana, 1965.

McNeal, Thomas A. *When Kansas was Young.* Topeka, 1934.

Marshall, James L. *Santa Fe—The Railroad that Built an Empire.* New York, 1945.

Masterson, Vincent V. *The Katy Railroad.* Norman, 1952.

Mathews, John J. *The Osages: Children of the Middle Waters,* Norman, 1961.

Mayhall, Mildred P. *The Kiowas.* Norman, 1962.

Maynard, Theodore. *De Soto and the Conquistadores.* London, 1930.

Mencken, Henry L. *The American Language.* New York, 1938.

Menninger, Edwin A. *Fantastic Trees.* New York, 1967.

Millbrook, Minnie Dubbs. *Ness: Western County, Kansas.* Detroit, 1955.

Miller, Mary. *A Pillar of Cloud.* Hesston, Kans., 1959.

Mitchell, S. Augustus. *Mitchell's Ancient Geography, designed for Academies, Schools, and Families.* Philadelphia, 1860.

Mitchell, William A. *Linn County, Kansas, A History.* Kansas City, 1928.

Monaghan, Jay. *Civil War on the Western Border.* Boston, 1955.

Mooney, Volney Paul. *History of Butler County, Kansas.* Lawrence, 1916.

Moore, Charles F. *Parade of the Presidents.* New York, 1928.

Moore, H. Miles. *Early History of Leavenworth, City and County.* Leavenworth, Kans., 1906.

Morgan, Lewis H. *League of the Ho-De-No-Sau-Nee or Iroquois.* 2 vols., New Haven, 1954.

Morrill, Edmund N. *History and Statistics of Brown County, Kansas.* Hiawatha, Kans., 1876.

Maurois, André. *Olympio; the Life of Victor Hugo.* New York, 1956.

National Geographic Society. *America's Historylands.* Washington, 1962.

Neff, Maggie. "History of Old Runnymede," in *Condensed History of the City of Harper, Kansas, 1877–1961.* Ed. by Ray E. Carr. Harper, 1961.

Nelson, Edward G. *The Company and the Community.* Lawrence, 1956.

Newman, E. M. *Seeing England and Scotland.* New York and London, 1930.

Newman, Tillie Karns. *Black Dog Trail*. Boston, 1957.

Nichols, Alice. *Bleeding Kansas*. New York, 1954.

Nyquist, Edna. *Pioneer Life and Lore of McPherson County, Kansas*. McPherson, Kans., 1932.

Orpen, Adela E. R. *Memories of the Old Emigrant Days in Kansas, 1862–1865*. New York, 1928.

Oskison, John M. *Tecumseh and his Times*. New York, 1938.

Owsley, F. L., O. P. Chitwood, and H. C. Nixon. *Short History of the American People*. Toronto, New York, and Boston, 1948.

Paden, Irene D. *The Wake of the Prairie Schooner*. New York, 1943.

Parrish, Randall. *The Great Plains*. Chicago, 1907.

Peattie, Donald C. *A Natural History of Trees*. Boston, 1950.

Perkins, Jacob R. *Trails, Rails, and War, The Life of General G. M. Dodge*. Indianapolis, 1929.

Phillips, William A. *The Conquest of Kansas by Missouri and her Allies*. Boston, 1856.

Ploughe, Sheridan. *History of Reno County, Kansas; its People, Industries, and Institutions*. Indianapolis, 1917.

Pottawatomie County Historical Research Committee, *Early History of Pottawatomie County*. N.p., 1954.

Prentis, Noble L. *A History of Kansas*. Kansas City, Mo., 1899.

Prescott, William H. *Conquest of Peru*. 2 vols., New York, 1898.

Pride, W. F. *History of Fort Riley*. N.p., 1926.

Raser, Margaret Haun, and Ina Rumford, compilers. *A History of Hodgeman County*. Jetmore, Kans., 1961.

Rath, Ida Ellen. *Early Ford County*. North Newton, Kans., 1964.

Rennie, Helen Ward. *A Tale of Two Towns*. Dallas, 1961.

Rich, Everett, ed. *The Heritage of Kansas*. Lawrence, 1960.

Richardson, Albert D. *Beyond the Mississippi*. Hartford, 1867.

———. *The Secret Service, the Field, the Dungeon, and the Escape*. Chicago, 1865.

Robley, T. F. *History of Bourbon County to the close of 1865*. Fort Scott, 1894.

Roenigh, Adolph. *Pioneer History of Kansas*. Lincoln, Kans., 1933.

Root, Frank A., and William E. Connelley. *The Overland Stage to California*. Topeka, 1901.

Ross, Harry E. *What Price White Rock?* Burr Oak, 1937.

Ruley, A. N. *A. N. Ruley's History of Brown County*. Hiawatha, Kans., 1930.

Rydjord, John. "The Conquistadores Come to Kansas," Vol. I, 1–20, in *Kansas, The First Century*. Ed. by John Bright. 4 vols. New York, 1956.

———. "French Frontier and the Indian Trade," Vol. I, 21–46, in *Kansas, The First Century*. Ed. by John Bright. 4 vols. New York, 1956.

———. *Indian Place-Names*. Norman, 1968.

Sageser, A. Bower. "The Rails go Westward," Vol. I, 221–54, in *Kansas, The First Century*. Ed. by John Bright. 4 vols. New York, 1956.

Sandburg, Carl. *Abraham Lincoln: The War Years*. Vol. I. New York, 1939.

Sanders, Gwendoline and Paul. *The Harper County Story*. North Newton, Kans., 1968.

———. *The Sumner County Story*. North Newton, Kans., 1966–67.

Sandoz, Mari. *Cheyenne Autumn*. New York, 1953.

Savage, Isaac O. *A History of Republic County, Kansas*. Beloit, 1901.

Schmidt, Heinie. *Ashes of My Campfire; Tales of Old Dodge City*. Dodge City, 1952.

Schulz, J. F. *Newest Guide Through Prague*. Prague, 1869.

Shackleton, Bernice C. *Handbook on the Frontier Days of Southeast Kansas*. Pittsburg, Kans., 1961.

Shelton, Lola. *Charles Marion Russell, Cowboy, Artist, Friend*. New York, 1962.

Shirk, George H. *Oklahoma Place Names*. Norman, 1965.

Shriner, Charles A., compiler. *Wit, Wisdom and Foibles of the Great*. New York and London, 1918.

Smith, Arthur D. H. *Old Fuss and Feathers, the Life and Exploits of Lt. General Winfield Scott*. New York, 1937.

Smith, C. Henry. *The Coming of the Russian Mennonites*. Berne, Ind., 1927.

Smith, Mortimer. *The Life of Ole Bull*. New York, 1947.

Smith, R. F. *Doniphan County, Kansas, History and Directory for 1868–1869*. Wathna, 1868.

Smyth, Bernard B. *The Heart of the New Kansas*. Great Bend, 1880.

Southey, Robert. *The Complete Poetical Works of Robert Southey*. New York, 1860.

Spaeth, Sigmund G. *A History of Popular Music in America*. New York, 1948.

Spring, Leverett Wilson. *Kansas, The Prelude to the War for the Union*. Boston, 1890.

Stewart, George R. *Names on the Land*. Boston, 1958.

Stokes, Will E. *Episodes of Early Days*. Great Bend, Kans., 1926.

Storey, Moorfield. "Charles Sumner," in *American Statesmen*. Ed. by John T. Morse. New York, 1900.

Stratford, Jesse P. *Butler County's Eighty Years, 1855–1935*. El Dorado, Kans., 1934.

Streeter, Floyd B. *Prairie Trails and Cow Towns*. Boston, 1936.

Sullivan, Frank S. *History of Meade County, Kansas*. Topeka, 1916.

Sunder, John E. *Bill Sublette, Mountain Man*. Norman, 1959.

Teale, Edwin W. *Journey into Summer*. New York, 1960.

Tennal, Ralph. *History of Nemaha County, Kansas*. Lawrence, 1916.

Thomas, Alfred B. *After Coronado*. Norman, 1935.

Thomas, Sister M. Evangeline. *Footprints on the Frontier: A History of the Sisters of Saint Joseph, Concordia, Kansas*. Westminster, Md., 1948.

Thomson, Matt. *Early History of Wabaunsee County, Kansas, with Stories of Pioneer Days and Glimpses of our Western Border*. Alma, Kans., 1901.

Throckmorton, George, *et al. First Hand Historical Episodes of Early Coffey County*. N.p., n.d.

Toepfer, Amy Brungarat, and Agnes C. Dreiling. *Conquering the Wind*. Garwood, N.J., 1966.

Tolsted, Laura Lu, and Ada Swineford. *Kansas Rocks and Minerals*. Lawrence, 1957.

Toothaker, Mrs. Pearl. *The History of Sheridan County*. Hoxie, Kans., 1961.

Tuttle, Charles R. *A New Centennial History of the State of Kansas*. Madison, Wis., 1876.

Van Gundy, John C. *Reminiscences of Frontier Life on the Upper Neosho in 1855 and 1856*. Topeka, 1925.

Van Osdel, A. L. *Historic Landmarks*. N.p., 1915.

Vestal, Stanley. *The Old Santa Fe Trail*. Boston, 1939.

———. *Queen of Cowtowns: Dodge City*. New York, 1952.

Villard, Oswald Garrison. *John Brown, 1800–1859*. Boston and New York, 1910.

Von Engeln, O. D., and Jane McElway Urquhart. *Story Key to Geographical Names*. New York, 1924.

Wallace, Berniece Boyd. *History of Paola, Kansas, 1855 to 1955*. N.p., 1955.

Waters, L. L. *Steel Trails to Santa Fe*. Lawrence, 1950.

Whittemore, Margaret. *Historic Kansas*. Lawrence, 1954.

———. *One-Way Ticket to Kansas; The Autobiography of Frank M. Stahl*. Lawrence, 1959.

Wiebe, David V. *They Seek a Country: A Survey of Mennonite Migration*. Hillsboro, 1959.

Wilson, Robert R., and Ethel M. Sears. *History of Grant County, Kansas*. Wichita, 1950.

Wolle, Muriel Sibell. *Stampede to Timberline*. Denver, 1949.

Woodward, William E. *Meet General Grant*. New York, 1928.

Young, Otis E. *First Military Escort on the Santa Fe Trail*. Glendale, 1952.

Zornow, William F. *Kansas, A History of the Jayhawk State*. Norman, 1957.

VII. GUIDES AND MISCELLANEOUS MATERIALS

American Name Society, *Bulletin* No. 2, March, 1966; No. 3, July, 1966; No. 14, April, 1969.

Barthalomew, John George. *Gazetteer of the British Isles*. Edinburgh, 1963.

Baughman, Robert W. *Kansas Post Offices*. Wichita, 1961.

Benedictine Monks of St. Augustine's Abbey. *The Book of Saints*. New York, 1966.

Blackie, C. *A Dictionary of Place-Names.* London, 1887.
Blackmar, Frank W. *Kansas, A Cyclopedia of State History.* 2 vols. Chicago, 1912.
Brewer, E. Cobham. *The Reader's Handbook.* Philadelphia, 1904.
Burch, C. S. *Handbook of Elk and Chautauqua Counties, Kansas.* Chicago, 1886.
Catholic Encyclopedia, 15 vols. New York, 1907.
Diamond Jubilee, Coldwater, 1959 (pamphlet).
Dawson, Frank. *Place Names in Colorado.* Denver, 1954.
Dictionary of American Biography. Ed. by Allen Johnson and Dumas Malone, 20 vols. New York, 1928–1937.
Douglas, J. D. *The New Bible Dictionary.* Grand Rapids, 1962.
Edwards, John P. *Historical Atlas of Sedgwick County, Kansas.* Philadelphia, 1882.
———. *Historical Atlas of Rooks County, Kansas.* Philadelphia, 1887.
———. *Historical Atlas of Sumner County, Kansas.* Philadelphia, 1883.
Edwards Brothers. *An Illustrated Historical Atlas of Miami County.* Philadelphia, 1878.
Ekwall, Eilert. *The Concise Oxford Dictionary of English Place-Names.* Oxford, 1960.
Ellis County, *Golden Jubilee Report,* 1926.
Encyclopedia Americana. 30 vols. New York, 1965.
Encyclopedia Britannica. 24 vols. Chicago, 1962.
English Place Name Society, *The Place-Names of Sussex.* Cambridge, Eng., 1924.
Ewen, C. L'Estrange. *A Guide to the Origin of British Surnames.* London, 1938.
Failing, Ann Jacobs. *Shoo Fly City.* Oxford, 1960.
Federal Writers' Project. *A Guide to Salina.* Salina, n.d.
———. *Iowa, A Guide to the Hawkeye State.* New York, 1938.
———. *Kansas, A Guide to the Sunflower State.* New York, 1939.
———. *New Jersey: A Guide to its Present and Past.* New York, 1939.
———. *North Dakota: A Guide to the Northern Prairie State.* New York, 1950.
———. *Utah, A Guide to the State.* New York, 1954.
Fitzpatrick, Lilian L. *Nebraska Place-Names.* Lincoln, 1960.
Franklin County Historical Society. *Reflections of Franklin County and Chautauqua Days.* Ottawa, 1961.
Funk & Wagnall's, *Standard Dictionary of Folklore, Mythology, and Legend.* 2 vols. New York, 1949.
Gannett, Henry. *American Names: A Guide to the Origin of Place Names in the United States.* Washington, 1947.
Gudde, Erwin G. *California Place Names.* Berkeley and Los Angeles, 1949.
Hackett, Charles W. "Policy of the Spanish Crown regarding French

Encroachments from Louisiana, 1721–1762," *New Spain and the West,* Ed. by George Hammond, 2 vols. Lancaster, Pa., 1932.
Jobes, Gertrude. *Dictionary of Mythology, Folklore, and Symbols.* 2 vols. New York, 1961.
Kane, Joseph Nathan. *The American Counties.* New York, 1962.
Kingman County Diamond Jubilee Souvenir Historical Program. Kingman, Kans., 1958.
Lambert, Eloise, and Mario Pei. *The Book of Place-Names.* New York, 1959.
Landman, Isaac, ed. *The Universal Jewish Encyclopedia.* 10 vols. New York, 1939.
Leduc, Alberto, and Lewis Lara y Pardo. *Diccionario de Geografía, Historia, y Biografía Mexicana.* Paris and Mexico City, 1910.
Lewis, Richard W. *Early Days History of Home City.* Marysville, 1949.
Lippincott, Grambo & Company. *Gazetteer of the United States.* Philadelphia, 1853.
Miller, Madeleine S., and J. Lane Miller. *Harper's Bible Dictionary.* New York, 1961.
Missouri Pacific Lines. *The Empire that Missouri Pacific Serves.* St. Louis, (n.d.).
Moulton, Charles Wilson, ed. *The Library of Literary Criticism.* 8 vols. Gloucester, 1959.
National Cyclopedia of American Biography. 51 vols. New York, 1898–1969.
Neibarger, Walt. *Sunflower Petals.* Tonganoxie, 1938.
Overman, William D. *Ohio Town Names.* Akron, 1958.
Partridge, Eric. *Name into Word.* London, 1949.
Paullin, Charles O. *Atlas of the Historical Geography of the United States.* New York, 1932.
Pine, L. G. *The Story of Surnames.* Rutland, Vt., 1966.
Pioneer Atlas of the American West. Chicago, 1956.
Reaney, P. H. *The Origin of English Place-Names.* London, 1960.
Remsburg, George J. *Scrapbook.* 4 vols. KSHL, Topeka.
Ruth, Kenneth. *Colorado Vacations.* New York, 1959.
Sanchez, Nellie Van de Grift. *Spanish and Indian Place Names of California.* San Francisco, 1930.
Santa Fe Railway. *Along Your Way.* Chicago, 1946.
Shankle, George Earle. *State Names, Flags, Seals, Songs, Birds, Flowers, and other Symbols.* New York, 1934.
Shillinglaw, T. G. Speech on "History of Taloga," September 25, 1887, KSHL, Topeka.
Smith, Eldon C. *The Story of Our Names.* New York, 1950.
Southwick, Albert P. *Wisps of Wit and Wisdom or Knowledge in a Nutshell.* New York, 1968.

Stillwell, L. *The Giant Elm*. Erie, 1918.
Stites, Lester. *History of Ionia, Kansas*. Cawker City, Kans., 1956.
Taylor, Isaac. *Names and their Histories*. London, 1898.
Tenney, Merrill C., ed. *The Zondervan Pictorial Bible Dictionary*. Grand Rapids, 1963.
United States Board of Geographical Names. *Sixth Report . . . 1890 to 1932*. Washington, 1933.
Upham, Warren. *Minnesota Geographical Names*. Saint Paul, 1969.
Vincent, Benjamin. *Haydn's Dictionary of Dates and Universal Information relating to all Ages and Nations*. New York, 1884.
Vogel, Virgil J. *Indian Place Names in Illinois*, Illinois State Historical Society, Pamphlet Series No. 4. Springfield, 1963.
Wagner, Leopold. *Names: And their Meaning*. London, 1893.
Walsh, William S. *Heroes and Heroines of Fiction, Modern Prose and Poetry*. Philadelphia, 1914.
Webster Dam Dedication. Stockton, October 6, 1956 (pamphlet).
Webster, Daniel. *An Address Delivered at the laying of the Corner Stone of the Bunker Hill Monument*. Boston, 1825.
Wheat, Carl Irving. *Mapping the Transmississippi West, 1500–1861*. 5 vols. San Francisco, 1957–1963.
Wilder, D. W. *Annals of Kansas*. Topeka, 1886.
Writers' Program. *The Origin of Massachusetts Place Names*. New York, 1941.

INDEX

Abbeyville: 471
Abelincoln (Oklahoma): 7
Abilene: 35, 226
Achilles: 210, 212
Acme: 209
Acres: 85
Ada: 11, 468
Adam: 224
Adams, John Quincy: 29
Admire, Jacob V.: 367
Adobe: 79
Advance: 409
Aeolia: 207
Aethelstane: 147
Aetna: 219
Afton: 162
Agolat: 489
Agnes City: 468
Agra: 199
Agricola: 85, 220
Agua Perdida: 14
Ailanthus: 48
Air: 484
Ajax: 213
Akron: 26, 49, 209, 273
Aladdin: 198
Alameda: 57
Albany: 152, 263
Albers Station: 473
Albert: 182
Albion: 135
Albright: 339
Alcove Springs: 16
Alden: 444
Alembic: 483
Aleppo: 227
Alexanderwohl: 173
Alexis, Grand Duke: 64
Alfalfa: 87
Aliceville: 466
Alioth Ranch (Hering-
  ton): 453
Allen County: 273, 316, 322
Alliance: 261, 448

Allodium: 85
Alma: 195, 287
Almelo: 182
Alpha: 205
Alta: 101
Altair: 10
Altamont: 101
Alta Vista: 101, 135, 209,
  412
Alton: 282
Altoona: 267
Alum Creek: 80, 101
Amazon: 102
Amber Creek: 80
Amboy: 266
America: 90
American Revolution: 6
Ames: 291, 466
Amherst: 254
Amiot: 75, 458
Amity: 481
Amo: 279, 481
Amy: 470
Anatomy Hill: 26, 484
Andale: 7, 34
Anderson County: 304,
  309, 311, 314
Andover: 250, 254
Angelus: 232
Anglessey: 165
Angola: 201
Annelly: 473
Anness: 472
Anson: 287
Antelope: 66
Anthony: 328
Antioch: 10, 227
Antrim: 168, 360
Appomattox: 6, 384, 410
Aral: 196
Arapaho County: 337, 430
Arbor: 44
Arcadia: 205
Arcola: 16, 217

Arcona: 195
Argentine: 75
Argonia: 34, 213
Argos: 210
Argyle: 152
Arikara River: 33
Arion: 207
Arizona: 298
Arkaketah (Oto chief):
  436
Arkansas City: 108
Arkansas River: 12, 14, 22,
  91, 108
Arlington: 255
Arma Post: 76
Armourdale: 84
Armstrong: 424
Aroma: 485
Arrington: 474
Artesia: 11
Arthur: 359
Artois: 126
Arvonia: 165
Ash Creek: 56
Ashland: 51, 356
Ash Point: 52
Ashtabula: 273-74
Ash Valley: 34, 48
Assaria: 153, 187
Ast: 181
Astor: 365
Atchison: 347
Atchison, David R.: 106
Atchison County: 304, 309,
  322
Atchison, Topeka, and
  Santa Fe (railroad): 439
Athelstane: 141
Athens: 205, 210
Athol: 156, 161
Athy: 170
Atkinson, Henry: 413
Atlanta: 206, 302
Atrato (Panama): 97

Attica: 205, 213
Aubrey, Xavier: 67, 95, 122
Auburn: 263, 370
Augusta: 469
Aulne: 126
Aurora: 207, 285
Austerlitz: 128
Austin, Moses: 99
Avila: 279
Avon: 141
Axtell: 459
Ayersburg: 293
Ayr: 152

Babcock: 29
Bachelor: 87, 476
Baden: 143, 180
Badger Creek: 64, 68
Bagdad: 198
Baileyville: 331
Baird, Obadiah: 96
Baker's Store: 304
Bala: 166
Balboa, Nunez de: 97
Bald Buttes: 46
Bald Eagle: 335
Baldwin: 8, 198, 247
Ballard Falls: 18
Baltimore: 302
Bangor: 165, 257
Banner: 372
Bannock: 432
Banwell: 132
Baptiste Springs: 17
Barber County: 321
Barnard: 444
Barnes: 456
Barnes, Earl: 45
Barrel Springs: 14
Barrett: 453
Bartles, Jacob (Bartles-
    ville): 421
Barton County: 385, 464
Basel: 131
Base Line: 10
Batchellor: 7, 18
Bath: 143, 208
Battleax: 409
Battle Corners: 409
Battle Creek: 409
Battle Hill: 32, 404
Bavaria: 178
Baxter Springs: 16, 202,
    247, 327, 417
Bayne: 332
Bayneville: 336

Bazaar: 468
Bazaine, Marshal Achille
    Francoise: 129
Bazine: 129
Beanville: 87
Bear Creek: 67
Beattie: 459
Beaubien Creek: 121
Beaumont: 130, 141
Beaver: 33, 64, 66, 70, 72,
    80, 477
Beaverton: 60, 70
Beckley Spur: 462
Becknell, William: 122
Bedford: 138
Bedlam: 378
Bee: 59
Beech Grove: 47, 415
Beecher, Henry Ward: 244
Beersheba: 228
Belfast: 170
Bell, John: 39, 56, 59, 63
Bellaire: 131
Bellefont: 125, 130
Bellegarde: 194
Belle Grove: 130
Belle Meade: 130, 390
Bellemont: 130
Belle Plaine: 130
Belle Prairie: 37, 130
Belle Springs: 131
Belleville: 130, 468
Belmont: 130
Beloit: 287
Belpre: 4, 37
Belvidere: 222, 285, 330
Belvue: 4
Ben Allen: 271
Bendena: 36, 473
Bender Mounds: 28, 121
Benecia: 100, 296
Benedict: 242
Bennett, James Gordon:
    64, 363, 365
Bennington: 6, 256, 259
Benton: 369
Benton, Thomas Hart
    (Senator): 310
Bentley, O. H.: 454-55
Berea: 230
Berlin: 179
Bern: 131, 132
Berwick: 152, 154
Bethany: 229, 460
Bethel: 229
Beto Junction: 489

Beulah: 234
Beverly: 255
Bible names: 24, 223
Bickerdyke, "Mother": 385
Bienville, Jean Baptiste: 109
Big Bend: 349, 433
Big Blue: 16, 24
Big Bow (Kiowa chief):
    432
Big Coon Creek: 69
Big Cottonwood Grove: 58
Big Creek: 417
Bigelow: 459
Big Flats: 33
Big Hill: 33
Big Indian Spring: 13
Big John Creek: 13
Big Muddy: 107
Big River: 91
Big Soldier: 410
Big Springs: 13
Big Timbers: 44, 49, 106
Big Woman Creek: 478
Billings, N.H.: 406
Birch: 47
Bird City: 60, 368
Bird Creek: 60
Birmingham: 144
Bismarck: 45, 180
Bison: 65
Bitter Creek: 20
Bittertown: 178
Black Bear Pawnee: 433
Black Hawk: 63, 435
Black Hills: 30
Black Jack: 49, 77
Black Kettle: 28, 82, 419
Black Warrior: 410
Black Wolf: 67
Blaine, James G.: 361, 388
Blair, Charles W.: 413
Blaze Fork: 20
Blood Creek: 4, 409
Bloom: 269
Bloomington: 39
Blue Earth River: 115
Blue Hill: 24
Blue Hills: 22, 23, 29, 32
Blue Jacket's Crossing: 29
Blue Juniata: 260
Bluemont: 24
Blue Mound: 29
Blue Mount Hill: 266
Blue Stem: 20, 23, 37, 38
Bluff City: 27
Bluff Creek: 27, 111

Bluffville: 27
Blumenthal: 173
Blunt, James Gillpatrick: 419
Boat Mountain: 25
Boaz: 292
Bodarc: 131
Bogue: 452
Bogus Legislature: 6, 244, 308, 323, 344, 377, 427, 429
Bohemian names: 192
Boicourt: 131
Boissiére, E. Valentin: 47, 124
Bolivia: 98
Bonaccord: 4, 482
Bonair: 484
Bonanza: 77
Bonasa City: 62
Bonita: 100
Bonner, James: 366
Bonner, Robert: 82
Bonner Springs: 13, 119
Bonnie Doon: 162
Boon: 85
Boone, Daniel Morgan: 85, 119
Boone, Napoleon: 128
Boone, Nathan: 47
Boonville: 85
Border Ruffians: 28, 377
Bosland: 83, 213
Boston: 250–51, 260
Botolph: 250
Bottoms: 33
Boudinot, Elias: 123, 429
Bourassas: 123
Bourbon: 119, 125, 308, 327
Bourbonnais Creek: 121
Bourgmont, Etienne, Sieur de: 106, 431
Bowling: 37
Bowling Green: 39, 274
Boyle: 452
Boys Creek: 476
Brazil: 103
Brazilton: 102
Breckinridge: 308, 315, 343, 345, 414
Breezy Hill: 11, 27
Bremen: 177
Brewer: 467
Brewery Creek: 483
Brewster: 454
Bricktown: 79
Brighton: 143

Bristol: 138
Britain: 134
Britons: 167
Broadbent, Albert Jefferson: 353
Broderick County: 319
Bronson: 457
Brooklyn: 8, 264
Brooks, Preston: 346
Broughton: 283
Brown, Gallatin: 48, 366
Brown, John: 381
Brown County: 319, 322
Browne, Orville H.: 319
Brownell: 460
Brown's Grove: 48
Brownsville: 263
Brudenthal: 174
Brue's map: 106
Brunot Creek: 124
Bryan, William Jennings: 147
Bryant, Edwin: 16
Buchanan: 242, 269, 345, 358, 414
Buck Creek: 66
Buckeye: 56, 274
Buck Run: 66
Buckner: 445
Bucyrus: 199, 275
Buda: 194
Bueffel Au: 232
Buena Vista: 6, 99, 338, 382
Buffalo: 65
Buffalo City: 65, 416
Buffalo County: 65, 330
Buffalo Mound: 30
Buffalo Park: 454
"Buffelow Crick" (De Mun's): 69
Buffville (Buffton and Buffington): 474
Buhler: 173
Bull City: 83, 216, 282
Bull Creek: 83
Bull, Ole: 90
Bull Run: 6, 410
Buncomb: 301, 373
Bunion Creek: 484
Bunker Hill: 6, 250, 253, 259, 277
Bunker's Addition: 277
Burdett: 48
Burdick: 474
Bureau: 373
Burlingame: 357

Burlington: 250
Burnett, Abraham (Pottawatomi chief): 33
Burns: 441
Burns, Robert: 153, 162, 370
Burr Oak: 50
Bush City: 338
Bushong: 458
Bushton: 86, 88
Butler County: 316, 322, 348
Butler, Andrew Pickens: 346
Butterfield Stage: 14, 31, 58
Butterfield Trail: 418
Butterfly: 59
Buttermilk Creek: 483
Byers: 200, 455
Buzick, William C.: 47
Buzzard's Island: 419

Cable City: 101
Cactus: 42
Cad: 411
Cadillac, La Moth: 124
Cadmus: 205
Cadue, Peter: 121
Cain: 38, 225
Cairo: 200, 283
Calcutta: 199
Calderhead: 155, 336
Caldwell, Alexander: 333
Caledonia: 151
Calhoun County: 316, 322, 355
California: 5, 16, 90, 295
Calista: 469
Calmar: 123, 187
Calorific: 11
Calybeate: 15
Cam: 137, 139
Camargo: 99, 382
Cambrian: 163
Cambridge: 137, 250
Camchester: 139
Camden: 259, 266, 462
Cameron: 79, 139
Camp Alert (Fort Larned): 417
Camp Beecher (Wichita): 244
Campbellton: 448
Camp Center: 380
Camp Crawford: 327
Camp Crily: 373
Camp Fletcher: 417

Camp Mackay: 413
Camp Scott: 379
Camp Sturgis: 417
Campus: 463
Canaan: 226
Caney: 7, 42, 87
Cannonball (stage line):
452
Canton: 197, 200, 260, 276
Canville Trading Post: 121
Capioma (Kapioma): 434
Cappaqua: 365
Capper, Arthur: 143
Captain: 409, 411
Cavalry: 409
Caravan Grove: 45
Carbon: 76
Carbondale: 34, 76, 267–
69, 415
Carden: 466
Cariboo: 72
Carlisle: 161, 466
Carmel: 228
Carneiro: 80, 101
Carolina: 301
Carr Creek: 8
Carson, Kit: 45, 122
Carter Creek: 485
Carthage: 201, 205, 219
Caruso: 221
Carvel: 361
Carver, George Washing-
ton: 32
Cash City: 88
Castañeda, Pedro de: 91
Castle Rock Creek Station:
31
Castleton: 256
Catalpa: 55
Cathedral of the Prairies
(Victoria): 147, 175
Catherine: 147
Catlin: 114
Cato: 205, 220
Caucus: 373
Cavagnial, Fort de: 119
Cavalry Creek: 82, 286
Covert Creek: 8
Cave Springs: 15, 159
Cawker City: 489
Cayot, John and Mary: 124
Cayuga: 259
Cedar: 50; Bluff, 324;
Creek, 43, 46; Mountains,
30; Cedars of Lebanon,
50; Point, 58

Cedron: 231
Centennial: 371
Center: 375–76
Centerville: 376
Central State (Kansas): 374
Centralia: 376, 380
Centropolis: 213, 242
Cerro Gordo: 6, 99, 380,
382
Cessna Aircraft Co.: 88
Chain Lakes: 20
Chalk Mound: 30
Chantilly: 126, 300, 392
Chanute: 112, 448
Chapman: 139, 169
Chapman's Creek: 52, 422
Chardon: 436
Charity: 480
Chase: 447
Chase, Salmon Portland:
277, 348
Chase County: 273, 277,
348, 367
Chautauqua: 14, 22, 261,
437
Chávez (Jarvis Creek): 47,
101
Chellis: 143, 208
Chelsea: 137, 250, 252
Chemung: 259, 261
Chenango: 259
Cheney: 441
Chepstow: 143
Cherokee: 429
Cherokee County: 316, 327
Cherokee Lowlands: 22
Cherry: 28, 47
Cherryvale: 47
Cheshire: 139, 273
Chester: 139
Chetopa (Osage chief):
435
Cheyenne Bottoms: 4, 22,
60, 431
Cheyenne County: 430
Chicago: 261, 283–84, 448
Chico: 101
Chicopee: 255
Chikaskia: 110
Chile: 99
Chiles: 320
Chillicothe: 273, 425
Chingawassa Springs: 12
Chippewa Hills: 33
Chisholm Trail: 83
Chitolah: 106

Chouteau (family): 112,
119, 120, 433; Island, 33,
120; Trading Post, 120
Christian: 174, 190
Chrysler, Walter P.: 404
Churchill: 488
Climax: 25
Cicero: 205, 220, 259
Cimarron: Crossing, 93;
Redoubt, 416; River, 14,
81, 92, 111; Springs, 14
Cimbri: 164
Cincinnati: 260, 273, 276,
384
Cipriano, Mary: 121
Circleville: 275
Civil War: 6
Claflin: 467, 475
Clarence: 54
Clarenden: 292
Clark, Mrs. Olive A.: 49
Clark, William: 115
Clark City: 304
Clark Creek: 416
Clark(e) County: 320, 400
Clay, Henry: 356
Clayton: 79
Clear Creek: 69
Clearwater: 110
Cleburne: 459
Clements: 446
Cleveland Station: 359, 466
Cliff: 449
Clifton: 456
Clonmel: 169
Cloud County: 365
Cloud, William: 395, 397–
99
Clover Cliff Spur: 463
Cloverdale: 87
Clyde: 155, 273, 482
Clydesdale Spur: 463
Clymer, Rolla: 23
Coal: 76
Coal Center: 458
Coats: 442
Cody, Buffalo Bill: 26, 64,
122
Cofachique (Cofachiqui):
306, 470
Coffey County: 311, 313,
317, 322, 377
Coffeyville: 314
Cognac, France: 131
Coin: 88
Cokedale: 76

Colby: 368
Cold Spring: 17, 286
Cold Water (Cow Creek):
    65
Coldwater: 286, 411;
    Grove, 48
Cole, Ame: 62
Colfax, Schuyler: 349
Collano: 488
Collar's Flats: 33
College Green: 39
Collet Creek: 124
Collyer: 246
Colokan: 487
Coloma: 296
Colony: 23, 278
Colorado: 294
Columbia: 89
Columbus, Christopher: 89
Colusa: 296
Colwich: 487
Comanche: 106, 430
Comet: 9, 482
Comisky: 458
Como: 218
Concord: 250, 253, 482
Concreto: 77
Conda River: 410
Conesburg: 441
Conelley's Map: 351
Conkling, Roscoe: 361
Conquest: 409
Constant: 481
Conway: 165, 334
Cooke, Col. St. George: 13
Cooks Ford: 32
Cool, Joseph: 11
Coolidge: 14, 440–41
Coon Creek: 11, 69
Coon Hollow Camp: 13
Cooper, James Fenimore:
    430
Copeland: 445
Copper Creek: 75
Cora City: 405
Corinth: 205, 305, 410
Corliss: 338
Cornell: 128
Cornhill: 86
Corning: 259, 455
Cornwall: 281
Coronado: 29, 36, 46, 89,
    91, 93–95, 238, 324, 397,
    470; Heights, 23, 94, 106,
    411

Cortez, Hernando: 90, 94,
    97
Cosmosa: 9
Cottage Hill: 27
Colton's Map: 345
Cottonwood: 43; City, 57;
    Falls, 135, 441; Station,
    177
Coues, Elliot: 92, 106, 108,
    113, 115
Council City: 357
Council Grove: 13, 45
Council Oak: 45
County names: 375
Courtland: 88, 259, 264
Covert: 44
Cowboy: 84
Cow Creek: 65, 83
Cow Island: 380, 412
Cowland: 83, 216
Cowley, Mathew: 403
Cowskin: 84
Coyne Creek (Rogler
    Creek): 86
Coyote: 68
Cayuga: 262
Cracklin, Joseph: 97
Crawford, Samuel Johnson:
    327, 395, 405, 418
Crawfordsville: 446
Cremona: 221
Creola: 481
Cresson: 452
Cresswell (Arkansas City):
    109
Crestline: 275
Criley, John D.: 440
Critzer: 452
Croghan, George: 412
Crooked Creek: 52, 83
Cromwell: 147
Crow: 63
Croweburg: 76
Crystal Springs: 16
Cuba, names: 89, 96
Cumberland: 164
Cummingsville: 238
Cunningham: 110
Curlew: 61
Curtis, H. Zarah: 417
Custer, George A.: 232,
    286, 419
Cuter: 485
Cutler: 98, 357
Cutts: 145
Cuyler: 481

Cyrus: 198
Czech: 192

Dakota sandstone: 31
Dale (Andale): 7, 34
Dale's Oil Spring: 16
Dalrymple: 474
Dalton: 457
Damar: 452
Danube: 161, 192, 472
Danville: 275
Dapport, J. W.: 41
Darien: 97
Darwin, Charles: 148
Davis: 49; Jefferson, 94,
    116, 303, 379, 393, 405;
    County, 308, 314, 322,
    324, 394
Dayton: 275, 461
Decatur County: 369, 407
Deception Creek: 19
Deep Hole: 416
Deer Creek: 66
Deerfield: 66, 447
Deerhead: 66
Deerton: 66
Defiance: 409
Delano: 153, 358
Delavan: 283
Delaware: 265, 424, 426;
    City, 139; River, 60
Delhi: 199
Delia: 469
Delila: 234
Delisle's Map: 92, 105
Deliverance: 35
Dell Ray: 155
Dellvale: 34
Delphi: 108, 208
Delphos: 210, 273
Densmore: 474
Delta: 159, 205
DeMun, Jules: 69, 120
Denison: 51, 188, 275
Denmark: 188
Denton: 148
Dent's Spur: 462
Denver: 191, 294, 326
Derby: 146
Derry: 170
Desire: 481
De Soto, Hernando: 94,
    252, 306
Detroit: 107, 124
Devil: 235
Devil's Backbone: 25, 235

Devil's Tower (Wyoming): 432
Devize: 222
Devon: 78, 148
Dewdrop: 11
Dewey, George: 421
Dexter: 82
Diablo, El Lugar de: 102, 235
Dial: 9
Diamond: City, 13; Island, 74; Springs, 13, 74
Diego: 101
Difficult Creek: 101, 487
Dighton: 407
Dinner Creek: 482
Discord: 7, 9, 482
Divide: 23
Dixie: 307
Dixon's Lone House: 285
Dodge, Granville: 397, 415
Dodge, Henry: 378, 415
Dodge, Richard I.: 64, 415
Dodge City: 397, 416
Dogtown (prairie dog): 71
Dolese Spur: 462
Donegal: 131, 168
Doniphan County: 304, 309, 322, 377
Donner Party: 16
Dorn, Jackson: 113
Dorn County: 317
Dorrance: 281
Douglas: 106, 335, 344, 346, 378
Douglass: 346
Dover: 142, 255; England, 135
Downer, James P.: 418
Downs: 41, 460
Dragoon: 409, 412
Dresden: 178
Drinkwater, O. H.: 51
Druids: 49, 165
Drury: 136
Dry Creek: 61
Drywood Creek: 44
Dublin: 168, 170
Dubuque: 123
Duck Creek: 62
Dudley, Robert: 158
Dunkirk: 130
Dull Knife (Cheyenne chief): 70, 430
DuLuth, Grayselon: 123
Dumun's Creek: 41

Dundee: 156
Dunkirk: 259, 265
Dunlap: 26, 338
Dupont: 145
Du Pratz, Le Page: 74
Duquoin: 123
Durfee's Ranch (Wichita): 49
Durham: 140
Dutch Creek: 177
Dutch Flats: 33
Dutch Henry's Crossing: 177
Duver: 85
Dyer's Town: 260

Eagle Point: 62
Eagle Tail: 63, 226
East Norway: 154
Easton: 269, 368
Ebenfeld: 173
Echo: 485
Eclipse: 10, 285
Economy: 87
Eden: 223
Eden Prairie: 37
Edgerton: 444
Edmund: 489
Edna: 471
Edson: 488
Edwards County: 330
Edwardsville: 452
Effingham: 455
Ego: 7, 481
Egypt: 201
Ehrsams: 132
Eight Mile Creek: 19
Eisenhower: 480
Elba: 128
Elbing: 174
Elbow: 484
El Cid: 95
Eldora: 54
El Dorado: 7, 20, 97
El Frio: 286
Elga: 153
Elgin: 152
Elgo: 168, 190
El Greco: 95
Elinor: 469
Elizabeth: 468
Elk: 66; Creek, 155; Falls, 18; Rapids, 143; River, 66
Elkader: 271
Elkhart: 279
Elkhorn Creek: 66

Ellen: 470
Ellinwood: 444
Ellis: 401, 403
Ellsworth: 6, 402
Elm: 456, 465; Grove, 45; Mill, 46
Elmdale: 43, 46
Elmo: 372
Elmont: 46
El Paso: 100, 146
El Río de San Pedro y San Pablo: 91
Elsimore: 189
Elsmore (Elsinore): 189
Elston: 101
Elwood: 40
Elyria: 275, 487
Emerald Hill: 168
Emerson: 468
Emery: 15
Eminence: 216, 481
Emmeram: 176
Emmett: 170
Emory's Map: 57
Empire: 76, 88
End-o-Track: 463
Englewood: 284
Ensign: 411
Enterprise: 87
Equity: 88
Escansaques: 105
Eschs Spur: 463
Eskridge: 328
Erie: 259, 267
Esperanza: 100, 480
Essex: 140
Eudora: 425, 478
Eugenia: 128
Eureka: 207, 481
Eustis: 279, 385
Evangeline: 112
Eve: 224
Everson: 143
Everest: 455
Ewing, Thomas: 335
Example: 479
Excelsior: 265
Exe: 142
Exodusters: 201
E-ya-no-sa (Kansas chief): 79

Fact: 485
Fairfield: 240, 336
Fairmount: 24
Fairview: 4, 130, 454

Fall River: 18
Falstaff: 5
Falun: 186
Fame: 481
Fancy Creek: 485
Fanning: 458
Farland: 20, 186
Farmer: 85, 88, 281
Farms: 85
Fargo Springs: 17
Far West: 484
Fawn: 66, 479
Fayette: 280, 283
Federal: 373
Fenwick: 141
Fern: 42
Feterita: 86
Fiat: 373
Fidelity: 481
Fillmore: 358
Fingal: 152
Finn, William: 393
Finney County: 330, 337
Finns: 145
Fitch, Julian R.: 14, 31, 76
Five Mile Creek: 19
Flats: 33
Flat Top Hill: 28
Flavius: 220
Fletcher, Thomas C.: 417
Flint Hills: 18, 22, 37, 63
Floersch: 180
Floral: 39
Florence: 114, 215, 470
Florida: 90
Flower Pot Mound: 39
Flush: 180
Folsom: 76
Fontana: 13
Foote County: 337, 408
Forbs Air Force Base: 463
Ford County: 397
Forest: 44
Formosa: 200
Fort Atkinson: 53, 413, 420
Fort Coffee: 232
Fort de Cavagniale: 119
Fort Dodge: 65, 397, 416
Fort Downer: 417
Fort Ellsworth: 403
Fort Expedient: 413
Fort Fletcher: 417
Fort Harker: 403
Fort Hays: 417
Fort Insley: 413
Fort Larned: 416

Fort Leavenworth: 378, 413
Fort Lincoln: 342
Fort Mann: 413
Fort Monument: 417
Fort Riley: 379, 380, 414
Fort Scott: 379, 413
Fort Sumner: 413
Fort Village (Kaw): 119
Fort Wallace: 14, 82, 417
Fort Zarah: 417, 432
Forty-Niners: 89, 97, 295, 312, 398
Fossil: 12, 400
Four Houses: 119
Four Mile Creek: 15, 19, 271, 327
Fourth of July Creek: 271
Fowler, George: 54
Fox: 68, 474
Frachet, Michael: 124
Fragrant Hill: 27, 484
Frankfort: 177, 179
Franklin: 8, 61, 322, 353
Franklinton (Columbus, Ohio): 89
Frederickstown: 165
Freedom: 372, 481
Free Will: 480
Fremont: 13, 480
Frémont, John Charles: 24, 59, 71, 394, 414
French: 4, 119; Bottoms, 33; Ford, 123; Ridge, 33, 124
Friend: 447
Friendship: 482
Frisco: 101, 297
Frizell: 338
Frog Creek: 71
Frontenac: 123
Fruitland: 47
Fulda: 181
Fuller Springs: 17
Fulton: 38, 281, 343
Funston, Frederick: 414
Furley: 454

Galatia: 227
Galena: 76, 281
Galesburg: 280, 282
Galileo: 221
Galt: 189
Galva: 187, 280
Game Creek: 66
Garden City: 39

Garden City, Gulf and Northern: 447
Garden of Eden: 38, 223
Garden Valley: 38
Gardner: 357
Garfield: 65, 211, 273, 330, 358, 375
Garland: 486
Garrison: 457
Gas City: 80
Gass, Patrick: 105
Gazette: 370
Geary: 54, 325, 327, 342
Geddesburg: 168
Gem: 74
Genesee: 259
Geneseo: 284
Geneva: 132, 259, 265
Geographical Center: 376
Georgia: 306
Gerlane: 488
Germania: 176
Germans: 172
Germantown: 176
Gettysburg: 288, 410
Geuda Springs: 15, 78
Gideon: 233
Giles, Frye W.: 118
Giles City: 467
Gilfillan: 157
Gillespie: 447
Girard: 120, 269, 327
Girls Creek: 475
Glacier Uplands: 32
Glade: 452
Gladstone: 148, 363
Glasco (Glasgow): 155
Glen: 156
Glen Burn: 155
Glendale: 34, 156
Glen Elder: 55, 156
Glen Grouse: 61, 156
Glenloch: 155
Glenwood: 17, 156
Glick: 222, 330
Globe: 9, 352
Gnadenau: 173
Gnadenfeld: 173
Gnoton: 138
Goddard: 444
Godfrey County: 317, 343
Goessel: 174
Goff: 455
Gognac: 131
Golden Belt: 64, 87
Golden Gate: 298

Goldenrod: 41
Good Intent: 480
Goodland: 279, 293, 385
Goodnow, Isaac: 59
Good Will: 481
Goose Creek: 62
Gopher: 71
Gordon: 442
Goshen: 225, 232
Goss and Glenn: 489
Gotland: 186
Gould, Jay: 457
Gourock: 135
Gove: 401, 403
Government Siding: 373
Graff: 137
Graham, John L.: 400
Grainfield: 87
Granada: 95
Grand Prairie: 36, 130
Grand River: 112
Grand Saline: 77
Grand Summit: 25
Granite Bluff: 27
Granite Falls: 18
Grant, Ulysses Simpson: 281, 330, 349, 382-86
Grant County: 330, 377
Grass: 36
Grasshopper: 18, 59, 265
Gray County: 319, 337, 445
Great American Desert: 423
Great Bend: 22, 91
Great Spirit Spring: 14
Greek: 7, 26, 204ff.
Greeley, Horace: 8, 44, 52, 67, 70, 79, 325, 363, 378, 419
Greeley Center: 212
Green, Nehemiah: 328
Greene, Max: 24, 27
Green Elm: 43, 46
Green Garden: 38, 87, 466
Greenleaf: 45, 455
Greensburg: 451
Green Valley: 38
Greenwich: 9, 141
Greenwood County: 317, 322
Greiffenatein, William: 33, 433
Gretna: 161
Gridley: 165, 257
Griffin: 205
Grinnell: 14, 117, 364, 420

Groomer: 372
Gross Cote: 33
Groton: 138
Grouse Creek: 61
Grove: 48
Gruenfeld: 173
Guadalquivir: 91, 433
Guelph: 215
Guess, George (Sequoah): 429
Guilford: 301, 410
Guitard: 123
Guthrie, Nancy: 426
Guthrie Mountain: 25
Guy: 141
Guzzler's Gulch: 483
Gyp Hills: 77
Gypsum: 22, 77

Hackberry Creek: 48
Hackberry Mills: 53
Hackney: 481
Haddam: 257, 339
Hagaman's Town: 482
Hail Ridge: 11
Halcyone: 205, 207
Hale, Edward Everett: 46, 106
Half Moon: 452
Half Mound: 30
Halford: 455
Halifax: 144
Hallowell: 339
Halstead: 363, 365
Hamburg: 178
Hamilton, Alexander: 352, 435
Hamlin: 330, 344
Hammond: 458
Hancock: 417
Hanover: 177
Hanston: 149
Haphazard: 479
Happy: 482
Hard-Crossing Creek: 76, 412
Hardesty: 14
Harding: 458
Hardpan: 85
Hardscrabble: 88, 147, 409, 487
Harlan: 336
Harley, David: 19
Harmonia: 205
Harmony: 482
Harper: 397, 404

Harrison: 360
Harry, "Horned Toad": 19
Hartford: 138, 257
Harvey County: 124, 328
Harveyville: 245, 328
Harwoodville: 17
Haskell, Dudley C.: 430
Haun Creek: 247
Havana: 96, 282
Haven: 257
Havens: 459
Haverhill: 138, 250, 254
Haviland: 245, 474
Hawk: 63
Hawkeye: 291
Hawkswing: 63
Hawley: 337
Hawthorne: 370
Hay: 38, 277
Hayes: 358, 385
Haytown: 331
Hazelton: 247
Hazelwood: 55
Healy: 460
Hebron: 228, 232
Hecla: 189
Hector: 205, 210, 212, 365
Heisler: 474
Helen: 210
Helianthus: 39
Hell: 235
Hell's Bend: 235, 374
Hell's Half Acre: 235
Helmick: 247
Helvetia: 132
Henderson, Cash: 88
Henning: 413
Henryville: 83
Herkimer: 177, 181, 259
Herington: 453
Herndon: 194, 344, 388
Hertha: 189
Herzog: 147, 174
Hesper: 207
Hesperia: 208
Hesperus: 167
Hess: 173, 471
Hesston: 174
Hewins: 102, 338
Hiawatha: 36, 292, 436
Hibbard: 444
Hibernia: 167
Hickory Creek: 43; Grove, 52; Point, 8, 37
Highhill: 24
Highland: 24, 32, 280

High Plains: 22, 34
Highpoint: 25
High Prairie: 37
Hill City: 26, 202
Hill Gove: 65
Hillsboro: 26
Hillsdale: 27, 34
Hillside: 27, 85
Hilltop: 25
Hodgeman: 401, 420
Hodgson's Hill: 26
Hoffman's Mill: 87
Hofnungsau: 173
Hofnungsfeld: 173
Hoganville: 239
Hog Back Point: 25
Hog Creek: 84
Hoisington: 338, 382
Holcomb: 442
Holland: 182, 285
Hollenberg: 57, 177
Holliday, Cyrus K.: 118, 250, 440
Hollis: 10
Hollyrood: 156
Holton: 288
Holy Cross: 238
Holyoke: 170, 254
Home: 5, 85
Home on the Range: 72
Homer: 210, 259, 370
Homestead: 84
Homewood: 44
Honek: 178
Honey Creek: 59
Hooker: 329
Hope: 128, 285, 480
Hopefield: 480
Hopper: 456
Horace: 212, 364
Horeb: 226
Horse Creek: 67, 82
Horton: 336
Hot Hill: 11
Hourglass: 9
Howard: 202, 343, 389, 392
Howe: 175
Howell: 446
Howes, Cecil: 8
Hoxie: 460
Hoyt: 328
Hudson: 154, 287
Hufbauer: 100
Hugoton: 127
Hull: 144
Hullco Spur: 463

Humboldt: 180
Hundred Head Canyon: 83
Hungry Hollow: 482
Hunnewell: 441
Hunter County: 300, 308, 315
Hunt's Station: 445
Huron: 273, 275, 427
Hurricane Hill: 11
Hurst: 303
Hutchinson: 246, 256
Hutchinson-Medicine Lodge Trail: 335
Hyacinth: 176, 205
Hygienic: 484

Ianthe: 205, 210
Iatan: 431
Idana: 473
Igo: 101, 242
Illinois: 280
Independence: 292, 371
India: 199
Indiana: 278
Indianapolis: 279
Indian Guide Hill: 32
Indian Hills: 32
Indian Mission, Irvin's: 32
Indian Mound: 33, 120
Indianola: 307
Indian removal: 3
Industry: 88
Ingalls, John J.: 21, 36, 333, 347, 374
Inman, Henry: 20, 29, 84, 122, 232, 421
Ino: 205
Insley (fort): 414
Invermay: 156
Inyo: 296
Iola: 469
Iona: 205
Ionia: 210
Iowa: 63, 290, 436
Ireland: 167
Irish Valley: 168
Iron Buttes: 23
Iron Mound: 30
Irving, Washington: 89, 95, 120, 134, 204, 214, 351, 369
Isabel: 471
Island City: 381
Isle au Vache: 412
Italia: 215
Itasca: 279, 293, 385

Iuka: 305, 404, 410
Iva: 223
Ivanhoe: 160
Ivy: 42

Jackson, Andrew: 355
Jacob's Mound: 28
Jamestown: 455
Janesville: 451
Jaramillo, Juan: 91, 93
Jarbolo: 102, 235
Jarvis Creek: 47, 101, 487
Jasper: 11
Jay Hawk: 96
Jayhawkers: 377
Jefferson (Cimarron River): 92
Jefferson, Thomas: 300, 308, 353, 371
Jelinek, George: 80
Jenkins' Ferry, Battle of: 403
Jericho: 229
Jersey Creek: 266
Jerusalem: 228
Jetmore: 401, 420, 445
Jewell, Lewis R.: 397
Jewell City: 406
Jingo: 409
Joe Field's Snake Prairie: 71
John Brown Spring: 17
John Brown's Mound: 28
Johnny Cake (Delaware Indian): 53
Johnson, Thomas: 424, 446
Johnson County: 308, 311
Joliet: 104
Jones, "Buffalo": 39, 64
Jones' Spring: 13
Joppa: 229
Jordan Springs: 230
Journalists: 363ff.
Joy: 482
Joy, James F.: 447, 460
Juanita: 478
Jumbo Spring: 13
Junction: 463
Juniata: 260, 267, 436
Juniper Bottoms: 203

Kalamazoo: 286
Kalida: 143, 208, 273
Kalloch: 246
Kalula: 415
Kalvesta: 208

Kanado: 487
Kanopolis Dam: 213
Kanorado: 40, 487
Kansa Indians: 424
Kansas, naming: 31, 105;
  topography, 20
Kansas Centre: 374
Kansas City, Kansas: 213,
  418, 426
Kansas City, Missouri: 119
Kansas County: 423
Kansas Falls: 18
Kansas-Nebraska Bill: 344,
  346, 378, 451
Kansas River: 22
Kansasopolis: 213
Kansopolis: 139
Kanwaka: 487
Kapioma (Kickapoo
  chief): 434
Kara: 421
Katherinenstadt (Russia):
  174
Kaw, Quans, Caw, and
  Cah: 24, 105
Kearny County: 330, 377,
  391, 392
Keats (Wild Cat): 69
Keats, John: 97
Kechai: 433
Keighley: 138
Kelley, Daniel E.: 72
Kelley, Mrs. R. M.
  Zamora: 95
Kelly: 459
Kelso: 161, 192, 461, 472
Kendall: 95, 122
Kenilworth: 158
Kennebec: 258
Kennekuk (Kickapoo
  chief): 434
Kensington: 136, 156
Kent: 143
Kentucky: 303
Keokuk (Sauk and Fox
  chief): 435
Kerwin Dam: 452
Keystone: 139, 270
Key West: 298, 306
Kickapoo: 16, 124, 434
Kitkehakis (Pawnees): 116
Kill Creek: 8, 409
Kimball: 457
Kincaid: 461
Kinderhook: 355
Kingman, Samuel A.: 335

Kingsdown: 145
Kinsely: 443
Kiowa County: 430, 432
Kipling, Rudyard: 441
Kipp: 209
Kirikquis (Wichitas): 91
Kismet: 199
Kit Carson Oak: 45
Kitley: 135
Klaine: 394, 400
Klink: 182
Kong: 201
Kosciusko: 195
Kossuth, Louis: 194
Kuka: 201
K.X. Siding: 463

La Bette: 104, 120, 369
Lac La Biche (Itasca): 293
La Clede: 119, 304
Laconia: 214
La Crosse: 387
La Cygne: 7, 61
Ladder Creek: 477
Ladonia: 159
Ladore: 142, 370, 461
La Fayette, Marquis de:
  127, 259
La Fontaine: 128
La Grange: 123
La Harpe, Bernard de: 105
Lais, Louis: 125
Lake City: 20, 370
Lake Farland: 20
Lakeview: 20
Lake Waconda: 14
Lakin: 446
La Loma Azul (Blue
  Hills): 24
Lamar: 360
Lamb, William: 124
La Mont's Hill: 264
Lanark: 152, 155
Lancaster: 139, 270
Lane: 52, 177, 331, 343, 349
Lane, Jacob B.: 11
Lane County: 332
Lanesfield: 444
La Ness: 487
Lane's Trail: 331, 367
Langham, Angus L.: 118
Lansing: 121, 286
La Paz: 98
Lapland: 190
Laredo: 100
Larkin: 339

Larned: 417
La Salle: 123
Las Animas, El Rio de: 131
Lasita: 486
Latham: 458
Latin: 7
Latitia: 474
La Touche de La Côte
  Bucanieus: 106
Latter Day Saints: 46
Laura: 360, 469
Laurel: 55
Lava: 75
Lawrence: 253
Lawton, Henry W.: 42
Leavenworth County: 6,
  322, 377
Leawood: 340
Lebanon: 50, 225, 304
Le Bête, Pierre: 120
Lebo, Joe: 422
Lee, Robert E.: 100
Lecompton: 62, 334
Leeds: 142, 144
Le Grande (Neosho): 113
Lehigh: 267
Lelande, Baptiste: 122
Lena: 283
Lenape: 265
Lenexa: 425, 478
Lenora: 472
Leon: 57, 292, 480
Leona: 470
Leonardville: 458, 483
Leota: 61, 470
Leoti: 61, 85, 460
Leoville: 241
Lerado: 100
LeRoy: 151, 283
LeRoy, John Baptiste: 130
Levant: 225
Level Creek: 19
Lewelling, Lorenzo: 163
Lewis: 370
Lewis and Clark: 67, 71,
  105, 107, 119, 121, 290,
  371, 475
Lewis and King Map: 111
Lexington: 6, 252
Liberal: 372
Liberty: 371
Lickskillet: 327
Liebenthal: 34, 175
Light: 9
Lightning Creek: 11
Lily: 41

Lima: 98, 280
Limestone Creek: 79
Limestone Pastures (Flint Hills): 23
Lincoln: 324, 341, 387
Lincoln, Abraham: 7, 32, 45, 341, 388, 415
Lincoln-Douglas Debates: 345
Lincoln Memorial Elm, Kansas: 45
Lindsay, Dr. Thomas: 16
Lindsborg: 188
Linn County: 26, 304, 309, 312, 322
Linwood: 54
Lippard: 175
Lisbon: 102
Litchfield: 281
Little Arkansas: 108
Little Bear: 29, 33
Little Coon Creek: 69
Little Dutch: 26, 209
Little John Creek: 13
Little Oak: 50
Little Santa Fe: 102
Little Town: 262
Little Walnut (Dry Walnut): 56
Liverpool: 144
Locknane: 436
Loco: 101, 490
Locust Grove: 35, 47
Lodi: 125, 128, 217
Lodore: 142
Logan, John Alexander: 49, 381, 387
Logan County: 330
London: 135, 252
Lone Elm: 43, 45
Lone Hill: 24
Lone Rock: 32
Lone Star: 10, 306
Lone Tree: 44, 48, 51, 177
Long, Stephen H.: 3, 21, 423
Longfellow, Henry Wadsworth: 104, 108, 112, 251, 294
Longford: 168
Longton: 143
Lookout Mountain: 25
Loretta: 175
Loring: 455
Lorraine: 129, 467
Lost River (Cimarron): 93

Lost Springs: 14
Louis XIV: 125
Louisa Springs: 14
Louisburg: 125, 304
Louisiana: 8, 125
Louisville: 32, 131
Loup: 67, 104, 107
Love: 481
Lovejoy, Julia: 13
Lovewell: 453
Lowe: Percival and Thaddeus, 421
Loyal: 41
Lucas: 38, 305
Lucerne: 87, 132
Luctor: 182
Ludell: 161, 192, 472
Lum, Rev. Samuel Y.: 118, 254
Lund: 188
Luray: 473
Luther: 245
Luzerne: 132
Lykens County: 311
Lynden: 257, 471
Lyon, Nathaniel: 324, 327, 344, 394, 399

McCallaster: 373
McCamish: 332, 445
McCoy, Isaac: 59, 112, 120
McCracken: 171, 460
McCune: 9, 171, 447
McFarland: 171, 336
McGee County: 171, 308, 311, 316, 429
MacKay, Aeneas: 413
McKinley Lake: 20
McKinney Lake: 20
McLaren, "Uncle Dan": 69
McLouth: 171
Madison: 315, 354, 375
Madura: 199
Magna City: 80
Magnesia Mound: 411
Mahaska: 291, 436
Mair's Springs: 15
Maize: 86
Mallet Brothers (Pierre and Paul): 109, 117
Malvern Hill: 166, 392
Manchester: 139
Manhattan: 24, 59, 260
Manila: 200
Mankato: 293, 375, 398
Mann, Marietta: 126

Mansard Buttes: 30
Mansfield: 277
Manter: 447
Mantua: 217
Maple: City, Grove, and Creek, 54; Hill, 27
Mapleton: 54
Marais des Cygnes: 4, 41, 61, 112, 164
Marak: 193
Marble Falls: 18
Marcou, Stephen G.: 124
Marena: 149
Marengo: 128, 130
Margaretta: 469
Mariadahl: 186, 466
Marienburg: 174
Marienthal: 176, 466
Marietta: 126
Marion: 9, 277, 308, 352, 367, 397
Mariposa: 41, 59, 100, 296
Marmiton: 104, 114
Marquette: 104, 107, 123, 286
Marshall: 304, 309, 311, 322, 441
Martin, George: 91
Martin Creek: 124
Martinsburgh: 444
Marymount (college): 24
Marysville: 467
Marvin: 452
Mashema (Kickapoo chief): 434
Mason: 216
Massillon: 125
Matanzas: 96
Matfield Green: 138
Mathew Sutter: 107
Mathews: 115
Mathewson, "Buffalo Bill": 46, 64, 460
Matoon: 282
May Day: 325, 486
Mayfield: 462
Mayo: 168
Mead, James R.: 39, 64, 67, 70, 433, 443
Meade County: 377, 390
Mecca: 276
Medary, Samuel: 323, 336, 464
Media: 198
Medina: 197, 276

Medicine Lodge: 366, 430, 432
Medora: 475
Medway: 264
Melrose: 160
Melvern: 166
Memphis: 200, 302, 486
Mencken, H. L.: 8
Mendota: 274, 384
Menno, Simon: 171
Menoken: 435
Mentor: 211, 275
Mercer, David W.: 138
Mercier: 177
Meriden: 256
Merriam: 448
Merrick: 444
Merrill Springs: 15
Merrimac: 255
Metz: 129
Mexico: 6, 89
Miami: 428
Michigan: 285
Mid-Continent (Topeka): 118
Midian: 198
Midlothian: 152, 159
Milan: 215, 218, 273
Milberger: 176
Mildred: 472
Milford: 7, 78
Military: 6, 377, 397; City, 409; Road, 32
Militia Hill: 409
Mill Creek: 78
Miller, Sol: 60
Millerton: 39
Milo: 86, 205
Milwaukee: 287
Mine á Breton: 99
Mine Creek, Battle of: 76, 418
Mineral: 47, 75
Mineral Point: 75, 458
Minersview: 76
Minersville: 75
Minerva: 221
Mingo: 430
Minneapolis: 293
Minneha: 293
Minnehaha: 292
Minneola: 463
Miocene: 12
Mirage: 485
Mississippi: 91
Mississippi Town: 203

Missouri: 107, 304; City, 242; Flat, 33
Missouri River: 92
Mitchell, William D.: 401
Mizpah: 232
Modena: 218
Modoc: 296
Mole Hill: 71
Moline: 282
Monecato: 115
Money Creek: 88
Monica: 204
Monitor: 486
Monjour: 176
Monmouth: 141, 259, 281
Monmouth, Geoffrey: 164
Monotony: 7, 463
Monrovia: 354
Montana: 294
Monte Casino: 232, 242
Monterey: 100, 296
Montezuma: 94, 411
Montgomery, James: 166
Montgomery, Richard: 167, 381
Montgomery City: 371
Montrose: 159
Monument: 31, 463
Moody Springs (Moody-ville): 17
Moonlight: 418
Moore, A. A.: 140
Moore, Ely, Jr.: 62
Moorehead: 449
Moore's Ranch (Marion): 140, 278
Moore's Summit: 25
Moorestown: 282
Moose Hill: 72
Moran: 171, 457
Moray: 152, 154
Morehead: 443
Morgan, Lewis H.: 117
Mormon Grove: 46
Morrill, Edmund N.: 330
Morris: 84, 444
Morris County: 336
Morrow: 339
Morse and Gaston Map: 92
Morton: 202, 279, 297, 350
Moscow: 99, 195
Mosquito Creek: 59
Mound: City, 27; Creek, 28; Hill, 34; Springs, 31; Valley, 28
Moundridge: 28

Mount Auburn: 264
Mount Ayr: 153
Mount Gilead: 22, 24, 231, 278, 364
Mount Helen: 472
Mount Hope: 22, 480
Mount Horeb: 24
Mount Ida: 211, 213, 472
Mount Jesus: 232
Mount Nebo: 231
Mount Oread: 24, 253
Mount Padilla: 94
Mount Pisgah: 231
Mount Pleasant: 35, 47
Mount Roy: 130
Mount Scholastica: 24
Mount Sinai: 231
Mount Sunflower: 40
Mount Tabor: 231
Mount Tamalpais: 43
Mount Vernon: 22, 352
Mount Zion: 25
Mouse Creek: 71
Mudge, Benjamin Franklin: 12
Mud Springs: 16
Mulberry: 47
Mule Creek: 82
Mullins (Terra Cotta): 79
Mullinville: 337
Mulvane: 442
Munden: 177
Munger: 433
Murat: 365
Murdock, Marsh: 108, 369, 433, 441, 443
Murdock, Thomas Benton: 369
Muscotah: 4, 37, 434
Musser's Bottoms: 33
Mustang Creek: 82
Mystic: 486

Naniompa: 262
Napawalla: 137
Napestle (Arkansas River): 92, 108
Napoleon: 128
Narka: 466
Narrows: 23
Nashville: 303
Nathan: 241
Natrona: 205
Navarre: 126
Naw Bone: 138, 250
Neal: 460

Necodemus: 26
Neighborville: 482
Nekoma: 436
Nemaha County: 320, 423
Ne Miskua (Grand
 Saline): 77
Nemo: 232
Neodesha: 435–36
Neosho: 18, 113, 282, 470
Neosho County: 423
Nepaholla (Solomon
 River): 109
Nescatunga (Little Red
 River): 111
Ness County: 397, 407
Nesuketong (Cimarron
 River): 92
Netawaka: 428
Netherland: 182
Nettleton: 444
Neuchatel: 132
Neutral City: 422
Neva: 196, 372
Nevada: 298
Ne Wakonda: 40, 109
New Albany: 152, 279
Newark: 266
New Basel: 132
New Bedford: 138, 250
New Boston: 253, 260
New Brighton: 143
New Buffalo: 65
Newbury: 149
New Cambria: 164
New Cincinnati: 221, 260
New Chicago: 261
New Elam: 182
Newell's Mill: 291
New England: 249
New Gottland: 186
New Haven: 257
New Lancaster: 259
New London: 136
New Memphis: 10, 34
New-Obermunjour: 176
New-Port: 124
New Post: 413
New Salem: 283
New Scandinavia: 185
New Schwanau: 133
Newton: 250
New Town: 418
New Windsor: 136
New York *Tribune*: 363
Niagara: 259, 261
Nicodemus: 201

Nickel: 88
Nickerson: 440
Niger: 91
Niles, Hezekiah: 366
Nimrod: 233
Ninnescah: 110
Niota: 489
Niotaze: 489
Nirvana: 200
Nish-co-ba (Deep Water):
 422
Niter: 80
Niutachi (Missouri River):
 107
Noble: 480
Nolan: 168, 463
Nonchalanta: 7
Nonpareil: 481
Norcatur: 487
Norfolk: 140
North, Frank: 117
North Branch: 245
North Cedar: 51, 275
Northern Mystery: 91
North Pole Mound: 23, 30
Norton County: 405
Nortonville: 446
Norway: 190
Norwegian Ford: 190
Norwich: 140
Norwood: 244
Nottingham: 144
Nova Albion (California):
 135
Novelty: 480

Oak: 27, 50, 155
Oakland: 50
Oakley: 161, 466
Oasis: 12
Oatville: 87
Oberg: 188
Oberlin: 277
Obermonjour: 175
Ocena: 206
Ocheltree: 368
O'Connel Air Force Base:
 170
Octagon City: 483
Odell: 169
Odense: 189
Odessa: 196, 210
Odin: 7, 189, 280, 282
Offerle: 125
Og: 234
Ogden: 268, 380, 404

Ogdensburgh: 420
Ogeese Creek: 114
Oglala: 436
Ohio: 273
Oil: 80
Oketo: 436
Oklahoma: 56
Olathe: 4, 425
Old English: 7
Old Ireland: 251
Old Maid's Fork: 476
Old Ulysses: 384
O'Laughlin, John: 52
Ole: 187
Olive Branch: 422
Olivet: 229
Olmitz: 193
Olney: 149
Olpe: 178
Olsburgh: 187
Olympia: 205
Omaha: 290
Omio: 200
Onaga: 427
One Hundred and Forty-
 two Mile Creek: 19
One Hundred and Ten
 Mile Creek: 19
Oneida: 259, 284, 472
One Mile Creek: 19
Oneonta: 262
Onion Creek: 42
Onondaga: 259, 261
Ontario: 427
Ophir: 98, 230
Opolis: 213
Orbitello: 60
Orchard: 47
Oread: 253, 327
Oregon: 295; Trail, 8, 121
Orinoco: 97
Oriole: 63
Orion: 207
Oro: 74, 98, 230, 406
Oronoque: 97
Osage: 4, 22, 107, 281;
 City, 112; County, 423;
 Cuestas, 22; Mission, 123,
 239; Plains, 22; Rock, 33;
 Trail, 433
Osage Indians: 111
Osawatomie: 487
Osawatomie Brown: 17
Osborne: 397, 404
Oscar: 188
Oskaloosa: 291, 436

Osma: 208
Osopolis: 213
Oswego: 259, 262
Otis: 284
Otoe: 423, 436
Otsego: 259, 261
Ottawa: 428
Otter Creek: 64, 69
Ottumwa: 291, 436
Outlaw's Corral: 154
Overbrook: 269
Overland Park: 449
Overland Trail: 449
Over Muncha: 176
Ovo: 60
Owl: 63, 101
Oxford: 135, 137
Ox Hide: 84
Ozark: 22, 108
Ozawkie: 434

Pacific City: 97
Padilla, Fray Juan de: 94
Padouca: 106, 431
Page City: 187, 291
Pa-ha-bee (Bluff Creek): 27
Pahuska (Osage chief): 112
Paint Creek: 29
Painted Rock: 37
Pakitanoui: 107
Papaya: 55
Palacky: 193
Palco: 452, 487
Palo Alto: 99, 382
Palmetto: 301
Palmyra: 8, 37, 197, 204, 247
Pani Pique: 433
Pansy: 41, 480
Panther Creek: 64
Paola: 429
Paradise: 63, 223, 235
Parallel Trail: 10
Pardee: 206, 246
Pardonnet, George: 124
Paris: 6, 119, 126, 210, 304
Park City: 9, 45
Parks Fort: 454
Parkville: 260
Parma: 218
Parnell: 421
Parsons: 461
Pashqua: 427
Passaic: 266
Pattonville: 480

Pauline: 463
Pawnee: 414; Indians, 116; Flats, 33; County, 423; Rock, 4, 31
Paw Paw: 55
Peabody: 174, 441
Peace: 422
Peach Creek: and Grove, 47
Pearl: 471
Peas Creek: 87
Peck: 445
Penalosa: 94
Pendennis: 144, 370
Penfield: 207
Pennsylvania Dutch: 182
Penokee: 288, 410
Penquite: 467
Penseneau, Paschal: 121
Pensineau Springs: 121
Peoria: 429
Perings Spur: 463
Perry: 454
Perryville: 197
Pershing, John J.: 422
Perth: 152, 159
Peru: 98, 280
Pesth: 193, 344
Peters: 49; City, 443; Creek, 63
Petersburg: 121
Petersburgh: 443
Petrea: 197
Petrolia: 80
Pfeifer: 175
Philadelphia: 108, 269
Phillips, William A.: 110, 363
Phillipsburg: 322, 366
Phillips County: 321
Pickwick: 142, 370
Piedmont: 130
Pierce: 447, 463
Pig Creek: 84
Pike, Zebulon M.: 3, 21, 23, 36, 63, 72, 75, 101, 106, 122, 135, 412, 423
Pilot Grove: 46
Pilot Knob: 32
Pilson: 192
Pine: 48, 54
Pinnacle: 31
Pinon: 48
Pioneer: 72, 84
Piper: 459
Piqua: 273, 424

Pisgalis Heights: 232
Pittsburg: 267
Pittsburgh: 268
Pixley, Rev. Benton: 113
Plain: 33
Plainville: 34
Plato: 214
Pleasant: 454, 484; Dale, 35; Green, 39; Grove, 48; Hill, Plain, Ridge, Run, Spring, Valley, View, 35
Pleasanton: 99, 418
Plevna: 193
Pliny: 77, 227
Plow Boy: 85
Plum: 46, 48, 52, 334
Plum Creek Flats: 33, 46, 466
Plymouth: 252
Plympton: 252
Podunk: 490
Poe: 447
Point Rocks: 31
Poland: 194
Pole Cat Creek: 54, 68
Poleska: 195
Poliska: 260
Pomeroy, Samuel C.: 310, 331
Pomme de Terre: 16, 117
Pomona: 47, 222
Pond Creek Station: 388
Pontiac: 428
Pony Creek: 82
Popcorn Creek: 86
Pope: 418
Poplar Hill: 27, 57
Porcupine Creek: 69
Portis: 460
Portugal: 102
Possum Hollow: 69
Post: 5
Post Office Oak: 45
Potato Mound: 28
Potosí: 26, 98
Potawatomi: 427
Pottawatomie: 17, 28, 427
Potter: 35, 365
Poverty Ridge: 80, 88
Powhattan: 436
Prairie: 8, 31, 35–37, 463
Prairie Chicken Creek: 61
Prairie Dog Creek: 69
Prairie du Chien: 131, 288
Prairie Quadrangle: 81
Prag: 192, 472

Prather's Creek: 68
Pratt: 395, 404
Pratt, J. Fenton: 145
Prattsburg: 404
Prescott: 458
Prescott, William H.: 89, 98
Pretty Prairie: 4, 37
Pride: 7, 481
Princeton: 274, 283
Prisoner of Zenda: 140
Proof: 485
Prospect: 88, 456
Prosper: 38, 88
Protection: 409, 486
Providence: 255
Provo: 294
Pumpkin Creek: 34
Punished Woman's Creek: 70, 477
Punkin Center: 489
Purcell: 443
Purity: 481
Pursely: 122, 168
Putnam: 440

Quaker: 245, 463
Quality Hill: 404
Quarantine Trail: 154
Quarry: 18
Quartelejo, El: 94
Quenemo: 435
Quindaro: 327, 426, 478
Quinter: 246
Quito: 99
Quivira: 64, 90, 93, 123, 433

Rabbit Creek: 71
Rackensack: 108
Radical City: 372
Radium: 79
Radley: 76
Raemer's Creek: 181
Rainbelt: 11
Rainbow: 12
Raleigh, Sir Walter: 97
Ramona: 370, 436
Randall: 410
Rand McNally Map: 365
Randolph: 263
Range: 84
Ransom: 420
Rantoul: 255, 356
Rapture: 481
Rattlebone Flats: 203

Rattlesnake: 71
Ravanna: 216, 277
Ravenna: 216, 273, 277
Rawlins: 377, 389
Raymond: 441
Reading: 270
Red Bluff: 27, 416
Red Bud: 56
Red Clover: 87
Redford: 288
Red Fork: 22, 92, 111
Red Hills: 22
Red Jaw Valley: 181
Redmondsville: 203
Redoubt: 416
Redpath: 85, 363, 367
Redwing: 60
Redwood: 55
Reece: 148
Reeder, Andrew H.: 116, 323, 326, 346
Reid, Whitelaw: 365
Remington, Frederic: 46, 79
Reno County: 381, 391
Republican County: 372, 423
Republican River: 104, 116
Rest: 88
Rex: 283
Rexford: 288
Rhine: 177
Rice County: 381, 391
Rich: 88
Richardson, Albert: 41, 67, 106
Richardson County: 308, 311, 317, 322
Richfield: 86, 297
Richland: 86
Richmond: 453
Richter: 452
Riga: 195
Ritchie: 372
Riley: 171, 380
Riley County: 6, 300, 377
Rio de S. Francisco (Arkansas River): 92
Rio Grande del Norte: 91
Rising Sun: 10
Rivière de la Fleche (Saline): 100
Roanoke: 302
Robber's Cave: 154
Robber's Roost: 31
Robidoux: 112, 123

Robinson, Charles: 7, 327, 414, 426
Robrodal, El Rio del: 92
Rochester: 139
Rock-a-By: 479
Rock: Creek and Point, 31; City, 32; Springs, 16
Rockford: 282
Rockwell City: 487
Rocky Ford: 32, 411
Rocky Hill: 27
Rogler Creek: 86
Rolla: 305
Rolling Green: 39, 135
Rolling Prairie: 37
Romance: 481
Rome: 205, 215, 218, 417
Rooks County: 6, 397, 408
Roosevelt, Theodore: 361
Roper: 457
Rosalia: 467
Roscoe: 361
Rose: 40; Bank, 40; Hill, 40, 282; Vale, 40
Rose Bud Creek: 40
Rosedale: 40
Roseland: 40
Rosemont: 40
Rosenfeld: 173
Rosenort: 173
Roseport: 40
R. O. Siding: 463
Ross, Edmund G.: 109, 349, 368
Ross, John: 29
Rossville: 368
Rotterdam: 182
Round Grove: 456
Round: House, Mound, Top, 30; Prairie, 37
Round Tree Grove: 45
Roundup: 84
Roxburgh: 152
Roxbury: 158, 161
Rozel: 467
Runnymede: 145–47, 191
Rural: 85
Rural Free Delivery: 8
Rural Springs: 71
Rush Bottom: 33, 89
Rush Center: 56
Rush County: 402
Russell: 12, 395, 399
Russell, Charles: 66
Rutland: 302
Ryan: 171, 454

Ryanville: 398
Rydal: 142

Sabetha: 232
Sac (Sauk): 434
Saffordville: 336
Saint Benedict: 242
Saint Bernard: 242
Saint Bridgit: 240
Saint Clere: 240
Saint Cloud: 241
Saint Fidelis: 175
Saint Francis: 239, 468
Saint George: 241
Saint Helena: 128
Saint Jacob's Well: 241
Saint Jerome: 92
Saint Joe: 240
Saint John: 388
Saint Julian: 240
Saint Leo: 240
Saint Louis: 125, 128, 241, 304
Saint Mark: 181, 240
Saint Marys: 240
Saint Nick: 238
Saint Patrick: 168
Saint Paul: 239, 429
Saint Peter: 239
Saint Philibert's Day: 55
Saint Sophia: 240
Saint Theresa: 240
St. John, John P.: 329
Salamanca: 95
Salem: 228
Salina: 77
Saline River: 92, 104, 109
Salisbury: 146
Salmon (Solomon): 109
Salt: 15, 77, 111
Salurian: 12
Samaria: 226
Samson: 234
Sand Creek: 31, 75
Sand Ford (Derby): 100
Sand River (Smoky Hill): 106
Sandago: 101
San Francisco, Rio Grande de: 92
San Luis Potosí: 98
San Pedro y San Pablo (Arkansas River): 238
Santa Fe: 4, 6, 102, 298, 439
Santa Fe Ridge: 30
Santa Fe Trail: 8, 13, 19, 31, 45, 57, 61, 65, 67, 74, 82, 89, 92, 102, 122, 351, 412, 421, 439
Satanta (Kiowa chief): 102, 432
Sappa: 115, 277, 436, 483
Sarcoxie: 425
Saratoga: 259, 262, 404
Sargent: 440
Satank (Kiowa chief): 432
Sauce: 483
Sauk: 434
Saurian Creek: 12
Savannah: 300
Savonburg: 188
Sawlog: 53, 78
Saw Mill: 48
Sawyer: 441
Saxe-Coburg: 136, 174
Say, Thomas: 115
Scammon: 76
Scandia: 185
Scandinavia: 185
Schoenchen: 175
Schoharie: 263, 407
Schoolcraft, Henry M.: 108, 293
Schulte: 176
Schwanau: 133
Scipio: 220, 279
Scotch Flats: 152
Scotland: 151, 157
Scott, John B.: 151
Scott, Sir Walter: 157, 270, 391
Scott, Winfield: 100, 329, 377–80
Scottsville: 151
Scranton: 267–69
Sears: 446
Secondine: 266
Section: 85
Security: 486
Sedan: 129
Sedgwick: 381, 392–94, 433
Sego: 41
Seguin: 307
Selkirk: 152, 161, 259
Selzer Springs: 15
Seneca: 32, 220, 259, 273, 275
Sequoyah: 330, 423, 430, 437
Seth: 225
Seven Cities of Cibola: 95
Seven Mile Creek: 19
Seven Springs: 15
Seventy-Six: 371
Severance: 454
Severy: 442, 457
Seward: 343
Shady Bend: 58
Shallow River: 106
Shallow Water: 18
Shannon: 171, 323, 393
Sharon: 226
Sharon Springs: 63
Shawnee: 308, 320, 423, 426
Shell Rock: 12, 18
Sherdahl: 191
Sheridan, Philip H.: 64, 377, 381, 384–86
Sherlock: 441
Sherman: 279, 335, 349, 377, 381, 384–87, 398
Shermanville: 177, 332, 386
Sherwin Junction: 463
Sherwood: 63
Shibboleth: 234
Shiloh: 6, 230, 305, 410
Shingawassa: 17
Shintown: 284
Shirley County: 398, 465
Shoo Fly: 129, 285, 436
Short Creek: 77
Shotgun Ridge: 154
Shunganunga: 33, 82
Sibley, George: 13, 45, 105, 412
Siding: 463
Silica: 27, 75
Silkville: 47, 124
Silver: Creek, 61, 445; Hill, 27; Lake, 20, 74
Silverdale: 74
Simancas: 89
Simmons, William R.: 62
Sinai: 226
Singleton: 202
Sing Sing: 265
Sitka: 298
Six Bulls: 113
Six Mile Creek: 13
Sixth Principal Meridian: 10
Skellyville: 80
Skelton: 145
Skiddy: 267, 461
Skidmore: 390
Skunk Creek: 67
Skull Creek: 98
Skull Springs: 17

Slabtown: 378
Slate Creek: 68, 77
Sleigh's Hill: 26
Slough Creek: 59
Smallwood: 338, 407
Smith, Captain John: 3, 55, 69, 436
Smith, Nathan: 399
Smith Center: 375
Smoky Hill: 12, 22, 106
Smoky Hill Buttes: 30, 94
Smoky Hills: 22
Smoky Hill Spring: 14
Smoky Hill Trail: 11, 417
Smolan: 186
Snake: 72
Snow: Creek and Hill, 11
Sodville: 79
Soldier: 409–11
Soldier Cap: 23, 30, 411
Solomon River: City and Rapids, 18, 109
Solvay: 160
Somerset: 266
Sonora: 99
Sorghum: 86
South Haven: 285
Soutrelle (grasshopper): 59
Southwick Glen: 39
Sparks: 32
Sparta: 205, 214
Spatterdock Creek: 41
Spearville: 443
Speed: 349
Spencer: 446
Spica: 86
Spivey: 441
Splitlog: 53, 78
Sprattsville: 179
Spring: 21; City, 472; Creek, 16; Hill, 76, 305; Lake, 11, 17; Place, 17; River, 16, 117; Valley, 17
Springdale: 34, 291
Springfield: 13, 17
Springvale: 16
Springville: 16
Spur: 462
Squatter City: 378
Stafford: 402
Stanley, Henry M.: 366
Stanton: 325, 357
Stanton, Edwin McMaster: 348
Star: 10
Stark: 281

Star Valley: 10, 34
State Line: 213, 440
Station Number 9: 11
Sterling: 422
Stevens County: 349
Stevenson, Robert Louis: 8, 295
Stilson: 76
Stilwell: 264, 452
Stockdale: 83
Stockholm: 187
Stockrange: 83
Stockton: 83, 375
Stolzenbach: 177
Stone: City, Corral, Mound, 32
Stony Hill: 27, 32
Stranger: 53
Stranger's Wife Creek: 478
Straw Hill River: 38
Stripville: 76
Strong, William Barstow: 58, 441
Studley: 144
Stuttgart: 178
Sublette: 102, 121
Success: 88
Sundial: 9
Sugar Bowl Mound: 29
Sugar Loaf: Mound, Valley, and Creek, 54
Sugarvale: 54
Sullivan: 168
Sulphur Springs: 15, 80
Summerfield: 459
Summit: 25, 209
Sumner, Charles: 346, 349, 360, 377
Sumner, Edwin V.: 413
Sumner City: 148
Sun: 10
Sunbeam: 10
Sunday: 10
Sunflower: 39
Sunland: 10
Sun Rise Heights: 404
Sunset: 10, 297
Sunshine: 10
Sunny Dale: 10
Sunnyside: 10
Sunny Slope: 10
Superior: 480
Surprise: 384
Survey: 10
Sycamore: 52

Sylvan Dale: 34, 48; Grove, 44, 48
Sylvia: 9, 444, 466
Syracuse: 205, 219, 259, 263
Syria: 198
Swan: 61
Swansea: 165
Sweadal: 186
Swede Center: 186; Creek, 186
Swedeland: 185
Switzler Creek: 19

Table Rock: 31
Tabor: 232
Taft, William Howard: 362
Table Mounds: 25
Tailholt: 487
Talleyrand: 127
Talmadge: 247, 453
Talmo: 489
Taloga: 31, 297, 489
Tampa: 306
Tank Farm Spur: 463
Taos: 298
Tapage (Pawnees): 116, 118; *see also* Topeka
Tasco: 99
Tatonka: 435
Tauromee: 260
Tea Pot Dome: 29
Tecumseh: 425, 440
Tel Aviv-Yafo: 229
Templin: 179
Ten-Mile: 90
Tennessee Town: 203
Tennis: 447
Terra Cotta: 79, 217
Terrapin: 71, 85
Tertiary: 12
Tescott: 7, 151, 488
Texas: 306
Thayer: 131, 288, 447
Thomas County: 377, 387
Thompson Creek: 19
Thresher Machine Canyon: 86
Thoreau, Henry David: 49
Thunderbolt Creek: 11
Tice: 445
Tickle Hill: 484
Tidy: 479
Tilden: 358, 384
Timber Hill: 44, 47, 179
Time: 9

Timken: 181
Tioga: 259, 448
Tippinville: 51
Tixier, Victor: 113
Toledo: 95, 273
Toluca: 99
Tonganoxie (Delaware chief): 425
Tong's Watermill: 292
Tonovay: 38
Tontzville: 240
Topeka: 117, 440
Topeka Trail: 480
Topsy: 244
Toronto: 427
Toulon: 128
Touzalin: 446
Towanda: 259
Townsdin's Point: 155
Townsend's Point: 482
Tractor: 85
Trading Post: 167, 418
Traer: 292
Tree of Heaven: 48
Trego: 400
Trent: 217
Trenton: 28, 259, 266
Tribune: 212, 364
Troublesome Creek: 487
Trousdale: 173
Troy: 205, 211, 213
Truesdale: 34
Trust: 481
Turkey Creek: Spring, Running, Standing, 61, 374
Turner: 85
Turin: 215
Turon: 217
Twin Buttes: 80
Twin Falls: 18
Twin Groves: 47
Twin Mounds: 24, 29
Twin Springs: 16
Two Mile Creek: 19
Tyro: 479
Tyrone: 168, 270, 365

Ukia: 263
Ulibarri (Uribarri), Juan de: 92
Ulysses: 102, 210, 252, 382, 384
Underwood: 148
Union: 373
United States Board of

Geographic Names: 105, 123, 269
Upland: 32
Uphill Creek: 19
Upola: 82
Urbana: 282
Ute: 294, 431
Utica: 201, 205, 219
Utopia: 7, 476, 481

Valeda: 222
Valencia: 95
Valhalla: 7, 189
Valley: 34; Center, 9; Falls, 18, 34, 60; Grove, 26
Valparaiso: 99
Van Buren, Martin: 355
Vashti: 446
Vassar: 264
Vera: 466
Verbena: 41
Vegetarian Creek: 113, 484
Verdi: 29, 221
Verdigris: 18, 104, 115, 371
Vermillion: 116, 123
Venice: 215, 218
Vernier: 455
Vernon: 453
Versailles: 126
Vesper: 232
Vesta: 222
Veteran: 411
Vial, Pedro: 24, 92
Valverde: 94
Vicker's Sod House: 402
Vicksburg: 410
Victoria: 147, 475
Victory: 409
Vidette: 411
Vienna: 179
Vieux, Louis: 121
Villisca: 133, 292
Vine Creek: 42
Vining: 456
Vinland: 191
Viola: 282
Violet: 41
Virgil: 205, 220, 259, 263
Viva: 103
Vliets: 335
Voda: 193
Volland: 191
Voltaire: 126, 279, 385
Von: 182
Vulture Creek: 63

Wabash: 279
Wabaunsee County: 285, 318
Wabaunsee (Potawatomi chief): 427
Wabun: 104
Waco: 84, 433
Waco Wego: 434
Wadsworth Mound: 28
Wagnerville: 474
Wagon Bed Springs: 13
Wagram: 128, 285
Wah Wah Suk: 427
Wakarusa: 8, 30, 253
Wakeeney: 7, 488
Wakefield: 50, 146
Wakon: 104
Waldeck: 178
Waldo: 454
Waldseemüller, Martin: 90
Wales: 163
Walla Walla: 294
Walker: 323, 325, 364, 419
Walker, "Big John": 73
Walkersburg: 466
Walker's Mound: 28
Wall Street: 88
Wallace: 6, 8, 388
Walnut: 48, 52, 56
Walnut City: 108, 402
Walsburg: 57, 488
Walton: 441
Wamego: 428
Wano: 468
Ware, Eugene: 16, 56
Warwick: 141, 453
Waseca: 440
Washington: 9, 45, 300, 308, 341, 351
Waterford: 168
Waterloo: 128
Waterville: 263
Wathena (Kickapoo chief): 434
Watunga Creek: 394
Waverly: 157, 279
Way: 440
Wayside: 440
Wea: 16, 80, 429
Won-zop-peach (Tar Springs): 80
Weaver: 489
Webster: 33, 118, 259, 324, 356
Weibly Bluff: 27
Weimar City: 179

Welcome: 484
Welda: 179
Weller County: 319
Wellington: 10, 101, 129, 135, 147
Wells: 446
Wellsford: 422
Wellsville: 79
Weskan: 487
Wesleyan: 245
Westfield: 277
West Mound: 31
Westphalia: 6, 178, 292
West, Sir Thomas: 139, 265
Westminster: 135
Westmoreland: 270
West Plains: 34
West Point: 409
Wetmore: 65, 455
Wheatland: 87
Wheaton: 47
Whipperwill Creek: 63, 121
Whiskey Creek: 483
Whiskey Point: 381, 409, 483
White Church: 248
White City: 461–62
White Clay Creek: 371
White Cloud: 291, 436
White Hair: 112, 262
White Oak Bluff: 51
White Mound: 28, 79
White River (Neosho): 113
White Rock: 25, 79, 117
White Water: 60, 477
White Woman's Creek: 18, 106, 476

Whitfield: 139
Whitman, Walt: 46
Whiting: 467
Wichita: 74, 91, 353, 433, 443
Wichita Eagle: 62
Widerange: 84
Wiedefeld: 173
Wier City: 76
Wilburton: 474
Wild Cat: 64, 68, 147
Wilder: 363, 367, 445
Wild Horse: 81, 452
Williamsburg: 445
Williamstown: 85
Willis: 338
Wilmington: 277
Wilmot Proviso: 310
Wilroads: 340
Wilson: 83, 308, 317
Wilsonton: 474
Wilsonville: 457
Winchester: 139, 300
Windom: 293, 360, 469
Windhorst: 180
Windsor: 135
Winfield: 247–48
Winifred: 466
Winkler: 181
Winona: 71, 292, 437, 478
Winterset: 149
Wise County: 300, 308, 315, 322
Wolf River: 67
Wolverine: 72
Wonsevu: 67
Wood, Samuel N.: 58, 277, 324, 367
Woodbine: 42
Woodhull: 475

Woodland: 44
Woodlawn: 44
Woodsdale: 44
Woodson County: 308, 312
Woodstock: 44, 159
Woodston: 44, 408, 488
Worcester: 253
Work: 88
Wright: 339
Wyandot: 424, 426
Wyckoff Bottoms: 33
Wynot, Neb.: 81
Wyoming: 98, 259, 267

Xavier: 242
Xenia: 38, 208, 273, 277
XYZ Affair: 128

Yates Center: 143
Yocemento: 77, 101
Yoder: 173
Yost, I.M.: 102
Young America: 479
Youngsville: 474
Yuba City: 297
Yukon: 91
Yuma: 65, 297

Zamora: 95, 122
Zeandale: 34, 86, 209
Zenda: 140, 370
Zenith: 9, 209
Zenobia: 198
Zephyr: 11
Zimmerdale: 34
Zion: 235, 329
Zorro: 490
Zulu: 6, 197, 201
Zurich: 133
Zutphen: 184
Zyba: 184, 490

The paper on which this book is printed bears the watermark of the University of Oklahoma Press and has an effective life of at least three hundred years.